FASCISM FROM ABOVE

FASCISM FROM ABOVE

The Dictatorship of
Primo de Rivera in Spain
1923–1930

SHLOMO BEN-AMI

CLARENDON PRESS · OXFORD
1983

Oxford University Press, Walton Street, Oxford OX2 6DP
London Glasgow New York Toronto
Delhi Bombay Calcutta Madras Karachi
Kuala Lumpur Singapore Hong Kong Tokyo
Nairobi Dar es Salaam Cape Town
Melbourne Auckland
and associates in
Beirut Berlin Ibadan Mexico City Nicosia

Oxford is a trade mark of Oxford University Press

Published in the United States
by Oxford University Press, New York

British Library Cataloguing in Publication Data
Ben-Ami, Shlomo
Fascism from Above: the Dictatorship of Primo de Rivera in Spain, 1923–30.
1. Rivera, Miguel Primo de 2. Spain—Politics and government—1886–1931 3. Spain—History—Alfonso XIII, 1886–1931
I. Title
946.08 DP243
ISBN 0–19–822596–2

Set by South End Typographics, Pondicherry
Printed in Great Britain by
Hazell, Watson & Viney Ltd.
Aylesbury, Bucks.

To the memory of my father

PREFACE

On 13 September 1923, General Miguel Primo de Rivera, the captain-general of Catalonia, seized power in Spain by means of a classic pronunciamiento. He established a seven-year dictatorship of which so far no systematic study has been undertaken. The present work is the first attempt to fill this yawning gap. The opinion has been widely held that Primo's *coup d'état* was a response to a so-called 'disintegration' of the political system of the Restoration, and therefore, only marginally, if at all, related to an economic or social crisis.[1] More recently it has been argued that the general's rebellion was a defensive reaction of the military caste against the threats to its corporate interests.[2]

Yet the question remains whether Primo de Rivera was just the successor to generations of 'Spanish' praetorians. Is the fact that a general takes over the reins of power violently, or that a court favourite seizes power through a palace *coup de main*, *per se* indicative of the nature and significance of his rebellion?[3] The mechanism of the take-over might not have changed, but its response to the challenges of a structurally changing society, its incisive identification with the terrified well-to-do classes, the would-be dictator's affinity with European anti-parliamentarian trends, and the presence of the 'communist' scare in the minds of his conservative supporters might perhaps be indicative that something new and more in tune with European post-War anti-democratic tendencies was being born in September 1923. To see the emergence of Primo de Rivera's Dictatorship as just a classic manifestation of military corporatism or syndicalism would be to reduce it to the dimensions of 'one more' pronunciamiento.

Primo de Rivera has been too frequently dismissed as a national

[1] Javier Tusell y Genoveva García, 'La Dictadura de Primo de Rivera como régimen político. Un intento de interpretación' in *Cuadernos Económicos de I.C.E.*, (henceforth *Cuadernos*) no. 10, 1979, pp. 39–44.

[2] This is a valid emphasis competently argued by Carolyn Boyd, *Praetorian Politics in Liberal Spain* (The University of North Carolina Press, 1979), pp. 236–71.

[3] Such is the minimizing treatment given to Primo's *coup d'état* by two contemporary analysts: Carlo Sforza, *European Dictatorships* (London, 1932); Curzio Malaparte, *Técnica del golpe de estado* (Barcelona, 1958).

Father Christmas, a Haroun-el-Rashid issuing decrees right and left, or a sympathetic Andalusian determined to force upon a whole nation his primitive and over-simplistic political philosophy. He was portrayed as a coffee-house politician, a prototype of the mass of Spaniards in which there were probably millions of potential dictators who could do nothing but applaud the anarchic spirit and eclectic policies of their well-intentioned hero.[4] Jacques Bainville wrote that Primo 'somewhat resembled the toreros of his native country. When the bullfight is over, all they think about is love-making.'[5] Some contemporaries, mainly in Latin America, dismissed him as 'a general *à la mejicana*, who only thinks of drawing his machete, and who lives between adventures and gambling'.[6] Devoid of any doctrinal basis, the Dictatorship, argued its critics, was an old-style autocracy, almost *pouvoir à l'état pur*. Himself a product of liberal politics, the Dictator could not betray his democratic spirit in order to become the herald of a new system.[7] His whole experiment was nothing but a 'parenthesis' with few, if any, important effects on Spanish life.[8]

What is, one may ask, the validity of a term such as historical 'parenthesis' at all? History is about change; and it is the task of the student of history to detect it. To stick to the 'folkloristic' traits of *Primoderriverismo* would hardly advance historical research. It certainly would not enhance our understanding of the period here under consideration and its place in the history of twentieth-century Spain. One can easily write, for example, the 'other history' of Italian Fascism, the anecdotes of Mussolini's showmanship, stories of ludicrous goings-on and sexual melodrama. Indeed, as Luigi Barzini seems to imply in a witty and amusing chapter on Mussolini, this 'other history' is not only relevant but might even be the real one.[9] But, whatever one's historiographical approach might be, the 'serious' Primo de Rivera has still to be unearthed if a valid conclusion

[4] G. Brenan, *The Spanish Labyrinth* (Cambridge, 1964), p. 79; H. Buckley, *Life and Death of the Spanish Republic* (London, 1940), pp. 18–19; Salvador de Madariaga, *España* (Buenos Aires, 1964), pp. 322–4. 343–4; S. Payne, *Falange* (Stanford University Press, 1962), pp. 5–7.

[5] Jacques Bainville, *Dictators* (London, 1937), p. 229.

[6] A staunch enemy of the Dictator, Sánchez Guerra, disputed the validity of this image; see *La Nación*, 28 Aug. 1926.

[7] Amadeu Hurtado, *Quaranta anys d'advocat. Historica del meu temps* (Barcelona, 1964), vol. 2, pp. 187–9; Joaquín Arrarás, *Historia de la segunda república española* (Madrid, 1964), vol. i, p. 153; Tusell, 'La Dictadura . . .'.

[8] Javier Tusell, *La crisis del caciquismo andaluz 1923–1931* (Madrid, 1977), p. 231.

[9] Luigi Barzini, *The Italians* (London, 1966), pp. 133–56.

about his regime is to be drawn. His was not the regime of an oriental despot or a benefactor devoid of any conceptual orientation. Nor was he the elementary kind of nineteenth-century Caudillo. His rule was to be imbued with ideological ingredients and with institutional components whose affinity with 'modern' dictatorships should not be disregarded.

There is no denying that much of the criticism of Primo de Rivera, especially that referring to his personality, was right. It will not be claimed here that his regime was wholly immersed in an all-embracing *Weltanschauung*, as was the case with modern totalitarian regimes. Nor will it be argued that the Dictator possessed a coherent, or systematic body of doctrine. He was the first to admit his spirit of improvisation, his pragmatism and syncretism. 'All my life I have been changing my views,' he declared in a speech at the National Assembly, 'sometimes I reject today what I accepted only a week ago.'[10] But the expedient traits of the Dictatorship should not be allowed to overshadow its novelty. No 'man on horseback' before Primo de Rivera had developed in Spain the notion of a New State to the degree that he did. He was not the sword of party vying for power, nor just a rudimentary embodiment of the barracks' political philosophy, but the protagonist of an entirely new kind of politics. Nor should one underestimate the Dictatorship's elevation of anti-democratic traditionalism to the status of an official guide-line. Under Primo de Rivera, moreover, the Catholic criticism of democracy started to attune itself to the mainstream of counter-revolutionary European thought; it acquired a strong flavour of what some considered to be the *Zeitgeist*.

This book is an attempt to re-examine Primo de Rivera's rise to power and his regime, and to see to what extent he went beyond his originally conservative intentions to acquire the touch of a 'modern' dictator. It is essential in this context to examine the civilianization of his regime, which had initially looked like a sheer military adventure; and to study the extent to which the general's rebellion against 'decadent' liberalism advanced the cause of a new political deal. Did the Dictator establish a new economic and social approach? Protectionism and economic interventionism came to Spain long before Primo de Rivera. But at no time before him had economic nationalism been institutionalized with such zeal and doctrinal

[10] Primo de Rivera, *Intervenciones en la Asamblea Nacional* (Madrid, 1930), p. 40.

conviction. Moreover, in the past there seems to have been a certain tension and dichotomy between the politically liberal state and its submission to protectionism.[11] Under Primo the dichotomy disappeared, as both politics and the economy complemented each other as two facets of a dictatorial, nationalist enterprise. Primo's was the first coherent essay made in Spain by a military ruler to establish a developmental dictatorship, of which we have had many examples in this century. An important aspect of the question of whether or not Primo de Rivera should be considered the herald of a Spanish 'new state' is the extent to which, by his drive to acquire a working-class *point d'appui* for his regime, he had moved away from his conservative loyalties and ceased to be committed at all costs to the sanctity of vested interests. Not all of Primo de Rivera's approaches went beyond the realm of intentions and the declarative stage. They should therefore be evaluated accordingly. Thus, for example, his social achievements did not always live up to his boastful claims. Nor were his promises to vindicate the greatest 'regenerationist' dream, the revitalization of local life and institutions, exactly fulfilled. Primo de Rivera should certainly be credited with relieving Spain from the nightmare of the Moroccan wars. He failed, however, in his pretentious, even ludicrous, attempt to secure for Spain the status of a world power. But, a *révolution manquée*, as the Dictatorship eventually proved to be, it nevertheless deserves the attention of students of history if only because it put the lid on a system that had provided a workable framework for parliamentary politics in Spain for the preceding fifty years, and inaugurated policies that were to become corner-stones of the Spanish right and eventually of the Francoist state. The Dictatorship anticipated the most essential ingredients of both the 'blue era' and the National-Catholic phase of Francoism. An attempt is made, through select comparative insights, to place the Spanish Dictatorship within a wider European context.

I have already dealt with some aspects of the Dictatorship in a previous book and in subsequent articles. The present study will therefore not elaborate too extensively on topics such as the Socialists' 'collaborationism' and Primo's confrontation with the Artillery Corps, with the universities, and with the dynastic and the Republican opposition. Inevitably, these issues are referred to when they are indispensable for the understanding of the broader picture, or when a fresh observation about them can be advanced.

[11] Raymond Carr, *Spain 1808–1939* (Oxford University Press, 1970), pp. 394–7.

It is a special pleasure for me to acknowledge the debts of gratitude which I inevitably incurred throughout the preparation of this book. I should especially like to thank those friends and colleagues who took the trouble to read, and comment on, all or part of the text: Dr Frances Lannon of Lady Margaret Hall, Oxford; Mr Raymond Carr, the Warden of St. Antony's College, Oxford; Professor Gabriel Jackson of the University of California, San Diego; Professor José Andrés Gallego, Madrid; and Dr Joaquín Romero Maura, whose comments were, as always, extremely thought-provoking. I have greatly profited from my conversations with Dr Paul Preston of Queen Mary College, London, as well as from the seminar under his direction to which I had the opportunity of presenting the main theses of this book. Dr José Varela Ortega has been a most stimulating interlocutor during my frequent visits to Spain; and Professor Stanley Payne of the University of Wisconsin has kindly read, and commented on, the proposal upon which this book is based. Professor Joan Connelly Ullman of the University of Washington has been helpful in her remarks; and so was Professor Walter Laqueur.

I should also like to extend my thanks for the help given by the staffs of the Archivo Histórico Nacional, the Biblioteca Nacional, and the Hemeroteca Nacional in Madrid; and the Bodleian Library in Oxford. Special thanks are due to Ms Rosemary Campbell, the librarian of St. Antony's College, for her constant help in tracing indispensable items.

It is a pleasant duty to thank the Warden and Fellows of St. Antony's College for electing me to a Visiting Fellowship, without which this book could hardly have been accomplished. Sir Isaiah Berlin has been helpful in many ways. The unfailing assistance of two friends and colleagues, Professor Zvi Vaavetz and Professor Gaby Cohen, both of the University of Tel Aviv, and of Ms Nitza Drori of the American Friends of the same university, has been indispensable throughout the preparation of this study.

S. B.

CONTENTS

ABBREVIATIONS

ACN de P	Acción Nacional de Propagandistas
CAMPSA	Compañía Arrendataria del Monopolio de Petróleos, S.A.
CEDA	Confederación Española de Derechas Autónomas
CNT	Confederación Nacional de Trabajadores
CONCA	Confederación Nacional Católico-Agraria
FUE	Federación Universitaria Escolar
LAM	Liga de Acción Monárquica
PSOE	Partido Socialista Obrero Español
PSP	Partido Social Popular
SNA	Secretariado Nacional Agrario
UGT	Unión General de Trabajadores
UM	Unión Monárquica
UMN	Unión Monárquica Nacional
UP	Unión Patriótica
UPC	Unión Patriótica Castellana

NOTE ON TERMINOLOGY

THE main terminological problem a book on Spain presents is that of the anglicization of Spanish terms. This has been approached in this work in the following way:

I. The names of parties and institutions are used according to their most familiar sound. Thus 'Unión Patriótica' is preferred to the English 'Patriotic Union', and 'Unión Monárquica' is preferred to 'Monarchist Union'. But the 'Socialist Party' is preferred to the official Spanish name 'Partido Socialista Obrero Español'. Institutions like *Ayuntamiento* (City council) and *Diputación Provincial* (provincial council) are best known in their Spanish form, and have, consequently, been used in that form. As for place-names, only five have been anglicized: Catalonia for Cataluña, Biscay for Vizcaya, Seville for Sevilla, Castile for Castilla, and Andaluçia for Andalucía.

II. The following usage of capital letters has been adopted:
   1. For the official name of institutions and corporate bodies.
   2. For denoting the institutional aspect of a term. Therefore, Fascist, 'Communist', 'Socialist', and 'Anarcho-syndicalist' determine an organization or the affiliation to a body, whereas the same words with small letters denote the abstract concept of the terms.

III. When in the translation of Spanish citations a divergence of meaning arises between the two languages, an attempt has been made to retain the original Spanish flavour.

INTRODUCTION

The Mixed Blessing of Neutrality

THE meaning of Primo de Rivera's Dictatorship cannot be separated from the fact that the general did not stage his rebellion in an immobile society. He 'caught' his country in the midst of a process of transition, whereby the old social and political order was being challenged by an emerging bourgeoisie and a radicalizing working class. It was the dangerous questioning of the established order, not just the professional interests of the army, that were at stake in September 1923.

Spain's neutrality in the Great War did not render her immune to its impact. Not only did the war years witness great economic and social changes in Spain, but in their aftermath the country was also thrown into acute class warfare that, together with the escalating manifestations of separatism, the tensions over the Moroccan campaign, and the difficulties encountered by the parliamentary system in its attempts to respond to the new challenges, made the term 'post-war crisis' in Spain as living a reality as elsewhere.[1]

Carried away by what was clearly a circumstantial 'boom', a specialized economic organ claimed in 1919 that the war had at long last turned Spain into an industrial nation. 'Industry', it went on, 'now plays the main role in Spain.'[2]

Neutrality, and the consequent convenience of exporting to the belligerent countries, opened golden opportunities for the Spanish economy, the volume of whose benefits, admittedly not always related to an increase in production, but rather to rising prices, reached unprecedented heights in almost every sphere. Thus, for example, the mining industry trebled the value of its production (462,193,129 pesetas in 1914; 1,387,097,669 in 1918).[3] Though the increase in coal output (4,424,400 tons in 1914; 7,237,500 in 1918)[4]

[1] François Denjean, 'Le mouvement révolutionnaire en Espagne' in *Revue de Paris*, 1 Nov. 1921, pp. 176–8.

[2] *El Financiero*, 4 July 1919.

[3] *Anuario Estadístico de España*, 1929, p. 117. Cf. Jean Baelen, *Principaux traits du développement économique de l'Espagne de 1914 à l'avènement du directoire militaire* (Paris, 1924), p. 86.

[4] *Anuario*, 1929, p. xxii. Cf. 'El presente y el porvenir de la industria hullera en España', in *El Sol*, 11 May 1921.

was such that it enabled Spain to reduce to an unprecedented minimum its import of British coal, the production of other important mining items, such as iron and copper, actually decreased.[5] The profits and the consequent accumulation of capital were mainly due to the vertiginous rise in prices caused by increasing demand. The big mining and industrial concerns of the country, companies such as Altos Hornos, La Papelera Española, Sociedad General Azucarera, Metalúrgica Duro-Felguera, and scores of new minor concerns[6] alongside bigger new enterprises such as Minero-Siderúrgica de Ponferrada, shared in the intoxicating festival of profits. Particularly colossal profits seemed to have been made by the big Basque shipping companies.[7] The fairly intensive activation of industry was also accompanied by an increase of about 37 per cent in the production of electric energy between 1914 and 1917. Its consumption by industry almost doubled during the war.[8]

For the first time in its history, the Catalan textile industry became a major exporter to Europe. The total export of woollen tissues rose from 3.7 million pesetas in 1913 to 162.5 million in 1915, dropping to 108 million in 1916, and 70 million in 1917. That of cotton tissues went up from 53.3 million pesetas in 1913 to 138.4 million in 1915, dropping to 105 million in 1917.[9] Overwhelmed, indeed intoxicated, by these unexpected profits, a Catalan textile manufacturer spoke of the war as 'a fantastic period, a prodigious dream in which all the business deals were smooth and prosperous, all ending in a real orgy of profits . . . In that period of our exporting fever we felt confidence in our capacity to conquer the entire world.'[10]

The war 'boom' had also accelerated the process of de-archaization of the country's social structure. Internal migration to the industrial centres of Biscay and Catalonia, combined with a substantial drop in the number of Spaniards who emigrated to foreign work markets

[5] Baelen, pp. 110–111; *Anuario*, 1929, p. xxii.

[6] For new companies see Santiago Roldán *et al.*, *La formación de la sociedad capitalista en España 1914–1920*, (Madrid, 1973), vol. 1, pp. 46–7; Joseph Harrison, *An Economic History of Modern Spain* (Manchester University Press, 1978), pp. 94-5.

[7] Tuñón de Lara, *El movimiento obrero en la historia de España* (Madrid, 1972), pp. 546–8; Harrison, *An Economic History*, p. 94.

[8] Baelen, p. 142.

[9] Albert Mousset, *L'Espagne dans la politique mondiale* (Paris, 1923), p. 309. Baelen, p. 128, gives the following figures for the total export of cotton goods: 1913—50,325,000 pesetas; 1915—155,078,972; 1917—130,300,060.

[10] Pedro Gual Villalví, *Memorias de un industrial de nuestro tiempo* (Barcelona, 1922), pp. 105–6, 226.

(down from 151,000 in 1914 to 20,168 in 1918),[11] had brought about a reduction of the percentage of the active population engaged in agriculture from 66 in 1910 to 57 in 1920. Likewise, the share of the active population employed in the industrial sector rose from 15.82% to 21.94%, and that engaged in the services from 18.18% to 20.81%.[12] The build-up of the industrial proletariat was a discernible process from 1910. The number of workers in the mining industry went up by 47% in the years 1910–18 (from 90,000 to 133,000. Their number more than doubled in Asturias: from 18,000 to 39,000); that of those employed in the metallurgical sector more than trebled (from 61,000 to 200,000); the textile industry almost doubled its workers' population (it went up from 125,000 to 213,000); while the transport industry employed in 1918 37% more workers than in 1910 (an increase from 155,000 to 212,000).[13] The internal migrations had, as a matter of course, increased the proportion of the urban population in Spain. 9.01% of the Spainiards lived in 1910 in cities of more than 100,000 inhabitants; in 1920 the ratio was 12.5%. 35% lived in 1910 in towns of more than 10,000 inhabitants; in 1920 the ratio was 39%, that is an increase of 1,190,060 inhabitants.[14]

An inevitable by-product of such structural changes was the substantial growth of the trade unions. These usually tend to swell at times of prosperity when their bargaining power is on the increase. Consequently, the strength of the Socialist *Unión General de Trabajadores* increased from 393 sections and 119,144 affiliates in 1914 to 1,078 sections and 211,342 affiliates in 1920.[15] The Anarcho-syndicalist *Confederación Nacional de Trabajadores*, always ahead of its Socialist counterpart when the conditions existed for a dramatic

[11] Baelen, p. 20. The bulk of the emigration came from the crisis-hit orange region of Valencia and Levante. 85,497 out of the 125,825 people who emigrated to France during the war came from this region; see *Información sobre emigración española durante la guerra* (Madrid, 1919), p. 51.

[12] *Estadísticas Básicas de España, 1900–1970* (Madrid, 1975), p. 369. Tuñón de Lara, *Panorama actual de la economía española* (Paris, 1962), p. 26. Martínez Cuadrado, *La burguesía conservadora (1874–1931)* (Madrid, 1976), p. 113, claims that, in absolute terms, the number of those employed in industry and in the services increased by 527,357 and 275,000 respectively.

[13] Cf. Bruguera, *Histoire contemporaine d'Espagne* (Paris, 1953), p. 334; Baelen, pp. 99, 128. For Asturias, see A. Shubert, 'Una revolución de autodefensa: La radicalización de los mineros de Asturias 1921–1934', in *Sistema, Revista de Ciencias Sociales*, Jan. 1982, p. 105.

[14] Juan Díez Nicolás, *Tamaño, densidad y crecimiento de la población en España, 1900–1960* (Madrid, 1971), pp. 22–30; *Anuario*, 1929, p. xx.

[15] *Anuario*, 1929, p. 478.

growth, surpassed in 1919 the figure of 700,000 members, about half of which were concentrated in industrial, and soon socially turbulent, Catalonia.[16]

Social turbulence was to be stimulated basically by inflation, or, more precisely, by the increasing gap between the wages of workers and those of the professional sector on the one hand, and galloping price increases on the other. In terms of national average, wages rose during the war by 25.6%, while prices did by 61.8%.[17] The economist Paris Eguilaz calculated that the real wage of workers dropped by an average of 20% in the years 1914–20.[18] The index of the cost of living of a working-class family had gone up from 117.6 in September 1914 to 161.8 four years later. An examination of the price movement of some fundamental food items would show even more dramatic price rises. Moreover, in big urban centres such as Madrid, and especially Barcelona, the capital of Anarcho-syndicalism, prices tended to be even higher.[19]

It was not exactly revolution, but mainly wage demands that the upsurge in the number of strikes came to reflect. 212 strikes were officially recorded in 1914, their number rose to 237 in 1916, 306 in 1917, and 462 in 1918. 1,819,295 working days were lost by the 109,168 strikers that took part in the strikes during the war.[20]

But not every strike was just a labour dispute. Conservative opinion, and indeed the entire political system of the Restoration, was seriously shaken by the chain of lower-middle- and working-class strikes that took place in the summer of 1917. These elements joined forces with sections of the Catalan and Asturian upper bourgeoisie in a circumstantial alliance—much like that which brought down Louis Philippe in 1848 in France—aimed at a readjustment of the division of political power in the country that would take into account the ascendancy of the bourgeoisie.[21] The lower classes were, however, mainly motivated by the deterioration of their living conditions. Early effects of the 'post-war crisis' began to

[16] Cf. A. Balcells, *El sindicalismo en Barcelona 1916–1923* (Barcelona, 1968), p. 130; Meaker, *The Revolutionary Left*, p. 235. Salvador Seguí's figures in *El Sol*, 4 Sept. 1920 (about one million members) look too generous.

[17] Balcells, *El sindicalisme a Barcelona 1915–1923* (Barcelona, 1965), p. 170.

[18] H. Paris Eguilaz, *El movimiento de precios en España* (Madrid, 1943), p. 159.

[19] *Anuario*, 1929, pp. 494–7. Wholesale prices doubled during the war: Lacomba, *Ensayos*, p. 118.

[20] *Número de huelgas de que ha tenido conocimiento el Instituto de Reformas Sociales desde 1905 a 1920,* (Instituo de Reformas Sociales, Madrid, 1920).

[21] Juan Antonio Lacomba, *La crisis española de 1917* (Madrid, 1970).

be felt in the summer of 1917, as France and Great Britain started to protect their currencies by restricting exports from Spain, thus undermining the profits of Spanish exporters,[22] as well as their relative flexibility in dealing with the unions.

The movement of the *juntas de defensa* was not exactly a 're-generationist' endeavour. Rather, it was a professional syndicate of low- and middle-rank officers aggressively concerned with status and income, and as such, highly representative of the grievances of the urban lower-middle classes and civil servants in a period of galloping inflation. The impact of the *juntas*, however, was far-reaching. Within a few months of their creation—officially in May 1917—they had been legalized, and had eventually turned into the maker and the deposer of Spanish cabinets. After 1917, the Canovite system was virtually held hostage by the ever-present threat of praetorianism.[23]

The revolutionary alignment of the summer of 1917 failed because the *juntas* ceased their flirtation with the civilian revolution once their demands had been met and their position as the moderators of Spanish politics had been consolidated. It failed also, perhaps mainly, because Cambó's assumption that the political bait that he had held out to the industrial proletariat—the democratization of the Canovite system—would avert the latent social revolution rested on fallacious ground. Once the political leaders of the Catalan upper bourgeoisie realized that they were actually the allies of a street revolution as reflected in the revolutionary general strike of mid August, they lost no time in deserting the movement and returning to the fold of the 'discredited' Canovite system. The tactical unity achieved by the two most powerful unions in the country, the CNT and the UGT, threatened to become, in the eyes of the conservative classes, the prelude to an eventual inplantation of the dictatorship of the proletariat in Spain.[24]

A legacy of Spain's 1917 *révolution manquée* was to deepen the mistrust between the organized working class and the bourgeoisie, and to strengthen the latter's disposition to endorse, or even actively help in bringing about, a system of 'law and order' to quell the threat, real or imaginary, of social revolution. Furthermore, the events of August 1917 had taught the Catalan bourgeoisie that the

[22] Exports started to drop in 1917: 1,361,548,000 pesetas in 1916, 1,311,314,000 in 1917; see Mousset, pp. 301, 306.

[23] Boyd.

[24] Denjean, pp. 174–5; Lacomba, *La crisis*.

army, which assisted in vigorously suppressing the working-class rebellion (the toll of repression was seventy-one killed and hundreds injured),[25] was its natural ally when it came to defending its most vital interests. 1917 had also shattered the remote possibility of a *rapprochement* between the army and social radicalism. There was a message too for the political class in Madrid. The use of the military by shaky governments as strike-breakers and quellers of disturbances not only aroused the military's resentment at being used in the undignified role of policemen, but also exposed, in their eyes, the incompetence of civilian rule, a necessary pre-condition for its eventual overthrow by the army.[26]

If anything, the post-war economic crisis only exacerbated the social fears of the owning classes. Employers had now to face, under conditions of economic retrenchment and depression, the rising expectations, soon to turn into violent desperation, of a highly and massively organized proletariat. The liquidation of the anarcho-syndicalist militant unions was to become one of the most cherished dreams of the Catalan employers.

The end of the ephemeral 'boom' was connected with the evaporation of the favourable conditions that prevailed during the War. The positive trade balance of about 400 million pesetas in 1918 was gradually eroded until it turned into a deficit of 403,300,000 pesetas in 1920, and into staggering ones of 1,256,200,000 and 1,396,800,000 pesetas in 1921 and 1922 respectively. True, except for 1920, the total volume of exports did not diminish; in fact, it even increased, 1921 turning out to be an exceptionally good year for exports.[27] But it was the key mining and heavy industries of the north and the Catalan textiles that were most adversely affected by the end of the war. The value of manufactured goods exported by Spain went down from 565,200,000 pesetas in 1916 to 471,300,000 in 1919, 322,700,000 in 1920, and 224,600,000 in 1921.[28] 13,544,165 kg. of cotton goods were exported through the port of Barcelona in 1919. A year later, a dramatic drop of 55% (8,728,746 kg.) in exports was

[25] Juan Pablo Fusi, *Política obrera en el país vasco* (Madrid, 1975), p. 376.

[26] This was not a unique Spanish phenomenon. See S. E. Finer, *The Man on Horseback. The Role of the Military in Politics* (New York, 1962), p. 27; Eric Nordlinger, *Soldiers in Politics. Military Coups and Governments* (New Jersey, 1977), pp. 90–1.

[27] Cf. Santiago Roldán *et al.*, *La formación*, vol. 1, p. 25; Mousset, p. 306; *Anuario*, 1929, p. 189. Exports developed as follows: 1918—1,009,000,000 pesetas; 1919—1,310,600,000; 1920—1,020,000,000; 1921—1,579,600,000; 1922—1,319,300,000.

[28] Mousset, p. 306.

recorded. But worse was still to come. The export of cotton goods dropped in 1921 by 76.8% in relation to the previous year, and that of 1922 by 66% in relation to 1921.[29] 'The panic', wrote a textile manufacturer, 'was acquiring epidemic dimensions', as huge stocks of textile goods were sold at 'almost zero prices'. For many industrialists, all this heralded 'the rough awakening into reality from a prodigious dream of grandeur'.[30]

Nor did the Basque industry escape the crisis. As in Catalonia, prosperity was somehow maintained until the beginning of the recovery of the European economies in 1920. But then the crisis became evident. The export of iron ore dropped dramatically by more than 400% between 1920 and 1921. And, though the next two years were to witness a gradual recovery, this fell drastically short of catching up with the figures of the good years. The total value of Spain's mining production reached its lowest level in 1922; it dropped by 45.6% in relation to the previous year. In the Biscayan mines, the total output dropped by 57.8% between 1916 and 1921. Within the next year alone it was to drop by a further 59.3%.[31]

The workers were, of course, anything but immune to the impact of the crisis. It is true that the general downward trend of both industrial and agricultural prices[32] reflected itself in a substantial drop in the index of the cost of living of working-class families. From its peak in September 1920 (202.6) it went down to 175.1 in March 1921, where it remained stable until the summer of 1922, and then descended again to 164.2 in March 1923.[33] But all this was poor consolation to, for example, the 120,000 textile workers in the province of Barcelona whose employers could not think of a better way of coping with the crisis than by resorting to redundancies, dismissal of workers, and a cut in wages. In the Asturian coal-mines, 3,000 workers had lost their jobs by 1919, and many others were made redundant. The situation was not different in the mining

[29] *Anuario*, 1929, p. 217.

[30] Pedro Gual, pp. 12–17, 222–3, 216, 218. The textile wholesale price index went down from 148 in 1920 (1913=100) to 94 in 1921 and 87 in 1922: *Anuario*, 1929, pp. 300–1.

[31] *Anuario*, 1929, pp. xxii, 219; Fusi, pp. 449–50; Mousset, p. 309. The coal output dropped by 32% between 1919 and 1922; see Baelen, pp. 101–3, and *Anuario*, 1929, pp. xxii–xxiii.

[32] The wholesale price index of industrial products dropped from 237 in 1920 (1914=100) to 199 in 1921, and 177 in 1922. Wheat prices went down by about 30% between 1920 and 1923; see *Anuario*, 1929, pp. 296–7, 300–1, 304, 306; Bruguera, p. 364.

[33] *Anuario*, 1929, pp. 496–7.

and industrial districts of Biscay. Mines were being shut down, some had introduced a shorter working week, and others resorted to mass dismissal of workers. In the metallurgical industry of Biscay alone, 40% of the jobs were lost between 1920 and 1922. And, where jobs were preserved, wages were cut. Altos Hornos did it by 20%, to be followed by the Asturian coal-mine owners.[34] In April 1921, a businessmen's organ described this gloomy panorama in the following words:

> Unemployment at the mines, unemployment at the factories, in agriculture and in every branch of national production! Unemployment is expanding across the country; and from the mountains of Cartagena, where the mining of lead has been paralysed, over to Bilbao where that of iron is decreasing, there is hardly any province where the workers have not started to feel the depressing effects of the crisis.[35]

The crisis of industry was enough to explain the tougher attitude now displayed by the employers in industrial disputes,[36] the rather docile behaviour of that part of the working class that followed the 'responsible' lead of the Socialists, who now completely abdicated the revolutionary leadership to the CNT,[37] and the intense social warfare that erupted in Barcelona where the frustrated expectations of the Anarcho-syndicalists clashed with the unyielding postures of an employers' class in crisis. The latter's behaviour, however, was not determined only by actual conditions. It was nourished by a growing, sometimes disproportionate, fear of an imminent Communist take-over. Primo de Rivera and those who paved his way to power, did not fail to seize, and indeed play, upon the 'Soviet menace' to justify the Dictatorship.

There is no intention to dispute Stanley Payne's claim that the degree of convulsive mass politics reached by Italy in 1921–2 came to Spain only in 1931–6. This should not entail, however, the dismissal of the 1917–23 crisis[38] as only marginally, if at all, relevant

[34] Marcelino Graell, *Resumen de la situación económica de España. Surgimiento de la clase media* (Barcelona, 1923), pp. 36–7; Shubert, 'Una revolución . . . ,' pp. 105–6. Baelen, pp. 103, 112; Fusi, pp. 446–8, 454, 458.

[35] *Correspondencia de España*, 30 Apr. 1921.

[36] Denjean, p. 178.

[37] The drop in the number of strikes after the war (1920 – 1,060; 1921 – 373; 1922 – 488; 1923 – 458: Tuñón, *El movimiento*, p. 726) reflected the unions' awareness of the erosion of their bargaining power.

[38] '. . . if that is the word for it', Payne would say. See his 'Spanish Fascism in Comparative Perspective' in Henry Turner (ed.), *Reappraisals of Fascism* (New York, 1975), p. 167.

to the search for the roots of Primo de Rivera's Dictatorship. Historical causation might be a more complex matter than political scientists and quantifiers like us to think. Assuming one can really form a comparative scale of political convulsiveness, how does one measure in quantitative and comparative terms the *panic* of the Catalan bourgeoisie? How does one evaluate the intensity of its *determination* to undermine the foundations of the liberal state? Even assuming that anarcho-syndicalist radicalism was far less menacing than working-class violence in Italy, what is in quantitative terms the *impact* of its *atentados*, as well as of the terrifying influence of the Russian Revolution, on the upper bourgeoisie? What is the sense at all of quantifying a 'natural average' of convulsiveness, when the real problem was not what happened in Cuenca or Soria, but in Barcelona; not in Sicily, but in Milan? Whatever the intensity of the social struggle in Catalonia may have been—and it was highly intense—in the last resort it was, as Royo Villanova was aware, 'the bitter restlessness caused by the reflections of syndicalism and bolshevism upon us', that counted.[39] Reality may not have been all that awesome, but it nevertheless activated, as Ossorio y Gallardo acknowledged in March 1919, 'the muse of fear, the diligent companion of the conservative classes, to suggest in these direful hours long madrigals and ballads in tribute to social order. Social order before anything else! Everything should be sacrificed on the altar of social order!'[40] A 'climate', a 'state of mind', may be as important as actual conditions in determining the prospects of either revolutionary or counter-revolutionary change.[41]

Immediately after the War, and before the famous 'trienio bolchevista' was inaugurated in Barcelona, the Andalusian countryside went through a sudden social commotion. The organizational fever that overtook in 1918–19 the small peasants and landless labourers in Andalusia, where hundreds of new syndicates spread as if by magic, was a response to wartime price rises, as well as a reflection upon the brutally depressed Spanish countryside of the apocalyptic expectations aroused by the Bolshevik Revolution. Governmental repression, the return of the Socialists to reformist

[39] Royo Villanova, *Bolchevismo y sindicalismo* (Madrid, 1920), pp. 61–2. For a similarly alarmist account, see Juan Francisco Correas, *El bolchevismo en España* (Madrid, 1920).

[40] *El Debate*, 18 March 1919.

[41] Cf. the case of the French Revolution: J. Talmon, *The Rise of Totalitarian Democracy* (Boston, 1952), pp. 69–70.

tactics, and the exhaustion of the movement's energy combined to extinguish the whole rebellion by early 1920. Yet its impact upon the conservative classes of the south was to strengthen their attentiveness to the social danger. Throughout the turbulent events, panic-stricken employers' associations spread across Andalusia to confront the radicalizing peasant unions, young bourgeois set up their own private militias 'to asssist' the authorities in curbing the 'bolshevik' wave, and Catholic syndicates were launched to neutralize the 'contaminating' influence of the 'red' unions.[42]

Revolution failed in 1917, and again in 1918–19, but the 'red scare' and the phantom of bolshevism were there to stay. The Russian example and the effects of the social outbursts in Spain were to remain a traumatic memory for Spanish conservatives up to Primo de Rivera's *coup d'état* and beyond. An over-reacting bourgeoisie, always predisposed to make a mountain out of a molehill, started to see even in purely labour conflicts the hands of communist agitators determined to undermine the very foundations of society.[43] Unamuno observed, on the morrow of the frustrated 1917 revolution, that 'the reaction [to the events of August] is evident and showy. The terrified Spanish bourgeoisie has lost its senses; one has only to listen to the strange rumours that are being propagated by self-styled men of order in the streets, squares, and casinos.'[44]

The 'red scare' was responsible for bringing the Spanish right to indulge in dictatorial dreams. In Catalonia, the Lliga Regionalista's gradual breakaway from parliamentary politics, and its drift into a position where it virtually created the pre-conditions for Primo de Rivera's take-over, were determined, to a great extent, by its social fears.

These were further nourished after the war by the breakdown of labour relations in Catalonia. The CNT's congress of Sants, in July 1918, had revolutionized the structure of Anarcho-syndicalism by establishing industrial unions for each major branch of production (*Sindicatos Únicos*) to replace the old craft organizations. The

[42] Jean Costedoat-Lamarque, *La question agraire en Andalusie* (Paris, 1923), pp. 19-27. Díaz del Moral, *Historia de las agitaciones campesinas andaluzas* (Madrid, 1973), pp. 364–76.

[43] Burgos y Mazo, *El verano de 1919 en Gobernación* (Cuenca, n.d.), p. 181 and *passim*.

[44] 'El Mercantil Valenciano', 9 Sept. 1917, quoted in Lacomba, *Ensayos*, p. 288. Madriaga was quick to draw a parallel between the revolutionary potentialities of Russia and Spain, see his 'Spain and Russia: A Parallel', in *New Europe*, 30 Aug. 1917.

Sindicatos Únicos reflected the CNT's decision to centralize and make more effective its struggle against capitalism in such a way that would tend to escalate every industrial dispute into a general confrontation with the employers.[45] The new structure, as the moderate Cenetista Salvador Seguí observed, was expected to enable the CNT to carry out a 'genuine, really revolutionary policy'.[46] The equally moderate Angel Pestaña was also overwhelmed by an apocalyptic mood about the imminence of the revolution's victory. 'The bourgeois world is sinking,' he said in 1918, 'we only have to push it a bit in order to pull down the rotten prop that still sustains it.'[47]

The forty-four-day 'Canadiense' strike—'the best-organized strike in the world' according to an enthusiastic Peirats[48]—that erupted in February 1919, and soon developed into an overwhelmingly general strike, demonstrated before a terrified Catalan bourgeoisie the efficiency of the new structure. The Catalan industrialists, and with them bourgeois opinion in Barcelona, drifted into a state of panic. 8,000 bourgeois volunteers, convinced that it was an issue of life and death to curb the revolutionary unions, joined the Somatén to help to crush the proletarian menace.[49] That 'formidable strike' suddenly confronted the so-called *clases acomodadas* with 'the fearful enigma of syndicalist tactics', with its 'astonishing discipline'. A Russian-type Communism was seen knocking at Spain's doors with an unprecedented vehemence,[50] while the state's citadel was being guarded with alarming laxity by petty politicians, entirely out of tune with the gravity of the crisis. The *Federación Patronal* pointed in frustration at the government's conciliatory approach to the workers' demands—it had approved the eight-hour day—as detrimental to the industrialists who had now to face, with higher costs of

[45] José Peirats, *La CNT en la revolución española* (Ruedo Ibérico, 1971), vol. 1, pp. 25–36; Ángel Pestaña, *El terrorismo en Barcelona. Medios y fines del sindicalismo en Cataluña (Conferencias dadas en Madrid el dia 4 de Octubre de 1919)* (Barcelona, 1978), pp. 25–6, 45–7.

[46] Quoted ibid., p. 71.

[47] Quoted in García-Nieto *et al.*, *Bases documentales de la España contemporánea*, vol. 6 (Madrid, 1972), pp. 151–2.

[48] Peirats, *La CNT*, i, p. 194.

[49] Peirats, *Los anarquistas en la crisis política española* (Buenos Aires, 1964), p. 17; Rosa Martínez Segarra, 'Grupos económicos en el Somatén' in *Cuadernos*, pp. 213–14. 'Anti-bolshevism' was becoming a major rallying cry for this traditional bourgeois institution, see José Fontán Palomo, *El Somatenista español* (Barcelona, 1924), p. 128.

[50] Gual Villalví, pp. 161–8. S. Carr, 'Industry and Society: Barcelona 1914–23' (Oxford D. Phil thesis), p. 132.

production, a declining, in fact a vanishing, foreign market. The government was explicitly accused of fuelling working-class rebelliousness.[51]

The 'Canadiense' strike enhanced the determination of the Catalan employers to fight back.[52] Romanones, the prime minister during the strike, was convinced they would not settle for less than the total annihilation of Syndicalism.[53] The *Federación Patronal*, founded in 1914, responded violently—these were Cambó's words—to the Syndicalist rebellion.[54] Such a fighting employers' organization, not the Spanish liberal state, was viewed by *La Veu de Catalunya*, the Lliga's organ, as the indispensable instrument for preventing the death of Catalan industry.[55] A gang of gunmen paid by the employers was then formed under the guidance of an ex-German spy, Baron de König, and a retired Spanish policeman, Bravo Portillo, with the explicit mission of liquidating syndicalist trouble-makers. By the end of the year, 200,000 workers were laid off by a co-ordinated lock-out put into practice by a combative employers' class determined to do away with revolutionary unionism.[56] The lock-out marked the start of a drift towards unrestrained *pistolerismo*, to which both sides contributed their share.[57]

After November 1920, official terrorism was introduced in Catalonia. It was orchestrated by the new hard-line Civil Governor of Barcelona, General Martínez Anido, the designation of whom was implicitly demanded by the Barcelona business community when it put pressure on Dato's government to dismiss his 'weak' predecessor, Carlos Bas. Only a strict, decisive policy of 'law and order' could restore the confidence of businessmen in the performance of the liberal state. Under Carlos Bas, according to a common protest of Catalan economic corporations, 'the public authorities' disregard of the essential functions that are supposed to justify their existence, is notorious and intolerable'. 'Barcelona refuses to submit

[51] Pedro Gual, p. 174.

[52] Ibid., pp. 202–3.

[53] Romanones, *Notas de una vida, 1912–1931* (Madrid, 1947), p. 162.

[54] García-Nieto, vol. 6, p. 180. See also Pestaña, *El terrorismo*, pp. 55–7, and S. Carr, pp. 37–8.

[55] Quoted in García-Nieto, vol. 6, p. 189.

[56] The Federación Patronal stood behind both terrorism and the lock-out: Albert Pérez Baró, *Els 'feliços' anys vint. Memóries d'un militant obrer, 1918–1926* (Palma de Mallorca, 1974), pp. 26–44; Pestaña, *El terrorismo*, pp. 8–13, 30–5; S. Carr, pp. 134–54.

[57] For the terrorist struggle, see José León-Ignacio, *Los años del pistolerismo* (Barcelona, 1981); and the evidence of Pestaña, *El terrorismo*, p. 12; *Lo que aprendí*, pp. 163–6, 172–80.

to death', they continued, it 'demands, it exacts that public authority lives up to its mission. Otherwise, let it confess publicly that it refuses, it does not know how to, or it cannot, put an end to the rule of terrorism in our city.'[58]

Martínez Anido's swift response to this challenge could not have been more pleasing to the employers. Thousands of militant Syndicalists were arrested by the agents of the new governor, hundreds of *atentados* were carried out under his orders, and the number of syndicalists gunned down by this official brand of white terrorism increased substantially. Many were shot by the cynical application of the *ley de fugas* 'while trying to escape'.[59] The assassination of Prime Minister Dato in March 1921 by an anarchist gang was a desperate protest against a government that shielded the murderous agents of Martínez Anido.[60] But the business community, the military, the police, the *requetés*, the Somaténes could not have been more delighted at the decisive way the governor had 'hoisted the flag of order'.[61] As far as Cambó was concerned, 'there is no government that, in this moment, could have conducted a better policy than that of Martínez Anido'.[62]

Encouraged and suported by both Martínez Anido and the *Federación Patronal*, the Sindicatos Libres, one of the manifestations nearest to fascism that grew up on Spanish soil prior to the Republic,[63] now came into being in Barcelona. Founded in October 1919 by a shop assistant with a Carlist background, Ramón Sales, the Libres' recruiting ground was among petty-bourgeois and lumpenproletariat

[58] J. Oller Piñol, *Martínez Anido, su vida y su obra* (Madrid, 1943), pp. 43–7.

[59] There is more than one version of the number of victims. López de Ochoa, *De la Dictadura a la República* (Madrid, 1930), p. 45, suggests that more than 400 people were killed in *atentados*. But the Dictatorship's organ *La Nación* (29 Apr. 1929), keen as it certainly was to exaggerate the scale of pre-dictatorial chaos, gave nevertheless lower and more reliable figures: 252 people were killed and 382 were wounded in social crimes throughout the years 1918–23. These figures broadly coincide with those of Farré Morego, *Los atentados sociales en España* (Madrid, 1922): 241 people were killed, and 576 were injured in Barcelona alone in the years 1917–23. But the number of *atentados* was obviously higher; 1,259, according to Francisco Cimadevilla, *El general Primo de Rivera* (Madrid, 1944), p. 55. For the white terror, see also Peirats, *La CNT*, i, pp. 31–6.

[60] A Socialist manifesto protested that the government had 'legalized the armament of the bourgeoisie'; quoted in Largo Caballero, *Presente y futuro de la UGT* (Madrid, 1925), pp. 154–5.

[61] For the widespread support among businessmen and conservatives, see Oller, pp. 64, 77–8, 93–6.

[62] Quoted ibid., p. 74.

[63] F. Cambó, *Las dictaduras* (Barcelona, 1929), p. 118; Pastor, *Los origenes del fascismo en España* (Madrid, n.d.), pp. 18–23.

sectors, defectors from Anarcho-syndicalist unions, ex-Traditionalists, and mere adventurists. The platform of the new organization rested on such typical principles as anti-internationalism, a condemnation of 'Jewish money', an élitism of a sort, a vague 'spiritual conception' about 'the history of life' as the answer to the confessional principles advanced by the Catholic syndicates, a demand for a restructuring of society along organic lines, and, what was most welcome by the *Federación Patronal*, a determination to meet in the streets the 'enemy from within', i.e. Marxists and Anarcho-syndicalists.[64] Though their mouthpieces tended to deny their 'yellowness', the Libres' street-fights against the Únicos as well as the postures they adopted in labour conflicts seemed to be usually in concurrence with the wishes of both the employers and Martínez Anido.[65] 'I have personally recommended to the Libres', the general was later to say, 'that for each of their dead militants they should go out and kill ten Syndicalists.'[66]

Bourgeois hysteria was not to disappear along with the exhaustion of the CNT. Not until Primo de Rivera had seized power and officially done away with the temporizing approach of the liberal state towards the revolutionary unions were the Catalan employers really tranquillized. Neither the crisis of their industries nor their mental attitudes had predisposed them to accept an alternative policy of social reforms, which in 1918, and again in 1919, Cambó had thought was 'the only way' to avoid a social catastrophe.[67]

But one of the effects of the war upon Spain was that it underlined, and gave a sense of urgency to, the need to tackle the deficiencies of its social and political system by non-traditional means. 'Who would be so fatuous as to think that the excessively long and depressive *siesta* of our nation should be prolonged', asked a contemporary, who also thought that society in Spain had changed to such an extent that it justified, among other things, the concession of women's suffrage.[68] Cambó was not the only one to press for a

[64] F. Baratech Alfaro, *Los sindicatos libres de España, su origen, su actuación, su ideario* (Prólogo de Ramón Sales) (Barcelona, 1927), pp. 66–104; Oller, pp. 34–40; Juan José Castillo, *El sindicalismo amarrillo en España* (Madrid, 1977), pp. 68–9.

[65] Pedro Gual, p. 204.

[66] Quoted in García Venero, *Historia de las Internacionales en España* (Madrid, 1957), vol. ii, p. 348.

[67] Quoted in Solá Cañizares, *Luchas sociales en Cataluña 1812–1934* (Madrid, 1970), pp. 40, 42–3.

[68] José Francos Rodríguez, *La mujer y la política españolas* (Madrid, 1920), pp. 11–13.

social 'revolution from above'. The Duque del Infatado had warned in 1918 that the monarchy and conservative institutions would be overthrown in a violent convulsion unless a real effort were made to improve social conditions.[69] And, in the heydays of anti-syndicalist repression, a progressive bourgeois, Rafael Gasset, warned that only social reforms could still dam the approaching Soviet avalanche.[70]

In effect, the assertion of Social-Catholicism after 1920—the *Partido Social Popular* was then formed—and its formula of social reforms was precisely an attempt 'to build a dike' against the spread of social radicalism. The PSP represented an attempt from the right to revitalize the politics of the Restoration. Inspired by the Italian Partito Popolari, the founders of the PSP—people from the ACN de P, ex-Traditionalists, and Mauristas of the kind of Ossorio y Gallardo—dreamt of a 'modern' multi-class party, one that would not manifest its existence only on the eve of elections, but would constantly appeal to, and mobilize, the masses. Absorbing as it did a moderate brand of regionalism, the PSP was also an attempt to curb the growth of radical regionalist groups. In the span of time that the PSP was allowed to operate, before the Dictatorship came to anaesthetize Spanish politics, it undoubtedly exhibited an intense degree of political activity. It was the only non-leftist group in the country to seriously indulge in mass politics in the months that preceded Primo de Rivera's take-over. It definitely was the most meaningful challenge to the Canovite system from the right.[71]

The challenges of the post-War crisis had also brought to bear upon the political class in Madrid the message that the prospects of survival of the Canovite system might be determined by its ability to cope with a changing society, if only because the electorate was becoming far less manageable than in the past. True, the disintegration of the dynastic parties into personalistic factions did not make the task any easier. But it was the gradual withdrawal of the ministry of the interior from election-'making', and the objective difficulties that it encountered in forcing its will upon an increasingly

[69] Frederick Pike, *Hispanismo 1898–1936* (University of Notre Dame Press, 1971), pp. 252–5.

[70] Rafael Gasset, *La humanidad insumisa. La revolución rusa, el problema social en España* (Madrid, 1920), pp. 243–51.

[71] Oscar Alzaga Villaamil, *La primera democracia cristiana en España* (Barcelona, 1973), pp. 141–246, 231, 255; José Montero, *La CEDA. El catolicismo social y político en la II republica* (Madrid, 1977), vol. i, pp. 9–88, 551, vol. ii, p. 99.

independent electorate, that determined the crisis of adaptation of the system.[72]

El Sol's dream of having in Spain 'political groups composed of clear heads and executive temperaments, free of fetichisms for the old, quick to cut out decayed institutions, ossified structures, prejudices'[73] did not materialize. But the political system was nevertheless showing a greater degree of responsiveness to public opinion. The proposal of the Romanones government in 1919 to concede an autonomous regime to Catalonia was a bid for the integration of the Catalan middle classes in the national political system.[74] Simultaneously, Romanones made a *démarche* towards the working class by decreeing the eight-hour day, and by pledging to set up arbitration committees where 'all the workers' aspirations could be satisfied'.[75]

In view of the need to preserve the Canovite system through measured changes, the Conservative Dato made his own bid for making it acceptable by the left. When he formed, in May 1920, his own government, he set out to promulgate some social and labour legislation. For the first time a ministry of labour was created in Spain, the CNT was again allowed to operate legally, and many of its arrested militants were set free. But as the leftist wing of the Catalan bourgeoisie had wrecked Romanones's attempts at a political conciliation with Catalonia, so did the bitter social reality in Barcelona Dato's *démarche*. The scale of the social conflict was not such that could be solved by cosmetic reforms. Dato's conciliatory policies soon changed into repressive tactics. Both the Catalan and the social issue remained a standing invitation for a would-be saviour of the *patria* to 'solve' them.

The same was true of the Moroccan problem. Dato's assassination in March 1921 was followed by the formation of a colourless Conservative government that was to witness, three months later, one of the most undignified military defeats in the annals of Spain's colonial history. The collapse of the Melilla military command left on the fields around Annual the corpses of more than 9,000 Spanish

[72] The British ambassador was impressed to see that 'for the first time in many years elections uninfluenced by official pressure were held in Spain', quoted in S. Carr, p. 249. For the post-war elections, see Martínez Cuadrado, *Elecciones y partidos políticos de España 1868–1931* (Madrid, 1969), vol. ii, pp. 799–816, 820.

[73] *El Sol*, 7 Oct. 1918 quoted by Meaker, *The Revolutionary Left*, p. 119.

[74] Pabón, *Cambó*, vol. ii, pp. i, 15–17.

[75] See the decrees of 15 March and 3 April, 1919 in *Legislación sobre la jornada máxima de 8 horas* (Instituto de Reformas Sociales, Sección de Legislación y Publicidad, (Madrid, 1924), pp. 3–10.

soldiers slaughtered by Abd-el-Krim's Rifian rebels, and deserted by many of their officers.[76] 191 million pesetas were spent by the government in Morocco in 1920, a year later, it was 519 million; 35 per cent of the national budget was then consumed by the army.[77] Inefficiency, corruption, and embezzlement of funds undermined the army's performance in the protectorate.[78] Another 'government of concentration' was now formed under the senior statesman of Spanish politics, Antonio Maura. But it failed to elaborate an effective Moroccan policy that could both please the army and still the increasing clamour for an investigation into the 'responsibilities' of the 'disaster'. Maura stepped down in March 1922 in favour of his Conservative colleague Sánchez Guerra. His was the seventh Conservative government in less than four years, and like its predecessors, it lacked a workable parliamentary majority.

Sánchez Guerra's rule, however, was characterized by a discernible responsiveness to leftist pressure. In Catalonia, he aroused the anger of the Catalan employers by sacking Martínez Anido and inaugurating a highly conciliatory approach towards the syndicalists,[79] whose unions were again permitted to operate freely. As for the Moroccan issue, he made a significant step towards conciliating leftist opinion by casting upon parliament the task of investigating the 'responsibilities' of the Moroccan disaster. Yet the Conservatives' reluctance to look into the civilian responsibilities, as opposed to the military shortcomings that they were ready, albeit half-heartedly, to punish, eventually paved the way for the formation in December 1922 of García Prieto's government of 'Liberal concentration'.

More than anything else, it was the clamorous campaign by liberals and Socialists for the investigation into the 'responsibilities' of the political establishment that had now brought the Liberals to power. Unacceptable as it certainly was to conservative and military opinion, this original sin was not unrelated to the fact that García Prieto's cabinet eventually turned out to be the last constitutional government of the monarchy.

[76] Francisco Bastos Ansart, *El desastre de Annual. Mellila en Julio de 1921* (Barcelona, 1922); D. Woolman, *Rebels in the Riff* (Stanford, 1968), pp. 80–102.

[77] Bruguera, p. 368.

[78] See, for example, Rafael López Rienda, *El escándalo del millón de Larache* (Madrid, 1922).

[79] Oller, pp. 150–6.

CHAPTER I

The Stage is Set

'The ruling classes conceded universal suffrage only as long as they could manipulate it. Little by little the people began to wake up, we began to know that a nation called England and another called France existed; we were starting to read and learn something. But in a rather exotic way, without proper schools or education, so that we were only able to guess the value of the vote. When we discovered it, they took it away and brought in the Dictatorship of Primo de Rivera, which lasted seven years.'

Juan Moreno, a sixty-four-year-old (in 1973) shoemaker in an Andalusian village: Ronald Fraser, *The Pueblo. A Mountain Village on the Costa del Sol* (London, 1973), p. 50.

'Remember the 13th of September 1923! Parliament was then starting to behave like a parliament!'

Juventud. Revista semanal, 23 Feb. 1930.

1. *The System and its Enemies*

THE pronunciamiento of Primo de Rivera came precisely at a moment when the parliamentary system was showing signs of becoming genuine, thus turning parliamentary politics into a real threat to the monarchy's previously undisputed position and to the prerogative status of the military.

The Cortes of 1923 exercised its functions with greater conscientiousness and energy than at any time since the Restoration. It was precisely when the government was displaying, in the words of the Socialist Prieto—certainly no friend of the prevailing system—'an exquisite and extraordinary respect towards the sovereign function of parliament',[1] and the Cortes was about to apply, in the words of a Socialist communiqué, 'the double principle of publicity and responsibility for everyone without any exception, thus assuming

[1] Prieto's speech on 21 November 1922 is in Indalecio Prieto, *Discursos fundamentales* (Madrid, 1975), pp. 64–5.

effectively a democratic function that so far had been exercised as a sarcastic sham'[2] that its life was ended abruptly. The parliamentary debate on the 'responsibilities' for the defeat at Annual was, again according to Prieto, 'a symptom of the redemption of Spanish parliament'. The radical republican Eduardo Ortega y Gasset went even further. The debate on the 'responsibilities', he said on the morrow of the *coup d'état*, did not reflect merely an institutional improvement of the Spanish parliamentary system, rather it represented a process of 'national maturity' and a 'profound purification' curtailed by the military.[3] An avowed democrat and the president of the Cortes, the Reformist Melquiades Álvarez, saw this fundamental betterment in the work of parliament expressed in every field of its activity. He thought that the Cortes' plenary sessions in which the 'responsibilities' issue was debated did 'honour to the parliamentary regime'. 'The Cortes', he said, 'started to acquire the sense of being an organ of opinion on the very morrow of their formation.'[4] Which is why, the republican Marcelino Domingo rightly argued, 'the Cortes became too rebellious an institution for the autocratic powers'.[5]

Authoritarian minds and hard-liners observed indeed with dismay how the unprecedented vigour and efficiency of Socialist opposition within parliament and in street gatherings was being alarmingly successful in undermining authoritarian policies, a success well reflected, as the Socialist Teodomiro Menéndez put it proudly, in the dismissal in October 1922 of Martínez Anido, and his chief of police, Arlegui, and in the very designation of the 'responsibilities committee'. The *coup d'état*, he concluded, did not emerge simply in order 'to expel old political parties from office', but in order to nip in the bud a promising process for Spanish democracy.[6] The vociferous campaign that from the spring of 1922 was being led by

[2] Andrés Saborit, *Julián Besteiro* (Mexico, 1961), p. 247. For a similar view that Primo de Rivera caught the parliamentary system in the middle of a promising process of democratization, see Práxedes Zancada, *Los problemas constitucionales de España* (Madrid, 1930), p. 265.

[3] Unamuno Archive: Eduardo Ortega y Gasset to Unamuno, 3 Dec. 1923. Eduardo Ortega, *España encadenada. La verdad sobre la Dictadura* (Paris, 1925), p. 507.

[4] *ABC*, 5 July 1923; Joaquín Maurín, *Los hombres de la dictadura* (Madrid, 1930), p. 133.

[5] Quoted in Ramiro de Maeztu, *Liquidación de la monarquía parlamentaria* (Madrid, 1957), pp. 11–15.

[6] *XII Congreso del partido socialista obrero español, 28 de junio al 4 de julio de 1928* (Madrid, Gráfica Socialista, 1929), p. 74.

Socialists, Communists, Anarcho-syndicalists, and Republicans in public meetings, through the press, and in the Cortes, where the faults of the military command, accused by *El Socialista* of 'civil cowardice',[7] and of the political establishment in the 'disaster' of Annual were being investigated,[8] brought conservatives to forecast 'grave difficulties' for the regime.[9] The Partido Social Popular warned that if the 'responsibilities' committee continued to unleash 'rebellion and despair'—the leftist Catalanist Luis Companys had just called for a campaign that would 'sweep away all of you, together with the king'—a solution would have to be found to the crisis either 'from within or outside parliament'.[10]

That the Cortes—once generally considered a docile and 'manageable' institution—should have engendered such an anti-establishmentarian protest was a rather novel phenomenon, and no wonder that 'a deep hatred towards parliament' should have developed in conservative circles.[11] An outstanding conservative, Gabriel Maura was in a position to observe that it was the modernizing trends in parliamentary politics that were responsible for turning the constitutional machine into a 'rickety and useless' apparatus. 'Not only was the numerical superiority of the government's supporters becoming tinier and tinier because of the persistent and considerable diminution of the influence, once almost omnipotent, of the ministry of the interior', he wrote, 'but also a more accurate estimation of Spanish life prevented the confusion of the parliamentary majority with the national.'[12]

What really happened was that the 'two-party system' no more represented, assuming that it ever had, the complex political and social expectations of a changing society. And, even when governmental

[7] *El Socialista*, 31 Aug. 1923. Among the members of the 'responsibilities' committee there were staunch anti-dynastic figures such as Prieto, Marcelino Domingo, and Fernando de los Ríos: *ABC*, 11 July 1923.

[8] For the pacifist campaign of the Socialists, see the reports on monster gatherings in *El Socialista*, 31 Aug., 1, 3, 7, 9 Sept. 1923. For the Socialist pressure in the 'responsibilities' committee, see *ABC* 4, 7 July 1923. For the leftist campaign for 'responsibilities', see also Marcelino Domingo, *¿Qué espera el rey?* (Madrid, 1930), p. 11; Meaker, *The Revolutionary Left*, pp. 437–8. The Ateneo, a liberal, intellectual club, initiated sharp debates on the same issue; see, for example, Cándido Ruimar, *¿Quién mató a Meco?* (Ateneo de Madrid, conferencias pro-responsabilidades, 13 de junio de 1923).

[9] *ABC*, 11 July 1923. See also La Cierva's speech in *ABC*, 4 July 1923.

[10] Companys in *ABC*, 5 July 1923; the PSP in *La Acción*, 28 July 1923.

[11] Carlos Blanco, *La Dictadura y los procesos militares* (Madrid, 1931), p. 3.

[12] Gabriel Maura, *Bosquejo histórico de la dictadura* (Madrid, 1930), p. 9.

coercion was exerted elections ceased to produce amenable majorities. Public opinion, as the British ambassador observed, was becoming aroused to take a real interest in questions of internal politics, 'and has unmistakably made itself felt'.[13] Therefore, governments would have to rely increasingly on reformist programmes rather than on an exclusive dispensation of official favours in order to survive.[14] The rule of the Liberal Bloc, that governed the country under the leadership of Premier García Prieto during the nine months that preceded Primo de Rivera's take-over, was indeed characterized by its attempts to respond to popular demands. This last government of the constitutional monarchy was actually brought into power to respond to, as the prime minister put it, the pressures of 'Spanish opinion that is increasingly determined to see us exacting ministerial responsibilities'. This 'vehement desire' of the public, explained the deputy Álvarez Valdés, could no longer be ignored. Even a die-hard conservative such as La Cierva had to acknowledge that the whole issue of the 'responsibilities' had 'the virtue of elevating the spirit of the people'. He feared, though, that the government's policies were 'too leftist'.[15]

It embarked indeed upon a process of democratization and reform alarming vested interests. The Reformist platform of Melquiades Álvarez was for the first time incorporated into a government programme. The reforms now proposed included an agrarian law, which the Socialist minority in parliament, now strongly committed to agrarian reform in order to placate its increasing rural membership,[16] made every effort to advance. Santiago Alba, the controversial foreign secretary in this government, had been since 1916 pressing for a fairly radical land reform. His idea was to introduce a fundamental tax reform, especially affecting large urban and rural properties, that would expand agricultural production and create funds for social reforms. García Prieto's government tried in 1923 to give a renewed momentum to this democratizing drive.[17] Its agrarian projects, however, were to pass into oblivion together with democracy.

[13] The ambassador quoted by S. Carr, p. 283.

[14] Martínez Cuadrado, *La burguesía*, pp. 376–81, 402–11, 416.

[15] See a report on the Cortes' plenary session in *ABC*, 4 July 1923.

[16] E. Malefakis, *Agrarian Reform and Peasant Revolution in Spain. Origins of the Civil War* (Yale University Press, 1970), pp. 159–60.

[17] For the attempts at agrarian reform in the years 1917–23, see ibid., pp. 432–6; and Costedoat-Lamarque, pp. 112–15.

The reformist zeal of the government produced also a radical proposal such as taxation of extraordinary war profits. This was also a motion already advanced by Alba when he acted as finance minister in 1916. It was obviously seen as an onslaught of the representative of agrarian–Castilian interests, Santiago Alba, on Catalan big business. In 1916 the motion was withdrawn thanks to the clamorous protests of the Catalan business community and to the strong parliamentary position of the Lliga.[18] Its return to the agenda in 1923, when the political power of Catalan capitalism was clearly in eclipse, was bound to increase the Lliga's feeling that it could no more defend the vital interests of Catalan capitalism by means of traditional politics.

Nor were reform proposals such as the establishment of the freedom of cults, a suffrage reform introducing proportional representation, a new scheme of public works to be financed by a more judicious tax system, a democratization of the Upper House, and a legalization of all labour organizations palatable to vested interests.[19] As far as the Upper House was concerned, the idea was to transform it into some kind of corporative Chamber as a means of curbing the hegemony of the big landowners who had only recently blocked a proposal of the Lower House aimed at fighting the colossal scale of tax evasion in the countryside.[20] It was now also proposed that the government should no longer be allowed to decree the suspension of constitutional guarantees without the previous consent of parliament. Both Alba and the Minister of Labour, Chapaprieta, seemed to be opting for a social-interventionist policy, which the former claimed was inspired by Lloyd Geroge's social liberalism. Proposals such as obligatory arbitration, and the *Instituto de Reformas Sociales*' demand to allow the workers a share in their employers' profits, as well as to have the latter contributing to a fund for workers' obligatory retirement, were all viewed with alarm by business sectors. The IRS, some claimed, 'is disturbing the peace of Spain'.[21] The proposal to abolish religious education altogether and to tax religious

[18] Joseph Harrison, 'Big Business and the Failure of Right-Wing Catalan Nationalism, 1901–1923' in the *Historical Journal*, vol. 19, no. 4 (1976), p. 912.

[19] For the government's reform programme, see García Venero, *Santiago Alba, monárquico de razón* (Madrid, 1963), pp. 172–7; Zancada, pp. 268–9.

[20] Calvo Sotelo, *Mis servicios al estado. Seis años de gestión* (Madrid, 1931), p. 255.

[21] Pierre Malerbe, 'España entre la crisis económica de posguerra y la Dictadura' in *Cuadernos*, pp. 66–8, 81–2.

property was viewed by the right as an inadmissible breach of Article XI of the constitution, upon which a delicate equilibrium between Catholics and liberals had rested for the last fifty years. This, and García Prieto's emphasis on the need to 're-establish a respect towards the freedom of conscience', were utterly opposed by the king, who succeeded in staving off the anti-clericalist projects of the government.[22]

But, whatever the practical results of the government's new deal—and they were, admittedly, meagre—,they succeeded in arousing the fears of conservatives. An organ of the *Unión Patriótica* was to recall in 1926 that the anti-religious proposals of this government were an unbearable onslaught on 'the Church's privileges', that in itself justified the *coup d'état*. Alba would be long remembered as the initiator of an offensive against 'religion, property, and the army'.[23] It was not decay, but reform and change, that was on the agenda when Primo de Rivera put the lid on the constitutional regime. García Prieto's government represented a most clear-cut, albeit, frustrated, essay at a democratization of the Spanish monarchy.[24]

The king, a central pillar of the Canovist system, was not too happy with the transformation of Spain's political machine. He was increasingly disturbed at the loss of control by his governments over the election-'making' process.[25] Alfonso had been for years exhibiting absolutist tendencies. He developed a strong desire to rule without parliament, a rigid undemocratic court etiquette, and a sickly admiration for the army, in the promotion of whose officers he was the major arbiter.[26] This he had done, as a parliamentary committee alleged in 1931, not unjustly, in order to mobilize the

[22] Zancada, pp. 268–9; Alcalá-Zamora, *Memorias* (Barcelona, 1977), p. 82.

[23] *Unión Patriótica*, no. 3, 1926; *Patria Española. Todo por Dios y para Dios*, 7 Sept. 1928.

[24] Tusell, *La crisis*, pp. 16–20, challenges the democratization thesis. It is not argued here that the Liberal government had a massive support of opinion, but rather that its policies were clearly directed at breaking beyond its traditional narrow power bases. Natalio Rivas—the cacique of the Alpujarras—on whose memoirs Tusell bases his view is right on one essential point. He considered the plans of García Prieto's government 'excessively radical' (Tusell, op,cit., p. 17). For a defender of the *caciquista* system they were indeed.

[25] Ortega y Gasset observed at the time that this was further pushing the king to adopt reactionary postures. See Javier Lalcona, *El idealismo político de Ortega y Gasset* (Madrid, 1924), pp. 206–7.

[26] E. Ortega, pp. 22–23; Alcalá-Zamora, pp. 74–7. See also Burgos y Mazo *¿De la república a . . . ?* (Madrid, 1931), pp. 20–30, relating his experience as a minister.

army's support for his aspiration to establish himself as an absolute ruler.[27] This impatience with the parliamentary system increased after 1921. Parliament, he believed, had seriously obstructed the material development of the country, and, by cutting the army budget, was responsible for the disasters in Morocco. One of the most remarkable utterances of a constitutional monarch is undoubtedly that made by King Alfonso in a speech in May 1921. 'Parliament', he said, 'is not living up to its duties . . . There is profuse debate in which the desire to improve the project does not appear, but rather the desire that it shall not prosper, for the better service of political purposes . . . '. 'It may be thought by those who hear me', he reckoned, 'that I am infringing upon the constitution . . . I feel the necessity for the provinces to start a movement in support of the king.'[28] A year later, in a speech in Las Palmas, the king reiterated his views in no less emphatic terms.[29]

These remarkable speeches helped cultivate the image of the king as a patriotic martyr kept captive by a bunch of corrupt politicians, from whose treacherous hands it was necessary to rescue him if the country was to be saved.[30] No one was to put it in a more figurative way than Primo de Rivera himself. 'The thick net of grasping politics has caught, indeed sequestrated, even the royal will in its meshes', he was to write in his manifesto.[31] In a speech to the Barcelona garrison in 1922, the king almost invited it to come to his rescue, and 'become the spark which moves the whole army'.[32]

Yet it seems clear that what motivated King Alfonso to flirt with an extra-parliamentary 'solution' was the resurrection of Spanish parliamentarism rather than its degeneration. The public debate on 'responsibilities' and Socialist anti-Alfonso propaganda—the most violent expression of which was Prieto's unprecedentedly bitter denunciation of the king in a much publicized speech on 17 April 1923[33]—could not but become an unbearable nuisance to the monarch. The projected session of the Cortes on 2 October 1923 to

[27] Romanones, *Notas*, pp. 242–55.

[28] *The Times*, 2 Feb. 1924.

[29] H. Vallotón, *Alfonso XIII* (Madrid, 1945), p. 142. His anti-parliamentarian views were deeply held; see Pedro Saínz Rodríguez, 'Educación de Alfonso XIII' in *ABC*, 16 Apr. 1978.

[30] *La Acción*, 26 Feb. 1923.

[31] *La Vanguardia*, 13 Sept. 1923.

[32] Robert Sencourt, *Spain's Uncertain Crown* (London, 1932), pp. 326–7.

[33] Indalecio Prieto, *Con el rey o contra el rey* (Mexico, 1972), pp. 201–63.

deal with the responsibilities committee's report, presumably incriminating the king himself, was a nightmare to him.[34] Julián Besteiro, a member of the committee, was later to reveal in an interview to *The New York Times* that his committee saw solid documentary evidence of the king's 'responsibility' in the Moroccan disaster. This was the reason, he believed, the king 'invited' the Primo de Rivera '*à la Mussolini* dictatorship'.[35] Indeed, this was presumably to be the reason for the precipitate seizure by the 'pronouncers' of the Picasso Committee archives on the morrow of the *coup d'état.*[36] For the first time since the Restoration, parliament and one of its committees had simply become incompatible with the royal will, was later to note General López de Ochoa, himself a member of the conspiracy that wiped out parliament with the cry of 'Long Live the King!'[37]

Yet the popular rebellion on behalf of the longed-for royal dictatorship was not forthcoming, and Alfonso had to cultivate the traditional anti-constitutional devices. In July 1923, he told a minister, Salvatella, that 'it is going to be very difficult to prevent the formation of a military government that should be free of those obstacles that hinder, for certain actions, the work of constitutional government'.[38] A month later, the king openly confessed to Antonio Maura his readiness to lead a *coup* personally.[39] No wonder then that the would-be 'pronouncers' should have looked to the king as a potential accomplice in their schemes to overthrow the parliamentary system. How else could the bizarre meeting between the monarch and the future 'pronouncers', in which the latter briefed him on their plans, ten days before they rose in arms, be explained?[40]

Members in the so-called 'military family' had reasons of their own to despise the parliamentary government. They were extremely

[34] Indalecio Prieto, *De mi vida, recuerdos, estampas, siluetas, sombras* (Mexico, 1968–70), vol. i, pp. 158–9.

[35] *Hojas Libres*, Nov. 1927. This view is widely accepted by contemporaries. See, for example, Joaquín Chapaprieta, *La paz fué posible. Memorias de un político* (Barcelona, 1972), p. 135; and *La Libertad*, 13 Sept. 1923.

[36] *The Times*, 25 Sept. 1923. General Picasso had conducted a thorough investigation of the Moroccan 'responsibilities'. His report was expected to be the basis for a parliamentary debate.

[37] López de Ochoa, p. 43.

[38] *ABC*, 19 Sept. 1930; E. Ortega, p. 43. Alcalá-Zamora, pp. 90–1, says the king also approached him when he was minister of war.

[39] G. Maura, *Bosquejo*, pp. 20–1, 27.

[40] The king told Austen Chamberlain about this meeting with the generals; see FO/371/10593/Rumbold to MacDonald, 28 Mar. 1924. See also Guillermo Cabanellas, *Militarismo y militaradas* (Madrid, 1933), pp. 93–4.

unhappy with the fact that the full weight of the 'responsibilities' campaign had been, so far, felt exclusively by the military, a complaint that was also echoed by the civilian, 'patriotic' supporters of the army.[41] The famous Picasso Report had exposed the faults of a great number of officers in the Annual disaster. At the beginning of January 1923, Colonel Francisco Jiménez Arroyo had been condemned by the superior military court to eighteen years in prison for negligence during the Moroccan campaign; a few week later, General Navarro was put on trial on similar charges; and, simultaneously, the military courts in Melilla had been passing severe verdicts on many other officers. Among others, General Echagüe, the chief of the Melilla military command, was dismissed from his post.[42] Generals Dámaso Berenguer, whose brother Federico was an important figure in Primo de Rivera's conspiracy, and Cavalcanti, also a key member of the conspirators' inner circle, were both expecting trial for their 'responsibilities'.[43] The army as such had every reason to put an end to the 'responsibilities festival'. The military organ *La Correspondencia Militar* expressed the state of mind of the army over the unfair deal the military were getting:

> The major problem of our rulers of today and tomorrow is that of restoring to the nation its confidence in her army, and closing the gulf between the military and public opinion . . . It is essential to prevent a repetition of the disaster; this can be done only by punishing those who brought it upon us and then failed to take due vengeance. But, *all* should be punished and not only those who have already expiated part of their guilt through captivity and martyrdom.[44]

Indeed, the appointment by the government, in July 1923, of a parliamentary committee to investigate the responsibilities of the 'various ministries'[45] was an unavoidable response to the pressing need to bridge the dangerous breach that was developing between civilians and the military.

But the aversion of the 'military family' towards the whole idea of 'responsibilities' reflected, in fact, a wider protest against the hegemony exercised by 'civilian criteria' in the running of public affairs, especially the Moroccan war. In other words, theirs was a

[41] *La Acción*, 31 July 1923.
[42] Mask, *Hacia la España Nueva* (Madrid, 1925), p. 94.
[43] Victor Ruiz Albéniz, *Las responsabilidades del desastre. Ecce Homo . . .* (Madrid, 1922), pp. 522-30.
[44] *La Correspondencia Militar*, 4 Feb. 1923.
[45] *ABC*, 7 July 1923.

protest against the threat to their privileged position, a threat inherent in the democratization of the Canovite system, and in the civilian priorities advanced by the government. The military had been conducting an unrestrained campaign against both the 'eternal petty politics' and 'politicians' as a whole during the months that preceded the *coup d'état*. Alba, the Minister of Foreign Affairs, was singled out for his pacifist policy in Morocco, and for depriving the army of the post of high commissioner in the protectorate, a post which he gave to a politician, Luis Silvela. The failures of Mr Alba, warned the military, 'will drag the government to perdition'.[46]

The military, both in Morocco and in the peninsula, felt deeply humiliated by the fact that, rather than by a military operation, their brothers in arms were ransomed from Abd-el-Krim's prisons by the huge sum of four million pesetas. A group of Artillery officers at the Madrid garrison responded to the humiliating deal with a manifesto calling for an attack on Alhucemas Bay as a retaliation against Abd-el-Krim's treatment of the Spanish prisoners. The Captain-General of Madrid, General Orozco, did not disavow the rebelliousness of his officers; in fact, he endorsed it publicly. 'What happens', he said to the press, 'is that there exists in the army a mood of displeasure because of the commentaries that are publicly being made of its faults.' Rather than opening an 'honourable' outlet to the army's grievances, the government further oppressed its 'dignity' by a special royal order stipulating that no military operation the commanders in Morocco thought necessary could be undertaken without the previous consent of the civilian high commissioner.[47]

Moreover, the government made it clear that the Moroccan issue did not occupy the highest priority in its plans. 'We should look first at the problems of the peninsula before diverting our attention beyond the straits', said the government's official communiqué on 6 April 1923, and it went on: 'We should condition the accomplishment of our international commitments [in Morocco] to the previous fulfilment of our obligation towards Spain and the Spaniards here in the interior.'[48] High Commissioner Luis Silvela dealt an additional blow to the revanchist aspirations of the *Africanistas* and their

[46] *Ejército y Armada*, 2, 4, 8, 14 Aug. 1923. For the new civilian emphasis on the running of the protectorate, see also Romanones, *Responsabilidades políticas del antiguo régimen* (Madrid, third edition, n.d.), pp. 114–15.

[47] *Gaceta de Madrid*, 20 Feb. 1923. For the military's agitation at this time, see *Folletín de El Sol* (henceforth *Folletín*), pp. 5–9.

[48] *El Sol*, 6 Apr. 1923.

patriotic admirers in the peninsula when he spelled out that it 'it was up to the Majzen, rather than the Spanish army to impose itself in Morocco'. 'In sum', he added, 'what is more important now is to stress that we are for a policy of pure protectorate' as opposed to one of military occupation.[49]

The mood of the *Africanistas* was understandably becoming one of exasperation and rebelliousness, and some of them even had expressed their sympathy with Mussolini's March on Rome. They enjoyed the support of 'patriotic' entities in the peninsula such as *Acción Ciudadana*, whose manifesto of 12 February 1923 had accused the government of treason, and called for an end to 'the paralysis of our military forces by superior orders'.[50] For ardent *Africanistas* to abandon Morocco was as calamitous as 'succumbing to the secessionist pressures of the Basque and the Catalan nationalists'.[51] Even in the Church one could hear voices such as that of the chief military vicar and the patriarch of Las Indias who said that a nation 'does not deserve to belong to the civilized family of nations if, cowardly and egotistically, it refuses to wash with blood the odious offence that has been inflicted upon it'. The Moroccan war was, he added, 'a sacred crusade'.[52]

The Melilla military governor confessed in a telegram to Minister of War Alcalá-Zamora,[53] following the above-mentioned royal order of 20 February, that a whole body of officers under his command was contemplating 'the most reckless and illegal enterprises'. And, like the Captain-General of Madrid, he also could not but condone his subordinates' indiscipline. 'They had become embittered', he said, 'because of the unjust attacks they have suffered.' He there-

[49] Ibid., 5 May 1923.

[50] *La Acción*, 13, 15 Aug. 1923; *El Sol*, 12 Feb. 1923. *Acción Ciudadana* was a body of counter-revolutionary action that operated under the auspices of bourgeois and Catholic organizations. Together with *Defensa Ciudadana*, created by the Marqués de Comillas to combat socialism, and *Unión Ciudadana*, closely connected to the Catholic syndicates, it was an additional display of the conservative classes' determination to defend their interests in the streets, parliamentary politics being no more instrumental. See Castillo, *El sindicalismo*, pp. 266–9, and his *Propretarios muy pobres, sobre la subordinación política del pequeño compesino* (Madrid, 1979), p. 339. The CONCA officially proposed to the king an extra-parliamentary solution.

[51] Ruiz Albéniz, *Estado actual del problema de España en Marruecos* . . . (Conferencias dadas en el Ateneo de Madrid, 29 y 31 de Mayo de 1922), p. 70.

[52] Manuel Cuenca, 'Panorama de la iglesia española del 1914, hasta el 1931', in Vicente Cárcel Ortí (ed.), *La iglesia en la España contemporánea* (Madrid, 1979), p. 328.

[53] The telegram is quoted in M. Fernández Almagro, *Historia del reinado de Alfonso XIII* (Barcelona, 1934), p. 421.

fore exhorted the government to ban the 'anti-Spanish and anti-patriotic' press campaign against the army, and to stop any further investigation into the Moroccan 'responsibilities'. It was up to the government, he concluded, to make clear before public opinion that the army had not completed its glorious counter-offensive after Annual because of explicit orders from the civilian authority, rather than because of any performance failure of the military, for which leftist opinion had been accusing them since the inauguration of the debate on 'responsibilities'.[54]

The leniency displayed by the government towards Corporal Barroso, who led, in August, a soldiers' mutiny in Málaga to prevent the embarkation of conscripts to the battlefields of the protectorate, further demonstrated the government's lack of determination over the war. It obviously infuriated the military and their 'patriotic' supporters among civilians. Primo de Rivera was later to say that his 'patriotic resolution [to seize power] was enhanced by the Málaga mutiny': 'The acquittal of Barroso made me grasp the full dimensions of the horrible abyss into which Spain had been thrown.'[55] The Málaga mutiny was seen by the military not as a simple act of insubordination. Rather, it was the reflection of the collapse of law as a deterrent, and of a general atmosphere of 'defeatism' cultivated by 'anti-patriotic separatists, Communists, and Syndicalists'. So, while military tribunals should punish the mutineers, 'military justice' should act 'also against the others', i.e. the anti-patriotic civilians. It was up to the army to educate the civilian community and to imbue it with a 'Spanish' set of values.[56] The conservative *La Vanguardia* followed suit in what was almost a wishful prediction: the vacillation exhibited by the government in the Barroso affair, it claimed, would have 'dangerous consequences in internal politics'.[57] To exasperate further the military, who feared the mutineers might 'contaminate' other sections of the army, *ABC*—whose hysterical campaign against the 'disintegration' of the state helped create the appropriate climate

[54] For an example of a sarcastic denunciation of the military, see Prieto, *Discursos*, pp. 110–16, 129.

[55] Interview in *L'Étoile belge*, 9 June 1926.

[56] *Ejército Español*, 24 Aug. 1923. The 1964 'pronouncers' in Brazil were said to be strongly motivated by the failure of Goulart's government to punish the leaders of a sailors' mutiny. That the law and the precepts of military discipline ceased to be a deterrent was an irresistible challenge for the military. See Alfred Stepan, *The Military in Politics. Changing Patterns in Brazil* (Princeton University Press, 1971), pp. 204–7.

[57] *La Vanguardia*, 2 Sept. 1923.

for the *coup d'état*—published a picture of Barroso fraternizing with two officers.[58]

Not only had the army's dignity suffered a mortal blow by the 1921 Annual defeat—in itself a sufficient reason for it to follow in the footsteps of the Greek officers that seized power (1922) after the flagrant defeat of Smyrna[59]—but also its corporate interests were clearly at stake throughout the months that preceded Primo de Rivera's take-over. This was emphatically reflected in a public communiqué by the government, at the beginning of April, in which a radical reduction of army cadres was announced. 'The country cannot sustain an army of such big dimensions', declared the government, while promising that military modernization would follow the cuts in military expenditures.[60] These cuts were anyway consistent with the government's civilian and reformist priorities. But, coming at a moment when the army's frustration was approaching its peak, this communiqué could not but be interpreted as yet an additional 'aggression' against the corporate interests of the military.

'The sad reality' was, according to a military organ, that the army's needs were being utterly neglected by the civilian authorities. 'Not even one voice in Parliament has been raised' to sympathize with hundreds of *alféreces* and lieutenants who had been for years expecting their legally deserved promotion, and with 4,000 sergeants who earned 'a ridiculous salary'. No less 'shameful', presumably, was the fact that the African army had been demanding for years in vain a more up-to-date weaponry 'to cope with the necessities of modern warfare'.[61] Small wonder that another military organ should claim, on the morrow of the *coup d'état*, that Primo's pronunciamiento was the inevitable response to the 'injustice that has been done to the army'.[62] Unamuno was later to observe accurately that this collective feeling of frustration, and the determination of the military to

[58] For the role of the conservative press in creating the climatic pre-conditions for the *coup d'état*, see Armiñán Oriozola, *Francia, El Dictador y el moro. Páginas históricas* (Madrid, 1930), pp. 27–42; and Hernández Mir, *Un crimen de lesa patría. La dictadura ante la historia* (Madrid, 1930), pp. 15–17. See also FO/371/9390, Howard to Curzon, 15 Sept. 1923.

[59] Doros Alastos, *Venizelos, Patriot, Statesman, Revolutionary* (London, 1942), pp. 220–1.

[60] *El Sol*, 6 Apr. 1923. For the cuts proposed by Alcalá-Zamora as minister of war, see his *Memorias*, p. 73. See also Mousset, pp. 317–18.

[61] *Ejército y Armada*, 18 Aug. 1923.

[62] *Ejército Español*, 13 Sept. 1923.

safeguard 'the honour of their class' had always lain at the root of their political interventionism.[63]

National issues, however, were always emphasized by the military as their cardinal preoccupation. Though frequently acting as a syndicate they preferred to pose as the altruistic champions of the national will. The vindication of Spain's honour and dignity by an offensive strategy in the protectorate seemed now to be the army's priority.

At the beginning of August 1923, a group of generals, including Primo de Rivera, now taking great pains in order to get rid of his 'abandonist' image, met at the *Casino Militar* in Madrid to manifest the army's combative mood. They supported General Martínez Anido's offensive plan for Morocco and protested against the government's damaging inactivity in the protectorate. They pointed out the growing rift between the government and the 'military family'. The army, the government was warned, 'would no longer tolerate being a toy in the hands of opportunistic politicians'.[64]

By the beginning of September, however, the government endorsed the recommendations of the General Staff, i.e. not to withdraw from the present lines in Morocco; and army circles even praised the government for 'removing the obstacles' from military planning.[65]

For a while it seemed as though military–civilian relations had entered a harmonious phase. The resignation of the Ministers Villanueva, Chapaprieta, and Gasset—all of them strong supporters of economies in Morocco and hence of a pacifist policy[66]—was hailed by *El Ejército Español*, which had not ceased to harass the government throughout the last months, as a victory for the 'highest interests of the country'. It even had warm words of praise for Alba:

> Mr Alba, more conscious of his duty as a statesman, has abandoned for the time being the project of which he had been the champion. He has demonstrated that he possesses a political sense lacking in his dissident colleagues.

[63] 'Hablemos al ejército' in *Hojas Libres*, June 1927. Political scientists argue, rather convincingly, that the defence of the military's corporate interests has been a major motive of military *coups*; see, for example, William Thompson, *The Grievances of Military Coup-Makers* (Beverly Hills, 1973), pp. 12–26, 32–9.

[64] *Ejército y Armada*, 2, 4, 8, 14 Aug. 1923; *El Ejército Español*, 21, 30 Aug. 1923. For Martínez Anido's plan, see Romanones Archive, Leg. 28, n. 9: *Plan de operaciones presentado por el general Martínez Anido al alto comisario de España en Marruecos, en 12 Julio de 1923*.

[65] *Ejército Español*, 3, 4 Sept. 1923.

[66] Chapaprieta, pp. 135–40.

As for the prime minister, he deserved 'an unconditional applause'.[67] The king, however, was rather displeased to have to interrupt his vacation in San Sebastián and come to Madrid in order to swear in the thirty-third government (altogether more than 400 ministers) of his twenty-one-year reign.[68]

But the Moroccan problem was not the only issue that separated the parliamentary government from its enemies. The constitutional regime was not really granted a breathing-space by its opponents. The conservative *ABC* preferred to see in the last ministerial crisis 'a depressing spectacle' which reflected the 'political disorientation' that characterized the whole system.[69] Armed robberies in Barcelona and Gijón, terrorism and violent separatist demonstrations in Barcelona (in which there were uttered slogans such as 'Muera España' and 'Viva la República del Rif'), infuriated, to put it mildly, the military and the 'patriots'.[70] The 'extreme criteria' that seemed to be prevailing in the committee of responsibilities[71] further fuelled the hysterical press campaign against the government. Conservative and 'españolista' organs such as *ABC* and *La Vanguardia* wrote about the 'collapse of the whole system' and attacked the 'criminal lack of patriotism' of the ministers.[72] *Ejército Español*, which a few days earlier had praised the government, now warned that 'if its feebleness goes on, it would be necessary to place upon the *good Spaniards* the task of correcting so many insults'.[73]

2. *A Terrified Bourgeoisie: Catalonia*

The 'good Spaniard' who was to save his country from 'anarchy' and redeem its national honour emerged from the tense atmosphere of Barcelona. It is indeed in Catalonia that the immediate origins of Primo's take-over should be looked for. It was there that the bourgeoisie created a hysterical atmosphere that surrounded Primo de Rivera with the halo of a 'saviour', and placed his rebellion, as a

[67] *El Ejército Español*, 3 Sept. 1923.

[68] Ana de Sagrera, *Miguel Primo de Rivera, el hombre, el soldado y el político* (Jerez de la Frontera, 1973), p. 221.

[69] *ABC*, 1 Sept. 1923.

[70] *Ejército y Armada*, 12 Sept. 1923. For terrorism and separatist demonstrations, see daily reports in *La Vanguardia*, 2–13 Sept. 1923. A separatist congress was held in Barcelona two days before the *coup d'état*, see Ramón Xuriguera, *Els Exiliats acusens* (Barcelona, 1930), pp. 155–8.

[71] *El Ejército Español*, 12 Sept. 1923.

[72] *La Vanguardia*, 6, 9 Sept. 1923; *ABC*, 7–9 Sept. 1923.

[73] *El Ejército Español*, 12 Sept. 1923.

contemporary observer had noted, in the general context of the anti-Bolshevik reaction that had overtaken other European countries as well.[74] Cambó, a genuine representative of the Catalan high bourgeoisie, 'the theoretician of the Spanish Dictatorship', as Maurín called him,[75] put in blunt terms his class's yearning and responsibility for the Dictatorship:

The Spanish dictatorship was born in Barcelona and was the product of the ambience of Barcelona where syndicalist demagogy possessed an intolerable intensity and chronicity. All the normal ways of defending society and all the conventional measures of government have failed to cope with this syndicalist demagogy . . . A society in which the demagogic avalanche puts in grave danger ideals and interests would submit itself to anything in order to feel protected . . . The instinct of life and defence would be given first priority, and the troubled society would clamour for a dictator, it would demand him unconditionally; it would not even ask him to serve or respect its ideal. It would only ask him to maintain order, to secure the possessive state . . . or a degree of civilization that the demagogic surge threatens to devour.[76]

This does not mean, however, that there was a real danger of social revolution on the eve of Primo's take-over. The *trienio bolchevista* had resulted in the virtual liquidation of Anarcho-syndicalism as a potential revolutionary threat. Moreover, 1923 was the first year since the end of the War to witness clear signs of economic recovery. Thus, for example, Spain's minero-metallurgic production started to approach again the high levels it had reached during the boom years of the War. The coal output which fell to its lowest level in 1922 (4,776,000 tons) surpassed in 1923 the 1919 peak, reaching the figure of 6,323,000 tons. A similar promising trend occurred in the production of iron ore (1922—3,240,000 tons; 1923—3,954,000), lead (1921—168,000 tons; 1923—182,000), cement (1921—540,000 tons; 1923—863,000), and copper (1922—25,539 tons; 1923—45,266). The value of the whole minero-metallurgic production in Spain which had reached its peak in 1919 (1,019,000,000 pesetas) and was at its lowest ebb in 1922 (751,000,000 pesetas) recovered dramatically in 1923 (1,119,000,000 pesetas).

[74] Luis de Araquistain, *El ocaso de un régimen* (Madrid, 1930), pp. 204–5.

[75] J. Maurín, p. 79.

[76] Cambó, *Las dictaduras*, pp. 144–5. Similar passages can be found in abundance also in Gual Villalví, *passim*. Cf. Alfred Cobban, *Dictatorship. Its History and Theory* (New York, 1971, first edition 1939), pp. 200, 254–7, 297–8 on the 'appropriate' atmosphere for the emergence of dictatorships.

The overall volume of production of the Biscayan mining industry went up from 1,287,301 tons in 1922 to 1,642,693 in 1923. Understandably, the shares of companies such as Altos Hornos of Biscay and Metalúrgica Duro-Felguera improved their position on the stock exchange (Altos Hornos—89 in 1922, 114 in 1923; Duro Felguera—37 in 1922, 49 in 1923). It was not only heavy industry that started to recover from the crisis. The Catalan textile manufacturers saw with pleasure how the 1921 protective tariffs had enhanced their production and improved their marketing potentialities. Improved conditions in Europe, moreover, enabled the Spanish economy to increase the volume of its exports from 1,096,000,000 pesetas in 1920 to 1,319,747,850 in 1922 and 1,596,006,728 in 1923. It clearly seemed as though the Spanish economy was about to enter, indeed together with the whole of Europe, a period of stability and renewed expansion.[77]

The economic crisis and retrenchment of the years 1919–22 had brought about a gradual drop in the number of industrial conflicts and strikes: 1920—1,060; 1921—373; 1922—488. Retrenchment had also entailed a consistent fall in the general index of the cost of living of a working-class family: from 175.1 in October 1920 to 165.1 in September 1923. The drop in the cost of living was even more accentuated in the villages: from 185.5 to 173.3.[78] So were wages dropping, however. This and unemployment came as a logical concomitant to the slow-down in economic activity. Skilled workers might have been able in some cases to preserve their average income, but the mass of unskilled and redundant day labourers could find no comfort in the drop of prices. Moreover, those among them who lived in Barcelona, the focus of working-class agitation, had to put up with one of the highest costs of living in the country. A working-class family with two children in the Catalan capital needed in 1922 58.45 pesetas per week for a living compared with 50 in Madrid and 58.85 in Bilbao. This meant that a day-labourer had to earn per day the impossible wage of 9.75 pesetas in Barcelona, 8.33 pesetas in Madrid, and 9.80 pesetas in Bilbao.[79]

A scientific argumentation that would prove that the 'social

[77] See data on the economy in *Anuario*, 1929, pp. xx–xxvii; Tuñón, *El movimiento*, pp. 673–5. For the textile industry, see Pedro Güal, p. 228.

[78] *Anuario*, 1931, and Tuñón, *El movimiento*, p. 726.

[79] Ibid., pp. 673–81.

danger', especially after the 1923 economic recovery, was a gross exaggeration of biased conservative propaganda should not overshadow the relevancy to the search for the origins of Primo de Rivera's dictatorship of the widespread feeling, real or imaginary, among the Catalan bourgeoisie that a social catastrophe was imminent unless a dictatorship was brought to power. In Italy, Fascism came to power under similar improved conditions, and after the 'revolutionary threat' had become highly hypothetical. Moreover the March on Rome came just in time to stave off a consolidation of parliamentary government; a Socialist-Popolari coalition seemed, at long last, imminent.[80] Mussolini was the first to dismiss the 'red danger'. He said in July 1921: 'To say that a bolshevist peril still exists in Italy is to accept a few disgraceful fears as the truth. Bolshevism is beaten.'[81] But, as Trevor-Roper pointed out, Fascism was born of fear.[82] It would be likewise inaccurate to claim that Napoleon I had saved on the 18th of Brumaire the French well-to-do classes from any real extreme revolution, the danger of which had already been eliminated by the Directory. What he did, however, was to capitalize on the *fear* of a Jacobin revival. The same can be said of Napoleon III who came to power exploiting to the fullest the panic fear of anarchy and socialism which had already been crushed by Cavaignac in the 'June days'.[83] In that sense, Jacobinism and Socialism played the part which fear of bolshevism was later to play in pre-Mussolini Italy and on the eve of Primo de Rivera's seizure of power.

It was the 'red danger' that was to be prevented as the major rationale of the *coup d'état*. Against the background of conservative and bourgeois hysteria the myth had been created by Primo de Rivera's panegyrists that he took power because 'his country was threatened by the same catastrophic chaos that existed in Italy just before Mussolini took over the reins of power'.[84] The British

[80] Renzo de Felice, *Fascism. An Informal Introduction to its Theory and Practice. An Interview with Michael Ledeen* (New Jersey, 1977), pp. 58–9. G. Salvemini, *The Origins of Fascism in Italy* (New York, 1973), p. 368.

[81] Quoted by A. Rossi, 'The Rise of Italian Fascism', in N. Greene (ed.), *Fascism. An Anthology* (New York, 1968), p. 51.

[82] H. R. Trevor-Roper, 'The Phenomenon of Fascism', in S. J. Woolf (ed.), *European Fascism* (London, 1968), pp. 23–4.

[83] A. Cobban, pp. 85–8, 101.

[84] See examples of a vast literature, Martín Riumbau Lazcano, *El levantamiento militar, sus causas y efectos* (Palma, 1923), pp. 29–40; Martínez de la Riva, *Las jornadas triunfales de un golpe de estado* (Barcelona, 1923), *passim*.

Ambassador in Madrid, Lord Howard of Penrith, who too frequently used the 'Latin' and 'Spanish temperament' as a handy explanation for the complexities of the Spanish scene, did not cease to see from every corner and under any bed the imminent 'revolution from below'.[85] Primo de Rivera used this hysteria to justify his rebellion. His 'revolution', he said, came right on time to prevent 'a revolution on Soviet lines'.[86] It was, he insisted, 'the social character' of the upheavals in Barcelona that had challenged him 'to save' Spain from 'complete ruin' by means of 'drastic surgery'.[87] His panegyrists were later to sharpen this kind of argumentation: Had he not emerged to save Spain 'civil war would have ensued and a Moscow-inspired revolution . . . chaos and destruction would have been unleashed'.[88] The Bolshevik phantom was an appropriate background to Primo's *coup d'état* just as it was a fabricated décor for the March on Rome.[89] In both cases the urban and agrarian bourgeoisie welcomed the 'last-moment' salvation from the 'red' danger.[90]

In Spain, members of the Lliga and employers' organs in Barcelona had been blaming working-class rebelliousness on 'Bolshevik agitators' well before the Russian Revolution. Their fears were, if anything, exacerbated after the events of Petrograd.[91] That the final aim of Syndicalism is the instauration of a Communist regime, which was to say 'the end of civilization', as Cambó put it before a restless audience of industrialists in late 1919,[92] was a tangible common feeling among the well-to-do classes of Barcelona. 'We are marching directly towards bolshevism', such was the standard fear of the conservative classes, a Barcelona industrialist, who was later to be a member of Primo de Rivera's Council of National

[85] FO/371/9490, Howard to Curzon, 21 Sept. 1923. See also his introduction to Charles Petrie, *Alfonso XIII and his Age* (London, 1963).

[86] Quoted in FO/371/9490, Howard to Curzon, 15 Sept. 1923.

[87] Interview in *L'Étoile belge*, 9 June 1926.

[88] C. Duarte Fernando, *España: Miguel Primo de Rivera y Orbaneja (Dos palabras por prólogo de Benito Mussolini)* (Madrid, 1923), pp. 67–8. For a presentation of the *coup* as the inevitable response to the Soviet threat, see also Yanguas's prologue to E. Tarduchy, *Psicología del dictador* (Madrid, 1930), p. 15; Cimadevilla, pp. 53–5; Manuel Gandarias, *Perfiles síquicos del dictador y bosquejo razonado de su obra* (Cádiz, 1929), pp. 19–21; Mask, pp. 88–93.

[89] Roland de Mares, 'Les étapes de la dictature espagnole', in *Revue de Paris*, 1 Dec. 1927, pp. 566–7. The defenders of the old system obviously minimized the importance of the social threat; see Romanones, *Las responsabilidades*, pp. 214–15. For a sarcastic dismissal of the 'bolshevik' threat in Italy, see G. Salvemini, *Under the Axe of Fascism* (London, 1936), pp. 167–8.

[90] See pp. 81–7.

[91] S. Carr, pp. 73–4, 95–100, 189.

[92] Quoted in García-Nieto, pp. 173, 174.

Economy, remarked in 1922. Only 'strong, rigorous, repressive laws' explicitly demanded by the possessing classes in Barcelona 'out of an instinct for self-preservation' could set their minds at rest.[93] They were totally disillusioned by the way successive parliamentary governments had handled the social conflicts in Barcelona. The Confederación Patronal had explicitly demanded a dictatorship that would bring an end to the liberal practices of solving labour disputes.[94]

It is, moreover, significant to note that the reactivation of the economy, precisely in the months that preceded Primo de Rivera's take-over, had, if anything, brought about a renewed and discernible radicalization of the class struggle in Catalonia, after months of relative calm. 3,027,026 working days were lost in the first nine months of 1923, 354,459 more than in 1922, a year that witnessed thirty strikes more than in 1923.[95] This indicated that the 1923 strikes were of longer duration because of the tougher line now taken by the employers against the wage demands of, and the manifestations of solidarity by, the workers. The latter's renewed combative spirit was simply enhanced by their belief that the economic recovery was bound to improve their bargaining power. The employers rightly feared that economic prosperity, unless accompanied by dictatorial repression, might result in dramatic strengthening of the unions. In Barcelona alone there were 103 strikes in each of the years 1922 and 1923, while their number in 1921 was only 20. Moreover, most of the strikes were now 'defensive', that is, attempts by the workers to prevent the increasingly adamant employers from undermining such social achievements as the eight-hour day, or cutting wages.[96] It should also be stressed that the workers' renewed agitation was not unrelated to the fact that, as a concomitant of economic reaction, the very months that preceded the *coup d'état* witnessed a renewed, albeit slight, rise in the general index of the cost of living (from 164.2 to 165.1 in the capitals, and from 170 to 173.3 in the villages), and quite a substantial rise in the price of basic necessities such as cooking oil (from 133.3 to 137.6), sugar (from 155.1 to 164.6), eggs (from193.8 to 207.6), rice (from 139.7 to 141.4), and chick-peas (from 148.1 to 158).[97]

[93] Pedro Güal, pp. 170, 191, 196.
[94] S. Carr, pp. 253–6, 258–9, 266–7.
[95] *Avance estadístico de huelgas correspondiente al primer semestre de 1923* (Madrid, 1924), pp. 11–13; Tuñón, *El Movimiento*, p. 726.
[96] S. Carr, pp. 78–81, 86–7. This was also true of the situation in the Asturian Mines, see Shubert, 'Una revolución . . . ', pp. 110–11.
[97] *Anuario*, 1931.

The Anarcho-syndicalists in Catalonia did not limit their protest to industrial action. After the restoration of constitutional guarantees by the Sánchez Guerra government in April 1922, indeed to the dismay of the Lliga, which lost no time in withdrawing its man, Bertrán y Musitu, from the government as a protest, terrorism started to acquire such a renewed vitality that *El Sol* talked about an incurable 'epidemic of terror'.[98] So much so that the government suggested the dismissal of General Martínez Anido, the hard-line civil governor of Barcelona, referred to by the Catalan bourgeoisie as the Spanish Mussolini that would save her from the communist chaos, as the only way to appease the Anarcho-syndicalists.[99]

It is noteworthy, however, that the Lliga, though obviously delighted with Martínez Anido's policy of law and order, was increasingly at odds with the general's *españolista* zeal. To their dismay, the leaders of the Lliga started to realize that their flirtation with Martínez Anido was undermining their support among Catalanist opinion, and they therefore decided to support the government in getting rid of this idol of the conservative classes.[100] What the Lliga yearned for was a saviour that would promise it the best of all worlds, a strong-handed policy of law and order and autonomy for Catalonia. Such exactly would be Primo de Rivera's bait.

Martínez Anido's dismissal in October 1922, to the loud protests of powerful big business organizations such as, among others, the *Fomento del Trabajo Nacional,*[101] only stimulated the belligerence of the Syndicalists. In Barcelona alone there were 34 deaths and 76 injuries from *atentados* carried out in the first five months of 1923.[102] A future panegyrist of the Dictatorship, José Pemartín, admittedly willing to exaggerate the dimensions of pre-dictatorial chaos, claimed that 813 *atentados* took place in Barcelona in the nine months that preceded the pronunciamiento[103] The public impression, however, counted more than accurate statistics. For the cartoonist

[98] *El Sol*, 27 July 1922.

[99] G. Meaker, *The Revolutionary Left*, pp. 456–60. Martínez Anido's official biographer described him as 'a supporter of the national-socialist and fascist doctrine', Oller, pp. 69–70.

[100] Oller, pp. 120–1, 129.

[101] Joseph Harrison, 'Big Business', p. 917; Oller, pp. 122–8; 164–5.

[102] *Folletín*, p. 11; Oller, pp. 131–6, 175.

[103] José Pemartín, *Los valores históricos de la dictadura española* (Madrid, 1928), p. 96. Stanley Payne, *The Spanish Revolution* (London, 1970), pp. 57–61, calculates as 154 the number of killings in the first ten months of 1923. Bainville, p. 227, exaggerates in speaking of 320 employers killed in Barcelona in 1923.

of *El Sol*, 'Saint Gunman' had become the unholy 'patron of Spain'.[104] The general transport strike of May–June 1923[105] in Barcelona was an additional manifestation of the Anarcho-syndicalists' renewed vitality.

It was, moreover, fairly evident that, in the CNT, the terrorist line represented by *Los Solidarios* group of Durruti, Ascaso, and García Oliver, though rejected as an overall strategy in the Zaragoza national congress, was now asserting itself.[106] This was well reflected in the swelling wave of *atentados*. The assassination of Cardinal Soldevila and of the governor of Bilbao, Regueral, and the assault of the Bank of Spain in Gijón acquired special notoriety. The assassination of Soldevila in Zaragoza, the stronghold of *Los Solidarios*,[107] was a climactic point in the violent struggle between employers and Anarcho-syndicalists, especially as Soldevila was identified as the protagonist of a strong-handed policy against social extremism.[108] The process of renewed radicalization in the CNT had already become evident in September 1922, with the removal of the CNT's National Committee from Barcelona, where the moderate line of Pestaña and Seguí prevailed, to Zaragoza where the extremists held the upper hand.[109] This radicalizing process was obviously enhanced by the assassination in March 1923 of Salvador Seguí, the moderate and anti-terrorist leader of the CNT.[110]

When Primo de Rivera rose in arms on behalf of 'law and order' not only had terrorism acquired a renewed vitality, but the CNT was certainly being torn apart by tensions between irreconcilable extremists and compromising moderates.[111]

[104] Ana de Sagrera, p. 208. [105] See below, pp. 51, 52.

[106] For the tendencies in the CNT in the years that preceded the *coup d'état*, see Gerald Meaker, 'Anarquistas contra sindicalistas: Conflictos en el seno de la Confederación Nacional del Trabajo, 1917–23', in Stanley Payne (ed.), *Política y sociedad en la España del siglo XX* (Madrid, 1978), pp. 45–107. The 'political' wing led by Seguí and Peiró received a set-back in Zaragoza.

[107] For *Los Solidarios*, see Abel Paz, *Durruti. Le peuple en armes* (Bordeaux, 1972), pp. 53–71. See also Carlos Forcadell, 'El asesinato del cardenal Soldevila' in *Tiempo de Historia*, IV, no. 47, Octobre 1978, pp. 19–21.

[108] Loc cit., pp. 16–23. For Soldevila's wishful prediction of a *coup d'état*, see *Heraldo de Aragón*, 5 June 1923. [109] Brademas, p. 19; Carlos Forcadell, p. 19.

[110] Anarcho-syndicalists tend to claim that the employers' federation was responsible for the assassination, as it was interested in encouraging the extremists in the CNT. Only thus could the pre-conditions for an authoritarian take-over be properly created. See, for example, Adolfo Bueso, *Recuerdos de un cenetista* (Barcelona, 1976), pp. 169, 175–6. A similar claim is advanced by Maurín, p. 133.

[111] Angel Pestaña, *Lo que aprendí en la vida* (Madrid, 1934), pp. 100–1, 186–9. Pestaña laid the blame for the advent of the Dictatorship at the door of the terrorist wing.

'Law and order', 'as the best guarantee for business', was indeed the cry that sprang from the ranks of the Catalan conservative classes,[112] a cry which accompanied and contributed to the collapse of the government's 'soft' policy. 'Too many crises', 'excessive atomism', 'an urgent need to have new and honest men in politics', 'an assault on the Salisachs firm', 'aggression against the agent of a depot', 'alarm at the Paralelo', 'the government fails to find an adequate civil governor for Barcelona', 'guns found in a Church'—this is a sample of headlines in *La Vanguardia*, a Barcelona conservative organ, and *La Veu de Catalunya*, the Lliga's mouthpiece, whose editorials had been undermining throughout the last months the government's authority by a systematic and overdone exposure of its 'feebleness' and its 'criminal lack of patriotism'.[113] Following a series of *atentados* in March 1923, the *Jaimistas* of Barcelona warned that 'since the facts demonstrate that we cannot rely upon the powers that be . . . we are willing to take justice into our hands and to deliver a hundred blows for every one dealt to us'.[114] In such a violent atmosphere, the judicious and compromising attitude of the new Civil Governor, Sr Raventos, an attitude so strikingly at variance with that of his tough and pro-employers predecessor, Martínez Anido, was condemned to a resounding failure. The employers managed to get rid of Raventos by completely avoiding any contact with him while looking to Captain-General Primo de Rivera for guidance and salvation.[115] With an even more emphatically pro-working-class policy, the new Civil Governor, Sr Barber, fell short of succeeding where his predecessor failed. The pressure of the employers on behalf of martial law[116] could not but increase once Barber declared, at the beginning of June, that unless the several-month transport strike that had paralysed the city and immersed its streets in garbage was ended by an agreement he would hand over to the workers the transportation system in order to reactivate the city's life.[117] The thousands of *Somatenistas* and employers who booed Barber as the 'agent of the Sindicato Único'

[112] A. Jutglar, *Els burgesos Catalans* (Barcelona, 1966), p. 345.
[113] *La Veu de Catalunya, La Vanguardia*, 15 Aug.–12 Sept. 1923.
[114] Quoted in *Folletín*, p. 11.
[115] A. Lerroux, *Al servicio de la república* (Madrid, 1930), pp. 216–18.
[116] Maurín, p. 133. See also a survey of the employers' relations with the civil governors in *Folletín*, pp. 11–12.
[117] The strike finally died out because of the workers' exhaustion, see Bueso, p. 177.

during the funeral of a *somatenista* murdered the day before[118] manifested clamorously their rejection of the legitimacy of orders emanating from any civilian authority representing the constitutional government, which they were convinced intervened in social conflicts always 'against capital'.[119] Prime Minister García Prieto should hardly have been surprised to see that, after Barber's removal, he could not find any candidate ready to assume the ungrateful job of the *ciudad condal*'s civil governor.[120] Barcelona had no civil governor when Primo rose to fill the vacuum of authority.

There is no special reason to think that Cambó's ferocious denigration of the Spanish state in October 1919 ceased to reflect the real mood of the Catalan bourgeoisie in 1923. He then said, amid the clamorous ovations of his audience of industrialists in the Palacio de la Música Catalana:

> The performance of the state has been characterized by its incongruity, a constant incongruity in its policy, directed to cajole, stimulate, exploit the Syndicalist—mainly when it sees him as a means to weaken . . . Catalan spirituality. Today neither the workers nor the employers have any confidence in the state. They all want to exploit it; none wants to serve it; and everybody is tired of having served it in the past . . . I accuse, gentlemen, the public power of the state for the violence created here in Catalonia . . . Today in Catalonia, we have the feeling that any power that does not spring from here is not ours . . . The State, gentlemen, with its performance, disturbs us.[121]

The panic-stricken high Catalan bougeoisie was thrown into a defensive posture in the months that preceded Primo's take-over. Under the stress of class warfare and the dangers to its vital interests, the Lliga accelerated its drive to strengthen its links with a 'strong', counter-revolutionary Spanish state while relegating its autonomist aspirations to a secondary position. This left the flag of autonomism available for more popular and extreme forces to hoist. The Lliga's position as the hegemonic political power in Catalonia was being

[118] *La Vanguardia*, 9 June 1923.

[119] Maura, *Bosquejo*, p. 17.

[120] *La Voz*, 12 Sept. 1923.

[121] Quoted in García Nieto, *Bases documentales . . . Expansión económica y luchas sociales*, pp. 178–9. Even before the post-War crisis had pushed the Catalan bourgeoisie to assume combative postures, Cambó made remarks in the following vein: 'The public power that is being imposed on the nation is a synthesis of impotence and unconsciousness'; see Francesc Cambó, *Actuació regionalista* (Barcelona, Publicacions de la Lliga Regionalista, 1915), p. 7. For similar utterances in 1922 see Pedro Güal, *passim*. Likewise, a manifesto issued by the Federación Patronal on 5 September 1919 blamed the government for the 'present situation of social disorganization'; quoted in Solá Cañizares, *Luchas sociales*, p. 44.

persistently undermined by a more extremist brand of Catalanism, which tried to divorce the movement from its early conservative garb, and to acquire a wider social base than the plutocratic foundations upon which the Lliga rested.[122] This was a development that could hardly increase the Lliga's confidence in its ability to preserve its hegemonic position in the area. Nor did it add to the peace of mind of those *españolistas* who now saw 'the material dismemberment of the grand patria' as closer than ever.[123]

The electoral strength of the Lliga had been on the decline since 1918. It then gained 57.7% of the Catalan votes. In June 1919 it lost 10% of its strength, and in February 1920 a further 9%. It recuperated in December 1920 (64.4%), but only thanks to the divisions and the abstention of its enemies. It dropped again in February 1923 (46.11%). In the April 1923 general elections it suffered an additional set-back. It was also defeated in the elections to the Barcelona *Diputación Provincial* in June, Acció Catalana and Lerroux's Radicals obtaining three seats each while the Lliga scored only two.[124] Humiliated and frustrated, Cambó, the Lliga Chief, resigned from parliament and, indeed, from any overt political activity. 'The hostility aroused by me, and which adversely affects the fortunes of the Lliga' had compelled him, he said, to quit politics.[125] Faced with 'social chaos', having lost its political hegemony in Catalonia to lower-middle-class extreme Catalanism, and frustrated by its inability to influence the Madrid government into conducting a Lliguista policy in Catalonia, the Lliga had nothing to expect from 'politics'. On the other hand, the would-be dictator, Primo de Rivera, promised the best of all worlds: autonomy, high tariffs, and social order.[126] The 'crisis of parliamentarianism' and the need to 'interpret' the national will rather than just 'represent' it, were soon to become standard concepts in the Lliga.[127]

In his pathetic defence of his father's memory in 1933, José

[122] For Acció Catalana, see Bofill i Mates, *Una política catalanista* (Barcelona, 1933), pp. 7–14, 40–2. For Estat Català, see A. Maseras, *La nostra gent. Francesc Macià* (Barcelona, n.d.).

[123] Benito Mariano Andrade, *Castilla ante el separatismo catalán* (Madrid, 1921), p. 5; Magdaleno de Castro y Hernández, *Nacionalismo, humanismo y civilización (La constitución interna de España y la ideología catalanista)* (Madrid, 1922).

[124] Tuñón, *El movimiento*, p. 696; S. Carr, p. 273; García Venero, *Historia del nacionalismo catalán* (Madrid, 1967), vol. ii, p. 301.

[125] Pabón, *Cambó*, vol. ii, pt. i, p. 449; Gaziel in *El Sol*, 30 Oct. 1925.

[126] See Puig i Cadalfach in *La Veu de Catalunya*, 27 Feb. 1930.

[127] Luis Durán y Ventosa, *Los políticos* (Barcelona, 1928), pp. 17–18, 41–3.

Antonio Primo de Rivera did not fail to point out the collective responsibility of the privileged classes, in Catalonia and elsewhere, to the coming of the Dictatorship. 'The privileged classes', he said, 'saw the coming of the dictatorship with jubilation. They realized that their beloved old *políticos* were too weak an instrument to cope with the changing times; and they expected the rule of a general to strengthen that which certain people call by the name of order.'[128] The breakdown of business, social chaos, and a genuine awareness of their weakness and disorganization combined to popularize among Catalan businessmen the idea that, as a textile industrialist put it in 1922, 'we need a dictatorship to restrain the exuberance of present society'.[129]

The 'illegitimacy' of the government cannot but be stressed in the eyes of the would-be pronouncer once he realizes the erosion of the government's image among the politically minded and economically powerful community. Primo de Rivera would later argue that on 13 September he was nothing but the tool of 'the public sentiment that prevailed at the time' and of the 'general judgement' according to which the government was exercising power 'weakly and sluggishly'.[130] Probably few are better suited than Melquiades Álvarez, the leader of the constitutional Reformist Asturian bourgeoisie, to demonstrate the dimensions of the legitimacy erosion suffered in the eyes of the middle classes, by the constitutional regime on the eve of Primo de Rivera's seizure of power. He declared in a speech by the middle of 1922:

> Everything in Spain is in crisis, everything is crumbling, from the sovereign authority of power down to military discipline . . . Above rules arbitrariness; below, disorder; violence everywhere . . . Profaned, sneered at a thousand times the constitution by the government . . . Little by little the eclipse of the constitutional regime is being prepared.[131]

Under such conditions, he would view the Dictatorship as an

[128] *Acción Española*, 16 Mar. 1933, p. 101.

[129] Pedro Güal, pp. 141–3. It was this basic weakness of the bourgeoisie that had caused it to abandon liberalism in order to espouse the cause of authoritarianism and fascism in Latin Europe. Cf. 'John Brown', 'The Legitimacy Problem in Latin Europe' in Gwyn Harries-Jenkins and Jacques van Doorn (eds.), *The Military and the Problem of Legitimacy* (London, Beverly Hills, 1976), p. 60; Franz Neumann, 'Notes on the Theory of Dictatorship' in his *The Democratic and the Authoritarian State* (The Free Press, Glencoe, 1957), p. 250.

[130] Miguel Primo de Rivera, 'The Last Four Articles', *The Times*, 20 Mar. 1930.

[131] César González Ruano, *Miguel Primo de Rivera, La vida heróica y romántica de un general español* (Madrid, 1935), pp. 63–4.

inevitable 'heroic measure to prevent a social threat'.[132] His participation in the 1923 reformist government was Melquiades Álvarez's contribution to slow up the slide towards dictatorship.

Alarmed liberals such as Melquiades Álvarez, or, for example, a nucleus of friends on the editorial board of the Liberal organ *El Imparcial*, who had been pressing for a civilian dictatorship, did not reject out of hand the prognosis of conservatives, such as Gabriel Maura, who believed 'an efficient authority' would be welcomed by public opinion even if that entailed 'a temporary loss of civic liberties'.[133] On the right, the PSP had advanced, in January 1923, the idea of a civilian dictatorship that should rest on the combined forces of the Lliga, Maurismo, and Social Catholicism. The Social Popular leader, Ossorio y Gallardo, did not discard the possibility that his party might even welcome a fascist solution. When the civilian dictatorship failed to materialize, *El Debate*, the patron of the PSP, openly demanded a military one.[134]

The representatives of the Catalan bourgeoisie, at least, did not wait passively for the Dictatorship to come as *deus ex machina*; but rather actively contributed in paving its way. Puig i Cadalfach, the Lliguista president of the Catalan Mancomunidad, was indeed to confess that 'we believed that the captain-general would resolve the problem of public order, and helped him'.[135] They helped him, according to a well-informed Gabriel Maura, by financing his preparations for the *coup*,[136] for which he even promised them ministerial posts.[137] Eduardo Ortega y Gasset, a passionate opponent of the Dictatorship, was even more explicit.[138] He wrote that, on the eve of his *coup d'état*, Primo met at the Front Romeu hotel in Barcelona the Lliguista magnates Puig i Cadalfach and Junoy. They promised him the support of the Catalan plutocracy in exchange for a promise to protect their industries and to meet Catalonia's aspiration

[132] See his introduction to Carlos Blanco, pp. xiv–xvi.

[133] Maura, *Bosquejo*, p. 10. See the contacts made throughout 1923 by a group on the editorial board of *El Imparcial* on behalf of the implantation of a civil dictatorship in José Félix Huerta, *Sobre la Dictadura* (Madrid, 1930), pp. 37–69.

[134] For the PSP, see *El Debate*, 13 Jan. 1923. Ossorio in Soldevilla, *Año político 1923* (Madrid, 1924), p. 111. *El Debate*, 6 July 1923 (on military dictatorship).

[135] Isidre Molas, *Lliga Catalana* (Barcelona, 1972), vol. i, p. 146. For the Lliga's help, see also Aiguader, *Cataluña y la revolución*, pp. 28–9; Xuriguera, pp. 106–7; García Venero, *Historia del nacionalismo catalán*, vol. ii, pp. 306–10.

[136] G. Maura, *Bosquejo*, p. 33. See also Emilio Mola, *Obras completas* (Valladolid, 1940), p. 53; Eduardo Ortega, pp. 59–61.

[137] This was confirmed by the Lliguista leader Ventosa i Calvell in *El Sol*, 21 June 1930.

[138] E. Ortega, pp. 327–32.

for autonomy. In a later meeting at Junoy's villa in Puigcerdá a treaty was allegedly signed between both sides. It was approved at an additional meeting in Barcelona in which the Catalan magnates were represented by such figures as the opulent Vizconde de Cusso (the president of the powerful industrialists' confederation Fomento del Trabajo Nacional), Marqués de Comillas, one of the wealthiest personalities in Spain, who throughout the night of the *coup d'état* would not move from Primo de Rivera's side,[139] and the Conde de Güell, and Milá y Camps. Whether such concrete arrangements did actually take place is hard to prove. What is beyond reasonable doubt is that there did exist a profound affinity between Primo de Rivera and the Catalan upper classes that made such arrangements feasible.[140]

That a political party should inspire, and even be an active accomplice in, a *coup d'état* was actually an inherent characteristic of the Spanish pronunciamiento throughout the nineteenth century.[141] The present one, however, was backed, in fact carried to power, by a clearly defined class: the upper Catalan bourgeoisie, the same class that in 1898–9, being in a deep crisis of confidence, claimed 'the country wants a real dictatorship, it detests parliamentarianism'. Then, it failed to enthrone its hero, General Polavieja, as a national leader. Primo de Rivera was a modern and more determined version of Polavieja.[142] He harboured, moreover, a rather novel hope; in case his *coup* failed through lack of military support, he believed an anchor of salvation could be found in the Catalan bourgeois militia, the Somatén, the commander of which was to be a member of the inner circle of the conspiracy.[143]

Primo's alliance with the Catalan bourgeoisie, it should be noted,

[139] García Venero, *Torcuato Luca de Tena* (Madrid, 1961), p. 298; *Historia del nacionalismo catalán*, pp. 306–7. For the Marquis's counter-revolutionary activities, see Castillo, *El sindicalismo amarrillo*, pp. 253–73; Miguel Cascón, *Luz sin sombra. El Marqués de Comillas* (Comillas, 1926).

[140] See also Fernández Almagro, *Catalanismo y república española* (Madrid, 1932), p. 116; Isidre Molas, p. 146. Only Durán i Ventosa among the Lliga's leaders did not support the *coup*. The Fomento del Trabajo tried to curb local protests against Primo's performance as captain-general lest the government followed the pattern applied to Martínez Anido, and dismissed him; see S. Carr, pp. 278–9.

[141] Julio Busquets, *El militar de carrera en España* (Barcelona, 1971), p. 45; Mola, p. 951.

[142] For Polavieja and Catalan big business, see J. Romero Maura, *La rosa de fuego. El obrerismo barcelonés de 1898 a 1909* (Barcelona, 1975), pp. 20–3, 27.

[143] Santiago Alba, *Para la historia de España* (Artículos publicados en Mayo de 1930 por *El Sol*), p. 22. For the commander of the Somatén, see below. p. 55.

was sealed by his promise to provide Catalan industry with high protective tariffs.[144] This was precisely one of the reasons why the industrialists had been alienated from the last constitutional government, which had negotiated the reduction of tariffs on products imported from Belgium, Norway, Switzerland, Great Britain, Germany, France, and the USA, with the view of favouring the average consumer.[145] Such a tariff cut amounted to a revolutionary reversal of the pro-Catalan tariff policy of the post-War years, a policy best reflected in the tariffs elaborated throughout 1921 by the *Junta de Aranceles y Valoraciones* in close collaboration with Cambó. It protected almost hermetically both light and heavy industry in the region to the detriment of the average consumer, merchants, as well as the exporters of agricultural products. *El Imparcial* spoke on behalf of the latter when it equated 'the catastrophe of the new tariffs' with the Moroccan disaster.[146] Inevitably, however, the 1921 tariffs were the most precious and ferociously guarded conquest of Catalan industry. Had it not, for the first time since the end of the war, increased national consumption in such proportions that 'all of our production was absorbed' as a textile manufacturer confessed?[147] This was also true of the Basque heavy industry, thanks to Cambó's tariffs no longer threatened by Belgian and German competition.[148] It can hardly be surprising that the Barcelona Chamber of Industry protested bitterly against the revision of Cambó's tariffs. It accused the government of abandoning the interests of industry in favour of 'the pitiful agriculture and the so-called interests of the consumer'.[149]

A couple of days after having seized power, Primo de Rivera was frank enough to say in a press conference that his commitment to a high tariff policy was a major reason for his *coup d'état*. The Liberal government's drastic reduction of tariff rates was such a 'criminal' decision, he said, that in itself 'justified whatever we have done' and especially 'our decision to dissolve the Cortes', which had ratified the 'criminal' tariffs.[150]

[144] López de Ochoa, p. 27.

[145] *The Economist*, 26 Nov. 1927; FO/371/9490, Howard to Curzon, 21, 29 Sept., 31 Oct. 1923; Azaña, *Obras*, vol. i, p. 547. See the protest of the Lliga against the new tariffs in *ABC*, 11 July 1923.

[146] See the pamphlet by Blas Vives, *La Política arancelaria de España* (Madrid, 1928); *Libertad*, 4, 10 Oct. 1921; Mousset, pp. 323–41 (quotes *El Imparcial* on pp. 326–7).

[147] Pedro Güal, p. 228; S. Carr, p. 274.

[148] Baelen, pp. 28–3, 105.

[149] Joaquín Juliá, *El proteccionismo y sus resultados* (Madrid, 1924), p. 39.

[150] *El Sol*, 18 Sept. 1923; Alba, *Para la historia*, p. 24.

3. *The Viceroy of Catalonia*

Primo de Rivera's position as a potential 'saviour' of Spain was established only after the candidature of General Aguilera, the president of the supreme military court, had been eliminated, at the beginning of July, when the Conservative leader, Sánchez Guerra, slapped him for insulting the honour of civilians.[151]

The immediate reaction of the military was to rally round their insulted colleague. Some seemed to have called for a manly bid to save military honour, and, as Aguilera's house was inundated by high-ranking officers, conspicious among whom were the four generals who were to be Primo's main supporters in Madrid, the Captain-General Muñoz Cobos had to warn the officers of the capital's garrison against indulging in rebellious activities.[152] Aguilera himself said that now it was up to 'people from outside parliament' to step in and solve the crisis. The severe verdicts passed by military courts against officers 'responsible' for the Moroccan disaster had initially turned General Aguilera into the uncrowned caudillo of the protest movement, so much so that he boastfully warned the government that he was followed by the whole nation. His commitment to seize power was becoming common knowledge, and early in July Deputy Arsenio Martínez Campos denounced in parliament the conspiracy he said was being prepared under Aguilera's auspices.[153]

Yet, finally, the would-be pronouncers realized they could not rely on a general whose fame rested on his unyielding punishing spirit against his military colleagues. Nor was Aguilera's 'soft' attitude towards civilians, so illustratively and, indeed, so ludicrously manifested in the 'slap affair', indicative that he was made of the stuff real 'pronouncers' are made of.[154] The cool relations that were said to exist between the king and Aguilera[155] were not instrumental either in consolidating the general's position as the potential leader of the impending *coup d'état*.

A 'strong' general was now available in Barcelona in the figure of Captain-General Muñoz Cobos had to warn the officers of the

[151] *La Correspondencia Militar*, 5 July 1923. [152] *ABC*, 6 July 1923.

[153] *Diario de Sesiones del Congreso de los Diputados*, 5 July 1923.

[154] For the significance of the 'slap affair' in ruling out Aguilera's leadership of an imminent 'eighteenth of Brumaire' (this was Romanones's term: see his *Notas de una vida*, p. 210), see *El asunto Sánchez de Toca-Aguilera* (Madrid, Imprenta de 'El Financiero', 1923); Ricardo de la Cierva, 'La dialéctica de las bofetadas' in *Historia y Vida*, no. 12, March 1969.

[155] FO/371/9498, Howard to Curzon, 15 May 1923.

Andalusian city of Cádiz in 1870 into a military family. His formation was completed in the atmosphere of the *ancien régime*, in whose social circles he had moved congenially and from whose practices of favouritism he had profited in order to advance his military career and his political ambitions. Levantine, non-respectful, undisciplined, bold, 'populachero', and unable to dominate his own passions, he was now about to act as the 'iron surgeon' of twenty million Spaniards to whom he would promise regeneration, renovation, and discipline. He had been a senator on behalf of the Conservative Party, and later he failed to get the 'blessing' of the Liberal cacique in Cádiz to stand again for a seat in the Senate. In 1917 and again in 1921 he made public his abandonist posture towards the Moroccan protectorate. He thought of some deal in which Spain would exchange its North African possessions with Gibraltar,[156] an idea that had been toyed with also by some British naval experts.[157] 'To have a soldier on the other bank of the straits entails a strategic weakness for Spain', he said on 25 November 1921. Such remarks cost him in 1917 the military command of Cádiz and in 1921 the captain-generalcy of Madrid. Yet he stuck to his abandonism. In February 1923, he had even supported Alba's 'undignified' peaceful release of the Spanish prisoners held by Abd-el-Krim.[158]

It is therefore fairly evident that Primo de Rivera could hardly be considered as the potential champion of a combative, annexationist policy in Morocco. That he nevertheless became the leader of a conspiracy among whose members there were generals such as F. Berenguer, Saro, Dabán, Cavalcanti (this 'quadrilateral' formed the Madrid branch of the conspiracy), and Sanjurjo, all of whom were conspicuous in their support of an offensive policy in the protectorate, was due to his ability to play down his abandonist posture once he began to conspire[159] just as he did to his centralist spirit when he came to seal his alliance with Catalan autonomism.

[156] M. Primo de Rivera, *Recuperación de Gibraltar* (Madrid, 1917).

[157] R. Gay de Montellá, *Valoración hispánica del mediterráneo* (Madrid, 1952), pp. 323–5.

[158] For Primo's Moroccan postures, see Armiñán Oriozola, *Espistolario del dictador* (Madrid, 1930), p. 129; Araquistain, p. 215; Alba, *Para la historia*, p. 15. For a complete biography, see Ana de Sagrera. All the existing biographies of Primo are highly eulogistic and frequently unreliable. For a brief portrait, see Rafael Salazar, 'Perfil humano de Primo de Rivera', in *Historia y Vida*, iii, no. 22 (1970), pp. 58–65.

[159] General Cándido Pardo González, *Al servicio de la verdad* (Madrid, 1931), pp. 359–60; Hernández Mir, *Un crimen* pp. 30–1.

But a serious confrontation with militant *Africanistas* over his fundamentally 'abandonist' strategy would finally break out during the bloody compaign of 1924 in the protectorate.[160] On the issue of 'responsibilities', however, he did not need to pretend. He was as determined as anybody else to stop the vindictive campaign against his fellow officers,[161] the members of what he himself used to call 'the caste'.

But, to say the least, Primo de Rivera's wavering posture over the Moroccan issue indicates that the sort of expectations that he might have embodied were of another kind. He was the only general among the conspirators with a civilian power base and with the halo of a tough protagonist of 'order'. Since the middle of 1918 he had been urging a determined policy against the civilian 'enemies of the patria'. Spain's major problem did not lie in Morocco but, as he wrote on 18 June 1918, in the fact that 'the whole national body is sick of laxity and faintness'.[162] It was during his service as captain-general of Valencia in 1920, as he later confessed, that working-class radicalism ('of a revolutionary, communist colour') 'terrified' and first brought home to him the message 'about the necessity to Spanish politics of methods different from the usual'. The 'atmosphere of pessimism and demoralization' that overtook Valencia's middle classes and 'the shameful and painful anarchy' his 'poor country' had been thrown into filled the captain-general 'with shame', because he felt he represented an impotent authority.[163]

On 14 March 1922, he became captain-general of Barcelona, where the renewed vitality of terrorism, especially following the dismissal of the 'tough' Martínez Anido and Arlegui, helped turn the flamboyant captain-general, who professed to cater to the needs of the Catalans, into a combination of Mussolini and Polavieja. He did not lose any time in seconding the business community's protest against the dismissal of Martínez Anido.[164] He won immediately, acting as if he was a viceroy—as the Socialist Prieto called him in parliament—the full support of the Catalan bourgeoisie for his uncompromising attitude against terrorism.[165]

[160] See below, pp. 112–13.

[161] Ana de Sagrera, p. 207.

[162] Quoted in ibid., p. 189. See also M. Primo de Rivera, *Opinión emitida ante un redactor del periódico El Ejército Español con motivo del orden público en los actuales momentos* (Guadalajara, 1919).

[163] Primo de Rivera, 'The last four articles', *The Times*, 20 Mar. 1930.

[164] Oller, p. 165.

[165] *ABC*, 4 July 1923. See also Alba, *Para la historia*, pp. 6–7.

During the transport strike in Barcelona, Primo de Rivera's popularity among the 'law and order' classes in the Catalan capital reached its peak. Wherever he went through the city people would look out from their windows and applaud him enthusiastically.[166] He would later write when recalling those days: 'What should I say of the mood of those who only in me had put their confidence inciting me to do something, to proceed in whatever manner so long as I release Catalonia from the hell that so evidently threatened it?' He took great pains to persuade the government against solving the strike in favour of workers. He was thus, he believed, 'faithfully interpreting the feeling of Barcelona that viewed [the strike] not as an economic issue, but as a clearly revolutionary enterprise'.[167] Primo's role during the transport strike—a strike that was started when the employers refused to honour the May Day Sabbath—was hailed by the Barcelona Chamber of Industry as totally opposed to the 'destructive' attitude of the government in Madrid. Primo was becoming the anchor of salvation of a business community that chose to see in the recent labour conflict 'a monstrous campaign of hatred' being launched by the working class.[168] That Primo de Rivera became the would-be saviour of the Catalan bourgeoisie was anything but a secret; and as early as March 1923 the Anarcho-syndicalists in Barcelona were talking of a general strike to stave off the imminent seizure of power by the captain-general in the name of his bourgeois clients.[169]

It should be noted, moreover, that Primo de Rivera's 'abandonist' positions in Morocco coincided conspicuously with those of the Catalan business for whom Morocco represented a burden, rather than an economic asset, which they were reluctant to sustain with their taxes. Cambó opposed the massive expenditures in a non-remunerative protectorate as much as he was aware of the radicalizing influence of the war upon working-class militancy.[170]

In June, a month after his ambition to become the Liberal senator for Cádiz—a position from which he might have expected to move

[166] His private secretary, José Ibáñez, as quoted by Ana de Sagrera, pp. 202–3.

[167] Ibid., pp.204–5. See also Primo's article in *The Times*, 20 Mar. 1930.

[168] For the strike, see *ABC*, 6, 7 July 1923; S. Carr, pp. 178–82, 285–6.

[169] Pardo González, vol. i, p. 361.

[170] For the attitude of Catalan business, see S. Carr, p. 285. The fall of Maura's government in March 1922 had been actually precipitated by Cambó's tough opposition to the plan of landing at Alhucemas Bay: see José Ramón Alonso, *Historia política del ejército español* (Madrid, 1974), p. 482.

into the ministry of war—had been thwarted by *caciquista* manipulations, Primo was summoned to Madrid by the government to be told that he should stop undermining the government's policy in Catalonia as faithfully executed by Civil Governor Barber. Primo's claim that only a declaration of Martial Law would end the transport strike, terrorism, and separatist demonstrations was rejected out of hand by the government which, however, lacked the stamina to dismiss the restless general.[171] That on his return to Barcelona from this visit to Madrid Primo de Rivera was enthusiastically acclaimed by an ecstatic crowd, the Somatén bourgeois militia, and 'the highest personalities of Catalan life'[172] was further reflective of the fact that Catalonia had become the anti-government power-base of this would-be saviour of Spain.

The failure of Primo de Rivera's mission to Madrid meant that there was no way, short of overthrowing it by force, that the constitutional government could be diverted from its policy of class conciliation in Catalonia, or indeed from its reformist path and its bid to apply new standards of accountability to the running of public affairs. It certainly refused to succumb to the captain-general's pressure, on behalf of his Catalan clients, to endorse repressive measures against the unions and, probably, legalize a possible resurrection of Martínez Anido's practices. Parliamentary politics had, then, failed to cope with the social menace as they had with the Moroccan problem, and with the threat to the integrity of the patria. If these burning issues were to be tackled efficiently, parliamentary politics should be done away with altogether.

[171] *Folletín*, p. 13.

[172] Ana de Sagrera, p. 204.

CHAPTER II

The Seizure of Power

1. *The Technique*

WHILE in Madrid, Primo started, as he later wrote, 'to conspire in broad daylight'. He met the king and Generals Saro, Dabán, Federico Berenguer, Cavalcanti, and the Duke of Tetuan, who were then still hoping that Aguilera would lead them into a seizure of power. And, in Zaragoza, on his way back to Barcelona, he managed to enlist the full support of General Sanjurjo, the military governor of the Aragonese capital.[1] Major Cruz Conde was appointed to be the liaison officer between Primo and Sanjurjo, for which he would be later compensated with the mayorship of Córdoba.[2] On 23 June Primo was back in Barcelona. As soon as he settled in his office at the captain-generalcy he started to write to his most intimate friends in garrisons all over the country. The answers when they came were anything but encouraging. 'Look, Ibáñez,' said the would-be dictator to his private secretary in those days, 'in order to rise I do not need to be followed more than by a cavalry squadron.'[3] In subsequent visits to Madrid, he strengthened his links with the 'quadrilateral', though he failed in his endeavour to enlist Aguilera. He also found the time to make a short and mysterious trip to San Sebastián, where the king was having his vacation.[4] On 7 September, on his way back to Barcelona from his last visit to Madrid, he again met Sanjurjo to tie up the last strings.[5]

The final preparations were now under way. He managed to enlist generals with command in Catalonia, like Barrera and López de Ochoa, as well as General Mercader, 'a courtier and an intimate friend of the king'.[6] These, in addition to Sanjurjo and the 'quadrilateral' in Madrid, were the only officers fully committed.

[1] Emilio Esteban-Infantes, *Sanjurjo* (Barcelona, 1958), pp. 68–9.

[2] E. Ortega, pp. 85–96.

[3] Quoted in Ana de Sagrera, p. 204.

[4] The information on this trip comes, however, from a source hostile to both Primo and the king, López de Ochoa, who participated in the conspiracy but later became disenchanted with the new regime; see his *De la Dictadura*, pp. 22–6.

[5] Primo describes his preparations in his posthumous articles in *The Times*, 20 Mar. 1930.

[6] López de Ochoa, p. 26.

Primo de Rivera's agents to other military posts in Spain and in the protectorate were met with a reserved sympathy towards the idea of establishing an *ad hoc* military regime, but with no operational commitments.[7] In the case of the prestigious senior General Weyler, an uncompromising rebuff was the answer.[8] As for the army of Africa, Primo was said to have briefed it about his plans 'out of comradeship and courtesy', but without asking it to intervene in his 'political movement'.[9] At last, Primo de Rivera decided to cast the die in what looked like a calculated gamble. He 'pronounced' on the morning of the 13th of September, thus advancing his plan by twenty-four hours.

The main reasons for the advancement of the *coup* were that the conspiracy was no longer a secret. Primo himself had a few days earlier briefed Spain's ambassadors in the main European capitals of his intentions;[10] Minister of Labour Portela Valladares was on his way to inaugurate a furniture exhibition in Barcelona and probably to prevent the *coup* everyone in the Catalan capital knew was scheduled for 15 September; and the Minister of War, General Aizpuru, had even tried to dissuade Primo in a telephone call. However, Aizpuru, an intimate friend of the rebellious general[11] did not make any serious effort to curb Primo's activities. Furthermore, he seemed to have deliberately provided the 'pronouncers' with arguments against the government by recommending an amnesty for Corporal Barroso, who had led the soldiers' mutiny in Málaga against the Moroccan campaign.[12] Last but not least, the separatist demonstration held in Barcelona on the occasion of Casanova's annual homage on 11 September, in which the Spanish

[7] Hernández Mir, *La dictadura en Marruecos. Al margen de una farsa* (Madrid, 1930), pp. 37–8; Pardo González, vol. i, p. 364; Cabanellas, p. 96.

[8] Julio Romano, *Weyler. El hombre de hierro* (Madrid, 1934), pp. 179–86.

[9] Alfredo Kindelán, *Ejército y política* (Madrid, 1947), p. 195.

[10] FO/371/9490, Howard to Curzon, 21 Sept. 1923. Diplomatic exchanges, even before the *coup* takes place, aimed at assuring the continuity of the country's international relations are frequently resorted to by *coup*-makers. See Edward Luttwak, *Coup d'État. A Practical Handbook* (Penguin Books, 1969), p. 214. Romanones knew of the *coup* well in advance. See his *Notas*, quoted in Tomas Echeverria, *Sobre la caída de Alfonso XIII* (Seville, 1966), p. 440.

[11] Ana de Sagrera, p. 205.

[12] Chapaprieta, p. 44. López de Ochoa, an active conspirator, claims Aizpuru was also a member of the conspiracy; see his *De la Dictadura*, p. 29. Primo was later to promote him as a reward, see Armiñán Oriozola, *Epistolario*, p. 115. For Aizpuru, see also the verdict of the Republic's responsibilities committee, *Las responsabilidades políticas de la Dictadura. Un proceso histórico . . . La sentencia* (Madrid, 1933), pp. 112–13.

flag was ostentatiously abused, incited the general to act immediately, before it was too late to stave off the separatist tide.[13] How could Primo de Rivera remain passive, a panegyrist of the Dictatorship was later to write, when a Catalan figure such as Rovira i Virgili claimed in a public rally that 'we do not want to be Spaniards'?[14]

On 12 September, then, Primo's sister, María, summoned for 9.30 a.m. the conspirators in Barcelona to her brother's office. Six generals—among them the military governor César Aguado Guerra and his chief of staff Juan Gil y Gil, the Commander-in-chief of the Somatén Plácido Foreira Morante, and López de Ochoa—eleven colonels and one lieutenant-colonel were there to receive the final instructions.[15] Subsequently, at dawn, September the 13th, the garrisons of the four Catalan provinces declared martial law and took over the main telephone exchanges in the area.[16] At five o'clock in the morning the civil government building was seized without any difficulty and General Losada, the military governor of Barcelona, immediately took over the functions of the civil governor. Actually, the porter was the only person on the spot, and he handed the keys willingly to the troops.[17] A similar scenario was enacted in the Aragonese capital, Zaragoza, and in Huesca: banks, prisons, telegraph and telephone centres were seized without any opposition being displayed by the government's officials, and the civil governors were replaced by their military counterparts.[18] The Captain-General of Aragón, Palanca, was not a member of the conspiracy, but Sanjurjo persuaded him to 'abstain' from intervening against it.[19]

Primo de Rivera's manifesto 'to the army and to the nation',[20] made public simultaneously with the seizure of strategic points in

[13] Revesz, *Frente*, p. 23; Primo in *The Times*, 20 Mar. 1930. For the homage to Casanova and the tense climate it created in Barcelona, see *La Vanguardia*, 12–13 Sept. 1923.

[14] Cimadevilla, p. 35. Cambó (*España, Cataluña y la nueva constitución* (Buenos Aires, 1929), p. 24, thought that separatism helped in creating 'the propitious ambience for the *coup d'état*'.

[15] Ana de Sagrera, pp. 209–10; López de Ochoa, pp. 24–32.

[16] Archivo Histórico Nacional (henceforth AHN), Gobernación, serie A, the civil governorship of Barcelona to the minister of the interior, 13 Sept. 1923, telegram no. 443, 3.20 a.m.

[17] Ana de Sagrera, p. 214; Mask, p. 97.

[18] AHN, Gobernación, serie A: governor of Huesca to the minister of the interior, 13 Sept. 1923, no. 490, 24.00; governor of Zaragoza to the minister of the interior, 13 Sept. 1923, no. 450, 9.00 a.m.

[19] Ana de Sagrera, p. 233.

[20] *ABC*, 14 Sept. 1923.

Zaragoza and Barcelona, was imbued with the classical rhetoric of pronunciamientos while detailing, in an attempt to reflect the widest possible political expectations of the nation, the challenges to which his rebellion was a response. It was high time, emphasized the boisterous general, to save the country from the hands of those 'professional politicians' who since the 1898 'disaster' had been ruling it for their own benefit.[21]

That Alba was pointed out as the personification and the scapegoat that should pay for all the evils of the old regime, is explicable by several reasons. Firstly, the *coup d'état* originated in Barcelona where Santiago Alba was seen as the embodiment of Castilian centralism and of the policy that subjugated the Catalan economy to the 'selfish' interests of the 'parasitic' and 'moribund' centre. His 'suspicious tariff policy' and 'the orientation he gave to the commercial treaties' were unbearable in the eyes of the Dictator or rather, of his Catalan clients. 'In Barcelona, gentlemen, the atmosphere was fatal', Primo de Rivera told a reporter of *La Correspondencia de España* on the morrow of his *coup*, 'all the industrialists and merchants who came to see me complained in alarming terms against Alba. "He is a thief, he is a thief", they used to tell me.'[22] Secondly, Alba applied civilian and diplomatic criteria in his approach to the Moroccan issue, an issue the military preferred to solve 'with bayonet-thrust'.[23] Thirdly, he personified more genuinely than any other minister a determination to enable representative institutions to check the military's autonomy. (For example, he had demanded, on 29 August 1923, the dismissal of Primo de Rivera from his post as captain-general of Catalonia because of his insubordination.) Fourthly, he exhibited a tough attitude against the excessive profits of those companies which did business with the army as well as against tax evasion by religious orders. By the standards of the time,

[21] Cf. Luttwack, pp. 85, 169; the denigration of 'corrupt politicians' is a familiar element in almost every military take-over. See, for example, the manifesto of the Greek Colonels in Richard Clogg and Yannopoulos (eds.), *Greece Under Military Rule* (London, 1972), p. 37.

[22] Quotation from *Folletín*, p. 46. See also *El Imparcial*, 15 Sept. 1923; *The Times*, 19 Sept. 1923.

[23] General Franco was to relate how his soldiers in Morocco, on conquering an enemy position, did it under the cry of 'Long Live Spain! Death to Alba!'; see Tusell, *La crisis*, p. 18.

Santiago Alba was a committed and almost 'revolutionary' liberal.[24]

The illegitimacy of the government thus exposed, it had no moral claim to stay in power, and the *coup d'état* was not only fully justified but also 'legal'. 'We represent', said Primo de Rivera in his manifesto, 'the true discipline.' 'We have not conspired,' he added, 'we have hoisted in broad daylight the flag of popular aspirations.' Rather than the army's representative he was the product and the self-imposed interpreter of an anti-parliamentarian atmosphere and of a weariness with 'politics'.[25]

Primo's initial intentions, as reflected in his manifesto, would probably classify him as a 'guardian-type praetorian' who strives to stave off political change and maintain public order by controlling the government directly, though promising to return it to civilians once the 'surgical operation' has ended. Yet there were also indications in Primo's early declarations that he contemplated, albeit hesitantly at this stage, becoming a 'ruler type',[26] that is the founder of a decidedly authoritarian regime imbued with a spirit of dynamism and change, for which he would have to resort to popular mobilization, grandiose economic schemes, and the establishment of a new political legality.

He surely thought that it was the military who should rule until things were again in order and civilians 'imbued with our morality and doctrine' were found to govern 'under our protection'. This was a rather novel approach. Primo de Rivera was the first 'pronouncer' who immediately thought of ruling without the parties, and indeed paved the way for what he considered to be a new political culture. His predecessors during the Isabeline era were either the instruments

[24] Vicente Blasco Ibáñez, *Alfonso XIII Unmasked. The Military Terror in Spain* (London, 1925), p. 115; García Venero, *Alba*, pp. 179, 186; Alba, *Para la historia*, pp. 6–7, 24.

[25] The exposure of 'the legitimacy deflation' of civilian governments has been a facilitating pre-condition for the success of military *coups*. The loss of legitimacy by a constitutional government has nothing to do with its parliamentary strength; it is rather the consequence of its performance failure as exposed by the military and their noisy supporters among the civilians. For a general discussion of the problem of 'legitimacy' and the military's disposition to intervene in politics, see Eric A. Nordlinger, *Soldiers in Politics. Military Coups and Governments* (New Jersey, 1977), pp. 92–5; Jacques van Doorn, 'The Military and the Crisis of Legitimacy' in Harries-Jenkins and van Doorn (eds.), *The Military*, pp. 17–39. For Primo's declarations, see Revesz, *Frente*, p. 84.

[26] For a definition of the two 'types', see Nordlinger, pp. 21–7.

of the existing parties or their allies. They did not think in terms of breaking away from the established political system.[27] True, Primo spoke of his rule as a 'parenthesis of curing' that would last 'fifteen, twenty, thirty days', but he also promised to 'establish a new regime', and a 'new kind' of parliament, 'truly representative of the national will'. The present parliament, he said, should be closed down for ever.[28]

Yet, like most praetorians, he also believed that complex problems can be easily overcome by a head-on policy. Gordian knots should be cut rather than untied. In flamboyant medical metaphors he promised a short rule in which the treatment of the gravely ill nation would be one of 'amputating the gangrened limbs'. 'We are performing radical surgery', he said, 'but we are not physicians, and once the patient is convalescent we shall carry him to a sanatorium where he can get stronger and be definitely cured.'[29] Several urgent tasks were to be accomplished in the immediate future by a military directory: national security would be ensured by the establishment of a national militia (the Catalan Somatén being the example to imitate), and the Moroccan problem, it was vaguely promised, would get a 'swift, worthy, and sensible solution'.

Whatever his final intentions might have been, during the 13th and the first hours of the 14th of September, Primo was fully aware of his military isolation, 'for not having taken the pains to consult even the most characteristic generals or the most sensible section of the officer corps', as General Queipo de Llano put it. Queipo himself was approached by fellow General Montero, to counter-pronounce against Primo.[30] General Muñoz Cobos, the captain-

[27] Cf. F. Fernández Bastarreche, *et al.*, 'El acceso de los militares al poder político', in J. M. Jover, *Historia de España. La era Isabelina y el sexenio democrático (1834–1874)* (Madrid, 1981), pp. 521–50.

[28] *ABC*, 15 Sept. 1923; *El Sol*, 16 Sept. 1923.

[29] *ABC, El Sol*, 18 Sept. 1923. That their rule is temporary is claimed by most *coup*-makers, see Finer, p. 36. The 'iron surgeon' metaphor had been popularized in Spain by Costa. Yet it is very familiar among political generals in other countries as well. See, for example, the declaration of General Park upon seizing power in Korea (1961) quoted in Nordlinger, *Soldiers*, p. 204. Romero Maura, *La rosa*, pp. 33–6, is convincing in claiming that Costa's real legacy was democratic rather than authoritarian. The 1898 generation should not be seen as yearning for 'a dictatorial genius' to save it; see Ángel Ganivet, *Spain: An Interpretation* (London, 1946), p. 128. Primo, however, preferred to capitalize upon the widespread misrepresentation of Costa.

[30] Antonio Olmedo Delgado and José Cuesta Monereo, *General Queipo de Llano, aventura y audacia* (Barcelona, 1957), p. 63; E. Ortega, p. 65.

general of Madrid, wavered, and not until the king had made his position clear, did he join the movement.[31] Zabalza, the captain-general of Valencia, refused to support the *coup*, though Gil Dolz del Castellar, the local Military Governor, García Trejo, his colleague in Castellón, and Colonel Lillo, the Tetuan Regiment commander, managed to take over strategic points in what amounted to a mini-*coup d'état* against Zabalza.[32] The Artillery corps exhibited a passive attitude, and Colonal Marchesi, the future director of the Artillery Academy, refused demonstratively to attend the reception of Primo de Rivera when he arrived in Madrid.[33] General Acha of the Artillery and General Montero of the Corps of Engineers even urged Captain-General Muñoz Cobos 'to sustain the legitimate power' for which they promised him their support.[34] And, in Palma de Mallorca, where the local captain-general's attitude was one of 'complete support of the government', General Weyler put his military talent and prestige in the service of the government, if and when this was ready to fight the rebels.[35] The government took up Weyler's challenge by appointing him as captain-general of Catalonia and by sending a battleship to transfer him to Barcelona. Admiral Aznar, the Minister of the Navy, however, though he made clear his corps supported the legal government, joined in the 'negative pronunciamiento' by discarding a bloody naval attack on the Barcelona rebels.[36] The Captain-General of the Navy, Admiral Fernández de la Puente, who rushed to Madrid as soon as he knew of the *coup*, manifested the non-committed attitude of his corps. 'I came', he said, 'to put myself at the orders of either the old or the new government.'[37] The Captain-General of Andalusia, the Infante Don Carlos, was probably, as Reuter announced, sympathetic

[31] *The Times*, 14 Sept. 1923; López de Ochoa, pp. 30–1; Primo bore a grudge against Muñoz Cobos for his wavering position on that fateful day, see Primo de Rivera's letters to Admiral Magaz, 20 June 1925, and to the Duke of Tetuan, 23 June 1923, in Armiñán, *Epistolario*, pp. 220–1, 241.

[32] Vicente Marco Miranda, *Las conspiraciones contra la Dictadura* (Madrid, 1930), pp. 11–18; Alcalá-Zamora, pp. 97–8. The ultimate success of the *coup* in Valencia depended much on the 'trabajos' done by Lieut.-Col. Joaquín Tirado. He was later to be one of Primo's most dedicated *delegados gubernativos*, see Payne, *Politics*, p. 229.

[33] *Hojas Libres*, July 1927.

[34] E. Ortega, pp. 115–16.

[35] AHN, serie A, the governor of Palma to the minister of the interior, 14 Sept. 1923, no. 496.

[36] Hernández Mir, *Un crimen*, p. 85. An *attentiste* attitude such as Aznar's has usually favoured the *coup*-makers everywhere, see Luttwack, pp. 105–6.

[37] Quoted in Rubio, p. 33.

to the royalist *coup*, but being a genuine liberal and constitutionalist, he refrained from extending any active support to the rebels, despite the pressure coming from officers in the Seville garrison.[38]

Moreover, except for Barcelona, Zaragoza, and probably also Bilbao, where General Viñe supported the *coup*,[39] there was no indication that any other garrison in the country was ready to follow actively in the rebellious general's footsteps. Military Governors across the country expressed, throughout the 13th of September, their full loyalty to the constitutional government. That of Mahón, for example, declared that an assembly of all the officers in the province had decided 'not to second the garrison of Barcelona and to recognize the legally constituted government'. Similar statements poured on to the minister of the interior's desk from the military governors of Cáceres, Burgos, Logroño, Málaga, Pamplona, Santander, and Toledo ('in a meeting of officers celebrated this morning in this garrison it was decided to remain faithful, loyal and disciplined, remaining therefore at the government's disposition'.)[40] General Losada, the military governor of Oviedo, personally supervised the fulfilment of his order that the local garrison should be confined to its barracks.[41] General Querol, the military governor of San Sebastián, and General Molto, the Captain-General of Pamplona, disregarded the pronouncers' orders to arrest Santiago Alba.[42] Nor was the attitude of the Civil Guard one of rebellion. The *Benemérita* in Albacete, for example, was even ready to be put on alert in order to neutralize a possible rising of the local garrison;[43] and the commander of the Guardia Civil in Barcelona made it explicit that, though his forces would not take sides in the present contention ('our contingents will remain aloof'), they would continue to 'lend service as usual'.[44] Coming from Barcelona—the focal point of the rebellion—this was an almost pro-government assertion.

[38] *The Times*, 14 Sept. 1923; Hernández Mir, *Un crimen*, pp. 90–3.

[39] *The Times*, 14 Sept. 1923.

[40] AHN, Gobernación, serie A, Leg. 42: telegrams to the minister of the interior (13 Sept. 1923) from the governors of Mahón (no. 469), Cáceres (no. 487), Logroño (nos. 461, 480), Málaga (no. 471), Pamplona (no. 477), Santander (no. 451), Toledo (no. 481). There is nothing to indicate that those military governors whose position is not recorded in the ministry of the interior did not support the government.

[41] *La Región* (Oviedo), 14 Sept. 1923.

[42] Alba, *Para la historia*, pp. 7–8.

[43] AHN, Gobernación, serie A, Leg. 42; governor of Albacete to the minister of the interior, 13 Sept. 1923, no. 46 and no. 459.

[44] Ibid., governor of Barcelona to the minister of the interior, 13 Sept. 1923, no. 444. See also an expression of loyalty from the Guardia Civil in Huelva, ibid., the governor of Huelva to the minister of the interior, 13 Sept. 1923, no. 451.

Yet Primo de Rivera's bluff succeeded. Firstly, he managed to create the impression that he was master of the situation. On the 13th, when everything was still unclear, he was giving a confident interview to the press attacking the 'ex-government' and tracing a detailed programme of his future government. As if he was the incarnation of the legal government and not a mutinous officer, he inaugurated a furniture exhibition in Barcelona with the acclamation of a euphoric audience, before which he paid a demonstrative homage to the Catalan language. In an order of the day to his soldiers he warned the 'ex-government' of a military confrontation, and made clear his intention to fight to the bitter end.[45] Secondly, the first reaction of the press and public opinion was favourable or indifferent to this rebellion against 'anarchy and political professionalism'. It was an 'attempt at a national regeneration', claimed the conservative *La Vanguardia. ABC* spoke about the 'calm expectation' of the public, and *El Sol* was convinced that the pronouncers would maintain their position 'at any risk'.[46] Thirdly, the government lacked the stamina to fight back. Alba's insistence that Primo should be dismissed was disregarded, and he rushed to save his skin by crossing the French border.[47] Finally, the 'abstentionist' posture assumed by the bulk of the army, unquestionably uncommitted to Primo's *coup*, amounted to a 'negative pronunciamiento'. Not to split the army and not to shoot at fellow soldiers remained a categoric imperative for the military.[48]

Nor did the government make a determined attempt to mobilize the loyal military. Though maintaining that it could only be dissolved by force, it meanwhile waited for the *deus ex machina*, the king, to arrive from San Sebastián and to solve an issue which the government had complete authority but no confidence to deal with alone.

[45] *La Vanguardia*, 14 Sept. 1923. See also Martínez de la Riva, *Las jornadas*, pp. 44–9.

[46] *La Vanguardia, ABC, El Sol*, 14 Sept. 1923. For a survey of the press's reaction, see Martinéz de la Riva, *Las jornadas*, pp. 101–9.

[47] Alba, *Para la historia*, pp. 4–9; *El Ejército Español*, 13–14 Sept. 1923; García Venero, *Alba*, pp. 179–84.

[48] The Kapp *putsch* in Germany (1920) gained initial success thanks to such an attitude of military solidarity by Von Seeckt, the army's commander. 'Troops do not fire on troops . . . when Reichswehr fires on Reichswehr, then all comradeship within the Officer Corps has vanished', he told the Minister of Defence Herr Noske. See J. W. Wheeler-Bennett, *The Nemesis of Power, The German Army in Politics 1918–1945* (London, 1967), pp. 75–6.

The government might also have feared a violent confrontation with the civilian population of Barcelona, upon which they knew Primo would rely if it came to that.[49]

It should, however, be stressed that the government was anything but indifferent. As has been demonstrated, it was in constant touch with the military governors all over the peninsula, and, on 13 September, it ordered General Muñoz Cobos to arrest the 'quadrilateral', an order which he refused to fulfil unless countersigned by the king. Indeed, for all practical purposes, Muñoz Cobos acted as if he were a member of the conspiracy. He was reluctant, he said, to fight the pronouncers so as not to divide the army and cause 'another Alcolea'.[50]

In order to gauge the full weight of the decisive role played by the king in Primo de Rivera's *coup d'état*, one should emphasize that not only did most of the captain-generals, military governors, and garrisons refrain from supporting the rebels but also, up to the last moment before its resignation, the civilian regime counted upon the full support of its administrative machine, whose officials did not fail to respond to the government's orders. These included, for example, measures to secure the supply of food in case a general strike was declared by the unions,[51] and an order to maintain 'public order', to which the Barcelona chief of police, for example, responded faithfully.[52] The civil governor of Valladolid even interrupted the rebels' communications by intercepting, on explicit orders from the government, a telegram from Primo de Rivera to the captain-generals of Burgos, La Coruña, and Valladolid;[53] and, on 14 September, a couple of hours before the government's resignation, the minister of the interior was still in full control of the country and was able to

[49] George Dwelschauvers, *La Catalogne et le problème catalan* (Paris, 1926), pp. 117–18.

[50] *Las responsabilidades políticas de la Dictadura*, pp. 112–14. Alcolea (28 Sept. 1868): a battle between Prim's rebel forces and the loyal army which toppled the monarchy.

[51] AHN, Gobernación, serie A, Leg. 42; a circular of the minister of the interior to the civil governors, 13 Sept. 1923, no. 320. See the swift response of the civil governor of Huelva in his telegram to the minister of the interior, 13 Sept. 1923, no. 451.

[52] Ibid., the civil governorship of Barcelona to the minister of the interior, 13 Sept. 1923, no. 445.

[53] Ibid., the governor of Valladolid to the minister of the interior, 13 Sept. 1923, no. 462.

marshal the 'forces of order' against the strike declared in Bilbao by the communists.[54]

That the government shrank from exercising its authority against the rebellious garrisons of Barcelona and Zaragoza was due to its failure to get the king to endorse such a step. 'It is the government's intention', telegraphed the minister of the navy to his officers, 'to punish the rebels.'[55] This, however, was not the king's policy. In fact, the last constitutional government of the monarchy was overthrown by a withdrawal of support from the king rather than by an objective collapse of its authority. Within the constitutional practice of the Restoration system the king was the supreme source of power, and an attempt by García Prieto's government to fight in order to stay in power without the king's backing would have been as revolutionary a step as that of Primo de Rivera, whose *coup d'état* would soon end in a familiar *crisis oriental*.[56] Nor is there any special reason to think that García Prieto believed that on the day of his resignation he was actually contemplating the funeral of the old regime. What is more probable is that he had no doubt the whole matter was nothing but a 'crisis'.[57] The fresh precedent of the removal of King Constantine and the execution of the Gounaris government in Greece (28 November 1922) by a rebellious military regime for incompetence and deliberate organization of military defeat could not but encourage García Prieto in his decision to step into oblivion.[58]

With Primo lacking the unanimous support of the army and with a paralysed government in office, it was then for the king to make the fatal decision. 'Everything depends now on the king', wrote *La Región* of Oviedo.[59] The rebellious general, just as much as the government, passively awaited the king's verdict. 'There remains

[54] Ibid., the minister of the interior to the governor of Bilbao, 14 Sept. 1923, 11.15 a.m., no. 322. For the strike, see below, p. 80.

[55] AHN, Gobernación, serie A, Leg. 42; the minister of the navy to the corps' officers, 13 Sept. 1923, no. 312. See also Alcalá-Zamora, pp. 97–8.

[56] In that sense, Malaparte, pp. 143–9, was right in considering Primo's *coup* as a palace manœuvre. Mussolini's *coup*, however, also ended in a traditional *Transformista* government crisis that would, moreover, be solved with a rather traditional coalition. *Crisis oriental*: a ministerial crisis during the Restoration, usually solved by the crown's intervention; the Palacio de Oriente was the king's residence.

[57] Giolitti, like García Prieto in Spain, viewed the whole affair as a 'temporary crisis'. See Adrian Lyttleton, *The Seizure of Power. Fascism in Italy 1919–1929* (London, 1973), pp. 94–102, 124.

[58] Hurtado, vol. ii, p. 189; Alastos, pp. 225–6.

[59] *La Región*, 14 Sept. 1923.

nothing but to wait and resist', he said to his fellow mutineers when he realized his isolation.[60] When Primo published his manifesto with the cry of 'Long Live the King' and with a ruthless attack on politicians for whom the king had no sympathy, Alfonso's position as the master of the situation was reaffirmed. In his long and deliberately slow journey from San Sebastián to Madrid—a journey whose 'slowness is incompatible with the gravity of the situation', as the Socialists put it[61]—he 'compared the data and clarified his doubts', and, when he arrived in the capital on the morning of the fourteenth, he was already convinced that most of the garrisons in Spain, though loyal to the government, were ready to obey his decisions, and that no active civilian or military movement on behalf of the government had emerged. He therefore rejected the government's demand that he should reconvene the Cortes on 17 September—the 'responsibilities' report was scheduled to be discussed now in parliament—and to dismiss the 'pronouncers',[62] who, on the other hand, were pressing him to make a quick decision under the threat that 'this revolution, though still moderate, may soon assume a bloody character'.[63] The government, consequently, resigned, and Primo was summoned to form a government, and 'throw the ministers out of the window', as he had asked the king to give him the authority to do in a telegram he had sent to him in San Sebastián on 13 September.[64]

Alfonso sanctioned with his authority the victory of force. His mother, the Regent María Cristina, had been able to manœuvre out of the 1898 crisis without resorting to a military solution—the presumed hero of which was, in the eyes of the Catalan bourgeoisie, General Polavieja—mainly because parliamentary politics were then still 'manageable', the middle classes were not that hysterical, and the working class was in a pre-organizational stage. There was no tangible, imminent menace to the continuity of the regime.[65] Such was not the view King Alfonso had of the Spanish scene when he placed himself in an extra-parliamentary position.

By his adherence to rebellion against constitutional legality, the

[60] *La Vanguardia*, 14 Sept. 1923.

[61] *El Socialista*, 14 Sept. 1923. See also E. Ortega, pp. 107–9, on the king's journey.

[62] See the government's communiqué in *ABC*, 15 Sept. 1923.

[63] Fernando Díaz-Plaja, *La España política del siglo XX en fotografías y documentos. Tomo segundo: de la Dictadura a la guerra civil, 1923–1936* (Barcelona, 1970), p. 10.

[64] Quoted in Petrie, p. 175.

[65] Romero Maura, *La rosa*, pp. 37–8.

king had helped to create the myth of his 'responsibility' for the Dictatorship. It is anyway hardly conceivable that the army would have abided by a rebellion that had not been sanctioned by the king, the supreme commander of the army and the embodiment of the nation. A *coup* without the king's consent 'would have been completely impossible'.[66] The king's defenders alleged that he had sacrificed himself to prevent a dangerous split of the army into two antagonistic factions, a split which, he feared, would end in a civil war. Alfonso was aware he had violated the constitution but, he asked rhetorically a journalist of the French *Le Temps*, 'what is better, to keep the constitution alive or let the nation die?' 'Does one really need to have an election in order to gauge the real will of the people?'[67] Whatever the truth may be, the myth prevailed. The fate of the king and his throne was from now inextricably linked with that of the Dictatorship.

2. *The Concept*

Primo de Rivera did not introduce any new pattern or theory of pronunciamientos. The 'theoretical' framework remained that of a general rebelling against a government which, though legal, consisted of a bunch of corrupt 'politicians'. It was for the 'pronouncer' to interpret the national will at a moment of crisis, while the king was, in Primo's case, to provide the necessary source of legitimacy. Like all previous pronunciamientos, the present one too was to be interpreted by its military protagonists as yet another 'sacrifice' of the army for the sake of the *patria*. Furthermore, it was also considered, within the traditional conceptual framework of pronunciamientos, as 'the army arrogating to itself the right that the people possess in a democratic regime to veto the government's decisions'.[68] A sincerely altruistic enterprise, the *coup* had little to do with the *juntas de defensa* movement which, *Ejército Español* claimed, was 'nothing but a simple riot' intended to 'satisfy petty vanities'.[69]

[66] Hoyos y Vinent, p. 217. This was emphatically underlined once again in the February 1981 frustrated *coup*, see José Oneto, *La noche de Tejero* (Barcelona, 1981).

[67] See select examples of a vast panegyrist literature: Cortés-Cavanillas, *Alfonso XIII, vida, confesiones y muerte* (Barcelona, 1966), pp. 19, 131, 286–9; Salvador Canals, *Spain, the Monarchy and the Constitution* (London, 1925), pp. 95–8. The interview in *Le Temps* is quoted in Lerroux, *Al servicio*, pp. 255–6.

[68] Bueno, p. 122. Cf. for the theoretical framework of pronunciamientos R. Carr, 'Spain: Rule by Generals' in Michael Howard (ed.), *Soldiers and Governments*, pp. 135–48.

[69] *El Ejército Español*, 14 Sept. 1923.

Primo de Rivera belonged to the 1898 military generation whose major, and deeply frustrating experience, was the loss, to the overwhelming supremacy of the United States, of the remnants of Spain's empire. This was a generation permeated with a profound sense of humiliation and defeat as well as with a feeling of alienation towards civilian society, a society either unwilling or unable to comprehend, or to identify with, the military set of values (loyalty, discipline, devotion, patriotism, sacrifice, order, unity, etc.). Primo de Rivera's rebellion was anchored in this typically Spanish sort of militarism determined by inward-channelled nationalism rather than by unrealistic expansionist dreams; it therefore set about fighting the enemy from within—syndicalism, socialism, communism, separatism, politics, etc.—rather than a non-existent foreign foe.[70] It was to the Nation, not to any given 'temporary' government that the military came to feel they owed allegiance.[71]

Yet, if the mechanism of the pronunciamiento and the inbred praetorian philosophy to which it responded were not new, the public atmosphere that surrounded it, its incisive identification with a terrified bourgeoisie in the socially turbulent Catalonia, its leader's awareness of, and affinity with, European anti-parliamentarian trends, and the presence of the 'communist' fear in conservative minds[72] were indicative that perhaps something new and probably more up to date with European post-War anti-democratic tendencies was being born. In other words, was Primo de Rivera only a successor of generations of 'Spanish' pronunciamientos or was his take-over also indicative of his country's incorporation into horizontal European socio-political processes such as the so-called 'crisis of democracy'? A panegyrist of the Dictator had a positive answer to advance: 'The *coup d'état* and the Dictatorship are not the consequence of a caprice of General Primo de Rivera, but a response—in addition to the factors that are specific to Spain—to the general current being now manifested throughout the world against parliamentary democracy and for a strong, durable and independent executive power.'[73]

[70] Busquets, pp. 137–9; Kindelán, pp. 179–88.

[71] Cf. the case of the Prussian army in Wheeler-Bennett, pp. 5, 200. MacArthur and Perón seemed to have shared a similar conception of loyalty, see Finer, pp. 26, 35.

[72] Araquistain, pp. 224–5.

[73] Revesz, *Frente*, p. 60. *The Economist*, 22 Sept. 1923 was aware of the overall implications of Primo's *coup*; it was 'a further blow to the stability of Europe, because it will lower by several points more the prestige of parliamentary systems of

The concept that a rebellion against a 'dissolving' constitutional legality is a patriotic move rather than a punishable rebellion was basically inherited from the traditional *golpista* philosophy. It now acquired, however, an up-to-date sophistication. For the 'catastrophist' right of the Second Republic, Primo de Rivera, rather than the nineteenth century's pronunciamientos, would be the example to imitate and improve upon. The Dictatorship would be remembered by *Acción Española* as a *révolution manquée*.[74] But the view would be rejected that it was 'the consequence of the myth of Don Juan'. Rather, it would be claimed, it was 'a mysterious nationalist reaction, an avant-garde of that which is now looming, with greater violence in the Spanish horizon'.[75] Primo de Rivera was 'the real herald and imitator of the movement of patriotic exaltation now redeeming us. He was the propagator of the anti-democratic practices, now so fashionable.'[76] Mussolini had set the pattern. Primo's was 'the second attempt made in Europe to advance the primacy of moral, social and economic problems, and put aside merely political issues'.[77]

That a general takes over violently the reins of power should not *per se* be indicative of the nature and historic significance of his act. The technique of the *coup d'état* might not have changed, but the social cleavages, and the bitterness of the political contest to which his rebellion was a response, developed in such a way that they helped mould a novel type of military rule. A similar transformation in the set-up of military intervention can also be noticed in some countries of South America, the classic continent of pronunciamientos, after World War I. As in Spain, the Great War had transformed many South American economies and polities by enhancing the role of industry and urban capitalism, by intensifying the migration from the countryside to the cities, by increasing the

---

government'. Cf. Menéndez Pidal, *Los Españoles ante la historia* (Madrid, 1971), p. 225: he saw the trend towards dictatorship in Spain in the 1920s as an assertion of Spanish traditional exclusivism, that was further enhanced by the inspiration received from European models.

[74] Raul Morodó, 'Una revisión de la Dictadura: Acción Española' in *Cuadernos*, pp. 91–108.

[75] *Acción Española*, 1 Feb. 1932, p. 429. See also ibid., 16 Mar. 1933, pp. 99–106.

[76] F. Bonmati, *El principe Don Juan de España*, quoted in Bernardo Díaz Nosty, *La irresistible ascención de Juan March* (Madrid, 1977), p. 113.

[77] Aurelio Joaniquet, *Calvo Sotelo, Una vida fecunda, un ideario político, una doctrina económica* (Santander, 1939), p. 56. See also the appreciation of people like Albiñana and Ledesma for Primo, in Pastor, *Los origenes del fascismo*, p. 101.

political expectations of the middle classes and the discontent of the urban proletariat, and by bolstering the cause of economic nationalism as the 'best' way to safeguard sectoral interests in an economy in transition. Against such a background of a structurally changing society, military interventionism had started to acquire new characteristics. Whereas the nineteenth-century primitive Caudillo thought in terms of simple authoritarian solutions, his post-War descendant became, under the stress of the 'modernizing' processes and the influence of European fascism, a violent advocate of a 'strong' and 'hierarchic' executive as the indispensable instrument for restraining the 'social chaos', while at the same time enacting a controlled social legislation, a sort of 'revolution from above'. The combination of an anarchic mob and the revolutionary pressure of internationally inspired unions with the presumed inadequacy of democratic practices to meet the dangers inherent in the new situation was a direct challenge to military values and, indeed, a standing invitation to a general or a junta to seize power.[78]

Likewise, the rather traditional mechanisms of seizure of power resorted to by some royal dictatorships in the inter-war period should not exclude them automatically from being considered as potential founders of 'modern' dictatorships, that is dictatorships that respond to crises inherent in modernizing pressures, and that rather than a system of *pouvoir à l'état pur* set up a regime based on practices of mobilization and controlled national consensus.[79] One might say that, like the regimes of Metaxas in Greece, King Alexander's dictatorship, and Stojadinović's proto-fascist essay in Yugoslavia, and similar attempts in inter-war Romania under the auspices of King Carol, *Primoderriverismo* started as an attempt to uphold by means of violence and through non-democratic methods, gradually assuming fascistic traits, the interests of the propertied classes, the unity and the 'dignity' of the fatherland. And, like the

[78] For Latin America, see John J. Johnson, 'The Latin American Military as a Political Competing Group in Transitional Society'; Edwin Lieuwen, 'Militarism and Politics in Latin America'; Victor Alba, 'The Stages of Militarism in Latin America' in John J. Johnson, *The Role of the Military in Under-Developed Countries* (Princeton University Press, 1964), pp. 91–129, 131–63, 165–83. Andrés Nin, *Las dictaduras de nuestro tiempo* (Madrid, n.d.), pp. 179–80, admits that the mechanism of Primo's *coup* was strictly traditional, the novelty lay in that, as in Italy, it responded to deep social cleavages.

[79] Franz Neumann wrote about the 'simple dictatorship' that exercises power through absolute control of the traditional means of coercion (the army, the police, the bureaucracy). This limitation is due less to self-imposed restraints than to the absence of any need for more sophisticated and extensive controls, to which dictatorships that emerge out of a crisis of democracy would have to resort. See his 'Notes on the Theory of Dictatorship', in Neumann, pp. 235–6.

Greek, Romanian, and Yugoslav dictatorships, Primo de Rivera's initial success rested upon active royal support, indeed upon a violation of the constitution by a monarch fearful and scornful of democratic procedures.[80]

Dictatorships such as these came to power during, and indeed were the product of, the transition of their countries from tradition to modernity. Rapid structural changes—enhanced by western investments, and reflected in industrialization, railroad building, the emergence of a market economy and of urban middle and working classes—were taking place in Balkan societies during the first quarter of the twentieth century.[81] The old socio-political order was being undermined by industrialization and its concomitant social changes, but the new one had not yet been established. It was the dangerous questioning of the legitimacy of the old order that brought these regimes to power. Under the impact of demographic changes, social pressures, and the emergence of new political forces resting on mobilized, rather than on manipulated, opinion, it became evident in countries such as Spain, Greece, Yugoslavia, and Romania—to mention only select examples of countries where dictatorships were produced by a threatened establishment in order to stave off or control change[82]—

[80] See a comparison between Alfonso and King Alexander of Yugoslavia in *Folletín*, p. 18. For the origins of the Romanian royal dictatorships, see Henry L. Roberts, *Rumania. Political Problems of an Agrarian State* (Archon Books, 1969), pp. 170–260; Robert Lee Wolff, *The Balkans in our Time* (Harvard University Press, 1967), pp. 101–18, 126–32; Eugene Weber, 'Romania' in Hans Rogger and Eugene Weber, *The European Right. A Historical Profile* (University of California Press, 1966), pp. 550–2. For the Yugoslavian case, see J. B. Hoptner, *Yugoslavia in Crisis 1924–1931* (New York, 1962), pp. 32–4; Vladimir Dedijer *et al.*, *History of Yugoslavia* (McGraw–Hill Book Company 1974), pp. 513–46. For the origins of Metaxas's seizure of power, see the excellent study of Harry C. Cliadakis, 'Greece 1935–1941: The Metaxas Regime and the Diplomatic Background to World War II' (Ph.D. dissertation, University of New York, 1970), pp. 47–74.

[81] For the structural changes, see L.S. Stavrianos, 'The influence of the West on the Balkans', and Stoianovich, 'The Social Foundations of Balkan Politics 1750–1941', in Charles and Barbara Jelavich (eds.), *The Balkans in Transition. Essays on the Development of Balkan Life and Politics since the Eighteenth Century* (University of California Press, 1963), pp. 184–226.

[82] For a short discussion of the problem of 'transitional dictatorships', see Howard J. Wiarda, *Dictatorship and Development. The Methods of Control in Trujillo's Dominican Republic* (University of Florida Press, Gainesville, 1970), pp. 188–9. He has Trujillo's dictatorship as the model. In Argentina, the example would be General Uriburu—rather than Perón—who in 1930 seized power in order to stave off the democratizing processes unleashed by the rule of the bourgeois Radicals. A brand of fascism imposed from above would be his device to cope with the requirements of a rapidly changing society. See *Argentina 1930–1960* (Buenos Aires, 1961), pp. 21–31; Arthur Whitaker, 'Flourish of Trumpets. Enter the Military 1930–43' in Joseph Barager (ed.), *Why Perón Came to Power?* (New York, 1968), pp. 141–4.

that politics could no more be exclusively resolved in terms of personalities and electoral rigging. Parliament was palatable to conservative minds in these countries so long as it did not try to play British or French kinds of politics. Sections of the ruling establishments, by over-exaggerating the puissance of the social menace, felt they would be unable to cope with it if they restricted themselves to parliamentary politics. The dictatorships they produced were the last gasp of a conservatism fearful of the social and political strains that accompanied industrialization.[83] To put it in the words of a contemporary enemy of the Spanish dictator: 'The military rebellion of Primo de Rivera was not just one of those many devices adopted by the old regime in order to preserve its authoritarian pre-eminence; it also responded to the transformation of Spain. It was the last-ditch defence of a retrogressive social state.'[84]

Which is why *Primoderriverismo*, like the Balkanic 'establishment fascist' regimes,[85] at least in their initial stages, rested on the conservative establishments, whom they pretended to guard against the threats of change. Whereas fully-fledged fascism emerged as a revolution from below, the recruiting ground of which was among alienated, revolutionary elements, these regimes did not come to power through mass mobilization, but rather by means of traditional devices such as *coups d'état* or palace manœuvres. They started, as did indeed also Francoism,[86] as a counter-revolutionary, defensive reaction, which would finally bet on a revolution from above to neutralize that of below.

Such leaders as Metaxas, Stojadinović, Călinescu, and Primo de Rivera looked to Mussolini for inspiration probably also with a

[83] This 'model', sometimes applied to the origins of Mussolini's rise to power, seems to me more emphatically relevant to the cases mentioned in this paragraph. Cf. Barrington Moore, *Social Origins of Dictatorship and Democracy* (Boston, 1967), p. 445; John Kautsky, *The Political Consequences of Modernization* (New York, 1972), p. 210; Alan Cassels, 'Janus: The Two Faces of Fascism' in Henry Turner (ed.), *Reappraisals of Fascism* (New York, 1975), pp. 69–92. A. F. K. Organski, *The Stages of Political Development* (New York, 1965), makes the useful distinction between the syncretic fascism that emerged in newly industrialized nations and the totalitarian National Socialism.

[84] Rodrigo Soriano, *A los hombres con verguenza*, in Romanones Archive, *Leg. 54, no. 20.*

[85] The term is used by Professor Pribicevic to define the inter-war dictatorships in the Balkans, see Centre for Mediterranean Studies, American Universities Field Staff, *The Identification of Pre-Fascist elements in Certain Modern Societies. Summary of Seminar Proceedings* (Rome, 1971), pp. 62–5.

[86] Cf. C. Viver-Pi Sunyer, *El personal político de Franco (1936–1945)* (Barcelona, 1978), pp. 55–6.

spirit of mimicry. 'Please convey to His Majesty the king of Italy, to Mussolini, and to the Italian navy', asked Primo de Rivera, on the day of his *coup d'état*, from Alberto Pizzo, 'my sympathy for the example they have set to all the peoples who know how to save and redeem themselves.'[87] He owed much to Mussolini's influence, he declared on another occasion. Actually, he said, it was 'Mussolini's seizure of power' that showed him what he 'ought to do' in order 'to save' his own country.[88] King Alfonso complemented the analogy by comparing his role in Primo's *coup d'état* to that of Vittorio Emmanuele in Mussolini's seizure of power. He accepted the Dictatorship, he said—'just as Italy took refuge in Fascism from the communist threat'—in order 'to curb anarchy' and 'the licentiousness of parliament'.[89]

The nakedly military character of Primo's take-over, to use the words of a contemporary British observer,[90] has been over-emphasized as a point of difference from Mussolini's civilian revolution. Yet, without under-estimating the powerful civilian momentum of Italian Fascism, was it not the sympathy Mussolini enjoyed in military circles and in the royal court which paved the way for the Fascist take-over, the March on Rome being no more than a fiasco? It is often forgotten that Mussolini's seizure of power had all the aspects of a *coup d'état*; the military Quadrumvirate that supported it in Rome, the army's decision not to oppose actively the *coup*, Mussolini's ability to pose as a loyal monarchist—these were no less important to its success than the famous Fascist 'élan'.[91] The same British observer argued surprisingly that 'had there been a parallel movement in Spain, its centre of gravity would have been in the industrial region of Catalonia and its headquarters in Barcelona, as Signor Mussolini's are in Milan' [*sic*]. In fact, precisely this is a strong point of analogy between Primo's 'revolution' and that of Mussolini.[92] A panegyrist of the Spanish Dictatorship was later to

[87] Martínez de la Riva, *Las jornadas*, p. 58.

[88] *L'Étoile belge*, 9 June 1926.

[89] Quoted in Cortés-Cavanillas, *Alfonso XIII*, p. 290. Vittorio Emmanuele, like his Spanish counterpart, had been showing increasing irritation with the parliamentary system which escaped his control. 'In 1922', he later said, 'I had to call upon these people [the Fascists] because all the others, in one way or another, had abandoned me.' See A. Lyttleton, *The Seizure of Power*, pp. 35, 90–1.

[90] *The Economist*, 22 Sept. 1923.

[91] See D. J. Goodspeed, pp. 144–71.

[92] *The Economist*, 22 Sept. 1923. *Le Gaulois* as quoted in Riumbau Lazcano, p. 22, points to the similarities in the process of seizure of power between Primo and the Duce. Like Milan, Barcelona harboured the 'virus of communism'; Nicola Pascazio, *La rivoluzione di Spagna* (Rome, 1933), pp. 46–9.

equate the role of Barcelona in Primo's seizure of power with that of Covadonga in the Reconquest. It was from the Catalan capital that 'the *reconquista* against the invasion of liberal doctrinarism' had started.[93] In less figurative terms, to curb or liquidate proletarian militancy, an ideal for which Spain's business community had made plainly clear it was ready to engender a dictatorship, was a major *raison d'être*—just as it was in the case of Mussolini—for Primo's take-over.[94] Nor did Catalan industry, scattered as it was in under-capitalized, small family firms, differ from that class of small and medium-sized industrialists who, finding themselves in acute economic difficulties, provided Mussolini with a power base in northern Italy.[95] It was, moreover, the breakdown of Giolittian democracy in Italy and the shaking of the mythical omnipotence of a parliamentary system based on 'oligarchy and *caciquismo*' in Spain, as well as the transition, admittedly more discernible in Italy than in Spain, of both regimes from exclusively manipulatory tactics to mobilizing practices, that created the pre-conditions for a dictatorial take-over in both countries.[96]

It should be stressed, however, that Primo de Rivera was to be the founder of a syncretic dictatorship. His historical mentors were also various. He combined his military tradition, the regenerationist myth of Costa's 'iron surgeon', Maura's 'revolution from above', and the 'urgent' need to 'disarm anarchist syndicalism that was just about to take possession of our homes',[97] in order to produce a 'revolution' that amalgamated archaic with up-to-date models.

Primo was presented as the legitimate executor of the regenerationist myth: 'He who comes to cure the sick has started already to operate; politicians and political parties are being uprooted from power and the enterprise of recuperation has started.'[98] Like Pavía's *coup* against the politics of the 'anarchic' Republic and Sidonio Paes's rebellion against the Byzantine politics of the Portuguese Republic, and, indeed, like Franco's drive 'to solder the nation' that had been 'divided by the political parties', Primo de Rivera's

[93] W.G. Oliveiros, 'La nueva Cataluña en la nueva España', *La Nación*, 1 June 1927.

[94] See Sergio Vilar, *Fascismo y militarismo* (Barcelona, 1978), pp. 152–8. See also Fernando Duarte, p. 69.

[95] Renzo de Felice, p. 62.

[96] For the breakdown of Giolittian parliamentarism, see Christopher Seton-Watson, *Italy from Liberalism to Fascism 1870–1925* (London, 1967), pp. 596–612; Lyttleton, *The Seizure*, pp. 15–41.

[97] Bueno, pp. 121–2, 142; Gandarias, p. 27.

[98] *Ejército y Armada*, 14 Sept. 1923.

pronunciamiento was imbued with an overwhelming passion against 'politics' and 'políticos'.[99]

He ruled out immediately upon his arrival in Madrid the possibility of setting up a government of 'political men', not just because this would have been inconsistent with his attempt to mount a campaign of diverted mobilization, the scapegoats of which were the *políticos*; but also because this would have entailed a non-radical solution in the eyes of the people, eager to see a 'revolution from above'. 'Revolution from above', Primo observed, was 'a phrase that reflected the ideas that Antonio Maura had inculcated in the popular conscience.'[100] So far, such a revolution had been thwarted by parliamentary liberalism; Primo would give it a renewed chance to succeed. He did not fail to seize upon the legacy of Maura—who the Traditionalist Vázquez de Mella had hoped vainly would become 'a Mussolini before Mussolini'—in order to present his rule as the culmination of a respectable movement of opinion committed to the restructuring of the Spanish state on healthy foundations of citizenship, controlled mobilization, a local government law based on a corporative franchise that might 'solve' the Catalan problem, and a campaign against the vices of petty politics. Significantly, Maura's 'revolution from above' was also a source of inspiration to the future leader of Spain's brand of 'dynamic fascism', José Antonio Primo de Rivera.[101]

Maurismo developed basically into a formula for leading the country in its transition from a pre-industrial, non-mobilized society to a modern polity while sterilizing the threats to the foundations of traditional society. Young Mauristas came closest to a modern right by advancing the synthesis of the best of the legacies of the right and the left, in order to stave off the socialist republic.[102]

Viewed thus as a mobilizing-from-above movement aimed at coping with the imperatives of a changing society, Maurismo sheds the appearance of a reformist, national authoritarian movement

[99] For the origins of Sidonio Paes's seizure of power, see Jesús Pabón, *La revolución portuguesa, de don Carlos a Sidonio Paes* (Madrid, 1941). For Pavía, see Payne, *Politics and the Military*, pp. 36–7. Franco in Pi-Sunyer, p. 65.

[100] Primo's article in *The Times*, 20 Mar. 1930.

[101] Juan Beneyto Pérez and José María Costa Serrano, *El Partido* (Zaragoza, 1939), p. 77.

[102] Carr. *Spain*, pp. 373–5, 430, 487–9; Stanley Payne, 'Spanish Conservatism' in *Journal of Contemporary History* henceforth *JCH*, vol. 13, no. 4, Oct. 1978, pp. 780–3; see also an instructive account by a young Maurista: José Gutiérrez Ravé, *Yo fuí un joven Maurista* (Madrid, 1946).

upon whose legacy Primo de Rivera's 'transitional' dictatorship could claim to dwell. His *Unión Patriótica* would indeed manipulate clear Maurista metaphors.[103] But, how does a dictatorship cure what the Mauristas considered to be Spain's grand illness, namely 'the congenital atrophy of the noblest organ of national life, *civismo*'?[104] In the last analysis, this would be, Antonio Maura would claim, the standing challenge of Maurismo, which the Dictatorship fell short of responding to.

Ortega y Gasset, an outstanding protagonist of the revolution from above, saw the reason for Spain's tragic 'invertebration' in the lack of directing élites. A disenchanted liberal, Ortega was also popularized by the Dictator for his own needs. The military were long convinced of the futility of 'politics'. The instability of the parliamentary system as reflected in the 'endless' series of 'crises' was there to prove their point.[105] Ortega, of course, was no supporter of a *cuartelazo* as the adequate response to the 'crisis of parliamentarism'. Yet, in February 1920, he expressed his view that 'a government of the military would have the advantage of putting an end to this parliamentary farce that so disgusts us'. 'It is up to the military', he continued, 'to impose silence and order upon this political gibberish, smiting the ministerial counsels, and taking hold of power if the crown is reluctant to grant it to them in goodwill.'[106] In his vigorous demand for a regime based on 'unity, agility, competence and personal responsibility'—'virtues that are alien to the parliamentary organism'—Ortega enabled the military to claim intellectual legitimacy for their anti-parliamentarianism. Parliaments, Ortega would argue, had been invaded by 'la populacheria', 'turbulence', and by a 'plebeian taste for scenes of cheap dramatics'. This was the reason why the high and small bourgeoisie, he wrote, wanted nothing 'but to see the boat sailing', and they would rather have at the helm a 'strong hand'.[107]

[103] See Chapters IV–V.

[104] Duque de Maura, *Discurso ante la Real Academia Española, el 18 de enero de 1920*

[105] Fifteen different cabinets served in the years 1917–23. Especially politically unstable were the months that preceded the *coup d'état*. The result of the switching of chairs was that when Primo de Rivera put the lid on the parliamentary system only three of the ministers had been in office from the beginning of October 1922. See Maura, *Bosquejo*, pp. 18–19. Cf. Zancada, pp. 55–7. Primo de Rivera showed a certain interest in Ortega's views, Lalcona, pp. 115–16.

[106] *El Sol*, 13 Feb. 1920.

[107] Ortega y Gasset, *Invertebrate Spain* (London, 1937); 'Vieja y nueva política. Conferencia en el teatro de la Comedia, en Madrid, el 23 de marzo do 1914' in José Ortega y Gasset, *Discursos políticos* (Madrid, 1974), pp. 63–102. Ortega's views on a

Would the Dictatorship create the élite pleaded for by Ortega to replace sterile parliamentarism? On the morning of 14 September, when an ecstatic crowd accompanied the would-be Dictator to the train which was to take him from his Barcelona military and civilian power-base to assume power, under the king's invitation, in Madrid, everything seemed possible. But, the task of making 'the boat sail with a strong hand at the helm' could, and would, be immediately put into practice.

3. *The Consolidation of Power*

The Military Directory appointed by the king on the morrow of the *coup d'état* paid lip-service to the constitution, which it promised to restore after a 'short parenthesis' during which 'people, uncontaminated by the vices which we attribute to the political organization' would emerge to rule the country.[108] Primo de Rivera actually swore allegiance as prime minister in a wholly legalistic and constitutional ceremony, presided over by the last government's Minister of Justice, Conde de López Muñoz.[109] This care to seize power without breaking the legal channels, or rather to legitimize the rebellion by a swift incorporation into established legal procedures, was, as Malaparte had noted, a Bonapartist innovation in the technique of the *coup d'état*, which was imitated by figures such as Kapp, Pilsudski, and Primo de Rivera. He might just as well have added Mussolini to this 'Bonapartist' list. The Duce came to the royal palace on 22 October 1922 as a respectable politician rather than as a Fascist street rebel.[110]

Yet the legal façade could not be preserved for very long. Primo de Rivera abandoned it much earlier than Mussolini. The Directory was empowered to legislate by decrees with 'public weal' as the sole criterion. Primo de Rivera was the only member of the Directory

---

revitalized political system and his criticism of liberal parliamentarism were further developed by him in 1924. See his articles in *El Sol*, 29 June, 12, 19 July 1924. For the problem of the lack of élites, see also Menéndez Pidal, pp. 101–7.

[108] *Gaceta de Madrid*, 16 Sept. 1923; *El Sol*, 16 Sept. 1923.

[109] Fernando Duarte, p. 23.

[110] Malaparte, pp. 143–9. For Mussolini's swift incorporation into the legal framework of the 'old regime', see Giuseppe Rossini, 'Fascism between legality and revolution 1922–1924' in Roland Sarti (ed.), pp. 33–40. Franz Neumann is in that sense aware of the 'Caesaristic' traits also of such figures as Savonarola, Cromwell, Perón, and Mussolini himself. See his 'Notes on the Theory of Dictatorship' in Neumann, p. 243.

enjoying ministerial status while the other seven members were nothing but administrative functionaries. Rather than genuine representatives of their respective corps they were there on a personal basis and as disciplined soldiers fulfilling the general's orders.[111] The representation conceded by Primo de Rivera to all the corps of the army in the Directory was not just a cynical attempt to incriminate the whole army in the military *fait accompli*, but also a genuine step to reunite the army, the divisions in which were running deep since the *juntas de defensa* emerged in 1917. The split between the 'bureaucratic' *junteros* and the combative *Africanistas* had been the cause of such bitter tensions that in November 1922, the legendary mutilated hero of Africa, General Millán Astray, declared he would retire from the army because 'two opposing authorities are running it'. His protest was supported by outstanding figures such as Generals Cabanellas, Franco, Mola, and Sanjurjo.[112] Primo de Rivera himself had never been a member of the *juntas* and he would persistently deny any affinity of his regime with them;[113] but he cultivated carefully his good relations with whatever remained of them. The conspicuous appointment of General Nouvilas, a leading member of the *juntas*, as secretary of the military directory, was consistent with such an orientation.[114]

Primo de Rivera was undoubtedly overwhelmed by the enthusiastic reaction to his *coup d'état* both in Barcelona and in Madrid. This was the reason why, he said, he responded with a frenetic series of decrees intended to 'clean up swiftly' the corrupt system. The king, who conferred upon him the right to submit to his signature 'whatever decrees that were convenient for public safety', was soon to be overwhelmed by the dictator's indomitable energy. He knew he should be radical to please the 'people who were anxious for a revolution from above'.[115]

[111] For the status of the members of the Directory, see Admiral Magaz in *El Sol*, 11 Dec. 1925; and *Responsabilidades por el golpe de estado. Segundo directorio*, in Romanones Archive, Leg. 63, no. 40. The members of the Directory represented the eight military regions of Spain. Admiral Magaz was there to represent the navy: see *El Sol*, 16 Sept. 1923.

[112] Kindelán, pp. 190–1; Ricardo de la Cierva, *Historia de la guerra civil española*, vol. i, p. 71.

[113] See, for example, *El Sol*, 1 Jan. 1924. For allegations of the Dictator's affinity with the *juntas*, see *Manchas en la historia de España* in Romanones Archive, Leg. 52, no. 47.

[114] Félix Huerta, pp. 48–9, 66–9; Ana de Sagrera, p. 18.

[115] Primo de Rivera, 'Revolution from the Top: Morocco', in *The Times*, 21 Mar. 1930; Calvo, p. 248.

Conspicuously, he started by pleasing his allies of the Catalan bourgeoisie. The appointment of the hard-liners General Martínez Anido as under-secretary of the interior and Arlegui as general director of the security police as well as the institutionalization of the Somatén were steps in absolute concurrence with the Lliga's wishes.[116]

Other energetic steps were then taken by the Directory in order to establish the new regime. Martial law was declared all over the country; jury trial was abolished; as a reward for having paved the way for the success of the rebellious take-over, General Aizpuru was invested with full powers in Morocco 'to vindicate the honour of the army'; the fifty civil governors of the previous regime were replaced by army officers, and the eight captain-generalcies were put under the rule of military committees in which all the main corps of the army were represented. The Cortes was immediately dissolved. Had the Cortes been a genuine 'expression of the popular will', claimed the Dictator, he would have followed 'Mussolini's example in Italy' and would not have dissolved it. A special decree warned public servants that they would be dismissed if they neglected their duties. Hard work and expediency were to replace 'politics'.[117] Many mayors and other civil servants did not wait to be dislodged by the new rulers; they resigned by the hundreds.[118] For the near future, the Dictator promised to rationalize the administrative system by getting rid of superfluous functionaries, to designate 'prestigious magistrates' to pass verdict on the 'responsibilities'—meanwhile, however, the archives of the Picasso committee, in which incriminating evidence against many officers and civilians was concentrated, were seized and never heard of again[119]—to 'solve' the Moroccan problem by means of 'diplomacy and war combined together', to exhibit a strong hand in matters of public order, to make 'a new administrative, governmental, judicial and possibly even military layout', and to create 'robust regions'. 'Catalonia', he promised, 'would not regret our coming to power.'[120]

[116] Azaña, vol. i, p. 547; *Gaceta de Madrid*, 18 Sept. 1923.

[117] For the breathtaking initial measures of the new regime, see *Gaceta de Madrid*, 16, 17 Sept. 1923; *The Times*, 17 Sept. 1923; and an exhaustive survey in Martínez de la Riva, *Las jornadas*, pp. 28–160. The comparison with Mussolini was drawn by Primo in an interview with *La Correspondencia de España*, quoted in Rubio, p. 37. The abolition of jury trial was to be viewed by the liberal opposition as a bitter attack by 'reaction' against democratic justice. See Pemartín, *Los valores*, p. 380.

[118] See a great number of reports on this in *El Sol*, 15–20 Sept. 1923.

[119] *The Times*, 25 Sept. 1923.

[120] *La Vanguardia*, 14 Sept. 1923.

4. *Long Live the Chains!*

The public reaction to the *coup d'état* was on the whole favourable. The rapidity with which the parliamentary government fell at the mere issue of a manifesto took away the breath of the country, as *La Región* of Oviedo put it when describing the atmosphere in that city.[121] And then came a feeling of relief because there had been no bloodshed. A citizen of Niebla (Huelva) saw how 'in all the cafés, clubs and other meeting-places' the new directory was spoken of favourably by people of all social classes '. . . because it is cutting off at the roots the innumerable immoralities from which our administration suffered!'[122] Francisco Villanueva, who was in Madrid on the day of the *coup*, was struck by the 'absolute indifference' with which the man in the street received the news of the pronunciamiento.[123] People were fed up with the social and political crises of the last years and seemed to long for a period of stability. A frustrated Jiménez de Asua was later to write: 'I thought that the Directory would be confronted by a vigorous liberal opinion; but I found only apologists, even amongst the sophisticated . . . People looked for the salvation of the patria in the untamed generalcy.'[124] Primo's attack on, and the subsequent measures he took to prosecute, the politicians were a successful appeal to the gallery, as Ortega y Gasset noted,[125] and the crowd applauded enthusiastically. Nothing could be more appealing to the acclaiming crowd than the cheap denunciation of 'the ostentatious private life' of Alba and his 'limitless political ambitions'. This was, the Dictator would rationalize, 'the last straw that broke the back of social consciousness'.[126] A couple of years later he contemplated the possibility of isolating the Rifian leader, Abd-el-Krim, by a similar exercise of diverted mobilization. He wrote to Sanjurjo:

We should carry on, in that country, with the natives, a revolution similar to that we have made here on 13 September, bringing home to the population

[121] *La Región* (Oviedo), 14 Sept. 1923.

[122] *The Times*, 29 Sept. 1923. *El Imparcial*, 28 Sept. 1923, wrote: 'public opinion views with a certain rejoicing the collapse of men and procedures that have failed.'

[123] Francisco Villanueva, *La dictadura militar* (Madrid, 1930), pp. 31–2. For a similar impression, see E. Ortega, pp. 187–8.

[124] Jiménez de Asua, *Política, figuras, paisajes* (Madrid, n.d.), p. 29.

[125] *El Sol*, 27 Nov. 1923. See the decree that laid the legal foundation for the prosecution of politicians in *Gaceta de Madrid*, 18 Jan. 1924.

[126] Quoted in *Folletín*, p. 46.

the message that it is Abd-el-Krim who should take the blame for all their frustrations and misfortunes.[127]

The so-called 'neutral mass' had no special reason to mourn the mishap of the 'políticos' who—at least in the public image—had been governing the country by 'corruption and camaraderie', and by the 'promotion of family *clientelae*'. Primo de Rivera had promised 'to get things done', and that was a convincing platform for many.[128] Azaña noted soberly: 'So long as the shopkeeper does not defraud the weight, and the functionaries go to the office to do their job properly the coffee-house frequenter cares for nothing.'[129] Primo's manipulation of 'regenerationist' catchwords made people think that, at long last, 'justice will be done' and *caciquismo* eradicated.[130]. That the new regime came to power by a *coup de force* was not that disturbing in the eyes of its passive supporters. Their posture was best expressed in Gómez de Baquero's words in *El Sol*: 'If the Directory rules well and overcomes the problems, it doesn't really matter that it originated in a pronunciamiento.' A leading article in the same liberal organ was almost euphoric in welcoming 'a Spain more noble and fertile than the old and ruinous one which we were born'.[131] *El Liberal* followed suit: 'In the depth of each citizen's consciousness there is a blossom of gratitude for those who have put an end to the rotation of greed and lust.[132]

Primo de Rivera's *coup d'état* proved to be the last Spanish pronunciamiento that proceeded so passively to a seizure of power. To be sure' the mixture of public applause and paralysis which greet a *coup d'état* should not necessarily indicate an absolute lack of political awareness in the population. The 1943 *coup* in Argentina, for example, came in the midst of deep modernizing socio-politicl changes, but was met with indifference.[133] Nor was the seizure of

[127] Primo de Rivera to Sanjurjo, 30 June 1925, in Armiñán, *Epistolario*, p. 349.

[128] Un Español Neutral, *Réplica al Conde de Romanones sobre las responsibilidades del antiguo régimen* (Madrid, 1925), pp. 16–17.

[129] Azaña, vol. i, pp. 143, 549. For the tough measures against merchants and shopkeepers who gauged prices, see *Boletín Oficial de la Cámara de Comercio de Madrid*, Oct. 1923.

[130] Primo's desk was inundated by telegrams about this style, see AHN, P. G. Legs. 52–4.

[131] *El Sol*, 13, 23 Sept. 1923.

[132] *El Liberal*, 18 Sept. 1923.

[133] For the profound changes in Argentina prior to the 1943 *coup*, see Gino Germani, 'Transformation of the Social and Political Structure'; and Arthur Whitaker, 'Flourish of Trumpets: Enter the Military', in Joseph Barager (ed.), pp. 110-50.

power by the Greek colonels, after a period of intensive political turmoil, exactly met with popular clamour.[134] The use of force can have a paralysing effect indeed.[135] The Spanish reaction to the 1923 *coup* is of course also explicable by the fact that the system that Primo came to replace did not enjoy mass support.[136] Indeed, an indispensable pre-condition for the success of military *coups* has been everywhere the predominance of 'machine' parties upon a basically manipulated electorate.[137] In Spain, this docile democracy had been consistently eroded since the Great War. But the process of transition to a fully-fledged mobilizing system fell short of consummation; and the reformist programme of the last constitutional government was not allowed to materialize and to possibly produce the wide degree of popular support that might have saved the system from such an inglorious end. It is only after the treatment of political anaesthesia administered by the Dictator had ended that the process of political change was again unleashed, and, eventually, came to fruition during the Second Republic. Which is why the pronouncers of 1936 would have to step into power upon the corpses of union members and party affiliates to whom the Republic was worth defending.

Now, however, the reaction of the organized proletariat was not a revolutionary one. The Anarcho-syndicalists, although they had been warning for months against the impending *coup d'état*, were completely taken by surprise when it finally came. The article Pestaña wrote for *Solidaridad Obrera* on the night of the pronunciamiento dealt with the need to reform the . . . paper's orthography. Many *Cenetistas* simply waited passively for the authorities to come and close their locals. The CNT was exhausted by years of brutal repression. It was now almost useless as an instrument of combat. The general strike it declared was inefficient, and could hardly be expected to stave off the widely acclaimed seizure of power.[138]

As for the Socialist movement, this was led by a fundamentally reformist leadership. And not before the grand disappointment of the working-class and grass-roots militants at the Second Republic's

[134] Clogg, p. 59.

[135] Cf. Sforza, p. 132.

[136] See Indalecio Prieto, *De mi vida, recuerdos, estampas, siluetas, sombras* (México, 1968–70), vol. ii, p. 160. Prieto, it should be recalled was one of the most outstanding believers in the democratization of the system that Primo had come to destroy. See above, pp. 19–20.

[137] Luttwack, pp. 137–8; Cambó, *Las dictaduras*, pp. 57–68.

[138] Bueso, pp. 202–3; Brademas, p. 24.

resounding failure to alleviate social conditions would a meaningful radicalization of Spanish Socialism take place. It was not at all impossible that many of the working classes were now genuinely satisfied with the prospect of a strong government that would secure them against the threats of extremists and from actual attacks of the gunmen of rival syndicates.[139] The executives of the PSOE and the UGT embodied this spirit of complacency when they warned their members against joining any revolutionary initiative (such as the failing strikes declared by pockets of Communists and Anarcho-syndicalists in Bilbao and Madrid) 'which can only serve as a pretext for repression', as *El Socialista* put it. 'Sterile movements' of opposition in order to save a rotten oligarchic regime had no promising prospects in the eyes of the Socialists, for whom the resounding failure of their 1917 revolutionary strike was still a vivid trauma as well as a constant warning not to endanger any more their carefully built unions by audacious policies. The Socialists, however, were genuinely disturbed by the euphoric support accorded to Primo de Rivera by the 'employers' class' which, they feared, might induce him to disregard labour legislation and the social 'conquests' of the proletariat. Yet the Socialists' worries were not to be translated into revolutionary action. Rather, they motivated an emphatically 'collaborationist' policy with the new regime. On 22 September, an order was issued to party members who were city councillors and members of Diputaciones Provinciales to stay at their posts rather than opt for 'false revolutionism'.[140]

Among the upper classes of society the enthusiasm was most discernible, as was observed by the British ambassador at the time. The conservative classes' euphoria, noted Ossorio y Gallardo, stemmed from their conviction that a new Narváez was born to safeguard their social interests.[141] The army was definitely acclaimed as 'the executor of the patria's will'.[142]

Small wonder that the Catalan business community should have

[139] Cf. *El Sol*, 18 Sept. 1923.

[140] For the Socialist reaction to the *coup d'état*, see *El Socialista*, 14, 18, 22, 27 Sept. 1923; Ben-Ami, *The Origins*, pp. 105–6. It should be noted, however, that the UGT had nevertheless carried out a rather successful twenty-four hour general strike in Bilbao; see Fusi, p. 493. This local strike explains why the Socialist national leadership was so eager to curb the uncontrolled militancy of local unions lest it drag the whole movement to a frontal clash with the new regime.

[141] FO/371/9490, Howard to Curzon, 21 Sept. 1923; Ángel Ossorio y Gallardo, *La España de mi vida* (Buenos Aires, 1941), p. 73.

[142] *La Vanguardia*, 14, 20 Sept. 1923.

set the euphoric tone. The Chambers of Commerce and Industry of Catalonia were the first to greet the Dictator. They actually extended to him their support even before it was clear at all that his 'movement' had succeeded. They knew it was a gamble on their part, and that in the case of failure, 'there might be severe consequences for the Chamber'.[143] The *Institut Agrícola Catala de San Isidre*, which represented the bulk of the region's large landowners, and whose members, together with those of the *Liga Industrial y Comercial* and *Fomento de Trabajo Nacional*, formed the big business basis of the Lliga, rushed also to congratulate the rebellious general. The Fomento expressed its 'spiritual and sentimental solidarity with this brave army'. Cambó himself was alleged to have said that the *coup d'état* was 'the only sweet we have been able to taste in a bitter year'. Nor did the Lliga's organ, *La Veu de Catalunya*, conceal its 'satisfaction' at the fall of the 'old regime'.[144] Puig i Cadalfach followed suit, saying that of an 'illegal *coup*' and the 'corrupt politics' of the present liberal system, the Lliga chose the former.[145]

Its members and the Somatén—the guardian of Catalan bourgeois peace and the anti-Syndicalist strike-breaker—accompanied *en masse* the would-be Dictator to the Barcelona railway station. 'We can safely affirm that we have never witnessed a similar phenomenon of this kind', explained an editorial of *La Vanguardia* when reporting the euphoric acclamation of the rebellious general upon his departure for Madrid. The platform was practically flooded, recalled a Cenetista eyewitness, by 'the most outstanding elements of reaction in Barcelona, all the monarchists, the bishop, the traditionalists, and a substantial delegation of both the Lliga and the Federación Patronal'.[146] Primo de Rivera was, so the Catalan bourgeoisie believed, to establish 'social order', to favour the Catalan economy, and to confer an advanced statute of autonomy upon their region.[147]

The *Unión Monárquica Nacional*, an *españolista* high-class Catalan party under the leadership of Alfonso Sala, seconded the Lliga's lead. 'More than just supporting this regenerating movement,

[143] Ibid., 18 Sept. 1923.

[144] Ibid., 15, 18 Sept. 1923; Rubio, p. 37. Cambó is quoted in Lerroux, *Al servicio*, p. 264; *La Veu de Catalunya*, 18 Sept. 1923.

[145] *La Vanguardia*, 19 Sept. 1923; *El Sol*, 15 May 1930.

[146] *La Vanguardia*, 15 Sept. 1923; Bueso, p. 201.

[147] *La Veu de Catalunya*, 15, 16 Sept. 1923; Pabón, *Cambó*, vol. ii, pt. I, pp. 452–3; *The Times*, 15 Sept. 1923, headlined the news of the *coup d'état* with 'Home rule to Catalonia'.

we form an indivisible part of it since its very beginnings', was the UMN's official reaction to the *coup d'état*. 'Bearing in mind that our emblem is that of the unity of the fatherland, the monarchy and social order, and those being precisely the principles that have come out victorious' through Primo's movement, the UMN could not hesitate 'to join the consolidation of the political and social regime just initiated'.[148]

A couple of months after the seizure of power, *Correspondencia de España*, an organ of Catalan industrialists, still applauded the rebuff with which the chairmen of both houses of parliament were met when they demanded to reconvene the Cortes. It was not parliamentarian purism that was at stake, but pressing social and budgetary problems, and the Moroccan issue. If the Dictatorship could solve them, obviously by dictatorial methods, it would deserve the warm support they had withdrawn from the failing democratic system.[149] Even the Barcelona Bar Association, a presumably 'legalistic institution', accepted the *coup d'état*, 'believing that it would at least resolve the disturbing social agitation'.[150]

Bourgeois euphoria was not limited to Catalonia. Spain's business community as a whole was in a festive mood. It was 'the mercantile and employer classes', noted *El Liberal*, that set the tone for the acclaiming public.[151] The pronunciamiento, argued *La Economía Moderna*, was 'a rebellion in the name of law' (*sic*), since it was aimed at imposing discipline on an anarchic polity.[152] The *Confederación Patronal Española*, essentially an association of medium-sized industrialists, which since the end of the war had been clamouring for a nationalistic economy to protect its shaky businesses, well illustrated the enthusiasm of businessmen. It did not even bother to wait for the resignation of the constitutional government before committing itself publicly to co-operate with 'the military movement' in 'demolishing at a stroke the putrid matter that, against all justice and morality, is leading the country slowly, but inexorably, to the most unfathomable precipice'.[153] The Zaragoza Chamber of Commerce had high hopes that the new regime would once and for all rationalize the labyrinthine, inefficient, and parasitic administrative system ('a population of millions of

[148] *La Vanguardia*, 19, 30 Sept. 1923.
[149] FO/371/9490, Howard to Curzon, 22 Nov. 1923.
[150] Hurtado, vol. ii, p. 171.
[151] Quoted in Rubio, p. 38.
[152] Riumbau Lazcano, p. 18.
[153] *El Sol*, 14 Sept. 1923.

employees') that the productive classes had been sustaining for years.[154] Such capitalist corporations as the powerful *Fomento Nacional del Trabajo* and the *Confederación Patronal Española* seemed, moreover, as the Socialists feared, to have expected the Dictator to follow in Mussolini's footsteps and crush the unions against which they had been battling since the War.[155]

The smaller entrepreneurs associated in the *Confederación Gremial Española* confessed, on their part, that the coming of the Military Directory is acclaimed 'by our class'. They expected the new regime 'to finish with the ruling oligarchies'.[156] At the same time, the Church-sponsored *Confederación Nacional Católico Agraria* foreshadowed the solid backing that conservative small and medium sized farmers were to provide the new regime with—they were to form, for example, the cohesive nucleus around which the *Unión Patriótica*, the regime's official party, was to be erected[157]—by welcoming every step planned by the Directory and aimed at 'strengthening authority, social discipline, and moral recovery'.[158]

This general middle-class confidence in the new regime resulted immediately in a sharp rise in the peseta's exchange rate and in the stocks of Spanish companies in the international market. The favourable reaction of the finance market to the *coup d'état*—viewed by the king himself as yet an additional justification for the support he extended to the pronouncers—amounted actually to a blessing given to the Dictatorship by the possessing classes.[159]

Ecclesiastical circles joined in, as could indeed be expected, the concert of acquiescence and applause. Vidal i Barraquer, the distinguished Cardinal of Tarragona, obviously expressed a Church view, as much as Catalan conservative opinion, when he praised 'the noble effort' of 'the most eminent General Primo de Rivera'.[160] The Church as a whole viewed the Dictator as *homo missus a Deo*.

[154] Ibid., 16 Sept. 1923.

[155] *El Socialista*, 14 Sept. 1923; Maurín, pp. 134–5. That such were the expectations of the employers was likewise confirmed by Aunós, Primo's future minister of labour. See his *La política social de la Dictadura* (Madrid, 1944), p. 44.

[156] *Confederación Gremial Española, Memoria de 1925*, Madrid, pp. 417–19.

[157] See below, pp. 126–9, 145–7.

[158] *El Debate*, 16 Sept., 18 Oct. 1923; *El Eco del Pueblo*, 27 Oct. 1923.

[159] *The Times*, 28 Sept. 1923. The king used the favourable reaction of the stock exchange as an *ex post facto* justification for the *coup d'état*; see Romanones, *Notas*, pp. 227–8.

[160] Ramón Muntanyola, *Vidal y Barraquer, el Cardenal de la paz* (Barcelona, 1971), p. 106.

And parish priests all over the country rushed 'to associate themselves with the regenerating movement' which, they hoped, would 'control for a long time the destinies of Spain'.[161] The Jesuit *El Debate* accurately reflected Catholic feelings, when it expected the Dictator to run 'a campaign of moral regeneration by banning gambling, pornography, alcoholism, and other social vices'. A Catholic organ in Córdoba echoed these expectations, but went even further in seeing the emerging new regime as the last-ditch attempt to save Spain from barbarism. 'Organized order' would surely be the consequence of Primo's success; his failure, God forbid, would pave the way to 'the overflowing torrent of bolshevism'.[162]

The new regime was warmly acclaimed also by the right-wing opponents of the constitutional system. Thus, for example, many Mauristas, the protagonists of the 'revolution from above', hailed the Dictatorship, 'whatever may be the anomalies of its origins'. They saw 'the resurgence of Spain', so persistently pleaded for by their mentor, Antonio Maura, coming closer than ever.[163] And the Carlist pretender, Don Jaime, conceived the *coup d'état* as 'a convergence towards our doctrines, the expression of a purely traditionalist spirit'.[164] For Victor Pradera, now an active member of the PSP, the *coup*, 'though illegal, was necessary'. Primo's, he said, was not a military take-over, but 'a national movement'. The PSP as a whole, with Ossorio's notable exception, subscribed to the view that the Dictatorship might eventually implement its own corporatist and neo-Maurista platform.[165]

Nor did the 'old' parties mount the barricades. The dynastic establishment, harrassed by the continuous threats from the military and their civilian allies, and outflanked by the challenge of the left, both in and outside parliament, seemed to be relieved by Primo de Rivera's bid to anaesthetize Spanish politics temporarily. The

[161] See, for example, AHN, Presidencia del Gobierno, Leg. 326, telegram from parish priests in Soria (23 Nov. 1923), Larache (8 Dec. 1923), Valladolid (11 Dec. 1923), Orense (14 Dec. 1923).

[162] *El Debate*, quoted in Rubio, p. 33; *El Defensor de Córdoba*, quoted in Tusell, *La crisis*, p. 33. For a survey of the Church's view, see Félix Huerta, pp. 80–3. See also Lerroux, *Al servicio*, p. 260.

[163] For the Maurista reaction, see *La Vanguardia*, 28 Sept. 1923. Maura, *Bosquejo*, pp. 54–5. The Maurista Benito Andrade claimed that 95 per cent of the Mauristas acclaimed the Dictatorship: *La Epoca*, 30 Oct. 1930.

[164] *Estampa*, 29 Apr. 1930; Maura, *Bosquejo*, p. 33.

[165] Tusell, *Historia*, pp. 115–17.

complacent attitude of the 'politicians' towards the coming of the Dictatorship must also be understood in the context of the political culture of which they were an inextricable part. Willing to democratize the system as some of them certainly were, none was yet ready to challenge the indisputable position of the king as the creator and deposer of cabinets. In the last analysis, the *coup d'état* was conceived by some 'politicians', wrongly as it turned out to be, as a 'crisis' which they were expected to solve in a gentlemanly manner, and within the established framework of 'crisis management' of the system, just as they had done with so many others in the past. They behaved as if they were sure that their position would be restored during the next 'crisis' within a few months. Tired, even exhausted, ex-Premier García Prieto could therefore see no difficulty in adding Primo de Rivera to his list of Saints for having removed from him 'the burden of the government'.[166]

ABC, which throughout the last months had been consistently eroding the authority of the constitutional government, did not represent the dynastic parties—although it probably reflected the king's feelings—when it claimed to see no reason for mourning 'the funeral of old politics'. 'Whatever now lies in ruins surely deserved its fate', it added.[167] It was more in resignation than in euphoria that the 'politicians' accepted the king's verdict. The organ of the Conservatives, *La Epoca*, said in an editorial: 'All those among us who have been demanding throughout the last years to let govern those who did not let others to do so, must now leave them to develop whatever capacity to govern God may put in their hands.' It is, moreover, noteworthy that such a complacent attitude by the Conservatives was their response to the 'evident and understandable . . . sympathy with which many and very considerable conservative elements' saw the new regime. The Conservative Party, which, at least officially, professed to hold 'monarchist, constitutional, and parliamentarian convictions in face of this act of rebellion', simply could not turn its back upon the clamórous support the conservative classes accorded to their long-awaited dictator.[168] The Liberal *El Diario Universal* proceeded along the same lines. 'We do not doubt', it said, 'that this triumphant movement is inspired by the purest

[166] Quoted in Ramos Oliveira, *Historia de España* (Mexico, 1952), vol. ii, p. 459.
[167] *ABC*, 14 Sept. 1923.
[168] *La Epoca*, 17 Sept. 1923. José Sánchez Guerra, *Al servicio de España. Un manifiesto y un discurso* (Madrid, 1930), p. 13.

ideals; and it is therefore right to expect from this movement the good of Spain.'[169]

Undoubtedly, Primo de Rivera's take-over aroused a wide range of hopes and yearnings among die-hard conservatives, right-wing would-be 'regenerators', and the so-called *clases acomodadas*. But it should also go down in history as responsible for cutting short what looked like a promising process for Spanish democracy. Many of the subsequent enterprises of the Dictatorship amounted to an attempt, however frustrated, to institutionalize this breach with parliamentary democracy.

[169] *El Diario Universal*, 17 Sept. 1923. For the Liberal reaction see also *El Imparcial*, 28 Sept. 1923. Romanones accepted this line: *El Socialista*, 17 Sept. 1923.

CHAPTER III

The Test of an Iron Surgeon

1. *To bring 'into the laws and habits . . . healthy ethics . . . morality and equity . . .'*

A COMBINATION of Costa's longed-for iron surgeon, and the self-appointed executor of Maura's 'revolution from above', Primo de Rivera always insisted upon the 'regenerationist' message of his regime. Maurismo was 'the theoretical generator' of the Dictatorship,[1] and Maura its 'guiding spirit'.[2] Looking back at his regime's achievements, the Dictator said to a plenary session of the National Assembly that his regime had marched along the lines traced by Maura, and had 'revolutionized everything'.[3]

Whoever may have been the historical mentors of Primo de Rivera, one thing is clear. The Military Directory that governed the country until December 1925 was an operational device deeply rooted in the tradition of 'parenthetical' military regimes that strive 'to put things in order' and, then, put the army back in barracks. Initially, the Directory met every day to deal with almost every aspect of the nation's life in an extremely well-intentioned and frequently ingenuous way. During the first months in office it had dealt with 18,920 matters, 7,814 of which were 'settled'; 8,122 transmitted to the ministerial departments, and 3,614 personally reported on by a general.[4] The deluge of decrees was usually accompanied by long *notas oficiosas* in which the Dictator exhibited his *bonhomie*, his fervent patriotism, and his almost mystical belief in his 'intuition' as the lever with which he would 'reconstruct' and 'regenerate' the 'decaying' Spanish state.

With practically no opposition to face, the Directory had no need to resort to brutal repression. Francisco Villanueva, an enemy of the new regime, reckoned that 'the Dictatorship did not shoot

[1] Primo in *La Nación*, 24 Dec. 1927. [2] Ibid., 6 Sept. 1927; 23, 24 Sept. 1929.

[3] *Diario de Sesiones de la Asamblea Nacional*, 26 July 1928, p. 986. For the inheritance of Costa's legacy by the spokesmen of the dictatorship, see also *Amor Patrio*, 20 Mar. 1927, and Emilio Vellando, 'Costa era mas grande', in *La Nación*, 25 Sept. 1929.

[4] *The Times*, 22 Dec. 1923.

people; the revolution from above did not send wagonloads to the guillotine'.[5] It was a 'revolution' carried out through the *Gaceta Oficial*.

The frenetic devotion of the Dictator to his work of 'reconstruction' and his discovery—a not unusual one among military rulers—that the government of a country is, after all, a more complex affair than that of commanding a regiment, or even a division, created the need for him to prolong his rule beyond the three-month limit that he had promised. A year after he took over, he confessed that 'we have still a long way to go'. Neither had the Moroccan problem been solved, nor had 'the political organ which should replace the Directory', that is the UP, had enough time to take off from the ground. 'The caciques still cling to their nests', he said, and the work of *saneamiento* (cleaning up) was still pending.[6] He was even frank enough to admit, in a speech in January 1925, that a complete solution had been found to none of the four major problems that lay at the root of his *coup d'état*, that is separatism, revolutionary syndicalism, the 'grave economic situation', and the Moroccan problem.[7] The Dictatorship had then to continue, for, as he explained in July 1925, 'there remains a lot of work to do'.[8]

Already upon the expiry of his self-imposed three-month 'parenthesis', the Dictator set out to reorganize the work of his Directory in a way that dissociated it from its primitive, exclusively praetorian image. This was also an attempt to meet much of the criticism which was making itself heard on account of the length of time during which the military government had remained in power without apparently making any effort to draw civil elements into the administration. A decree of 21 December therefore reorganized the Directory in such a way that its members would no longer be personally in charge of ministerial departments; these would be handled by civilian under-secretaries who might, depending on the case, take part in the Directory's meetings. The Directory, moreover, would cease to meet daily, and would be convened by its president like any other regular government.[9] In January 1924, the wave of anonymous denunciations, which had been initially encouraged by

[5] Francisco Villanueva, *La Dictadura militar* (Madrid, 1930), p. 111. One sometimes forgets, however, that the very existence of a dictatorship is a deterrent that makes brutal repression superfluous. Cf. the Portuguese case in Tom Gallagher, 'Controlled Repression in Salazar's Portugal' in *JCH*, vol. 14, no. 3 (1979), pp. 396–400.

[6] *The Times*, 15 Sept. 1924.

[7] *ABC*, 25 Jan. 1925.

[8] *The Times*, 18 July 1925.

[9] *El Sol*, 21 Dec. 1923.

the new regime as a cheap device to acquire public acceptance, was curbed, as a special decree forbade the authorities to act automatically upon such accusations.[10] Three months later, a new decree reinstituted the office of civil governor in Spain's fifty provinces. The military governors who had assumed the authority of their civil counterparts were now confined to carrying out their original military duties only.[11] In July 1924, an additional step towards 'normalcy' was taken as all the members of the Directory were empowered to countersign the decrees handed in for the king's approval. So far only the Dictator possessed the right to countersign decrees, and the present amendment was tantamount to elevating the members of the Directory to ministerial status.[12]

The image of the 'iron surgeon' was, however, something that could not be delegated. It was the exclusive patrimony of the Dictator who did not cease to operate upon the 'sick' nation from the moment he came to power. In an effort to fight corruption and *caciquismo*, politicians and public servants were forbidden to act as company directors.[13] This decree, which affected ex-prime ministers, ex-chairmen of parliament, and ex-ministers who had based their power on the manipulation of favours and the distribution of largess, was an important demolishing manœuvre against the power-bases of the old regime, just as it was a successful appeal to the gallery which applauded the humiliation of the *políticos* affected by the decree.[14]

'A period of Catonian morality and severity is now being inaugurated', boasted the Dictator upon issuing his decree.[15] But, as was the case with other 'regenerating' measures of the new regime, the implementation of the new law did not always live up to its spirit. For one thing, the vacancies that were now created on the managing boards of public companies became a bait with which to attract adherents to the new regime.[16] In addition, Primo was personally to give dispensation to some people affected by the decree from the obligation to abide by it. Moreover, an order of July 1927 exempted corporations created by the Dictatorship from the jurisdiction of the law of incompatibility. The latter's spirit was further undermined by the fact that many of the people affected by the decree could, and did, delegate their posts as directors to their associates and

[10] Villanueva, *La Dictadura*, pp. 123–4.
[11] *Gaceta de Madrid*, 4 Apr. 1924.
[12] *The Times*, 4 July 1924.
[13] For this so-called 'decree of incompatibilities', see *Gaceta*, 13 Oct. 1923.
[14] Villanueva, *La Dictadura*, pp. 110–11.
[15] *El Sol*, 14 Oct. 1923.
[16] Maura, *Bosquejo*, p. 40.

relatives.[17] It was the top figures of the old regime, people such as Sánchez Guerra, Marqués de Lema, Duque de Rubi, Romanones, and Sánchez de Toca, whose 'dignity' did not allow them to circumvent the new law, who were left to bear its brunt.[18] A key official of the Unión Patriótica, José Gabilán, later resigned his post in a state corporation in a step that looked, more than anything, like a propaganda exercise.[19]

Primo de Rivera did not live up to the high expectations he had initially aroused concerning his eradication of *caciquismo*. His regime certainly cultivated, indeed it rested upon, its image as an anti-*caciquista* crusade. Primo's civil governors and his mayors took care to spread the myth about the Dictatorship being the staunch enemy of *caciquismo*.[20] It was symptomatic that one of the most warmly applauded slogans during the procession of 5,000 mayors that came to the capital in 1925 to pay homage to the Dictator was a rhyme exclaiming:

> Bravo! my general
> Down with all the caciques
> To all of whom you should apply
> The sane martial law.[21]

In his own Catechism of the Citizen, Primo de Rivera put special emphasis on his anti-*caciquista* mission. And, when early in 1924 he thought that he might hold new elections, his instructions were for strictly 'clean' elections. He had also stipulated, in a special decree, that government departments should not issue 'recommendations' or exercise any other kind of nepotistic practices.[22]

This 'regenerating' aura of the new regime as well as the petty ambitions of private citizens unleashed, in the early days of the Dictatorship, a wave of denunciations against municipal functionaries. Panic-stricken by what looked like an unmerciful purge of the civil service, some secretaries of Ayuntamientos went so far as to commit suicide.[23] Others rushed to find shelter under the umbrella

[17] Tusell, *La crisis*, pp. 66–73.

[18] *The Times*, 15 Oct. 1923; Romanones Archive, Leg. 20, no. 22: Marqués de Cortina to Romanones, 13 Oct. 1923.

[19] *La Nación*, 28 Dec. 1928.

[20] See, for example, *Senara, semanario defensor de los intereses morales y materiales de Ciudad Rodrigo*, 10 Feb. 1926: 'Nidales de la vieja política en Ciudad Rodrigo'.

[21] Ana de Sagrera, p. 261.

[22] Tusell, *La crisis*, pp. 36–58; Primo in *La Nación* 7 Jan. 1928.

[23] *Folletín*, pp. 51–2; Manuel Benavides, *El último pirata del mediterráneo* (Barcelona, 1934), pp. 256–7.

of the new masters by shouting as loudly as they could their support for the new regime and their hatred of *caciquismo*.[24] There were also those who did not lose any time in returning the municipal treasury funds which they had embezzled in the past.[25]

The Dictator might have failed to eradicate *caciquismo*, but he certainly scored a propaganda victory. The population as a whole was by no means sorry to see former municipal councillors and caciques being arrested by their dozens, nor to know that ex-deputies and senators, for whom they had little or no respect, had been deprived of their privileges, such as the right of travelling free on the railways of Spain, that numbers of useless officials, who drew their pay without ever entering their offices, had been dismissed, thus effecting considerable economies, and that food speculators were being strictly punished.[26]

It was not long, however, before the 'purifying' momentum was lost. The wave of denunciations died out as the Dictator himself started to discourage it. *Empleocracia* and *enchufismo*—eternal maladies of Spain's administrative system—were not wiped out despite the Dictator's utterances to the contrary. It is hard to accept the claim that Primo had reduced by 25 per cent the number of civil servants.[27] The Dictatorship was a highly 'interventionist' regime that, if anything, expanded the bureaucratic network.[28] As for *enchufismo*, Primo de Rivera himself resorted to 'recommendations' in order to place his favourites in comfortable positions. Probably no more than fifty functionaries were fired throughout the country for holding more than one job.[29] The new director-generals and heads of departments in ministries such as Public Instruction, Communications, Development, Labour, and Local Administration were not always entirely 'new men'; the old connections of some of them could easily be traced.[30] Clearly, Primo de Rivera did not engender a radical reform of the civil service. What he certainly did was to maintain a certain tension in its ranks by periodically warning public funtionaries against neglecting their duties.[31] In one case, he declared that any official, whether civilian, military, or clergyman,

[24] Duarte, pp. 35–7. [25] Pemartín, *Los valores*, p. 247.

[26] For these and other measures of the kind, see *ABC*, 17 Oct. 1924; *The Times*, 22 Sept. 1923, 22 Oct. 1923, 13 Apr. 1925; FO/371/9490, Howard to Curzon, 9 Nov. 1923.

[27] Roland de Mares, 'Les étapes de la dictature espagnole', in *Revue de Paris*, 1 Dec. 1927. [28] See below, pp. 242–4. [29] *Folletín*, p. 39.

[30] Ibid., p. 40. [31] *La Nación*, 18 Sept. 1926.

could face dismissal if his performance showed that he did not love his patria [*sic*].[32]

Primo de Rivera was the victim of a fallacious illusion, namely that his paternalistic counsels would suffice to turn lazy functionaries into industrious ones, to make them punctual, honest, intelligent, and heroic defenders of state interest. The shortcomings of the old regime's administration were at least exposed to the criticism of public opinion through parliament and a free press, while the clumsiness and structural maladies of Primo de Rivera's administration were concealed behind a wall of censorship and mountains of flamboyant oratory about 'rejuvenation' and 'regeneration'. Symptomatic cases of *pluriempleo* and calamitous inefficiency were, however, subtly uncovered by the press. To the Dictator's embarrassment,[33] cases were unearthed such as that of a certain functionary who held eighteen jobs at the same time(!), others who earned two salaries in the ministry of public instruction and one in the ministry of foreign affairs; a certain individual who earned two salaries in the ministry of development (20,000 pesetas altogether), a 7,000 peseta salary in the ministry of education, and a 4,000 peseta monthly income from the ministry of labour. There were hundreds of other people with a more 'modest' accumulation of jobs and positions.[34] This could hardly be otherwise when the excessive, indeed suffocating, 'interventionism' of the government had brought about the creation of dozens of regulating committees that had to be staffed by 'reliable' people.[35] It was no surprise, therefore, that, while recognizing that many of the deficiencies in the Dictatorship's administration were inherited from the old regime, the 1928 annual report of the Supreme Tribunal of the Treasury concluded that 'the growing number of expense accounts, compensations, gratuities and other kinds of emoluments which, without really having the character of a salary, are being received by officials, both civilian and military', created such a labyrinthine situation in the public service that the Tribunal considered it 'impossible to carry out its controlling mission'.[36]

A blow to *caciquismo* was also intended by the dissolution of 9,254 town councils all over the country. The relevant decree provided for the election of the new city councils by tax-payers. But, again, the result was not very edifying. The government had reserved

[32] Ibid., 26 Jan. 1925.
[33] Primo de Rivera in *La Nación*, 23 Apr. 1928.
[34] *Folletín*, pp. 745–9.
[35] See pp. 240–4.
[36] *Gaceta de Madrid*, 18 Oct. 1928.

to itself the right to appoint directly the mayors in cities with a population of more than 100,000 inhabitants. Furthermore, the fact that the decree explicitly cast upon the local military authorities 'to supervise and to intervene in' the formation of the new councils indicated that the whole process was not an autonomous affair in the smaller municipalities either.[37] In practice, there were cases—in Andalusia for example—in which old *caciquista* connections continued to determine the composition of the new Ayuntamientos.[38] 'Everybody knows', *ABC* was to write in February 1929, not without some slight exaggeration, however, 'that in the immense majority of villages the political leadership is now embodied in exactly the same people who had previously used practices of *caciquismo*.'[39] Otherwise, it was a new brand of governmental favouritism that was substituted for the old system of patronage and *clientela*, as was indeed manifested when, on 1 April 1924, the new Ayuntamientos were constituted all over the country.[40] City and provincial councils as well as civil governments were now to be filled with members of the official party, the UP.[41]

The most complete adoption by the Dictatorship of the decentralizing philosophy of Maurismo was reflected in the Municipal and Provincial Statutes elaborated by José Calvo Sotelo, a young disciple of Antonio Maura, who came to serve as the new regime's director-general of local administration, Primo de Rivera's 'revolution from above'. Assisted by a team of ex-Mauristas and authoritarian Catholics such as Gil Robles, Conde de Vallellano, Pi y Suñer, Vidal Guardiola, and Jordana de Pozas,[42] Calvo Sotelo produced a project that was intended to be the fulfilment of Primo's promise to create 'robust regions' ruled by local 'fuerzas vivas'. The Municipal Statute was based upon the free election by corporate bodies of the mayor and his council, both of whom would be allowed to exercise their functions autonomously, thus, supposedly, manumitting local government from the grip of *caciquismo* and governmental coercion. It was also stipulated that the Ayuntamientos would be free to decide their own developmental priorities. 'Home rule', a restoration of 'the national sense of autonomy', and the revival of 'pure municipal democracy'—such were the high expectations embodied by the government in its municipal

[37] Ibid., 1 Oct. 1923. [38] Tusell, *La crisis*, pp. 58–64.
[39] *ABC*, 27 Feb. 1929. [40] *Folletín*, p. 124. [41] See below, pp. 151–4.
[42] José María Gil Robles, *No fué posible la paz* (Barcelona, 1968), p. 30.

reform.[43] No less grandiose were the promises brought forward by the Provincial Statute. This, in Calvo Sotelo's words, rested upon 'a generic formula: the region would be able to exercise, in addition to the powers of the *diputaciones provinciales*, those state faculties which do not involve its sovereignty, but are rather of a regional nature . . .'.[44]

However, the reality did not live up to the dream, and the Statutes were never allowed to function. Nor was the designation in October 1923 of army officers as *delegados gubernativos* attached to municipal and provincial councils exactly a formula for the 'revitalization' of local life. Throughout the last months of 1923 and the early months of 1924, about 1,400 such military delegates were scattered all over the country to supervise, in an atmosphere of panic among the local functionaries of the old regime, the substitution of complacent, designated Ayuntamientos for the old, elected ones.[45] It was not long before Primo de Rivera could safely claim that the local leadership 'supported' him. It would demonstrate it by, among other things, paving his future visits in the provinces with popular triumphal processions.[46] The regime consistently resisted the challenge of those who demanded municipal elections. It claimed to be satisfied with the 'moral and physical energies' of its arbitrarily appointed councils.[47] Primo's 'revolution' at the local level seemed to have reached its limits.

The *delegados gubernativos* were expected to strike at the roots of the *caciquista* strongholds of the old regime, the municipalities. They were called upon to replace old pressures and intimidations by 'honesty and uprightness'; they were strictly forbidden to accept honours and bribery; and they were urged to improve the lot of 'both the poor, and the lower middle classes' by curbing the rise of the cost of living. This should be done, it was suggested, by cutting down the brokerage gap, that tended to increase retail prices, and by supervising weights and measures. To these prosaic tasks of the *delegados* others, somewhat more 'poetic', were added, such as the

[43] *Gaceta de Madrid*, 9 Mar. 1924. See also Aurelio Joaniquet, *Calvo Sotelo*, pp. 67–98.

[44] Calvo, pp. 72, 76.

[45] *Gaceta de Madrid*, 21 Oct. 1923; Cabanellas, p. 99; Duarte, pp. 35–7.

[46] For information on the new Ayuntamientos and their support for 'the saviour of Spain', see AHN, P.G. Leg. 337; 'Dependencias del estado—Ayuntamientos, 1923–1924'; ibid., Gobernación, serie A, Leg. 12; 'Ayuntamientos, 1923–1932'.

[47] *La Nación*, 21 May 1926, responding to challenges from *El Debate* and *El Socialista*.

'organization' of local units of the Somatén, troops of boy scouts, associations of physical culture, and lectures on the principles of 'good citizenship'. They were likewise to help to promote the fight against illiteracy, and, in short, 'everything that tends to fortify and refine the soul of the citizen'. All these tasks, explained the Dictator, constituted the most important mission of his regime and one which would have 'the most far-reaching implications'. 'It is upon your actions', he appealed to his delegates, 'that the success or the failure of this regime, that has come to save the patria, depends.'[48]

Flamboyant oratory and an almost religious sense of mission could also be found among some of the *delegados*. This is how one of them introduced himself to the citizens of his district:

> Oh beautiful, fertile, blessed land that should have been a paradise on earth, but failed to ascend to the position it deserves because of disunity, passivity, lack of public spirit, the excess of passion, and the stupidity of its sons! Speaking to you is one who knows your virtues and your defects. It is highly urgent to stimulate the former and correct the latter. Which is why I start my mission by shaking your spirits with this message, because if we really are to be cured of our vices, it is necessary that we start by acknowledging them . . . I am a conscience and a will-power; a man who loves good . . . I come to collaborate with you; to be one more brother that will work for the progress of your villages without dismay or lassitude.[49]

José Fernández Navarro, the restless and enterprising *delegado* of Cañete, a town in the province of Cuenca, had in mind even more sublime missions, such as that of imbuing the local population with 'the legendary virtues of the Hispanic race', and fighting 'the ridiculous pacifism that is the cause of effeminacy and degeneration'.[50]

Ardent patriotism and flamboyant phraseology, however, could not conceal the fact that hundreds of officers had rushed to seize what was for many nothing but a golden opportunity to live lavishly on two salaries, one from the army and the other (plus expenses) from the local authority to which they were attached.[51] Soon, a long waiting-list of officers expecting an appointment as *delegados gubernativos* appeared; many were to inundate the authorities with petitions and recommendations. Some thought that by exposing the

[48] *Gaceta de Madrid*, 21 Oct. 1923; AHN, P.G. Leg. 331: 'Delegados Gubernativos, Oct. 1923'; Casas Ramos y Moraleda, *Dos años de directorio militar* (Madrid, 1925), pp. 527–9.
[49] Quoted in Tusell, *La crisis*, p. 94.
[50] *El Magisterio Castellano, Revista de Instrucción Pública* (Cuenca), 1 Mar. 1924.
[51] For the financial conditions, see the royal order of 10 Dec. 1923 in AHN, P.G. Leg. 331.

failures of a *delegado* they would increase their own chances of replacing him.[52] Even retired officers came to demand their share in the unexpected bonanza.[53] A case such as that of the *delegado gubernativo* of Sanguesa, who demanded to be sent back to active duty in Africa,[54] was not exactly a usual phenomenon.

Though often well-intentioned, the *delegados gubernativos* brought local life under a suffocating tutelage. Some of them were certainly conscientious figures who believed sincerely that their mission was, as Celestino Cárcamo, the energetic *delegado* of Motril, put it, 'the last card we are allowed to play, because if we let this opportunity slip instead of seizing it decisively, we shall be inevitably condemned to chaos'.[55] However, the overall picture that emerges from the evidence is one of *delegados gubernativos* who came to save the municipalities from the paralysing tyranny of the old caciques, but ended by substituting their own brand of arbitrary management for the favouritism of the old 'political friends'. They supervised the creation of new city councils[56] and dissolved them brutally when they seemed to act in a 'seditious manner', as was the case of the Ayuntamiento of Leire in the province of Orense.[57] They encouraged slander as 'a laudable manifestation of the public spirit'. The *delegado gubernativo* of Morón, for example, urged the local population to inform him of any republican activity they might have knowledge of.[58] The *delegados* interfered, in a most patronizing manner, in local development policies,[59] in the regulation of economic activities down to their most minute details—the government had instructed them to encourage the breeding of rabbits, fowls, bees, and silkworms (*sic*)[60]—in the establishment of new schools,

[52] See selected examples from a mountain of letters sent to the Dictator: from Capt. Cándido Manzanares, 12 Dec. 1923; Capt. Emilio Abarca, 15 Feb. 1924; Col. Carlos Piero denigrating Capt. Enrique Sánchez Casero, 12 Jan. 1924; a group of officers, 13 Apr. 1924; General Leopoldo Saro recommending Lieut.-Col. José Ferrer, 14 Nov. 1924—AHN, P.G. Leg. 331.

[53] Ibid., Alesbán Pérez to Primo de Rivera, 8 Nov. 1923.

[54] Ibid., 14 Sept. 1924.

[55] *Al Pueblo de Motril y los de su Distrito*, 2 de Marzo de 1924, in AHN, P.G. Leg. 331. For an account of a conscientious, hard-working *delegado*, see E.T.L. *Por pubelos y aldeas. De las memorias de un delegado gubernativo* (Madrid, 1928).

[56] See hundreds of reports in AHN, P.G. Leg. 331.

[57] Ibid., Civil governor of Orense to Primo, 7 Feb. 1924.

[58] Ibid., order of 5 Mar. 1924.

[59] See examples in *El Día de Cuenca*, 19, 26 Feb. 1924. See also the protest sent by the civil governor of Ciudad Real to Primo de Rivera against the intervention of the *delegado* in the running of the mines of Almadén, AHN, P.G. Leg. 331, 27 June 1927.

[60] *Folletín*, p. 124; Casas Ramos, pp. 527–9.

and even in the appointment of new teachers.[61] They were the censors of public morality, the guardians of cleanliness in public premises, the champions of more humane treatment of animals, and even the peacemakers among quarrelling couples.[62] They were likewise involved in the 'education' of the citizens according to rigorously patriotic norms, such as those elaborated by the *delegado* of Albuñol, Juan Banquerí Martínez, in his 'Catechism of the Citizen'.[63] It goes without saying that the *delegados* were there also to mobilize the population for pro-regime demonstrations; they encouraged people to subscribe to the regime's mouthpiece *La Nación*; they enlisted new recruits to the UP;[64] and they staged public protests against the 'un-patriotic' calumniators of the regime, such as the republican novelist Blasco Ibáñez.[65] 'Spain', wrote with indignation an opponent of the regime, 'was thus subjugated to a regime similar to the African protectorate, since the mission of the *delegados gubernativos* was no different from that of the administrators of the Moroccan tribes.'[66]

Clearly, the *delegados gubernativos* were becoming a source of embarrassment to the regime. Frequently ignorant in the fields they were to act in as advisors, they became an intolerable burden on the local budget and aroused the hatred of the population, who saw them as the agents of a new system of 'bureaucracy and *caciquismo*'.[67] Yet, popular opposition and growing resentment in the army at being used as an instrument of political and administrative control fell short of bringing this failing institution to an end. Contrary to what is sometimes assumed, *delegados gubernativos* continued to function until the very last day of the regime.

For one thing, this remained throughout a handy solution for the employment of superfluous officers, many of whom were left without any occupation even after all the vacancies of *delegados gubernativos* had been filled. This was the reason for an explicit order by Primo de Rivera, in March 1927, to employ superfluous officers in the various branches of the public service.[68] For another, throughout their years in office many *delegados* had established a network of

[61] AHN, P.G. Leg. 331, May 1924.
[62] E.T.L., pp. 91–7.
[63] AHN, P.G. Leg. 331, Apr. 1924.
[64] Ibid., hundreds of reports throughout 1924 and 1925.
[65] Ibid., Dec. 1924.
[66] Eduardo Ortega, pp. 293-8.
[67] José García Benítez, *Algunas reflexiones sobre ética militar* (Madrid, 1931), pp. 20–2; Cabanellas, pp. 99–103; Calvo, pp. 24–7.
[68] *The Times*, 28 Mar. 1927.

congenial 'working relations' with powerful vested interests, who, consequently, exerted pressure on behalf of their 'own' *delegado* or against the idea of abolishing the institution altogether. Thus, for example, by sacking Tomas Aparisi, the *delegado* of Motril, Primo had invited dozens of protests that poured in from chambers of commerce, agricultural associations, and 'people of all social classes'.[69] Similar pressure was brought to bear on behalf of Captain Blanca, the *delegado* of Rua, when 'old-time caciques' almost managed to get rid of him. The *delegado* of Jerica was strongly supported by the local Sindicato Agrícola,[70] and his colleagues in Belorado, Cambados, Montellano, Alganitas, Villalba, Andújar, and Garriguella, to mention only a few out of hundreds of cases, were sustained in office by the local branches of the UP and the so-called 'fuerzas vivas'.[71]

In 1925, Primo started to show signs of weariness with the *delegados gubernativos*. He was dismayed to see them behaving like grand caciques, and ordered that any vacancies should be filled by those who had already served as *delegados*, so as not to swell the ranks of this new powerful syndicate. He had seriously considered doing away altogether with the institution, but, when in 1927 he asked the civil governors for their opinion most of them counselled against such a step. A decree was therefore promulgated on 28 December 1927 to the effect that 'given the efficacious labour they are carrying out', the *delegados gubernativos* should remain in office. Their total number, though, would be reduced to 'the strictly indispensable level', and they would have to work under the orders and supervision of the governors.[72] However reduced in number, the *delegados gubernativos* would only disappear into oblivion together with the regime. On the eve of the Dictator's final débâcle, he still found time to order that the *delegados gubernativos* continue, 'for the time being, to exercise their functions'.[73]

Primo de Rivera had intitially boasted that he would 'restore the independence of the judiciary', as part of his anti-*caciquista* 'crusade'.[74] But it was soon made clear that, in his endeavour to

[69] AHN, P.G. Leg. 331, 2 Feb. 1924.

[70] Ibid., mayor of Rua to Primo, 7 Feb. 1924; Sindicato Agrícola de Jerica to Primo, 15 Feb. 1924.

[71] Ibid., Leg. 354: telegram of 17 July, 7, 11, 12 Nov., 6, 28, 31 Dec. 1924. Such appeals were still pouring in by February 1925.

[72] Ibid., Leg. 332—The entire Legajo deals with this inquiry and its conclusions.

[73] Ibid., Leg. 332, 7 Jan. 1930.

[74] *El Sol*, 2, 10 Oct. 1923.

'regenerate' the nation, the 'iron surgeon' should not be hampered by legal or legalistic considerations. It was probably in the patronizing and arbitrary procedures applied to the judicial system that the Dictatorship most resembled an archaic, old-style autocracy. In this sphere, Primo behaved from the very beginning as a Sultan administering justice at the town's gates or as a gallant, equitable knight with a Robin Hood sense of mission.[75] Like any benevolent caliph, he was no stranger to the concept of justice; but he was totally devoid of any deference to juridical procedures. The appearance in March 1927 of the periodical *Audencia Pública* was an attempt at helping 'to put a limit to the excesses'[76] in judicial matters. It reflected the pre-occupation of liberal minds with what was probably the most notorious feature of the Dictatorship, its contempt for due process of law. Primo de Rivera's local and provincial officials applied the same *caciquista* practices to the designation of judges as had been known under the old regime.[77]

A 'regime of illegal fines' as Unamuno called it,[78] the directory arrested its opponents and exiled them, sometimes without even bothering to bring them before a judge, as in the case of the lawyer Arturo Casanueva.[79] No less arbitrary were the procedures according to which the republican militant Álvaro de Albornoz was arrested while appearing as a solicitor in court,[80] or those by which the Marqués de Cortina was exiled in retaliation for an article which he had published in *Actualidad Financiera* criticizing a recent tax on the shipping industry.[81] In September 1924, Rafael Sánchez Guerra was placed in custody for writing a critical article in a foreign newspaper,[82] and the ex-leader of the Partido Social Popular, Ossorio y Gallardo, was arrested for 'spreading rumours' that might undermine military discipline, a crime the authorities obtained knowledge of by intercepting his private correspondence.[83] Likewise, the 'outrageous concepts' contained in a private letter of Unamuno,

[75] Menéndez Pidal, p. 68: Primo represented a common disrespect for law among Spaniards.
[76] *Audencia Pública*, 19 Mar. 1927.
[77] Casas Ramos, pp. 529–30; Alonso Salazar, *La Justicia bajo la Dictadura* (Madrid, 1930), p. 19.
[78] Romanones Archive, Leg. 63, no. 6: Unamuno to Jiménez de Asua, 8 Aug. 1926.
[79] *Hojas Libres*, 1 May 1927.
[80] *El Socialista*, 3 July 1924. For Primo's systematic affront to lawyers and judges, see *Escrito de Benigno Varela a Don Santiago del Valle, fiscal del supremo*, 8 Feb. 1930, and 'El general rebelde ante la justicia', in Romanones Archive, Leg. 68, no. 39.
[81] *The Times*, 8 Jan. 1924.
[82] *El Sol*, 21 Sept. 1924.
[83] *The Times*, 12 Sept. 1924.

where he criticized the Dictator for interfering on behalf of a prostitute (nicknamed 'La Caoba') in a matter which was *sub judice*, brought about the professor's exile and eventual dismissal from his chair at the University of Salamanca.[84] Sometimes the Dictator would simply dictate the verdict to the judge, as was the case in the notorious trial of La Caoba,[85] and in that of Primo's intimate friend Conde de los Andes, whose judge, Arcadio Conde, was ordered to 'show leniency'.[86]

If there was a novelty in the approach of the civilian directory to legal issues, it lay in its attempt to invest lawlessness with legal status. A decree of May 1926 enabled the government to decide on exceptional measures even when these were 'incompatible with the law'.[87] A month later a decree was promulgated that empowered the government to impose, without any restrictions, 'administrative and disciplinary sanctions, even when they contradict existing laws and regulations'.[88] In October of the same year an additional decree appeared that allowed the government to suspend the verdicts of the supreme court. It could also disregard the decisions of the tribunal of administrative disputes, a right which the government could also exercise retroactively, thus depriving the citizens of any constitutional defence against administrative abuses.[89] When, in December 1928, the Dictator signed a decree which in one stroke did away with judicial immovability,[90] he also took the opportunity to explain his legal philosophy. Such measures, he said, were demanded by the public weal and by the need 'to complete the dictatorial enterprise of *saneamiento*'. Only then, he promised, would Spanish society be allowed again to exercise its legal rights. He went on reasoning:

> The very essence of a dictatorship is its right and its duty to substitute, when it conscientiously believes it to be proper, the moral for the written law, as well as, while responding to circumstantial imperatives, to prefer the supremacy of the executive power over any other. A dictatorship ought never to

[84] Miguel de Unamuno, *De Fuerteventura a Paris* (Paris, 1925), p. 16. For scores of other cases, see Ramiro Gómez Fernández, *De la Dictadura al poder. La Dictadura me honró encarcelandome* (Madrid, 1930).

[85] Blasco Ibáñez, *Alfonso XIII Unmasked. The Military Terror in Spain* (London, 1925), pp. 117–18. López de Ochoa, pp. 67–9. See another such case in Maura, *Bosquejo*, p. 358.

[86] Primo to General Adolfo Vallespinosa, 12 June 1925, in Armiñán, *Epistolario*, p. 163.

[87] *Gaceta*, 16 May 1926.

[88] Jiménez de Asua, *Notas de un confinado* (Madrid, 1930), pp. 95–104.

[89] *Gaceta*, 15 Oct. 1926.

[90] Hurtado, vol. ii, pp. 250–1.

be accountable for breaches of the law: this would contradict its very essence. It should be accountable, however, for breaches of moral norms.[91]

2. *Regeneration Through God—The Genesis of the National-Catholic State*

The myth of the iron surgeon was essentially a secular one. Primo de Rivera, however, was strongly attached to Catholic, traditionalist values. In fact, his regime amounted to a clear anticipation of the era of National-Catholicism under Francoism.[92] It was a regime that equated nationalism with the Catholic legacy of Spain, viewed religious events with utmost reverence,[93] and strongly upheld the moral interests of the national Church, for which it deserved its full and most enthusiastic support.

The hierarchy had warmly welcomed the *coup d'état*. Bishops were seen embracing the Marqués de Estella publicly in the streets; and they appealed to the believers to pray—as the Bishop of Madrid-Alcalá put it—'for all those who now govern our beloved Fatherland'.[94] There can be little doubt that from the point of view of the hierarchy *Primoderriverismo* was a Golden Age. And even those parish priests who did not derive any material satisfaction from the new regime[95] understood that it was an indispensable promoter of National-Catholicism. It was not with any great reluctance that hundreds of priests throughout the country were to join the state-manipulated campaign against the 'anti-patriotic defamations' being launched by some 'wrongly called Spaniards abroad'.[96] The parish priests of the Ayuntamiento of Vega de Valcarcel in the province of León expressed their choice in the clearest terms possible. They protested, they said, against the government's disregard of their poor material conditions, but they also

[91] Quoted in Cambó, *Las dictaduras*, pp. 40–1.

[92] Cf. S. Ben-Ami, *La revolución desde arriba: España 1936–1979* (Barcelona, 1980), pp. 77–81.

[93] See, for example, the reference to Easter in *La Nación*, 1, 2 Apr. 1926; 14, 15 Apr. 1927.

[94] Verax, 'Quelques Maîtres du destin: Le général Primo de Rivera', in *Revue des deux mondes*, Paris, 1 June 1928, p. 515. Lerroux, *Al servicio*, p. 260; *The Times*, 18 Aug. 1928. See also Manuel Cuenca, 'Panorama', in Cárcel Ortí (ed.), pp. 286–7.

[95] For the living conditions of the lower clergy, see below pp. 302–3.

[96] AHN, P.G. Leg. 326, Dec. 1924: 'Escritos del Cabildo Catedral de todas las de España protestando de la campaña difamatoria de algunos mal llamados españoles en el extranjero'.

knew that the fundamental interests of the Church demanded that 'the Directory continues in power for an indefinite time'.[97] Having put an end to anarchy and secular disintegration, Primo de Rivera earned from the Church the same ecstatic eulogies it would later shed upon the leader of the 1936 'crusade'. The Marqués de Estella was hailed as 'the illustrious Caudillo of our Spain', the 'saviour of the Fatherland', 'the restorer and the strengthener of the Christian monarchy'. The only wish a true Christian could make on the fifth anniversary of the new regime was to be allowed 'the pleasure of many more such anniversaries'.[98]

It was Alfonso XIII himself, a modern transfiguration of the Catholic monarchs, who had set the pattern of the regime's relations with the Church in an ultramontane speech with strong medieval overtones, which he delivered at the Vatican in November 1923. Allegedly written by the Jesuit Father Torres, the speech concluded with an anachronistic commitment to turn Spain into the spearhead of a new crusade, should this be declared by a modern Urban II. If such a crusade were started, promised King Alfonso to the Pope, 'then Spain and its king, always loyal to your orders, would never desert the place of honour which its glorious traditions in fighting for the Cross dictate'. Now, as in the past, Spain was conceived by its king as 'the soldier of religion'.[99]

The religious were of course thankful to God for having given Spain such a profoundly Catholic monarch. But, since it was a complete negation of the 'other Spain', the anachronistic religious fanaticism displayed by the king shocked enlightened opinion. Liberals would have 'preferred' Fascism to obscurantism, since the former had at least shown that, even in the country of the Holy See, a certain degree of liberty of conscience could still be respected.[100]

Primo's rule amounted to a fundamental breach with the precepts of the liberal state in that it encouraged clerical obscurantism, and officially endorsed it as its educational and cultural guide-line. As in the case of the Dictatorships of Franco, Salazar, and that of the Greek colonels, Primo's regime was to be imbued with a spirit of religious and moral conformism, and with a rejection of 'intellectual

[97] Ibid.: 'Escrito de D. Bonifacio Saavedra y varios mas párrocos del Ayuntamiento de Valcarcel', 17 Oct. 1925.

[98] Conónigo J. Montagut, *El Dictador y la Dictadura* (Barcelona, 1928), *passim*; Father Manuel Jover Mirá, *La España inmortal* (Madrid, 1930), *passim*.

[99] *ABC*, 20 Nov. 1923.

[100] Menéndez Pidal, pp. 225–6; *El Sol*, El Liberal, La Libertad, 24, 25 Nov. 1923.

audacity'. In spite of Primo's somewhat *machista* image, he had a fundamentally Catholic vision of a morally and sexually ascetic society, in which the teachings of the Church, rather than the 'spirit of the new times', should set the standard of public conduct.[101] The Dictator, as well as his Minister of Education Sr. Callejo, had stipulated that education should be religious and patriotic.[102] 'We have been accused of being clericalists', said the Dictator to an audience of municipal representatives in January 1925; and he did not take the trouble to refute this accusation. His educational philosophy, he explained, rested upon the 'utmost reverence for religious communities', and he would, therefore, make any effort to prevent 'the snatching of children away from religious educational institutions'. His anti-intellectual concept of education demanded that: 'We should canalize cultural development along the paths that are most convenient to the state. Extravagant and original philosophers may utter whatever soliloquies they like; but they should never be allowed to teach. No culture at school will be permitted that is not religious and patriotic.'[103] This was essential for 'the formation of the race', he explained on another occasion.[104] Sr. Suárez Somonte, the general director of primary education, made clear that he supported 'the intervention of the priest in curricular as well as in extra-curricular education in order to warn youth against perverted ideas'.[105]

Consequently, educational inspectors and provincial governors were urged, as the governor of Cuenca, José Balcells, put it in a circular letter, 'to imbue the educational system with an immaculate religious and patriotic sentiment'. A decree of February 1924 had ordered the dismissal of any teacher who 'teaches his pupils such doctrines as are opposed to the unity of the patria and are offensive towards religion'.[106] A textbook, compiled and printed by the government and whose content was in absolute accordance with Church precepts, became the fundamental educational instrument in schools.[107] This book, as the regime's mouthpiece was happy to

[101] Cf. Rodis Roufos, 'Culture and the Military' in Clogg (ed.), pp. 148–52; F.C.C. Egerton, *Salazar, Rebuilder of Portugal* (London, 1943), pp. 163–8; Luis Ramírez, *Vie de Francisco Franco, régent du royaume d'Espagne par la grâce de Dieu* (Paris, 1966), *passim*.

[102] *La Nación*, 26 Jan. 1925, 29 March 1926.

[103] *Folletín*, pp. 195–6. See also *The Times*, 26 Jan. 1925.

[104] Primo de Rivera, *Intervenciones*, p. 334.

[105] *La Nación*, 12 June 1928.

[106] *Hojas Libres*, May 1927, Oct. 1928.

[107] Melchor Fernández Almagro, *Historia del reinado de Alfonso XIII* (Barcelona, 1934), p. 496.

point out, 'closed the spiritual field of education to well-known and very harmful speculations'.[108] Consequently, in Lérida a teacher was suspended for recommending to his pupils 'excommunicated' books: Unamuno's *Recuerdos de niñeza y mocedad* was considered to be such a book. As a result of ecclesiastical pressure, teachers in Orense and in Ávila were dismissed for spreading liberal doctrines; an inspector of primary education in Granada was fired for refusing to gather schoolchildren at the entrance of the city in honour of the archbishop; and orders were issued to make it obligatory for teachers and pupils to attend mass.[109] Not just administrative inefficiency, but also clerical pressure, may well account for the fact that in 1929 thousands of classes at primary level had no teachers, while 4,000 teachers were still vainly waiting for their assignments.[110]

Liberal educational centres such as the *Museo Pedagógico, Las Normales del Instituto Escuela*, and *La Escuela Superior del Magisterio* were also severely scrutinized; and the activities of the enlighted *Junta para Ampliación de Estudios* were channelled into reactionary paths by introducing clerical figures into its ranks.[111] Traditionalist and ecclesiastical minds could not bear to see the disciples of the *Institución Libre de Enseñanza* educating 'a generation of pedants, declamatory pessimists devoid of any patriotic sentiment and addicted to all that is un-Spanish'.[112]

The introduction of the textbook, in which the French Revolution was dismissed in one page as a meaningless episode and the Counter-Reformation was given one hundred pages, was only one aspect of the clerically oriented reform of the educational system. Whereas Religion had so far been a voluntary subject at school, it now became obligatory; and others such as Christian Doctrine, the Social Doctrine of the Gospel, Apologetics, and Morals acquired a privileged status in the curriculum together with 'patriotic' subjects such as the geography and a traditionally interpreted history of Spain.[113] Both patriotism and religion complemented each other,

[108] *La Nación*, 17 Nov. 1927.

[109] *Hojas Libres*, May 1927, Oct. 1928. For Unamuno's book, see AHN, P.G. Leg. 358: civil governor of Orense, 17 Dec. 1925.

[110] *El Magisterio Español*, 26 Feb. 1929.

[111] Madariaga, *España*, p. 336.

[112] *La Lectura Dominical*, Oct. 1926.

[113] 'Notas explicativas de un proyecto de decreto para la reforma de la segunda enseñanza, Junio de 1926', in AHN, P.G. Leg. 358. This project was in absolute concurrence with the conclusions of the First National Congress of Catholic Education held in April 1924, *The Times*, 24 Apr. 1924.

while liberalism and permissiveness were tantamount to anti-patriotism and 'disintegrating' tendencies.[114]

It was hardly surprising that the regime's mouthpiece, *La Nación*, launched a campaign against the new 'immoral' fashions of women's clothing.[115] It was likewise to be expected that a sympathetic ear would be lent by the authorities to appeals such as that of the parish priest of Cumuñas against the 'obscene literature being displayed in the kiosks of Madrid'; that of a lady from Zamora demanding the removal of young teachers from classes of teenage girls—'only immoralities could arise from such an encounter', she warned—that of a certain Dr A. Fernández, who protested against the nomination of the liberal Salvador Vila to the Chair of Hebrew at the University of Salamanca; that of the Acción Católica of Palencia interpreting the demand of three hundred organizations on behalf of religious education,[116] that of *Associaciones de Padres de Familia* demanding 'rigorous laws against immoral lectures' and against 'dealers in works that incite to evil', and those of scores of other organizations urging the government to ban pornographic films and publications.[117] The Minister of the Interior, the notorious Martínez Anido, issued in February 1927 an explicit order to confiscate any pornographic publication to be found in the post offices, that is, before it reached its destination.[118] In fact, this order was the reiteration of a previous one whereby special agents were to supervise the public premises to make sure that 'women are respected and that decency does not suffer from phrases or gestures of bad taste'. Street soliciting by prostitutes was also to be curbed;[119] public spectacles and music-halls were likewise strictly scrutinized to make sure that artists abided by 'moral norms',[120] and games of chance were forbidden.[121]

[114] 'La necesidad patriótica de la enseñanza religiosa', in *El Noticiero* (Cáceres), 30 Nov. 1927.

[115] *La Nación*, 21 Sept. 1926.

[116] AHN, P.G. Leg. 326, 20 June 1925; Leg. 358: 'Una Zamorana', Oct. 1926; Dr A. Fernández , 28 Nov. 1927; Acción Católica Palentina, 15 Apr. 1928.

[117] AHN, serie A, Gobernación, Leg. 48, Exp. 6: Pornografía, 7 Apr. 1927, no. 147; 24 Apr. 1927, no. 331; 21 Apr., no. 454; 23 Apr., no. 491.

[118] AHN, Gobernación, serie A: The minister of the interior to the director-general of communications, 5 Feb. 1927. During the second half of 1925 15,911 pornographic publications had been confiscated, *La Nación*, 21 Jan. 1926. See the material in AHN, Gobernación, serie A, Leg. 48; 'Pornografía, 1927'.

[119] See a variety of instructions in AHN, Gobernación, serie A. Leg. 52; 'Prostitución'.

[120] *Gaceta de Madrid*, 10 May 1924. See also AHN, Gobernación, serie A. Leg. 13; 'Blasfemia, 1924'.

[121] See AHN, Gobernación, serie A. Leg. 40; 'Juegos 1924–1925'.

Voluntary bodies such as the League Against Immorality, and the National League for the Defence of the Clergy, were keenly encouraged by the government to fight the danger of 'moral dissolution'.[122]

The supervision of public morality according to a pious Catholic code was to be the main task of the *juntas ciudadanas* that were set up in every provincial capital under the auspices of the governor, the captain-general, the local UP president, the mayor, and a Church delegate. Created in mid 1927, the *juntas* were conceived as the guardians of 'the vigour of Primo de Rivera's revolution'.[123] In their periodic meetings these Civic Juntas issued instructions to local officials about ways 'to curb prostitution and to preserve morality', and about how 'to combat blasphemy and punish the breach of the law of Sunday Observance'.[124] They likewise examined ways of fighting alcoholism among youngsters.[125] There were even cases in which *juntas* functioned as provincial courts for 'moral crimes', imposing fines on evil-doers. Such was the case in Barcelona of a humble fisherman, Salvador Masgrans, who was punished for a certain 'crime' committed by his daughter.[126] The organization of pro-government demonstrations, mainly following after the usually abortive conspiracies of the regime's enemies, or when the government looked for public support for its constitutional schemes in 1929, were also frequent endeavours of the civic *juntas*.[127] They thus represented a total conception of what constitutes 'a good citizen'. He should combine in his daily life the tenets of nationalism and Catholicism. He should be a law-abiding Catholic with a somewhat puritan morality. The unity of the *patria* and the support of the government were the only cases that could justify his 'political' mobilization.[128]

The ecclesiastical establishment flourished under the favourable conditions provided by the Dictatorship. In the 1920s the religious orders maintained over 900 professional and other colleges and catered for the education of half the children who received any formal education in Spain.[129] The number of religious communities

[122] *La Nación*, 12 Nov. 1927.

[123] Ibid., 4, 6 July 1927.

[124] AHN, P.G. Leg. 338; reports from the *junta ciudadana* of Álava, 3 Oct., 15 Dec. 1927, 14 Aug. 1928.

[125] *La Nación*, 22 July 1927.

[126] AHN, P.G. Leg. 338; a report from the civic junta of Barcelona, 15 Nov. 1927.

[127] Ibid., reports from Álava, 19 Feb. 1929, and Castellón, 10 Sept. 1929.

[128] Ibid., Legs. 383–6 are a mine of information on the activities of the juntas all over the country.

[129] *The Times*, 24 Apr. 1924; 18 Aug. 1928.

went up from 4,490 in April 1923 to 4,980 (1,946 of which were dedicated to educational tasks) in December 1930. The religious orders that numbered 71,815 in 1923 reached the figure of 81,400 in 1930. By then the secular clergy amounted to 32,607 priests.[130] Just as the Dictatorship had created a congenial and receptive atmosphere for the institutional consolidation of Catholicism, it stymied the activities of other Christian sects, such as the Evangelicals, for example, who were harassed for professing their faith or their beliefs in public.[131] Not more than 131 non-Catholic priests were operating in Spain in 1930.[132]

The ambitions of the Church extended beyond the sphere of mere service, for they included proselytism. It spread its doctrines and exercised a socio-political influence through such lay institutions as Acción Católica and the Confederación Nacional Católica Agraria (which claimed in the twenties 5,000 syndicates and 600,000 affiliates)[133] that was described in 1929 by Cardinal Segura, the Primate of Spain, as 'the best achievement of the Catholics at the present moment'.[134] The small and medium-sized farmers who formed the backbone of the CONCA would, eventually, constitute the initial power-base, indeed the founding nucleus, of Primo's *Unión Patriótica.*[135] A wide variety of other Catholic entities, *Patronatos* of every sort, ladies' associations, organizations of *Padres de Familia*, as well as urban Catholic syndicates were also there to further the cause of Catholicism and the social teachings of the Church, as opposed to the class concepts of socialism and those of liberal individualism.[136]

3. *'A Quick, Dignified, and Sensible Solution', or A Conqueror* malgré lui

One of the central promises of Primo de Rivera's pronunciamiento

[130] Cf. *Anuario*, 1931, pp. 664–5, 667–8; Jiménez de Asua, in *Diario de Sesones de las Cortes Constituyentes*, 13 Oct. 1931.

[131] *The Times*, 20 July 1929.

[132] 'Censo de población de 1930', *Anuario*, 1931.

[133] *El Imparcial*, 8 Nov. 1930, Castillo, *Propietarios*, pp. 114–21, 294–9, competently disputes these figures as highly exaggerated.

[134] *Boletín Oficial de la Acción Católica Española*, 25 Feb. 1929.

[135] See below, pp. 126–9, 145–7.

[136] For the CONCA as a bulwark of support for the Dictatorship, see Castillo, *Propietarios*, pp. 337–59. The aims of Catholic syndicalism are clearly formulated in Agustín Revuelta Martín, *Ventajas que la sindicación católica reporta a la clase agraria* (León, 1928). For the efforts of the Church to organize, at local level, rural workers and keep them away from harmful socialist doctrines, see *El Labrador, Revista quincenal con licencia eclesiástica*. For the widespread activities of Catholic lay institutions, see *Boletín de la Acción Católica Española*, 1929.

was that of bringing a 'quick, dignified, and sensible' solution to the Moroccan problem. He then boasted of possessing the formula that would relieve Spain, once and for all, from the Moroccan nightmare. Even his enemies were prepared to justify 'an event so unjustifiable as a *coup d'état*' if the Dictator had indeed cut the Gordian knot of the Moroccan dilemma.[137] But, as far as Morocco was concerned, Primo started as anything but the elaborator of a determined, strong-handed policy.

In fact, he fell back on his well-known 'abandonist' postures. During the first months of his rule, he took virtually no steps to fulfil his boastful promises. The conditions of the Africanist 'quadrilateral' for supporting Primo de Rivera had focused on the necessity of finding a military solution to the Rifian rebellion. However, a month after having seized power, Primo boldly deceived his Africanista supporters by claiming that 'an invasion of Alhucemas is no longer an urgent matter'.[138] And, as if further to emphasize a non-bellicose strategy for the protectorate, he started in November 1923 to release early thousands of draftees.[139] Moreover, instead of opting for a 'dignified' military solution, the Dictator simply returned to the thoroughly discredited, 'civilian' policy of peaceful negotiations with the rebels, for which the last constitutional government had been so severely castigated by the military.[140] As late as June 1925, when preparations for an invasion of the protectorate were well under way, Primo was still eager to keep alive the diplomatic option, as he continued to hope that a peaceful agreement might avoid the need for a military showdown.[141]

Primo's abandonism was matched only by his absolute lack of any vision concerning the economic potentialities of the protectorate. In Morocco, he was anything but the executor of Costa's grand colonial dream. The Dictator was probably further encouraged to stick to his abandonist postures by the fact that the very business community that had yearned for his seizure of power did not seem to have shown any keen interest in the economic exploitation of the protectorate. There were no real, powerful economic concerns to applaud or to put pressure on the regime to adopt an aggressive

[137] Villanueva, *La Dictadura*, p. 185.

[138] *El Sol*, 11 Oct. 1923.

[139] Ibid., 23, 28, 30 Nov. 1923.

[140] Hernández Mir, *La Dictadura en Marruecos. Al margen de una farsa* (Madrid, 1930), pp. 57–125, *Folletín*, pp. 119–20.

[141] Primo's letters to Magaz, 18, 21 June 1925; to Jordana, 26 June 1926, in Armiñán, *Epistolario*, pp. 205–8, 227–31, 236.

colonial policy in Morocco. Actually, loud voices were heard being raised against a futile and non-remunerative enterprise. When, in March 1924, the Rifian offensive seemed to be gaining momentum and there was a possibility that the government might mobilize all its military force to curb it, the country's Chambers of Commerce advanced their view that such a reaction by the government would be economically unwise. It certainly was not likely to satisfy their demand for budgetary stringency as the best way to alleviate the burden of taxation.[142] Now they argued that:

> The public treasury will never find in Morocco a compensation for the expenditures it has had to make in order to finance the war. On the contrary, it may happen—actually it is already happening—that the products of the protectorate will become our keenest competitors in both the home and foreign markets.[143]

It is significant that, once identified with Primo's abandonism, such a representative of Catalan capitalism as Cambó should have condemned the Dictator when, in the summer of 1925, the latter seemed to be opting for a strategy of total military occupation. Cambó failed to see in the protectorate that kind of promising colony waiting to be exploited by energetic enterpreneurs that other European bourgeoisies allegedly saw in Africa and Asia. For Cambó, northern Morocco was a useless, barren land, a superfluous and unnecessary burden on Spain's limited financial resources. In his view, evidence showed that those countries which possessed no colonies were also those 'whose currency is the soundest', while the colonial powers 'are being constantly weakened'. Cambó, like the Chambers of Commerce, saw in abandonism a great hope for a balanced budget, and hence of an alleviation of the burden of taxation. A retreat from Morocco would consequently also bring about 'an international revaluation of the peseta'.[144]

If indeed imperialism had been elsewhere the last or superior stage of capitalism, in the present Spanish case one would have to look for its origins in strictly political and strategic motives, or ones

[142] Such an argument was a central theme in the criticism of business sectors against the financial policy of the Dictatorship, see pp. 328–30, 349.

[143] *El Socialista*, 19 Mar. 1924.

[144] For Cambó's views, see his letters to the Dictator on 17 August and 16 October 1925 in *Folletín*, pp. 268–70. See also Cambó in *La Veu de Catalunya*, quoted ibid., p. 291; and Cambó, *España, Cataluña y la nueva constitución* (Buenos Aires, 1929), pp. 117–18; Hernández Mir, *Del desastre a la victoria (1929–1926). El Rif por España* (Madrid, 1927), p. 18.

that were closely connected with national honour and dignity as some perceived them. In fact, in his answer to Cambó, after the successful landing at Alhucemas, the Dictator did not deny the irrelevancy of economic arguments as an explanation of Spain's Moroccan enterprise. 'I do not think that there is any Spaniard who seriously believes that these 20,000 km² of arid terrain of the Rif and Yebala can be a [remunerative] colony for us. We should consider the value of this coastal strip of Northern Morocco in the light of entirely different concepts.'[145] King Alfonso was even more explicit in outlining the motives of international prestige that underlay Spain's actions in Morocco. He said in an interview with *El Imparcial* of Montevideo:

> This war is costing Spain a million pesetas a day . . . This is money that we could well have invested in our schools for the better education of our people. But to abandon the fight would be tantamount to the suicide of the white race, it would mark the beginning of the expulsion of the white man from North Africa, a severe blow to western civilization, that would certainly have repercussions in all other colonies . . . Spain cannot afford to be the first to fold the flag of the white race in Africa.[146]

It was, then, the myth of Spain as the sentinel of the west that prevented it, whatever the cost, from succumbing to the pressures of 'barbarian rebels'. They would have to be subdued by Spanish soldiers, many of whom came from villages where the advantages of western civilization were as unknown as in the Rif mountains.

Not even after Spain's hold of the protectorate had been secured in 1926–7 did the Dictatorship seem to have gone to too much trouble in order to satisfy the demands of some businessmen and romantic colonialists for a policy of investments and development in Morocco. Africanist organs did not cease to urge the government to launch programmes of agricultural and industrial development in the protectorate. Spain had in Morocco, it claimed, the markets it had been vainly looking for in other parts of the world. But neither this argument nor the Africanistas' contention that 'our zone in Morocco has the potential to produce more than the whole of Algeria' seemed to have moved the Dictator and his officials to conduct a real policy of colonization and economic exploitation of the protectorate.[147]

[145] Primo's letter to Cambó, 21 Oct. 1925, in *Folletín*, pp. 270–2.

[146] Quoted ibid., p. 273.

[147] *España en Africa*, 15, 31 Jan., 15 Feb. 1927; 15, 30 June 1928; 15 June, 15 Aug. 1929. See also almost every issue of *Revista Hispano-Africana. Liga Africanista Española*, 1923–9.

Primo de Rivera had always been ready to contemplate a peaceful, negotiated evacuation of the protectorate. What he could by no means afford was to be compelled to do so by a military defeat. Abd-el-Krim's offensive in the spring of 1924 was a challenge not only to Primo's Moroccan strategy, but to the very credibility and 'dignity' of his regime. The government had therefore no choice but to make clear its decision to fight the Rifian aggression 'regardless of our criterion or final purpose in Morocco'. In May 1924 General Sanjurjo, a famous Africanista, was precipitately moved from his Zaragoza assignment to the post of commander-in-chief of the Melilla sector. The decision was made to fight 'whatever the cost might be'.[148]

Such combative language was forced upon the Dictator not only by the pressure of the rebels, but also by that of his Africanista officers. In his visit to the protectorate in the summer of 1924,[149] the Africanistas brought home to him an unequivocal message. Regardless of what may have been Spain's real interests in Morocco, an abandonist policy or an undignified performance by the Dictatorship in the protectorate would put in serious danger the very survival of the regime. As was the case under previous civilian governments, Morocco was not an issue that Primo could afford to tackle in a way that was unacceptable to the military, and yet survive politically. Now as always, the Moroccan problem was fundamentally an internal issue.

The fierce opposition of his élite troops[150] was no less a threat to Primo's rule than the futile Moroccan war. The Africanistas were scandalized to realize that their military dictator was toying with the same ideas as his civilian predecessors, and that his major concerns in elaborating his Moroccan strategy were issues such as the need for a balanced budget, and the pressure of civilian opinion yearning for peace. The Africanistas could not but feel dishonoured by Primo's 'Jewish plan' of withdrawal. The growing grudge against the plan among Africanistas was such that the Commander-in-Chief, General Aizpuru, had to threaten any officer with capital punishment who criticized the government's plan. 'Ours is not a revolutionary army in which decisions are made by suffrage', he stated.[151]

[148] See Primo's official note of 1 July 1924 in *ABC*.

[149] *El Sol*, 18 July 1924.

[150] Hernández Mir, *La Dictadura*, pp. 126–82.

[151] 'Orden general para oficiales del día, 12 de Junio de 1924', in Romanones Archive, Leg. 58, no. 8.

It did credit to Primo de Rivera's leadership that, in spite of the hostile atmosphere that surrounded his plan of withdrawal, he still managed to make the Africanistas abide by it. But he seemed to have succeeded in setting their minds at rest only by accepting that the retreat should be a tactical rather than a strategic step. This was a clear shift of emphasis from views he had previously defended; and the Ben-Tieb incident had much to do with it.[152] Upon his return to the peninsula he confessed that he had heard in Morocco 'loyal and sincere views opposed to mine, which I had, therefore, to modify partly'.[153] And, on the first annivarsary of his *coup d'état*, a few days after he arrived for the second time to inspect the situation in the protectorate, his message to his fellow countrymen was that 'there is no other way in Morocco than to fight until the enemy is defeated'. 'Otherwise', he said, 'as a race we should be losing our virility, and as an army our prestige.'[154]

But prestige can sometimes be a costly affair to enhance. The autumn and winter of 1924 were perhaps the gloomiest hours of Primo de Rivera's rule. The retreat of his forces from their advanced positions in the protectorate sometimes turned into a rout. The retreat from Xauen was the bloodiest operation of them all.[155] A strict censorship was imposed on any news coming from Morocco, as the 'quick, dignified, and sensible' solution was anything but forthcoming, and the 'pessimist augurs' among the Africanistas were again displaying their dissatisfaction.[156] When, by mid December, a total of 180 Spanish military posts had been abandoned, the so-called Primo de Rivera line that was now formed could defend hardly anything beyond the communications between Tangier, Tetuan, and the French zone.

It does seem, moreover, that once the new Primo de Rivera line had been stabilized, the dictator started to toy again with 'abandonist' ideas. He explained that Spain would not give up its civilizing mission in the protectorate, it would only change its method of

[152] Mola, p. 1024; FO/371/10593, Gurney to Ramsay MacDonald, 2 Aug. 1924. At the Legion's camp of Ben-Tieb, the Dictator was almost assaulted physically by the furious Africanistas. For that tense encounter, see 'Ben-Tieb — relato de un testigo', in Romanones Archive, Leg. 58, no. 44.

[153] Official note of 23 July 1924 in *ABC*.

[154] *El Sol*, 13 Sept. 1924.

[155] For reports on the retreat, see *El Sol*, 13, 24 Sept., 12 Dec. 1924; Hernández Mir, *La Dictadura*, pp. 183–244; Woolman, Chapter 9. For Xauen, see Shannon and Ann Fleming, 'Primo de Rivera and Spain's Moroccan Problem, 1923–1927', in *JCH*, vol. 12, no.1, 1977, pp. 180–7.

[156] 'Orden general del día, 30 Nov. 1924', in Romanones Archive, Leg. 58, no. 48.

exercising it. The new approach would combine direct military rule in the area protected by the new line, and rule through friendly local chieftains in the zone beyond that area. Sporadic military operations might be needed to strengthen the authority of these local allies.[157] Whereas he had previously hinted that the retreat from advanced positions was fundamentally a tactical exercise—that is an avenue to total occupation—he now seemed to have fallen back on it as a strategic move. He was no longer sure 'whether we should extend our operations to the other zone or not'. The purpose was now to elaborate a Moroccan policy that would be 'compatible with the economic possibilities of Spain'.[158]

Yet, as far as the Moroccan problem was concerned, Primo de Rivera displayed anything but dogmatism. Considerations of an international nature[159] and the emergence of favourable conditions for Franco-Spanish co-operation against the common Rifian foe finally made the Dictator opt for a policy of total military occupation. He also developed a fear that Abd-el-Krim was about to set up a puppet state either under communist influence or subservient to the interests of the Germans, who might eventually turn it into an air and submarine base against Spain. Primo's conviction that Morocco was becoming the launching ground of 'an Islamic–Bolshevik' offensive against the *patria* he had just rescued from 'red barbarism' was an important factor in his switch of policy.[160]

Yet, not until the agreements with the French had been sealed did Primo de Rivera give up hope of reaching a peaceful arrangement with Abd-el-Krim. Since the conclusion of the withdrawal to the new line, the Dictator had been negotiating with the rebels through the good services of the Basque millionaire Horacio Echevarrieta. On 20 June, three days after the Franco-Spanish conference opened in Madrid, Echevarrieta met Abd-el-Krim for a last-moment attempt to bridge the gap between the two sides. His proposal now consisted of the recognition by Spain of an autonomous entity in the Rif that would even have its own army, albeit one under direct Spanish command.

But, if Primo de Rivera still needed a reason to stick to common strategy with the French, Abd-el-Krim provided it by his bold

[157] *Folletín*, p. 172.

[158] Primo's speech at a pro-government rally in December 1924, quoted ibid., p. 195. [159] M. Martín, *El colonialismo español en Marruecos* (Paris, 1972), p. 82.

[160] Primo to Sanjurjo, 4 June 1925, in Armiñán, *Epistolario*, p. 125. See also his declarations in *La Nación*, 25 May 1926.

rejection of Echevarrieta's terms. He would have nothing less than full independence.[161] Abd-el-Krim is an extreme example of a national leader who doomed his movement to perdition by refusing to accept the limits of his power and of his potentialities for manœuvre. By mid August 1925 both the Spaniards and the French had definitely given up their attempts to reach a peaceful solution to the crisis. 'Abd-el-Krim has made peace impossible', now exclaimed the Spanish Dictator. Therefore, at a meeting on 31 August between himself and General Pétain in Algeciras, the final touch to the common military plan was added.[162]

The carefully planned and successfully executed Spanish landing at Alhucemas Bay on 5 September 1925 came simultaneously with a French attack against Abd-el-Krim's republic. The Spanish press was obviously inundated with euphoric and eulogistic reports of the heroic operation. This could not be otherwise when the censorship banned any news of the organizational deficiencies and logistic shortcomings of the landing, news that circulated clandestinely among the opposition in Spain.[163] Nothing succeeds like success, however, and, notwithstanding numerous deficiencies, the landing was a decisive breakthrough towards ending the Moroccan 'nightmare'. A massive concentration of fully equipped men, artillery batteries, aeroplanes, and warships, eight among them French, launched its full strength upon the northern coasts of Morocco.[164] Victory, as Primo de Rivera assured his soldiers, was imminent, because 'We are bound to fight, as Spanish citizens and soldiers . . . We can and should be proud of being a sublime race, a vigorous people, a well-organized and well-governed nation.'[165] Alhucemas was then as much a test for the regime as a challenge to the army.

It was not, however, until the beginning of October that the government was able to announce that 'the villages around Axdir', Abd-el-Krim's capital, had been occupied.[166] And not even then could it be said that the war was over. In fact, even after Abd-el-Krim had surrendered to the French on 27 May 1926, large areas of

[161] For these latest attempts to reach a peaceful settlement, see *Folletín*, pp. 235–6; Primo to Magaz, 18, 21, 23 June 1925, in Armiñán, *Epistolario*, pp. 205–8, 227–31, 236.

[162] *Folletín*, pp. 243–7.

[163] 'Noticias sobre la toma de Alhucemas', in Romanones Archive, Leg. 23, no. 6; Armiñán, *El Dictador*, pp. 153–89.

[164] See the accounts of the landing in *ABC*, 9 Sept. 1925; Woolman, Chapters 12–13.

[165] *Folletín*, p. 245.

[166] *El Sol*, 2 Oct. 1925.

the protectorate still remained insecure for the Spanish forces.[167] Not until the occupation of Xauen in August 1926 could the war really be considered to be over.[168] Furthermore, the financial cost of the war did not diminish substantially after Alhucemas. Only 50 million pesetas less than in 1925–6 were spent on the protectorate in 1927 (350 million compared with 400 million). Even in 1928, the expenditures in Morocco were still fairly high—314 million pesetas—though a greater portion of this money was now spent on civilian tasks.[169] Throughout 1926 the government still found it very difficult to accept petitions by parents who demanded the repatriation of their sons 'now that the war is over'.[170] Bloody encounters between Spanish soldiers and Rifian rebels were not uncommon until the spring of 1927.[171]

But Primo's was a regime of patriotic exaltation and festivals. When the battlegrounds of Morocco were still anything but quiet, Madrid started to celebrate. Generals Saro, Sanjurjo, Despujols, and Fernández Pérez, who commanded the four main columns at the landing, were promoted early in October. The Dictator himself was hailed as the greatest military commander of modern times. He was awarded the highly prestigious Gran Cruz Laureada de San Fernando and the Gran Cruz de Mérito Naval. The relevant decree asserted that 'Every difficulty has been overcome by the iron will, the serene courage, the prodigious intelligence, the insuperable military competence of General Primo de Rivera [who] . . . managed to crown with undisputed success the most arduous enterprise ever to be carried out by a colonial army.'[172] Pompous oratory apart, the aura of the pacifier of Morocco undoubtedly belonged to the Dictator. He had made the dream of every civilian government since 1909 come true: peace with honour. On 4 July 1927, the vicious cycle of frustration, humiliation, and defeat was closed, as the Dictator demonstratively allowed himself to go back on his earlier solemn promise that the Moroccan 'responsibilities' would be dealt with. A complete amnesty was signed on that day for all

[167] For the surrender of the rebel and the final peace negotiations, see *La Nación*, 27 May 1926; Hernández Mir, *Del desastre*, pp. 5–90.

[168] *La Nación*, 11 Aug. 1926.

[169] For the cost of the war, see Primo to Sanjurjo, 13 Aug. 1926, in Armiñán, *Epistolario*, p. 383. Maura, *Bosquejo*, p. 224, Benítez de Lugo, *Obra económica, financiera y monetaria de la Dictadura* (Madrid, 1930), p. 22. For public works, see *La Nación*, 24 May 1928.

[170] AHN, P.G. Leg. 348.

[171] *The Economist*, 30 Apr., 7 May 1927. *La Nación*, 24 Aug. 1927, wrote that the war had only now ended.

[172] *Gaceta de Madrid*, 6 Oct. 1925.

those who were convicted for their faults in Morocco, among them General Berenguer.[173] Annual was no longer the tomb of Spanish military dignity, it was just the kind of temporary 'set-back that occurs in the best of armies': Spain had finally rescued her honour. 'We can now say with Castelar that Spain starts in the Pyrenees and ends in the Atlas mountains', wrote a euphoric panegyrist of the regime.[174]

4. *Spain, Great . . .*

The Cuban disaster of 1898 had shattered whatever pretensions some Spaniards might have harboured in relation to the status of their country as a world power. Defeated and humiliated, Spain was exposed to the whole world as a backward country suffering from inefficiency and misgovernment, a stagnant, agrarian society not yet ready to face the challenges of the twentieth century. 'Regenerationism' was about curing the structural maladies of the Spaniards and their country, developing its economy, educating its people, and reforming its government, in short, 'restoring Spain's pulse'. Only when this grand design of national reconstruction was completed could Spain's international aspirations inspire credibility. Primo de Rivera wrongly believed that this stage had now been reached, and he embarked upon diplomatic adventures that could not be sustained by Spain's real power. The long overdue victory over the Rifian rebels was a great achievement. It did not suffice, however, to turn Spain overnight into a world power.

Primo's ambitions were now directed towards the international city of Tangier. He asked for nothing less than its full incorporation into the Spanish protectorate, a demand inconsistent with a Spanish–French–British agreement of 1923 that conceded the French special prerogatives in the administration of the city. The 1923 agreement had actually been presented to Spain by the British and the French almost as a *fait accompli.*[175] Primo de Rivera tabled, early in 1924, a series of reservations to the treaty. His demands consisted of an extension of the Spanish zones of Melilla and Ceuta, and the concession of additional prerogatives to the Spanish officials in the city's administration. These demands were unceremoniously

[173] Maura, *Bosquejo*, p. 77.

[174] Gandarías, p. 63.

[175] Marqués de Mulhacén, *Política mediterránea de España 1704–1951* (Madrid, 1951), pp. 329–45; Gay de Montellá, p. 322.

turned down by the French, who would only agree to have one Spanish official in the city's customs service but refused to allow any privileges to the Spaniards in the actual administration of Tangier.[176]

But once the Moroccan war was over, and 'Spain has succeeded in asserting, and in invigorating its international personality',[177] Primo launched a new, and more determined, bid for a Spanish Tangier. It was not only Alhucemas that had now entitled Spain to assume the position of a world power. Foreign Minister Yanguas also mentioned in this context the daring Spanish flight across the ocean, the invention by La Cierva of the *autogiro*, and the resumption by Spain of her leadership of the Latin American nations. Spain had definitely broken 'the parenthesis of scepticism', and she demanded a prominent place in world politics.[178]

The Dictator's 1926 boastful initiative over Tangier was also launched amid a fabricated upsurge of patriotic feelings backed by petitions of Africanists and Spanish merchants, as well as by the Spanish community in the international zone.[179] It suited the political aims of the regime to turn Tangier into a national issue. It had the potential to extend and emphasize 'the coincidence between the nation and its government'. Tangier had the great virtue of 'making of all the Spaniards one Spaniard'; it was an 'admirable agglutinative'.[180] Indeed, the Dictatorship anticipated here the kind of patriotic exaltation and *mise-en-scène* that was later to be engineered by Franco in his bid to incorporate Tangier into the protectorate.[181]

There was, throughout, an element of the ludicrous in the search for grandeur and international prestige of Primo de Rivera's foreign policy. His diplomatic offensive over Tangier provided him with the opportunity to run an experiment in *Weltpolitik*. Foreign governments were bombarded with applications to support Spain's demands over the international city.[182] The Minister of War, the Duke of Tetuan, assured British and French opinion that Spain would grant full equality to the non-Spanish citizens of Tangier, and would never fortify the city so that it became a strategic threat to other

[176] *Folletín*, pp. 103–4. [177] *La Nación*, 18 Mar., 6 May, 16 Aug. 1926.

[178] Ibid., 24 Mar. 1926.

[179] AHN, P.G. Leg. 320: Comisión de Centros Comerciales Hispano-Marroquíes, 18 Aug. 1926; *España en Africa*, 31 Jan. 1927.

[180] *La Nación*, 17, 23, 31 Aug. 1926.

[181] Cf. Charles and Carolyn Halstead, 'Aborted Imperalism: Spain's Occupation of Tangier 1940–45', in *Iberian Studies*, vol. vii, no. 2 (Autumn 1978), pp. 53–71.

[182] AHN, P.G. Leg. 346; Embajadas y Asuntos Internacionales.

powers. Moreover, he asserted, no country was better equipped than Spain, because of the nature of her regime, to fight off any 'bolshevik propaganda' that was likely to emerge in the international zone.[183] In concrete terms, the Spanish argument—the king echoed it in an interview with *Le Figaro*, and the Dictator in a letter to Briand— was basically that as long as Tangier remained outside the Spanish protectorate, it would continue to be a base of hostile operations against both the Spanish and French possessions in Morocco. Its incorporation in the Spanish zone was therefore in the best interests of the French as well.[184] Indeed, *La Nación* preferred to present the Spanish demand for Tangier as 'a sacrifice that we make for civilization'.[185] But, as far as the Dictator was concerned, it was the international prestige of Spain and of his regime that was at stake. Tangier was to be the test case of Spain's pretensions to be considered as a world power. Primo put it in a characteristically outspoken and figurative way: 'Spain, glorious Spain, the mother of one hundred nations, cannot afford to sit in the gallery of the world theatre, not even in the stalls. She needs to have a seat in the box.'[186] Spain, claimed *La Nación*, had enough political and economic power to sustain such a grand dream.[187]

After the failure in February 1927 of a Franco-Spanish conference to work out a bilateral solution to the crisis, a new conference was opened on 20 March 1928 at the Quai d'Orsay, this time with the participation of Spain, France, Britain, and Italy. The Spanish position in the negotiations was clearly vulnerable. Spain had virtually no international support for changing a status quo to which she had subscribed not long before. Moreover, the French government and opinion were infuriated by what they saw as a Spanish attempt to pave the way, for reasons of 'dictatorial solidarity' as well as in an attempt to enlist additional pressure against the French, for the Italians to have a say in the issue of Tangier.[188] Actually, the policy of inviting Italy to the Tangier negotiations in the hope that the Mediterranean Latin 'sister' would play an important role in Spain's

[183] An interview with Clara Candiani, Dec. 1926; manuscript in AHN, P.G. Leg. 346.

[184] The king's interview with Clara Candiani, ibid. For the message to Briand, see Primo to Spain's ambassador in Paris, 15 Aug. 1926, ibid.

[185] *La Nación*, 3 Sept. 1926.

[186] Gandarías, p. 75.

[187] *La Nación*, 2 Sept. 1926.

[188] AHN, P.G. Leg. 442; Spain's ambassador in Rome to Primo de Rivera, 25 Mar. 1924.

favour was inaugurated by the last constitutional government.[189] What the Spaniards refused to understand was that Mussolini was anything but prepared to play the game of others. He had his own: the Italian *mare nostrum*. In August 1926, the Duce had made it clear that his government would not back the incorporation of Tangier in the Spanish protectorate. The Italians argued that 'the Spanish petition might be conducive to a radical change in the Moroccan situation as established by international treaties and might have repercussions upon both Italian interests and the general aspect of the Mediterranean'.[190] The 'ineradicable suspicion of Italy and what might be behind the Italian demands', which Primo had developed in the course of the negotiations over Tangier,[191] was eventually vindicated. The Italians proved to be of no help to Spain; they were as active as the French in blocking any attempt to alter in any substantial way the status of the international city.[192]

The mountain had given birth to the mouse. The final agreement on Tangier fell far short of fulfilling the Dictator's grandiose aspirations. An improvement of the mechanism for the prevention of arms traffic in the international zone, and the concession to the Spaniards of the post of the city's chief of police, were all the success that Primo could claim.[193] Somehow he still thought that the whole affair had 'enhanced the dignity of Spain'.[194]

But the Dictator harboured still greater dreams. In fact, his diplomatic offensive over Tangier was also a cumbersome tactical device aimed at blackmailing Britain and France into accepting his grand aspiration to a permanent seat for Spain in the League of Nations' Security Council, i.e. the concession to Spain of the status of a first-rate world power.[195] Spain, according to the Dictator, was entitled to such a status 'because of its history, its size, the number of its inhabitants, the fact that it possesses two rich archipelagos and

[189] *El Sol*, 1 Sept. 1923.

[190] AHN, P.G. Leg. 346; Spain's ambassador in Rome to Primo de Rivera, 26 Aug. 1926.

[191] Chamberlain quoted in G. Carocci, *La Politica Estera dell'Italia Fascista (1925–1928)* (Bari, 1969), p. 217.

[192] AHN, P.G. Leg. 346; Merry del Val (London) to Primo, 21 Apr. 1927; Spain's ambassador in Rome to Primo, 25 Aug. 1926.

[193] For the final agreement, see Marqués de Mulhacén, pp. 347–51; Gay de Montellá, pp. 322–3.

[194] *Folletín*, p. 726.

[195] In their internal discussions the Spaniards confessed that such indeed was their tactics: AHN, P.G. Leg. 438: Yanguas to Spain's ambassadors in London and Rome, 28 July 1926.

a modest colonial patrimony; because of the fact that it also exercises a protectorate of world interest . . . and because of the race that it represents'.[196]

But a permanent seat in the League's Security Council was reserved, under the Locarno agreement, for Germany; and, as early as September 1924, she had made it clear that she would refuse to be accompanied by Spain or by any other nation (Poland and Brazil also advanced their candidacy) in her ceremonial return to the family of nations.[197] Germany's position was strongly supported by Sweden, herself a member of the Security Council, which, rather than be content with the role of a passive opponent to the Spanish *démarche*, actively campaigned against it.[198] As for the French, they consistently avoided a clear commitment to extend their co-operation with the Spaniards in Morocco to the issue of the League of Nations.[199] The Dictator's official visit to Paris to celebrate the official end of the Moroccan war,[200] and the exchange of medals between himself and General Pétain may have reflected mutual appreciation between the two armies, as Foreign Minister Briand noted,[201] but this fraternity would not bring France to go out of its way in order to defend Primo's diplomacy of brinkmanship in Geneva. Initially, it was the readiness of France and Britain at least to 'consider' the Spanish demand that resulted in the appointment of an international commission to work out a compromise. This consisted of a proposal to create three new non-permanent seats in addition to the six already in existence. This was a clear attempt to meet Spanish pretensions half-way, and, indeed, one that provided Spain with a dignified way out of the impasse into which she had manœuvred herself. But it was a feature of the Dictator's foreign policy that it was conducted with a total, almost quixotic disregard of the limits of power, of the relation between goals and means. It was beneath his dignity to accept a 'mutilated' membership of the Security Council, and he ordered his delegate at the League to reject the compromise.[202]

196 *L'Étoile belge*, 9 June 1926.

197 AHN, P.G. Leg. 349; Spain's ambassador in Berlin to Primo, 24 Sept. 1924.

198 Ibid., Leg. 438; Spain's ambassador in Stockholm to Primo, 3 Apr. 1926.

199 The Spaniards approached their French allies over the League issue and received only evasive answers: ibid., Yanguas to Spain's ambassador in Paris, 20 Feb. 1926, 10 May 1926.

200 See the euphoric reports in *La Nación*, 12, 14 July 1926.

201 AHN, P.G. Leg. 346; Primo to Spain's ambassador in Paris, and France's ambassador in Madrid to Primo, 22 July 1926.

202 *Folletín*, pp. 343–53.

Primo's bold policy of all or nothing[203] lost him the support of most of the Council's members. Moreover, it helped to underline the fallacy of his 'Latin–Mediterranean' friendship with Italy as well as of his pretension to speak in world politics in the name of Spain's Hispano-American 'daughters'. Sciajola, the Italian delegate, did not leave any doubt as to his country's refusal, 'under the actual circumstances', to back the Spanish demand.[204] This was a serious set-back to Spain, since it was the Italians who in 1924 had encouraged the Spanish government to advance its candidacy for a permanent seat in order to counterbalance Germany's expected entry to the League with the status of a world power.[205] Argentina and Uruguay were hardly more forthcoming than the Italian 'ally'.[206] Indeed, the support of Spain's position in the international arena by the Latin American countries should not have been taken for granted by the Dictator, overwhelmed though he may have been by the torrent of rhetoric about Iberian fraternity that flew from both sides of the ocean.[207]

On 2 September 1926, the League's special commission went a step further towards Spain by recommending that some of the non-permanent members of the Security Council could become *de facto* permanent if, upon the expiry of their respective terms, they were again elected by the League. It was proposed that this procedure could go on indefinitely. The British and French foreign ministers, Chamberlain and Briand, now appealed personally to Primo de Rivera to accept this latest compromise, which indeed reflected an optimal attempt to meet Spain's demands. But the Dictator would accept nothing but a ceremonial entry, through the front door, to a permanent seat. He knew it would have been wise diplomacy to accept the compromise, but he could not bring himself to relinquish the grand role he had cast for himself in his own script.[208] He wrote to Chamberlain and Briand: 'My personal inclination is that of immediately accepting the invitation. But I am bound by my duty to watch over the prestige of this old, glorious, and beloved Spain which, when relegated to a position that is

[203] Primo left no doubt that such was his approach, *La Nación*, 15 June 1926.
[204] *Folletín*, pp. 343–53.
[205] AHN, P.G. Leg. 439: Spain's ambassador in Rome to Primo de Rivera, 13 Oct. 1924. Mussolini again supported the idea in 1925, ibid., 27 Aug. 1925.
[206] *Folletín*, pp. 343–53.
[207] For the regime's showpiece of Hispano-Americanism, see pp. 202–5.
[208] *Folletín*, pp. 343–5.

inferior to the one she is entitled to, is left with no choice but to resort to a dignified abstention.'[209] Carried away by his own vanity and by the 'patriotic' pressure of Spanish Ayuntamientos and conservative corporations of all sorts,[210] a pressure which he had himself consciously unleashed and stirred up, Primo went even beyond 'abstention' to declare, on 8 September 1926, Spain's total withdrawal from the League.

This rather grotesque exhibition of national pride was resorted to only after blackmail diplomacy had failed. Earlier in the year, Primo had vainly attempted to change Sweden's 'absolutely intransigent' attitude by threatening to revise Spain's commercial treaty with her.[211] In the middle of August, he gave a renewed and artificial sense of urgency to the issue of Tangier as a way of accelerating Spain's entry into the Security Council. He warned that 'Europe and the entire world would not recover their tranquillity in relation to Tangier, unless Spain is given complete rule over the city'.[212] At the same time, he warned that the failure of the powers to acquiesce to his demands over Tangier would result in the immediate withdrawal of Spain from the League of Nations.[213]

Primo de Rivera had definitely succeeded in arousing the indignation of European opinion. In characteristically restrained style *The Times* rejected Spain's policy over Tangier and the Security Council as 'incompatible with the principles of the League of Nations'.[214] The *Daily News* was outspoken. Spain, it editorialized, was trying to blackmail the other powers by playing off Tangier against Geneva. She had thus placed herself in an impasse where compromise had become a virtual impossibility.[215] The French *Journal des débats* accused Primo de Rivera of trying to ease the pressure of his overwhelming internal difficulties by artificially creating an external crisis.[216] *L'Humanité* maintained that the very reputation of the League had been challenged by the Spanish Dictator, and it should therefore by no means succumb to his blackmail.[217] The torrent of criticism only increased when Spain's withdrawal from the League was finally announced. The influential *Journal de Genève* wrote:

[209] Ibid., p. 348.
[210] See hundreds of telegrams in AHN, P.G. Leg. 438: Asamblea de Naciones, 1926.
[211] Ibid., Spain's ambassador in Stockholm to Primo, 27 Feb. 1926.
[212] *El Sol*, 15 Aug. 1926.
[213] *Folletín*, p. 350.
[214] *The Times*, 20 Aug. 1926.
[215] *Daily News*, 29 Aug. 1926.
[216] *Journal des débats*, 31 Aug. 1926.
[217] *L'Humanité*, 31 Aug. 1926.

This step by General Primo de Rivera is to be totally condemned . . . a miserable country is that in which its leaders do not ask for her opinion, and which is not in a position to express it. Its future is being mortgaged by people whose total authority rests on sheer force. Yet the legitimate distinction that ought to be drawn between the Spanish people and its rulers should not diminish the anger of the League of Nations . . . [The countries involved in the Tangier issue] should now refuse to enter into any negotiations with a government that does not deserve any international confidence whatsoever.[218]

Primo's experiment in world politics was, then, a total failure. He had lost both Tangier and Geneva. And, what was perhaps even graver, as *L'Œuvre* observed, 'Spain has separated herself from Europe at the very moment when Europe is about to reconstruct herself.'[219]

The failure of Primo's initiatives over Tangier and the League also had internal repercussions. They brought into the open a divergence of views between Yanguas, the foreign minister, and his master, the Dictator. On 20 February 1927, the 'ministerial crisis' ended with the latter personally assuming the portfolio of foreign affairs: a very 'Mussolinian' way of solving cabinet disputes, Gabriel Maura was to note.[220] Primo de Rivera probably also expected that the forthcoming international conference on Tangier might result, thanks to his introduction of Italy into the forum of nations directly concerned with the status of the city, in a breakthrough in Spain's favour, and he wanted to be there alone to reap the success. A vain hope, as it turned out.

In March 1928, Primo de Rivera's humiliation was completed. The guardian of Spain's dignity returned then to the fold of the League of Nations without even pretending to impose preconditions. 'The government accepts thankfully', he wrote to Sr. Francisco José Urrutia, the president of the Security Council, 'and without conditions or reservations, your honoured invitation [to return to the League], with the confidence that the General Assembly will determine in due course the status that is compatible with Spain's special position as a great neutral power during the last war, and with her lineage as the mother of peoples and civilizations.'[221]

When a dictatorship daily claims that one of its major endeavours, and indeed achievements, is that of enhancing Spain's international

218 *Journal de Genève*, 11 Sept. 1926.

219 *L'Œuvre*, 12 Sept. 1926.

220 Maura, *Bosquejo*, p. 227. See also *The Times*, 20, 22 Feb. 1927.

221 *El Sol*, 22 Mar. 1928. See also AHN, P.G. Leg. 438; Primo to his ambassadors in London and Paris, 23 March 1928, asking them to notify Briand and Chamberlain of his decision. No further explanations were given or assurances demanded.

prestige, it obviously faces a resounding set-back when its grandiloquent initiatives are rebuffed and it is overwhelmingly denounced by European opinion. International politics may be cynical, but they have their rules, one of them being that they cannot be run by decrees and royal orders in the way the Spanish people were. It might be right to suggest, as *The Economist* did, that the rebellion of the artillery corps against the Dictatorship, a rebellion that coincided with Spain's diplomatic initiative, 'does not suggest that Spain possesses the combination of qualities which is required by her international pretensions'.[222] But a dictator's whims can be imposed on the international community, even when he is opposed at home, provided he possesses the force to back them. Primo suffered from two basic disadvantages: he had an opposition, and no force to impose his will beyond his frontiers. But if he played for high stakes with inadequate resources—to borrow A. J. P. Taylor's characterization of Hitler's foreign policy—it was because his entire regime rested on an incessant appeal to improve, change, and redeem his country. He intuitively maintained, that for a dictatorship to survive, it must keep going, or at least pretend to. Antonio Maura likened this predicament to the riding of a bicycle; once you cease to pedal you fall over . . .

[222] *The Economist*, 11 Sept. 1926. For the artillery, see pp. 362–3.

CHAPTER IV

'The Second Stage' *The Politics of Controlled Mobilization*

PRIMO DE RIVERA was never too happy with the view of his regime as a mere military adventure. He consistently strove to give it a solid civilian basis and a political philosophy. 'The word pronunciamiento', he said, 'does not flatter us at all.'[1] It is possible to discern in his rule the foundations of a civilian 'new state', which he consistently advanced in his search for a new source of legitimacy and for an alternative power-base to that of the bayonets and the crown.

1. *One Party*

(a) *The Origins of the Unión Patriótica.* The Unión Patriótica, about whose 'artificiality' everything has already been said, constituted an important landmark in the crystallization of Spanish agrarian fascism. The UP's emergence as a party (Primo would always prefer to see it as a national 'anti-party', or a 'League of Citizens')—the former being a Mussolinian concept later utilized also by the founders of *Renovación Española* and *Acción Nacional* in Spain, while the latter characterized the *Action Française*[2]—was as natural as that of any political organization claiming to possess a social basis. This was evident enough for the Dictator to acknowledge later that 'the Unión Patriótica was born spontaneously, with the advent of the Directory, in Castilian lands'.[3] It started life in Valladolid, the Catholic capital of the middle landowners and corn-growers of Old Castile: the same socio-geographical setting that later bred under the Republic the *Juntas Castellanas de Actuación Hispánica* and the

[1] Primo de Rivera, *Actuación ciudadana que corresponde al ejército* (conferencia pronunciada . . . en el Casino de Clases de Madrid, el día 26 de octubre de 1927, Madrid, 1927), pp. 15–21.

[2] Sometimes the term 'falange' was used to describe the UP; see *Unión Patriótica*, 1 Mar. 1929.

[3] His speech in El Palacio de Hielo, *La Nación*, 19 Oct. 1925. See also José María Pemán, *El hecho y la idea de la Unión Patriótica* (Madrid, 1929), pp. 11–12, on the Castilian spontaneous origins of the UP.

Juntas de Ofensiva Nacional Sindicalista, both of which eventually found their way into the Falange. It was also among this social class that the *CEDA*, whose future leader Gil Robles was very active in launching the UP during its initial steps,[4] found its most solid mass support.

Moreover, the very idea of founding the *Unión Patriótica Castellana* originated in the same circles—those of the Catholic organ *El Debate*, the *Acción Nacional de Propagandistas*, and the *Partido Social Popular*, and under the same initiative, that of Ángel Herrera,[5] that was to generate in 1931 *Acción Nacional* and, eventually, the *CEDA*. *El Debate* had actually demanded the creation of such a party on the very day Primo de Rivera was summoned by the king to take over the reins of power. These were no mean expectations that *El Debate* harboured in relation to the new party. It was anticipated that this would be the instrument for putting into practice the dreams of Maura's 'revolution from above', and would institutionalize the PSP's drive to break away from the old system of political *clientelae* in favour of one of civil mobilization and social emphasis, on the lines of the Italian *Partito Popolare*. The proposed party should not limit itself simply to lending the Dictator a body of organized popular support, but should also prepare itself for the task of becoming the mass party on the right that would some day succeed the Dictatorship. This longed-for movement, editorialized *El Debate*, like any political party, aspired 'to conquer power'.[6] 'An enormous body of opinion is now supporting' the new regime, explained Ángel Herrera by mid November, but it remained a diffuse and highly inefficient force so long as it did not crystallize into 'new and sane political organizations'. Herrera's urge came in a meeting in Valladolid of Catholic Propagandists, from which actually sprang, on that very day, the organizing committee of the new party.[7]

This Catholic–agrarian circle launched the UPC as an association of small and medium-sized farmers in support of the newborn regime, and as a bulwark against anarchy in case it failed to survive. The UPC's socio-political physiognomy was accurately reflected in the personal background of those who subscribed to its founding manifesto in Valladolid: figures such as Agustín Ruiz, the president

[4] Gil Robles, p. 29.

[5] For Herrera's initial moves towards the establishment of the UPC, see *El Debate*, 13 Nov. 1923.

[6] *El Debate*, 15, 19, 21, Sept., 8 Dec. 1923.

[7] Ibid., 13 Nov. 1923.

of the Catholic Syndicate of Railwaymen, Francisco Pérez, the head of the Valladolid branch of the same syndicate, Rafael Alonso las Heras, the president of the Federation of Catholic–Agrarian Syndicates, and his deputy Armando Valentín Aguilar, as well as Antonio Jimeno, a distinguished member of the *Casa Social Católica* of Valladolid. Prominent and highly active among the members of the UPC's founding nucleus was Eduardo Callejo, Primo de Rivera's future minister of education.[8]

The example of Valladolid was soon to be followed elsewhere in Castile, as throughout the last months of 1923 the UPC was hectically staging, all over the region, mass gatherings in which crystallized a commitment to uphold 'Catholic values', 'social justice', and 'agrarian interests', as well as to bring about 'a dignified solution' to the colonial war in Morocco. In Ávila, Burgos, and Palencia, it was Gil Robles's persistent propaganda that must be credited with the establishment of UPC branches on 8 and 13 December 1923 and in late February 1924, respectively. The politico-social colour of the founders was always similar: presidents of *Casas Sociales Católicas*, of Catholic–Agrarian federations, and of Catholic syndicates.[9]

In some cases, the groups that were founded responded to a vague and diffuse aspiration of regeneration or to the opportunistic need to join the bandwagon of the victorious Dictator. That this was not always an automatic response to a central initiative is perhaps reflected in the variety of labels adopted by each group. For example, in Torre Alhaquime (Cádiz) the local mayor constituted the *Unión Ciudadana*; in Garrucha an *Asociación Patriótica* was founded, while the teachers' union in Salamanca claimed to have joined the local *Unión Patriótica Nacional*.[10]

In March 1924, still before the government's efforts to institutionalize the new movement had gained momentum, UPC branches were founded in Segovia, Logroño, Toledo, and Cádiz. The latter was not the first Andalusian centre of the UP; the PSP had founded a branch in Seville as early as mid December 1923.[11] In April, there followed suit Valencia, Ciudad Real, Badajoz, Santander, and, of course, the important branch of Madrid, in whose founding committee there gathered Catholic Propagandists, members of the PSP,

[8] Ibid., 2 Dec. 1923.

[9] Ibid., 8, 13 Dec. 1923; 12, 26 Feb. 1924.

[10] AHN, P.G. Leg. 354: Pedro Villalba to the prime minister, 30 Mar. 1924; and telegrams from Garrucha and Salamanca, 13, 27 Mar. 1924.

[11] *El Debate*, 17 Dec. 1923. For the mushrooming of UP centres at this early stage, see 'origen y desarrollo de la UP', *Unión Patriótica*, 1 Nov. 1926.

and officials of the Confederación Nacional Católico–Agraria. The founder of the ACN de P and the president of the CONCA, José Manuel de Aristizábal, was prominent, together with Gil Robles, among those who launched the branch in the capital.[12]

The founding manifesto of the Madrid UP laid down the right-wing traditionalist ideology of the new movement, and eventually of the new regime, an ideology emphatically protective of agrarian property and values. Organic democracy was substituted for decaying parliamentarism. Actually, the authors of this manifesto professed to be responding consciously to an earlier appeal by the Dictator to the embryonic UP, in his speech of 25 January at the Teatro del Centro, to assist him in elaborating 'a clear and concrete definition of our doctrine'. Primo de Rivera had by then been showing an eagerness to replace the bayonets with a civilian ideology and movement as the main *point d'appui* of his regime. Those who drew up the Madrid manifesto provided him with the relevant 'doctrine'. They acclaimed the Dictatorship as the last-ditch defence of Spain before it 'drowns in the chaos of a bloody anarchy'. Standard Maurista slogans were also resorted to, such as the revitalization of local life and institutions. Spain's chronic malady—civic anaemia—was to be cured by opening up the public channels for 'constructive' political activity. An important, and conspicuously strong, emphasis, was also placed on urging the Dictatorship to uphold the unity and the integrity of the *patria*. Society should be reformed on the basis of 'Christian morality'. Therefore, pornography and blasphemy should be ruthlessly repressed, the integrity of the Spanish family, alarmed by the threat from the challenges of modern society, should be enhanced, and the ecclesiastical network of social and educational institutions keenly favoured. The family should, moreover, become the fundamental nucleus of the future political constitution, as it was upon it, as well as upon corporative bodies, that what Santiago Fuentes Pila referred to as a new 'organic democracy' should rest. The 'defence of property' should be reconciled with the need to promote the 'working-class' standard of living.[13]

While contemplating a possible institutionalization of the UP, the Dictator had before him, however, two, rather than one, spontaneous

[12] *El Debate*, 13 Apr. 1924. The Madrid branch was actually started in mid March; see *El Sol*, 14 Mar. 1924.

[13] For the manifesto, see *El Debate*, 13 Apr. 1924, and Mask, pp. 138–56. For Fuentes Pila, see *El Debate*, 15 Apr. 1924.

initiatives. Barcelona, like Valladolid, had its own independent civilian movement in support of the Dictatorship. *La Traza* was a small group of 'blue-shirt' imitators of Italian Fascism founded early in 1923. It had enjoyed the encouragement of at least one of the generals involved in Primo de Rivera's conspiracy, López de Ochoa. A month after the *coup de'état* it changed its name to *Federación Cívico-Somatenista*, and seemed to be enjoying strong official favour.[14] Early in November and again in December, Primo de Rivera had even openly declared he would like it to extend its organization to the whole of Spain. Then, he said, 'Spain would possess a civil force of undisputed strength.'[15]

But it seems fairly clear that it was the simultaneous Castilian initiative that gained the most substantial momentum and was thus able to provide the organizational nucleus and the ideological creed for the civilian movement now crystallizing around the victorious Caudillo. The powerful network of Catholic syndicates, newspapers, and ecclesiastical lay associations that supported the initiative of the Catholic Propagandists could certainly not be matched by the sporadic and dispersed cells of fascist lunatics in Barcelona.

An open contest did nevertheless take place between the Cívico-*Somatenistas* and the Catholic Propagandists, throughout the first two months of the new regime, over the hegemony of the now imminent dictatorial party. Indeed, the somewhat precipitate, even hectic steps of the Castilians in founding their own branches reflected their eagerness to create a *fait accompli* that would relegate the *Cívico-Somatenistas* to the margin of the pro-dictatorial popular movement. At the same time, the Castilians also traced their view as to the political colours they would have liked the new regime to wear; these should by no means be the blue shirts of the Catalan fascists. Fascism—and *La Traza*, claimed Ángel Herrera, being 'inspired by fascism'—might have been 'convenient' for the highly agitated region of Catalonia, but it certainly provided no solution for the whole of Spain. Instead of a genuine, revolutionary mass mobilization in the fascist style. Ángel Herrera and his Propagandists had in mind a selective and controlled mobilization of 'directing minorities', inspired by the traditionalist spirit, that would lead the country away from decadent liberalism,[16] and stave off a

[14] Ibid., 31 Oct., 4 Nov., 1 Dec. 1923.
[15] Ibid., 2 Nov. 1923; *La Vanguardia*, 2 Dec. 1923.
[16] *El Debate*, 26 Oct. 1923, 13 Nov. 1923.

revolutionary take-over by either the extreme left or the extreme right.[17] Yet the Dictator would not exclude anybody from what he expected to be an all-embracing movement; and *La Traza*, or the *Federación Cívico-Somatenista*, finally joined the UP at about the time it had been institutionalized.[18]

Clearly, the Dictator was becoming aware of the need to find a civilian popular colouring for what might have been dismissed as a sheer military adventure. Already upon the expiry of his self-imposed three-month 'parenthesis', he grasped in as determined a manner as he could that if he wanted to extend his rule he would have to look for additional, civilian sources of power rather than base himself on the exclusive will of the king or the grudging sympathy of the military. The Dictatorship had to 'fascisize' itself from above if it wanted to survive.

In a way, Primo de Rivera was led to adopt such a posture by some of the steps he had been taking since he came to power. Such, for example, was the decree of 22 November 1923 which dismissed Romanones and Melquiades Álvarez, the chairmen of both houses of parliament, who had been pressing him to return to constitutional practices, of which the reconvening of the Cortes no later than three months after it had been suspended was an essential one.[19] By this bold step against the constitution and the sovereignty of parliament, the Dictator had created a vacuum of legitimacy that the most important of his future political endeavours, such as the Unión Patriótica, the National Assembly, and two plebiscites, came to fill.

Clearly, however, the Dictator's official visit to Italy in November was a crucial landmark in his decision to transform his regime. The Duce left an electrifying impression on both the king and 'his Mussolini'. He who spoke frequently about his 'movement' as a 'virile' endeavour was struck by the irresistible 'virility' of Mussolini's system. The Italian dictator was greeted by 'his Spanish prototype', as the British ambassador in Rome chose to call Primo de Rivera,[20] as the founder of the doctrine of 'Mussolinism' which had now converted Spain. 'Your figure is not just an Italian one', said Primo to the Duce at the Palazzo Venezia. 'You are the apostle of the

[17] The fear of revolution is reflected in most of the founding manifestos of UP in Castile, as well as in the speeches of its initiators. See for example, ibid., 12 Feb. 1923 (Gil Robles in Palencia), 8 Dec. 1923 (UP of Ávila).

[18] Ibid., 23 Apr. 1924.

[19] *El Diario Universal*, 15 Nov. 1923.

[20] FO/371/9493, Grahame (Rome) to Curzon, 23 Nov. 1923. He later corrected himself: 'I cannot say that His Excellency impressed me as being a second Mussolini.'

world campaign against dissolution and anarchy.' In an interview with the Italian journal *Impero*, Primo de Rivera went as far as expressing the hope that 'Spain would follow in the footsteps of Italian Fascism', and that 'Spanish fascism' would assist him in 'liberating the country from harmful elements'. 'Fascism', he continued, 'is a universal phenomenon that ought to conquer all nations . . . Fascism is a living Gospel.'[21] 'Mussolinism', the Spanish Dictator claimed upon returning from his visit, had become 'the guide of Spain' and it was about to transform its face.[22]

On the day of his return from Italy, huge columns in the press were devoted to the figure of the Duce and to Fascism, asserting that the Directorate meant to take Italy for their model.[23] The National Association of Teachers saluted the Dictator with the slogan 'Long live Latin Fascism!'[24] To those who came to greet him in Barcelona, Primo explained that he had not gone to see artistic and historical Italy, but the Duce's Italy which, he said, 'has set an example to Spain'. From that example, he continued, he had learnt that he had been too lenient until then in the punishment of those responsible for Spain's ills; but he would lose no time in remedying the error, and a 'new Spain' would arise, a Spain of discipline and order.

Moreover, whereas in his first days in power Primo de Rivera, like any elementary military caudillo, seemed to believe that he might be able single-handed—the hand that signed an endless number of decrees—to cure Spain's maladies, he now spoke of the need to mobilize 'the assistance of the country'.[25] 'In the very near future', he said in an official note a few days after his return to Spain, 'there would start the second stage of our mission, a mission to which it would be absurd and imprudent to fix a limited timetable. It would last for as long as we enjoy the confidence of public opinion.'[26] He would now set out to organize a system of public acquiescence.

[21] Duarte, pp. 197–8. For the interview in *Impero*, see Rubio, p. 73.

[22] Full reports of the visit were given in the diplomatic dispatches: FO/371/9493, Howard (Madrid) to Curzon, 24 Nov. 1923; Graham (Rome) to Curzon, 23 Nov. 1923; Cecil Dormer (The Vatican) to Curzon, 21 Nov. 1923.

[23] FO/371/9493, Howard to Curzon, 8 Dec. 1923.

[24] Quoted in Rubio. p. 73.

[25] For his speeches upon his return from Italy, see Maura, *Bosquejo*, pp. 53, 55. See also Duarte, pp. 209–14; and FO/371/9493, Howard to Curzon, 7 Dec. 1923.

[26] *El Sol*, 5 Dec. 1923.

(b) *Institutionalization and Recruitment*. The Dictator's decision to gather the wide variety of local 'patriotic' initiatives under official control seemed to take definite shape only in early April 1924. The decision was also consistent with a whole range of measures taken at around the same time with a view to laying the foundations of what might eventually become a civilian regime.[27] Thus, for example, it was during the first days of April that the renovation of all the municipal councils of Spain was started on the basis of a restriction of the so far almost dictatorial powers of the *delegados gubernativos* over the Ayuntamientos.[28] The civil governors—among whom the number of the military was now also reduced substantially[29]—were to nominate the new municipal councillors; admittedly, a practice still a long way from the corporative system of election promised in the recently promulgated Estatuto Municipal. However, a special royal order of 10 April, that started the preparation of a new electoral census,[30] indicated that the Dictator was at least contemplating putting into practice those clauses of the Municipal Statute referring to elections. The process of 'civilianization' of the Dictatorship was further bolstered by the Socialists' decision to accept posts in the new municipal councils as long as they were themselves allowed to designate their own delegates.[31]

A circular letter sent by Primo de Rivera to the *delegados gubernativos* on 5 April 1924, urging them 'to unite and organize all men of goodwill',[32] constituted the first practical step towards the institutionalization of the UP.

Subsequently, the Dictator took up the cudgels for recruiting the 'vital forces' of two key regions, Catalonia and the Basque Provinces. At this initial stage, he clearly expected the UP, and indeed his entire rule, to rest upon the traditional triangle of economic and political power, Valladolid–Barcelona–Bilbao. He believed that the mobilization on behalf of his regime of the economically powerful and politically influential productive classes of these regions would administer the final *coup de grâce* to the 'old system', and, hardly less important, would assist the Dictatorship in its grand 'bourgeois' task of modernizing Spain's economy.[33] In spite of frequent flattering allusions to the working class, the Dictator's present initiative

[27] That such was the background against which the new regime set out to institutionalize the UP was later acknowledged by the Dictator himself; see his *Disertación Ciudadana* (Madrid, 1926), p. 34.

[28] *El Sol*, 29, 30 Mar. 1924.

[29] *El Debate*, 13 Apr. 1924.

[30] *El Sol*, 11 Apr. 1924.

[31] *El Socialista*, 14 Apr. 1924.

[32] Casas Ramos, p. 527.

[33] See Chapter VII.

responded to his more genuine belief in the virtues of the middle classes, in their supposedly pious manners, in the stability of their family life.[34]

Thus, it was during a visit to Barcelona in mid April 1924 that Primo de Rivera first revealed the text of a decree 'establishing' the UP, that was to appear in the *Gaceta* only a fortnight later. He now spoke of the idea of organizing 'a party of patriotic union' which would embrace all those who 'yearn for the ideals of patria and order'. He expected this UP, eventually, to put forward candidates, who would be supported by the government, in the forthcoming elections.[35] In a passionate appeal to the Catalan employers who, he said, had stood by him on the fateful thirteenth of September, and whose support he now pretended to institutionalize, he asked them, and Catalan opinion as a whole, to reach their own conclusion by comparing the present order with the dreadful 'derangement . . . of economic activities' by 'the waves of terrorist Syndicalism' that had made his *coup d'état* inevitable.[36]

A few days after his appeal to Catalan opinion, Primo took yet another step in his now consistent campaign of surrounding his regime with civilian acquiescence. On 25 April, he explained to the civil governors that he would now like to see the formation of 'a big party under the name of Unión Patriótica' that would, hopefully, one day gain 'a strong majority' in the future Cortes. The civil governors were left in no doubt as to the role they were expected to play in this endeavour: 'to protect' and closely supervise the organization of the new party.[37]

Primo de Rivera's personal campaign on behalf of the UP was renewed during an official visit he made to Bilbao early in May. Prior to his visit, a decree heavily protecting national industry was promulgated.[38] While in Bilbao, he expected that the Federation of National Industries, with whose leader, Ramón Bergé, he negotiated his political plans, would 'reciprocate' by extending its support to the incipient UP. In a meeting with the respectable members of the *Club El Sitio*, the Dictator explained that 'the best way for you to fulfil your patriotic aspirations is by supporting the nascent

[34] *La Nación*, 9 Aug. 1928.

[35] *El Debate*, 15 Apr. 1924. The decree appeared in *La Gaceta de Madrid*, 29 Apr. 1924.

[36] A declaration to *El Noticero Universal*, quoted in *Folletín*, pp. 125–6.

[37] AHN, P.G. Leg. 380: Primo's circular to the governors and the *delegados gubernativos*, 25 Apr. 1924.

[38] *La Gaceta de Madrid*, 1 May 1924.

Unión Patriótica'. But the immediate response of the Basque upper classes to Primo de Rivera's *démarche* was less than encouraging.[39] However, this was by no means due to their refusal to support the new regime. The *Liga de Acción Monárquica*, the natural home of the Biscayan oligarchy, would provide a solid backbone to the Dictatorship throughout.[40] Rather, it stemmed from the natural inclination of businessmen to exert their influence through the traditional channels used by pressure groups.[41] Their sceptical attitude towards the UP was also due to a calculated reluctance to be identified with a party whose prospects were anything but clear. The future would prove the validity of their judgement, if only because they were perfectly able to promote their vital economic interests without having to stand for that purpose at the forefront of the UP. As in the case of Franco's political personnel, being in power under Primo de Rivera did not necessarily mean possessing it.[42]

Yet, Primo de Rivera did not run out of ideas on how to promote his party. Contrary to what had clearly been the intention of the Castilian initiators of the UP, he now emphasized, and this was already evident in his appeal to Catalan opinion on 14 April, his will to 'de-ideologize' the UP, so as to make it acceptable to as wide a public as possible. Potentially divisive, ideology became an impediment to the consolidation of a one-party system; and legitimacy had to be built upon principles as eclectic as possible.[43] Among other things, the Dictator now promised that the UP's creed would not contradict the 1876 constitution, and he underlined the vaguest possible and most non-controversial slogans it would stand for, such as administrative efficiency, Spain's unity, social and military discipline.[44]

Not unlike other cases of parties mobilized from above,[45] the UP was to be explicitly conceived as an eclectic body. It asked nobody

[39] See a report on Primo's contacts in Bilbao in *Folletín*, pp. 129–31.

[40] Javier de Ybarra y Bergé, *Política Nacional en Vizcaya* (Madrid, 1948), pp. 579, 594–7.

[41] This fundamentally prudent, and indeed opportunistic, attitude of the business magnates towards politics characterized some of the Catalan big-business associations in the years that preceded the Dictatorship. See S. Carr, *passim*.

[42] Pi-Sunyer, p. 34.

[43] For a comprehensive theory of this pattern, see Samuel Huntington, 'Social and Institutional Dynamics of One-Party systems', in Huntington and Clement Moore (eds.), *Authoritarian Politics in Modern Society: The Dynamics of Established Party Systems* (New York, 1970), Chapter 1. The Mexican PRI is a case in point.

[44] *El Sol*, 16 Apr. 1924.

[45] See below, pp. 394–7.

'Where do you come from?' or 'What ideals do you cherish?' as long as these did not contradict 'the cause of social order and the country's fundamental institutions'. It appealed to all those who, 'in spite of sticking by the most antagonistic philosophical conceptions, the most conflicting social doctrines, and the most irreconcilable political views, were ready to give preference in their hearts to the patria'. One did not even have to abandon one's beliefs as long as one was ready to harness one's energy, as Primo put it, 'to the illegal, but patriotic, movement of the 13th of September'. There was no binding 'doctrinal orthodoxy' in the UP, he explained.[46] Some years later, Ángel Herrera followed a similar pattern. Acción Nacional, he would say, was 'a formula of understanding and a link between citizens of disparate ideologies'.[47]

To increase the bait, the Dictator did not hesitate to undermine the halo of an anti-*caciquista* 'regenerator' that surrounded his seizure of power. He started his own brand of *caciquismo* by favouring *Upetistas* for the jobs of city and provincial councillors.[48] Consequently, the institutionalization of the UP heralded a change in its physiognomy, and in the political culture that it represented. Artificial branches mushroomed under the guidance of the government's delegates; and an army of yes-men, flatterers, and those who had been protected by the old *caciquista* system came to find shelter under the Dictatorship's protective umbrella.

They were encouraged to do so by the unrelenting propaganda and *caciquista* blackmail of local and provincial officials. Conceived as an apolitical League of Citizens open to 'all men of goodwill whatever their ideological beliefs', it was now up to the civil governors and their local officials such as the *delegados gubernativos* and the mayors to set up the UP. For that purpose a thorough revision of the population census was carried out throughout the summer of 1924.[49] Local 'committees of organization' were then formed and thousands of manifestos were printed and distributed urging the population to join in. One such manifesto, reflecting the expectation of recruiting as eclectic a public as possible, ran as follows:

[46] *La Nación*, 9 Jan. 1926, 3, 8 Aug. 1927, 2 Jan. 1928.

[47] Montero, i, p. 149.

[48] See below, pp. 152–4.

[49] For the instructions to the provincial officials in relation to the organization of the UP, see 'Luis Hermosa del Directorio Militar a los gobernadores civiles sobre la UP. Julio de 1924', in Romanones Archive, Leg. 63, no. 74; and *La Gaceta de Madrid*, 29 Apr. 1924. See also Primo in *La Nación*, 8 Aug. 1927.

Worn away the old political parties, buried for good. We must now seriously consider an entirely new and definitive system of government. No one will be asked where he came from; we are not interested in knowing anything but what his feelings and thoughts are. Honesty, good faith, a sane willpower—these are the only credentials we demand from those wanting to join this new Association, which will defend no bastard interests, wants no favours nor advantages of any kind, and has no ideal other than that of the general good, and prosperity and the aggrandizement of our beloved patria.[50]

Yet such pompous invitations fell short of doing the job alone. Special instructions had to be issued on more 'practical' techniques of recruitment.[51] Consequently, the *delegados gubernativos*, sometimes the mayors, simply 'ordered' the setting-up of UP branches and designated their officials; an arbitrary practice, which was applied not without arousing local animosity among local *Upetistas.*[52] Throughout the second half of 1924, the Dictator's desk was virtually inundated by reports from governors, *delegados gubernativos*, and mayors providing endless details on the UP centres they had helped to establish, the juntas they had appointed to run them, and data on affiliates.[53] Sometimes, holders of official positions were 'registered' into the UP *en bloc* without even being previously consulted; in one case, a meeting of the mayors in a given province arbitrarily decided upon the enrolment into the UP of all their city councillors.[54] At Quintanar de la Orden, the town's major taxpayers were 'persuaded' by the local *delegado gubernativo* to join in 'for their own benefit'.[55] Nor, of course, were the humbler citizens spared, and fifteen years later a day labourer in an Andalusian village still remembered how he had been offered a job by the local cacique if he joined the UP,[56] a case which there is no special reason to think was an exceptional one. The *delegado gubernativo* of Arandigoyen, a certain Lieut.-Col. Munárriz, was so overwhelmed by the smooth way in

[50] *Unión Patriótica de Sacedón—Al Pueblo*, 19 Sept. 1924, in Romanones Archive, Leg. 75, no. 6.

[51] AHN, P.G. Leg. 354; 'Circular a los gobernadores civiles dando instrucciones relacionadas con la UP', 28 Aug. 1924.

[52] AHN, P.G. Leg. 354: 'Vecinos de Aracena a Primo de Rivera', 19 June 1924.

[53] See, for example, AHN, P.G. Leg. 354; reports from the *delegado gubernativo* of Cabra, 17 Dec. 1924; from the civil governor of Santander, 5 Oct. 1924 (he said that branch had now 6,319 members), from the *delegado gubernativo* of Valls (Tarragona), 4 Sept. 1924; and from the mayor of Sarria, 13 Apr. 1924.

[54] AHN, P.G. Leg. 354: 'Carta de Fernando Álvarez sobre admisión de elemento oficial en UP', 25 Aug. 1924.

[55] AHN, P.G. Leg. 354; report from *delegado gubernativo* of Quintanar de la Orden, 8 Aug. 1924.

[56] Fraser, p. 59.

which he had been able to enlist 1,490 members to the local UP branch, that he took the liberty of advising General Martínez Anido, who had been supervising the 'creation' of the UP from his desk at the ministry of the interior, that 'the present regime can easily continue, without Cortes or elections, for a long time'.[57]

Evidently, the Directory seemed to be recruiting members for the UP by those familiar methods with which the old home office had 'made' the elections. Indeed, the decree that 'officially' created the UP stated explicitly that the *Consejo Nacional de Unión Patriótica*, that was to supervise the party's 'organization and statistics', should reside in the ministry of the interior, the traditional focus of political manipulation.[58]

The 'rank and file' of the old parties—they were referred to by Royo Villanova as 'a mass of familiar faces'[59]—were not absent from the UP.[60] Sometimes a whole branch of a dynastic party would join.[61] In many provinces, especially in the predominantly agrarian ones where *caciquismo* rather than being eradicated was enlisted to serve the new cause, the UP was to be directly controlled and promoted by the old familiar faces. Such were, for example, the cases of Albacete, where the UP's provincial president was the ex-Ciervista José Mañas Guspi; Cádiz, where the ex-Maurista Luciano Bueno became the first chief of the party in the province; and Jaén, where the Dictator's minister, once a Conservative deputy for Linares, Yangüas Messía, was the UP's prime mover. Among the leaders of the UP in Granada one could find the ex-Conservative Miguel Rodrígues and the ex-Liberal Conde de las Infantas. This was also the case in Málaga where the Liberal ex-deputy Juan Rodríguez Muñoz became the UP's provincial chief. His deputy was the ex-Conservative senator Felix Saenz Calvo. As a whole the UP in Andalusia was swelled by Conservatives, Liberals, Ciervistas, and Mauristas. In the very province of the Dictator, Jerez, the new party was almost the private fief of the ex-Maurista Conde de los Andes, who filled it with 'his men'; while the UP of Jaén was to be torn apart by old feuds between the 'men' of grand caciques such as

[57] AHN, P.G. Leg. 354; Lieut.-Col. Munárriz to Martínez Anido, 31 May 1924.
[58] *La Gaceta de Madrid*, 29 Apr. 1924.
[59] *Intervención de Antonio Royo Villanova en la discusión de la memoria del Sr. Roig Ibáñez 'sobre el porvenir político de España' en la Academia de Jurisprudencia*, Romanones Archive, Leg. 45, no. 52.
[60] *Nueva España*, 30 Jan. 1930.
[61] See the case of the Círculo Dinástico de Reus, in AHN, P.G. Leg. 354, 11 May 1924.

Saro and Yangüas. The grand cacique of the UP in Ávila was the Conservative ex-senator Marqués de Benavites who enrolled in it most of his 'political friends'. The Conservative ex-deputy for Tarragona, Conde de Asalto, became the leader of the UP in that province, a job that was manned in Castellón by the Conservative ex-deputy Marqués de Benicarló, and in Gerona, by a cacique who had served in the past both Liberals and Conservatives, Federico Bassols Costa. Galicia was to witness an almost total disbandment of old groups who rushed to jump on the UP's bandwagon. In the Canary Islands, the new party was led by the very caciques who had been ruling the islands on behalf of the dynastic parties from early in the century.[62]

With no special credentials to present, it was hardly surprising that almost every political group in the country was represented in the UP; ex-Mauristas who had the illusion that they were seeing their 'revolution from above' nearer than ever,[63] Carlists who were tempted to see in the antiliberal revolution of Primo de Rivera a convergence towards their own traditionalist doctrines (and in the UP tenets of Religion, Patria, and Monarchy a variation on their own: God, Patria, and King),[64] ex-Liberal opportunists,[65] and ex-Conservatives with an authoritarian cast of mind.[66] They would be joined by eternal *pretendientes* for governmental jobs,[67] official nominees at all levels of the administration, and Catholic petty intellectuals (an eminent writer such as Azorín bluntly declined the editorship of the regime's organ).[68]

It was no mere coincidence that in July 1924, amidst the influx of

[62] A mass of data on the establishment and leadership of UP branches in the agrarian provinces of the South where *caciquismo* was stronger as an agent of recruitment to the new party reached Primo de Rivera's desk, see AHN, P.G. Legs. 354, 358. See also FO/371/10593, Rumbold to MacDonald, 14 Aug. 1924; Vicente Risco, *El problema político de Galicia* (Madrid, 1930), pp. 185–7; and a special study on Andalusia in Tusell, *La crisis*, pp. 134–48. For a thorough investigation of the role of old caciques in the UP, see José Luís Gómez Navarro-Navarrete, *Unión Patriótica (Aproximación al estudio de un partido dictatorial)* (Memoria de Licenciatura, Madrid University, 1979), pp. 126–30. Some important information on the same issue emerges alo from Publicaciones Patrióticas. *La Asamblea Nacional. Biografía y retratos de los 400 Asambleistas y numerosos datos del mayor interés* (Madrid, 1927).

[63] Lerroux, *Al servicio*, pp. 259–60. [64] Primo in *The Times*, 4 Oct. 1927.

[65] Belmonte to Romanones, n.d., in Romanones Archive, Leg. 28, no. 35.

[66] See the speech by Burgos y Mazo, the grand Andalusian cacique, in Romanones Archive, Leg. 28, no. 27. His political fief in Huelva completely disintegrated, see *El Socialista*, 3 Apr. 1924. See also 'Declaraciones de Bugallal', 13 June 1925 in Romanones Archive, Leg. 75, no. 6. [67] Hurtado, ii, p. 243.

[68] *The Times*, 23 July, 16 Oct. 1925.

old *clientelae* into the ranks of the UP, the Liberal leader, Romanones, and his Reformist counterpart, Melquiades Álvarez, should have petitioned the Dictator to allow them to address their followers. It was a desperate attempt on their part to stop the defections from their respective parties to the newly born and officially protected UP.[69] A similar purpose—that of blocking off a landslide from constitutional monarchism towards the politics of a one-party system—was expected to be served by the abortive attempt of a group of right-wing intellectuals to set up a *Liga de Intelectuales Monárquicos*. This collective initiative of Saínz Rodríguez, Rafael Altamira, and Gómez de Baquero, launched early in 1925, did not really get off the ground. It serves, however, as an additional demonstration that the recruitment to the UP was undermining the potential base of parliamentary monarchism in favour of what Saínz Rodríguez feared might become an extreme, ultramontane right.[70]

The *caciquista* connections of the UP cannot be denied. But *ABC*'s comment that the local leadership of the new party 'is embodied in the very same caciques of the past'[71] should not be taken at its face value. The UP was not entirely devoid of sincere adherents.

Calvo Sotelo, no keen supporter of the UP, had to recognize that its ranks were also filled by 'gentlemen of the ideal' and by 'gentlemen of industry, men of serene moral lineage'. But the officialization of the party unavoidably meant, as Calvo Sotelo was to acknowledge, that the UP became instrumental as a breeding-ground for the personal ambitions of 'a wide variety of people who held disparate, albeit basically right-wing, ideologies'. Many defended no ideology whatsoever; they represented an army of opportunists, 'soup and spoon men'.[72] Others viewed the new party as a channel through which pressure could be brought to bear on behalf of legitimate economic and social interests. The UP thus became the focal point for disparate interests: industrialists and agriculturalists were there to advance the cause of protectionism, while merchants came to defend the opposite cause; consumers joined in to call for lower prices, while the producers were there to assert their need for comfortable profit margins.[73]

[69] Ibid., 14 July 1924; *Folletín*, pp. 133–5.
[70] Pedro Saínz Rodríguez, *Testimonio y Recuerdos* (Barcelona, 1978), pp. 351–2.
[71] *ABC*, 27 Feb. 1929. [72] Calvo, pp. 331–2. [73] Maura, *Bosquejo*, p. 134.

But there was an important element in the UP which in a rather crude way conceived the new party as the instrument of a right-wing revolution in whose ranks they were eager to serve. Gabriel Maura described the profile of this element as 'a mass of opinion . . . more extensive and numerous, but much less civic-minded than Maurismo, though also attractive to elements that would otherwise have gone to Maurismo: the messianic, the anti-*políticos*, the pseudo-conservative who, by vulgarizing the etymology, thought that *tranquilidad* derives from *tranca* [stick], and a great multitude of Spaniards of good faith, devoid of any juridical sense.'[74]

Furthermore, the case of the predominantly rural provinces, where *caciquismo* managed to take over the UP and turn it into 'the old regime in disguise', tells only part of the story. Many were the provinces where new people, unblemished by old political connections, and not necessarily representing the so-called 'traditional oligarchy', ascended to positions of leadership in the UP, or formed its committees. This was usually achieved not without local squabbles between antagonistic factions.

Let us examine the case of the Barcelona UP branch. Its founding nucleus consisted of the *La Traza* group. The *Tracistas*, who parodied in their organization the Fascist squadrons,[75] were later joined by others who believed sincerely in the 'regenerating' mission of the new regime, as well as by the detritus of the old parties. Some members of the local Liberal Party, such as the well-intentioned Dr Soler y Roig, joined the party without even consulting their leaders. But there were other Liberals who were explicitly encouraged to join by their local leaders, so that they could be used as 'spies in the enemy camp'. Very soon, however, the Barcelona UP was torn by internal quarrels as the *Tracistas*, now led by Soler y Roig and a certain Captain Gimeno, the first secretary of the local UP, referred to themselves as the 'pure Unión Patriótica'. The 'non-authentic' element came from the upper-class, patriotic, and *españolista* Catalans of the Unión Monárquica, people such as Alfonso Sala, Marqués de Foronda, Milá y Camps, Manuel Monach, who later became the president of the Barcelona UP's provincial committee, and the secretary of the city's Chamber of Urban Property, the

[74] Gabriel Maura, *Recuerdos de mi vida* (Madrid, n.d.), pp. 181–2.

[75] In January 1924 they acclaimed the Dictator in Barcelona with something like a Fascist parade, see *El Sol*, 9 Jan. 1924.

lawyer Andrés Gassó y Vidal.[76] Though careful to preserve the autonomy of their own organization, these people flirted with Primo's regime—Sala was said to be contemplating the marriage of his son with the daughter of the Civil Governor-General Miláns del Bosch—in order to consolidate their social position and eventually succeed the Lliga as the predominant political force in the region.[77]

Primo de Rivera, however, seemed to be aware that the social basis that could have been given to his regime by *Umenista* circles was too narrow. This, then, was why he manned the administrative network of the province of Barcelona not necessarily with *Upetistas*; so much so that Gassó y Vidal complained in a letter to the Dictator that 'UP affiliates are being denied legitimate assistance' since in key provincial organs 'the UP lacks any representation whatsoever'.[78] Rather than those of the UP, Gassó y Vidal seemed here to be defending the interests of the *Umenista* nucleus within the UP. Primo's officials in the region, such as the Military Governor General Emilio Barrera, were better disposed towards the 'authentic' middle- and lower-middle-class UP. The abolition of the Catalan Mancomunidad[79]—a key power-base of Sala and his UMN—responded to the more radical philosophy of 'one country' backed by the 'purist' *Upetistas* and their mentor General Barrera.[80] The leadership of the former consisted now of the triumvirate Dr Menacho, Dr Soler y Roig, and a certain Sr Lacoma who was later ennobled by the Dictatorship to become Barón de Minguella. Both Menacho and Soler y Roig were also promised a reward for their patriotic labour. This later came in the form of positions at the University of Barcelona.[81]

Barcelona's UP, of course, had no monopoly of internal squabbles between antagonistic factions of the regime's supporters. The interesting thing about it was that it reflected the fact that the UP had not become the exclusive domain of the old social and economic oligarchy. Rather, in those provinces in which old *caciquismo* did

[76] AHN, P.G. Leg. 354; A report from the president of the UMN of Viliví del Panadés, 6 Feb. 1924. See also *Biografía y retratos*, *passim*.

[77] *Heraldo de Madrid*, 15 July 1925.

[78] AHN, P.G. Leg. 446; Gassó y Vidal to Primo de Rivera.

[79] See below, pp. 197–99.

[80] AHN, P.G. Leg. 354; José Graneé, president of the UP of Balaguer, 14 Feb. 1925.

[81] A thorough report on the UP of Barcelona can be found in the document; Belmonte (oficina del Partido Liberal de Barcelona) to Romanones, 13 June 1925, Romanones Archive, Leg. 35, no. 6.

not 'conquer' the new administration and the UP network, relatively new and exclusively middle- and lower-middle-class figures, who had not served the old regime, came to the fore as the local and provincial leaders of the UP.

Biscay, where the UP was to acquire a special strength,[82] is another case in point. Primo de Rivera pressed for the incorporation into it of the *Liga de Acción Monárquica*,[83] an *españolista* corporation of potent economic magnates. The LAM, however, refused, probably with the king's encouragement, to throw in its lot with the ephemeral UP.[84] It was not a problem of moral scruples, but of sheer opportunism. The result of the Basque plutocracy's obstinacy was that the local UP had to be manned by people of a humbler lineage, such as González Olasso, Luis Arana, Federico de Moyua y Salazar, and Esteban Bilbao, all of whom would eventually occupy the key posts in the Ayuntamiento of Bilbao and in its Diputación Provincial. The prime mover of the UP in Biscay and its eventual chief was the president of the Biscayan Mutualist Association of Employees, Eduardo Sotés Ortiz. The economic interests of the LAM, just like those of the UMN in Barcelona, remained unchallenged; but its men were dismissed from administrative posts and its regional political hegemony was shattered in favour of those *Upetistas* who emerged from lower social echelons.[85] The Dictator was left with no choice but to make a principle out of his failure to hoist the Basque upper bourgeoisie on to the UP's bandwagon. His reshuffle of the administration in Bilbao, he said, was an indispensable 'purifying operation', without which the Biscayan administration could not be the 'determined auxiliary of the regime's regenerating enterprise' that he wanted it to be.[86]

As is usually the case with *partidos únicos*, the UP accelerated the political decline of the traditional élites, and created the channels for the emergence of a new political class.[87]

Barcelona and Bilbao were not in an exclusive position as far as the political ascension of *homines novi* was concerned. That part of the middle-class and the lower provincial bourgeoisie which had come to dislike politics *à l'ancienne* and had not enjoyed conspicuous

[82] García Venero, *Historia del nacionalismo vasco* (Madrid, 1969), p. 460.
[83] See below, p. 198.
[84] Calvo Sotelo, *Mis servicios* (edition of 1974), p. 225.
[85] The Bilbao conflict about posts and the UP is covered in *El Sol*, 20 Feb.–7 Mar. 1926. See also *Biografía y retratos*, *passim*.
[86] *El Sol*, 24 Feb. 1926.
[87] Cf. Maurice Duverger, *Les Partis politiques* (Paris, 1951), p. 288.

privileges under the old regime emerged now as the new 'political class' of the Dictatorship. There were provinces and localities in which the UP became completely dominated by previously politically uncommitted figures, people of liberal professions, representatives of small and modest economic concerns, presidents and members of local Chambers of Urban Property, Chambers of Industry and Commerce, and small savings banks.

Such were the cases, for example, of UP local and provincial chiefs such as Manuel Hernández Marín in Teruel, Arturo Yllera in Valladolid, the eloquent vice-president of the Chamber of Commerce and Industry of Huesca, Manuel Banzo, who eventually became one of the petty ideologues of the new regime, the merchant Enrique Fraga Rodríguez in La Coruña, the industrialist Leandro Nagore in Pamplona, the lawyer Gonzalo López Montenegro y Carvajal in Cáceres, the physician José Pérez Agote in Álava, the lawyer José María López Cepero y Murn in Seville, the physician Segundo Gila in Segovia, the jurist Miguel Allué Salvador in Zaragoza, the pedagogue Emilio Orfila in Igualada, and the physician Andrés García in Salamanca. At a lower level, that is as simple members, rather than presidents of local and provincial juntas, the presence of many others of the same social standing and of a similarly obscure or non-existent political past was even more discernible.[88]

It was this middle class that formed the hard core of *Upetistas* in the provincial capitals and towns. UP meetings would usually, as *La Nación* confessed, 'bear the mark of our middle classes, those that in every country constitute the salt of the earth'. In spite of Primo's professed wish to make the UP into a socially all-embracing national movement, he put special emphasis on the appeal to the same middle classes, 'so keen on preserving the virtues of our race, so unwilling to change their attitudes to the tenor of the latest fashion'. They were, in his view, 'a highly stable social element in their family life, in their dedication to work, and in their romantic faith in the future and prestige of the patria'.[89]

The UP was a revolutionary organization in the sense that it gave political expression and provided the channels through which, for the first time, a right-wing movement in Spain had been able to mobilize the provincial urban and agrarian bourgeoisie that had so

[88] AHN, P.G. Leg. 324; *Biografía y retratos, passim*. A thorough examination of this issue can be found in Gómez Navarro-Navarrete's excellent thesis, *Unión Patriótica*, pp. 100–11, 144–7.

[89] *La Nación*, 5 Sept. 1927, 8 Aug. 1927.

far been mainly the target of the demobilizing politics of *caciquismo*. An obvious practical reason for that was that these weaker sections of the Spanish middle classes, unlike the Basque and Catalan plutocracies, were simply not strong enough to exert pressure on the government through other channels, and they welcomed the golden opportunity to fill the political vacuum created by the 'abstentionism' of the oligarchy. They were happy with their new-found role as *the* political class of the Dictatorship, whatever this may have meant in terms of practical influence.

The participation of the Catholic–Agrarians in the UP exemplified this political change. As a whole, Catholics, or, more specifically, those inspired by the ACN de P, remained loyal to the Dictatorship throughout.[90] Members of the PSP in Andalusia, for example, were prominent among those who obtained positions in the official UP.[91] Moreover, one can even argue that the incorporation of the Social Catholic elements—the challengers of the Canovite system from the right—into Primo's *partido único* further underlined the UP's breakaway from the old political class. Whereas in the southern rural provinces the UP tended to be taken over by *caciquismo*, in the agrarian centre and north, 'new men', mostly agrarian bourgeois and officials of Catholic corporations, took over. It is significant, though, that as in the case of the urban plutocracy, the higher aristocracy tended to keep aloof from the UP;[92] its ranks, however, were ornamented with a number of provincial nobles.

However, humbler landowners and tenants among the members of the Confederación Nacional Católico–Agraria moved to key positions in the official UP, as well as in the regime's administrative apparatus. CONCA's officials manned a great number of juntas and committees of the UP at the local level. Such were the cases of the president of the Agrarian Syndicate of Benavente (Zamora), who became the UP's provincial chief in Zamora; José Santos Fernández, the president of the Catholic Agrarian Federation of Santander, who became the UP chief in that city; his counterpart in Murcia, Martínez García, led the party in that city; the branch in Orense was to be headed by an official of the local *Círculos Católicos de Obrerors*; and that of Burgos by a member of the local Catholic–Agrarian Syndicate, José María de la Fuente. Their counterparts in

[90] Montero, i, pp. 133–4, 393.

[91] Tusell, *La crisis*, pp. 126–7.

[92] The nobility's role in the UP was studied by Gómez Navarro-Navarrete, pp. 100–3.

Logroño, Lugo, Teruel, and La Coruña, to mention only select examples, became key activists and leaders of the UP in their respective provinces. This was also the case with some PSP officials. Conde de Vallellano was a prominent figure in the Madrid UP, and, eventually, the capital's mayor. His colleagues in the PSP, Santiago Fuentes Pila and Conde de Bilbao, also became UP activists in Madrid, while José Gabilán rose to the position of secretary-general of the whole party. The PSP militants Manuel Banzo in Huesca and José Ibáñez Martín in Murcia were the presidents of the UP in their respective provinces, as well as something of party ideologues.[93]

A Castilian organization of small and medium-sized farmers which, after having been active in the foundation of the UPC, continued to maintain a close affinity with the official UP, was the *Secretariado Nacional Agrario*, under the conspicuous presidency of the Dictator's brother, José Primo de Rivera. 'There is not so much as one word said by us or one step made by our organization which contradicts the tenets of the UP', declared, as late as January 1929, the SNA secretary at a large gathering in which speakers defended the idea that only a 'robust and confident peasantry' could constitute the spinal cord of a truly 'Hispanic' regime.[94]

It is likewise significant that in Galicia also it was an association of small and medium-sized farmers, the *Confederación Regional de Agricultores Gallegos*, that provided the UP with its main popular support in the region. Fundamentally anti-liberal and permeated with contempt for 'politicians' that had neglected the interests of agriculture for so many years, small and medium-sized landholders in Galicia came to the UP in search of salvation. The leaders of their syndicates were to be rewarded with positions in the city councils of Galicia.[95]

But history will not come to regard Primo de Rivera as the great mobilizer of Catholicism in Spain. This is the role of the founders of the CEDA, Ángel Herrera and Gil Robles. The Dictatorship—as opposed to the Republic—was a Nationalist-Catholic regime that tranquillized the strata from which the militancy of the CEDA was later to draw its strength. Catholic religious and lay activities were

[93] Castillo, *Propietarios* pp. 345–9; Gómez Navarro–Navarrete, pp. 130–7; Tuñón, 'En torno a la Dictadura de Primo de Rivera', in *Cuadernos*, p. 19. Much information is contained in *Biografía y retratos*.

[94] See the reports in *España Agraria*, Jan.–Apr. 1929. The UP's president in Toledo, Conde de Casa Fuerte, was an official of the SNA.

[95] Risco, p. 210.

complementary to and in conformity with—rather than in antagonism to—the regime's fundamental precepts. Just like Fascism, militant Catholicism was nourished by conflict. *La Nación* explicitly suggested that once the UP had been established there was no need for the attempts to create a Christian Democratic Party (the PSP) based on 'popular Catholicism' to continue. No one would deny, it went on, that the regime's 'traditional spirit' combined with its 'fertile dynamism' had made superfluous the need for a separate Social-Catholic movement.[96]

Now, moreover, it was politically anaesthetized and harnessed to the service of a Dictatorship for which mobilization from above was essentially an instrument of demobilization. The climax of the UPC's propaganda campaign was the mass gathering of Medina del Campo, on 24 May 1924.[97] Special trains transported to this very Castilian town about 30,000 people to hear the Dictator promise that, with their assistance, he would be able to bequeath to his children 'a purified Spain'. Eduardo Callejo, the UPC's president, manifested his organization's readiness to be institutionalized in the service of the new regime. The aim of the UP, he said, was that of 'organizing public opinion around the government', of 'creating a movement of civic assistance' to the new regime. Callejo was thus implying that the UPC was ready to be an auxiliary, rather than an independent, movement. Its ideology, as was repeated in another mass meeting, this time in Santander, was consistent with the April manifesto of the Madrid branch, and hence fully in tune with the Dictator's broad aims.[98]

Not surprisingly, the initiators of the authentic, ideologically inspired, Castilian UP started to feel ill at ease in the company of the residues of *caciquismo* within the new UP. The 'officialization' of the party had, they felt, suffocated their grand aspiration to create a real, genuine civilian alternative to the Dictatorship. Those among the PSP leaders who, like Ossorio y Gallardo, had warned from the very beginning that no neo-Maurista purposes would be served by the Dictatorship were now vindicated.[99] As early as April 1924, *El Debate*, which had passionately supported the UPC, started to echo concern about the party's detachment from its original Social-Catholic

[96] *La Nación*, 5 Apr. 1926. Cf. D. Benavides, *El fracaso social del Catolicismo español. Arboleya Martínez 1870–1951* (Barcelona, 1973), p. 64.

[97] *El Sol*, 26 May 1924.

[98] For the Santander meeting, see *El Sol*, 30 Oct. 1924; Pemartín, *Valores*, pp. 621–3.

[99] Alzaga, *La primera*, pp. 278–91.

basis.[100] Later, *El Debate* was to leave little doubt as to its wish to see the emergence of a new Catholic party, the UP having only perpetuated what it called 'civic stagnation'.[101] The Dictatorship's rejection of parliamentarianism, it argued, was a step in the right direction. But, it had failed to create, in *El Debate*'s opinion, the longed-for 'party of order' that could represent 'conservative Spain' in its entirety.[102]

The institutionalization of the UP entailed the need to centralize its organization through strict hierarchical control, a structure suggested by the Dictator as early as August 1924. He thought of a pyramid on top of which he would stand as *Jefe Nacional*—a position he would indeed assume 'by acclamation' in May 1925. To assist him there were to be a National Directory, under the presidency of the subservient José Gabilán, and an Assembly, the membership of which would be limited to the UP's provincial chiefs, 'university professors, merchants, agriculturists, and other persons of extraordinary prestige'. Beneath these national bodies, a network of fifty provincial assemblies and directories and hundreds of local branches, as well as youth and women sections, was, eventually, to be spread all over the country—a structure closely resembling that which the Falange later adopted.[103]

The definitive structure was reached at a special meeting of the Grand National Junta in July 1926. This body, 'a genuine representation of the vital Spain', according to *La Nación*, consisted of the UP's provincial presidents, 'the gentlemen of the new political ideal', 'the paladins of the new social regime'.[104]

Primo de Rivera himself, as undisputed *Jefe Nacional*, was 'the supreme authority', and it was up to him and him alone to set the norms and the guide-lines for the party. He would preside over all the party's national organs, and would have the exclusive right to appoint their members as well as to dismiss them. The *Jefe Nacional* would be assisted by a *Gran Junta Directiva Nacional* and by a *Comité Ejecutivo Central*. The former was of course to be presided over by Primo himself, who would appoint a vice-president—this

[100] *El Debate*, 20 Apr. 1924.

[101] Quoted in *La Nación*, 21 Oct. 1929.

[102] *El Debate*, 20, 24 Feb., 2 May, 16 Aug., 23 Sept., 1929.

[103] *Unión Patriótica*, 1 Nov. 1926; AHN, P.G. Leg. 354; a circular letter on the setting-up of the UP's Junta Central. There were also some UP branches abroad; see *Boletín de la Asociación Patriótica Española*, Buenos Aires, Dec. 1928. Primo encouraged these centres: *La Nación*, 7 Mar. 1928.

[104] *La Nación*, 5 July 1926.

would be his loyal servant José Gabilán—and a secretary-general, a post first held by Luis Benjumea and later by Gabriel de Aristizábal, the brother of the president of the CONCA. All the fifty *Jefes Provinciales* and an additional body of twenty-one members directly appointed by Primo de Rivera would man the *Gran Junta Directiva*.[105]

The UP machinery was entirely controlled by Primo de Rivera or, what amounted to the same thing, by his watch-dog José Gabilán. No deviation, doctrinal or administrative, could even be contemplated under such circumstances. One could hardly expect an organization so attentive and subservient to orders emanating from above to develop an independent initiative, a vitality of its own, a drive or change.

The completion of this organizational process was seen by Primo de Rivera as a sign of maturity of the UP. He therefore ordered the civil governors to refrain from interfering in the work of the party. The UP should from now on, he said, run 'an organically independent life'[106] But, professed intentions apart, the truth was that the civil governors, many of whom were in their job precisely because they were *Upetistas*, never ceased to exercise a high degree of influence on the running of local and provincial branches. After all, the very statute of the party had given them an official standing within the UP's machinery.[107]

A *partido único* needs to have its own press organs. *La Nación*, which first made its appearance on 19 October 1925, was—like similar newspapers elsewhere[108]—an officially initiated and constantly sponsored mouthpiece. Its editor, Manuel Delgado Barreto, was an apprentice of fascism who was later to be the initiator of the Falange's organ *El Fascio*. *La Nación* was launched in order 'to spread the UP's ideals,[109] and to argue against those who combat us', as Primo de Rivera put it in a letter to Alfonso de Lara, the civil governor of Albacete. He asked him, as he probably did forty-nine other provincial governors, to approach people of 'strong economic position' to buy shares of the projected organ.[110] Simultaneously,

[105] For the structure of the UP, see *Unión Patriótica, Estatutos y Reglamentos para su régimen* (Madrid, 1927).

[106] *Unión Patriótica*, 15 Feb., 6, 15 Aug. 1927, 15 June 1928.

[107] See *Unión Patriótica. Estatutos y Reglamentos*: they were directly responsible for the 'election' of the *juntas provinciales* and their chiefs.

[108] See the example of Trujillo's 'La Nación', in Wiarda, *Dictatorship*, p. 125.

[109] *La Nación*, 29 Mar. 1926.

[110] AHN, P.G., Leg. 358; Primo to Alfonso de Lara, 21 July 1925.

the *delegados gubernativos* started to prepare lists of potential subscribers, and indeed to 'recommend' to them the new official organ. It does not seem that many people lined up to buy *La Nación*'s shares. Consequently, as an appeal, on 25 September 1925, to the Provincial Deputies of the province of Bilbao seems to indicate, state functionaries had to be urged to become shareholders of the regime's mouthpiece.[111] Martínez Anido's office at the ministry of the interior was also to ensure that the official views propagated by *La Nación* received the greatest possible circulation.[112]

The nature of *La Nación* as a daily newspaper was such that it could not devote much space to reports on the routine of the UP's activities. For that purpose, a special bi-weekly magazine, *Unión Patriótica*, was launched on 1 October 1926. About seventy other provincial organs also took good care to provide the country with information on party activities.[113] A strict, at times awkward and inconsistent, censorship of the Spanish press was further expected to guarantee the regime's monopoly of information. The censorship, however, left to the liberal press a certain *embarras de choix*. One could not attack the Italian dictatorship, but it was possible to denounce dictatorships in general by attacking, for example, the Russian or the Greek dictatorships.[114] Sometimes foreign newspapers were bribed to cater to the Dictator's public relations and to surround his regime with an aura of international legitimacy.[115] The UP's *Junta de Propaganda Patriótica y Ciudadana* also launched special newspapers abroad for similar purposes.[116]

The carefully elaborated statute of the UP was not intended to prevent the party from being used as an avenue to, and as a battleground for, power. Indeed, as is usually the case with *partidos únicos*, the members of UP tended to become the personal clientele

[111] *Folletín*, p. 285.

[112] AHN, Gobernación, serie A, Leg. 49; 'Telegramas, circulares del ministerio y respuestas sobre difusión de artículos publicados en La Nación'. The newspaper claimed a daily circulation of 55,000 copies.

[113] The number 70 appears several times in *Unión Patriótica*. For an example of a local organ, see *Unión. Órgano de la Unión Patriótica de Mataró* (Barcelona, 1926).

[114] Celedonio de la Iglesia, *La censura por dentro* (Madrid, 1930).

[115] Romanones Archive, Leg. 63, no. 91; 'Informes sobre la estancia de Primo en Paris'; *Folletín*, p. 545; Maura, *Bosquejo*, p. 188; Xuriguera, p. 14. *Hojas Libres*, no. extraordinario, in Romanones Archive, Leg. 2, no. 48.

[116] See, for example, *La España de Hoy. Periódico editado en español, francés, alemán e inglés, para propagar en todo el mundo el resurgimiento actual de España*, 1929; *La España Nueva*, 1929.

of the Dictator.[117] He was the supreme distributor of largess. This was by no means peculiar to Barcelona or Bilbao. After all, had not a special order of Primo de Rivera's explicitly stipulated that 'public corporations should be almost exclusively composed of affiliates to the UP'?[118] The civil governors were, moreover, explicitly urged to appoint *Upetistas* as city councillors.[119] Being, as they were in at least a third of Spain's provinces, members of the UP, the governors[120] did not need much encouragement to abide by such instructions. Cases were not infrequent like that of Orense, whose civil governor was picked from the local UP and subsequently became instrumental in placing his party colleagues in all kinds of positions. In Ares (La Coruña) the UP organized a campaign against the taking-over of the Ayuntamiento by 'old caciques'. Whether or not they were successful is not known.[121] But *Upetistas* in Almería, for example, who were shocked to see that the civil governor had bypassed them when filling the vacancies in the administration of the province, seemed to have won their case. They complained directly to Primo de Rivera, who intervened in the dispute in such a way as to legitimize the concept that administrative posts should be the fief of local *Upetistas*.[122] In practice, this was a pattern already applied in the UP's cradle, Valladolid, where the provincial leaders, people like Eduardo Callejo and his successor as president of the provincial branch Blas Sierra, and the Catholic-Agrarian circles that supported them, virtually took over the province's administration from the old *Albista* caciques.[123]

As the UP evidently failed to become that 'purifying civic crusade' with a vitality of its own and devoid of 'bastard ambitions', that the Dictator dreamt of,[124] he was led to turn it into a wide club of friends

[117] Duverger, p. 290. This would not be different if the UP is defined as a *parti unifié*—that is, an amalgamation of disparate elements—rather than as a strictly disciplined *parti unique*; for the distinction, see Juan Linz, 'Una interpretación de los regímenes autoritarios', in *Papers. Revista de Sociología* (Universidad Autónoma de Barcelona), no. 8, 1978, p. 16.

[118] Primo de Rivera, *Disertación*, p. 35; *Unión Patriótica*, 15 Nov. 1927, 1 July 1928.

[119] Primo, ibid., 15 Nov. 1928.

[120] Gómez Navarro-Navarrete, pp. 141, 156.

[121] AHN, P.G. Leg. 354: Unión Patriótica of Orense, 3 Oct., 18 Dec. 1924; ibid.: La Coruña, 16 Oct. 1925.

[122] Romanones Archive, Leg. 31, no. 46; Carta al gobernador civil de Almería, 11 May 1926.

[123] José Luis Gómez Navarro *et al.*, 'Approximación al estudio de las élites políticas en la Dictadura de Primo', in *Cuadernos*, pp. 187–8, 192–5.

[124] Primo in *El Sol*, 17 Oct. 1925; and *La Nación*, 9 Aug. 1928.

that would share among themselves the benefits of power. In instructions he issued in March 1926, Primo legalized the position of the UP as 'the zealous legion that must keep an eye on the investiture and prestige' of those who actually exercise power in the provinces. It was up to it to denounce to the authorities those functionaries whose performance had been one of 'imprudence and partiality'.[125] Soon, however, the UP would be promoted from just the position of a watch-dog. In June 1926, *La Nación* had to state in rather apologetic terms that municipal functions were being exercised 'in no small proportion by people who do not belong to the UP'. But a year later, the same organ changed the syntax: 'only in very few cases, and even those must be carefully justified, can people exercise public functions who are not members of the UP. The UP was, after all, born in order to assume the leadership and administration of Spain.'[126]

The Dictator was even more explicit. In November 1927, amid frequent rumours that the UP would soon be called to succeed to the Dictatorship, he made it clear that it was 'indispensable that the Diputaciones and Ayuntamientos should be manned predominantly by members of the UP, which is the civic organization upon which the collective responsibility of this administrative stage is cast'. 'In any case', he added, 'and with only rare exceptions, the presidents of the Ayuntamientos and Diputaciones must be *Upetistas*.'[127]

The provincial chiefs of the UP, in one of their monthly meetings in Madrid with Primo de Rivera and other eminences such as Generals Martínez Anido, Barrera, and Miláns del Bosch, expressed their keen interest that such instructions should be zealously put into practice.[128] They did not have much reason to be dissatisfied. After all, as *La Nación* itself acknowledged, it was 'from within the UP that most of the new executive officials' were picked.[129]

It was precisely with the hope of sharing in the spoils of power that an influx of members came to the UP—in July 1927, the party claimed a membership of 1,700,000[130]—the green banner of which could now be seen in every village throughout the country followed by lusty bands of adherents. It is significant that when Francisco de

[125] Ibid., 29 Mar. 1926.

[126] Ibid., 19 June 1926, 27 Sept. 1927.

[127] *Unión Patriótica*, 15 Nov. 1927.

[128] *La Nación*, 16 Feb. 1928.

[129] Ibid., 9 Mar. 1928.

[130] *Unión Patriótica*, 15 July 1927. There are no reliable statistics, however. In January of the same year, Primo was shocked to realize that only 5,000 affiliates were registered in the Madrid branch, see *La Nación*, 8 Jan. 1927.

Cossío wanted in April 1931 to illustrate the giddy republicanization of the masses following the establishment of the Second Republic, he would compare it with this superficial 'Upetization'.[131] One could almost speak of the 'camisas viejas' of the 'auténticos' and the 'camisas nuevas' of the 'arrivistas' as the party organizers started to get impatient with the avalanche of new recruits.

The Dictator himself was not unaware that the material bait he had displayed threatened to undermine whatever authenticity the UP had possessed in its initial days. As early as May 1926, he contemplated preventing the party from admitting to its ranks 'those who think that belonging to the UP conferred upon them certain advantages'.[132] A year later, he warned against turning the party into 'an agency of advantages and job distribution (*colocaciones*)'.[133] But to no avail. Disappointed, he realized that UP local and provincial chiefs 'are quarrelling with greater frequency than is desirable' with the mayors and the civil governors over honours, favours, and *enchufes*.[134]

To shore up what he now viewed as a degenerating process within the UP, Primo de Rivera thought of following in the footsteps of the Italian Fascist party, which between the years 1922–5 had strictly controlled the influx of new members, the so-called *fascisti del pane*, and in 1925 had definitely closed its lists. In June 1928, he appealed to local branches to replace those among their leaders who had displayed 'lukewarmness of faith' by others 'more capable, enthusiastic, and less selfish' because, he said, 'our League should never give thanks to official favour'. 'The UP', he said, 'had reached its coming of age', and should therefore keep away those who came to it 'in search of personal favours'. He ordered that the party should now leave its lists open for only three more months to allow in new members, after which the lists would be closed.[135] A couple of months later he stipulated that 'before admitting a new recruit, the UP must examine with the greatest scrupulosity the purity of his performance as a citizen'.[136]

But the limits of this sudden civic purism were set by the fact that the UP's monopoly over positions in the public administration was not really challenged. The civil governors were instructed to continue drawing from within its ranks their candidates for official jobs.

131 *El Sol*, 28 Apr. 1931.
132 *La Nación*, 17 May 1926.
133 Ibid., 8 Aug. 1927.
134 Maura, *Bosquejo*, p. 237.
135 *La Nación*, 11, 22 June 1928.
136 Ibid., 9 Aug. 1928.

There was not much substance to the Dictator's promise that the UP's hierarchy would from then on exercise stricter control over the performance of its members in municipal and provincial offices.[137]

Nor was the 'selectionist' approach maintained for very long. True, on 13 September 1928 the Unión Patriótica's lists were closed, in order to take a census that would enable the classification to be made of those who had joined before that date, putting them in a category different from those who might join later.[138] But the enthusiasm generated by the celebrations of the regime's quinquennium persuaded the UP to make yet another effort to capitalize upon what looked externally like the rejuvenation of the regime. It decided, therefore, to keep open its lists for new members until 1 January 1929. Primo de Rivera 'had opened wide the doors of the UP', exclaimed with a measure of bitterness a 'purist' *Upetista* organ.[139] Nor was the material bait removed altogether as neophytes continued to be welcomed, and an order was issued that stipulated that four-fifths of the seats in any provincial and local corporation should be strictly preserved for *Upetistas.*[140] *La Epoca*, the Conservative organ, was totally right in deducing from the symbiosis between the UP and official power that 'the UP is nothing but the powerful civic nucleus which uncompromisingly supports the present situation, that which we have always called, here and elsewhere, the governing party'.[141]

To be sure, the Dictator and his official organs were always ambivalent when referring to the political future of the UP. On 21 August 1924, Primo reiterated his view that the UP 'is not a political party', yet 'its mission' was that of succeeding to the Directory. On 20 February 1925 he suggested a new path. The UP itself should not be a party, he said, but 'the mother of parties . . .'.[142] It would generate, or eventually turn into, an authoritarian 'modern party'.[143] Yet, in June 1928, on the eve of the regime's quinquennium and amidst a euphoric, albeit fabricated, atmosphere, the Dictator, who could see nowhere the emerging 'new parties' and who was approaching the moment of truth in which he could no longer afford to waver about the political future, returned, rather in desperation, to

[137] Ibid., 27 Aug. 1928.

[138] *The Times*, 13 Sept. 1928.

[139] *Patria Española*, 7 Sept. 1928.

[140] *El Republicano*, 20 Nov. 1928. See Primo's declaration in *El Sol*, 4 Oct. 1928.

[141] *La Epoca*, 22 Feb. 1929.

[142] Revesz, *Frente*, pp. 89–90.

[143] *Unión Patriótica*, 1 Nov. 1926, 15 Jan. 1927.

his original formula. The UP, he now said, 'is something which I created in order to provide the nation with an organ of government'.[144]

(c) *The Organization of Public Support.* Whatever the uncertainties about the UP's future may have been, it was upon its present that the emphasis was put. As the *partido único* of the regime it anticipated the most important ingredients of the Republic's extreme right. To begin with, the UP was the first right-wing movement in Spain after Maurismo which took to the streets to stage grand gatherings and monster parades, unknown to the traditional parliamentarian right. Like Franco's *movimiento*, the UP was conceived as a means to turn the Dictatorship into a 'national movement'. It was a 'constant expression of public acceptance', 'organized conduct'. 'A dictatorship', explained the party's ideologue José María Pemán, 'needs to be daily stimulated by the heat of living and lively national opinion.' The UP was needed, he said bluntly, 'in order to say yes' to the Dictatorship. Pemán believed that a major task of the UP was to neutralize the 'negative' and 'destructive' aspects of mass politics. In other words, its mission was to demobilize people through false and controlled mobilization or, that is, to canalize the political instincts of the masses into 'constructive action'. Sheer tyranny was excluded because of 'the actual level of democratic sensitivity'. 'In a modern state', a dictatorship, he believed, must not and cannot rest exclusively on the official and bureaucratic apparatus of the state.[145]

However for another ideologue of the regime, José Pemartín, the UP was more than just a façade. Canovism had failed, he argued, precisely because it lacked popular support. The lesson for the Dictatorship was clear: to use 'all available means' in order to create 'a *real* mass movement imbued with a profound and essential ideology'. Nothing less than the fate of future generations of Spaniards depended on this enterprise.[146] Only such a 'civilian militia' could guarantee 'the definite irreversibility' of the 'formidable transformation' brought about by the Dictatorship. This did not mean that the UP should be allowed to develop an independent, uncontrolled life.[147] In a series of exhaustive articles,[148] Pemartín

[144] *La Nación*, 12 June 1928; *Unión Patriótica*, 15 June 1928.
[145] Pemán, *El hecho*, *passim*.
[146] Pemartín, 'El ejemplo de Cánovas', in *La Nación*, 15 Mar. 1928.
[147] Pemartín, 'El orden subvertido', in *La Nación*, 17 Feb. 1928.
[148] See, for example, 'Hacia la nueva ciudadanía. Las dos escuelas', in *La Nación*, 4 Apr. 1928.

disputed the view of the so-called rationalist school that the masses should be allowed to mobilize for their own ends. His was the approach of the anti-rationalists, 'Christian and others', who maintained that 'there are values which are external to the masses' and which might even have to 'prevail against the masses'.

A difference between the UP in Spain and traditional conservatives is that the former was mobilized in the name of an apocalyptic fear that reactionary values were about to be undermined by new and aggressive forces that the traditional right either did not understand, and hence was unable to cope with, or forces that were simply not strong enough to pose a meaningful threat. The UP proposed to substitute for lethargic nostalgia an emphatic awareness of the need to manipulate mass society, and to harness it to the nationalist cause. Even propaganda was referred to as a kind of war. 'The speech is also a struggle, and we must struggle indefatigably in order to win', said Manuel Banzo in a UP meeting. 'In life, just as in war, indifference is the cardinal sin', wrote the *Upetista* columnist Carlos Wilf in a clear allusion to the 'delicate right' who had let the motherland collapse under the stress of 'the anarchist avalanche'.[149] The propagandist Juan Bonell Gómez urged the UP not to drift into passivity. It should, he said, 'constantly prepare its collective soul to meet the oncoming calamity'.[150]

Indeed, the UP machine was by no means lethargic. The Dictator himself cultivated it with great care as, he stated repeatedly, it was designed to assist him in reviving, 'as Italy had already revived' under Mussolini, 'the glorious traditions of Spain'.[151] The major role of the UP was that of spreading among the public the message of the new regime. It was the main organ of propaganda that Primo had at his disposal, and the most active one. The UP frequently appeared as a recruiting centre for adherents *ex populo* that could be used as a tub to thump on grand occasions such as the regime's anniversaries. Like Caesarism's festivals, the UP's *mises-en-scène* were to be an instrument of 'popular democracy'.[152] Its frequent

[149] *Unión Patriótica*, 15 May, 15 June, 15 July, 1928; 15 Sept., 1 Oct., 15 Nov., 15 Dec. 1929. For the distinction between the traditional and the new right, cf. Arno Mayer, *Dynamics of Counterrevolution in Europe* (New York, 1971), pp. 48–55; J. Weiss, *The Fascist Tradition: Radical Right-Wing Extremism in Modern Europe* (New York, 1967), pp. vii–xv, 1–30.

[150] Juan Bonell Gómez, 'Invitación a la fortaleza' in *La Nación*, 30 Mar. 1928.

[151] Quoted in Revesz, *Frente*, pp. 93–8.

[152] Cf. George Mosse, 'Caesarism, Circuses and Monuments', in *JCH*. vol. 6, no. 2, 1971, pp. 176–82.

gatherings and celebrations, like the many national meetings of the regime's official corporations (agricultural entities, professional organs, Ayuntamientos, etc.), were planned as a kind of 'political sport' to keep public opinion occupied.[153] Indeed, hardly a day passed without the UP staging propaganda meetings, conventions of women and youth sections, cultural events, or huge gatherings dedicated to paying homage to 'outstanding' figures. The Dictator's speeches on some of these occasions were broadcast, a significant novelty.[154] No less novel was the fact that the propaganda section of the UP produced a special film to spread the message of the regime's achievements.[155]

On given occasions, mainly after the regime's enemies had staged their usual abortive uprisings, or when the foreign press denigrated the regime, or a European statesman criticized its policies, or a political upheaval—such as that generated by the student rebellion—originated unfavourable comments abroad, the UP organized monster parades, and mass petitions of loyalty to the Dictator, in which millions of signatures (real or false) were collected.[156] Some of the UP's rallies, held in front of Primo's office at the Buenavista Palace which, like Mussolini's Palazzo Venezia, turned into the focal point of *Upetista* liturgy, reminded the British ambassador of Fascist gatherings.[157] On one such occasion, when the UP staged a demonstration in front of Primo's window, the Dictator had to address the public three times, with the help of a microphone, before they were ready to disperse.[158]

Upetista propagandists were eager also to demonstrate that Spain was not that decadent country that 'anti-Spanish literature' had invented.[159] Spain's greatness was recaptured on the battlefields of

[153] Maura, *Bosquejo*, pp. 154–5.

[154] The organ *Unión Patriótica* contains plenty of information on such events. See also on the activities of youth sections in *La Vanguardia*, 2, 3, 15 Jan., 14 Feb., 19 Mar. 1929. *The Times*, 17 Oct. 1925, pointed out the novelty of broadcasting.

[155] *The Times*, 27 Mar. 1926.

[156] *La Nación*, 21 Mar. 1929; *La Vanguardia*, 1, 6, 28 Feb., 19 Mar., 18 Apr. 1929; AHN, P.G. Leg. 354: information on UP's reaction 'against Blasco Ibáñez's accursed campaign', Legs. 313, 418; information on the reaction of the foreign press' 'anti-Spanish' campaign during the student troubles.

[157] FO/371/11936, Gurney to Austen Chamberlain, 14 July 1926.

[158] *El Sol*, 16 Apr. 1929. See also the women's demonstration in front of Primo's residence to thank him for the victory in Morocco: *La Nación*, 7 June 1926.

[159] An anticipation of what would later be the main themes of *Upetista* propaganda can be found in M. Siurot, *La emoción de España. Libro de cultura patriótica-popular* (Madrid, 1924).

Morocco and in an ecstatic racial-spiritual Hispano-Americanism. The victory in 1925 over the rebels of the Riff was, according to a special issue of the periodical *Unión Patriótica*, 'a demonstration of Spain's capability to repel any attack of whatever power'.[160] But it was the daring flight of two Spanish pilots in 1926 across the Atlantic to South America that generated the greatest enthusiasm. It was hailed in meetings and in a euphoric press coverage as an undisputable demonstration of 'Iberian vitality'. The national euphoria over the flight, however, was not just a *mise-en-scène*; it was genuine. The government's decision to bestow on the pilots a special gold medal was a response to public clamour.[161]

The anniversary of the Dictatorship was always the occasion for sending hundreds of propagandists to proclaim across the country the glory of the regime, while dozens of trains transported, free of charge, thousands of citizens to ceremonies and 'popular parades' in the capital. During the quinquennium, for example, an ecstatic campaign of propaganda preceded the celebrations as the UP's network was fully mobilized to urge the masses, men, women, and even children to take part in the events. The festival itself was a seven-day event in which hundreds of meetings and civilian parades were staged even in the remotest villages, in which the UP also distributed snacks and charity to the poor.[162] The climax was, of course, the celebrations in the capital, to which fifty trains transported about 100,000 people and where public buildings were used to accommodate the demonstrators. In a typical gesture, the Dictator lodged some of them in his own house.[163] The royal palace was inundated with postcards carrying Primo's picture and demanding the turning of the 13th of September into a national holiday.[164]

It was not without significance that the message of this organized enthusiasm was brought home to the palace. The king had

[160] *Unión Patriótica*, 15 June, 15 Oct. 1928.

[161] *La Gaceta de Madrid*, 4 Apr. 1926. See the ecstatic coverage given by the UP press: *La Nación*, 1, 5 Feb., 5–8 Apr. 1926; *Amor Patrio. Periódico inspirado por el progama de Unión Patriótica*, 5 Apr. 1927.

[162] *La Nación*, 2, 9, 16, 18 Aug. 1928; 4, 5, 8, 10, 11, 12 Sept. 1928; *Patria Española*, 7 Sept. 1928.

[163] *La Nación*, 13 Sept. 1928 (30,000 children paraded in Madrid); *Patria Española*, 7 Oct. 1928; *The Times*, 13, 14 Sept. 1928. 40,000 people paraded in Barcelona, *La Nación*, 17 Sept. 1928.

[164] Romanones Archive, Leg. 2: 'Comisión . . . del homenaje nacional al General Marqués de Estella'. Primo had wanted the celebration 'to show to our enemies' the extent of popular support enjoyed by the Dictatorship, *La Nación*, 23 June 1928.

deliberately chosen to stay away from Spain during the celebrations. This was his way of showing his growing displeasure with the Dictatorship. Indeed, the UP's demonstrative ceremonies can be seen as a means of pressure by the Dictator upon his royal sovereign; an assertion of his popular power base, a base independent of the king's will and hence immune from his notorious penchant for political intrigue. Significantly, *La Nación* referred to the popular celebrations as 'a clear and categorical plebiscitary demonstration'.[165] No statesman possessing such a wide and exalted following can be 'Bourbonized' through a familiar *crisis oriental*. Such tactics—incidentally, frequently resorted to by Mussolini and his Fascist party as well—were also used by Primo de Rivera when he wanted to put pressure on the king to sign some controversial decree. This was the case, for example, with the much-publicized plebiscite organized by the UP to exert pressure on the king to allow the creation of the National Assembly.[166]

It was essential for the Dictator to keep the public in a state of high tension. The consolidation of the Dictatorship demanded that the revolutionary menace to 'the foundations of Spanish society' be kept alive. It was there that the ultimate justification of the regime lay. Every conspiracy, real or fictitious,[167] was seized as an opportunity to mobilize support for the regime and underline the indispensability of its continuation. For example, when Blasco Ibáñez, the famous republican writer, published abroad his libel against the king and the directory,[168] all the resources of the regime were put on a war footing. A son of Martínez Anido was sent to Paris to commission the writer José María Carretero with the writing of the pro-regime response to Blasco Ibáñez's denunciations.[169] Dozens of regional and provincial delegates and the country's 9,000 mayors were brought by the UP from all over Spain to pay homage to the 'most popular king in history' and to 'the bravest general on earth'. The latter was also presented with fifty-one albums containing

[165] Ibid., 13 Sept. 1928.

[166] See pp. 212–16.

[167] The 'invasion' at Vera de Bidásoa was generated by the *agents provocateurs* of Martínez Anido. See the account of the commander of the force that 'contained the invasion', Juan Cueto, *Cuentos al Nuncio. Sobre derivaciones republicanas de los sucesos de Vera* (Madrid, 1933). For the maintenance of a permanent condition of stress as essential to the consolidation of dictatorships, see Alexander Gerschenkron, 'The Stability of Dictatorships', in *Continuity in History and Other Essays* (Harvard University Press, 1968), p. 315.

[168] Blasco Ibáñez, *Alfonso XIII Unmasked*.

[169] González Ruano, *El General Primo de Rivera* (Madrid, 1954), pp. 120–1.

more than three million signatures, collected throughout the provinces. Half a million medals of 'homage to the king' were also issued to the public.[170] Primo was delighted; 'this is great propaganda', he wrote from Morocco to his deputy in Madrid.[171] This whole series of demonstrations seemed to have left such a great impression on the British ambassador—not perhaps very familiar with ways of 'organizing' opinion—that he became convinced that 'General Primo, like Signor Mussolini, enjoys being dictator and the moment will never arrive when they will voluntarily resign. Neither will go till forced to do so.'[172]

2. *One Leader*

Primo de Rivera, just like Franco after him, with whom he also shared the conviction that the Spanish people 'are the easiest people in the world to govern', actually conceived of this sort of official homage as a daily plebiscite.[173] A rhetorical dialogue such as the one he conducted with the multitude at the anti-Blasco Ibáñez rally was tantamount to a general election. 'Do the people want me', he asked, 'to continue at the head of the government?' The response came in a clamorous ovation, some among the crowd suggesting a lifetime or a twenty-year term for his rule, and others proposing that he should govern the country till all the caciques had died. 'Do the people want us', he continued, 'to persevere though they cannot expect transcendental achievements before we consolidate the path of purification?' The answer 'did not leave any doubts' about 'the people's will'. Genuinely overwhelmed by such manifestations of fidelity, no wonder the Dictator exclaimed that 'after such a demonstration of support I feel I have the obligation to stay at the head of government until all my strength is exhausted'.[174] '99% of the Spaniards are with me,' he said in December 1926 to the French journalist Clara Candiani, 'how can I leave office in such circumstances?'[175] And, a couple of years later, conquered by the colourful parade of thousands of people who invaded the capital to celebrate the quinquennium of his regime, he declared:

[170] *The Times*, 22–4 Jan. 1925.
[171] Primo to Magaz, 14 June 1925, in Armiñán, *Epistolario*, p. 173.
[172] FO/371/11906, Rumbold to Austen Chamberlain, 29 Jan. 1925.
[173] *La Nación*, 10 May 1926. Cf. Francisco Franco Salgado-Araujo, *Mis conversaciones privadas con Franco* (Barcelona, 1976), pp. 274, 342.
[174] *La Nación*, 26 Jan. 1925; *Folletín*, pp. 192–7.
[175] AHN, P.G. Leg. 350.

Following the imposing manifestation of today, you can safely assert that an overwhelming majority of the Spanish people has pronounced [its support for the regime] in such proportions that the government should have no hesitation in claiming that it is accompanied and strengthened [by the people]. So enormous has been today's event that one can hardly remember another of similar dimensions . . . I shall not need to summon you on every anniversary; this would be an excessive inconvenience. But all you who hear me now, I do invite you for the 13th of September in five years time; and here we shall be, if not the same persons, certainly the same regime, with even more civic authority than today.[176]

There was no reason for the Dictator to think that only 'organized' opinion was on his side. The nation's will was reflected, he was confident, also in spontaneous demonstrations. A couple of months after the Civilian Directory was set up, he stressed this conviction while on a visit to Segovia:

If, when I walk through those villages, the women lift up their sons in order to recognize me and see in me—excuse me my immodesty—the saviour of the patria; if I have your affection; if, when I go out for a walk every Sunday, unescorted and on foot, through those streets wearing my Spanish cape, I receive the clearest and the most popular ovations; if it is on those days that I see joyful youngsters and seductive girls come to pull the fringes of my cape in order to see whether I am indeed General Primo de Rivera . . . if all this is true, which it is, we can affirm that the people are with us.[177]

Sometimes he would deliberately go out into the streets of Madrid to have his spirit cheered up by the spontaneous display of sympathy from the people. On one such occasion he decided to mingle with the people 'because I felt I no longer enjoyed the support of those elements without whose assistance it is impossible to go on'. But his walk through the crowded streets of the capital, he said, had fortified his spirit and injected an elixir of life into his determination 'not to spare any effort or sacrifice in order to serve till the very end a people so great and so noble as the Spanish'.[178] Such direct and simple contacts with grass-root people—during a visit to Santiago, for example, he walked through the streets, hit the target, was glad to be invited to *churros*, and happily shook hands with passers-by—were, he confessed an essential component of his style as a ruler.[179]

The 'noble people' could then also act without being previously mobilized by the UP's propaganda machine. Not infrequently, the

[176] *El Sol*, 14 Sept. 1928. [177] *Folletín*, p. 307. [178] *La Nación*, 3 Apr. 1926.
[179] Ibid., 26, 29 July 1926.

demonstrations in favour of Primo de Rivera were as spontaneous as they were striking; many of his visits to towns and pueblos turned into triumphal processions.[180] For example, on his journey along the east coast in January 1929, thousands of villagers filled his railway-coach with flowers and oranges, which he later offered to the shrine of Our Lady of Grace at Barcelona.[181] While on a visit to Medina del Campo and its surroundings, his railway-coach was hailed in a most enthusiastic way by people of all social classes free of the 'cold and restrained character' of fabricated demonstrations.[182] He would visit even the remotest villages, where he pronounced eloquent, pompous, sometimes embarrassingly banal speeches. For example, in Ampuero, a small pueblo of 448 inhabitants in the province of Santander, the population gathered to hear him praise the 'well-known' beauty of the local women.[183] The inauguration of a slaughterhouse in Porriño (Galicia) was the occasion for an ecstatic eulogy of the economic achievements of his regime.[184] Everywhere he would present himself as a providential leader whose thaumaturgic touch sufficed to solve his *patria*'s problems. In a meeting of the UP in July 1926, he recalled how he had promised the wheat-growers help in a moment of great stress the previous year, and, thanks to his alliance with heaven, the rain had come and the crops had been saved. He had promised help to the coal-miners, and the British strike had come, solving difficulties.[185] On his return from his provincial tours, these constant plebiscites as he and his panegyrists viewed them,[186] he told reporters how:

> villages and towns are burning with enthusiasm. They acclaim the government and shout '20 years more'. They do not worry about lost liberties which no one refused them, or parliamentary representatives, who in no way serve the general good. Work is being done pacifically everywhere. The roads are the best in the world; agriculture, industry, and commerce are protected, and there is citizenship, worship, national pride, and confidence in the present and the future . . . After all, it is very easy to govern such a noble people as the Spaniards.[187]

[180] Cortés-Cavanillas, *La Dictadura y el Dictador* (Madrid, 1949), pp. 53–66; FO/371/10593, Rumbold to Ramsay MacDonald, 14 Aug. 1924. See also Maura, *Bosquejo*, p. 283.

[181] *The Times*, 21 Jan. 1929. For a similar reception in Valencia, see *La Nación*, 29 July 1926.

[182] Ibid., 31 May 1927.

[183] *El Republicano*, 20 Sept. 1928.

[184] *The Times*, 5 Apr. 1928.

[185] Ibid., 9 July 1926.

[186] Juan de Castilla, 'Los viajes del presidente y el contacto del país', 'La fuerza de la Dictadura', in *La Nación*, 8 Nov. 1928, 11 Apr. 1929. See also *The Times*, 9 July 1926.

[187] *The Times*, 16 Aug. 1927.

It was during such visits, he said, that he came to grasp in the most lucid way how, under his guidance, the Spanish people were transforming the face of the country. He therefore came to identify the 'aggrandizement of the *patria*' with the continuation of his rule. After a sweeping tour of Extremadura he felt he should assure the mass of his supporters that

> to those who, in order to discourage you, tell you that I am old or exhausted, you should answer first that it is not true; that if the relentless years have made my hair grow white, and the burden of responsibilities and work has furrowed my brows, my intelligence has not weakened, my will is as firm as ever, and my heart beats in a youthful rhythm.[188]

What was the secret of Primo de Rivera's popularity with the masses? He undoubtedly possessed that unique charm—one which is not always susceptible of rational explanation—that makes some leaders well liked by the masses, and others, who lack it, equally disliked; *levitas popularis*, they called it in Republican Rome. This charm, however, had to be constantly cultivated by an always magnanimous, yet never condescending, intercourse with the people.[189] Clearly, Primo's paternalism, that was so repellent to the political opposition and the educated middle class, was highly appealing to the man in the street. The simplicity, sometimes even the vulgarity, of his manners, his Robin Hood sense of justice, his head-on approach to complex matters, his irresistible sympathy and *bonhomie*, his taste for celebrations, wine, women, and good food, his somewhat quixotic readiness to fight for what he sincerely thought was a noble cause—all that made up a constant appeal to the gallery, and the gallery applauded. He who confessed that he had learnt the art of government at the Casino of his natal town, Jerez, and through the 'science of life', was an amusing novelty to a people tired of legal-minded professional politicians. The flamboyant and good-humoured Dictator created a refreshing effect on the 'average' Spaniard; the coffee-house politician—a not negligible part of the nation—could easily identify with him. Primo was the personal mirror for many Spaniards. His sentimental, almost puerile patriotism could hardly have failed to generate a sense of identification with the public at large. It was his inarticulate, direct way of

[188] *La Nación*, 9 Oct. 1926.

[189] Z. Yaavetz, 'Levitas Popularis', in *Atene e Roma*, 1965, n. s. 10, iii, esp. pp. 103–10.

exposing his intimate feelings that was probably the most distinct feature of his dialogue with the people. Standing in front of Hernán Cortés's monument in his home town Medellín, he described the emotions that overtook him:

I took off my hat, and for a few moments I was irresolute, not knowing whether to pray as I would have done in the presence of a holy effigy, or to recite quietly in patriotic homage and intimate emotion the song of the flag. But the unique spectacle, incomparably touching, conquered me, subdued me, and ended my vacillations: I sang . . . I sang the virile, noble, and sincere hymn, strong and sonorous, like a cry of the race . . . [190]

The torrent of imposing oratory, written and spoken, which the Spanish Dictator poured upon his people might have been an inherent Spanish or Latin characteristic. But it also responded to the vital need of a dictator to be ubiquitous, persevering, and always assertive. It was also an exercise in political mimicry. It can be viewed as an attempt to imitate Mussolini, whose dominance of the Italian people was attributed to 'the magic of his hallucinatory oratory'.[191] Primo de Rivera, not unlike the Duce, with whom he clearly shared being the fairly genuine reflection of the man in the street, had a showmanship concept of politics.[192] For him politics were a *mise-en-scène*: the art of distracting and making the people rejoice. His whole style as a ruler amounted to a spectacle of magic or a juggling act with the whole nation as an audience. His official notes, in which he almost daily briefed the people on his policies and personal feelings (he would even tell them of his love for a lady whom he wanted to marry) in a language of embarrassing familiarity, were, as he was to write in his farewell *nota*, 'accountable for my constant communication with the Spanish people'. It was through these intimate notes, rather than through his decrees in the *Gaceta* that, he said, the people had really come to know him.[193] His *golpes de efecto*, his ingenious tricks, his appeals to the most elementary or childish sentimentality of the people, and his spectacular actions—all stem from his concept of the nature of politics and public opinion.[194] In effect, he believed that by his frequent participation

[190] *La Nación*, 9 Oct. 1926.

[191] *Folletín*, p. 508.

[192] Cf. Barzini, pp. 133–56. The similarities between Primo and the Duce are implied in a book by a panegyrist of the Dictatorship: Andrés Revesz, *Mussolini el dictator en pyjama* (Madrid, n.d.).

[193] See a selection of such notes in Dionisio Pérez, *La Dictadura a través de sus notas oficiosas* (Madrid, 1930); the last note in pp. 331–4.

[194] Cf. *Folletín*, p. 714.

in public meetings he was also asserting his personality as a statesman. 'I am used to attending meetings like this one', he said to a gathering of the UP, 'just like Poincaré and Mussolini do in their respective countries.'[195]

Caudillismo was not a new theme in Spanish history. But in the UP propaganda, Primo de Rivera's personality cult was cultivated as a combination of a modern *führerprinzip* and Caesarian apotheosis. He was credited with redemptive features borrowed from previous historical examples as well as from the realm of theology. It was an exercise in the secularization of religious metaphors and the sanctification of political terms.[196]

The Dictator was portrayed as the personification of the most perfect values of humanism, justice, piety, Christianity, and patriotism; he was an 'exceptionally talented' man, a leader 'by nature'. There hardly existed a short expression that could reflect his rich personality. He was the embodiment of the soul of Spain, the essence of 'españolismo'; he was permeated with a profound faith in God, in the *patria*, and in his own self. Among his noble qualities one should mention his humanity, justice, generosity, limitless optimism, frankness, and natural ability to get along with people, his firmness and energy, his talent for gaining rapid insight and vision into national problems, his ability to grasp the pulsation of the street, his incomparable personal courage, his unique capacity for work and his power of assimilation, his talent as an orator, and his capacity for changing his views. Primo de Rivera was actually a rare and complex personality: impulsive and reflective at the same time, 'hot-headed' and serene; the prototype of the Hispanic race and more.[197]

In a series of speeches, later published under the auspices of the Dictator himself, the army chaplain, Manual Jover, referred to his Caudillo as the 'saviour of the Fatherland', Joaquín Costa's longed-for 'iron surgeon', who had now emerged to cure the maladies of his country. Even classical mythology was enlisted to describe him as a 'Titan' fighting Jupiter, a one-eyed gigantic Cyclops forging Zeus' rays, and an Atlas who, 'with his stout unshakable shoulders avoided the collapse of the lofty roof of our beloved Fatherland'. He is a

[195] *El Sol*, 12 Mar. 1928.
[196] This practice is the central theme of an instructive article on Nazism by U. Tal, *Structures of German 'Political Theology' in the Nazi Era* (Tel Aviv, 1979).
[197] Cimadevilla, pp. 177–214.

'Christ', it was said, who carries the cross on his shoulders, a 'magician' and a 'genius'. His temper was made of steel; he was 'the Messiah who carries the sun of justice in his right hand in order to illuminate the beloved Spanish soil'. No wonder he had nothing to fear from comparison with the most distinguished figures in world history: 'What Alexander the Great called his hope, Caesar his luck, and Napoleon his star, Primo de Rivera called more modestly and accurately his divine help.'[198] That he escaped unharmed from an attempt on his life in August 1926 was of course due to 'the providential luck that protects the life of the notable Caudillo'.[199]

Primo de Rivera himself actually did not think 'the star' should be monopolized by Napoleon; he also had his own, he told a French journalist.[200] In a speech in July 1924 before an *Upetista* audience in El Ferrol he resorted to his 'divine connection', 'heaven's help', as the only possible explanation for 'this inspiration that I have, this excess of health of mine'. Even 'the effort that I made on the fateful 13th of September 1923 is not my exclusive work'; and in 'the virility that flows in my veins one cannot fail to see the presence of providence'.[201]

Nor was Primo de Rivera's calibre as a military genius inferior to that of Hannibal, Napoleon, or El Cid. The analogy of Spain's 'undefeated Caudillo'[202] with the latter was especially strengthened by the fact that both had acquired their fame in the war against the Moors. In the process Primo de Rivera proved himself 'a modern Caesar'. With Napoleon he shared the belief that 'every law can and should be violated when the destiny of the *patria* is at stake'.[203]

As in the case of Mussolini—with whom he also shared strong

[198] Jover Mirá, *passim*. See also Duarte, pp. 26, 30, 37.

[199] *La Nación*, 2 Aug. 1926.

[200] Interview with Clara Candiani in AHN, P.G.

[201] *Folletín*, p. 154.

[202] *Patria Española*, 7 Sept. 1928.

[203] For additional references to Primo's personality cult, see also *Álbum Primo de Rivera. Suplemento artístico de la revista 'El Imán'*, Barcelona; *El Buen Sentido. Gloria Nacional. Versos formados por Visitación Argumanez en alabanza de Primo de Rivera y Alfonso XIII*, in Hemeroteca Municipal, A/1697; *Unión Patriótica*, 1 Dec. 1927, 15 Mar., 15 May, 15 Nov. 1928. Of course, the achievements of the regime were entirely and almost exclusively the work of one man, the great Caudillo, see the euphoric reports on the successes of the Dictatorship in Emilio Zurano Muñoz, *Hagamos patria. La voluntad en acción (cultura, educación, trabajo)* (Madrid, 1927); Ramón Martínez de la Riva, *La España de hoy* (Madrid, 1926); Pemartín, *Los valores*; E. Díez-Retg, *España bajo el nuevo régimen. Cinco años de gobierno Primo de Rivera* (Madrid, 1928); José María Saseras y Batllé, *Dos años de Dictadura militar (homenaje a Primo de Rivera)* (Barcelona, 1925).

qualities of 'virility' and the 'vocation' of a journalist—the Spanish Dictator was a *Pater Patriae* who worked indefatigably into the night so that his people could enjoy untroubled the pleasures of life.[204] 'Spanish people,' said a leading article, 'your president is vigilant while you are asleep.'[205] Such a catch-phrase was frequently used by Dictators—such as, for example, Franco, Trujillo, and Mussolini—who had to think of devices with which to depoliticize the masses. The cult of a leader possessing an inhuman power of work, unlimited dedication and perseverence, and an intuitive, genial perception of political issues was intended to set the people's minds at rest and keep them away from politics.[206]

To compensate the Dictator for his devotion, and services to the *patria*, the UP awarded him the medal of work; he was decorated with valuable insignia of gold and diamonds; a precious baton of command 'with the most unique jewel that can be found' was bestowed on him; his picture was distributed to every member of the party, a proposal was made to confer upon him the title of 'Prince of Peace', the house where he was born in Jerez was presented to him as a gift by the town's population, and the colossal sum of four million pesetas was raised through public subscriptions in Spain and among Spanish communities abroad in order to honour him with a house in the capital—Caesar received a similar *Domus Publica*—since he had no money or time to spare for his own and his family's earthly necessities.[207] With 'modesty' and 'a spirit of self-sacrifice', the Dictator accepted the donation because, he said, he planned to house in it 'duly and without personal profit the offices and national centre of the UP and the Somatén'.[208]

It is noteworthy that the Dictator was not just a passive and reluctant spectator of this festival of honours, though he frequently went to great pains to display a fictitious modesty. He had to set, as

[204] See 'Primo de Rivera, a Slave of his Work' in *the Daily Mail*, 26 Apr. 1929.

[205] *Unión Patriótica*, 1 Apr. 1927.

[206] Cf. Wiarda, *Dictatorship*, pp. 132–7, 192; Christopher Hibbert, *Benito Mussolini, a Biography* (London, 1962), pp. 56–61; Luis Ramírez, *Vie de Francisco Franco*, pp. 246–58. A good article on Mussolini is Piero Melograni, 'The Cult of the Duce in Mussolini's Italy', in *JCH*, vol. 11, no. 4, 1976, pp. 221–37.

[207] Fernández Almagro, *Historia*, p. 510; Maura, *Bosquejo*, pp. 258–61; *La Nación*, 3 Oct. 1928. The public subscription for the house was successful only to a limited extent. Much of the money came from official corporations, see *Folletín*, pp. 804–5. Spaniards living abroad also contributed their share: *La Nación*, 21 Nov. 1928. Some of these honours were reminiscent of honours conferred upon Julius Caesar; see Stefan Weinstock, *Divus Julius* (Oxford University Press, 1971), pp. 163–281.

[208] *La Nación*, 3 Oct. 1928.

he put it when refusing an honour proposed to him by the king, 'an example of personal disinterestedness when serving the *patria*'.[209] But he could not bear to see figures other than himself attracting too much public attention and admiration. During the ecstatic celebrations in honour of the pilot Ramón Franco and his collegues, he was, just for a while, pushed off the centre of the public stage. He therefore arranged to be granted, at the very ceremony in which the pilots were decorated by the king, the Laureada of San Fernando for the second time.[210] After having received so many honours the Dictator could afford the luxury of paying lip-service to modesty. 'I demand', he said on the morrow of the quinquenniun, 'that all these moving manifestations of national love towards me should cease completely.'[211]

3. *An Anaemic Militia: The Somatén*

Just as the UP started as a Castilian natural growth later manipulated by the Dictator, so the Somatén, a traditional Catalan militia[212] of preservers of bourgeois peace, was institutionalized by Primo de Rivera in his search for national acquiescence. By extending the Somatén to the whole of Spain to become the champion of 'order, justice, morality and progress', the Dictator expected it 'to enlist and organize the well-to-do people so that their support can fortify us'. The guardian of bourgeois peace, the Somatén was conceived as a militia of people of middle, upper-middle class, and noble origin, people of 'proved morality', and those who 'exercise a profession in their respective localities'.[213]

The identification of the upper classes with the counter-revolutionary mission of the Somatén was the reason that the militia's commanding cadres in such places as Madrid, Seville, Granada, Barcelona, or Bilbao looked more like the governing boards of banks and companies, or like exclusive aristocratic clubs, than the nucleus of a potentially revolutionary militia.[214]

That these people joined the Somatén at all, in spite of the fact

[209] Official note of 16 May 1927 in *ABC*.

[210] *Gaceta de Madrid*, 6 Oct. 1925.

[211] *La Nación*, 3 Oct. 1928.

[212] For the origins and history of the Somatén, see J. M. March, *El Somatén, su origen y su naturaleza, su historia y organización. La salvación de España* (Barcelona, 1923).

[213] *Gaceta de Madrid*, 17 Sept. 1923.

[214] Rosa Martínez Segarra, 'Grupos económicos en el Somatén', in *Cuadernos*, pp. 217–22.

that the Dictatorship was there to set their minds at rest by reducing the possibility of a resurgence of the social threat of the past, was probably due to the fact that the 'red scare' had become not just a cliché of dictatorial propaganda but an immanent part of upper-class attitudes in Spain. The Somatén was in this respect 'the appropriate response to the international Communist menace', the champion of bourgeois values.[215] It was there to prevent the agents of the Comintern 'from infiltrating into the soul of youngsters' and 'from undermining our civilization' by, among other things, 'their use of women only as an instrument of pleasure which anybody could treat as he pleases'.[216]

The Somatén was organized from above by the captains-general (much in the same way as the civil governors 'organized' the UP), who were also the supreme commanders of the militia's units in their respective military regions.[217] Throughout the last months of 1923, reports poured on to Primo de Rivera's desk from captains-general or local commanders relating how Somatén militia were being established and expressing, as a matter of course, their members' fervent support for 'the principles of 13 September'.[218] Frequently, and especially in rural areas, the military commanders would not hesitate to use the good services of old caciques as agents of recruitment.[219]

Such a patronizing approach to recruitment meant that, rather than as a revolutionary, dynamic militia, the Somatén was conceived as an auxiliary of the authorities in their endeavour to preserve order and enhance the cause of 'good citizenship', and in the case of strikes to help sustain the economy and crush the 'revolutionaries' by running the paralysed public services.[220] A panegyrist of the Dictatorship indeed likened the Somatén to the Organization for the Maintenance of Supplies (OMS) which emerged in Britain from among the middle classes to curb the radical unions.[221]

[215] E. Díaz-Retg, pp. 113–18.

[216] 'El bolchevismo y la juventud' in *El Somatén*, Feb. 1928.

[217] AHN, P.G. Leg. 442; 'Capitanía General de la 8ª Región. Ciudadanos!', 21 Sept. 1923.

[218] Ibid., reports from the Canary Islands, 26 Oct. 1923; Algeciras, 6 Nov. 1923; Tafalla, 21 Nov. 1923; Coruña, 22 Nov. 1923.

[219] Tusell, *La crisis*, pp. 149, 152; Martínez Segarra, 'Grupos económicos', p. 218.

[220] For the constitution, organization, and development of the Somatén, see José Fontán, *El Somatenista español* (Barcelona, 1924), pp. 131–49; Francisco de P. Moreno Duarte, *Disertación Somatenista* (Zaragoza, 1928); AHN, P.G. Leg. 441: 'Objeto y organización del Somatén'. See also *La Nación*, 24 Apr. 1926.

[221] Mask, pp. 128–33. For the auxiliary missions of the Somatén, see also the reports in *El Somatén*, Feb. 1928.

The conformist precepts along which the Somatén was expected to operate were probably instrumental in turning it into the focal point for the small landowners of the CONCA,[222] the urban petty bourgeoisie, and all manner of conservative patriots. A certain forty-five-year-old bachelor peasant, Daniel Ansede from Pacios (Lugo), said that he came to the Somatén to 'fulfill the sacred obligations demanded by the military directory', obligations 'which are closely related to the teachings of the apostle Santiago'.[223] The Somatén was also attractive to citizens who expected, just as in the case of the UP, to gain official favours. Indeed, a struggle over prerogatives and petty honours was the reason for a number of disputes over positions in local Somatén units.[224]

Frequently looking like Dad's Army or, as in the case of the Hlinka Guard in Slovakia, like comic-opera actors,[225] Somatenistas became the laughing-stock of the population in many localities.[226] An old politician, the Vizconde de Eza, claimed that in order to be considered a fool by the educated Andalusian ladies one had to have a radio, play 'mah-jong' . . . and belong to the Somatén.[227] To protect themselves from the sarcasm of their fellow citizens, Somatenistas would appeal to the government to help them put an end to 'the outrages that are being committed against our honest institution'.[228]

It was indeed in order to 'elevate the authority of the Somatén in the public concept to a level it presently lacks' that a General Assemby of the Somatén was held in La Coruña in the summer of 1928. But, just as in the case of the UP, a way to get the Somatén off the ground was found in the concession of honours and prerogatives, which was exactly what the rank and file had been demanding.[229] In effect, the preliminary debates that preceded the meeting of the General Assembly showed that at least part of the blame for the lack of prestige of the Somatén had to be taken by the authorities

[222] Fernando Martín Sánchez-Juliá, *Ideas claras* (Madrid, 1954), p. 793.

[223] AHN, P.G. Leg. 442; Daniel Ansede to Primo, 18 Oct. 1925.

[224] Ibid., complaints from Ronaldo Simón Corchero, Somatén of Torrecilla de los Angeles (Cáceres), 14 Feb. 1924; from José Ropero Fernández, Somatén of Lagrosán (Cáceres), 12 Feb. 1924.

[225] Y. Jelinek, 'Storm-troopers in Slovakia: the Rodobrana and the Hlinka Guard', in *JCH*, vol. 6, no. 3, 1971, p. 104.

[226] Eduardo Ortega, p. 231.

[227] *La Nación*, 21 Aug. 1926.

[228] AHN, P.G. Leg. 442; 'Escrito en demanda de protección a su augustiosa situación por haber llegado a ser objecto de vajaciones, menosprecio y antipatías de sus convecinos', 22 Aug. 1925.

[229] For such demands, see ibid., Leg. 441: 'Propuestas'.

themselves which 'generally display towards us nothing but apathy, indifference, and lack of understanding'.[230]

Some of the Somatén demands were met when a special order allowed members of the militia to hunt in specified areas without the licence required of 'ordinary citizens'. And, 'as it had been done with the UP', a member of the Somatén in each provincial capital would represent his militia in the *junta ciudadana*, a position from which he could cater for the needs of his fellow Somatenistas. To make recruitment easier, it was decided that no financial obligations would be expected any more of the Somatenistas towards meeting their expenses, as these would now be taken care of by the municipal budgets.[231] The members of the militia would henceforth be exempt from searches by the police, a special medal of merit would be granted to those whose zeal in fulfilling their duty was exemplary, the tutelage so far exercised by the local military authorities over Somatén units would be relaxed as their 'natural chiefs', and not only the captain-general, would also be entitled to order their mobilization; and an authorization would be issued to allow Somatenistas to carry small arms.[232] The latter, though aimed at increasing the Somatén's prestige, was apparently also a response to a demand put forward for clear commercial reasons by the armaments industry of Eibar.[233]

But in spite of the frequent allusions of the regime's spokesmen to the Somatén as 'a reality that has taken deep root in the public conscience',[234] there is little evidence to prove that either propaganda or the distribution of privileges brought any notable change in the Somatén's strength and image.

Although foreign observers rushed to draw an analogy between the Somatén and Fascism,[235] there is very little proof to sustain such a conclusion. Yet Primo de Rivera could not always resist the

[230] Ibid.; Luciano Bohigas (member of the organizatory committee of the Somatén of the 8th region) to Primo, 3 Apr. 1928.

[231] Ibid.; 'Commandancia General de Somatenes de la 8ª Región', La Coruña, 5 May 1928.

[232] Ibid.; 'Modificaciones y aclaraciones mas importantes que con relación al reglamento actual le Somatenes se hacen en el confeccionado por la comisión designada a tal fin por la presidencia del Consejo de Ministros'. The tendency to separate the Somatén from the authority of the military command was a striking novelty, cf. Moreno Duarte, pp. 9–10.

[233] AHN, P.G. Leg. 441: 'Instancia que eleva la Cámara Oficial Armera . . . solicitando autorice a los Somatenes el uso ordinario del arma corta', Eibar, 24 July 1928.

[234] *La Nación*, 14 May 1928.

[235] FO/371/9490, Howard to Curzon, 18 Sept. 1923.

temptation of resorting to the same analogy. The Italian Fascist militia, he said early in 1924, was run by 'exactly the same criterion and regulations as those of the Somatén'. Both reflected a common determination 'to erect a dyke against unhealthy ideas'. In Primo's view, the Somatén was his regime's response to the social extremism against which he had pronounced on the 13th of September. He placed great hopes upon the Somatén, 'the big brother of the UP', whose '250,000' members (according to *official* sources) were expected to be the armed fist of his *partido único*. Primo de Rivera always spoke of the UP and the Somatén in one breath, as he clearly had in mind the fascist symbiosis between party and militia.[236]

Such a symbiosis, however, did not materialize. For one thing, Primo de Rivera himself lacked the revolutionary zeal and determination to bring it to full fruition. Furthermore, a dictatorial regime is in itself the answer to the threats that had produced the Fascist militia in Italy. The Dictatorship was an authoritarian regime whose very existence tranquillized those who would otherwise have gone to swell the ranks of fascism. It is indeed highly significant that the Somatén in Catalonia had before the *coup d'état*, that is when people joined it as a spontaneous response to the social threat, about 65,000 members. In 1926, after the Dictatorship had established 'social peace' and wiped out the 'communist danger', the number of affiliates went down to about 63,000,[237] a figure that would probably have been lower had not the government set out actively to enlist people to the Somatén. That the Somatén did not become a fascist militia is explained by the very nature of the Spanish Dictatorship. The revolutionary exaltation of the lower middle classes and the *déclassés* was not something it had come to encourage. Even Mussolini in Italy was, on the morrow of the seizure of power, to set out to tame and domesticate the militia. Primo de Rivera though, rather than use the Somatén, and for that matter the UP also, as the instruments for the seizure of power, established them only after he came to power in order to replace bayonets with 'the people' as his power-base. Primo manipulated an existing institution; he did not create an entirely new one. 'The Somatén belongs neither to the Directory, nor to Primo de Rivera,

[236] Primo in Duarte, pp. 209–14; and in Rubio, pp. 96, 392. For the membership of the Somatén, see FO/371/10593, Rumbold to MacDonald, 14 Aug. 1924. But two years later *La Nación* (21 Aug. 1926) spoke of only 200,000 members. In 1929 Primo himself gave the figure of 120,000, see Rubio, p. 392.

[237] Martínez Segarra, 'Grupos económicos', p. 221.

nor to anybody. It belongs to Spain,' such was the view exposed by a Somatenista propagandist,[238] a view hardly possible in a truly fascist militia fanatically linked with its national *jefe*. A revolutionary militia that springs as a spontaneous movement from below would have been as unacceptable to Primo de Rivera as were Rolao Preto's blueshirts in Portugal to Salazar. *El Sol* was right in observing that the Somatén was an organization of vigilantes that the regime thought had to be strictly watched lest it became a danger to its creator.[239]

238 Moreno Duarte, p. 30.

239 *El Sol*, 21 Sept. 1923.

CHAPTER V

Tenets for a New State

1. *The Prophets of the New Order*

THERE is no denying that anti-liberalism and anti-parliamentarism in Spain lacked the articulate, intellectual legitimacy they had acquired in Italy, for example.[1] Many of the *Upetista* utterances on the subject were frequently superficial slogans deficient in originality. One of the few intellectuals to support Primo de Rivera's regime, Ramiro de Maeztu, observed that precisely this superficiality would prove one of the causes of the Dictatorship's failure to strike deep roots in Spain.[2] José Antonio, the future founder of the Falange, shared Maeztu's frustration. Only the intellectuals, he argued, could have saved his father's enterprise from syncretism and political amorphousness; they could have provided it with 'the bearing of a strong and elegant doctrine'.[3]

Nevertheless, the lack of doctrinal basis of the Dictatorship has been overdone; its attempts to acquire intellectual legitimacy have been entirely ignored, and its unmistakable anticipation of the precepts of the 1930s extreme right in Spain has been completely overlooked.[4] The writers of *Acción Española*, however disappointed they might have been with the failure of the Dictatorship to erect a new system in accordance with their doctrines,[5] were the main doctrinal team of the UP. Figures such as Ramiro de Maeztu, Manuel Bueno, José Pemartín, José María Pemán, Vicente Gay, José de Yanguas, and a score of obscure propagandists came to

[1] *Acción Española*, 1 Feb. 1932, pp. 427–9; José Félix de Lequerica, in E. Vegas Latapié, *El pensamiento político de Calvo Sotelo* (Madrid, 1941), pp. 41–2.

[2] Ramiro de Maeztu, 'La lección de la caída', in *Liquidación de la monarquía parlamentaria* (Madrid, 1957), pp. 145–51; 'Unión Patriótica', in *La Nación*, 3 Nov. 1927.

[3] José Antonio in *Las responsabilidades*, p. 81; and his 'The Intellectuals and the Dictatorship', in Hugh Thomas (ed.), *José Primo de Rivera. Selected Writings* (London, 1972), pp. 35–40.

[4] See, for example, Payne, *Falange*, pp. 6–7. The Dictatorship is not even mentioned in B. Oltra and A. de Miguel, 'Bonapartismo y Catolicismo. Una hipótesis sobre los origenes ideológicos del franquismo', in *Papers*, no. 8, pp. 53–102.

[5] Raul Morodó, 'Una revisión', pp. 92–108.

national prominence as the prophets of a new state and an aggressive right in the service of Primo de Rivera. The 'pseudo-intellectuals' did not support the Dictatorship; but the latter enjoyed whatever intellectual legitimacy could be provided by the 'real intellectuals', the 'Catholics, the patriots, the nationalists'.[6] *Primoderriverismo* anticipated Francoism in inheriting and synthesizing the old traditionalist and reactionary tenets, such as the organic concept of state and society, and the idea of a unitary state loyal to its 'true' essence. Moreover, though it is certainly true that the UP's ideologues were not great luminaries, and they may have possessed an intellectual attitude or 'mentality' (*subjektiver Geist*), rather than an 'ideology' (*objektiver Geist*), they nevertheless formulated and transmitted a doctrinal message in which anti-democratic traditionalism acquired a strong flavour of what they considered to be the *Zeitgeist*. It is during the Dictatorship that the Integrist and Catholic criticism of democracy, the origins of which can be traced back to the conservative reaction to French Enlightenment,[7] started to tune itself with the mainstream of counter-revolutionary European thought. *Primoderriverismo*, in the process of breaking out beyond the philosophy of the barracks, came close to acquiring a political *Weltanschauung*. Its indifferent omission by historians presupposes a doctrinal wealth in Spain's 'authentic' fascism which it never really possessed.

As is usually the case with single parties in authoritarian regimes, the UP did not indoctrinate on a massive, aggressive scale.[8] The UP nevertheless constituted an abrupt breach with the 'civilized' parliamentarian right not only in matters of style, organization, and techniques of mobilization, but certainly also in its programme and ideology. After an initial stage of recruitment and organization within no strict doctrinal premises—on the contrary, an all-embracing vagueness was turned into a principle—the stage had come, thus rationalized Manuel Bueno, the monarchist sympathizer with the new regime, 'to elaborate an ideology just as Gentile did in Italy years after Mussolini had seized power'.[9]

A conspicuous novelty in the UP was that it tended to relegate the monarchy from its paramount status to a subsidiary or even simply representative and ceremonial position.

[6] *Acción Española*, 1 Feb. 1932, pp. 427–8.

[7] Cf. Javier Herrero, *Los origenes del pensamiento reaccionario español* (Madrid, 1973).

[8] Juan Linz, 'Una teoría del régimen autoritario. El caso de España', in Payne, *Política y sociedad*, pp. 228–33.

[9] *La Nación*, 17 Nov. 1925.

In the first years of the Dictatorship, not only did the king exhibit his full support for dictatorial measures but he also willingly posed as some kind of ideologue of the new Spain. When he returned from his state visit to Italy, where he had the opportunity to express his admiration for 'the wise and virile form of government' that was Fascism,[10] he defined the Dictatorship as 'the last card for the salvation of Spain'.[11] No less significant was the king's complete identification with the European 'new order'. The threat to western civilization posed by the Russian Revolution and its successors had convinced him that parliamentary government was no longer adequate for the defence 'of the actual order of things against the Soviet idea'. Italy had shown the road to follow, and 'Spain has, in her turn, reached her own conclusion'.[12]

But as Primo de Rivera's aura of the restorer of social peace and the victor of Alhucemas started to fade, the king became increasingly concerned with the precariousness of his crown if he persisted in his unconstitutional alliance with the Dictatorship. Even more important, the king's alienation from Primo de Rivera was determined by the latter's drive to institutionalize a regime based upon his own personal leadership and charisma and upon a civilian movement independent of the crown. Primo de Rivera now represented a challenge to the archaic practice that had allowed King Alfonso to manipulate *his* prime ministers; and this was more disturbing to the monarch than the actual violation of the constitution. As in the case of the relations between Metaxas and his king in Greece,[13] it was the threat to the personal rule of King Alfonso that lay at the root of his dissociation from Primo de Rivera's Dictatorship. He could no longer bear the loss of his most cherished prerogative, that of vetoing the initiative of the executive which had now, moreover, also absorbed the functions of the legislature. The king resented being pushed into the background while the Dictator occupied, in a most demonstrative way, the centre of the public stage.[14] 'The king is jealous of Primo de Rivera', reported the British ambassador.[15] Alfonso increasingly resented the company of the Dictator in his visits to the provinces, simply because on such occasions it was the

[10] FO/371/9493, R. Grahame (Rome) to Curzon, 23 Nov. 1923.

[11] *The Times*, 30 June 1926.

[12] Charles Petrie, *King Alfonso and his Age* (London, 1963), pp. 194–7. See also *El Sol*, 26 Apr. 1925.

[13] Cliadakis, pp. 113–14.

[14] Cf. Calvo, pp. 116–17; Blasco Ibáñez, pp. 151–2.

[15] FO/371/11936, Rumbold to Austen Chamberlain, 9 Sept. 1926.

general, rather than the sovereign, who attracted most of the attention.[16]

King Alfonso might initially have conceived of himself as a Spanish Vittorio Emmanuele,[17] but he now came to dislike the role. It simply did not suit his dominant personality to be the crowned fetish of 'his Mussolini'. He could nowhere see an organized body of opinion solidly behind the *monarchy*, while Primo de Rivera manipulated all available means to organize *Primoderriverista* opinion. The king became increasingly uneasy about the regime's ceremonies in which he seemed to be a secondary figure. On the fifth anniversary of the *coup d'état*, he simply 'escaped' on a state visit to Sweden in order to spare himself yet another embarrassing demonstration of complicity with the Dictatorship.[18] It was in this context that the king's entourage became busy spreading the rumour about the sovereign being 'a political prisoner' desperately looking for a way out of his cell in order 'to save the constitution'.[19] Primo de Rivera, however, would not let himself, as he boastfully said to a troop of journalists, be 'Bourbonized'.[20] The king was compelled to sign every decree he brought to him even though some of them, such as the decree dissolving the artillery corps and that creating the National Assembly, were strongly opposed by the monarch. If indeed Primo de Rivera had started, as Malatesta put it, as 'a courtier dictator', he did not rule as a 'servile courtesan'.

It was in line with Primo de Rivera's drive to assert his regime's independence of the crown that the UP invited into its ranks, as the Dictator put it in a speech in Valladolid early in 1925, 'all those who are not necessarily monarchists provided they respect the figure of the *Chief of State*'. He would even invite Republicans and anti-Alfonsist Carlists to join the party; even 'leftist elements' were said to be welcome in his 'civic crusade'.[21] The monarchy, as in the programme of Calvo Sotelo in the 1930s and later in Francoism, was, in spite of frequent expressions of monarchist sentiments, relegated to a secondary position. Not a word was dedicated by the Dictator to the monarchy in his article on his regime in the Parisian *L'Illustration*; and such an omission—it would be repeated in the political constitution adopted in June 1928 by the UP[22]—could not be

[16] Ibid., 22 Sept. 1927.
[17] Hurtado, ii, pp. 223–4.
[18] FO/371/13434, Grahame to Austen Chamberlain, 9 Nov. 1928; *El Republicano*, 20 Sept. 1928.
[19] Maura, *Bosquejo*, p. 29; *Folletín*, p. 801.
[20] Romanones Archive, Leg. 2, no. 31.
[21] *El Sol*, 26 Jan. 1925.
[22] *L'Illustration* (Paris), 28 July 1928; *Folletín*, p. 801.

accidental. A Spanish version of the *Führerprinzip* and the principle of 'Spain above all' became the paramount values, according to José María Pemán, the UP provincial Chief of Cádiz, and the author of a book on the UP.[23]

Primo was disappointed at the small amount of ground gained by the UP under the monarchist emblem, and though the term 'Monarchy' was never removed officially from the UP's credo its frequent evasion now reflected a conscious attempt to appeal to a much wider public than that which could be attracted by the programme of the Medina del Campo gathering. When establishing the UP, the Dictator had said that he expected it to absorb all those who were prepared to act 'within the fundamental principles of the 1876 constitution'.[24] Now, however, rather than a monarchist community, the UP came to be conceived as the *partido único* of the new regime,[25] as a 'national movement',[26] and as a *Primoderriverista* league at the service of its leader: 'The Unión Patriótica is something of *mine* which *I* have created . . . it is an integral part of the constructive labour *I* intend to carry out with power.'[27]

The UP anticipated the Falange's ecstatic denunciations of the philosophical conceptions of liberalism and democracy, and was the first right-wing movement in Spain to capitalize substantially on the myth of the Communist threat. This was not invented by General Martínez Anido in a notorious speech in La Coruña in the summer of 1928, as Ricardo La Cierva has implied.[28]

Primo may not have invented the Communist threat, but his regime was the first determined attempt to make it a point of departure for a new state. The Dictatorship had absorbed into its premises the paranoic fear of a 'Masonic Soviet' conspiracy to discredit Spain, and had institutionalized the Manichaean conception of the anti-Spain—a local version of the Action Française's anti-France and the Fascist anti-Nazione[29]—to which Pemán would later give a literary expression in his drama 'The Angel and the Beast'.[30]

[23] Pemán, *El hecho*, p. 115. See also Pemán in *Unión Patriótica*, 11 Nov. 1929.
[24] *Gaceta*, 29 Apr. 1924.
[25] Maura, *Bosquejo*, pp. 105, 274–5.
[26] Primo in *Unión Patriótica*, 15 Nov. 1927, 1 Jan. 1928.
[27] Ibid., 15 June 1928.
[28] Ricardo de la Cierva, *La historia perdida del socialismo español* (Madrid, 1972), p. 100.
[29] Cf. José María Albiñana, *Después de la Dictadura. Los cuervos sobre la tumba* (Madrid, 1930), pp. 68–9; Menéndez Pidal, p. 227.
[30] Pemán, *Poema de la bestia y el ángel* (Madrid, 1939).

In this context, the UP came to be conceived as the 'national constructive block' that would decide the outcome of the confrontation between 'subjective and individual rights', with the 'Soviets' on the one hand and the *patria* on the other hand, in favour of the latter. The Dictator actually anticipated Franco in his self-imposed task of 'sentinel of the west' against the Bolshevik menace, and enthroned his UP as the avant-garde of Christian society in its struggle for survival against Asian, pagan Communism. 'We have set an example to all the peoples of Southern Europe', he said, by erecting 'a wall' against the 'excessive appetite' of 'Anarchism and tyrannical Communism'.[31] Though 'evidently' Primo's seizure of power had averted an 'imminent' Communist take-over, the regime's spokesmen called for constant watchfulness, because 'the Soviet has not abandoned us'. 'The hand of the Soviet', warned *La Nación*, 'is behind the whole campaign of plots, clandestine literature, lies, and invention of rumours.' Spain had all the reasons not only to be 'vigilant', but was also fully justified in organizing its own 'crusade against Bolshevism'.[32]

Ramiro de Maeztu, whose major literary contribution to the cause of the new regime was probably his exhaustive series of articles in *La Nación* against the horrors of Communism, that new version of 'oriental despotism',[33] viewed the Dictatorship as the best, indeed the only, answer to the Soviet threat: 'Against Bolshevism, the Dictatorship! Against subversion, the bayonets! This is the formula of the day. And this is so because of the very nature of Bolshevism, which is nothing but the rebellion of the subhuman against civilization.'[34]

To make the war against Communism more efficient, an order was issued in July 1925 that concentrated in the hands of the *Dirección General de Seguridad* 'all the police services related with Communism'.[35] The ministry of the interior began a thorough investigation of Communist and 'other subversive sectarianisms'

[31] Primo, in *La Nación*, 5 Sept. 1927, and in his *Intervenciones*, p. 133. For Franco, see Luis de Galinsoga, *Centinela de Occidente. Semblanza biográfica de Francisco Franco* (Barcelona, 1956).

[32] *La Nación*, 23 July 1926, 22 Apr. 1927, 2 May 1927 ('Los Soviets en España').

[33] See, for example, 'Culturas y subhombres', 'El engaño querido', 'Los desperados', 'La nueva guerra', 'Defensa del occidente', 'El odio del nómada', 'La moral de Lenin', in *La Nación*, 21, 24 Feb. 1927; 10, 21 Mar. 1927; 7 Apr., 9 May, 16 June 1927.

[34] *La Nación*, 28 Feb. 1927.

[35] AHN, P.G. Leg. 438: Telegrama circular, 25 July 1925.

throughout the world.[36] The credentials of any Russian citizen who might happen to wish to come to Spain were most suspiciously examined.[37] The Spanish authorities were frequently placed on the alert against 'Communist agents', as Spain's ambassadors abroad virtually inundated their superiors with information on the subversive activities of the Comintern.[38]

But bolshevism was, according to *Upetista* logic, a direct outcome of democracy and parliamentarism, the imminent collapse of which tends always to pave the way for the 'extremist passions of groups determined to undermine the foundations of Christian society'. Like the Punic Gods, rationalism and its political consequences (liberalism and individualistic democracy) had devoured their worshippers, by producing the 'Russian tragedy'.[39] The dialectical conclusion, according to Vicente Gay, was to ban for ever universal suffrage. Professor Gay, later to be Franco's press officer and an enthusiastic propagator of the theories of fascism and national socialism, with German subsidies,[40] made his début in the UP press as the exponent of the scientific legitimacy for the liquidation of democracy and parliament. In an exhaustive series of articles heavily loaded with learned quotations he came to prove that it was high time 'to take leave of the illogical and sterile democratic ideal and to move towards new horizons'. Democracy, he argued, had always been in reality based on 'an electoral lie' that inevitably produced an 'aristo-democracy', that is, the exclusive rule of the plutocracy over the whole community. The 'new' and 'true' democracy would have to take notice of the fact that people were mainly concerned with practical policies and achievements. Such 'false Gods' as Rousseau could no longer satisfy the yearning of the masses for the advancement of their material needs. This was, he thought, the main legacy of the Great War; it had shattered the credibility of all past political philosophies. Instead of a system based on parties, Gay now proposed an Italian-type corporative democracy to cope with the new times.[41]

[36] AHN, Gobernación, serie A. Leg. 49, Exp. 11: 'Tercera International, Boletínes y Documentos'. See also ibid., Leg. 17: 'Communismo-Bolshevikismo, 1924–1930'.

[37] See, for example, ibid., Leg. 17, Exp. no. 5, Direcc. Gen. de Seg. to the ministry of the interior, 11 Jan. 1927.

[38] Ibid., 'Bolcheviques'.

[39] Pemartín, 'Ídolos y máscaras', *La Nación*, 26 Feb. 1927.

[40] Hugh Thomas, *The Spanish Civil War* (Penguin, 1977), pp. 335–6.

[41] See a selection of Gay's articles: *La Nación*, 6 June, 25 Aug., 19 Sept., 18, 26 Oct., 1 Nov. 1928, 29 Jan., 13 June, 25 May, 8 Oct. 1929.

It was not only institutional changes that the UP would strive to bring about; its pretensions were of a more total nature. Primo asked it to be the mentor of a new man, the catalyst that would help to moderate the habits and attitudes of the Spaniard, and inspire him with 'the sanest ethical principles and with a new attitude to hygiene'. The natural optimism and joyfulness of the Spaniard must not be touched; but it was essential that much of this national energy be converted into 'an insuperable example of diligence and the methodical life'. The '*Upetista* man', in Primo's vision, was to be imbued also with 'a romantic sentiment of life', with a chivalrous attitude towards women; he should read a lot and even be able to express himself in a poetic style . . .[42]

Admittedly, Primo de Rivera was anything but an articulate political thinker. Yet he contributed his share to the anticipation by his regime of later nationalistic propaganda, and helped to absorb into the premisses of the Spanish right a verbiage and ideological fragments to which his son, José Antonio, the founder of the Falange, was later to give intellectual sophistication. The Dictator claimed to be outraged by the 'counter-romanticism of the new times' and the cult of positivism that had eroded the old cohesion of society.[43] On a practical level, he started by promising to restore parliament after a short 'parenthetical' rule; but he gradually adopted the view that the parliamentary system had 'passed into history'. 'For what should we revive', he asked rhetorically, at a UP grand meeting in Alcalá de Henares, 'that artifice or gimmick called parliament' of which most nations are 'desperately trying to get rid? For What?' Political parties were disappearing everywhere, and he was confident they would never return to life. Especially encouraging was the Italian example. 'Like Mussolini,' he said, 'I also think that the influence of so-called public opinion upon the actions of the government should be limited.'[44] 'Like the Duce', he thought that the principle of freedom, 'so nice in theory', was 'useless as a norm for real life'. It therefore had to be replaced by the principle of authority. The 'True freedom', which he said he expected to establish in Spain, must express the hegemony of 'collective values', while being tyrannical towards the individual.[45]

[42] See the UP's platform in *La Nación*, 22 June 1928; Primo quoted in *Folletín*, p. 639.

[43] *La Nación*, 8 Aug. 1927.

[44] Primo in Revesz, *Frente*, pp. 17–18; and *La Nación*, 26 Apr. 1926, 12 June 1928.

[45] Primo in *L'Étoile belge*, 9 June 1926, and in *Unión Patriótica*, 15 May, 1 July, 15 Aug. 1928.

But it was only opinion as represented in parties and parliament which he despised. That of the festivals, receptions, anniversaries, and parades—in short, that of the 'daily plebiscites'—was the elixir of life of the Dictatorship, 'its principal support'. But the grand occasions had not to be the only means of cultivating the symbiosis between the people and the Dictatorship. Children should also be brought to see in the regime the formula for Spain's salvation. Schools and the Church, the teacher and the priest should combine together to inculcate 'love for the regime'.[46]

It is, of course, true that much of the UP ideology can be found in Spanish traditionalist and Catholic anti-democratic thought. But nostalgic and reactionary tenets such as monarchy, religion, authority, the social structure, hierarchy, the rejection of egalitarianism, and the nation were everywhere the source of inspiration that European fascists—like the UP in Spain—found in the ideological reservoir of the traditional right.[47] In Spain, moreover, the Spanish and the Catholic tradition were 'one and the same', as the UP ideologue José María Pemán observed.[48] Militant Catholicism was as 'legitimate' a term of reference for Spanish fascism as the Roman glories and symbols were for the Italian Fascists. It was not without significance that when Mussolini signed the Lateran agreements with the Holy See, the UP staged demonstrations of sympathy with the Duce, the message of which was that fascism was after all 'not incompatible with Catholicism'.[49] In order to build its political future according to 'its true nature', Spain had to look for inspiration in its Catholic past. Only thus, explained José Pemartín paraphrasing Maurice Barrès, could 'the regenerating virtue of the historical sense' be properly harnessed to the effort of erecting a new future.[50] Pemartín would later argue that even Spain's 'true' Fascist party, the Falange, can, in the last analysis, be reduced to a modern version of what he called 'the technique of Traditionalism'.[51] He might probably have subscribed to the view of the British Fascist who wrote that 'Fascism is militant Christianity.'[52] The 'new Spain',

[46] *La Nación*, 1 Jan. 1929. For education, see pp. 104–6.

[47] For the principles of the traditional right, see Robert Nisbet, 'Preface', in 'A Century of Conservatism', vol. 13, no. 4, Oct. 1978, pp. 629–34. For fascism being inspired by reactionary ideas, see Hugh Seton-Watson, 'Fascism, Right and Left' in *JCH*, vol. 1, no. 1, 1966, p. 185.

[48] *Unión Patriótica*, 15 Dec. 1929.

[49] *Estampa*. 5 Mar. 1929.

[50] Pemartín, 'Las ideas de nuestra política', in *La Nación*, 31 Jan. 1927.

[51] José Pemartín, *¿Qué es lo neuvo?* (Madrid, 1940), pp. 330–1.

[52] Ronald Coates, 'What is Fascism?', in The Italian Documents' Collection, at St Antony's College, job. no. 30, no. 014472.

wrote Ramiro de Maeztu, must be built upon old principles. These should recover, through propaganda and indoctrination, 'their seducing power'.[53]

The Catholic legacy, moreover, was taken up by UP ideologues only as a point of departure. Their propaganda and essays reflect the influence exercised upon them by modern Italian Nationalists and indeed by the living example of Fascism. The *Zeitgeist* was ever present in their attitudes. José Pemartín in fact thought that no political regime is viable that contradicts 'the major ideological currents of the time'.[54]

In line with the European new right, the 'damned wave of utilitarianism', 'positivism', 'materialism' or, in other words, 'the semitic conception of life' were now denounced over and over again by UP essayists. Hence, Ramiro de Maeztu viewed the Dreyfus affair as 'a spiritual civil war'. 'The victory of Fascism in Italy' was, according to Manuel Banzo, the UP provincial chief of Huesca, a great achievement in the struggle against 'destructive nineteenth-century philosophies'. The negation of the legacy of the French Revolution and of the liberal nineteenth century had everywhere been an intellectual point of departure for modern right-wingers and fascists. José Pemartín was among UP propagandists the most prolific and consistent challenger of the 'nineteenth century'. It was a century, he said, of absolute and categorical statements in science, society, and politics; whereas the present century was an age of relativism, applicable to science (Einstein), to political systems, and even to such axiomatic values as freedom. Reality in its changing varieties rather than eternal truths should now be the guiding light for the architects of political regimes. Pemartín paid an admiring tribute to his generation's 'new, young, concrete, and vital thought that strives to grasp reality in the most expedient way possible'.[55]

Pemartín frequently pegged his ideas on to Ortega y Gasset's great authority because his thought, he said, coincided with that of such thinkers as Spengler and Bergson who had broken the yoke of rationalism and dogmatic logic in favour of 'intuition, action, and vitalism'. Pemartín was delighted to see that Ortega's views on

[53] Ramiro de Maeztu, 'Los sectarios', in *La Nación*, 8 Dec. 1927.

[54] *La Nación*, 26 Aug. 1926.

[55] *Unión Patriótica*, 1 Oct., 1 Nov. 1926; 15 Jan., 15 Sept. 1927. The attack on Judaism as a reflection of rationalism, intellectualism, and capitalism was commonplace in Nazism, see U. Tal, *Political Faith of Nazism Prior to the Holocaust* (University of Tel Aviv, 14 June 1978), pp. 20, 25. Ramiro de Maeztu in *La Nación*, 18 Aug. 1927.

individual freedom fully coincided with those of the 'new European' currents of thought. Had not the 'great teacher' written that 'freedom is a value of a very problematic and highly equivocal nature . . . it is nothing but a scheme, a formula, an instrument for life. To subdue the former to the latter . . . is tantamount to idolatry'? An absolute tenet according to Ortega, as Pemartín was happy to discover, was heroism, 'this sublime sportsmanlike gesture in which man imperils his own life', and which possesses 'an unfading vital grace'.[56]

The Dictatorship was retrospectively presented as a rebellion against the greatest sin of the nineteenth century, universal suffrage. This time dwelling on the traditionalist Victor Pradera, Pemartín spoke of universal suffrage as 'an anti-human device, something like a bestial phenomenon; it is anti-intellectual and plutocratic'.[57] Numerical sovereignty was an absurdity because it could easily contradict the 'true' interests of the 'real' Spain, for example if it decided, in the most legal way, to set up a liberal republic or communist system. Real democracy did not necessarily entail 'individual equality', which is by definition indifferent to values such as national tradition and 'collective destiny'.[58]

Clearly, people like Pemán, Pemartín, Vicente Gay, Emilio Vellando, Carlos Wilf, and Ramiro de Maeztu dreamt of bringing the regime as close as possible to a totalitarian model.

Ramiro de Maeztu, who in 1927 was already viewed by Spain's most genuine fascist, Ernesto Giménez Caballero, as 'the most audacious Black Shirt that has so far raised his arm Caesar-like in the public life of Spanish letters',[59] confessed that Fascism 'is the supreme sign of Europeanness, of spiritual height'. An ardent supporter of the Dictatorship, he became Primo's ambassador in Argentina from late 1927, and would indefatigably lend his pen to the defence of his regime. Retrospectively, Maeztu castigated the UP for having failed to provide the backbone for a permanent new regime. He accused it of not being 'a real *fascio*'. Primo's, he wrote,

[56] Pemartín, 'Mas alla del racionalismo', 'La libertad colectiva', in *La Nación*, 14 June, 15 Oct. 1927. See also 26 Aug. 1926. Cf. Ortega y Gasset, *El tema de nuestro tiempo* (Madrid, 1923), pp. 139, 195.

[57] Pemartín's articles in *La Nación*, 18 Nov. 1926, 28 Jan. 1927.

[58] Pemartín, 'Los antiguos partidos políticos y el socialismo'; 'Del sufragio corporativo y de clases', *La Nación*, 11 Mar. 1927, 11, 15, 17 Feb. 1927. See also his articles in *La Nación*, 27 Oct., 10 Dec. 1926, 28, 31 Jan., 9 Apr., 23 July 1927.

[59] Miguel Ángel Hernando, *La Gaceta Literaria (1927–32), biografía y valoración* (University of Valladolid, 1974), pp. 21–2.

was 'a fascism without a *fascio*'.[60] An intellectual of the right, who represented himself as an anti-intellectual in so far as 'the hostility of our intellectual classes towards heroism prevails' and who dreamt of becoming the 'grand inquisitor' who would 'burn all the writers of the left', Ramiro de Maeztu expected the UP to be a fighting militia. He wanted it to impose, 'if necessary by bloodshed', a 'national' and 'total culture' that would be imbued with a spirit of 'compulsion and discipline' and strive to advance a total answer to all the expressions of national and existential life. A 'real fascism' was what he had in mind, the erection of a totally new world on the ashes of the one that had been shattered by the Great War.[61]

At the time, however, he said he was fascinated by the UP's 'patriotic orientation, its spirit of order and traditionalism', and he proclaimed his readiness 'to shed [his] blood together with the Somatén and the UP in the fight against communism'. He especially welcomed the UP's radical break with the old right as far as the issue of the unity of Spain was concerned. The UP, he wrote, had rightly understood that the worn-out means of traditional politics could no longer cope with separatism that threatened 'to break Spain vertically' and with communism that wanted to do so 'horizontally'. He supported the idea of not excluding non-monarchists from the UP. National unity, this was the paramount value. 'Unity or death!' he wrote. He viewed the UP as the potential catalyst of a modern *reconquista* aimed at reclaiming for Spain both the totality of its people and of its territory.[62] The Nation is the most elevated of 'natural societies', by no means a dissoluble, voluntary association. In this irrational, mystical Nation, man had ceased to be a separate being, he had become an inextricable, organic part of the natural, eternal communion of Spaniards.[63]

Force was, of course, the best instrument for imperial aggrandizement and expansion. Ramiro de Maeztu was euphoric at the performance of the Spanish army in carrying out its 'civilizing' mission among the Moors of North Africa, in proving that 'the smallest

[60] Ramiro de Maeztu, *El nuevo tradicionalismo y la revolución social* (Madrid, 1959), pp. 212–13.

[61] 'Los intelectuales', in *La Nación*, 28 Apr. 1927; 'El partido de la cultura', 'El fascismo real', 'Crisis de ideas', in *El Sol*, 22 Apr., 14 May, 16 Sept. 1924.

[62] See his articles in *El Sol*, 22 Apr. 1924, and *La Nación*, 7 July, 3, 7, 10, 14 Nov. 1927. See also his *Con el Directorio*, pp. 305–9.

[63] Ramiro de Maeztu's articles in *La Nación*, 14, 16 Feb., 28 Apr., 18 Aug., 5 Dec. 1927. See also *Con el Directorio*, pp. 272–6, 289, 293.

button on the uniform of a Spanish soldier represents the whole of Europe, Christianity, and civilization', whereas the cause of Abd-el-Krim was that of 'the desert, slavery, polygamy, and Islam'. The Spanish victory in Morocco had vindicated, he said, his condemnation of 'the soft abandonism of our intellectual circles', and their 'humanistic myth'. The war had proved that a nation cannot rely on its intellectuals and artists to secure for it a proper place in the world; for that it needs the imposing quality of 'the category of action'.[64]

Dwelling heavily on traditional values and attentive to the voices of the prophets of the European new order, it was only to be expected that *Upetista* philosophy should sound like an echo of the French and Italian progenitors of fascism.[65] The challenge to the ethos of universality, to the cult of rationalism, the onslaught against the forces of evil unleashed by the French Revolution, and the demand to return to a romantic, somewhat mythical past—all this was of course not unique, nor original, to the leading group of UP propagandists. Their insistence on the structure of society and the Nation as sacred values that are the product of history, even nature, and therefore unaffected by human choice, and their condemnation of free political action as the inherent cause of national dismemberment are elements that can easily be found in the premisses of the European radical right. Reason and choice should be replaced by the religious spirit of obedience. Faith should precede understanding, that was how Nazi political theology would put it.[66] That the permanent, spiritual destiny of the nation embodied in the figure of a royal, Catholic dictator should be the exclusive guiding star of the modern state was a key aspiration for Maurras just as it was an obsessive dream for Ramiro de Maeztu in Spain. The latter, however, laid special emphasis on the military, even militaristic, character of his longed-for royal dictatorship.

[64] *Con el Directorio*, pp. 141–6, 272–6; 'La contrarrevolución', in *La Nación*, 4 Apr. 1927; 'La immensa disolución', 'Acción de gracias', 'Crítica y credo', in *La Nación*, 24 Mar., 9, 18 Aug. 1927.

[65] Cf. Zeev Sternhell, *La Droite révolutionnaire 1885–1914. Les Origines françaises du fascisme* (Paris, 1978); J. S. McClelland (ed.), *The French Right from de Maistre to Maurras* (New York, 1971); Richard Griffiths, 'Anticapitalism and the French Extra-Parliamentary Right, 1870–1940', in *JCH*, vol. 13, no. 4, Oct. 1978, pp. 720–74; Adrian Lyttleton (ed.), *Italian Fascisms: From Pareto to Gentile* (New York, 1975).

[66] U. Tal, *Structures of German 'Political Theology' in the Nazi Era* (Tel Aviv, 1979), p. 21.

Counter-revolution must not fight Moscow alone. It should also fight the enemy from within, liberals, socialists, and libertarians.[67] Political rivals were thus turned into 'enemies' and internal politics into a potential battleground. Such a sharp departure from traditional right-wing politics had characterized fascism everywhere. *Upetistas* had now advanced the intellectual legitimacy for the destruction of any future Spanish democracy by force just as they had justified the wiping-out of the 1923 parliamentary system for the 'anti-national' process it had unleashed. Sedition against democracy—which was after all the outcome of nothing but the absurd whims of the multitude—was, then, a sacred duty rather than punishable rebellion.

In Spain, an overwhelmingly agrarian country, an important stem of fascism was to take root, as Déat and Doriot hoped it would do in France, among small and medium-sized landowners, the same class that formed the original Castilian backbone of the UP. As in the case of the Farmers' League at the turn of the century in Germany, the middle- and lower-middle-class agrarians that flocked to give *Primoderriverismo* its popular basis represented the transformation of a traditional conservative spirit into a pre-fascist drive.[68] This was both anti-capitalist and anti-socialist; it militantly advocated an integrationist, organic, and socially harmonious society—a euphemism for the suppression by force if necessary of the class struggle—in which 'reality' would prevail over 'thought'. Ruralism, the yearning for a lost natural agrarian heaven on earth, was a frequent topic of *Upetista* propaganda, a topic also shared in varying degrees of sincerity by European fascists.[69]

In Spain, the small Castilian peasants of the *Secretariado Nacional Agrario* helped to provide the Dictatorship with a ruralist ideology, as well as with the necessary encouragement for the struggle against 'socialist propaganda' in the countryside. Their spokesmen committed the small Castilian peasantry to support the grand endeavour of creating 'a Great, Strong, Resurrected and Immortal Spain', as the Dictator's brother, who was also the SNA's president, expressed it. In close collaboration with *Acción Católica* and the Church-sponsored peasants' union, the *Confederación Nacional*

[67] Ramiro de Maeztu, *Con el Directorio*, pp. 163–7.

[68] Cf. Hans-Jurgen Puhle, 'Conservatism in Modern German History', in *JCH*, vol. 13, no. 4, Oct. 1978; Castillo, *Propietarios*.

[69] Cf. Barrington Moore, *Social Origins*, pp. 449–52; Renzo de Felice, pp. 68–9; E. Weber, 'Romania' in Weber and Rogger (eds.), p. 569.

Católico-Agraria, and strongly encouraged by the regime's mouthpiece,[70] the SNA campaigned on a large scale in support of the implementation of a corporatist structure in Spain, and on behalf of 'agrarian virtues'.[71] The organization's secretary, Rafael de Roda, saw in the Dictatorship the martial, rural virtues that had produced elsewhere heroic regenerating movements: 'It is from the fields that the stoutest soldiers had always emerged. In critical hours, the Cincinnati had always left behind the plough, the Washingtons the plantations of Virginia, the Bismarks Windhorst, and the Von Moltkes the plains of Hanover and Brandenburg . . .'. Capitalism and urbanism, explained Rafael de Roda, were the generators of 'the greatest of all enemies', namely socialism. Parliament and universal suffrage were also a rotten product of urbanism and modernization, argued the UP official Francisco Fernández at an SNA meeting. Therefore, he maintained, the SNA's demand for an organic, corporate state should be supported as a 'barrier against the omnipotence of parliament', and as a vital instrument in the struggle against 'Rousseauist individualism'.[72]

Primo de Rivera and UP speakers responded generously to the 'ruralist' campaign by adopting the defence of agricultural interests and strongly upholding the mythical virtues of rural anti-liberalism and nationalism. 'Non-industrialized Spain', the Dictator declared nostalgically, 'is the true Spain, that which has in the past acquired an immortal imperial glory.' In his *Disertación Ciudadana* delivered in Toledo in the summer of 1929,[73] the Dictator reiterated his view that ruralism was not just a matter of economic and social policy, it was also an attempt to respond to 'centuries-old atavism', the reflection of a continuous quest for an idyllic Arcadia. José Pemartín praised the Dictator's approach as a bid to 'replant strongly and solidly Spanish individualism in its atavistic social earth, in its natal soil, in its modernized and fertile fields'.[74]

'Virile', sometimes vulgarly *machista*, the Spanish Dictatorship none the less paid lip-service to the virtues of womanhood. A special role was reserved for the Spanish woman in *Upetista*

[70] See, for example, 'El Secretariado Nacional Agrario, los problemas del campo y la eficacia de las organizaciones apolíticas', *La Nación*, 2 Oct. 1929.

[71] *España Agraria*, 1927–9, *passim*.

[72] Ibid., Feb. 1929.

[73] Primo de Rivera, *Disertación Ciudadana* (Conferencia pronunciada en el Alcazar de Toledo, Marzo 1929).

[74] For Primo's 'ruralism', see also Duarte, pp. 54–64; *La Nación*, 15, 23 Aug. 1929. See also *España Agraria*, 1929, *passim*.

propaganda. Primo de Rivera's frequent allusions to the virtues of the beautiful sex were generally dismissed as cheap flattery, which in a sense they were. Yet they also reflected, as was the case with the *madonna* myth in Fascism, an *Upetista* overall vision of a stable, anti-feminist society in which women would be 'the soul of the home and of the family, the religious mentors of their sons', as the propagandist Jose María María put it in a commemoration of the *Dos de Mayo*. The official articles of faith of the UP published in June 1928 promised that the constitution of the new Spanish state would 'surround woman with the greatest respect'. No doubt, it was Primo de Rivera's awareness of the Catholic, conservative attitudes of Spanish women, rather than his democratic spirit, which caused him to preach the integration of women into the politics of his regime either as members of the National Assembly, as patronesses of Somatén units, or as city councillors. In a typical remark, Primo de Rivera explained that the Municipal Statute's provision to allocate seats for women in Ayuntamientos was made with the purpose of 'preventing the men in the councils from conceiving insane ideas'.[75]

2. *Eulogy to an 'Era'*

There is no denying that Primo de Rivera was no Mussolini, and his regime no Fascism. The evident traits of *bonhomie*, the adornment of simplicity, modesty, and Spanish directness that characterized the Dictatorship, as well as its air of cordiality and accessibility stood in apparent contrast with the imposing *mise-en-scène* practices employed by the Duce. It is, moreover, self-evident that the regimes differed in a substantial way as to the comprehensiveness of the ideology to which they responded and also as to the role of the UP and the Somatén on the one hand, and the party and militia in Fascism on the other. Primo de Rivera erected a *partido único*, which he was right to point out was not 'an armed force like Fascism',[76] and an anaemic militia from a position of power to provide his rule with public support and the trappings of Fascism. The Duce, on the other hand, seized power with the assistance of the imposing popular energy of a well-structured Fascist movement and militia, which he, however, consistently tried to tame and domesticate

[75] Alberto Valero Martín, 'Las mujeres y el régimen', in *La Nación*, 26 Dec. 1929; *Unión Patriótica*, 15 May 1928; *El Republicano*, 20 July 1928; *Folletín*, pp. 196–7.
[76] *La Nación*, 9 Aug. 1928.

in the years that followed the March on Rome. The Fascist Party was far less easily managed by the Duce than was the UP by the Spanish Dictator. The revolutionary purists of the kind of Farinacci in Fascism and the local power of the party's *ras* was something Primo de Rivera did not have to bother with.

None the less, there was among *Primoderriveristas* an unmistakable admiration for Fascism and a proclivity to draw analogies between their regime and the Duce's. Both, they liked to claim, were the result of a rebellion of 'the conservative spirit' against Russian Bolshevism.[77] When the Italian deputy Carlos Barduzzi lectured in the Madrid Academy of Jurisprudence on the need to strengthen the links between the Latin nations, the Dictator's mouthpiece, *La Nación*, took the opportunity to emphasize that it was not just tradition, similarity of language, and religion that united Italy and Spain. Their respective regimes, it claimed 'are similar phenomena within the framework of comparative political biology; they belong to the same genus, a change of system, albeit by different ways: the middle class in Italy and the army in Spain. In both cases, it has been demonstrated that the energies and the resources of the Great Race were emphatically latent'.[78]

That the subject of the revolution (the middle class in Italy and the army in Spain) was different was less crucial than the fact that in both cases the goal was similar: to depart from the old concept of the State for that of the new one. Both regimes moreover, were building their respective systems upon the solid foundations of national tradition, that is upon an anti-individualistic legacy. Both regimes also made use of the advantages of the scientific and social progress brought about by individualism.[79] In other words, they both harnessed modernization to the cause of the united, organic nation and its traditional values.

Certainly, Mussolini was not a conservative but a revolutionary, Primo de Rivera himself reckoned, but, he added, the Duce's revolutionary spirit was 'nationalistic', that is 'respectful to tradition and dwelling upon it'. In that sense, argued the Spanish Dictator, 'we also are revolutionaries'. 'To Italy', he said, 'we are linked by race affinities as well as by a similar political system.'[80] Consequently, Primo de Rivera banned any attacks on Fascism in the Spanish press. And, in another context, he would not hesitate to impose a

[77] Ibid., 10 Apr. 1926.
[78] Ibid., 30 Apr. 1926.
[79] Ibid., 10 May 1926, 2 Mar. 1928.
[80] *L'Étoile belge*, 9 June 1926.

heavy fine on a Spanish firm, Masport, for refusing to do business with Italy on political grounds.[81] When, in early 1927, Primo de Rivera came out, through the pages of *La Nación*, in defence of press censorship, he took the opportunity to explain the nature of his regime's relations with Italy. He banned any attack on Italy in the Spanish press, he said, because otherwise

> Italy with its Fascist regime, notwithstanding the fact that it has a large number of sympathizers in Spain, would be bitterly attacked by its opponents, so that the most cordial relations that presently exist between the two countries and their governments would certainly be undermined . . . Many times the manœuvre of criticizing the Italian regime has been intended in order, in fact, to combat and injure our own . . .[82]

Primo de Rivera underlined this parallel in a conversation with the Duce's ambassador in Madrid. 'The prosperity and progress of the Fascist regime are vital for the survival of our own.'[83]

However, Primo de Rivera, who professed to admire Mussolini's 'tenacity, his faith', and 'his formidable work',[84] resorted to the analogy with Fascism more as a religion of rote, or for rhetorical purposes. More eager to give substance to this simile were people in his entourage, such as his energetic Minister of Labour, Eduardo Aunós, and the UP's ideologues Ramiro de Maeztu and José Pemartín. A meeting with Mussolini in the spring of 1926 turned Aunós into an ardent admirer of Fascism. The constitutional system, he explained upon his return to Spain, had finished its historical role. The example of Fascism had shown the necessity to strengthen the State with the assistance of corporative organs and a 'selected parliament'. As a conclusion of his study-tour in Italy, Aunós harboured no doubts as to the enviable success of Fascism: 'It has all the meaning of an essay that has fully succeeded, an essay we should all salute as a promise full of agreeable hopes. We should study it with great interest and fondness, because it is by the experience of Fascism that the future political evolution of the European nations should be inspired.'[85]

For Pemartín Fascism had already begun to leave its impact upon the Mediterranean nations. The latter had now all the aspects of

[81] FO/371/14165, Grahame to Henderson, 1 Oct. 1929; *The Times*, 4 Sept. 1928.
[82] *Folletín*, p. 626.
[83] Viola to Mussolini, 13 Nov. 1926, in *Documenti Diplomatici Italiani*, Seventh Series, 1922–35, vol. iv, no. 486.
[84] Primo's interview with Clara Candiani.
[85] *La Nación*, 8 May 1926.

vital 'panthers', resurgent nations, while the Nordic peoples were in evident decline. One could hardly fail to see how:

> Young Fascism is reviving the nostalgia for imperial Rome; the new *Valerysante* France is returning to Racine; and Spain is starting again, through its neo-classicism and Hispano-Americanism, its universalistic, and paradoxically also particularistic, enterprise . . . On the other hand, the pachydermic peoples of the north can only contemplate, once again, with their vitreous and lymphatic eyes the triumph of the Panther, the revival of art, science, action, politics, and life of the eternal Mediterranean civilization.[86]

Pemartín would not define himself as a fascist, but he confessed that 'the doctrines of fascism are on *this* side of the demarcation line'. Not only were there pragmatic considerations, he said, that 'make me well disposed towards fascism' (such as the defence against Bolshevism, and the Masonry), but also solid doctrinal tenets. Such a one was the rejection of popular sovereignty, and the belief in 'something which is external and superior to the will of the nation', and which provides it with organic continuity and cohesion.[87] Ramiro de Maeztu put it in blunter terms: 'The doctrine of Mussolini is the good one. Let no one diminish even one shred of the shadow that the Italian flag casts upon the world!'[88]

There was, however, a sense of unease tinged with a grain of envy in *Upetista* circles with regard to the analogy with Fascism. While hailing 'the virile affirmation of the principle of authority' common to both regimes, *La Nación* nevertheless acknowledged that they also differed 'in very important aspects', not least in the fact that the enthusiasm and exaltation that characterized the Fascist movement 'had not been manifested in Spain'. To make the analogy with Fascism more valid, a complete change of policy towards the press was, of course, needed. Opposition newspapers such as those published in Spain were inconceivable in Fascist Italy. It is, of course, doubtful whether the Spanish admirers of the Italian example really wanted to follow it in all its details. Even for Pemartín, the 'disciplined, active exaltation' of Fascism was excessive, the lack of any control over the actions of the government, 'so necessary in every state', too absolute, and Fascism's affronts to the Church hierarchy 'absolutely reprehensible'.[89] Unlike Carlism, the UP was not entirely

[86] Ibid., 11 May 1928. [87] Ibid., 6 Dec. 1928.

[88] Ramiro de Maeztu, 'Unidad y libertad', in *La Nación*, 20 June 1927.

[89] 'El discurso de Mussolini, el relieve del fascismo y la eficacia de los gobiernos fuertes', 'Ni fascio ni anti-fascio'; and Pemartín, 'Dime con quién andas', in *La Nación*, 7 June, 11 Oct., 6 Dec. 1928.

opposed to Fascism's display of social radicalism; nor did it harbour any reservations about the centralistic policies of the Fascist state, which the Carlists found to be entirely incompatible with their decentralistic philosophy. Yet *Upetista* and Carlist criticism of Fascism coincided in two essential points. Fascism's worship of the secular state and its dynamic and seemingly uncontrollable *élan* were repellent to both movements.[90]

More resolute and wholehearted was the defence of Dictatorship as such, and Spain certainly did not need Mussolini to discover for her the wonders of authoritarian rule. But the contemporary 'universal' tendency towards Dictatorship could not be, and was by no means, disregarded. On the contrary, it was a constant source of inspiration to the regime's supporters.

For one thing, as Jacinto Capella, a staunch panegyrist of the regime, wrote in a review of a book on Mussolini, 'the word Dictatorship that was in the past a cause for alarm to our parents, has now received naturalization papers in Europe'. The Spanish 'new democracy', its panegyrists were happy to point out, was not only adjusted to 'our psychology, our temperament, and our racial spirit', as Emilio Vellando put it, but also to 'the universal moment', that is, to the European dictatorial tide. The Mediterranean authoritarian regimes of Italy, Spain, and Greece, as well as those of Bulgaria and Hungary, were, in Aunós's view, a patent demonstration that 'the old system is no longer suitable for the new life'.[91] The Dictatorship's propagandists were eager to praise any such move towards authoritarianism throughout the continent. They acclaimed with jubilation the breakdown of the Portuguese Republic and the 1926 military take-over. It underlined the historical inevitability of the dictatorial tide; it was 'a natural fact' that 'is compatible with our ideology'.[92] Significantly, anti-Bolshevism soon became common ground upon which both dictatorships could build a bridge of friendship. Indeed, one of the first agreements reached between the two dictatorships was one that bound their respective police forces to co-operate in fighting the Communist threat.[93] The Spanish authorities also

[90] For the UP, see ibid., 20 Apr., 25 June, 27 Sept. 1926. Cf. Blinkhorn, *Carlism and Crisis in Spain 1931–39* (Cambridge, 1975), pp. 168–82.

[91] See *La Nación*, 26 Nov., 1 Dec. 1926, 16 Nov. 1927.

[92] Ibid., 1, 2 June 1926.

[93] *The Times*, 30 May 1927. For the application of the agreement, see AHN, P.G., Leg. 346: Spain's ambassador in Lisbon to Primo, 28 July 1927; AHN, Gobernación, serie A, Leg. 17: 'Bolcheviques'.

committed themselves to curbing the activities of Portuguese political refugees in Spain.[94] The Pangalos Dictatorship in Greece was hailed as yet another proof of 'the failure of parliamentarism', and advice for Pangalos was immediately put forward. When in 1929 King Alexander of Yugoslavia established his royal dictatorship, *La Nación* wished him 'the best of luck', because he had, after all, 'overthrown nothing but a fiction'. The Yugoslav dictatorship, claimed one of the clearest fascist minds in Primo de Rivera's camp, Vicente Gay, was yet another hopeful sign of the advance of Dictatorship and the retrogression of parliamentarism.[95]

3. *One Country*

No real headway was made by the regime in its wavering attempts to revive local and provincial life; its Municipal and Provincial Statutes remained virtually a dead letter. This was so because it was after all the unitary, centrifugal drive that proved to be the most powerful principle of the new establishment. Regionalism, to which there was always a danger decentralization might drift, was anathema. It was seen as the enemy of national unity, the obstacle to the creation of a national economy, a threat to Spain's international status, as well as to the aspiration of developing a 'truly Spanish culture', and reviving the Hispano-American commonwealth. How would regionalism coexist with the need 'to revive this imperial Spanish conscience, this glory of being a Spaniard which is the very negation of all movement of dissociation'?[96]

The unity of Spain, a country where separatist and autonomist feelings have always been strong, is rightly considered to be a major tenet of Spanish fascism. The dynastic parliamentarian right had never been happy with regionalism, yet its most notable figures, statesmen such as Silvela, Maura, and Romanones, had always striven to accommodate Catalan autonomist aspirations. *Upetista* propaganda, on the other hand, constituted an abrupt breach with that tradition of 'accommodation' with regionalism. 'Regionalist feelings are incompatible with a Great Fatherland', claimed the Dictator before a UP mass meeting where he also coined the slogan

[94] Ibid., Leg. 48: A circular of the minister of the interior to the civil governors.

[95] See the articles of Emilio Vellando, Albiñana, Vicente Gay, in *La Nación*, 28 Sept. 1928, 1 Mar., 2 Apr., 22 July, 9 Jan. 1929. See also articles, ibid., 12, 16 Apr., 8 May 1926; 8, 10 Jan. 1929.

[96] Pemán's articles in *La Nación*, 13, 23 Oct. 1928.

'Spain One, Great, and Indivisible'.[97] This, and the principle of 'better to have a red Spain than a broken one', which the Dictator espoused ('We can compound with Republicans, even with Anarchists, but never with those who consistently attempt to destroy the unity of the *patria*')[98] were to be bequeathed to and absorbed by Calvo Sotelo's *Bloque Nacional*, and, almost intact, by the Falange. 'Region? Province? the Nation above all!', Such was *La Nación*'s comment on Primo's Olimpia speech. The nation, an indivisible spiritual unity, should under no circumstances be a negotiable concept.[99]

That the political bait of automomy for Catalonia did not materialize was not for lack of a previous commitment to the Lliga. It simply proved to be inconsistent with the whole notion of 'one' country which was inherent in the basic philosophy of many Spanish generals, as well as of the new and aggressive right now in the making.[100] Primo's fellow conspirators in the Barcelona garrison, who had for years been harbouring strong anti-Catalanist feelings, must apparently also share the credit, or blame, for the Dictator's anti-Catalanist shift.[101] One should not forget, for example, that Martínez Anido, who had had a frontal clash with the Catalan autonomists during his term as civil governor of Barcelona,[102] was now in charge of internal affairs.

But most important of all, Primo de Rivera was carried on to a collision course with the Catalans also by the inner dynamics of his dictatorial regime. No dictatorship worthy of its name can afford the application of such concepts as 'decentralization' and 'autonomy'. These are incompatible with the very essence of its spirit, as they entail a diminution of dictatorial power.[103] Significantly, in Yugoslavia also the Croats hoped that King Alexander would grant them autonomy once he had got rid of parliamentary politics. But when he finally established his dictatorship in 1929, they had to share the same disillusions as their Catalan counterparts, and realize that, regardless of previous commitments, dictatorships are simply

[97] *El Sol*, 21 Mar. 1925; *Unión Patriótica*, 15 Sept. 1927.

[98] Primo's speech at the Olimpia, *La Nación*, 1 Feb. 1926.

[99] *La Nación*, 22 Feb. 1926.

[100] The Catalans blamed the king for the U-turn over Catalonia, see Ventosa y Calvell to Alba, 27 May 1930, in Santiago Alba Archive.

[101] Maura, *Bosquejo*, pp. 58, 121; García Venero, *Historia del Nacionalismo catalán*, p. 311.

[102] See p. 39.

[103] Cf. with the case of the Soviet Union, Gerschenkron, 'The Changeability of a Dictatorship', in *Continuity*, pp. 289, 290.

the wrong partners to negotiate autonomy with. A Serbian king, let alone a royal dictator, could not but strengthen the unity of Yugoslavia.[104] 'Sectionalism' and 'decentralization' were likewise anathema to such disparate dictatorships as Trujillo's in Santo Domingo and the Jacobins, for whom the 'République une et indivisible' was an ultimate value.[105] One need not, of course, embark on remote examples, as the Spanish case itself is self-evident; only democratic regimes such as that of the Restoration or the post-Franco system had ever given, or contemplated giving, an autonomous deal to Catalonia.[106]

As soon as he was firmly in the saddle, Primo de Rivera set out to decree measures and sanctions against separatism. No flag except that of Spain was to be flown under any circumstances; no language other than Castilian was to be used on any official occasion; all offences 'against the security and unity' of the Fatherland, and all attempts to 'disjoin or weaken it', were to be referred to military tribunals. Catalans would very soon find their cultural clubs closed down, their autonomist leaders arrested, and their professional corporations such as the Barcelona Bar Association severely scrutinized.[107] Municipalities were instructed to add street nameplates in Spanish to those already written in Catalan, shopkeepers were forbidden to advertise their goods in Catalan, and a public performance of *Els segadors*, a national song, was banned.[108] In December 1923, an additional decree forbade schools to teach any subject not included in the syllabus approved by the ministry of education.[109] This prohibition was tantamount to wiping out the Catalan historical and cultural legacy from the schools. Later on, in January 1928, an order was to be issued that made it obligatory for the Catalan press to publish government communiqués in Spanish rather than have them translated into Catalan.[110] 'New forms of resistance will be met by yet new punishments', such was the warning language of a decree of 18 March 1926.[111]

It was no surprise that Catalan institutions should have dissociated

[104] Sforza, pp. 131–2.

[105] Wiarda, *Dictatorship*, p. 112; J. Talmon, *The Rise of Totalitarian Democracy* (Boston, 1952), p. 110.

[106] S. Ben-Ami, 'The Catalan and Basque Movements for Autonomy', in Y. Dinstein (ed.), *Models of Autonomy* (New Bruswick, 1982), pp. 67–84.

[107] *Gaceta*, 19 Sept. 1923; Rossinyol, pp. 560–2.

[108] FO/371/9490, Howard to Curzon, 21 Sept. 1923.

[109] *El Sol*, 21 Dec. 1923.

[110] *The Times*, 16 Jan. 1928.

[111] *Gaceta*, 18 Mar. 1926.

themselves from the Dictatorship. A case in point was that of the Barcelona Bar Association which had started by applauding the *coup d'état*[112] but soon came to a frontal clash with the new regime. And when the board of the Association resisted an order to have the Judicial Guide of Catalonia published in Spanish, the government did not hesitate to put it behind bars, and to replace the rebellious board with a zealously *españolista* one.[113] The government was clearly ready to risk arousing Catalan hatred in order to implement its 'Spanish' policy.

Significantly, it was on the morrow of his return from his state visit to Italy and as part of his recently acquired determination to abandon the provisional character of his rule that Primo de Rivera began his campaign to do away with the Catalan Mancomunitat.[114] On 12 January 1924, a royal decree appeared which dissolved all the democratically elected Diputaciones Provinciales in Spain, with the notable exception of those in the Basque provinces.[115] A fortnight later, Puig i Cadalfach, the president of the Mancomunitat and an ardent supporter of the *coup d'état* in its initial stages, was sacked unceremoniously and replaced by Alfonso Sala, the *españolista* leader of the Unión Monárquica Nacional, a party closely linked with the Catalan UP. This appointment corresponded with Primo's endeavour to base his Catalan policy on quisling figures, people of 'social eminence and prestige' who had not been 'contaminated' by separatism, such as Sala, Roig i Bergadá, Rusiñol, Conde de Güell, and Milá i Camps.[116]

But not even Sala's untarnished *españolismo* would convince the Dictator to tame his centralizing spirit. Sala genuinely believed that his cordial relations with the new regime would enable him, as the new president of the Mancomunitat, 'to preserve and even advance all the genuinely Catalan institutions which do not infringe upon the sovereignty of the state or the unity of the Spanish nation'.[117] Primo seemed to put real trust in the 'good Catalans' like Sala whom he believed would be careful not to break the delicate equilibrium between the state and the region. On the other hand, what if one day,

[112] See p. 83.

[113] For the Bar Association affair, see Arturo Perucho, *Catalunya sota la Dictadura* (Barcelona, 1930), pp. 158–66; *Gaceta*, 6 Mar. 1926; Romanones Archive, Leg. 28, no. 47: 'Detención de la junta del Colegio de Abogados de Barcelona'.

[114] Maura, *Bosquejo*, p. 56. See also Puig i Cadalfach's article in *La Veu de Catalunya*, 4 Mar. 1930.

[115] *El Imparcial*, 13 Jan. 1924.

[116] See Primo's letter to Sala in Pabón, *Cambó*, vol. ii, pt. I, p. 472; *Gaceta*, 12 Jan. 1924.

[117] Sala in *El Sol*, 31 Jan. 1924.

when he, Primo, was no longer in office, the 'bad Catalans' were to take over the Mancomunitat and shatter this fragile equilibrium? Could he really afford to bequeath to future generations an institution that might one day become the breeding-ground of separatism?

The Dictator's wavering ended with the promulgation, on 12 March 1925, of the Provincial Statute which, as Sala rightly understood, amounted to a virtual dissolution of the Mancomunitat. Nor did Primo de Rivera leave any doubts as to the impact he intended the Statute should have on Catalan aspirations, or as to the nature of his up-to-date, and now definitive, policy over regionalism. This he was kind enough to explain in a long and, as usual, frank official note:

> Upon publishing the royal decree that inaugurates the new provincial system, I feel I have an obligation to explain to public opinion, especially to that of Catalonia, my strong support for this law which may seem to you to contradict certain tendencies which I have encouraged until very recently . . . I have totally rectified my judgements within a year and a half. I once thought that historical regionalism, while being instrumental in developing a decentralizing, efficient and economical administrative system, might also be conducive to the strengthening of the bonds of national unity in Spain. That was why I defended it sincerely. But . . . and that is the main reason for my complete change of opinion, I understood that to reconstruct the region, to strengthen its personality, to exalt its differential pride would be tantamount to destroying the great work of national unity and to initiating a highly disruptive process, such as can always be stimulated by human pride and egoism.[118]

The Mancomunitat, he later explained, had become a catalyst of 'real nationalism that threatened to undermine the very roots and foundations of Spanish nationalism'.[119] Primo's change of attitude towards the Catalan issue would be seen by his previous supporters in Catalonia as sheer treachery. For his staunch panegyrists, it was a manifestation of the kind of statesmanship that only Primo and the Italian Duce seemed to possess.[120]

The new Diputaciones Provinciales designated by the government were, not surprisingly, manned by *españolista* figures. All the functionaries of the Mancomunitat who wanted to keep their jobs in the Diputaciones would have to take an oath of *españolismo*.[121]

[118] *El Sol*, 21 Mar. 1925. For the shift in Primo's Catalan policy, see Calvo, pp. 66–7. Reversz, *Frente*, pp. 25–6.

[119] Primo, *Intervenciones*, pp. 39, 43–6, 52.

[120] *La Nación*, 17 Jan. 1928.

[121] Ibid., 15 Feb. 1926.

When Alfonso Sala understood that the Commission for the Co-ordination between the Four Catalan Provinces, to the presidency of which he was appointed, would by no means be allowed to develop into a renewed version of the Mancomunitat, he handed in his resignation to Governor Miláns del Bosch on 22 April 1925. Even Alfonso Sala 'with his proved *españolismo* had become incompatible with us', Primo de Rivera suspected people might rightly say of him.[122] The new president of the Diputación of Barcelona, Josép María Milá i Camps, who had inherited from his father, a one-time mayor of Barcelona (Josép Milá i Pi), a deep distrust towards Catalanism as an agent of political convulsions in the region, became the docile servant of the regime's centralistic policies.[123] Primo de Rivera's unitary spirit had finally prevailed as the 'nightmare' of the Mancomunitat was removed, and the foundations of an unyieldingly unitary state were laid down.[124]

In spite of his conscious reliance upon the Church to provide his regime and the Unión Patriótica with religious sanction, Primo de Rivera's unitary policy did not stop at the door of the Catalan Church either. In effect, his determination to suppress the use of the Catalan language even for liturgical purposes was soon to turn the Catalan clergy, as was also eventually to happen with the Basque and the Catalan Church under Francoism, into the champions of regional liberties and cultural autonomy. Already upon his return from his state visit to Italy, Primo de Rivera had disclosed to Puig i Cadalfach his intention 'to have recourse to Rome in order to prohibit the preaching in Catalan'.[125] Papal support for the banning of the Catalan language as a canon language was not forthcoming, however, and Primo de Rivera had to have a frontal clash with the Catalan clergy; which he could afford thanks to the full support he enjoyed from the 'Spanish' Church over this issue.[126]

Consequently, Cardinal Vidal i Barraquer, the bishop of Tarragona, who had been initially prominent in blessing the coming of the Dictatorship,[127] soon retreated to the neutral, vague ecclesiastical terminology about the need 'to obey the constituted power'.[128]

[122] Joaniquet, *Alfonso Sala* (Madrid, 1955), pp. 305–14; Armiñán, *Epistolario* (Primo's letter to Miláns del Bosch, 2 Apr. 1925), pp. 71–2.

[123] Hurtado, ii, p. 231.

[124] Primo in *El Sol*, 21 Mar. 1925, and *Unión Patriótica*, 15 Sept. 1927.

[125] Puig in *La Veu de Catalunya*, 4 Mar. 1930.

[126] Cuenca, 'Panorama', in Cárcel Ortí (ed.), p. 287.

[127] See p. 84.

[128] *La Vanguardia*, 7 Mar. 1924.

Attempts by the civil governor of Gerona, for example, to use the local clergy as a recruiting agent for the UP were curtailed by Vidal.[129] And when, at the beginning of February 1925, he participated in a meeting of support for the king, he made it clear this did not imply an acceptance of the regime but was just 'an affirmation of the principle of authority, and of social, familial and religious order'. 'We should co-operate with the state,' he went on, 'but in our own way, that is the Church as a Church, the State as a State, the municipality as a municipality, the Gallego as a Gallego, the Catalan as a Catalan, the Valencian as a Valencian.'[130] Vidal would not succumb to the *Primoderriverista* concept of the Patria-España, for which he would consequently be labelled 'anti-Spanish'.[131] Indeed, every effort was made to transfer the stubborn Cardinal to a bishopric outside Catalonia, but to no avail. However, every time a Catalan bishopric became vacant, as was the case with those of Barcelona, Tortosa, and Gerona, the government would lose no time in seizing the opportunity of filling the vacancies with 'Spanish' priests.[132] As for those Catalan priests 'who conducted conspiratorial activities'—Primo's euphemism for the expression of nationalist feelings—the orders were explicit: 'We must send them to serve in Andalusia.'[133]

Primo de Rivera would not even hesitate to risk open collision with the Holy See if that became necessary. 'We want Rome to decide between us and Catalonia', he said to Vidal i Barraquer in warning tones, 'and if it refuses to stand on our side, we should expel the Nuncio and move straight away to the constitution of a National Church.'[134]

That the Catalan hierarchy should have turned against Primo de Rivera was no surprise if one recalls the daily persecution of the Catalan prelates. 'The considerable data that I was able to collect', Manuel Brunet was later to write in a research article in *La Veu da Catalunya*,[135] 'permits me to state that there was no politician or

[129] See his letter to the Pope in Ramón Muntanyola, *Vidal y Barraquer, el Cardenal de la Paz* (Barcelona, 1971), p. 167.

[130] *Diario de Barcelona*, 3 Feb. 1925. See also Vidal to Primo, 4, 14 Jan. 1928 in AHN, P.G. Leg. 383.

[131] José Meseguer y Costa (bishop of Lérida), *Catecismo de la doctrina cristiana* (Lérida, 1929), p. 81; AHN, P.G. Leg. 326; 'Labor anti-españolista del arzobispo de Tarragona, 1924'.

[132] Muntanyola, pp. 120, 144, 167.

[133] Primo to Magaz, 5 June 1925, in Armiñán, *Epistolario*, p. 141.

[134] Muntanyola, p. 146.

[135] Manuel Brunet, 'L'eglesia Catalana durant la dictadura', in *La Veu de Catalunya*, 3 May 1930.

party in Catalonia that had been persecuted with such tenacity as the Catalan priests.'[136] The civic Junta of Barcelona was especially active in 'uprooting' separatism.[137] It was also utilized by the local authorities as the agent of *españolismo vis-à-vis* the Catalan clergy. For example, in August 1927, it ordered the dismissal of a Catalanist professor, Sr. Monserrat, from his teaching position at a local seminary without even bothering to consult the bishop of Barcelona. This was done because 'the atmosphere and the ideas prevailing in the seminary are of an exalted Catalanism', as Governor Miláns del Bosch put it at a meeting of the civic junta.[138] Even a seemingly minor issue such as the name of the ecclesiastical Catalan institution *Foment de la Pietat Catalana* became the object of the civic junta's policy of demolishing the most minor expressions of Catalanism. It demanded that the institution change its name to that of *Foment de la Pietat de Catalunya*, which was tantamount to saying that Catalonia was a geographic rather than a national entity.[139]

Primo de Rivera, just like Franco's prime minister, Arias Navarro, during the Añoveros affair,[140] did not really grasp that the rebellion of the nationalist Church was not just a problem of 'public order'; its judicial and political implications were more fundamental. This was understood by the Jesuit *El Debate*, when it decided to dissociate itself from the government's policy towards the Catalan Church. It supported the collective refusal of the Catalan episcopate, early in February 1928, to abide by the ban on the Catalan language. 'This is not a political question', commented *El Debate*, 'this is an ecclesiastical matter of faith, morality and discipline.'[141] Actually, *ABC* and *La Nación* were isolated in their support of Primo de Rivera's harsh treatment of the Catalan clergy. Primo's policy came thus under the fire of a strange coalition of liberals and Catholics.[142]

But Primo succeeded where Arias failed. He was far more successful than Franco's premier in bringing the Pope to acquiesce in his policy towards the nationalist Church. Admiral Magaz, the Dictator's ex-deputy, was especially sent to Rome to negotiate a

[136] See some examples in Muntanyola, pp. 123–37.

[137] AHN, P.G. Leg. 338; Reports from the civic junta of Barcelona, 17 Apr. 1928, 17 July 1929, 18 Nov. 1929.

[138] AHN, P.G. Leg. 383; 'Junta ciudadana de la provincia de Barcelona', 18 Aug. 1927.

[139] Ibid., Junta ciudadana to bishop of Barcelona, 18 Nov. 1927; the bishop to General Emilio Barrera, 19 Dec. 1927, Barrera to bishop, 15 Jan. 1928.

[140] Ben-Ami, *La revolución*, pp. 260–2.

[141] *El Debate*, 8, 13 Feb. 1928.

[142] *ABC*, 2, 8 Feb. 1928. See also Gaziel, quoted in Muntanyola, pp. 158–9.

workable compromise with the Holy See. Consequently, during the last year of the Dictatorship it became clear that the Vatican had decided to sacrifice the extremist wing of Catalan particularism in order to salvage its congenial relations with the most fervently Catholic, indeed ultramontane, regime in Europe. Since December 1928 the Vatican's instructions to the Catalan clergy had been in concurrence with the regime's unitary policies. Consequently, the order coming now from Rome was that no seminarist 'who is contaminated with Catalanism' could enter the priesthood; nor should any 'Catalanist professors' be allowed to teach in the seminaries. Under no circumstances, said an order of the *Sagrada Congregación del Concilio* (4 January 1929), should the 'legitimate love towards the *patria chica*' be allowed 'to infringe upon the canonic laws and to negate the love towards the entire *patria*, that is the *patria grande*'. Moreover, the Vatican, which understandably refused to break the explicit rule decided upon by the Council of Trent whereby the catechism should be taught in the vernacular,[143] none the less stipulated that the Catalan catechism should include special passages thereof, underlining the love for the *patria grande*. The same, of course, applied to the sermons of the local priests.[144]

The bitter reaction of the Catalan episcopate to the Vatican's orders clearly reflected the extent of Primo's success in having the Vatican legitimize his unitary policies.[145] Primo de Rivera would have certainly liked to ban the Catalan language absolutely; yet his compromise with the Pope was something he could really celebrate. Catalan particularism could get nothing but very limited support in Rome. Cambó, another of the prominent Catalan disenchanted ex-supporters of the Dictator, now saw with dismay how 'the Church, contradicting all its traditions, had put itself on the side of might against right'. This, he feared, might result in an anticlerical eruption when the Dictatorship was over.[146]

4. *The Hispano-American Commonwealth*

Hispano-Americanism, current coinage for nationalists and tradi-

[143] In 1927 there were in Barcelona 411,741 people whose parents were Catalans, and 411,827 whose parents were not Catalans, see AHN, P.G. Leg. 383: 'Junta ciudadana de la provincia de Barcelona', 15 Nov. 1928.

[144] For the new regulations issued by the Vatican, see Muntanyola, pp. 451–60.

[145] AHN, P.G. Leg. 383; 'Junta ciudadana . . .'. See also Maura, *Bosquejo*, pp. 314–15; and Muntanyola, *Vidal*, pp. 180–1.

[146] Pabón, *Cambó*, vol. ii, pt. I, p. 548.

tionalists in Spain, was an important showpiece of the Dictatorship. It did not entail, though, a revival of old imperialist dreams. Rather, it was compatible with Ganivet's claim, later even supported by such a militant writer as Ramiro de Maeztu, that Spain had exhausted her forces of material expansion, and should therefore concentrate on enhancing the spiritual union of the Hispanic peoples.[147] In effect, it was King Alfonso who first launched the new regime's aspiration to be the leader of the Hispano-American nations. In his visit to the Vatican, he presented himself to the Pope as the spokesman for the entire Hispanic race. He asked that 'the Spanish-American world', that constituted 'one-third of the earth's Catholics', might have greater representation in the Vatican. Spain's vehement aspiration, he said, was to renew and strengthen its 'tight embrace' with its ex-colonies, and to lead the Hispano-American race to new peaks of grandeur.[148] In his speeches, Primo de Rivera also addressed himself frequently to 'our brothers of the Iberian race'.

The daring flight of three Spanish pilots in 1926 across the Atlantic was, in this context, hailed by UP mouthpieces as an indisputable demonstration of 'Iberian vitality'; it was a providentially tempting repetition of the discovery of America by the Catholic Kings. The flight was turned, by government initiative, into an ecstatic propaganda tour throughout the entire South American continent, the governments of which responded enthusiastically to the exhibitions of fraternity of the 'madre-patria'. Cuba, for example, elevated its delegation in Madrid to embassy status under the impact of the excitement aroused by the daring flight.[149] The foreign minister of Panama exclaimed that every man in the continent was proud of belonging to 'that magnificent race, which had repeatedly given examples of courage and abnegation'. 'Our Mother Spain', he continued, 'does not need to make special efforts to bind herself with her American sons. Our blood, our vernacular, our religion and our whole civilization are inextricable ties . . . The flight is a kiss sent by the madre-patria to her sons in America.'[150] The excitement was such that the president of Uruguay protested that his country was excluded from the itinerary of the Plus Ultra. Ramón Franco had therefore to change the itinerary 'lest the Uruguayans be

[147] Ganivet, p. 120; Ramiro de Maeztu, *Defensa de la hispanidad* (Valladolid, 1938).

[148] The speech in *Folletín*, p. 76.

[149] AHN, P.G. Leg. 346; Spain's representative in Habana to Primo, 11 Feb. 1926.

[150] Ibid., Belisario Porras (Panama's ambassador in Paris) to Primo, 7 Feb. 1926.

offended'. 'The impatient population of the Argentinian Republic', he explained, 'can wait half a day until we finish our visit to Uruguay.'[151] The president of the 'impatient' Argentinians responded to the popular clamour when he decided to commemorate the flight by erecting a special monument to be financed by public subscription.[152] Overwhelmed by this display of affection, the Spanish government decided to grant the Plus Ultra as a present to the Argentinian people. To which the Argentinian president responded with a gesture of his own: he ordered the cruiser 'Buenos Aires' to take the pilots in a triumphal journey back to Spain.[153]

To justify its oratory of *hispanismo*, the Dictatorship launched frequent initiatives. Such was, for example, the Spanish exhibition held in Havana early in 1926 to celebrate the conclusion of a commercial treaty between the two countries.[154] In October 1926, a subscription was organized throughout South America for the erection in Madrid of a monument to Cervantes.[155] A year later, a Congress of the Latin Press was held in the Spanish capital.[156] Additional initiatives included the publication, under governmental auspices, of a special organ dedicated to the promotion of the 'Hispano-American spirit',[157] the establishment of a Spanish cultural centre in Chile, and the elevation of the Spanish delegation in that country to embassy status; the agreements signed with Peru and Panama for an exchange of scholars and students; the commercial treaties signed with Cuba and Argentina, and the agreements with Peru and El Salvador to have their Guardia Nacional trained by the Spanish Guardia Civil.[158] Late in 1929, radio-telegraph links and airmail services were established with Argentina, Brazil, Paraguay, Uruguay, and Chile. Earlier, in 1925, a Federation of Latin American students was set up in Madrid, its organ, *Patria Grande*, being

[151] Ibid., Ramón Franco to Primo, 7 Feb. 1926.

[152] *Boletín de la Asociación Patriótica Española*, Buenos Aires, Dec. 1928: 'El monumento al Plus Ultra'.

[153] AHN, P.G. Leg. 346; Spain's ambassador in Buenos Aires to Primo, 27 Feb. 1926. For the euphoric reception accorded to the pilots in South America, see *La* Nación, 1–11 Feb. 1926; *Glorias de la raza, La voz del pueblo y el raid Huelva–Buenos Aires* (Madrid, 1926).

[154] AHN, P.G. Leg. 346; Spain's representative in Habana to Primo, 4 Feb. 1926.

[155] Ibid., Spain's ambassador in Bogotá to Primo, 13 Oct. 1926.

[156] *Folletín*, p. 732; Conde de Santibáñez del Río, 'El hispanismo triunfador', in *La Nación*, 21 July 1927.

[157] *España Avanza. Órgano Mundial de las Ciudadanías Hispano-Americanas* (Madrid, 16 Sept. 1928). *La Nación* published a weekly supplement for South America: *La Nación, Edición Semanal para América*, 1926–9.

[158] Primo, *Intervenciones*, pp. 372–3; *La Nación*, 5 June 1928.

subsidized by the Spanish government. Primo de Rivera established a special desk at the Foreign Office to promote links with South America. He also ordered that no Latin American citizen who visited Spain should be considered a foreigner.[159] He even made a *démarche* towards the hostile Mexican government in an attempt to establish friendly relations, if not upon political grounds then upon the *hispanista* common denominator.[160] Certainly, the most spectacular showpiece of *hispanismo* was the Ibero-American Exhibition in Seville in 1929. It gave great publicity to cultural, artistic *hispanismo* as it also did to the economic potentialities of the Hispanic commonwealth.[161]

Cambó might have been right in warning against the naïve belief that *hispanismo* could provide the ground for a spectacular expansion of the economic ties between Spain and her former colonies.[162] But economic considerations were not uppermost in Primo de Rivera's mind. Whether this was sound economics or not, the historic and racial bonds with the Latin American countries were, in his concept, an inextricable part of Spain's destiny. Therefore, though he had initiated a *rapprochement* with Italy as part of his Mediterranean policy and because of his ideological affinity with the Italian dictatorship, he did not think that Italy should be given the same favourable status conceded to Hispano-American countries in their commercial treaties with Spain. There should be made, he argued, 'a justified' distinction between Italy and the South American daughters.[163] It was as a gesture of solidarity more than anything else that, in November 1928, the National Bank of Argentina came to the rescue of Spain with a fifty-million-peseta loan in agricultural products.[164] 1928 was the gloomiest year of the decade for agricultural production in Spain. A year before, it had been the Spaniards who made the Argentinians a loan of a hundred million pesetas to help them to finance their orders from the Spanish naval industry. Primo was not to be deterred by the rumours that Argentina had used part of the money to pay for her naval orders in Italy. 'I do not know whether we have profited or not from the sale of cruisers to Argentina', he explained, 'but we have certainly advanced the moral and spiritual relations that bind us to Argentina.'[165]

[159] Cimadevilla, pp. 294–9.
[160] Albiñana, *Despueś*, pp. 43–5.
[161] *Boletín de la Asociación Patriótica Española*, Buenos Aires, May 1929; *La Nación*, 8–13 May 1929.
[162] Cambó, *España, Cataluña*, pp. 114–17.
[163] AHN, P.G. Leg. 346: 'Notas sobre el tratado comercial con Italia', April 1924.
[164] *The Times*, 7 Nov. 1928.
[165] Primo, *Intervenciones*, p. 370; *Folletín*, pp. 590–1.

CHAPTER VI
The Constituent Phase

1. *Towards the Civilianization of the Dictatorship*

IN order to gauge the significance of the transition to civilian rule in December 1925, one must remember that such a process was not a unique *Primoderriverista* phenomenon. It had also happened elsewhere when military rulers started to be overwhelmed by the complexity of the socio-economic problems they had initially thought they could solve through head-on policies.[1] It is significant in this context that Primo de Rivera himself should have referred to the need to tackle complex economic issues such as, for example, his plan for the taxation of capital, as a relevant reason for moving to the civilian phase of his rule. Furthermore, the Dictator confessed that a civilian dictatorship would be more likely to inspire confidence in the business community as a whole, and among the banks in particular, a confidence without which he could not expect to carry through either his tax reform or his developmental schemes. The civilian directory heralded the accentuation of the developmental traits of the regime.[2] It was thus no mere coincidence that the appointment of the new government should have been made at a time when consultations with Spain's top economist, Flores de Lemus, brought home to Primo de Rivera the urgent message concerning the grave situation of the Treasury.[3]

Yet, consistent though it might have been with a well-known tendency among military rulers to rely on technocrats, 'unarmed bureaucrats',[4] the new civilian directory nevertheless heralded a new phase, not only in terms of policies and personalities, but also in the overall orientation of Primo's regime. It was now clear that the Dictator was ready to assume the task of a long-range, rather than *ad hoc*, restructuring of the Spanish state. The transition to civilian government, dismissed by some as a mere change of labels without touching the substance,[5] was in effect a conscious step towards a new kind of legality.

[1] Cf. Finer, pp. 14–17. [2] See Chapter VII. [3] *El Sol*, 2, 3 Dec. 1925.
[4] Cf. Nordlinger, pp. 119–22. [5] Brenan, p. 81.

For some time, the Dictator had been contemplating the possibility of transforming his originally military rule into a civilian dictatorship. As early as April 1925, he wrote from Morocco to his minister of war, the Duke of Tetuan, that as soon as he had solved the Moroccan problem he would set up his 'first civilian ministry'.[6] And to Calvo Sotelo, his future minister of finance, he even sent a general outline of the 'programme of reconstruction' to be undertaken by such a ministry.[7] Undoubtedly, the prospects of a victorious end to the Moroccan war only strengthened the Dictator's determination not only to stay in power, to the disappointment of those who expected him now to see his mission as completed,[8] but also, as he put it, to start 'the second stage' of his rule with a view of perpetuating it.[9]

Early in October 1925, that is after the crucial landing at Alhucemas Bay, Primo de Rivera returned, more determined than ever, to the schemes of his future civilian government, among which he included a law regulating labour contracts.[10] The Dictator had clearly in mind the necessity of perpetuating his rule (or in his own words, 'to take a step towards normal conditions'), that, so far, had been characterized by the *ad hoc* and 'parenthetical' features of the Military Directory.[11] Enormous economic and administrative problems, as well as a preoccupation with the constitutional amorphousness of his regime, as he had indeed confessed in a speech at the Mundial Cinema in Madrid, were the reasons that had brought him to propose 'a government of a more stable character and with longer prospects of life than the Military Directory'.[12] Early in November, Primo de Rivera explained to Luca de Tena, the director of *ABC* who had accompanied him during the Moroccan campaign, that his future 'normal government' would lay the ground for the new constitutional framework, replacing parliamentary democracy with a unicameral system based on corporative suffrage.[13] No wonder that the liberal *El Sol* was alarmed by such an abrupt departure from the very essence of a provisional military dictatorship. 'The Directory' it protested, 'is displaying a tendency to perpetuate itself'; and it continued:

The junta of generals who had come to sweep away old politics has now

[6] Primo to Duke of Tetuan, 2 Apr. 1925, in Armiñán, *Epistolario*, p. 80.
[7] Calvo, pp. 99–105. [8] Romanones, *Notas*, pp. 222–3; *La Nación*, 28 July 1928.
[9] *La Nación*, 8 Aug. 1927. [10] *The Times*, 6 Oct. 1925.
[11] *The Economist*, 2 Jan. 1926. [12] *The Times*, 17 Oct. 1925.
[13] *Folletín*, p. 292.

exceeded its initial mission far beyond what one would have assumed. It now tries to reconstruct the state by altering the very foundations of national life. The president of the Directory, according to his own declarations, is contemplating a reform of the constitution . . . and a revolutionary reform in our system of taxation . . . All this carries much more significance than the *coup d'état* of 13 September itself. The proposed reforms are not just police operations as was the *coup d'état*, nor can they be viewed as just an additional measure of *saneamiento*. [The transition to civilian rule] is tantamount to a revolution that reaches the very entrails of the nation, and affects the most inveterate institutions.[14]

The transition to civilian rule also meant that Primo de Rivera had now officially put the army back in barracks. 'The army is henceforth to abstain absolutely from taking part in politics', he decreed on the morrow of the designation of the new government.[15] Moreover, the royal decree establishing the Civilian Directory promised 'a reorganization of the armed forces', a task, it was explained, that only a civilian regime which adopts a broader approach to military issues than the strictly professional one, could cope with.[16] The civilianization of the regime was further emphasized by a decree stipulating that those military governors who still functioned as civil governors should thereafter confine themselves to their military assignments, while civilians were appointed to administer the provinces.[17] This, of course, did not mean that any relaxation of order and discipline would be allowed. Censorship was to be maintained, and the right of assembly and association would continue to be restricted as before.[18]

A striking novelty, hardly palatable to the liberal opposition, was also Primo's reference to the new directory as the government of his *partido único*, the UP. The latter, he said in the decree that set up the new cabinet, was 'a large political party' ready to assume power, and therefore, he added, addressing himself to the king, 'it is upon the UP . . . that your Majesty should now confer the task of governing the country'.[19] Indeed, most of the civilians in the new cabinet held prominent positions in the UP.[20]

[14] Ibid., pp. 292–3.

[15] *The Times*, 7 Dec. 1925.

[16] *Gaceta*, 4 Dec. 1925; *El Sol*, 3 Dec. 1925.

[17] *El Sol*, 2 Dec. 1925. The affected provinces were Oviedo, Orense, Valencia, Málaga.

[18] *Gaceta*, 4 Dec. 1925.

[19] *La Nación*, 3 Dec. 1925. *Unión Patriótica* (15 Nov. 1926, 15 July 1927) would usually refer to the new government as the government of the UP.

[20] For biographical and other data on the new ministers, see José de las Casas Pérez, *El régimen y sus hombres. Lo que me han contado a mí* (Madrid, 1930),

Primo de Rivera's new team included several technocrats, some lesser figures of the old regime, and prominent provincial chiefs of the UP. The new Minister of Work, Eduardo Aunós, helped to imbue the new regime with a corporative ideology. Much influenced by the Italian example, he became, among Primo's collaborators, one of the most committed supporters of a new constitution along Fascist lines. José Calvo Sotelo, who had in the past been the civil governor of Valencia and later under Primo the UP chief of Orense, and the elaborator of the much publicized reform of local administration, received the key ministry of finance. An ex-Maurista activist, Calvo Sotelo had joined the new regime to help to execute the longed-for 'revolution from above'. The ministry of education was conceded to Sr. Callejo, an obscure professor at the University of Valladolid and 'a deserter from the Maurista youth', whose main merit was that of having been a principle mover of the Unión Patriótica among Catholic-Agrarian sectors in Old Castile. Rafael Benjumea, the Conde de Guadalhorce, an engineer, who had gained his reputation as the builder of hydraulic complexes in the province of Málaga where he also later became the UP's provincial chief, was put in charge of the most pretentious ministry of the Dictatorship: the ministry of development. The portfolio of foreign affairs was given to a young professor, Yanguas Messía, who first put his talent to the service of the new regime as the organizer and eventual chief of the UP of Jaén. In 1936, he would draw up the famous decree that nominated Franco as the Nationalists' head of state.[21] The Duke of Tetuan was appointed the minister of war, probably not because of any outstanding military talent or irresistible authority, of both of which he was devoid. He was a long-time intimate friend of the Dictator, who was, in effect, the minister of war in all but name. That an obscure vice-admiral, Sr. Cornejo, should have been appointed as the minister of the navy was no novelty. Ministers of the navy had always been unknown figures in Spain. The same could hardly be said of General Martínez Anido, another future servant of Franco, whose 'efficiency' and reputation in matters of 'public

passim; and *Folletín*, p. 302. In a reshuffle early in November 1928, Conde de los Andes became Minister of National Economy; General Julio Ardanaz assumed the ministry of the army (a new title for the old ministry of war), and García de los Reyes replaced Cornejo in the navy: *La Nación*, 3 Nov. 1928.

[21] It was shown by Viver Pi-Sunyer, *El personal*, pp. 170–92, that the presence of *primoderriveristas* in Franco's early political personnel was overwhelmingly higher than either that of the political class of the Restoration or that of the Republic's 'bienio negro'.

order' was beyond dispute. He was put at the head of the ministry of the interior.

2. *'A Genuine Representation of the Nation': The National Assembly*

The transition to a civilian regime was no isolated insight. Simultaneously with its emergence there crystallized in Primo's mind the idea of carrying out a constitutional reform through a new corporative parliament.

In March 1924, three months after he had returned from Italy and precisely at the time when he started the institutionalization of the UP, the Dictator disclosed to a French journalist his plan 'to summon the nation according to its representative classes, that is universities, industry, commerce, workers, in sum, all the Spain that thinks and works'.[22] But urgent tasks, such as the Moroccan war, compelled the Dictator to shelve his plan. It came again to the fore in November 1925,[23] that is when victory in Morocco had been assured and the transition to a civilian government was imminent. Corporatism was not an idea for which Spain needed the Italian example to start implementing it; it was inspired by national traditions and by the teachings of the Roman Catholic Church.[24] Moreover, Primo de Rivera began to talk of a corporative chamber at a time when Mussolini had not yet got rid of the old *transformista* parliament.[25] But once the Duce had started to build his corporative state, the Spanish Dictator was further encouraged to pursue his constitutional schemes. Primo, according to his finance minister, Calvo Sotelo, was very much impressed by the Duce's recommendation, conveyed to him through Eduardo Aunós in 1926, that he should lose no time in setting up his own parliament. 'Parliament', explained Mussolini, 'is the indispensable costume which must be worn at the international soirée.'[26]

Independently of the Duce's advice, though, the Dictator and his spokesmen subscribed to the view that an entirely new political structure was vital if 'the decrepit parliamentarian organs' were to be replaced by more healthy institutions.[27]

Significantly, it was the national congress of the UP, held in July

[22] Quoted in Maura, *Bosquejo*, p. 55.
[23] *La Nación*, 19 Nov. 1925.
[24] Cf. Rafael María Sanz de Diego, 'La iglesia española ante el reto de la industrialización', in Cárcel Ortí (ed.), pp. 603–52.
[25] Cf. Lyttelton, *The Seizure*, pp. 121–48.
[26] Calvo, p. 336.
[27] *La Nación*, 7 Jan. 4, 15 June 1926.

1926, that took the first operational decision towards establishing a new, corporative parliament. Subsequently, the UP staged a national campaign aimed at mobilizing public support for the implementation of its decision. The regime's official mouthpiece liked to refer to the new parliament as being in tune with the 'trends of this century', and as a definite step out of 'this transitional regime' towards a new, permanent one. Originally, the UP's decision spoke of the National Assembly as the hierarchic summit of a society wholly structured along corporatist lines. Only thus could 'the durability of the foundations upon which the fabric of the new Spain is to be erected' be assured.[28]

Primo de Rivera subscribed to this vision of a vertically structured corporative Spain culminating in the National Assembly. In almost identical terms to those later used by Salazar, the Spanish Dictator envisaged a system, the spinal cord of which would consist of 'the main cellule of the nation, the municipality, and then the family with its ancient virtues and its modern civic concept. The province would be the nucleus, the principal vertebra that would guide and irrigate the entire state system.'[29] For Primo the National Assembly was an imperative deriving from what he viewed as 'the failure of the parliamentary system in its present form', a failure he was encouraged to see taking place also 'in the two countries most akin to Spain', Italy and Portugal. Carried away by the Italian analogy, he envisaged the Assembly as a Spanish *Gran Consiglio* that would assist him in creating 'a new Spain'. This is how he put it in a manifesto celebrating the third anniversary of his seizure of power:

> The government and the Unión Patriótica harbour the conception of a state of a new structure, strong, real, practical, democratic, and free of distorted philosophies and humiliating imitations. This [new structure] will have to be approved by a Grand Assembly that must be the genuine representation of the country and with whose assistance we intend to start the revolutionary labour demanded by the health of Spain, the changing times, and the exhaustion of all actual solutions.[30]

This document contained probably the clearest and sharpest departure so far of Primo de Rivera from the 1876 constitution, to whose precepts he had occasionally paid lip-service. How else could one interpret his promise 'to make a new Spain by throwing overboard all the medley and baggage of a legislation [that had]

[28] Ibid., 7, 22, 27 July, 4 Aug. 1926.

[29] *ABC*, 5 Sept. 1926; Salazar, p. 101.

[30] *ABC*, 5 Sept. 1926. See also Primo's declarations in *El Sol*, 13 Sept. 1926.

enthroned a legal tyranny, more fallacious and cruel than any recorded by history'?[31] Far from contemplating a swift end to his rule, the Dictator explained in an interview with a Belgian newspaper that 'after a century of misgovernment, we need at least half a century of strong government'.[32] The Dictatorship, illegal and 'parenthetical' in its origins, was about to embark upon a constituent process, at the end of which he expected Spain to have its own 'peculiar regime, typically national, well adapted to our needs, and clean from any exotic imitations'.[33] What Primo de Rivera called 'the executive phase' of his rule was, as he later explained to the constituent committee of the Assembly, over. The new stage was to be characterized by 'a change of the entire legislation of the country in both letter and spirit'.[34]

Primo de Rivera was careful to stress that the Assembly would not be the result of an impromptu decree; its origins—a decision by the UP—were democratic, and its eventual convocation would have to be emphatically demanded by the people through a national plebiscite. The latter was also an initiative of the UP, which expected it to be the expression of 'the nation's confidence in the government, especially in its president, as well as the people's will that a National Assembly be constituted to assist it in governing the state'. The 'glorious Caudillo' did not lose time in endorsing the UP's idea.[35]

Completely in tune with the regime's consistent drive to surround itself with an aura of public acceptance and legitimacy,[36] the plebiscite was now also part of an impressive campaign aimed at popularizing the idea behind the National Assembly. Coming at a time when the regime's authority was at a low ebb because of its grave collision with the entire Artillery corps,[37] the plebiscite was also expected to bolster up its declining prestige. No less important, by 'organizing' an overwhelming vote of confidence in his regime, the Dictator expected to overcome the king's reluctance to endorse the Assembly, which Alfonso rightly saw as a further nail in the coffin of the 1876 constitution. The monarch, whose line of defence

[31] *ABC*, 5 Sept. 1926.

[32] *L'Étoile belge*, 9 June 1926.

[33] Quoted in Calvo, p. 335.

[34] Quoted in M. García Canales, *El problema constitucional en la Dictadura de Primo de Rivera* (Madrid, 1980), p. 107.

[35] See the original document of the UP in AHN, Gobernación, serie A, 31 Aug. 1926.

[36] Cf. the role of the plebiscite in the regimes of Nasser, Napoleon, Primo, and Franco, Finer, pp. 18–19.

[37] See below, pp. 362–3.

with regard to his role in Primo de Rivera's *coup d'état* had always been that, by sanctioning the *fait accompli*, he had simply responded to the people's yearning, was now to be faced with an imposing expression of the 'national will'. As rumours about the king's weariness with the Dictator and about his will to 'Bourbonize' him (the expression is Primo's)[38] became widespread, the Assembly, as well as the plebiscite, were both conceived as the personal weapons of the Dictator in his fight for political survival. On 13 September 1923, the general was a political gambler dependent on the exclusive will of the king. Since then, however, he had been consistently cultivating through the UP, the Somatén, frequent propaganda tours across the country—and now the plebiscite and the Assembly—his personal popular power-base and source of legitimacy. He was eager to show that his power no longer rested exclusively on royal favour. The 'democratic liturgy and mass gatherings' could well serve this purpose. The Dictator's 'hunger for the masses'[39] was also shrewd political tactics.

On 3 September 1926, Primo de Rivera issued the appropriate orders to the authorities 'to facilitate every convenient and necessary assistance so that national public opinion could be expressed with the utmost liberty'.[40] The minister of the interior, however, was more explicit, as he put the state machine at the service of the plebiscite. He instructed the civil governors to give the greatest possible publicity to all manifestos urging the people to vote. Every propaganda effort was to be made so that 'all the Spaniards should know about the plebiscite, its significance and implications'. The governors were also instructed to curb any disturbances or hostile propaganda by imposing heavy fines upon, and 'if necessary even exiling', those who might attempt to stymie the whole effort.[41] Indeed, punishments along these lines were eventually carried out.[42] It was taken for granted that public functionaries would vote for the regime. What they were explicitly urged to do was 'to make their families and friends vote likewise'.[43]

[38] Probably by replacing him with General Berenguer, who had just been given the post of head of the king's military household, see Hurtado, ii, p. 230.

[39] González Ruano, pp. 7–8.

[40] AHN, Gobernación, serie A, Leg. 47, circular no. 15/067, 3 Sept. 1926.

[41] Ibid., circular to the civil governors, nos. 22 and 15/036, 2 Sept. 1926.

[42] See, for example, ibid., civil governors of Alicante, La Coruña, Gerona, Cádiz, and Las Palmas to Gobernación, nos. 413, 62, 272, 236, 267; 13, 16, 8, 7, 8 Sept. 1926.

[43] Ibid., circular no. 15/309, 8 Sept. 1926.

There can hardly be any doubt as to the freedom of choice given to the people in this plebiscite. Elections had always been rigged in Spain. What was strikingly novel about the plebiscite was the extent to which the government mobilized its machinery for propaganda purposes. UP propagandists spread all over the country to explain the significance of 'these hours of historical emotion' and to enlist popular support for 'this gigantic step in preparing the ground for the emergence of the young Spain'.[44] A large number of conservative women assisted the authorities by distributing manifestos and urging people to vote lest Primo de Rivera should leave the nation once more to the hazards of 'politics'.[45] 'Patriotic youth' of all sorts were also reminded that the time had arrived for them to show their love for Spain.[46] Nor was the Church idle. Members of the hierarchy joined in the chorus of support since, as the bishop of Tortosa put it, 'the plebiscite is not a political act', but an 'expression of gratitude for the government's labour on behalf of social, moral and religious interests'.[47] Active support for the government's efforts was also forthcoming from Martínez Anido's old allies, the Sindicatos Libres.[48]

The plebiscite was also conceived as a popular vote of confidence for the Dictator; indeed, it became the culminating point in Primo's personality cult. The Dictator himself set the tone of the campaign when he said that he had carried his mission so far 'according to the will of God'. 'When one works under such auspices', he added, 'not only has he the right to expect the success of the plebiscite, but also it would be improper for the nation not to extend to him its support.'[49] It was, therefore, to the man 'who had restored social peace', to the 'Caudillo of Alhucemas and the undefeated commander of Tetuan and Kudia-Tahar'. to 'the defender of Spain's international prestige', and to 'the guardian of order and morality in the public administration' that the UP asked the nation to give a vote of confidence. Mothers were asked to compensate the general for ending 'the black Moroccan nightmare'; workers were urged to remember that

[44] See reports on propaganda in *La Nación*, 9, 10 Sept. 1926.

[45] *El Sol*, 12, 14 Sept. 1926.

[46] 'Manifesto a las Juventudes Patrióticas de España', in *La Nación*, 8 Sept. 1926.

[47] AHN, Gobernación, serie A, Leg. 47; a report from the mayor of Tortosa, no. 363, 11 Sept. 1926. See also the support of the bishop of Madrid-Alcalá, Sr Eijo Garay, for the plebiscite, in *La Nación*, 14 Sept. 1926.

[48] AHN, Gobernación, serie A, Leg. 47: 'Sindicatos Libres de Tortosa', no. 396, 12 Sept. 1926.

[49] *El Sol*, 11 Sept. 1926.

it was Primo de Rivera who had first advanced a policy of public works and social justice; employers were reminded that it was thanks to the present regime that their plants had ceased to be battlegrounds. As for the lovers of democracy, they were told that 'the plebiscite is the most important step towards the people's participation in the government of the State' so far undertaken by any regime in Spain.[50]

The conditions under which the plebiscite was finally held between the eleventh and the thirteenth of September could hardly encourage the 'free expression of the national will'. Polling-stations were run by a personal delegate of the state-appointed mayor. He was assisted by six members, half of them designated by the local UP and half by the mayor. Nor did the actual voting procedure allow for much freedom of choice. Every citizen was asked to sign his name in front of the scrutinizing eyes of officials, on whose goodwill much of his daily life was dependent. To have the greatest possible number of signatures, suffrage was given to both men and women from the age of eighteen, and special mobile polling-stations moved from house to house to collect the signatures of those people who, for whatever reason, were unable to get to the polling-stations.[51] The latter were decorated with the king's and Primo de Rivera's portraits. In Barcelona, Martínez Anido's picture was added to the series to remind the 'neutral masses' of their salvation from social chaos by the 'strong hand' of the present regime.[52]

Whatever one may think of the efforts displayed by the government in staging the plebiscite, they fell far short of resembling the irresistible psychological coercion resorted to by totalitarian regimes on similar occasions. None of the latter would have sounded the clarion call for 'a vote of confidence' in which slightly more than 50 per cent of the electorate took part, as was the case with Primo de Rivera's plebiscite. 7,478,502 people, out of 13,110,897 who possessed the right to vote, finally responded to the regime's appeal and signed their support. Old-fashioned electoral frauds were also resorted to. In Palafrugell (Gerona), for example, a firm promised to send the signature of 300 of its employees; and the governor of Guadalajara instructed the mayors in his province to allow people

[50] *¡Plebiscito Nacional! ¡La UP de Madrid!* in Romanones Archive, Leg. 2, no. 28.

[51] AHN, Gobernación, serie A, Leg. 47: reports from Tenerife, no. 114, 4 Sept. 1926, and Huesca, no. 527. 18 Sept. 1928.

[52] For reports on polling-days, see *El Sol*, 12–14 Sept. 1926.

Votes cast in favour of the regime[53]

Province		*Province*	
Álava	42,178	Logroño	49,039
Albacete	120,022	Lugo	145,817
Alicante	201,657	Madrid	342,797
Almería	166,446	Málaga	186,730
Ávila	54,205	Murcia	327,977
Badajoz	227,812	Navarra	117,278
Baleares	128,835	Orense	146,805
Barcelona	500,351	Oviedo	117,539
Burgos	86,015	Palencia	67,004
Cáceres	151,735	Pontevedra	150,096
Cádiz	183,188	Salamanca	102,868
Canarias	227,319	Santander	106,982
Castellón	117,085	Segovia	61,053
Ciudad Real	211,783	Sevilla	205,770
Córdoba	180,264	Soria	59,338
Coruña	208,570	Tarragona	157,726
Cuenca	81,325	Teruel	82,203
Gerona	92,208	Toledo	142,500
Granada	197,887	Valencia	415,872
Guadalajara	57,770	Valladolid	99,830
Guipúzcoa	51,545	Vizcaya	110,749
Huelva	117,691	Zamora	92,384
Huesca	83,340	Zaragoza	135,283
Jaén	309,274		
León	159,437		7,478,502
Lérida	96,659		

to vote twice.[54] Sometimes, of course, the support marshalled by Primo's agents reflected genuine satisfaction with the regime. Such was the case of the province of Jaén where the high prices fixed for the local olive oil by a recent decree were said to have accounted, to a large extent, for the outstanding success of the plebiscite in that province.[55]

In the months that followed the plebiscite, the men of the regime turned their attention to the nature of the National Assembly and

[53] AHN, Gobernación, serie A, 'Plebiscito Nacional: datos definitivos de la votación'.

[54] Ibid., reports from Gerona, no. 272, 8 Sept. 1926, and Guadalajara, no. 441, 14 Sept. 1926.

[55] Ibid., reports from Jaén, no. 439, 14 Sept. 1926.

the new constitution it would be called upon to work out.[56] That the Assembly would express the organization of the state according to 'classes and professions' was evident to all.[57] Emilio Carreras, the president of the Federation of the Professional Syndicates of the South of Spain, echoed the support of the Sindicatos Libres for a Chamber that would be the sum of the professional assemblies and associations, the genuine expression of 'the vital' and 'vertebrate' Spain. The fate of 'anarchic liberalism', exclaimed Father José Gafo, the famous organizer of Catholic syndicalism, was about to be sealed.[58] Warm support for such a view was forthcoming also from Ramiro de Maeztu. He referred to the National Assembly as to a focus of opinion resting upon the four fundamental social pillars; Family, State, Religion, and Property. The method of election for the new organ should, he said, dwell upon the precept of 'the moral inequality of men'.[59]

José Pemartín expected the National Assembly to express the revival of a mythical, ideal past of 'social solidarity', a past in which order was 'intuitively' appreciated. By 'order', Pemartín meant a natural division of society whereby 'the inferiors did not collectively hate their social superiors'. This 'natural concept of servitude' should now be restored and harnessed for the sake of supreme national interests. A frequent popularizer of Ortega, Pemartín now enlisted the philosopher's concept of 'select minorities' to the cause of the forthcoming National Assembly. The aristocracy of title, 'blood and money', rather than the masses should set the tone in the new Chamber. Pemartín argued that the failure of Maura was due to the inherent incompatibility between his 'revolution from above' and 'parliamentarism from below'. The latter could by no means serve the former.[60]

A 'revolution from above' also implied an entirely new constitution, as Pemartín and Ramiro de Maeztu repeatedly explained.[61] The deference towards, or rather the lip-service occasionally paid by *Upetistas* to, the 1876 constitution, was abandoned altogether, as

[56] *El Sol*, 4 May, 5 Oct. 1927, was understandably disturbed by the regime's claim that the plebiscite had given it a mandate to impose a new constitution.

[57] *La Nación*, 21 Sept., 5, 6, 23 Oct. 1926.

[58] Ibid., 28 Oct. 1926, 3 June 1927.

[59] Ramiro de Maeztu, *Liquidación*, pp. 21–5, 41–5. See also his article in *La Nación*, 2 June, 19, 22 Sept. 1927.

[60] Pemartín, in *La Nación*, 31 Jan., 11, 15, 17 Feb., 6, 30 Aug., 20 Sept. 1927 ('Parliamentarismo desde arriba').

[61] See their articles ibid., 22, 25 June, 26, 29 Sept. 1927.

the regime's spokesmen advanced in a most emphatic way the elaboration of a new constitution as the fundamental task of the future National Assembly. 'Has the present constitution been, by chance, prepared by God that it should be considered unsurpassable and unreformable?'; asked *La Nación* sarcastically a few weeks after the plebiscite.[62]

Primo de Rivera shared his panegyrists' eagerness to have a new constitution. 'The seven million genuine votes' given to the regime in the last plebiscite granted him, he said, a full mandate to reconstruct the Spanish state.[63]

Clearly, such declarations were a direct affront to the king. They undermined the very concept of the Dictatorship as an interim affair. He therefore made every possible effort to thwart the Dictator's attempt to wear a parliamentarian costume. The king was opposed to any reform of the 1876 constitution and he rejected out of hand the Dictator's constituent aspirations.[64]

Evidently, the plebiscite alone fell short of smoothing the way for the Assembly. Primo's declaration late in October 1926 that 'next month the Assembly would be convened'[65] did not impress the monarch. The Dictator had therefore to continue softening up the resistance of the dynastic politicians and that of the king's entourage. Significantly, he did not try to reach his ends by playing down, or concealing, his real intentions. He was as outspoken as ever. He did not lose any opportunity to present his constituent schemes as a sound substitute for the old system that had turned the country into the 'bolshevik shipwreck'. Parliament, he said, was an 'exhausted and corrupt' institution, which 'has been taken over by audacious minorities'. It should not be given a new lease of life. He also tried to blackmail the king into signing the appropriate decree by frequently announcing that his signature was 'imminent' and that the Assembly would 'soon' be convened.[66]

To put additional pressure on the king, Primo de Rivera also endorsed a selective inquiry run by *La Nación*, in which scores of people expressed their support for the Assembly.[67] Thus the official

[62] Ibid., 7 Oct. 1926. See also 'Sobre la nueva constitución que ha de darsele a España para que termine el periodo constituyente', ibid., 29 Apr. 1927.

[63] *The Times*, 1 Feb., 14 Sept. 1927; *El Sol*, 1 June 1927; *La Nación*, 8 Aug. 1927.

[64] G. Maura, *Dolor de España* (Madrid, 1932), p. 69.

[65] *La Nación*, 27 Oct. 1926.

[66] See the Dictator's references to the Assembly in *El Sol*, 15, 20 Jan., 31 May, 4 June, 6 July, 15 Aug., 6, 22 Sept. 1927. *La Nación*, 30 May 1927.

[67] See Primo's letter to the editor of *La Nación*, 15 Nov. 1926.

organ's columns would host, after November 1926, the opinions of professors of public law justifying on scientific grounds the new enterprise; the view of 'a notable criminologist who had always supported parliamentarism' but now had come to accept the National Assembly; and the expressions of warm support from people such as the playwright Jacinto Benavente, the president of the General Spanish Society of Entrepreneurs, the director of the National Museum of Archaeology, a member of the Academy of Jurisprudence, the president of the National Library, and even a famous comedian, who said that he supported the Assembly on the grounds that it would increase public activity in the capital to the benefit of show business . . .[68]

It does seem, however, that the major obstacle to the summoning of the Assembly was the dynastic politicians, rather than the king.[69] Alfonso wanted them to participate in the new institution; he needed accomplices for his constitutional sins. In spite of the view of some of his supporters that 'those who have destroyed the country' should not be allowed to have any say in the future Assembly,[70] the Dictator did hope to see the 'políticos' in his parliament. He obviously expected that a reconciliation with the dynastic politicians would not only underline the legitimacy of the Assembly but also that of his regime as a whole. But this was precisely what most of the politicians refused to do.[71]

In the end, however, the problem was who would display a greater determination and perseverence, the king or his Dictator. The latter did. Moreover, the Dictatorship did not yet face the insurmountable difficulties that would challenge it in 1929; its position was still secure enough for a 'Bourbonization' not to be effective. The Dictator's last bid to get the king's signature was made on 5 September 1927 at San Sebastián, where the monarch was spending his summer holidays. He then declared: 'I take it for granted that His Majesty the king, always ready to approve governmental propositions when he is convinced of their utility to the nation, will soon subscribe to the present one.'[72] Pushed into a corner, and hoping he might still find the right opportunity to return, for the sake of his crown, to solid constitutional ground, the king finally signed, on the fourth anniversary of the regime, that is almost two

[68] Ibid., 8, 9, 10, 12, 29 Nov. 1926.

[69] See Tusell, *La crisis*, pp. 196–201.

[70] *La Nación*, 23 Sept. 1926.

[71] Ben-Ami, *The Origins*, pp. 165–8.

[72] *La Nación*, 5 Sept. 1927.

years after Primo de Rivera had first launched the idea of summoning a corporative parliament,[73] the decree setting up the National Assembly. To save face with the friends of the parliamentary monarchy, the king explained that the Assembly was 'a step towards normal conditions'.[74]

This was not, however, the significance attributed to the Assembly decree by the Dictator and his spokesmen. According to a euphoric *La Nación*, Spain was witnessing the culmination of 'a revolutionary process without precedent in world history'.[75] Only slightly less pompous, the Dictator announced the conclusion of the *saneamiento* stage of his regime. 'The time has now come', he added, 'to re-structure national life.'[76] For the liberal opposition the convocation of the Assembly was a reason for great concern; it grasped the revolutionary implications of this step. *El Sol* explained this concern in the following terms: 'Even in Italy, the cradle of present dictatorships, parliament has not yet been abolished. It continues to function, and to be elected by universal suffrage, albeit only in appearance. Until this moment, Spain is the only country where parliamentary institutions have been replaced . . .'[77]

Far more pedestrian in style than the magniloquent oratory of the past months, the decree, signed on the fourth anniversary of the regime,[78] set up the nature and limitations of the long-heralded National Assembly. It was not to be a parliament; therefore, it would neither legislate nor share sovereignty with the king. Like Salazar's Asamblea Nacional, it rested on the principle that the government alone would be invested with power of legislation.[79] Therefore, its task would be one of 'assisting and advising' the government, that is it would lack real power of initiative. Its major and most important assignment was that of preparing 'a general and complete legislation', that is a constitution that, when the Assembly's three-year term was completed, would be presented to 'a sincere debate by public opinion'.

There was, then, some confusion as regards the status of the Assembly. Though certainly denied the power to defeat the government and legislate—its members would not have parliamentary immunity, but would enjoy fringe benefits such as free travel in

[73] *The Times*, 19 Nov. 1925.
[74] See the king's interview with Clara Candiani in AHN, P. G.
[75] *La Nación*, 12 Sept. 1927.
[76] *Gaceta*, 14 Sept. 1927.
[77] *El Sol*, 11 Oct. 1927.
[78] *Gaceta*, 14 Sept. 1927.
[79] F. C. C. Egerton, *Salazar, Rebuilder of Portugal* (London, 1943), pp. 235–7.

trains—it was constantly requested to discuss—the decree even said 'criticize'—and approve the government's policies, and eventually to prepare an entirely new constitution. The Assembly was also expected to look into the 'responsibilities' of all governments since the start of the Moroccan war in July 1909, to study and propose economies in public spending, and to expose whatever deficiencies and irregularities it might discover in the public administration. To underline the Assembly's 'consultative' rather than constituent nature—an emphasis demanded by the king—it was stipulated that all its labour would have eventually to be submitted to the approval of a truly legislative chamber that would succeed the Assembly after its three-year term had expired.

In order to exercise its various functions, the Assembly would hold four plenary sessions each month, from October to July. Its main tasks, however, were to be carried out in its eighteen different committees, each consisting of eleven members. The first and most important of these was the committee for the preparation of 'projects of constituent laws'.

The Assembly was also conceived as an instrument for underlining the regime's popular basis. Yanguas Messía, the Assembly's president, put it, in his inaugural speech, in the following way: 'It has always been a policy of the government presided over by General Primo de Rivera to look for civic collaboration . . . Initially, it tried to get it in a vague and general way; later it did it through quasi-consultative organs; and now it does it by widening the circle of the advisory elements and by elevating to national dimensions the functions attributed to them.'[80]

A professed believer in 'a parliament that would integrate the various classes',[81] the Dictator was now given the opportunity of creating it. The Assembly was then to consist of between 325 and 375 deputies divided into three main categories: the representatives of the state, the provinces, and the municipalities, those of the various 'activities, classes and values', and a major bloc of UP delegates.

It is noteworthy that, just as when he contemplated the transition to a civilian regime, so on the eve of the convocation of the Assembly, Primo de Rivera intensified his efforts to present the UP

[80] *Diario de Sesiones de la Asamblea Nacional*, no. 1, 10 Oct. 1927.

[81] *La Nación*, 5 Sept. 1926; Francisco Villanueva, *El momento constitucional* (Madrid, 1929), p. 11.

as the backbone of the new endeavour. He therefore now ordered the preparation of a new census of the party to make it ready to assume the position of the main 'parliamentary' bloc in the Assembly.[82] To assure the authenticity of this bloc, UP branches all over the country were asked either to reiterate their confidence in, or remove it from, their respective chiefs, taking great care to overlook the 'arrivistas' who had joined the party 'at the last hour'.[83] There is no evidence, however, that grass-root members exercised any real influence on the nature of their representation in the Assembly. This consisted of the forty-nine provincial chiefs who obtained their seats automatically.

As for the second sector in the Assembly, 'organic' representation was given to economic corporations, agricultural and industrial alike. It was stipulated that not only the employers but also workers and technical personnel in such corporations would get their share of seats in the new chamber. In this category of 'activities, classes and values' seats were also allocated to cultural associations, royal academies as well as to the various levels of the educational network.[84]

The bloc of the state's representatives in the Assembly was to consist mainly of ex-officio nominees, such as directors-general of state corporations, captains-general, the archbishops, the public prosecutor, the president of the High Court, the members of the *Consejo de Estado*, the governors of state banks, the presidents of the Councils of Labour and Instruction, as well as the president and the secretary-general of the UP. To emphasize the centralistic nature of the regime, the capital, Madrid, was to have the prerogative of a special representation consisting of the bishop, the captain-general, the governor, the president of the Diputación, the mayor, the rector of the university, and the president of the Somatén's organizing committee. A certain, limited degree of election was allowed for choosing the representatives of the municipalities. Each province was expected to send two deputies to the Assembly, one representing the province and the other the city councils.

The result of all this was that the government was in a position to control the lion's share of the seats, and consequently to produce a conformist 'governmental' chamber. An internal document of Primo

[82] *The Times*, 6, 10 Aug. 1927.

[83] *La Nación*, 19, 23 Aug. 1927.

[84] *Gaceta*, 14 Sept. 1927. As early as February, an inspector of primary education demanded to be appointed as the representative of the education sector in the forthcoming Assembly: AHN, P. G. Leg. 358; Sr Chacón to Primo. 2 Feb. 1927.

de Rivera's office described, in February 1928, the Assembly's structure in the following way:[85]

		ought	*are*	*vacancies*
State	State Representatives	58	57	1
	Ex-officio members	61	55	6
	Representatives of the Provinces	101	98	3
Unión Patriótica		49	49	—
Activities, Classes, and Values		131	124	7
		400	383	17

Hardly any effort is needed to prove that the category of State Representatives, and that of the ex-officio members, were an entirely governmental team. Nor were the 147 representatives of the provinces outside the government's control. Each province sent to the Assembly three deputies, that is the UP provincial chief, one delegate for all the Ayuntamientos, and a member, usually the president, of the Diputación Provincial. Both the latter and the municipalities were under the exclusive control of the civil governors. Moreover, the instructions sent by the government to the civil governors as regards the election of provincial deputies, as well as the reports of the governors,[86] show that whatever scope of free elections was provided for by the Assembly decree, in practice the government limited it by imposing its own men.[87] As for the 49 UP provincial chiefs, these were the professed 'friends' of the regime, precisely the reason that had enabled them in the first place to assume their position.

We remember that Primo de Rivera had expressed his wish that the UP should constitute the major parliamentary bloc in the Assembly. At first sight, it might seem as though the Dictator's wish did not materialize, as only 51 people were in the Assembly in their capacity as *Upetistas* (49 provincial chiefs, the president, and the secretary-general). But in reality, as it has already been pointed out elsewhere, the UP was able, through explicit governmental policy and thanks to the 'good services' of the civil governors, to infiltrate and eventually take over the local and provincial administration.[88]

[85] AHN, P. G. Leg. 305; 'Asamblea Nacional', 6 Feb. 1928.
[86] AHN, P. G. Leg. 177; 'Asamblea Nacional'.
[87] See also AHN, Gobernación, serie A, Leg. 4; a circular of Martínez Anido.
[88] See pp. 152–4.

One may safely conclude that most of, if not all, the 147 provincial deputies were either *Upetistas* or people close to UP circles.[89]

Even the 124 deputies representing the 'activities, classes and values' were to a great extent akin to the government, if only because its opponents simply refused to legitimize the regime by their presence in the Assembly.[90] Moreover, the decree setting up the rules for the new Chamber explicitly stated that these representatives of economic, social, and cultural associations were to be appointed to the Assembly by the government, rather than by their respective corporations.[91] Clearly, Primo's Chamber became the focal point for the regime's acquiescent servants, those who accepted its political philosophy of 'organized conduct'. Opposition was an unacceptable concept.

But not quite. The Dictator did not rule out the possibility that, in a respectful and 'constructive' way, the Assembly would provide a floor for conflicting ideas. He was prepared to have in the Assembly mildly oppositionist figures such as Gabriel Maura, Saínz Rodríguez, Juan de la Cierva, the moderate Catalanist Sr. Ayats, and the outspoken representative of the small peasants, Sr. Monedero. The reason was explained by Primo himself in a speech at the Assembly. Referring to Sr. Monedero, he said

> We have brought him here to the Assembly in order that he should bridle the propaganda that he makes outside this Chamber. We thought that here his words would cause no damage because they are listened to by discreet people and serene spirits, mediating men who are about to intervene in the preparation of the laws. But, outside this building, I must warn him that . . . he must abstain from uttering the same words he has pronounced here.[92]

In Primo's concept, then, the Assembly was to provide a dignified forum for a domesticated opposition to give expression to its grievances. The Dictator would even have non-monarchists in the Assembly, as he said in his inaugural speech, addressing himself to the king. In his endeavour 'to sweep away' the old system, he explained, he thought he should not insist that deputies should be monarchists. 'Many of the deputies assembled here', he explained, 'have never let the monarchist institution enter their political credo;

[89] María Teresa González Calbet, *Aproximación al estudio de la Asamblea Nacional Consultiva de Primo de Rivera (1927–1930)* (Memoria de Licenciatura, Madrid, April 1976), pp. 61–2.

[90] For those who refused, see *Diario de Sesiones*, no. 2, 20 Oct. 1927.

[91] *Gaceta*, 14 Sept. 1927.

[92] Primo, *Intervenciones*, pp. 144–5.

but this is no reason why they should not be considered good Spaniards.'[93] Indeed, this approach towards non-monarchists, the regime's acceptance of a quasi-opposition within its premises, the internal division of the Assembly between the state, the corporations, and the *partido único*, as well as the absolute control of the working mechanism of the Assembly by the government amounted to an almost absolute anticipation of Franco's Cortes.[94]

The Dictator's allusion to non-monarchists can also be seen as an appeal to the Socialists. He was especially keen on having a substantial representation of the working class in his National Assembly. Already in February 1924, when he first started to toy with the idea of reforming the old senate along the lines upon which he later set up the Assembly, he expressed his view that, from such a reformed Chamber 'the workers' representation ought not to be excluded. In the context of the social harmony we seek, the working class constitutes a basic factor upon which the economic organism ought to rest. A perfect organization of the Republic [*sic*] counsels that this force should be duly represented in the government of the state.'[95]

But Primo de Rivera's wish to have a socially balanced Assembly did not materialize. Its social physiognomy inclined heavily towards the middle classes. As previous research has already shown,[96] this was clearly manifested in the socio-professional division of the 400 deputies.[97] Primo's Assembly did not represent a radical breach with the old Cortes as far as its feature of an exclusively middle-class club was concerned. No new class was absorbed into the Assembly that had been absent in the old legislative chambers. The main novelty of the Assembly lay perhaps in the fact that the number of practising lawyers reflected a sharp drop in relation with the old Cortes. They were matched in number by the fashionable sector of what had become an era of public works, engineering (each group dominated 9.5 per cent of the seats). A highly interventionist and centralist regime which, therefore, encouraged the growth of the

[93] *Diario de Sesiones*, no. 1, 10 Oct. 1927.

[94] Cf. Linz, 'Una teoría del régimen autoritario', pp. 205–63; José Amodia, *Franco's Political Legacy. From Dictatorship to Façade Democracy* (London, 1977), pp. 92–117.

[95] AHN, P. G. Leg. 330: 'Renovación del Senado', 25 Feb. 1924.

[96] J. Linz, 'Spanish Cabinet and Parliamentary Élites: from the Restoration to Franco', unpublished paper, pp. 81–100. Tuñón de Lara, 'En torno a la Dictadura de Primo de Rivera', in *Cuadernos*, p. 30; González Calbet. *Aproximación al estudio de la Asamblea*.

[97] Full personal data on the deputies is easily obtainable from *Biografía y retratos*; *Gaceta*, 5 Oct. 1927; *Boletín de la Asamblea Nacional*, Dec. 1928, vol. 3, pp. 603–25.

bureaucracy,[98] it was likewise not surprising that it should have given a substantial share of seats to its civil servants. Nor could Primo de Rivera, in spite of his eagerness to shift his power-base from the barracks to the civilian community, overlook the military origins of his rule as well as the crucial impact that the goodwill of the army could have upon the viability of his regime. The high number of military (between 10 and 12.75% of the seats), admittedly not all in active service, that received seats in the Assembly reflected this link. It is likewise notable that, in spite of frequent allusions to the hostility of the aristocracy to Primo de Rivera, it was fairly well represented (about 8.25%).[99] A conspicuous deficiency of the Asamblea was the absence from its ranks of any prominent intellectual, though universities were represented by a fluctuating number of professors (4.5–5.5%). All along, it remained an unglamorous body devoid of intellectual legitimacy. Like many modern dictators, Primo preferred 'doers' to 'thinkers'; hence his admiration for engineers such as Guadalhorce, and technocrats like Calvo Sotelo.

One would have expected that a regime that professed to dwell on Costa's legacy of reactivating and giving political power to Spain's *fuerzas vivas* would have given the lion's share of the seats in its Assembly to the producing sector. This was not entirely the case (entrepreneurs 9–9.5%, manual labourers, less than 1%; agrarian and urban proprietors 7%), if only because Primo de Rivera was also committed to other non-productive groups, such as the bureaucracy and the military, both of which, as Franco was also to realize during his first years in power, had to be relied upon if the system was to live up to its 'apolitical' and 'technocratic' image.[100] One should also bear in mind that the rejection of the Assembly by the Socialists had the effect of reducing the role of the working class in the new Chamber to that played by the representatives of the Free and the Catholic Syndicates. The latter were represented in the Assembly by people such as Antonio Monedero Martín for the Confederación Nacional Católico-Agraria and the *Liga Nacional de Compesinos*, Mariano Puyuelo Morlán, Antonio Larrañaga for the Confederación Nacional de Sindicatos Libres, and by a score of officials of local syndicates.[101]

[98] See pp. 242–4.

[99] (Marqués de) Hoyos, pp. 224–5, observed that Primo enjoyed the support and even admiration of the provincial aristocracy; that of Madrid did not lose any opportunity to show him its disdain.

[100] Cf. Pi-Sunyer, pp. 64–73.

[101] *Biografía y retratos*.

None the less, it cannot be argued that the business community was under-represented in the Assembly. An examination of 100 Asambleistas out of the 124 that were appointed from the category of 'classes, activities and values' shows that about 62 of them belonged in one way or another to active economic sectors: 14 to agriculture and cattle-raising, 21 to industry, 9 to the banking and insurance network, 4 to commerce, 5 to employers' associations, and 9 to syndicates.[102] Moreover, prominent representatives of both the powerful Catalan and Basque business communities did receive seats in the Assembly. One could see in Primo's Chamber people such as Juan Antonio Güell (Marqués de Comillas), one of the wealthiest men in Spain; the powerful Catalan banker, José Garriga-Nogues (Marqués de Cabanes); the secretary-general of the Fomento del Trabajo Nacional and textile magnate, Pedro Güal Villalví; the wealthy *Umenista*, Alfonso Sala; the president of the Barcelona Chamber of Urban Property, Juan Pich y Pon; and a prominent member of the board of that same corporation, Gassó y Vidal; the president of the Confederación Gremial Española, José Ayats Surribas, Antonio Lucio Villegas, the director of the important metallurgical concern Duro-Felguera; Carlos Prast, the influential president of the Madrid Chamber of Commerce who received the post of the Assembly's deputy-president, and a score of lesser entrepreneurs.

Agriculture was represented in the Assembly by such people as Jesús Cánovas del Castillo, the secretary-general of the *Asociación de Agricultores de España* and the owner of olive plantations; Octavio Elorrieta y Astaza, a member of the *Junta de Acción Social Agraria* who was linked with afforestation concerns; Francisco Marín y Beltrán de Lis (Marqués de la Frontera), a landowner who was also the secretary-general of the General Association of cattle-raisers; García Guijarro, an outspoken defender of the Valencian orange-growers; Baamonde Gracient, representing the wheat-growers and the flour producers; and Conde de los Andes, representing the wine merchants. There were, of course, others who did not come to the Assembly as the representatives of any particular agricultural corporation, but were nevertheless landowners attentive to the needs of agrarian property.[103]

To gauge the extent to which the Assembly gave a fair repre-

[102] González Calbet, pp. 64–8.

[103] For all personal details on the deputies, see *Biografía y retratos*.

sentation to vested interests one should look, for example, at the composition of its tariffs committee. Not that Primo de Rivera needed any pressure to turn him into the fanatic protectionist that he was. But to make sure that protectionism was duly defended, the committee included the textile industrialist, Güal Villalví; the president of Altos Hornos, Sr. Merlló; Sr. Picavea and Sr. Aresti from the Papelera, and the eminent protectionist economist, Flores de Lemus.[104]

The Assembly also provided Primo de Rivera with a golden opportunity to demonstrate his conception of 'state feminism'.[105] Instead of 'liberal feminism', that was conducive to the disintegration of the sacred cell that was the family, he proposed to incorporate women into public institutions without undermining their fundamental role as symbols of motherhood and social stability. He believed they would bring with them to public life a sense of restraint, responsibility, and balance. This, he claimed, they had already shown in the way they exercised the suffrage, for the first time in Spain's history, in the national plebiscite. Now they were allocated nine seats in the Assembly. A colourful and curious innovation, their activities in the Chamber were reported with pride and delight by the regime's spokesmen. Of course, it was not 'politics' that they concerned themselves with in the new parliament. Natividad Domínguez de Roger, a correspondent of *La Nación*, devoted her energies to matters of education; Carmen Cuesta intervened on behalf of women's 'civil rights'; the female worker María López Monleón was said to have tabled an entire programme concerning the protection of women's labour; while Srta. Díaz Rabaneda dealt especially with issues such as absenteeism and emigration; and the Marquesa de la Rambla busied herself with a campaign for obligatory religious education.[106]

The National Assembly shared a common feature with the UP. Both were new beginnings that set out to break with old politics and to open channels of political participation for people previously unknown in politics. Though lesser figures of the old regime had definitely found their way into the key institutions of the new

[104] Op. cit.; for the protectionist views of Flores de Lemus, see his speech in *Boletín de la Asamblea*, 20 Jan. 1928.

[105] *La Nación*, 24 May 1928.

[106] Other women in the Assembly were María de Echarri, María de Perales, Lópe de Sagredo, Peresa Luzatti. For the role of women in the Assembly, see *Boletín de la Asamblea*, Jan. 1928; Vicente Gay, 'La intervención femenina', in *La Nación*, 21 Apr. 1928. See also ibid., 24 May 1928.

regime, it is fairly evident that they had encouraged the emergence of *homines novi*. About 84 per cent of the deputies in the National Assembly (325 out of 400) had never served before in the Cortes.[107] Those sixty-five deputies who had been in the past members of parliament were generally obscure figures. Among the best-known 'old politicians' one could find political fossils such as the two octogenarian ex-ministers of education, Saturnino Miguel Esteban Collantes, Conde de Esteban Collantes, and the Silvelista Carlos María Cortezo y Prieto. The most prominent figures of the old regime who agreed to serve in the Assembly were Juan de la Cierva and Gabriel Maura. Both shared an authoritarian vision of politics which they expected would be enshrined in the new constitution that the Assembly was called upon to prepare. The Liberal ex-minister and 'friend' of Romanones, Baldomero Argente, joined the Assembly in order to defend, as he said, the principles of economic liberalism in a regime that leaned too heavily towards protectionism.

But the political élite of the dynastic parties was careful to keep aloof from the Assembly. It was the small, frustrated local politicians of the old regime that were happy to find their way into Primo's parliament. Therefore, people could be found in the Assembly who had held minor local and provincial positions under the auspices of the old dynastic parties. Thus, for example, supported by the Albistas, Gaspar Rodríguez Pardo became the mayor of Valladolid in 1919; Eliseo González Negro had used the same leverage to become the deputy-mayor of Zamora; Justiano Fernández Campa y Vigil-Escalera got the post of civil governor of Santander under Maura's national government; José Gabilán had served as a Maurista city councillor in Madrid; Manuel Clavijo Carrillo had been a Ciervista deputy-mayor of Murcia; Federico Bassols Costa was known as an old-time cacique for both the Liberals and the Conservatives of Gerona; and Juan Rodríguez Muñoz was the Liberal cacique in the province of Málaga.[108]

Conceived as a non-'political', 'constructive' chamber, the Assembly was expected to break away from the useless rhetoric of the old Cortes; and though deputies were encouraged to 'advise' and 'criticize' the government, they were called to order when they became too outspoken. The rigid working procedures of the Assembly were the main instrument for stifling criticism.[109] To

[107] *La Nación*, 7 Oct. 1927.

[108] *Biografía y retratos*.

[109] *Gaceta*, 14 Sept. 1927; *El Sol*, 13, 20., 1 Nov. 1927.

begin with, it was up to the exclusive initiative of the Assembly's presidency,[110] after previous consultation with the government, to table issues for debate in the different sections. When the sections had reached their conclusions, rather than to the plenum of the Assembly, these were to be presented to the government, which would decide whether to open a general debate, to endorse the conclusions, or to shelve them altogether. And even when a general debate in the plenum had taken place, it was up to the presidency, in accordance with the government, to allow any voting at all. The government, moreover, would in no case commit itself to abide by the vote of the majority.[111]

And if this were not enough, the Dictator, who made a special effort to participate in the debates, was there to sneer at those deputies whose criticism of the government was, in his opinion, excessive. He dismissed them as fossilized residues of old parliamentarism. 'The Assembly', he reproached an over-eloquent deputy who had surpassed the twenty-minute limit fixed for parliamentary speeches, 'is not a place where useless arguments can be initiated by means of witty sayings or inopportune remarks, but rather one where work should be seriously, correctly, and patriotically performed.'[112] If the price was a 'boring Assembly', as those who looked back with longing to the days of oratory, intrigue, corruption, and inefficiency had insinuated,[113] it was worth paying, as long as the result was 'the end of *politiqueo*'.[114] Primo de Rivera certainly contributed to the general 'boredom' that surrounded the Assembly, by imposing strict censorship on its proceedings.[115] One could not even address oneself to the gallery any more.

As a whole, the issues brought forward by the government for discussion in the committees were mainly of a social and economic nature.[116] These included issues such as the preparation of a new penal code, the reform of leasehold contracts of urban premises, the government's decree regulating the protection of national industries,

[110] The presidency consisted of *Upetistas* and 'governmentalists' such as Yanguas, José Gabilán Andrés Gassó y Vidal, Vicente Gay, Juan Bautista Guerra, Carlos Prast, Srta. Carmen Cuesta; see *Boletín de la Asamblea Nacional*, vol. i, Jan. 1928.

[111] *Boletín de la Asamblea*, vol. i, Jan. 1928. See also ibid., vol. iii, 1928, pp. 603–25: 'Reglamento definitivo de la Asamblea'.

[112] Primo, *Intervenciones*, p. 339.

[113] Hurtado, ii, pp. 247–8; Maura, *Bosquejo*, p. 256.

[114] *Unión Patriótica*, 1 Nov. 1927.

[115] *El Sol*, 19 Jan. 1928.

[116] *La Nación*, 25 Nov. 1927, 19, 21 Jan. 1928, was delighted that such was the case.

a reform project of university studies, and some of the government's public-work enterprises.[117] Some of the conclusions reached by the different committees were endorsed by the government, sometimes after introducing slight modifications in them. Such was the case with the reforms introduced in the penal code, and the new system of industrial and commercial regulations promulgated in July 1929.[118] There were also cases when the government took the liberty of deciding against the views that predominated in a committee or in the plenum itself. Such, for example, was the case with the decree regulating the leasehold contracts of urban premises which imposed limits on the rights of proprietors that were unacceptable to most deputies. This decree, however, can be seen as a victory for the merchants and the industrialists in the Assembly who wanted to pay as low rents as possible for their premises.[119]

The Assembly was not always just an acquiescent forum where the lackeys of the regime could applaud its policies and give them popular legitimacy. On frequent occasions, Assembly members used the platform to attack official policies on issues such as regionalism, as did the Catalan deputy Sr. Ayats;[120] the rigid and 'controlled' working procedures of the Assembly, as did Gabriel Maura and Saínz Rodríguez on several occasions; tariffs, as did the Marqués de Rozalejo when he asked to extend to the silk industry the same degree of protection enjoyed by the rest of the textile sector; education, as did Saínz Rodríguez and Fernando Pérez Bueno; and the status of the lower clergy, as did the Archbishop of Valladolid. Four deputies had even voted against the 1929 national budget that was presented to the Assembly in December 1928.[121]

An examination of the *Diario de Sesiones* or the *Boletín* of the National Assembly would show that in the overwhelming majority of the cases in which deputies used the platform it was in order to express the particular grievances of their respective corporations.

[117] For the deliberations in the committees, see *Boletín de la Asamblea*, vol. i, 1928, pp. 253–61, 435–40; vol. ii, 1928, pp. 209–13, 398–400; vol. iii, 1928, pp. 183–6; vol. i, 1929, pp. 221–2, 435–7; vol. ii, 1929, pp. 213–16, 422–4; vol. iii, 1929, pp. 172–5.

[118] *Gaceta*, 14 Jan. 1928, 30 July 1929.

[119] *Boletín de la Asamblea*, vol. i, Jan. 1928; *Gaceta*, 15 Dec. 1927.

[120] José Ayats Surribas, *El problema de Cataluña ante la Asamblea Nacional Consultiva* (Barcelona, 1930).

[121] See the debates in *Boletín de la Asamblea*, vol. i, Jan. 1928; vol. iii, Dec. 1928; *The Times*, 22 Dec. 1927; 17 Jan., 27 June, 18 Dec. 1928. Unable to express freely his views on university issues, Saínz Rodríguez finally resigned his seat in the Assembly; see his *Testimonio*, pp. 112–16, 347–8.

Antonio Monedero would frequently come out to defend the small farmers of the Liga Nacional de Campesinos; Gual Villalví would do the same on behalf of industry and protectionism. The latter was an issue frequently put forward by representatives of agrarian interests such as Luis García Guijarro for the orange-growers of Valencia, Fernando Palanco and González de Gregorio for the wheat-growers of Castile, Sr. Solés for the olive-growers of the south, and Marqués de la Frontera for the cattle-raisers. Protection was also the preferred topic of representatives of the heavy industry of the North, such as Lucio Villegas. A representative of electric concerns, Sánchez Cuervo, was there to demand state assistance for hydroelectric plants. Mariano Puyuelo concerned himself with an attempt to convince the plenary session of 18 January 1928 that the Sindicatos Libres, whom he represented in the Assembly, provided the perfect framework for the organization of the entire working class of Spain. It was also no surprise that he should have questioned the special prerogatives accorded to the Socialists in the Comités Paritarios. The deputy-president of the Assembly, Carlos Prast, who was also the head of the Madrid Chamber of Commerce, was indefatigable in his uphill struggle for free trade. Even the Somatén had its spokesman in the Assembly, Quintiliano Saldaña, an author of a book on the Somatén, who was outspoken in his demands for special privileges for the members of his institution.[122]

3. *A Constitution 'Clean of Exotic Imitations'*

In spite of the domination of the Assembly by corporate interests and economic debates, Primo de Rivera's Assembly will probably best be remembered by the constitution it elaborated. Surely, this was no secondary task it had been called upon to carry out. In his inaugural speech, Primo had made abundantly clear that the Assembly's main mission was to give 'a new constitutional structure to the country'.[123]

It was in June 1928 that the Dictator gave as definite a shape as he was able to to his new deal.[124] In a twenty-point political programme, which he then published, he called for the elaboration of an entirely

[122] See the debates in *Boletín de la Asamblea*, Jan., Mar., Dec. 1928, July 1929.

[123] Primo, *Intervenciones*, p. 14.

[124] This was, however, heralded much earlier; see an article inspired by the Dictator in *La Nación*, 12 Feb. 1926. For the new constitutional precepts, cf. ibid., 22 June 1928; *The Times*, 25 June 1928; *El Republicano*, 20 July, 5 Sept. 1928.

new constitution based on a single Chamber to be elected through corporative suffrage. The new constitution would sanctify the precepts of 'national unity' and 'state sovereignty', as opposed to the 1876 concept of the co-sovereignty of king and people. The monarchy was not even mentioned in the whole programme. It is conspicuous also that neither the crown nor the people nor the nation were presented as the institution to which the army—so far considered by King Alfonso as his private patrimony—should be subordinate. The army was presented as the 'efficient arm of the *State*'. The Dictator, after having contemplated with fictitious modesty how the UP pursued his personality cult, imbued his party with yet another fashionable Fascist tenet, the supremacy of the State. This up-to-date constitution would have to be approved by a national plebiscite. Direct democracy would thus replace the decaying politics of the system based on parliamentary representation.

The UP, explained the Dictator, would not confine its corporatist programme only to the system of political representation. As with Fascism, it was expected that 'all the activities of national life should be organized along corporatist lines'. The party system of the future would certainly be that of a one-party state. 'It is only our League that would enjoy [official] protection and would be imbued by the government with doctrinal belligerence.' The Socialist Party would, as the only exception, be tolerated, but only as long as it kept aloof from politics, and confined itself to its social and economic tasks. The Dictator had no vision of some kind of two-party system. The Socialist Party would not be expected 'to alternate' in power with the UP; it would be the domesticated working-class *point d'appui* of an otherwise bourgeois dictatorship.

That the Decalogue—a series of commentaries written by the UP ideologue, Pemán—unlike Primo de Rivera's twenty points, which overlooked the monarchy altogether—subscribed to the formula of a 'constitutional monarchy' was not to be viewed as an endorsement of 'vulgar', worn-out parliamentary concepts. What was meant by 'constitution', Pemán explained, was 'a respect for Spain's tradition', or rather for its 'internal constitution', the 'real way of being of the nation's organism'. A constitution was not a set of laws democratically arrived at, but the very organic essence of a nation.[125]

[125] José María Pemán, 'Comentarios al decálogo de la Unión Patriótica', *La Nación*, 17, 24 Aug., 20 Sept., 8, 31 Oct., 29 Nov. 1928; 26 Feb., 4, 8 Mar. 1929.

Not surprisingly, the two most outspoken *Asambleistas*, as far as the need to adapt Spain's constitution to 'the spirit of the times' was concerned, were the UP ideologues José María Pemán and José Pemartín. As members of the constituent committee, they were allowed a unique opportunity to implement their vision of a New State. 'A solution twentieth-century style' was needed, one that would seal Spain's integration into the all-European process of 'revision of ideas'. They called for the 'smashing of the idols of the past', and the complete rejection of the 'superstitious fascination with the liberal spirit of 1876'.[126]

A reflection of the importance attributed by Primo de Rivera to the constituent committee was that, contrary to the other committees which were generally manned by obscure *Asambleistas*, it consisted of the 'luminaries' of the Assembly.[127] Significantly, the most prominent figures of the old regime to have collaborated with the new one, Juan de la Cierva and Gabriel Maura, were also members of this important committee. They both went to great pains, in their respective memoirs, to conceal the fact that it was their authoritarian spirit and their will to do away with the liberal precepts of the old constitution which were the motives that had brought them to the Assembly in the first place.[128] It was, after all, Gabriel Maura who declared from the rostrum of the Assembly that 'the present Dictatorship is as legitimate as any other government in any other regime. Moreover, I am convinced that, at the present moment, no regime other than a dictatorship is possible in Spain.'[129] The two other ex-Mauristas in the constituent committee, Antonio Goicoechea and César Silió, were made of a clay similar to Maura's. They had both belonged to that wing of the Partido Social Popular which had broken away from the supposedly more liberal group

[126] Pemán, *El hecho*, pp. 330–41; Pemartín in *La Nación*, 28 Oct., 22 Nov., 30 Dec. 1927; 28 Jan., 3, 8 Feb., 9 Mar., 11 June 1928. Similar views on the future constitution were advanced by other *Upetista* luminaries, see, for example, Vicente Gay and Juan de Castilla, ibid., 11, 13 Feb., 10 Mar. 1928.

[127] For the members of the constituent committee, see *La Nación*, 15–22 July 1929. 'Luminaries' were Yanguas, Ramiro de Maeztu, Victor Pradera, Mariano Puyelo Morlán (secretary-general of the Sindicatos Libres), José Pemartín, Jose María Pemán.

[128] Cf. Juan de la Cierva, *Notas de mi vida* (Madrid, 1955), pp. 300–5; Gabriel Maura, *Recuerdos de mi vida* (Madrid, n.d.), pp. 184–5. See also AHN, Gobernación, serie A, Leg. 47; governor of Murcia to the minister of the interior relating how Cierva campaigned for the plebiscite among his friends.

[129] *Folletín*, pp. 739–40.

headed by Ángel Ossorio, in order to collaborate with the Dictatorship.[130]

The ex-Mauristas in the constituent committee were the staunchest protagonists of an entirely new constitution. Gabriel Maura did not accept the view of the dynastic politicians that the 1876 document was simply in a state of temporary suspension. As far as he was concerned, it had 'failed', 'broken down', like the parliamentary system itself. Consequently, he proposed a total separation between the executive and the legislative powers, as well as the creation of a compact advisory body to assist the monarch in co-ordinating the functioning of the various powers.[131] Goicoechea, who was consistently edging towards fascism, was even more outspoken than Maura. An admirer of Mussolini, he wanted to see the Spanish Dictatorship moving closer to the Italian model. No cosmetic reform of the parliamentary system would be acceptable to him. His formula was that of a durable dictatorship that would run the country with the assistance of a government of 'selected minorities' and a corporate Chamber. National sovereignty and universal suffrage were utterly rejected.[132] It was the radical approach of the Mauristas,[133] rather than La Cierva's view that only a limited reform of the 1876 constitution was needed,[134] that would win the day in the committee. Consequently, both La Cierva and the Marqués de Santa Cruz voted against the final draft that came out of the deliberations.[135] The vision that gained the upper hand was that of a new state, rather than that of a patched-up reform of the old one.

The new constitution was first made public on 5 July 1929.[136] Democratic principles such as the sovereignty of the people and the separation of powers were conspicuously absent from it. It endorsed three fundamental and immutable principles: the unity of the State, the Monarchy, and the King's power to legislate together with the

[130] For the views and the tendencies among the members of the committee, see Eduardo Ortega y Gasset, 'El fracaso del proyecto de constitución', in *Hojas Libres*, 1 Feb. 1928; García Canales, pp. 23, 99–101.

[131] See Maura's introduction to Jerónimo García Gallego, *La quiebra de nuestro sistema político y la gestación de un régimen nuevo* (Madrid, 1928).

[132] Antonio Goicoechea, *La crisis del constitucionalismo español* (Madrid, 1926).

[133] The common Maurista posture was manifested throughout the committee's deliberations, see AHN, P.G. 305–6.

[134] La Cierva in *Boletín de la Asamblea*, vol. i, Jan. 1928.

[135] E. Ortega, 'Fracaso del proyecto de constitución', *Hojas Libres*, 1 Feb. 1928.

[136] The complete text can be found in *Boletín de la Asamblea*, vol. iii, 1929, pp. 1–136.

Cortes. Moreover, it was upon the king rather than on the Cortes that the power to initiate constitutional reform was conferred; and no law could be promulgated by the Cortes without being ratified by the crown. The king was also the supreme head of the executive in possession of full powers to appoint and dismiss the ministers, and even to interfere with the judiciary. The king was thus both an 'extra-constitutional' and 'constitutional' figure at the same time.

As far as the legislative power was concerned, an important innovation was the articles establishing the *Consejo del Reino*. Like a similar organ in Franco's constitutional framework, this was to be a kind of Upper Chamber. It was to consist of between fifty and seventy-five members, half of them elected on a corporative basis and half appointed for life from among the social and administrative establishment of the state. Its task would be that of 'examining the laws approved by the Cortes' and assisting the king and the government 'in whatever consultations it might be entrusted with by either or both'. Rather than a defender of the people's sovereignty, the *Consejo del Reino* was conceived as a branch of the executive.

Nor did the Cortes proposed in this document constitute an encouragement to democratic minds. Only half of its members were to be elected by universal suffrage, while the other half was to be partly appointed by the king and partly elected by professional and cultural institutions, thus investing even the Lower Chamber with corporate traits. A conclusion drawn by *El Debate* was that the historic aristocracy was about to be replaced by a 'cultural and economic' élite.[137] Certainly, it was not the sovereign power of parliament that was to be enhanced by this new deal. The new Cortes was not even given the authority to scrutinize the actions of the executive; the government was made unaccountable to parliament. The legislative functions of the Cortes were not edifying either. Although it possessed, together with the king, the right to initiate legislation, there were spheres, such as foreign policy, constitutional reform, defence matters, and issues 'implying a reduction of taxation or an increase in public expenditures' from the discussion of which the Cortes was totally excluded. And any of its decisions could in any case be vetoed either by the *Consejo del Reino* or by the king.

The independence of the judiciary was also limited. Article 97 stated that it was the supreme court's right to appoint and dismiss

[137] *El Debate*, 25 Jan. 1930.

judges, and supervise the work of the tribunals, 'when this right is not entrusted either by the constitution or the laws to other entities'. This meant that a simple law was enough to turn the supervision of the judiciary into a function of the executive. The king's right to interfere with the judicial system was in fact enshrined in article 2 of the 'Organic Law of the Executive Power'. It stated that 'the king will have to discuss with his ministers the measures that he should take as participant in the exercise of legislative and judicial powers'.

The people were not mentioned even once in this constitutional draft. Sovereignty resided in the *State*. Although Spain was defined as 'a Nation constituted into a politically unitary State', this did not imply that the Nation exercised the sovereignty. It had irretrievably delegated it to a unitary and indisputably monarchist state. The citizen rights were also of a very limited character. For example, article 23 recognized the government's right to open the private correspondence of its subjects; article 22 made it a *duty* of the citizen 'to procure the discovery of public crimes', and, in fact, to participate actively in the persecution of the political opposition to the regime. The rights of professional, social, and cultural associations, as well as the articles that protected the citizen's right to 'freely express his ideas and opinions', could be arbitrarily annulled by the total suspension of constitutional guarantees, when the government decided on emergency measures.[138]

The anti-democratic spirit of the constitutional draft was compatible with Primo de Rivera's views. The Dictator had displayed great interest in the work of the constituent committee, and on various occasions had proposed guide-lines to its members. For example, he put special emphasis on the national and political unity of the state, while recommending a degree of municipal and provincial decentralization along the lines of his Municipal and Provincial Statutes. The negation of national sovereignty, the supremacy of the state, the latter's intervention in the economy and in society, and the organization of both along corporative lines were all basic precepts recommended to the committee by Primo de Rivera himself.[139]

[138] For an evaluation of the proposed document, see Enrique Martí Jara, *El rey y el pueblo* (Madrid, 1929), pp. 206–315. The most complete analysis of the constitutional draft can be found in García Canales, pp. 109–552.

[139] Raul Morodó, 'La proyección constitucional de la Dictadura: la Asamblea Nacional Consultiva', in *Boletín de Ciencias Políticas*, nos. 13–14, Aug.–Dec. 1973, pp. 89–91.

Yet, rather than a dictatorial diktat and in spite of its strong authoritarian flavour, the new constitution reflected a compromise between the residual liberalism of some members in the committee, and the corporatist, traditionalist concepts defended by others. Especially identified with the latter, Primo could not bring himself to endorse the entire document. He found some fundamental discrepancies in it, which he presented to the plenum of the Assembly in the bluntest possible terms. He rejected the bicameral provisions and called for one single chamber 'integrated by popular representations, some elected by direct suffrage, and others through professions and classes'. He also wanted a certain number of deputies to have their seats ex officio. He was likewise opposed to the excessive prerogatives granted by the proposed constitution to the Moderating Power. Thus, for example, he did not think that the king should appoint the prime minister; the latter should be directly elected by the Chamber, and should be invested 'with supreme attributions'.[140]

One cannot escape the conclusion that the *Consejo del Reino*, the prerogatives of the monarchy, and the excessive dependence of the government and its head on the king's will were Primo de Rivera's main reservations. As early as January 1928, he had warned the constitutional committee against granting the king too much authority. 'One of the errors of old politics', he wrote to Gabriel Maura, 'was to let the king play too big a role.'[141] Clearly, Primo was reinforced in his objections to the royal prerogatives by Mussolini's reservations with regard to the new Spanish constitution. Consequently, he confessed to the Italian ambassador in Madrid that, 'contrary to the cautious and wise Italian king [the Spanish monarch] has a tendency to act on his own initiative, and, therefore, his independence of action should be restricted'.[142] In an official note issued on the sixth anniversary of his *coup d'état*, Primo brought into the open his reservations. He pointed out 'the disequilibrium of powers' inherent in the new constitutional draft. It had, he said, 'cast upon the royal power too heavy a burden of functions', which would underline even further its position as an 'unaccountable

[140] Cf. Primo, *Intervenciones*, pp. 63–73; Primo in *La Nación*, 21 Feb. 1928; José María Pemán, *Mis almuerzos con gente importante* (Barcelona, 1970), pp. 33–6; Calvo, pp. 337–8.

[141] Primo to Gabriel Maura, 21 Jan. 1928, in Maura Archive, Leg. 86.

[142] *I Documenti Diplomatici Italiani*, seventh series, vol. viii, Medici to Grandi, 15 Nov. 1929, no. 156.

authority'. He accepted the 'moderating' nature of the king's power; he rejected its 'ruling' implications.[143]

Primo de Rivera, however, either failed to understand or lacked the imagination and the revolutionary decisiveness to implement the suggestion inherent in Mussolini's reservations: to turn the king into a symbolic and representative figure, while assuming for himself the 'excessive prerogatives' granted to the crown by the constitution. That the Dictator was unable, or unwilling, to impose on the country a constitution of his own making, was due to a complexity of reasons and to an accumulation of difficulties that were eventually to bring down his whole regime, and which will be dealt with in the last chapters of the present work. At this stage, it can be asserted that Primo de Rivera was conscious of the advantages of a system that combined parliament with Dictatorship. The general, who came to power with nothing but 'parenthetical' intentions, found himself gradually developing a political philosophy which, if stripped of its impulsive, simplistic, and naïve overtones, amounted to a discernible anticipation of a Spanish *Estado Novo*.

[143] *El Debate*, 13 Sept. 1929.

CHAPTER VII

Dictatorship and 'Development'

LIKE his 'regenerationist' mentors, Primo de Rivera was permeated with a deep frustration at Spain's economic *retraso*. The enhancement of production, the development both of the nation's economic resources and of its infrastructure, were essential if Spain was to be incorporated into the modern times.[1] As far as Primo was concerned, no regime was better equipped than a Dictatorship to put into practice the reform programme of the Aragonese 'regenerationist', Costa, announced in the two words 'schools' and 'larder'.[2] The Spanish bourgeoisie and the liberal state had failed to propel the country into the twentieth century; it was, then, up to a centralizing, coercive state to respond to the challenge, indeed to assume the historical tasks of the bourgeoisie.

But notwithstanding the evident increase of industrial production during the Dictatorship, a direct result of the reactivation of the economy by substantial government investment in public works, mainly in road construction, in public buildings, and in the overhauling of the railway system, Primo's was not the grandiose modernizing enterprise that his panegyrists claimed it to be. Rather, it was a fairly measured, even incipient, essay in development, or, should we say *fomento*, to use the more modest Spanish term. Perhaps a somewhat more remarkable feature of Primo's economic deal lay, however, in the fact that it rested on, and was instrumental in, formulating a fairly coherent economic ideology for the Spanish Right that was based on a 'productive' and nationalist approach as well as on corporatist and organic institutional schemes.

1. *Economic Nationalism and Big Business*

Autarkism and the suppression of liberal principles such as free trade and free competition reached unprecedented dimensions under the Dictatorship. Economic nationalism as such was no novelty in Spain, and throughout the Great War it even received substantial

[1] J. Costa, *Reconstitución y Europeización de España* (Huesca, 1924).
[2] Primo in *The Times*, 24 Sept. 1929.

encouragement.[3] But nothing that had previously been done was so absolutely interventionist and so zealously nationalist as were the policies of Primo de Rivera. They amounted, in the words of *La Vanguardia*, to a 'Spanish-Monroe doctrine—Spain for the Spaniards'.[4] Furthermore, never before had a regime in Spain been so consistent in its doctrinal defence of interventionsm. Primo de Rivera, as his finance minister was to observe, 'stimulated state interventionism with real unction'.[5] Economic liberalism was just as much anathema as was political liberalism; this was a profession of faith, not a capitulation to pressure groups. 'Nothing is free today in social life', commented *La Nación*. The 'tutelary action of the state', it argued, 'should embrace all the manifestations of national life'.[6]

Primo de Rivera would not have subscribed to the view of Salazar, himself hardly a liberal, who said in the thirties that he considered 'the modern tendency of unlimited state intervention to be a mistaken policy', and that 'the new economic nationalism' was 'so remote from the true interests of the nation'.[7]

Primo was a fanatic interventionist. He explained his philosophy in a speech before the National Assembly:

> Those who listen to me with attention may by now understand that I am insisting, each time more strongly, upon the theory of State intervention, because I believe that, under all circumstances, States, and especially modern States where the interests are so complex and contradictory, need to live under strict management . . . A government, besides its essential function to govern the country . . . is more than anything else a big board of directors. In the economic sphere, the government, with all its organs and advisory bodies, is the *consejo de administración* of the nation, and it should never allow either ravings or ambitions and egoism to impose themselves. Rather, it should see to it that everybody marches according to the rules . . .[8]

In Primo's concept, economic 'crisis' was an intrinsic product of a century of liberalism. Corporatism and interventionism were an indispensable safety-belt against 'ruinous competition'. The individual effort as such was in Primo's opinion of a 'plethoric' and 'overflowing' nature, and therefore tended only to enhance 'a competition which, when it is not illicit, is incapable and inconvenient'.[9]

[3] Roldán, *La formación*, vol. i, pp. 323–97.
[4] *La Vanguardia*, 14 Mar. 1929.
[5] Calvo, p. 260.
[6] *La Nación*, 16 July 1926, 8 Feb. 1927.
[7] Salazar, pp. 18–19, 122.
[8] Primo de Rivera, *Intervenciones*, pp. 98–9.
[9] Pemán, *El hecho*, p. 201–2.

Yet it was not only a problem of convenience or economic expediency that dictated interventionism, but also the need 'to bolster up our collective economic personality as against that of other countries'. In fact, the economic system was conceived by the regime as a battlefield. It was there that 'the most terrible battles', 'more disastrous than the bloody ones', were said to be taking place.[10] Everywhere, claimed a member of the Council of National Economy, 'the concept of national economy', and the awareness that 'every particular nation is a separate and perfectly defined productive and consuming entity' were being recognized. 'Economic independence', he said, had become the paramount national ideal. In this economic world war in which the principle of international co-operation was utterly neglected, it was crucial to Spain's very existence

> to bolster up national production even at the expense of great collective sacrifices, to exalt [its] productive activities, to bring about a harmonious development of all the resources of national wealth, to conquer new branches of production, to protect, regulate, and shelter [its] industries, to watch with great care [its] agriculture, to guard [its] cattle-raising, to stimulate [its] mines, to encourage [its] fishing industry . . .[11]

Primo de Rivera's views coincided absolutely with this approach. He professed 'an enthusiastic economic nationalism', which his finance minister, Calvo Sotelo, confessed to have favoured 'with the warmest zeal'. Both also agreed that those industries should be nationalized whose raw material was Spanish, and which were indispensable to Spain's political independence.[12] Such industries were, as a matter of course, to receive even greater favours—such as a reduction of taxes, for example—than the others.[13]

Spain's economy was then to be brought under an unprecedentedly high level of *dirigisme* and tutelage. State-assisted monopolies and a wide range of excessively bureaucratized regulating committees supervised economic activities down to their most minute details.[14]

Within the framework of the government's tutelary schemes, special attention was accorded, through strict supervision, to the

[10] José María Valverde, 'Amemos lo español', *La Nación*, 3 May 1927.

[11] José María Valverde, 'Unidad orgánica de la economía nacional', in *La Nación*, 4 Mar. 1927. For the Dictatorship's nationalistic approach to the economy, see Gregario Fernández Díaz, *La orientación nacionalista de la economía* (Barcelona, 1927).

[12] Calvo, p. 260.

[13] See a decree in *Gaceta*, 25 May 1926.

[14] See a list of committees in Román Perpiñá Grau, *De estructura económica* (Madrid, 1952), pp. 31–2.

promotion of industry. As early as April 1924, a special decree was promulgated that set up a series of auxiliary devices 'in order to stimulate the creation of new industries and to further develop those already existing'. Special favours would be granted to those industries whose products were directly related to national defence. In any case, state assistance would be given to firms only when their governing bodies were exclusively Spanish, at least 75 per cent of their capital came from Spanish sources, no less than 80 per cent of their personnel were local, and their sources of energy and other raw material were, whenever possible, Spanish. All such subsidized industries would, as a matter of course, 'be subject to the inspection of the Section for the Defence of Production of the Council of National Economy'.[15]

Also created in 1924, the Council of National Economy was the supreme instrument for the defence of national production,[16] a model for the future protagonists of a nationalist economy in the CEDA.[17] A strongly protectionist body,[18] presided over by the Dictator himself, it was only natural that it should include among its eighty-two members staunch protectionists such as the big magnates of Catalan and Basque industry, people such as the Conde de Caralt, Domingo Sert, and Federico Echevarría, and representatives of powerful agrarian interests, such as Luis García Guijarro and the Marqués de la Frontera.[19] It was indeed a feature of many of Primo de Rivera's interventionist organs that they were manned by representatives of the economic sectors directly concerned with the sphere of activities of each such institution. Hence, they became the channel through which industrialists and agriculturists would advance their particular interests. It can be argued that Primo's interventionism, inasmuch as it reflected an attempt to impose a planned economy from above for the sake of the national interest, amounted to a system for the defence of Spanish capitalism and the country's landowners.

All the various committees concerned with industry were in effect

[15] *Gaceta*, 26 Apr. 1924.

[16] For the CNE, its faculties and activities, see the evidence of its vice-president Sebastián Castedo, 'Un ideario económico', in *Actividad Financiera*, 20 Aug. 1925. *The Economist*, 26 Nov. 1927, was obviously concerned with the adverse effects that such an institution was having on British exports.

[17] Montero, vol. ii, p. 156.

[18] Cf. *Gaceta*, 11 Mar. 1929.

[19] *Memoria de la actuación del Consejo de Economía Nacional en el año 1927* (Madrid, 1928).

only the particular branches of a central, controlling leviathan, the Regulating Committee of Industrial Production, whose terms of reference explicitly stated that 'no society or industrial concern could be established, expanded or even transferred to some other locality without being properly authorized by the Committee to do so'.[20] The Committee would also control the volume of industrial production, prices, marketing policy, and the acquisition of machinery. Primo de Rivera viewed this organ as a last-ditch attempt to save Spanish industry from the whims of the free play of economic forces.[21] In effect, like similar measures enacted in Italy in 1933,[22] Primo's Regulating Committee amounted to a defence of big, established concerns against the competition of new and smaller plants. For the liberal *El Sol*, the creation of the Committee marked 'such an intensive degree of state interventionism that one might safely see it as a decisive step towards a regime of state socialism'.[23] So much so that even Calvo Sotelo started to question the wisdom of his master's interventionist zeal.[24]

But Primo was adamant. 'What stands between [the Regulating Committee of Industrial Production] and its opponents', he said in response to the reservations put forward by the *Círculo de la Unión Mercantil e Industrial*, an association of small and medium-sized entrepreneurs who rejected intervention as being exclusively favourable to big business, 'is a matter of principle, of doctrine. It is the government's conviction that the solution [to our economic problems] lies in a greater degree of state interventionism in all the facets of national life.'[25] The creation in November 1928 of a new Ministry of National Economy to co-ordinate all the services, advisory bodies, and controlling devices that had mushroomed since the coming of the Dictatorship to power was the peak of an ascending movement towards an optimal control of the economy.[26] Primo's was of course not an absolutist command economy—not even the Stalinist system was able to live up to such an ideal image[27]—but an attempt to curtail the liberal economy as incompatible with a developmental dictatorship, and to bring about a greater concentration of business by shielding powerful interests at the expense of the smaller entrepreneurs.

[20] *Gaceta*, 5 Nov. 1926.
[21] Primo, *Intervenciones*, p. 138.
[22] C. Schmidt, *The Corporate State in Action* (London, 1939), p. 159.
[23] *Folletín*, p. 326.
[24] Calvo, pp. 258–60.
[25] Primo in *Folletín*, p. 325.
[26] *The Times*, 5 Nov. 1928.
[27] Cf. T. Dunmore, *The Stalinist Command Economy. The Soviet State Apparatus and Economic Policy 1945–1953* (London, 1980).

The price of development, Primo reckoned, was to subsidize, heavily if necessary, what he maintained was the vehicle of prosperity, namely big business. Spanish capitalism, the powerful financial groups, and the close political allies of the regime profited directly from Primo's brand of economic nationalism, especially from his preference for monopolistic concerns. Primo left the country in no doubt that it was his policy 'to support and assist the big companies, from which spring the sources of our national wealth'.[28] The enemies of the system, smaller entrepreneurs and liberal minds, attacked state intervention as being frequently inefficient and always too costly.[29] But those who, like the economist Perpiñá Grau, thought beyond their own private interests, gave certain credit to the state for bringing about a degree of rational concentration of Spanish business, which private initiative had been unable to achieve. Such 'a change in Spain's approach to economic organization'[30] was, admittedly, accompanied by all kinds of abuses. Corruption tends to be a by-product of economic systems based on state control and subsidies and on a proliferation of bureaucracies. Primo de Rivera's Spain was no exception. Almost every concession of a monopoly was accompanied by a certain largess at the expense of public funds, and by 'an abuse of diets, gratuities and an accumulation of posts and salaries'.[31]

Powerful shipping companies, such as the Transatlantic and the Transmediterranean, received government subsidies that previous governments had continuously denied them.[32] That Sr. Dominé, the owner of the Transmediterranean, should have paid for the special trains that brought the crowds to Madrid for the December 1924 pro-regime demonstrations reflected his excellent 'working relations' with the Dictatorship, which accorded his company preferential treatment.[33] The Railway Statute of 1924 resulted in deeper commitments by the government to invest in the railway system[34] in such a way that always assured the companies a margin of profits at the expense of public funds, commuters, and merchants.[35] The largess in dealing with the railway companies was indeed exceptional.

[28] Quoted in M. Rubio, p. 144.

[29] See below, p. 322–4.

[30] R. Perpiñá Grau, 'Cómo se racionaliza España', *El Financiero*, Nov. 1930, pp 11–13.

[31] Marcelino Domingo, *¿Qué espera?*, pp. 149–52.

[32] *Gaceta*, 18 Dec. 1923, 6 Apr. 1925.

[33] *Hojas Libres (extraordinario)*, in Romanones Archive, Leg. 2, no. 48.

[34] *The Economist*, 26 June 1926.

[35] Dalmacio Iglesias, *Política de la Dictadura. La carestía de la vida: sus causas y remedios* (Barcelona, 1930), pp. 67–71.

70,000 free shares were distributed to brokers who mediated between the government and the British company that received the concession to construct the Ontaneda–Calatayud railway.[36] Lionel Phillips, the head of a group of British investors who received this concession, did not have any reason to complain either. 'The contract price was fair and profitable', he said.[37] The milking of public funds by this company was to continue well into the later years of the Dictatorship.[38]

Generous subsidies were also granted to those companies which were engaged in public works. For example, the company *Canalización y Fuerzas del Guadalquivir*, on whose board of directors there figured, conspicuously, the future minister of development Conde de Guadalhorce, was granted in April 1925 the right to exploit the hydraulic energy of the Guadalquivir river between Córdoba and Seville. The government committed itself to financing 50 per cent of the company's expenses.[39] A similar subsidy was received in March 1926 by the *Compañia de las marismas del Guadalquivir* which, in addition, was exempted from the profits tax.[40] Especially favourable treatment was also accorded to the *Unión Española de Explosivos* for its exploitation of the falls of the Carrión river, and to the *Electro Metalúrgica Ibérica* for developing the falls of the Alberche river.[41] It was no mere coincidence that such a favour should be shown to a company on whose board of directors the Minister of War, the Duke of Tetuan, was a member.[42] The Duke of Tetuan, as the upright Conservative ex-prime minister Sánchez Guerra was later to note with indignation, 'was a poor man when he entered office', but upon his death he was in a position to bequeath to his family the sum of four million pesetas.[43]

The Hispano-Portuguese Society for Electric Traction presided over by another friend of the regime, the Basque businessman Horacio Echevarrieta, who had been used by Primo de Rivera as a peace mediator with Abd-el-Krim, was conceded in August 1926 the authority to exploit, in co-operation with the Portuguese government, the falls of the Duero river. *The Eléctrica de Castilla*, owned by the financially powerful Urquijo family, received in April 1927 highly favourable conditions for its commitment to construct

[36] Maura, *Bosquejo*, pp. 343–4.
[37] *The Times*, 30 Sept. 1924.
[38] *El Sol*, 26 Feb. 1927.
[39] *Gaceta*, 29 Apr. 1925.
[40] Ibid., 5 Mar. 1926.
[41] Ibid., 25, 26 June 1926.
[42] Maura, *Bosquejo*, p. 184.
[43] López de Ochoa, p. 161.

the La Toba dam in the Júcar river. And in August 1928 a team of investors, among them the Marqués de Argelita, the Conde de Torrubia, Carlos Benjumea, the brother of the minister of development, and the Conde de San Antolín de Sotillo, was granted a heavy subsidy for the construction of the motorways Madrid–Valencia, Madrid–Irún, and Oviedo–Gijón. Even General Sanjurjo was to have his share in the generosity shown by the Dictatorship towards its opulent friends. An airways company owned by the Loring firm—the pioneer of Spanish aviation which also monopolized the construction of aircraft for the government—and presided over by Sanjurjo was granted in January 1929 the monopoly of air transportation in Spain. Martínez Baldrich, a son of the minister of the interior, received the monopoly of rat extermination and works of disinfection throughout the country.[44]

An especially scandalous concession that violated all established norms was that granted to the merchant adventurer, the millionaire Juan March, to monopolize the tobacco trade in Morocco. A notorious contrabandist was elevated by the Dictator to the status of an altruistic patriot. 'Whatever the origins of his huge fortune may be, one thing is certain', assured the general, 'Mr Juan March has put his wealth at the directory's disposition for patriotic and charitable endeavours.' But Juan March was not exactly a saint. The compensations he received for his 'display of patriotism' were by no means slight. The tobacco monopoly was granted to him for a period of fourteen years, and any violation by the state of the terms of the concession would have had to be fully indemnified.[45]

There was also a certain contradiction between the regime's professed economic chauvinism and the fact that various foreign companies or such as rested on a great deal of foreign capital—for example, ITT, AEG Ibérica, Construcciones Electromecánicas, Siemens Schukert Española—were granted generous concessions.[46] The American International Telephone and Telegraph Corporation received in August 1924 the monopoly of running and developing the telephone services in Spain. To pay tribute to national dignity, it was stipulated that the ITTC should act through its Spanish agents and associates—among them the Banco Urquijo and the Banco

[44] See a survey of these cases in *Hojas Libres (extraordinario)*, Romanones Archive, Leg. 2, no. 48.

[45] Bernardo Díaz Nosty, *La irrisistible ascensión de Juan March* (Madrid, 1977), pp. 116–49; Manuel Benavides, pp. 233–312.

[46] *El Debate*, 18 June 1929 complained against such concessions.

Hispano-Americano, both of which collaborated in this deal with the National City Bank of New York—under the label of *Compañía Telefónica Nacional*.[47] Outstanding among the exceptionally favourable terms of the concession were the clauses that exempted the Telefónica from all kinds of taxes, and stated also that if and when the state reclaimed the concession, it would have to pay in gold for all the company's installations in Spain. It was no mere coincidence that the Dictator's intimate allies in Catalonia, Güell and Comillas, were closely connected with the new enterprise.[48] The whole telephone-monopoly affair might have been 'a shameful business', as the enemies of the regime preferred to see it;[49] but there is little doubt that the services and technical know-how of the American company were absolutely essential to the development of a modern telephone network in Spain. This is the only way one could possibly reconcile the government's nationalistic oratory with its concessions to foreign capital.[50]

It is in the context of Calvo Sotelo's momentous failure to revolutionize Spain's tax system,[51] that his eagerness to establish the petroleum monopoly should be viewed. He was encouraged by the revenues the government was getting from the monopolies on tobacco, matches, and lotteries; and he expected that that of petroleum would surely surpass them.[52] Of course, the simple principle of economic nationalism was not absent either from the government's considerations. The CAMPSA that was to run this new monopoly was controlled by a consortium of Spanish banks, such as Banco Urguijo, Banco Hispano-Americano, Banco de Bilbao, and Banco Español de Crédito.[53] Imitating a similar monopoly established in Italy by Mussolini, the CAMPSA, which was to be strictly controlled by the government, strove to capture for the state the profits made by Standard Oil and Shell as well as to defend national interests—Primo believed the CAMPSA was essential for national defence—against the foreign companies that had been 'colonizing' Spain for years.[54]

[47] *The Economist*, 4 Oct. 1924.

[48] *Gaceta*, 28 Aug. 1924; Iglesias, pp. 83–4. It was also rumoured that the Dictator's son, José Antonio, received a position in the Telefónica thanks to his obvious links with the regime: *El Sol*. 12 Sept. 1924.

[49] *Impreso anónimo contra el Marqués de Estella*, in Romanones Archive, Leg. 63, no. 51.

[50] Cf. Roberto Carballo Cortina, 'El capital extranjero y la Dictadura: La I.T.T. en España', in *Cuadernos*, pp. 582–9.

[51] See below, pp. 270, 325–6.

[52] Calvo, p. 135.

[53] Benítez de Lugo, pp. 78–9.

[54] The relevant decree is in *Gaceta*, 22 Oct. 1927. See also Primo's declarations in *El Sol*, 23 June 1927, and in his *Intervenciones*, pp. 94–5. See also *El Debate*, 3, 8 July 1927.

The nationalization of the petroleum industry was to be achieved by the seizure with due compensation of all the installations in Spain of foreign companies, and by the stipulation that the CAMPSA should be Spanish in both capital and personnel, with the government owning 30 per cent of the shares.[55] It was this stipulation that made the CAMPSA acceptable to the great financial and industrial groups of the country. Initially apprehensive at the possibility that the new monopoly might pave the way for an encroachment upon the interests of the private sector, they changed their attitude once the CAMPSA proved, in effect, to be an alliance between the government and the most influential banks in Spain.[56]

The foreign companies that were taken out of the Spanish market were offered generous reparations, yet they threatened Spain with a boycott. This would have ruined the whole enterprise had not an agreement for the sale of petroleum been signed with the Soviet Union,[57] in itself a very curious 'betrothal' for a regime that rested on the myth of the Bolshevik threat to Spanish society. But then Russian petrol was far cheaper than that of the 'western imperialists'.[58] The French *Journal des débats* wrote sarcastically on the Spanish new petroleum monopoly: 'The Spanish government rejects any foreign collaboration. But it does not want to be labelled as xenophobe. It therefore ruins British, American, and our own interests in Spain, while at the same time bringing wide smiles to the face of the Soviets.'[59]

It must be acknowledged, however, that in dealing with the multinational oil magnates the Spanish government showed remarkable tenacity. Threats such as those of Sir Henri Deterding, the President of Shell, to the effect that 'in two or three years you will come to us on bended knees', were rejected out of hand.[60] A Valuation Commission was set up to assess the value of the

[55] *Gaceta*, 30 June 1927.

[56] Cf. F. Cabana, 'CAMPSA: La lucha entre el Banc de Catalunya y el grupo March', in Rafael Aracil and M. García Bonafé (eds.), *Lecturas de historia económica de España*, vol. 2, *siglo xx* (Barcelona, 1977), pp. 47–68.

[57] *The Times*, 9 Jan., 19 July 1929.

[58] See Robert Whealey, 'La diplomacia española del petróleo: De Junio de 1927 a abril de 1931', in *Cuadernos*, p. 522.

[59] Quoted in *La Nación*, 18 June 1928. It was the accusation that Spain had become 'the friend of the Communists' that was especially embarrassing for the regime; see *La Nación*, 25 Feb. 1928. For a violent attack on the petrol monopoly by a French writer, see J. Graudel, *Le Monopole du pétrole en Espagne* (Paris, 1935).

[60] Calvo, p. 202.

multinational companies' assets in Spain, and after exhausting negotiations the compensations matter was finally settled.[61]

As for the Dictatorship's nationalistic precepts, they certainly came triumphant out of the confrontation. 'The liberal thesis', rejoiced Primo de Rivera in the decree establishing the petroleum monopoly, had been replaced by 'a state monopoly that would constitute a positive advantage to . . . the Spanish economy'.[62] Another decree promulgated at about the same time further underlined the nationalist commitment. It authorized the government to nationalize other foreign companies in Spain.[63] In practice very little was achieved; but the decree enabled the government to boast that the regeneration of Spain by means of economic development was an exclusively national enterprise.

To their dismay, the multinational companies were to realize that their exclusion from Spain did not entail the collapse of the Spanish petrol industry. In fact, it was after the creation of the CAMPSA that 'the big petroliferous factories of the littoral were started . . . and the huge reservoirs, the gigantic tank-wagons, and the tankers made their appearance'. Moreover, in the years immediately after the CAMPSA came into being, it was able to supply an increasing demand for and consumption of petroleum by the transport network (in 1927 there were 135,000 cars in Spain; in 1930 this figure had almost doubled: 250,000 cars) and by the expanding industry,[64] while increasing the government's revenues from the petroleum industry.[65] According to *The Times*, the monopoly had brought in as revenue to the state more than double the sum by which the state formerly benefited under customs duties.[66]

2. '. . . *To Pursue Progress With the Utmost Celerity*'

The monopolies were not the only bait held out by Primo to Spanish capitalism. Also his plan of public works was in the interest of—indeed it was demanded by—industrialists and bankers. The latter were

[61] *The Times*, 19 July 1929. For a more comprehensive treatment of this issue, see A. Shubert, 'Oil Companies and Governments: International Reaction to the Nationalization of the Petroleum Industry in Spain: 1927–1930', in *JCH*, vol. 15, no. 4 (1980), pp 701–20. [62] *Gaceta*, 30 June 1927. [63] Ibid., 8 June 1927.

[64] For the effects of the new monopoly, see J. M. Benítez Toledo, *La política española del petróleo* (Madrid, 1936), pp. 130, 137–8; *El Debate*, 18 Jan. 1929, and *The Times*, 9 Jan. 1929.

[65] The revenues increased from 112,462,554 pesetas in 1928 to 148,939,516 in 1929; see Benitéz Toledo, pp. 144, 147–8. [66] *The Times*, 19 Jan. 1929.

especially anxious to invest, if possible under favourable conditions, the capital they had been accumulating since the Great War.[67] In fact, as early as 12 November 1923, six of the most powerful banks in the country, claiming to represent the business community as a whole, appealed to the government to initiate a plan of public works, for which they urged it to issue a colossal public debt of 5,000 million pesetas. They explained to the government that unless internal consumption was increased—and the public works were a means to achieve that—there was no real incentive for them to invest in the economy. A few days later, the Federation of National Industries—a group of mainly Basque and Catalan producers of iron, steel, and electricity—joined the bankers' campaign. A modern infrastructure was essential for the development of industry, in which they would then be ready to invest their excess capital.[68] When they were finally initiated, the public works were acclaimed by entrepreneurs as a major incentive to the development of Spanish industry, and as such they were initially applauded by business associations, such as the influential *Sociedad de Estudios Económicos*. Its president, Marcelino Graell, could not realize in 1926 that heavy expenditures might eventually act as a boomerang on the Spanish economy, and he welcomed enthusiastically the creation of the extraordinary budget[69] as indispensable for 'the reconstruction of the national economy'. 'It is about time', he said, 'that roads were constructed to transport our industrial and agricultural products, that the forests were resettled, that new ports were opened to maritime traffic, and that the waters of our rivers were rationally exploited.'[70]

But it would be misleading to present Primo de Rivera as exclusively concerned with the interests of big capital. In his public-works enterprise, the Dictator was not just acting as the tool or the agent of Spanish capitalism to which he, as some would say, presented on a silver tray the ideal conditions for its consolidation. For one thing, the working class was at least as interested in public works as the 'plutocracy'. Indeed, simultaneously with the demands of the business sector for infrastructural development, the Socialists had also put forward their view about the urgent necessity for launching a programme of public works.[71] The Dictatorship's pursuit

[67] For the accumulation of capital, see Roldán, *La Consolidación del capitalismo*, vol. ii, pp. 177–284. [68] *El Liberal*, 12–15 Nov. 1923. [69] See below pp. 348–9.

[70] AHN, P.G. Leg. 320; Marcelino Graell to Primo de Rivera, 23 July 1926.

[71] *El Socialista*, 14, 15 Nov. 1923; *El Liberal*, 15 Nov. 1923.

of economic modernization proved to be absolutely compatible with the Socialists' gradualist philosophy that had long advocated a bourgeois revolution as the indispensable pre-condition for socialism. Primo's policy also contained the touch of a great dream, a grand design of modernization. In this sphere as in many others, he viewed himself as the executor of the 'regenerationist' schemes of Costa, the architect of a gigantic effort to advance Spain into the twentieth century in a matter of years. And there was also this inherent feature of dictatorships which was to develop full steam ahead, no matter who was going to profit from such a development.[72] Calvo Sotelo, who was to collide more than once with 'the moneyed classes', later explained the Dictatorship's developmental fever in the following terms: 'A dictatorship, that is an executive and expedient government, could not undertake a programme of slow materialization *ad Kalendas Graecas*. It had to embark upon a rapid process so that the country could start to profit from the enterprise immediately after its initiation.'[73] To put it in Eduardo Aunós' words, the public works were conceived as likely to create 'an effective well-being' that would 'compensate' the people for 'the loss of the chimerical political liberties'.[74] But there was also the eternal topic of *retraso*. The situation of Spain, as the Dictator had himself observed one week after his seizure of power, 'is not such that allows us to go slowly. Rather, it compels us to pursue progress with the utmost celerity.'[75]

Primo de Rivera's rule would long be remembered, and rightly so, as an era of cement and roads. The regime's commitment to public works, or 'reproductive works' as it preferred to call them, was absolute. It would not be set back by the cost of its enterprise. Budgetary stringency was dismissed out of hand. By the end of June 1926, in the midst of an orgy of public spending, an official communiqué warned the people against 'false hopes concerning economies'. 'Spain', it explained, 'can by no means disregard her internal necessities, nor can she ignore the imperatives of her international rank and future.' Rather than a 'vulgar and inefficient policy of painstaking economies that would leave crucial needs unattended', it was the regime's commitment 'to increase wealth' at all costs.[76] Between financial thrift and what Primo viewed as the urgent task

[72] Cf. Sforza, p. 242.
[73] Calvo, pp. 394–5.
[74] E. Aunós, *España en crisis 1874–1936* (Buenos Aires, 1942).
[75] *El Sol*, 20 Sept. 1923.
[76] *Folletín*, p. 492.

of incorporating Spain into the twentieth century, the Dictator's choice was unambiguous.[77]

Four years after the coming of the Dictatorship, an official at the Ayuntamiento of Barcelona described the regime's achievements in so far as public works were concerned, in the following terms:

> Public works are gathering vigorous momentum in all the compasses of the nation. Gigantic plans for the construction of roads and railways, the reclamation of swamps, the building of canals, harbours, and urbanizations are being carried out across the peninsula . . . It seems as if the collective spirit has awakened from a centenary dream and has set out to reconquer swiftly its former glorious position in the world.[78]

The ecstatic oratory of the regime was never really matched by its actual achievements. But these flamboyant assertions nevertheless exemplify the paramount role that public works came to play in Primo de Rivera's new deal.[79]

Probably the most pretentious undertaking of the civilian directory, and indeed one which was greatly inspired by Costa's 'regenerationist' legacy,[80] was that concerning the development of the country's hydraulic system. For that purpose, the government set up early in 1926 special Hydrographic Confederations to 'exploit in a co-ordinated and methodical way' the country's hydraulic potentialities.[81] It should be stressed, however, that of all the Confederations only that of the Ebro under the directorship of the ambitious engineer Lorenzo Pardo had produced any significant results, among which was the establishment of a new irrigation network for 72,613 hectares of land and the improvement of that of another 109,136 hectares.[82] This the Confederation was able to achieve with the help of a direct subsidy of 52.5 million pesetas from the government, and another 125 million which it mobilized by issuing its own bonds.[83]

[77] Primo quoted ibid., p. 483.

[78] *Ayuntamiento de Molíns del Rey. Cuatro años de actuación. Memoria de la gestión realizada durante el cuatrienio 1924–1927, redactada por el secretario de la corporación municipal D. Feliciano Baratech Alfaro* (Barcelona, 1928), pp. 13–14. For an equally euphoric and highly detailed account of the development of the province of Barcelona, see *Avance de la Provincia de Barcelona en el último quinquenio de septiembre de 1923 a igual fecha de 1928* (Barcelona, 1929).

[79] For current information on public works, see *Revista de Obras Públicas*, 1923–30.

[80] Cf. *La Nación*, 22 Mar. 1926.

[81] *Gaceta*, 6 Mar. 1926.

[82] Lorenzo Pardo, *La Confederación del Ebro. Nueva política hidráulica* (Madrid, 1930), p. 39. See also Lorenzo Pardo's declarations in *El Sol*, 12 May 1928.

[83] Lorenzo Pardo, pp. 21, 112–16.

But in other regions of Spain the Dictatorship did not achieve anything more than just creating the appropriate Confederations. Over-bureaucratization, the refusal of the bigger landowners to collaborate with the projects, and the short span of time the Confederations were allowed to operate combined to thwart the chance of any tangible results being produced.[84]

The modernizing efforts of the Dictatorship were more successful in the fields of road-building and railway re-equipment. 9,455 kilometres of new roads compared with 2,796 in the five years that preceded the Dictatorship were built all over the country.[85] It should not be surprising that the Bulletin of the Chamber of Mechanical Transports was so euphoric in praising Primo de Rivera's roads, where there circulated, by the end of the Dictatorship, four times as many cars as in 1923.[86] Notwithstanding the Dictator's encouragement, the Spanish car industry (essentially in the hands of two firms, Hispano-Suiza and Industria Nacional Metalúrgica) was incapable of meeting the increasing demand, and imported cars were to be seen more frequently on the country's roads,[87] to the dismay of staunch nationalists and to the detriment of the balance of payments.[88] The staggering increase of 75% in the number of car accidents[89] and of 365% in that of the people who were injured in them in the years 1923–9[90] reflected the dramatic upsurge in traffic, rather than the bad roads.

In fact, the establishment of a network of new roads and the impressive increase in the number of cars and lorries[91] can be seen

[84] Nicolás Ortega, 'Política hidráulica y política colonizadora durante la Dictadura de Primo de Rivera', in *Cuadernos*, pp. 370–3. Moreover, the Dictatorship spent on irrigation far less than did the supposedly less 'developmental' Republic. See Malefakis, p. 234.

[85] Ceballos-Teresí, *Historia económica*, vol. 7, p. 383; 1923—67,963 km.; 1929—77,418 km. According to *Estadísticas Básicas*, p. 241, there were in 1931 12,174 km. of roads more than in 1925.

[86] *Boletín de la Cámara de Transportes Mecánicos*, Apr. 1928, Aug. 1931. About 180,000 cars were added during the Dictatorship, see *Estadísticas Básicas*, p. 253.

[87] *La Nación*, 9 Apr. 1928, acknowledged that only 10 per cent of the cars circulating in Spain were made in the peninsula. Primo nationalized the Spanish car industry (*Gaceta*, 3 Apr. 1928) with the hope that this would help to increase its production. Local production increased from 21,855 cars in 1925 to 36,928 in 1929 (68.9 per cent), see Calvo, p. 261.

[88] See p. 339.

[89] *Boletín de la Cámara de Transportes Mecánicos*, Aug. 1931.

[90] *Estadísticas Básicas*, p. 267; 14,381 people were victims of car accidents in 1929; 1,813 of whom lost their lives.

[91] The number of imported lorries increased from 3,587 in 1927 to 6,685 in 1928, and 9,067 in 1929. See Pierre Lefaucheux, *La peseta et l'économie espagnole depuis 1928* (Paris, n. d.), p. 152.

as partly responsible for what was perhaps only a modest increase of about 800 kms. of new rails. Commuters were clearly abandoning the train in favour of the car. The whole rail system, though, had been re-equipped and modernized, by means of direct state assistance or by the issue of special State Railway Debts. Though road transport started to pose a meaningful challenge to the supremacy of the cargo trains, the latter still dominated the field. The volume of freightage transported by train did not diminish under the Dictatorship, in fact it even increased by about 38 per cent between 1923 and 1928.[92] This, and generous state assistance, enabled the railway companies to claim, in spite of the car's competition, a constant increase in their revenues.[93] It likewise allowed them to increase the number of their employees during the Dictatorship by 14.3 per cent (from 101,327 to 115,829).[94]

The government's undertakings in the field of infrastructural development also included the investment of large sums (156 million pesetas until early 1927) in the modernization of some of the country's most backward harbours.[95] Special programmes of public works, that included the construction of roads, military bases, and telegraph services, were also approved for the Spanish zone of Morocco.[96]

One does not have to accept the view that Primo de Rivera's schemes of public works were mainly, or exclusively, conceived as an attempt to advance the interests of Spanish capitalism, in order to recognize that infrastructural modernization was indispensable to the development of industry. Not only could this operate better and more efficiently with the help of modern communications and a greater production of energy, but also its auxiliary branches such as, for example, the cement, and the iron and steel industries—both essential elements for the implementation of public works—received an unprecedented boost.

In an era of bridges and public buildings,[97] the Dictatorship witnessed the doubling of the production of cement in Spain from 863,354 tons in 1923 to 1,820,011 in 1929, and the near quadrupling

[92] For data on commuters, freightage, and new rails, cf. *Anuario*, 1929, pp. xxvi–xxvii; *Estadísticas Básicas*, pp. 244–5.

[93] *The Economist*, 26 June, 11 Dec. 1926; 'Los ferrocarriles en 1929', in *El Financiero*, Nov. 1930, pp. 87–91. For the massive state assistance, see Ceballos-Teresí, vol. 7, p. 232.

[94] Ibid., vol. 7, p. 375.

[95] Ibid., vol. 6, p. 233.

[96] Benítez de Lugo, p. 22; *The Times*, 6 Sept. 1929.

[97] See, for example, the case of capital, below, p. 315.

of its consumption (494,099 tons in 1923; 1,773,946 in 1929).[98] There was a stage in 1928 when the local production of cement fell drastically short of meeting the expanding demand. In a special decree of 15 November 1928, Primo's protectionist government was therefore compelled to reduce tariffs on foreign cement, thus allowing the import of 300,000 tons for the exclusive consumption of public works.[99] A significant increase could also be noted in the production of ingot iron that arose by about 60 per cent,[100] and that of ingot steel, that actually doubled (from 462,601 tons in 1923 to 926,034 in 1929).[101] But not even this increase in national production sufficed to meet the expanding needs of the public works, and ingot iron and steel had still to be imported.[102]

Practically all the available statistical data point to a substantial increase in industrial and mineral production. Industrial production alone increased between 1923 and 1929 from an index of 102.5 to one of 141.9.[103] Taken together, the output of Spain's mines and industry increased by 38.4% under the Dictatorship.[104] The production of iron ore went up by about 77%, most of which went to exports (an increase of about 48%). The production of copper ore increased by 76%, that of zinc by 41%, that of soft coal by 16%, that of coke by 32%, that of steel and wrought iron by about 112%, that of cast iron by 87%, that of copper by about 18%, and that of lead by 12%.[105] The overall value of mineral production increased by about 54% until 1928 (from 1,119,391,890 pesetas to 1,718,290,542).[106] It was not at all surprising that the mining industry should have employed about 25% more workers in 1929 than in 1923 (131,051–163,367).[107]

[98] Cf. *Estadísticas Básicas*, p. 218; Lefaucheux, p. 105; Velarde, *Polítíca económica*, pp. 133–4.

[99] 'La industria del cemento en España', *El Financiero*, Nov. 1930, pp. 119–20.

[100] From 400,270 tons to 640,425. See Luis Barreiro, 'La industria minerosiderúrgica española', in *Revista Nacional de Economía*, Jan. 1930, p. 70.

[101] Luis Barreiro, loc. cit., p. 71.

[102] Ibid., p. 71.

[103] Senen Florensa Palau, 'Economía y comercio exterior en la España de los años veinte. Un enfoque de la Dictadura de Primo de Rivera', in *Cuadernos*, p. 484.

[104] Velarde, *Política económica*, pp. 171–3. Paris Eguilaz, *Factores*, p. 432, calculated this in index terms: 1913—100; 1923—107.8; 1924—124; 1925—127.3; 1926—140.6; 1927—139.6; 1928—142.6; 1929—149.2.

[105] For absolute figures, cf. *Anuario*, 1929, p. 140; Luis Barreiro, 'La industria minero-siderúrgica', p. 72.

[106] Cf. *Estadísticas Básicas*, pp. 190–7; Ceballos-Teresí, vol. 7, p. 331.

[107] Cf. *El Financiero, no. extraordinario dedicado a 1929*, Nov. 1930, p. 178; *Anuario*, 1929, p. 117.

To keep pace with this discernible acceleration of industrial production, the output of electric energy more than doubled between 1923 and 1930 (it rose by 120%). Consequently the revenues of the treasury from taxation on the use of electricity increased by 44% in the first four years of the regime. It is indicative of the greater use of electricity in industry that, whereas in 1920 the private consumption of electricity was about 60% of that of industry, in 1930 industry consumed 360% more than the private sector. Electric traction for urban and inter-urban transport increased during the same time by about 150%. By 1929, there was hardly a provincial capital in Spain that did not have its network of electric tramways; while the electrification of the country's railways was in full progress. Ten per cent of the total production of energy was then consumed by the traction system.[108] It was not at all surprising that the balance of a company such as the *Unión Eléctrica Madrileña* showed an increase of 90% in net profits between 1923 and 1928.[109] Likewise, the Barcelona Traction, Light, and Power Company—a key enterprise in an industrial city like Barcelona—improved its positive balance by 100% within the first two years of the civilian directory. Another power company, the CHADE, of which Cambó was a major shareholder, also showed an improvement in its balance sheet of about 20% within one year of the launching of the civilian directory's development projects; while its gross profit went up by more than eight million pesetas within that same year.[110]

Industrial and mining concerns did not lag far behind. The Río Tinto copper company, for example, reported that in 1926 production had been satisfactory, so that it was able to pay 50% dividends in spite of the lower price-ruling for copper during 1926. And though the net profit of the company in 1927 came out £100,000 lower than in 1926, it continued to pay the same dividend due to the fact that the depreciation of copper was balanced off by an increase in the sales of pyrites and iron ore. The proliferation of public works presented golden opportunities for an engineering company such as Babcock & Wilcox, which had been able to do consistently well.[111]

[108] Cf. *Estadísticas Básicas*, p. 188; *Anuario*, 1929, p. 170; Juan Carlos Llorente, 'Producción y distribución de la energía eléctrica durante la década 1920–1930', *Cuadernos*, pp. 537, 539–40; 'El estado actual de la producción, distribución, y empleo de la energía eléctrica en España', *El Financiero*, Nov. 1930, pp. 33–51.

[109] *Anuario*, 1929, p 266.

[110] *The Economist*, 9, 16 Apr. 1927, 31 Mar., 7, 28 Apr. 1928.

[111] See the same reports, ibid.

The intensification of economic activities was also reflected in the huge profits now made by insurance companies. Their profits increased by 166% within five years, while during the whole decade prior to 1923 their profits had risen by only 36%.[112]

Indeed, almost every important company in the country profited from the boom. The net profits of a sample of five of the key concerns of heavy industry in Spain—Altos Hornos de Vizcaya, Española de Construcciones Navales, Duro-Felguera, Siderúrgica del Mediterráneo, Maquinista Terrestre y Marítima—showed an unmistakable growth of 51% between 1925 and 1929.[113] The net profits of the *Unión Española de Explosivos* rose by 173% between 1923 and 1928, those of *La Papelera Española* by about 38%, those of the *Sociedad General Azucarera Española* by 140%, and those of the *Unión Española de Construcción Naval* by 26%. This optimistic trend was also reflected in the constant advance of the main shares on the stock exchange.[114]

Agriculture presented a somewhat different picture. Primo de Rivera dreamt of a self-sufficient, autarkic Spain. Agriculture, he maintained, was the main source of Spain's natural wealth.[115] Yet his frequent rhetoric about 'rural awakening'[116] was not translated into the practical sphere of a structural renovation of Spanish agriculture. The prosperity of the latter, Primo should have known, was the basic condition for a balanced development of industry, whose main market was in agricultural Spain.[117] Like other developmental dictatorships in this century, his regime was much more committed to the glamorous task of industrial expansion than to the prosaic needs of agriculture.[118] Like Falangism, and unlike rurally oriented, reactionary Spanish Traditionalism, the Dictatorship was definitely committed to industrial and urban modernization.

Credit facilities were essential if an independent small peasantry was to emerge in Spain. But agrarian credit was not raised by

[112] 'Los seguros en España', in *El Financiero*, Nov. 1930, pp. 78–9.

[113] Luis Olariaga, *La crisis siderúrgico-metalúrgica en España* (Madrid, 1932), p. 12

[114] *Anuario*, 1929, pp. 266–7.

[115] *La Nación*, 22 Oct. 1926.

[116] See his *Prólogo al curso de ciudadanía* (conferencias de varios autores pronunciadas en el Alcazar de Toledo en Marzo de 1929) (ed. La junta de propaganda patriótıca y ciudadanía, Madrid, 1929), p. x.

[117] The Dictator's minister of labour was fully aware of this symbiotic link, see Aunós, 'La economía social del ministerio de trabajo' in *Revista de Acción Social*, I, no. 5 (Oct. 1928), p. 416.

[118] James Gregor, *Italian Fascism and Developmental Dictatorship* (Princeton, 1979), *passim*. This is also true of military rulers; see Nordlinger, pp. 166–70.

Primo de Rivera to the standards required for such a lofty aim. The *Servicio Nacional de Crédito Agrícola* established in 1925 operated with a fund of 100 million pesetas. The basis of its much-publicized enterprise consisted of modest loans of initially up to 5,000 pesetas, later raised to 10,000 pesetas, to small and medium-sized farmers. The loans were to be given against the guarantee of the borrower's crops.[119] Yet, in spite of the government's campaign to attract farmers to make use of these credit facilities, 'the mortgage loans did not seem to have assumed great importance' under the Dictatorship, as *El Economista* observed by mid 1929. Proprietors simply found the conditions too harsh. In 1927, 13,841,000 pesetas were borrowed by both independent peasants and agrarian corporations. The total sum of loans went up to 30,231,000 pesetas in 1928, and to 31,289,000 in 1929. The lion's share of the loans seemed to have been taken by wheat-growers. 6,739 of them borrowed in 1928 22,913,024 pesetas, an average of 3,400 pesetas each.[120]

Agrarian protectionism and interventionism were, however, high on the agenda. Gregorio Ledesma, the mayor of Toledo and a central member of the *Secretariado Nacional Agrario*, a Castilian organization of small and medium-sized farmers, expressed in 1929 his colleagues' delight at the fact that 'following the example of Mussolini's protectionist agrarian policy, the Spanish Dictatorship had provided agriculture with more effective state assistance and protection than it had ever enjoyed during one hundred years of economic liberalism'.[121] In September 1926, representatives of 122 agrarian entities in the area of Valencia had met in order to manifest their gratitude for the Dictator's 'agrarian policy'.[122] Though the wine industry suffered from a constant drop in consumption and from high costs of internal transport, Primo was always attentive to its needs, and some of the international commercial treaties he had engaged in were attempts to meet them. In April 1926, the wine-growers of Valencia, Levante, Aragón, and Catalonia thanked the Dictator for his consistent efforts 'to alleviate the crisis of vine-growing'.[123] A fervent protector of Spanish

[119] Servicio Nacional de Crédito Agrícola, *Folleto comprensivo de las disposiciones legales y formularios a los fines de la divulgación del servicio, ley, reglamento y reales decretos referentes al crédito agrícola* (Madrid, 1927).

[120] *El Economista*, 25 May 1929: 'El crédito agrícola en España'.

[121] See the official publication of this organization, *España Agraria*, Jan.–Apr. 1929.

[122] AHN, P.G. Leg. 320; Civil governor of Valencia to Primo.

[123] AHN, P.G. Leg. 320; Pascual Carrión to Primo, 20 Apr. 1926.

agriculture,[124] the Dictator assured minimal prices to wheat-growers and blocked with high tariffs the import of foreign agricultural products such as rice, wine, and oil. And when in 1926 the agriculturists in the Salamanca region complained of over-production, the Dictator did not hesitate to come to their rescue by opening to them, in a special decree, the Moroccan market.[125] The result of such attentive assistance was that the export of agricultural products was constantly on the increase during the Dictatorship,[126] while their imports showed a downward trend.[127]

Year	*Imports of Foodstuffs* (pesetas)	*Index*
1923	686,370,000	253
1924	476,650,000	176
1925	426,340,000	157
1926	364,290,000	134
1927	420,750,000	155

Imports of foodstuffs suddenly went up in 1928 to 614,000,000 pesetas because of a catastrophic frost that hit agricultural production, but they started to descend again in 1929: down to 554,000,000 pesetas.

But the Dictator could never please everybody. Mariano Matesanz, the president of the Spanish Association of Agriculturists, accused the government of consistently preferring the interests of industry to those of agriculture. In a country whose agrarian hinterland consumed 80 per cent of its industrial products, it was essential to opt for an emphatically agrarian orientation, he claimed.[128] The olive- and wheat-growers would always argue vociferously that they were not sufficiently protected, and that they were anyway less favoured by the regime than industry.[129] The wine-producers were especially disturbed by the excise tax that raised the price of their products artificially.[130] The wheat-growers demanded the same

[124] See an example of an enthusiastic recognition of this fact; 'Presidente Federación Sindicatos Católicos Agrarios Diócesis Osma eleva adhesión gobierno y agradecimiento por protección a la agricultura', 10 Mar. 1926, in AHN, P.G. Leg. 320.

[125] *La Nación*, 1 May 1926.

[126] For agricultural exports, see p. x.

[127] *Anuario*, 1929, pp. xxii–xxiii.

[128] *Actividad Financiera*, 4 June 1925.

[129] *Boletín de la Asociación de Agricultores de España*, Feb. 1929–Jan. 1930. See also Matesanz's protest in *Folletín*, p. 225, as well as that of the Sindicato Central de Aragón y Asociaciones Católicas, in AHN, P.G. Leg. 320; Civil governor of Zaragoza, 19 May 1926.

[130] *El Mercantil*, 15 May 1928.

export incentives as those enjoyed by industry and the mining sector, and even more hermetic tariffs than those they already enjoyed.[131] But the Dictator never did view wheat as an exportable item. Rather, it was an essential element for self-sufficiency in bread.

The ideal that Spain should be able to produce its *vital* necessities was uppermost in his considerations, even if that meant sacrificing some of the interests of agriculture. Therefore, when the representatives of the fruit-growers of Valencia in the National Assembly, Marqués Sotelo and García Guijarro, protested against the high tariffs that the government had imposed on the importation of sulphate ammonia, of which Spanish industry produced only 20,000 tons a year out of the 180,000 tons that agriculture consumed, the Dictator rejected their protest out of hand. He would not give in to their demands for lower tariffs for sulphate ammonia, he said, because he was determined to protect the young Spanish industry of nitrogen, which he claimed was crucial for 'national defence'.[132] Another case of favouring industry at the expense of agriculture was that of the excessively high tariffs that were imposed on the import of agricultural machinery. The Dictator would explain that this was essential for the protection of the local metallurgical industry.[133] Clearly, the orange-growers of Valencia were one section of agriculture who could not reconcile themselves with the high degree of protectionism introduced by the Dictatorship. Not especially worried by foreign competition, they would have preferred freer trade that would create the appropriate conditions for the absorption of their products in foreign markets.[134] As a fundamentally exporting sector, they also suffered from the Dictator's 'patriotic' policy of maintaining a high exchange rate for the peseta.[135]

As far as production was concerned, the achievements of agriculture did not always depend on official policies but on the arbitrary logic of 'good' and 'bad' years. This is why, contrary to the upward trend of industrial production, agriculture showed erratic results. 1928, for example, was a catastrophic year for agricultural production

[131] Ibid., 21 Apr. 1928; Gregorio Fernández Díez, 'La economia Castellana ante la Dictadura', in *Revista Nacional de Economía*, Jan. 1930, pp. 112–23.

[132] Primo, *Intervenciones*, pp. 163–7; *The Times*, 3 Nov. 1928.

[133] Juan Hernández Andreu, 'Algunos aspectos de la depresión económica estructural española: 1925–1934', in *Cuadernos*, p. 391.

[134] Luis Lucía Lucía, *En estas horas de transición* (Valencia, 1930), pp. 104–12.

[135] *Hojas Libres*, 1 May 1927.

because of frost damage, and 1929 was a year of over-production—both cases entailed difficulties for the agriculturists. In 1925, massive imports of wheat had to be allowed because of the drought.[136] Official indexes of agricultural production inevitably reflect a serpentine line: 1923—114.5; 1924—98.3; 1925—119.4; 1926—98; 1927—127.1; 1928—89.8; 1929—129.6.[137]

An important aim of the Dictator's economic policy was that of narrowing, or even eliminating, Spain's trade deficit. His major instrument for achieving that was by erecting high tariff walls. Foreign economic interests were obviously enraged by the fact that Spain shared with the Soviet Union 'the unenviable distinction of having relatively the highest tariff walls in Europe', and with Fascist Italy a chauvinistic approach towards national production.[138] A royal decree of 30 April 1924 had complemented the Law of Industrial Production of 1917. And subsequent measures, such as the decree of 1927 making it obligatory for Spanish protected industries to use 40 per cent of their coal from that produced in Spain, further underlined the protectionist zeal of the government.[139] The Catalan industry, especially its textile sector, was delighted. Not only had the Dictatorship done away with the threat of the last constitutional government to reduce tariffs, it had also decreed additional protection. Domingo Sert, the president of the powerful Fomento del Trabajo Nacional, was happy to acknowledge that government protection 'highly contributes to the promotion of Spanish sericultural wealth; not only does it defend the picker but also the spinning industry and that of the silk twist'.[140] Spain stood undoubtedly as an example of exceptionally extreme protectionism; the index number assigned to her tariff, 35, compared with one of 6 for Great Britain, and was exceeded only by that of the Soviet Union with 43.[141]

[136] *The Economist*, 4 July 1925.

[137] Cf. *Anuario*, 1931, p. 48; Velarde, *Política económica*, p. 198. Substantially higher indexes are proposed by Paris Eguilaz, *Factores*, p. 428.

[138] *The Economist*, 29 Oct. 1927. The League of Nations denounced Spain in 1927 as the most protectionist country in the world; Fontana and Nadal, 'Spain 1914–1970', in Cipolla (ed.), *The Fontana Economic History of Europe*, vol. 6, part 2 (Fontana Books, 1976), p. 472.

[139] Consejo Nacional de Combustibles, *Real decreto regulador de la obligación de consumir carbón nacional impuesta a las industrias protegidas* (Madrid, 1927). According to *La Nación*, 20 Aug. 1928, this measure saved the jobs of 35,000 workers.

[140] Domingo Sert to Primo, 16 Oct. 1926, in AHN, P.G. Leg. 320.

[141] *The Economist*, 29 Oct. 1927. See a summary of the protectionist measures introduced by Primo in Cambó, *Valoración*, pp. 281, 283, as well as Consejo de Economía nacional, Sección de Defensa de la Producción, *Prontuario de disposiciones protectoras de la producción e industrias nacionales* (Madrid, 1926).

By applying high tariffs, Primo de Rivera certainly did not inaugurate any new policy in Spain. It can even be argued that the Dictatorship did not alter the 'protectionist consensus' of the Restoration that rested on a defence of the Catalan and Basque industries and of Castilian agricultural products.[142]

But protectionism for Primo de Rivera was not just an opportunistic device aimed at placating Catalan big business and the coal mine-owners of Asturias, as was claimed by frustrated British exporters.[143] Rather, it was a doctrinal anti-liberal commitment fully consistent with the Dictator's political concepts.[144] When in July 1926 a decree was issued that zealously protected both industry and agriculture against foreign competition, *La Nación* hailed it as a long overdue manifestation of 'tariff patriotism'.[145] To those who attacked the 'rigidity' of his tariffs, Primo responded that they were 'a defensive weapon' that should 'under no circumstances' be removed.[146] The Dictator was convinced that protectionism—a key element in an interventionist economy—was Spain's 'major defence against social upheavals'. The experience of other nations, he explained, showed that 'industrial freedom' had caused 'millions of unemployed', while Spain's controlled economy enabled her to 'maintain her standards and even prosper modestly'.[147] Merry del Val, the Spanish ambassador in London, explained to angry British businessmen his master's policy in blunt terms. 'Spain', he said, '*believes* in protection, and she is determined to restore and increase her national wealth in proportion to her population.'[148]

To improve Spain's chronically adverse trade balance additional devices had to be introduced. Such were. for example, the export incentives given by mid 1927 to the textile industry in Barcelona and to the rice-growers of Valencia.[149] A kind of incentive was also the creation in 1928 of the *Banco Exterior de España*, that was to make credits and commercial facilities available as a means of fostering foreign trade, a special emphasis being laid on opening the South American market to Spanish products.[150] This bank, explained a columnist in *La Nación*, represented the government's policy of

[142] José Varela Ortega, 'El proteccionismo de los trigueros Castellanos y la naturaleza del poder político de la Restauración', in *Cuadernos*, no. 6, 1978, esp. p. 7.

[143] *The Economist*, 29 Oct., 26 Nov. 1927; *The Times*, 1, 12, 27 Dec. 1928, 23 Jan., 18 Feb., 26 Apr., 29 July 1929.

[144] Cf. Lefaucheux, pp. 176–7.

[145] *La Nación*, 16 July 1926.

[146] Primo, *Intervenciones*, pp. 92–3.

[147] Primo in *Folletín*, pp. 830–1, 862.

[148] *The Times*, 8 Mar. 1929.

[149] *La Nación*, 31 May 1927.

[150] *El Sol*, 6 Aug. 1928.

'active protectionism' that complemented that of 'defensive protectionism' based on high tariffs.[151]

A kind of 'active protectionism' was also the much-publicized Campaign Pro-National Production, the initiators of which were not in the government, though the latter obviously gave it its blessing, but in the Catalan business community. It was started in 1927 by the *Sociedad de Estudios Económicos* of Barcelona, and was immediately joined by the Biscayan League of Producers. The Catalan Church supported it, and the government contributed their share by exempting from the stamp tax all propaganda related to the consumption of national products. Slogans such as 'Let us prevent the national patrimony from falling into foreign hands: this is our best national frontier', 'Write on Spanish paper with Spanish ink!', or 'Buy national products even when they are more expensive!'[152] were spread all over.

To improve Spain's international trade balance, Primo de Rivera also resorted to a policy of commercial treaties. These treaties, however, had to be adapted to realities, hence they frequently reflected a departure from nationalistic principles. The agreement with the United States, for example, granted the Americans the status of a most-favoured nation in tariff matters. Such treatment was necessary to placate the Catalan textile industrialists who needed American raw cotton at as low a price as possible.[153] Some attempts were started to grow cotton in Spain. But Primo himself had to confess that, so long as Spain's cotton production fell so drastically short of meeting the demands of industry for raw material, 'it would be madness to stymie imports by putting up tariffs'.[154] A preferable status was also given to Cuban goods in the Spanish market with the view of preserving the favourable status enjoyed by Spanish products in Cuba.[155] Nor did Spanish industry seem to welcome the commercial treaty that was concluded with Germany. It favoured Spain's agricultural exports to the Weimar Republic in exchange for a more favourable treatment of specific German industrial products in Spain.[156] In his search for a market for Spanish agricultural products,

[151] Alterius, 'Proteccionismo defensivo y proteccionismo activo', in *La Nación*, 21 Aug. 1928.

[152] *La Nación*, 10 Aug. 1927; Carlos Velasco, 'Concentración e intervención en la Dictadura: hechos e ideas', in *Cuadernos*, pp. 148–50.

[153] *Folletín*, p. 591.

[154] Primo, *Intervenciones*, pp. 118–21.

[155] *El Sol*, 16 July 1927.

[156] See the support of dozens of agricultural corporations for the new treaty in AHN, P.G. Leg. 330, 28 June 1926.

the Dictator would even start commercial negotiations with the Chinese government.[157]

Of particular importance to Spanish agricultural exports was the commercial treaty signed with the French government early in 1924. It especially improved the conditions for the export of Spanish wines and oranges to the neighbouring Republic; and was, therefore, strongly defended by bodies such as the Export Syndicates of Catalonia, the Agricultural Chamber of Valencia, especially its section of orange-exporters, and the Syndicate of Wine Exporters in Villafranca del Panadés, the Catalan wine heartland.[158] Early in 1928, however, Spain's agricultural exports were severely hampered by the decision of the French government to put up its tariffs for Spain's wines and oranges, thus doing away with the favourable trade balance, of about 200 million pesetas, that the Spaniards had so far enjoyed in their commercial relations with France.[159]

As a whole, the Dictatorship years witnessed some improvement in Spain's trade balance (in pesetas):[160]

	Exports	*Imports*	*Balance*
1923	1,596,000,000	3,063,000,000	– 1,467,000,000
1924	1,791,000,000	2,947,000,000	– 1,156,000,000
1925	1,585,000,000	2,250,000,000	– 665,000,000
1926	1,606,000,000	2,154,000,000	– 548,000,000
1927	1,895,280,000	2,585,520,000	– 690,240,000
1928	2,183,000,000	2,004,000,000	– 821,000,000
1929	2,113,000,000	2,737,000,000	– 624,000,000

This improvement was evidently reached thanks to a not negligible increase of Spanish exports of about 33% between 1923 and 1929,[161] an increase for which agriculture should be mainly given the credit. Some improvement, though, was also discernible in the performance of Spanish industrial products in foreign markets. The export of raw material also witnessed an increase.

Contrary to what the protectionist zeal of the government might have led us to expect, the drop in imports was substantially lower than the rise in exports. In 1929 Spain imported only 4% less than it

[157] AHN. P.G. Leg. 346; Spain's delegate in Peking to the foreign minister.

[158] Ibid., Leg. 330 'Convenios Internacionales', Feb. 1924.

[159] Primo, *Intervenciones*, pp. 113–17.

[160] H. Paris Eguilaz. *Factores*, p. 208; *Anuario*, 1929, pp. xxii–xxiii; 'El comercio exterior de España in *El Financiero*, Nov. 1930, p. 92; and the data provided by the Council of National Economy in *La Nación*, 30 Apr. 1927.

	Cattle	*Raw Material*	*Industrial Products*	*Foodstuffs*
1923	3,890,000	369,880,000	344,560,000	877,910,000
1924	3,640,000	393,390,000	401,250,000	992,230,000
1925	3,380,000	340,730,000	456,410,000	784,130,000
1927	4,460,000	297,340,000	384,800,000	1,022,710,000
1928	2,000,000	426,000,000	387,000,000	1,303,000,000
1929	7,000,000	435,000,000	472,000,000	1,193,000,000

had in 1923. Reasonably low volumes of import were reached, however, in 1925, 1926, and 1927 (36%, 42%, and 18.5% respectively lower than in 1923). But then the public works went full steam ahead, and the import of machinery and raw material had to be accelerated. Throughout the period the main items in Spain's imports that could not be eliminated in spite of protection were industrial products, and such raw materials as were essential for development and for keeping industry going.[162] It was, however, precisely the rise in exports which seemed to have created the conditions for financing the hardly diminishing imports.[163]

But, the growth of exports was due to a great extent to official encouragement and intervention that, in its turn, made Spanish exports more expensive than they would have been otherwise. The government's careful policy of commercial treaties was evidently also instrumental in fostering exports. But protectionism might have slowed down the possible expansion of Spain's foreign trade. In 1927, for example, the volume of Spain's foreign trade per capita was 34 pesetas compared with 230 in Denmark, 217 in Switzerland, 195 in Belgium, 192 in England, 103 in France, and 91 in Germany. Even countries such as Estonia, Lithuania, and Greece did better than Spain.[164] Spanish merchants, who were obviously concerned by this phenomenon, did not fail to point to protectionism as being mainly responsible for the reduced volume of the country's international trade.[165]

3. *Financial 'Largess' and the 'Traditional Obstacles'*

It is a feature of public works that they underline a tension between the burden imposed on the community that has to finance them and

[162] *Anuario*, 1929, pp. xii–xxiii. See also Florensa Palau, 'Economía y comercio exterior' pp. 483–4. [163] Cf. Velarde, *Política*, p. 224. [164] Iglesias, p. 47.

[165] See the protest of the Chamber of Commerce of Madrid, in *The Economist*, 4 July 1925.

the benefits derived by entrepreneurs and workers. For a while it seemed as if the Dictatorship was ready to risk such a potentially dangerous discord between conflicting interests. It later succumbed, however, to the pressure of the owning classes and refrained from implementing a thorough redistribution of the burden of taxation. Yet the tension did not disappear altogether; indeed, it was to accompany the regime (as will be seen in the last chapters) right up to its downfall. The Dictatorship had clearly increased the tax pressure, especially upon the middle classes, which was why the latter were to feel increasingly alienated from it.

As soon as the military directory was firmly in the saddle, it launched stern measures against tax evasion. The directory's onslaught on tax evaders and the latter's fear of the strong hand of the military government had immediate results, and 'all over Spain the yield of all sorts of taxes increased outright'.[166] Industrialists, artisans, merchants, and big landowners lined up in their hundreds to settle their debts to the treasury.[167] For the first quarter of the 1924–5 fiscal year the receipts were 862 million against 830 million for the same period of 1923.[168]

But tax evasion was 'an accursed and inextinguishable plant',[169] and Calvo Sotelo realized, immediately upon assuming the post of minister of finance, that the measures taken by the military directory fell short of coping with the colossal dimensions of the problem. He was satisfied with the 'splendid' results of the more efficient inspection of tax collection which he had introduced.[170] But he was eager to implement more radical measures. This he tried to do by three subsequent decrees promulgated early in January 1926. Aimed at eradicating tax evasion in the business sector and among proprietors, his decrees immediately became the cause of a hysterical outcry by landowners and businessmen.

One of the decrees provided the measures of a new 'evaluation of rural and urban property'. It stated that most of the property in Spain was being undertaxed, because its value had so far been under-evaluated. From now on, this exceptionally radical decree warned that all property, whose owner had intentionally misled the authorities as to its real value and to the profits he drew from it, would be expropriated. It would be sold at a public auction in which special advantages would be accorded to the man who had

[166] Calvo, pp. 124–5.
[167] Ramón Garriga, p. 222.
[168] *The Economist*, 15 Nov. 1924.
[169] Calvo, p. 125.
[170] Ibid., pp. 137–8.

denounced the fraud to the authorities. Another decree, which concerned mainly the business sector, made it obligatory for businessmen, shopkeepers, and merchants to keep 'a special diary of industrial and commercial sales and operations' to provide the basis for tax assessment by special agents of the treasury.[171]

Clearly, Primo de Rivera was far less reluctant than Franco after him to contemplate an expansion of the tax basis of his budgets. Unlike the Caudillo, Primo had undermined his support among the middle classes, the business community, and the landowners by his attempt to shift the burden of taxation on to their shoulders. His appeal to the moneyed people 'to get used to the idea' that their behaviour as taxpayers should be inspired by 'civic morality',[172] was hardly to their taste. It was inconceivable, he said in support of Calvo Sotelo's decrees of January, that 'a proprietor whose income exceeds 250,000 pesetas per year, or someone in the liberal professions who might enjoy a similar revenue, should pay in taxes between 8 and 10 thousand pesetas in the former case, and between 3 and 4 thousand in the latter'.[173] Calvo Sotelo made it quite clear that the government's intentions were 'to modify the present distribution of the burden of taxation in such a way that will cast greater obligations upon the higher incomes'. The Dictator himself boasted that the recent tax reforms were tantamount to 'a complete revision which, being inspired by a sense of justice, augments the burden upon capital while diminishing that of labour'.[174] It is, he continued, 'an egalitarian tax system which some might call democratic and others even bolshevik.'

The 'democratic' spirit of the new tax deal proposed by the regime stemmed from the fact that an income tax was to be levied on workers' wages. This so-called utilities tax was said to be aimed at 'dignifying' the workers, and 'justifying the special care that the state displays towards the social sector'. This tax was not to be too vehemently combated by the Socialists because after all it did not really affect the manual workers. Applying to earners of wages higher than 3,250 pesetas per year, it mainly penalized people of the liberal professions, army officers, stock-exchange employees, notaries, and property registrars.[175] An essentially middle-class tax,

[171] *Gaceta*, 3 Jan. 1926. See also Velarde, 'Los terratenientes contra Calvo Sotelo', in *Sobre la decadencia económica de España* (Madrid, 1969), pp. 204–5.

[172] *El Sol*, 13 Sept. 1926.

[173] *La Nación*, 13 Jan. 1926.

[174] *Gaceta*, 18 Dec. 1926.

[175] Calvo, pp. 164–9; *La Nación*, 18 Dec. 1926.

it was bitterly denounced by Carlos Prast, the president of the Madrid Chamber of Commerce.[176]

'Finance', wrote the Third Marquess of Salisbury in 1864, 'is a contest between various classes waged for the purpose of resisting the imposition of what each considers an unfair proportion of that contribution from property by which the service of the state is carried on.'[177] It did not take long after the promulgation of his tax reform for Calvo Sotelo to come to terms with the political imperatives of such a definition. The pressure of the owning classes against the novel approach of the government to the issue of tax evasion was overwhelming.[178] 'Individualistic egoism', as *La Nación* observed, had 'launched a rebellion against distributive justice'.[179] Official assurances to the effect that the government did not intend to infringe upon the sacred rights of property, but only to fight 'the abuses of certain property owners',[180] failed to quell the rebellion; and Calvo Sotelo would have finally to waive his measures concerning the evaluation of rural property. He was compelled to acknowledge that those who had warned him 'not to go for the landowners' were right.[181] He realized, however, that proprietors would rather accept an increase in the existing taxes than abide by a radical change of the system. In a decree of July 1926 Calvo Sotelo did precisely this; he levied higher taxes on landowners.[182] But this of course did not suffice to meet the needs of the constantly expanding budget.

The Dictator dreamt of one simple progressive tax on capital, an idea that was nipped in the bud by the unfavourable reaction of the 'moneyed people'.[183] Calvo Sotelo proposed to base the national budget on a progressive income tax, on the heavy taxation of luxury goods as well as on an energetic campaign to eliminate, or at least reduce to a minimum, the epidemic of tax evasion. The revenues from the concession of monopolies, the imposition of financial punishments on absentee landlords and on 'the deficient exploitation of the land', the creation of a value-added tax, stamp duty, and a reform of the taxation system on inheritance—all these, he believed, would enable the government to reach 'a balanced national budget' in a way that would leave 'no area of the nation's needs untended'.[184]

[176] *Actividad Financiera*, 13 Aug. 1925.

[177] Quoted in A. Offer, *Property and Politics 1870–1914* (Cambridge University Press, 1981), p. 162.

[178] More on the landowners' attitude on pp. 325–6.

[179] *La Nación*, 12 Jan. 1926.

[180] Ibid., 28 Jan. 1926.

[181] Calvo, pp. 126–30.

[182] *Gaceta*, 1 July 1926.

[183] *La Nación*, 23 Mar. 1926; Calvo, p. 149.

[184] Calvo, pp. 104–5, 134, 142, 149.

Had Calvo Sotelo been allowed to implement all the tax reforms he had in mind, the Dictatorship would certainly have been remembered as the executor of a most radical redistribution of the burden of taxation. Such a reform, however, was not carried out. In the end, a fear prevailed in the government that heavy taxation upon proprietors and the higher income groups might inhibit capital investment and jeopardize the regime's developmental schemes. Yet although vested interests were successful in blocking some of the reforms, especially those relating to rural property, and Calvo Sotelo had every reason to be disgusted by 'the riot of the moneyed people', he was nevertheless successful in substantially increasing the treasury's revenues from taxes. A more efficient tax collection, a constant struggle against tax evaders, the real increase of taxes on items such as tobacco, matches, and spirits, the new stamp duties, the simplification of the assessment of the taxes levied on industry, the new tax on personal income, the concession of monopolies, and, no less meaningful, the expansion of economic activities, all these resulted in a substantial increase in the treasury's revenues from taxes.[185] It was no mean achievement, for example, that the number of taxpayers registered as industrialists and merchants increased by about 63%, and their contribution to the treasury's revenues from taxation increased by about 70% within five years, as against an increase of only 33% during the whole period between 1907 and the end of the Great War.[186] That the number of taxpayers registered as entrepreneurs should have increased within the first five years of the Dictatorship from 416,777 to 679,598 reflected not only the genuine expansion of the entrepreneurial classes, but certainly also the successes of the regime in its fight against middle-class tax evasion. Undoubtedly, the main burden of taxation, the pressure of which had been constantly on the increase,[187] lay now on the shoulders of the middle classes. It was also mainly they who were called upon to pay for the expanding expenditures of the municipalities of Spain which, in addition to their own issues of public debts, had to resort to a wide variety of local taxes—a contemporary counted about 110 such different levies—to balance their shaky budgets. 'We must thank God that we are not asked to pay a special tax for the right to breathe in public', sighed sarcastically the above-mentioned source.[188]

[185] Primo in *La Nación*, 2 Jan. 1928.

[186] *Anuario*, 1929, p. 387.

[187] Velarde (*Política*, p. 242) put the pressure in index terms: 922—83; 1923—86.6; 1924—104.5; 1925—94.6; 1926—95.5; 1927—108; 1928—129.5; 1929—119.6.

[188] Iglesias, pp. 122–7.

The overall increase in the treasury's revenues from taxation during the whole period of the Dictatorship was not a negligible one. The yield from the different taxes, state services, and monopolies showed an increase of about 50 per cent (2,411, 940,440 pesetas in 1922–3; 3,627,433,472 in 1929).[189] An examination of the particular types of taxes indicates that it was the share of the important economic groups in the overall contribution to the national budget that showed the most substantial increase.

Significantly, the yield from direct taxes, the main contributors of which were the middle classes, increased during the Dictatorship at a greater rate (49%) in comparison with indirect taxes, the yield of which had also shown a considerable increase (44%). And again, as far as the direct contributions to the treasury were concerned, the share of the industrial sector increased at a higher rate (85.62%) than that of the landowning sector. But, notably, the latter's direct tax contribution to the treasury, which in the twenty-three years that preceded the Dictatorship rose by only 38%, went up under Primo's seven-year rule by 58.31%. In absolute figures, the share of the landowners was substantially higher than that of the industrial sector (1922–3: 230,301,755–101,539,190; 1929: 364,597,920–188, 623,892). Equally significant is the fact that the utilities tax which mainly affected the higher income groups should have risen by about 25%, and that the tax on immovable property should have yielded in 1929 72.98% more than in 1923.[190]

As far as the revenues from indirect taxation were concerned,[191] it is not surprising that a protectionist regime such as the Dictatorship should have increased its revenues from customs by 29.87%. That the increase here was not even higher[192] was due to the fact that Primo de Rivera did not invent protectionism, and tariffs were high enough before he came to office. The highly substantial increase in the yield of the stamp duty (76.69%) is perhaps an explanation of why it was so vehemently condemned by businessmen. The increase of 52% in the revenues from the supply of lighting was reflective of the fact that electricity was becoming a widespread commodity. The services by the state and the monopolies it had created with the professed intention of increasing its revenues also showed a substantial rate of increase in the sums they yielded to the treasury (about 66%).[193]

[189] *Anuario*, 1929, p. 359. [190] Ibid., p. 353. [191] Ibid., p. 354.
[192] Benítez de Lugo, p. 62, claims the increase was 40%.
[193] *Anuario*, 1929, p. 355.

It should be seen, however, as a serious indictment of the Dictatorship, that the entire landowning class of Spain paid throughout the Dictatorship in taxes a sum far lower than that yielded to the government from the sale of lotteries. The same was also true of the industrial sector.[194] This, inasmuch as it reflects the Spaniards' mania for lottery, undoubtedly exemplifies the failure of the regime to carry out a surgical reform of Spain's tax system. It is this momentous failure to shift the tax burden on to the shoulders of the 'oligarchy' that made the appeal of the government to public loans inevitable if it still wanted to carry out its development projects.

It was of course to be expected that the increase of revenue should have been instrumental in narrowing the deficits of the ordinary budgets. Some optimistic sources even speak of surpluses after 1926.[195]

	Revenues	*Expenditures*	*Balance*
1923–4	2,617,047,068	3,048,386,042	– 431,338,974
1924–5	2,777,840,568	2,941,724,894	– 163,884,326
1925–6	2,755,288,568	3,092,538,991	– 337,250,423
1926*	1,478,092,334	1,445,518,525	+ 32,573,809
1927	3,073,378,604	3,139,441,153	– 66,062,549
1928	3,258,518,604	3,257,590,079	+ 928,525
1929	3,399,771,082	3,370,104,025	+ 29,667,057

* 2º semester

But this assessment of the government's expenditure seems to be quite unrealistic even for the years that preceded the introduction of the extraordinary budget. Morocco alone devoured in 1924–5 172,233,296 pesetas more than in 1923. 'Ruinous sums!' exclaimed the Dictator.[196]

Moreover, even if one is ready to accept these optimistic figures, one should reckon that they refer only to the government's ordinary budgets. The expenditure of the extraordinary budget turned every presumed surplus into an entirely fictitious one. Thus, for example, a contemporary source, whose figures as far as the treasury's revenues are concerned are similar to those of Dalmacio Iglesias,[197]

[194] Cf. Ibid., pp. 353–5: 1929: lotteries—413,280,647 pesetas; landowners—364,597,920; industry—188,623,892.

[195] Iglesias, pp. 107–8. *Estadísticas Básicas*, p. 332, proposes a surplus of 185.5 million pesetas for 1928, but a deficit of 366 million for 1929.

[196] See Villanueva, *La Dictadura*, p. 203; Primo to Sanjurjo in Armiñán, *Epistolario*, p. 361.

[197] *Folletín*, p. 823.

reminds us that if one is to take into account both the ordinary and the extraordinary expenditure of the government for 1929, it would amount to 4,405,429,590 pesetas. In other words, instead of a surplus of 29,667,057 pesetas, as the figures of Dalmacio Iglesias indicate, the government was faced in 1929 with a real deficit of 1,005,658,508 pesetas, which it had to try and cover by the further issue of public loans.

A large scale of capital mobilization was indispensable if the regime was to live up to its image as a developmental dictatorship. The government believed it had found a formula of salvation in the creation of an extraordinary budget which was expected to be covered by the surpluses of the ordinary one and to a much greater extent by public loans. In other words, it was the money-owners together with the modest savers who were expected to finance Spain's 'modernization'. Their readiness to do so would very much depend on the degree of confidence inspired by the regime. Not an exclusively Spanish phenomenon—Great Britain had in the 1920s its own extraordinary budgets, such as the Road Fund and the Unemployment Insurance Fund[198]—the extraordinary budget reflected a quasi-Keynesian approach; it was viewed by the regime as the indispensable instrument for carrying out 'at an accelerated rhythm enterprises of national reconstruction'. Consistent with its regenerationist imagery, it expected the budget to 'stir up the spiritual and material energies of the race, until now lethargic'.[199]

To be sure, the foundations of this policy were already laid down by the military directory, which in two years had mobilized from the public 1,734,355,000 pesetas, according to Calvo Sotelo, to finance extraordinary schemes of development as the supreme excuse of a dictatorship.[200] Side by side with the mobilization of public financial resources to pay for governmental enterprises, the military directory had encouraged the municipalities to engage in local developmental projects, for which the Bank of Local Credit was ready to grant generous loans. It does not seem that Ayuntamientos were always

[198] Cf. Donald Winch, *Economics and Policy. A Historical Survey* (Collins, 1972), p. 108. The difference was, of course, that in the Spanish case, there was no parliamentary or other public control of such budgets. *La Nación*, 17 July 1926, acknowledged that the extraordinary budget would have been impossible in a parliamentary system.

[199] *Gaceta*, 13 July 1926; *La Nación*, 20, 21 July 1926.

[200] For the generous issues of government bonds under the military directory, see *The Economist*, 19 Apr., 24 May, 20 Dec. 1924; Calvo, pp. 465–71.

eager to commit their modest treasury to large-scale operations. The government, however, had no patience with this house-keeping mentality. Thus, for example, when the city council of Gerona refused to abide by the governor's instructions to engage in a lavish plan of public works, the whole Ayuntamiento was dissolved and replaced by a more compliant one.[201] As a whole, however, city councils were happy to benefit from the sudden availability of money for building schools, for the renovation of their system of sanitation, or for the upkeep of streets and pavements.[202]

Nor was the budgetary jugglery which manifested itself in the way that the extraordinary budget was run, and in the arbitrary manipulation of data and figures, invented by the civilian directory. The abrogation by the military government, at a very early stage, of the Law of Accountancy[203]—which had prohibited the uncontrolled transfer of credits, limited the concession of supplementary funds for whatever state service or work, and, in brief, committed the government to stick to its original budget—removed any independent control over the executive's allocation of public funds. The national budget thus turned into a non-compulsory, arbitrarily elastic framework. The government had to look constantly for additional sources of income to fill the ever-increasing 'holes' in its budgets.[204] Such 'holes' were inevitable as the government, acting always as the nation's *consejo de administración*, took on increasing commitments.

With the transition to civilian rule and the creation, on 13 July 1926, of an extraordinary budget of 3,539 million pesetas to finance, for the next ten years, public works and other governmental enterprises,[205] thus, in effect, hiding a real deficit behind the apparent surpluses of the ordinary budget, the orgy of public spending gained momentum, so much so that the Treasury's Comptroller had to give up in depair his attempts to supervise public expenditure. The ministries, especially that of development, would simply not disclose the real figures.[206] Primo de Rivera himself was to confess

[201] *El Sol*, 23 Mar. 1925; *Folletín*, pp. 275–6.

[202] See the example of Madrid, *Miercoles Ciudadanos*, 14, 21, 28 Sept. 1927, 5 Oct. 1927; and that of Molíns del Rey, *Cuatro años*. See *El Debate*, 17 Sept. 1929, on the development in the small municipalities across the country.

[203] *Gaceta*, 19 Sept., 2, 5 Oct. 1923.

[204] Primo acknowledged this predicament in a letter to Magaz, 13 Apr. 1925, see Armiñan, *Epistolario*.

[205] *Gaceta*, 13 July 1926. Guadalhorce, however, said he worked with an extravagant budget of 5,200 million pesetas. See his testimony in Ceballos-Teresí, vol. 7, p. 22.

[206] Marcelino Domingo, *¿Qué espera el Rey?*, pp. 153–4.

publicly[207] the unreliability of his budgets when he 'forecast' a 'surplus' of 32.5 million pesetas for 1926–7.[208] To give an illustration, an amalgamation of both the extraordinary and the ordinary budgets of 1928—for the latter, Calvo Sotelo had claimed a surplus of 186 million pesetas—would show an overall deficit of 859.8 million pesetas.[209]

It was vital for the government that the first debt issue aimed at helping to finance the extraordinary budget should be a success. It therefore launched a propaganda campaign proclaiming the soundness of the Spanish economy and finances. The result was highly encouraging. The issue, on 16 November 1926, of an instalment of 225 million pesetas in funded debt was a real success, applications amounting to more than twice the amount offered.[210] It should be noted, however, that a key feature of the regime's debt emissions was that their success largely depended, as the government was fully aware, on the willingness of the public to participate in them, a willingness that would always be conditioned by the degree of confidence, both political and economic, inspired by the regime. A government that based its entire developmental enterprise on private money, mobilized on a voluntary basis, would be faced with an acute dilemma when the unsound state of its finances and the regime's lack of political prospects became common knowledge. However, this was not yet the case.[211] The big banks acquired an important share of the November 1926 issue, but the participation of the private saver in this enterprise was by no means negligible: 163 million pesetas.[212] In an earlier issue of 400 million pesetas between 60 and 70% of the bonds were acquired by small investors.[213] It is noteworthy that about 60% of the savings deposited in savings banks and pawn shops during the Dictatorship, that is about 1,125 million pesetas, went to the stock exchange,[214] where government bonds were negotiated alongside the shares of private companies.

The increasing availability of money in private hands in the twenties apparently encouraged individuals to buy government

[207] *Folletín*, p. 320. Another friend of the regime, Victor Pradera, did not hesitate to mock Calvo Sotelo's 'surpluses', see *Diario de Sesiones de la Asamblea Nacional*, no. 16, 17 Feb. 1928, p. 586.

[208] *Gaceta*, 1 July 1926.

[209] Benítez de Lugo, p. 38; *Folletín*, pp. 583–5, 661–7.

[210] *The Economist*, 11 Dec. 1926.

[211] It would be in the second half of 1929, see pp. 342–56.

[212] *Folletín*, p. 498.

[213] *La Nación*, 9 Apr. 1926.

[214] José Francísco Formés, 'El ahorro popular durante la Dictadura: Las Cajas de Ahorros y Montes de Piedad', in *Cuadernos*, p. 290.

bonds, especially as they were usually proposed with splendid conditions. The amount of money deposited in current accounts in private banks increased under the Dictatorship by about 50% (from 2,468,400,000 pesetas in 1923 to 3,694,100,000 in 1929).[215] Savings banks proliferated all over the country; their number increased in the same period from 163 to 216 in order to give services to 1,519,000 new savers. Private savings increased during the Dictatorship by 147% (from 1,616,800,000 pesetas to 4,000 million).[216]

The frenetic financial operations of the government had definitely elevated economic activities, and the stock exchange in particular, to become the focal point of public interest.[217] In tones that may be familiar to observers of the latter years of Franco's Spain, a high official of Primo's Council of Economy, José María Valverde, expressed his jubilation at such a phenomenon. 'The great spirits, and many small ones,' he wrote, 'are primarily concerned with economics, increasingly forgetting politics.'[218] This phenomenon, according to *La Nación*, reflected 'a high level of civic education' [*sic*].[219] Though the banks clearly dominated the field[220] the fever of investments in treasury bonds and shares had captured the small and average saver too. 'The fever of buying and selling has reached dimensions never before known; gainers and losers arrived frequently at a state of real delirium.' The desire to make easy money through stock-exchange transactions captured the imagination of the urban middle classes.

A contemporary observer described the festival of speculation of those euphoric days in the following terms:

> The banking inflation favoured by the frequent emissions and conversions of debt, and the entrance of foreign currencies and bonds are creating throughout the country a fever of speculation. People buy and sell on the stock exchanges of Madrid, Barcelona and Bilbao more than ever. People are no longer satisfied with a modest interest for their savings, not even with that of the bonds, shares and debentures they hold. In all the tertulias, those of aristocratic circles and bourgeois clubs, as well as in the bars and taverns, everybody speaks of business, of profits and of paid-up shares. What

[215] Nicholas Belford, 'El sistema bancario durante la Dictadura de Primo', in *Cuadernos*, p. 239.

[216] *Estadísticas Básicas*, p. 319: 'Depósitos en Cajas de Ahorro con especificacion de entidades, imponentes, y saldos'. Cf. data given by Primo de Rivera in *La Nación*, 10 Oct. 1929.

[217] Hurtado, ii, pp. 244–5.

[218] 'Política y economía', in *La Nación*, 26 Mar. 1927.

[219] Ibid., 21 Jan. 1927.

[220] *Folletín*, p. 598.

characterizes this period is that nobody thinks of Spain, exactly like the time of the intense fever that overtook the country following the loss of the colonies. All, now as then, think of establishing business, setting up factories, exploiting mines and farms. Everybody thinks of business deals, subsidized by the state, concluded by pulling wires within the government, and, if possible, by snatching money from the state.[221]

It is not hard to see how in such an atmosphere of stock-exchange fever any unfavourable rumour or political turmoil could have a devastating effect on the mobilization of capital by the government from the private saver.

As early as February 1925, a contemporary economist, Luis Olariaga, viewed the government's frequent appeals for public money as having an adverse effect on the prospects of Spain's ever achieving a sound economy. Spain's exports, he said, ran no real chance of competing successfully in the international market. The only real prospect for an expansion of Spanish industry lay in the intensification of national consumption. This, however, was hampered both by the high cost of internal transport and by the scarcity of public money for investments. He accused the government of mobilizing the public's savings to finance its own expenditure, and of excluding them from the business sector, thus advancing state capitalism at the expense of the private sector of the economy.[222]

This was not an entirely fair criticism. True, by the end of 1929 the Spanish government was responsible for about 75% of the total debt issues that were then in circulation (that is 20,260,050,118 pesetas out of 29,249,144,170). However, the direct responsibility of the Dictatorship, though indeed substantial, was more modest. During the Dictatorship, the government had been responsible for between 40 and 60% of the total amount of bonds issued, while in 1917, for example, it was responsible for only 22.6%.[223] But it is nevertheless highly indicative of the intensive reactivation of the private economy under the Dictatorship that the industrial sector (this includes banks, railways, electricity, and mining concerns) was able to mobilize in the years 1924–9 4,553,360,000 pesetas of public money. This was 141% more

[221] Ibid., p. 694.

[222] Luis Olariaga, 'La crisis económica. Esperando la acción del estado', in *La Nación*, 28 Feb. 1925. A similar criticism could be heard in business circles, see *Boletín de la Cámara Oficial de Comercio e Industria de Sabadell*, Nov. 1925.

[223] Ceballos-Teresí, vol. 7, p. 404; *Anuario*, 1929, p. 263.

than the sum mobilized by the same sector in the five years that preceded the Dictatorship.[224]

The apparent soundness of the government's finances, so crucial to the absorption of its loans by the public, and consequently, to the financing of the extraordinary budget, seemed to have been enhanced, early in 1927, by the largest consolidation of the floating debt ever achieved in Spain with such 'splendid results'.[225] The immediate effect of the conversion was to bring about a surplus of floating balances, great ease in the money market, and, consequently, a big rise in stocks and bonds.[226]

This general spurt of markets had been more the result of a psychological boost created by the successful conversion than of any real increase of money as the conversion operations were a mere exchange of paper, and did not set free a single peseta. For the government, the main significance of the conversion was political; it consolidated the Dictatorship and enhanced its prestige. For bankers and capitalists, it was a splendid business with which they co-operated out of sheer greed for profit, though the government, as usual, preferred to see in the success of its financial operations the result of the self-sacrifice of Spanish capital on behalf of national reconstruction.[227]

However successful the conversion may have been, by February 1928 the issue of public bonds by the government had already reached the large figure of 3,064,628,500 pesetas, about 60 per cent of which were channelled to cover the budgetary deficits.[228]

But even this was only part of the picture, for there were many debts that were not directly issued by the government, but were guaranteed by it as a way of indirect subsidy to industrial and public enterprises,[229] or to projects such as the construction of cheap housing.[230] To have an even more accurate picture of capital mobilization for public expenditures under the Dictatorship, one should also add the bonds issued directly, and with warm encouragement by the government, by Ayuntamientos and Diputaciones. When all this is taken into account, the following picture emerges:[231]

[224] 'Valores emitidos en 1929, comparados con el decenio 1919–28', *El Financiero*, Nov. 1930, p. 15.

[225] *The Economist*, 16 Apr. 1927.

[226] For the whole operation, see Calvo, pp. 155–9. Benítez de Lugo, pp. 85–7, 97, 103–4; *Folletín*, pp. 485, 568–70.

[227] Ibid., pp. 570–4; Benítez de Lugo, pp. 95–6.

[228] 'Revista de Economía y Hacienda' quoted in *Folletín*, p. 686.

[229] Such a practice was allowed in a special decree, *Gaceta*, 25 Jan. 1926.

[230] Benítez de Lugo, pp. 30–1, 108.

[231] 'Valores emitidos en 1929, comparados con el decenio1919–1928', *El Financiero*, Nov. 1930, p. 15; cf. *Folletín*, pp. 840, 841; *Anuario*, 1929, p. 362.

Public Bonds (pesetas)

	Issued by the State	*Issued by Corporations*	*Total*
Nov. 1923	333,726,500		333,726,500
1924	578,790,000	26,850,000	605,640,000
1925	500,000,000	63,510,000	563,510,000
1926	625,000,000	178,480,000	803,480,000
1927	300,000,000	138,460,000	438,460,000
1928	800,,000,000	429,240,000	1,229,240,000
1929	1,162,500,000	145,950,000	1,308,450,000
Total	4,300,016,500	982,490,000	5,282,506,500

That this sum was still 1,465,967,000 pesetas less than the amount of money mobilized by the state and its corporations in the five years that preceded the Dictatorship, was partly due to the fact that the Moroccan war had compelled the government to resort to exceptionally large-scale issues of public loans (in 1922, for example, 2,121,040,000 pesetas), and partly to the fact that the last constitutional governments had indeed anticipated Primo's policy of capital mobilization for development schemes. Put in perspective, the Dictatorship's financial effort was not that spectacular.

But to gauge the scale of local developmental enterprises during the Dictatorship one should add to the debt of the Ayuntamientos the 250 million pesetas of direct credit which they received from the Bank of Local Credit (between 1926 and 1929 they borrowed 213,647,100 pesetas from other sources). Moreover, the ordinary budgets of Spanish Ayuntamientos had increased in the years 1925–9 by about 123 million pesetas. As for the Diputaciones, their indebtedness increased during the Dictatorship by about 130 million pesetas, that is by almost 130 per cent.[232] Calvo Sotelo, in line with the policy already started by the military directory, did not leave any doubt as to the approach of the civilian government to the issue of municipal debts. It encouraged them to the extent that the capital thus mobilized was invested in public works.[233]

The upsurge of economic activities under the Dictatorship and the increasing requirements of capital created most favourable conditions for the expansion of the banking system in Spain. The

[232] *Anuario*, 1929, pp. 398–9; Benítez de Lugo, pp. 109–10. Calvo, p. 49, claims that the credit given by the Local Credit Bank amounted to just 215,411,574 pesetas. See the case of the Ayuntamiento of Priego (Córdoba): its expenditures increased by more than 80 per cent under the Dictatorship, José Tomas Valverde, *Memorias de un alcalde* (Madrid, 1961), p. 29 ff.

[233] Calvo, p. 47.

private banks, which during the Great War had greatly expanded their activities and accumulated huge amounts of capital, used the opportunities created by the Dictatorship to recapture the momentum of growth.[234] Some of the new banks were semi-state enterprises, whose activities catered for a wide range of the needs of the state-controlled economy as well as—in the case of the new Mortgage Bank, for example—for social endeavours such as cheap housing projects. The Bank of Local Credit was another example of a semi-state bank. Founded in 1925, it was expected to be the catalyst of the infrastructural development of the municipalities of Spain. In 1928, the Banco Exterior de España was started, by state initiative, to promote Spanish foreign trade. Such a bank had been demanded by industrialists in Catalonia since 1900.[235] They also welcomed the fact that the Bank of Industrial Credit, which had existed before the Dictatorship, now expanded its credit facilities. By 1928, its outstanding loans amounted to 460 million pesetas.[236]

In 1929, the inflationary effects of public spending, especially as they were accompanied by the political crisis of the regime, would become a serious problem for the government.[237] It is, however, essential to a balanced evaluation of the developmental effort of the Dictatorship to stress that, significant as it certainly was, in the last analysis it was by no means an extravagant adventure. Rather it was a fairly measured, even elementary enterprise that did not stretch the nation's financial burden beyond its productive and saving capacity. Nor can it be said that it had mortgaged the nation's future, as critics such as Benítez de Lugo tended to claim. For one thing, infrastructural investments were, as Calvo Sotelo hoped they would be, 'reproductive'; hence they were matched by a substantial, real increase in industrial production. For another, the acceleration of economic activities and the concomitant mobilization of capital

[234] Nicholas Belford, 'El sistema bancario durante la Dictadura de Primo', in *Cuadernos*, pp. 241–50. The Bank of Spain advanced during the Dictatorship an average of 4,500 million pesetas worth of loans per year; the average in the decade that preceded the Dictatorship was 500 million; see ibid., p. 253. The number of banks increased during the Dictatorship from 161 to 209, and their balances by 62 per cent (from 8,802.72 million pesetas to 12,196.11); Ceballos-Teresí, vol. 7, pp. 402–5.

[235] Harrison, 'Catalan Business and the Loss of Cuba 1898–1914', in the *Economic History Review*, vol. xxvii, no. 3, Aug. 1974, p. 440.

[236] For the banking system under the Dictatorship, see also Calvo Sotelo in Primo, *Intervenciones*, p. 368; and Idelfonso Cuesta Garrigos, 'Los grandes bancos españoles, su evolución (1922–1943)', in *Moneda y Crédito*, Dec. 1944, no. 11; Velarde, *Política económica*, pp. 207–10.

[237] See Chapter IX, sections b and c.

did not unleash any extraordinary rate of inflation in Spain. To be sure, Primo's economic system was anything but immune to inflation. The wholesale price index rose dramatically in the first two years of the Dictatorship (around 9 per cent), and prices did undergo sharp, short-term rises also in subsequent years.[238] Calvo Sotelo later acknowledged the 'high level of our internal prices', especially in 1929 when world prices had been dropping rather sharply;[239] this incompatibility between internal and external prices would have an adverse effect on the national currency.[240] But it was precisely after 1925, that is when the regime embarked upon its 'extraordinary' budgetary enterprise, that prices in Spain started to show a marked downward tendency; in 1928 they were even lower by 2.9 per cent than in 1923, the lowest point since 1917.[241] Significantly, the expansion of economic activities did not unleash a rise in wages. On the contrary, the overall tendency of wages was towards stability, and even depreciation; a trend that was made easier to digest by the working class precisely because the price index of basic food necessities had been consistently dropping after 1925.[242] Moreover, another possible indicator of the rate of inflation, the circulation of paper currency, did not show throughout the Dictatorship any extraordinary increase; in 1929 it was higher only by 4.14 per cent in relation to 1923.[243] As a whole, it does seem that Primo's 'new deal' was a reasonably balanced affair.

The Dictatorship had embarked upon unthrifty expenditure as one means of making itself widely acceptable to the Spaniards. Development and financial operations were substituted for 'accursed' politics. But no economic system, successful as it may apparently look, can be credibly maintained in a political void. Before long, the Dictator came to realize that his regime's lack of political prospects had done much to undermine his economic deal. But before examining this symbiotic link between the economy and politics in the context of the overall crisis that led to the débâcle of the regime, we must attempt to outline some of the social consequences of the Dictatorship.

[238] For prices, see below, pp. 306–8, 374–6.

[239] Calvo, p. 312. See also below p. 374.

[240] See below, pp. 338–40, 348–9.

[241] The wholesale price index of foodstuffs and industrial products (1913 = 100): 1923—172; 1924—183; 1925—188; 1926—181; 1927—172; 1928—167; 1929—171. See 'Los precios en España', in *El Financiero*, Nov. 1930, pp. 77–8; *Añuario*, 1929, pp. 296–7; Ceballos-Teresí, vol. 7, p. 353.

[242] See below, pp. 306, 374–5.

[243] Cf. Calvo, p. 186; Velarde, *Política*, pp. 206–7.

CHAPTER VIII

Primo de Rivera's Social Deal Between Change and Stagnation

1. *'Christian Socialism' and the Socialist Alliance*

PRIMO DE RIVERA's nationalist economic policy was in concurrence with his regime's fundamental political precepts, and both were complemented by a social approach that cast upon the state and upon corporative organs the task of creating a 'just society'. He was fundamentally motivated by an unsophisticated concern for the well-being of the working class, and he strove to achieve a 'Christian' and just equilibrium between the haves and the have-nots. This could be brought about, he believed, only by 'a harmonious association between Capital and Labour', the standard device of corporative systems. The alternative to such a harmonious system was, God forbid!, the Soviet example . . .[1]

The Dictatorship cannot be said to have been impregnated with the same cold indifference that characterized the attitude of Francoism towards the popular masses.[2] Rather than presenting himself as a staunch defender of the 'oligarchy', Primo did not lose time in 'shaking the obstinate quietism of the conservative classes', in order to advance the cause of a 'social revolution from above' that could prevent the more violent and radical one from below.[3] Immediately upon assuming power, he called on employers to sacrifice part of their profits in order to improve the living standards of their workers. In special appeals to the employers, he urged them to respect and abide by 'all the social conquests' so far made by the working class. He added the hope that 'the type of violent, greedy and arbitrary employer has disappeared from our society'.[4] Though himself a landowner, Primo claimed that he subscribed to the concept of the social function of property. Declarations apart, this

[1] See Primo's declarations on social issues in *El Socialista*, 29 Sept. 1923, 27 June 1928; *La Nación*, 1 June 1927; Revesz, *Frente*, pp. 104–10.

[2] Cf. Benjamín Oltra, Amando de Miguel, 'Bonapartismo y Catolocismo', pp. 75–6.

[3] Calvo, p. 127.

[4] *El Socialista*, 3 Oct. 1923; *La Nación*, 17 May 1926.

principle was never applied where it was most needed, in the countryside. In the cities, and for the cause of urban workers, the Dictator exhibited greater generosity. He would, as his finance minister later recalled, frequently react energetically against the excesses committed by employers.[5] The 'economically powerful classes', he warned, should not expect favours from his regime at the expense of 'the other classes'.[6]

As for the workers, 'the indispensable factor of national progress',[7] he promised them he would improve 'the imperfect regime under which the wage-earner lives' by guaranteeing better labour contracts, and by advancing programmes of professional promotion. He made it clear, however, that though he would definitely protect the workers, he drew a clear distinction between the 'bad'—Anarcho-syndicalists, Communists, or members of 'cells belonging to Masonic sects'—and the 'good' ones, those who followed the moderate teachings of Pablo Iglesias.[8] Primo de Rivera would accept a dialogue with Socialism only so long as it abandoned political action and stuck to a peaceful, trade-unionist line of struggle. 'Workers' associations? Yes; but only for cultural aims, for protection, mutualism, and even for sane politics, not for resistance and not by undermining production.'[9] Only the Socialists could be expected to live, at least temporarily, up to such an image. Primo was therefore determined to attract them to a *modus vivendi* with the state, both because it isolated the violent Anarcho-syndicalists and because he was desperately looking for a partnership with the organized working class that would guarantee the success of his development enterprises, and bring about a 'maximization of output'. The workers, he knew, were 'the most important sector in the life of the country, and one that could most influence its transformation and aggrandizement'.[10]

Primo de Rivera did not expect of course that the 'harmony between Capital and Labour' would be reached through a free concert of social forces. It was up to the state 'to see to it, with its paternal and neutral intervention, that the social conditions and the relations between Capital and Labour are effective'.[11] In fact, he

[5] Calvo, quoted in García Canales, p. 57.

[6] Quoted in Cambó, *Las Dictaduras*, p. 33.

[7] *La Nación*, 20 Mar. 1926.

[8] Primo in his *Intervenciones*, p. 301, in Aunós, *La Política social de la Dictadura* (Madrid, 1944), pp. 31–3; and in *Folletín*, pp. 788–9.

[9] *El Socialista*, 29 Sept. 1923.

[10] Ibid., 28 Sept., 2 Oct. 1923.

[11] Ibid., 2 Oct. 1923.

thought that a dictatorship was better equipped than any other regime for such a task. Or, as he put it in a speech welcoming Albert Thomas, the president of the International Labour Office, 'only a dictatorial democracy, or a democratic dictatorship such as the one that presently rules Spain . . . can reorganize the social and economic life of the country without any class bias'. Primo's Minister of Labour, Eduardo Aunós, declared on the same occasion that 'we are here putting into practice a real *official* socialism'.[12]

There is no evidence to sustain the view that Primo de Rivera wanted to have in Spain some kind of two-party system in which the UP and a moderate labour party might be able to alternate peacefully in power.[13] Rather than subscribing to such a socially orientated version of the *pacto del Pardo*, the Dictator preferred to keep the monopoly of power in unmistakably nationalist hands, while accepting the 'just' demands and 'legal' conquests of Socialism. Nor is there much evidence to support García Venero's view that Primo's alliance with the Spanish left was an opportunistic device aimed at strengthening his links with the *Cartel des Gauches* that came to power in France in May 1924.[14] Primo's working-class policy was a much more fundamental affair.

Clearly, Primo de Rivera had in mind the domestication of Socialism, or rather its 'nationalization', its absorption into the premisses of the nationalist state. For him, there was no fundamental divergence between socialism and the State. But then he had his own concept of socialism as being

> the most equitable and considerate enjoyment of earthly goods within the relativity of productive capacities, and conditioned by the existence of capital and talent. The temperate credo of socialism fits, then, into any political doctrine and any regime . . . Our monarchy . . . would be socialist inasmuch as it authorizes the government to realize in Spain an economic transformation that would bring about the union of the use of land with its possession, would guarantee the rights of the tenants against the whims and cupidity of the landowners, would protect labour, advance remedies against unemployment, and, in sum, meet with diligence and within a framework of absolute discipline and order whatever is just in 'revolutionary' demands.[15]

[12] *Folletín*, pp. 753, 754.

[13] For such a view, see Maurín, p. 187; J. A. Gallego, *El Socialismo durante la Dictadura* (Madrid, 1977), pp. 93–6, 131–4.

[14] García Venero, *Historia de las Internacionales en España* (Madrid, 1957), vol. ii, p. 415.

[15] *El Liberal*, 6 Jan. 1928.

Primo went so far as to claim that there was no fundamental divergence between the Socialist party and the UP. Their social doctrine coincided with each other, he said, almost completely.[16] What made the UP the appropriate agent of a state that would integrate socialism and nationalism was the fact that it was permeated 'by ideals of the right and the left alike'.[17] A UP ideologue, Pemartín, thought that without an advanced social policy, that is without 'absorbing the positive, constructive part of socialism', there was no solid prospect of success for Primo de Rivera's revolution. Nowhere in the world, he argued, was there now room for more than two parties, that is the Socialist and 'the other one'. In Spain, it was a crucial role of the latter to absorb the former. In other words, the Dictatorship was urged to defeat Socialism 'with its own weapons', that is by 'socializing', by 'improving conditions'.[18]

Though a populist leader of sorts, who anticipated the Falange's *Auxilio social* and the CEDA's *Asistencia Social* by patronizing the opening of workers' clubs and the distribution of free meals and clothes to needy people,[19] Primo de Rivera was no social demagogue. Summoning to his help social-Catholic tradition, he anticipated the Falange's integration of nationalism and socialism, as being the best way to curtail the advance of 'Communism'.[20] Neither Mussolini's nor Perón's socialism had much to do with the social teachings of the Church. But the former's integration of socialism and nationalism (he failed, though, where Primo de Rivera succeeded: the CGL rejected his appeals for collaboration), as well as the latter's solicitude for urban workers, whom he turned into a solid source of power without having to abandon ultranationalism, are patterns that recall to one's mind the Spanish Dictator's experiment. He domesticated labour by catering to the needs of the working class (a policy that was to end by alienating from his regime vested interests) without abandoning ultrapatriotism. In Portugal, Salazar also argued that his New Economy rested upon the authority of a vigorous state that protected society against both 'the excesses of capitalism' and the demands of 'destructive bolshevism'. But, unlike Primo de Rivera,

[16] Alfaro Baratech, *El Sindicalismo español en el momento actual* (Barcelona, 1929), p. 71.

[17] Primo in *La Nación*, 9 Aug. 1928.

[18] Pemartín, 'Los dos frentes de ataque. Ante la amenaza socialista', 'La transformación de los partidos', in *La Nación*, 14 Jan., 18 June 1928. See a similar thesis in Juan de Castilla, 'Izquierda y derecha', *La Nación*, 28 Mar. 1928.

[19] *Unión Patriótica*, 15 May 1929; *La Vanguardia*, 19 Jan. 1929.

[20] Primo in *Unión Patriótica*, 15 Jan. 1928.

the Portuguese Dictator rejected out of hand the possibility of building the fatherland in a consensual partnership with Socialists. He discarded the possibility of embarking upon social initiatives before economic recovery was achieved,[21] while Primo maintained that social emphasis was a prerequisite to economic development.

Primo de Rivera, unlike many military rulers who concentrated on catering for the budgetary and other needs of the army and refrained from flirting with social ideas,[22] inaugurated a social policy that, by striving to acquire a working-class *point d'appui* for his regime, was not committed at all costs to the sanctity of vested interests. In his instructions to his energetic minister of labour in 1925, the Dictator urged him to elaborate a comprehensive body of social legislation that would be the basis of a society in which the humble people could feel protected, and could profit from ever-increasing benefits.[23] As far as the allocation of funds for social purposes was concerned, there can be little doubt that the Dictatorship did not fall back on budgetary orthodoxy and stringency. Between 1920 and 1929, government expenditure on education increased by 58% (8,000 new primary schools were built, and school attendance increased by 22.9%), that on social benefits by 98%, and that on health services by 200%; whereas in fields such as infancy protection, public charity, and strictly social services the government spent in 1929 2,246%, 100%, and 800% respectively more than in 1920.[24] The government also keenly encouraged private charitable institutions to extend the scope of their enterprises.[25] It is not surprising that infant mortality and the general death-rate should have dropped during the Dictatorship by about 14%.[26]

Given the social commitments of the Dictatorship—these were made explicit about a fortnight after the seizure of power in a meeting between the Dictator and the leader of the Asturian miners, Manuel Llaneza[27]—and given the essentially pragmatic orientation

[21] Salazar, pp. 80, 144–5, 169.

[22] Nordlinger, pp. 171–6.

[23] Aunós, *El golpe de estado del general Primo de Rivera y sus primeras disposiciones de orden social* (Madrid, 1944).

[24] Admittedly, these are official figures: Calvo Sotelo, 'Orientaciones económicas y tributarias', in *Curso de Ciudadanía. Conferencias pronunciadas en el Alcazar de Toledo*, Marzo de 1929 (Depósito Geográfico e Histórico del Ejército, s.a.), pp. 323–31. Cf. Calvo, *Mis servicios*, pp. 479–81.

[25] See details and data in Ministerio de la Gobernación, Dirección General de Administración, *Estadística de la beneficencia particular en España correspondiente a los años 1926 al 1928 inclusive* (Madrid, 1930), pp. 87–126.

[26] J. Nadal, *La población española* (Barcelona, 1971), p. 188.

[27] *El Socialista*, 2, 5 Oct. 1923.

of both the Socialist Party (PSOE) and its attached syndical organizations (UGT), it is hardly surprising that the Socialists agreed to 'collaborate' with the Dictatorship, or as they would have preferred to say, to apply 'interventionist tactics'.[28]

I have studied elsewhere the topic of Socialist collaboration with the Dictatorship,[29] and there is no point in recapitulating. It is the regime's policies and attitudes, rather than the Socialist reaction, that should now be underlined. For Primo de Rivera, the Socialists' acquiescence in his regime was tantamount to working-class legitimacy for the Dictatorship. Highly satisfied, he even claimed that there was no need to think of reinstituting democracy in Spain, because Largo Caballero's presence in the *Consejo de Estado* meant that the workers' aspirations were being adequately represented in the institutions of the new regime.[30]

Indeed, rather than *directly* producing spectacular improvements, the social policy of the Dictator, just like his economic deal, resulted mainly in the formulation of new institutional schemes. Less than a week after he came to power, he appointed a committee to look into ways of bringing down the price of basic commodities,[31] and in subsequent decrees he set out a mechanism for price control. In April 1924, he created the institutional framework that was to advise the government on all matters of labour and social legislation. This he did by replacing the old Institute of Social Reforms with a Council of Labour, in which an equal representation was allotted to workers and employers.[32] This corporate approach was extended to other socio-economic institutions as the civilian directory embarked upon additional enterprises. The state, Socialist functionaries, and employers were to be represented also in such bodies as the Provisions Committee, the Committee of Subsistence, and in a variety of bodies concerned with economic and social planning such as the Council of National Economy, the Council of Telegraphic Administration and Information, The Comptroller Council of Accounts, and many others.[33]

It was in such bodies that much of the Dictatorship's social legislation, the wide publicity of which admittedly surpassed its rather modest application, was generated. In October 1924, a pretentious project for the construction of cheap houses for workers

[28] Ibid., 11 Nov. 1924; 10 Oct. 1926.
[29] Ben-Ami, *The Origins*, pp. 101–27.
[30] Primo in Revesz, *Frente*, p. 102.
[31] *Gaceta*, 18 Sept. 1923.
[32] Ibid., 30 Apr. 1924; Aunós, *Política social*, pp. 38–9.
[33] Aunós, op. cit., pp. 33–83.

was launched,[34] a project Aunós viewed as 'the main and most fundamental part of our ministerial enterprises'.[35] Subsequent decrees made available credits and subsidies to those companies that were contracted by the government to build cheap houses. The companies were to be exempt from taxes related to their work on such projects for a period of thirty years, and so would be the cheap houses' owners or tenants. Not only was the government itself to provide funds for the enterprise, 180 million pesetas until August 1928,[36] but city councils were also authorized to issue their own public debts for financing local projects of cheap housing. To attract money to the project, the government even allowed savings banks, public pawnshops, and funds of mutual and charitable character to constitute themselves into construction companies and thus benefit from the splendid conditions it had granted to those engaged in the building of cheap houses. These provisions were complemented in July 1925 by a special decree providing credit for the construction of Economical Houses. This new measure was aimed at extending the housing project to those who could not even buy a 'cheap house', and would be given favourable conditions for renting them.[37] Further subsidies and credits—70 million pesetas until the summer of 1928[38]—were made available for the project. The Chambers of urban landlords were especially disturbed by these measures that, they feared, might bring down rent rates.[39] This did not seem to be the case however. In Madrid, for example the number of flats available at less than fifty pesetas a month was, if anything, falling.[40]

According to Calvo Sotelo the Dictatorship had spent on cheap housing 261 million pesetas, as compared with only 8 million spent by governments in the ten years prior to 1923 on similar enterprises.[41] But the dream of 'constructing a house for every Spaniard', like a similar pretension embodied in Mussolini's project of *case popolari*,[42]

[34] Cámara Oficial de la Propiedad Urbana de Barcelona, *Las recientes disposiciones del Directorio encaminadas a impulsar la construcción de viviendas económicas* (Barcelona, 1924).

[35] Aunós, *Política social*, p. 79.

[36] *La Nación*, 22 Aug. 1928.

[37] For the case of Barcelona, see *La Epoca*, 19 June 1929.

[38] *La Nación*, 22 Aug. 1928.

[39] *Miercoles Ciudadanos*, 14, 21, 28 Sept., 5 Oct. 1927. For the whole issue of cheap houses, see also Aunós, *La política social*, pp. 39–79.

[40] 1910 = 90,595; 1930 = 67,369. See Aviv, A. and J., 'Ideology and Political Patronage: Workers and Working-Class Movements in Republican Madrid', *European Studies Review*, vol. ii, no. 4, Oct. 1981, pp. 492–3.

[41] Calvo Sotelo, 'Orientaciones', pp. 323–31. Far lower figures (111 million) have been suggested by A. Cotorruelo, *La política económica de la vivienda en España* (Madrid, 1960), p. 54.

[42] Gregor, pp. 280–1.

fell short of materialization. The Mortgages Bank, the Fund for the Enhancement of Small Property, and the frequent injections of money into the project could never cope with the colossal requirements.[43] It was mainly in the construction of houses for the military—a special *Patronato de Casas Militares* was set up to that effect—that substantial headway was made.[44]

Almost a pre-condition for the collaboration of the Socialists with the regime was their demand for advanced labour legislation. Funds were therefore allocated by the government for the professional promotion of workers, the conditions for which were set up in a special Statute of Professional Education that was promulgated on 31 October 1924. Research into social matters was to be encouraged by the Social School, which was provided with an appropriate archive and library. A special Fund of the Emigrant was created in September 1924 to provide protection to Spanish immigrants abroad as well as to create facilities for their repatriation.[45] By the middle of 1926, subsidies for prolific families were decided upon,[46] and legislation concerning the regulation of workers' retirement was promulgated.[47] By the end of the same year, Regulations Concerning the Implementation of the Law of Sunday Rest, that had been frequently ignored by employers, were issued. In 1927, measures were started to prevent women's night work as well as to regulate the provisions concerning work done in the home. In March 1929, social-insurance payments were extended to pregnant women.[48] A special measure had stipulated that no application by an entrepreneur for a state tender—and in an interventionist economy there were bound to be many of these—would be considered that did not specify what social benefits the workers would be granted by the company.[49] It was not always possible, or even feasible, to force employers to abide by existing labour legislation, especially when during periods of latent unemployment the workers themselves were not that keen on defending their rights. But the Dictatorship should at least be credited for rationalizing and gathering all labour legislation in a special Labour Code that contained all laws, and

[43] *Folletín*, pp. 698–9. According to *La Nación*, 14 Dec. 1928, only 1,600 families had so far got cheap houses.

[44] Iglesias, p. 101.

[45] Aunós, *Política social*, pp. 36, 44.

[46] AHN, P.G. Leg. 320; telegrams of support for the new law.

[47] Primo, *Intervenciones*, pp. 305–6.

[48] *La Epoca*, 25 Mar. 1929, acclaimed the new laws as likely to help curb the danger of socialism.

[49] Primo, *Intervenciones*, pp. 296–7.

specified the rights related to labour and apprenticeship contracts, accidents at work, and industrial tribunals.[50]

The climax of Aunós's policies, and one which the Socialists considered to be their major achievement, was the corporative organization established in November 1926 to deal with labour conflicts and social legislation through joint committees, *Comités Paritarios*, of workers and employers.

The idea had its precursors in Spain. Aunós himself recalled that his system was the culmination of traditional corporatism that had been applied in Spain since Roman and medieval times. The upsurge of labour conflicts in the twentieth century brought right-wing politicians and thinkers to revive this old idea as the best means of controlling the social process and damming the advance of the socialist formula based on confrontation. The teachings of Pope Leo XIII (especially his *Rerum Novarum*) and the corporatist views advanced by the Partito Popolare in Italy gave renewed relevancy to corporatism in the eyes of the Catholics.[51] The demand for a corporatist system that would neutralize the bitterness of labour conflicts only gained strength with the growth of working-class militancy under the impact of the post-war economic crisis. As early as 1917, Calvo Sotelo, Primo de Rivera's future minister of finance, had been involved in the elaboration of a programme for organic democracy in which labour relations were to be determined within an authoritarian, corporatist machinery.[52] A leader of the Catalan bourgeoisie, Puig i Cadalfach, viewed in 1919 the concept of mixed commissions of workers and employers as the *only* way, short of repression, of curbing the unprecedented upsurge of social conflicts.[53] Aunós himself, then a Catalan politician, had been active among Catholic groups in Catalonia in elaborating formulas to adapt old corporatist conceptions to modern society.[54] On an operational level, Prime Minister Romanones ordered, in March 1919, the creation all over Spain of '*consejos paritarios* in order to deal with issues affecting capital and labour'.[55] The application of this decree and another one of 5 October 1922, was, however, very partial. When, in 1926, Aunós came to establish his own corporative

[50] Aunós, *Política social*, pp. 50–1. See surveys of the Dictatorship's social legislation in *Boletín de Legislación Social*, 1926–9. For a convenient summary, see Alvaro López Nuñez, 'Previsión y seguros sociales' in *Curso de Ciudadanía*, pp. 93–118.

[51] G. Maura, *Jurados mixtos para dirimir las diferencias entre patronos y obreros y para prevenir y remediar las huelgas* (Madrid, 1901).

[52] S. Carr, p. 110.

[53] Ibid., p. 203.

[54] Pike, p. 266.

[55] Zancada, p. 264.

machinery, there were about twenty-six Comités Paritarios in Spain, most of them especially affecting white-collar commercial workers.[56]

Though acknowledging the Spanish roots of corporatism, as well as his debt to traditional Catholic thought, mainly that of La Tour du Pin,[57] Aunós was, however, hardly satisfied with past achievements in this field. He thought of creating a 'machinery organized in an integral way, that would amplify and perfect the wavering essays of corporatism so far made in Spain'.[58] The Fascist essay on corporatism was by then only in its infancy. In fact, it started at about the same time as Aunós's, with the creation in 1926 of the ministry of corporations, and culminated only with the establishment of the Chamber of Fasces and Corporations in 1939.[59] The Italian model might not have been there for Aunós to try to imitate it; but his visit to Italy in 1926 and his meeting with Giuseppe Bottai were a source of inspiration to him, though by then he certainly had already outlined the major details of the system he was to decree in November that same year.[60]

This does not mean that corporatism was not conceived by the Dictatorship as an attempt to come nearer to Fascist institutions and conceptions. Aunós viewed his new mechanism in terms of what he considered to be the *Zeitgeist*. He claimed it responded to the urgent need to avoid 'the atomistic disintegration' of society, and to 'relieve . . . labour from the amorphous anarchy where it had become bogged down by the sad errors suffered by humanity in the stage of civilization dominated by individualism'.[61] It was, moreover, 'the only barrier able to prevent liberalism from leading, as a most logical derivation, towards socialism'.[62] The new 'strong state' was to be based on 'the functional solidarity between all the elements of production' rather than on political parties, the embodiment of permanent civil war, and the breakdown of discipline and hierarchy.[63] Primo de Rivera himself was not alien to this concept. He was aware that 'the organic foresights' inherent in the new corporatist system were the best weapon available to defend the 'disarticulate collectivities' from 'disruptive seductions'.[64] In fact, responding to Ortega's challenge, *La Nación* argued that the proposed corporative

[56] Gallego, p. 207.

[57] Aunós, *La Reforma corporativa del estado* (Madrid, 1935), p. 130.

[58] Aunós, *La política social*, p. 57.

[59] R. Sarti (ed.), pp. 136–7.

[60] Aunós, *La política social*, pp. 58–9.

[61] *Gaceta*, 27 Nov. 1926.

[62] Aunós, *La reforma corporativa*, p. 87.

[63] Ibid., pp. ix, 182.

[64] *La Nación*, 3 Oct. 1928.

system was the instrument for the 're-vertebration' of Spain.[65] The Dictatorship's panegyrists always looked to the developing corporatism of Italy for inspiration. The 'vital *élan* of Fascism' combined with the advantages of 'the Corporatist State' were said to be reflective of an enviable 'passion for order' that was leading Italy to a prosperity which 'the countries that still stick to *laissez-faire* can never dream of achieving'.[66] The Fascist *Carta di Lavoro* of 1927 was hailed as precisely such an instrument of progress. Spain had every reason 'to follow attentively' the example of 'the sister nation', Italy.[67]

Aunós's system was not the obligatory, comprehensive, and all-embracing corporatist edifice that the Italian system pretended to be. But it differed from the 1919 corporatist essay in Spain in that it provided an ampler scope for dealing with both labour relations and labour legislation. Unlike the Fascist system that prohibited the independent existence of trade unions, in Spain, the latter's juridical personality was recognized; but, admittedly, only if and when they acted within the framework of the corporatist machinery. One was, then, free to belong to whatever syndicate one liked, but one's union could not effectively protect one's interests unless it sought representation in a Comité Paritario; this became the only legal channel of solving labour conflicts. Aunós was the first to acknowledge that this principle of 'free syndication within a system of obligatory corporation' was a key maxim of social-Catholic corporatism, that differentiated his system from the Italian model.[68] The result of this was that, whereas the Italian system came to seal the destruction of the Marxist Unions and replace them by official bureaucracies, Aunós's machinery was based upon, and created the conditions for, the consolidation and the expansion of the Socialist unions. Moreover, whereas in the Italian system Mussolini was able to carry out his promise to Signor Benni, the president of the Confederation of Industry (*Confindustria*), that 'so long as I am in power the employers have nothing to fear from the labour courts',[69]

[65] Ibid., 8 Nov. 1927.

[66] Vicente Gay in *La Nación*, 18 Feb. 1928.

[67] Alterius, 'Hacia una nueva forma del estado?', 'El estado corporativo fascista'; Vicente Gay, 'El gran contrato colectivo de trabajo'—*La Nación*, 15, 26 May 1927; 5 Mar. 1928.

[68] Aunós, *La reforma corporativa*, p. 130. Cf. Giuseppe Bottai, *Esperienza corporativa* (Rome, 1929), pp. 419–30; Lyttleton, *The Seizure*, pp. 322–33.

[69] Schmidt, p. 124 Primo gave a similar assurance only to his most intimate allies among the employers: the Marqués de Comillas and the owners of rightist newspapers; see the Marqués de Guad-el-Jelú, *Contestación al discurso leido por el Excmo. Sr. D. Eduardo Aunós en el acto de su recepción pública* (Real Academia de Ciencias Morales y Políticas, Madrid, 1944), p. 134.

in Spain, the verdicts of the Committees, thanks to the intervention of the state delegate, were usually favourable to the workers.[70]

As far as the structure of the system[71] was concerned, the country's economic activities were divided into twenty-seven spheres, ten of which covered the services sector, fifteen the so-called 'secondary activities' (that is industry, commerce), and two the 'primary activities', that is the mining industry and fishing. Agriculture was excluded altogether from the system.[72] Essentially, the system consisted of joint committees of workers and employers, from the local and professional level up to the regional and national, that dealt with both labour conflicts and matters of social legislation. The primary and basic cell was the local Comité Paritario, that is, a shop-floor committee. It consisted of an equal representation of workers and employers, while the chairman and his deputy were always state nominees. Clearly aimed at favouring the Socialists, the system by which the workers' representatives were to be elected gave all the seats to the union which obtained the majority of the votes. The Anarcho-syndicalists, whose organizations were dissolved, rejected the Comités Paritarios as opposed to the principle of 'direct action';[73] and the Catholic syndicates, which were, not unfrequently, also discriminated against in the Committees, could hope to have a substantial representation only in their strongholds in Barcelona and Navarra.[74] There were cases, however, as in the elections to the Comité Paritario of the metallurgical workers in Biscay, where even a coalition of Catholics, Libres, and Solidaridad de Obreros Vascos failed to take away the hegemony from the Socialists.[75] Thus, the Socialists acquired the lion's share of working-class representation in the Committees, and workers in the cities who wanted to be properly represented in labour conflicts had to do it through the UGT. Aunós was satisfied with this system of elections for the Committees because, as he explained, it was bound to create a coherent workers' delegation, rather than one split among contesting factions. Such a workers' representation was better equipped to prevent the employers from advancing their particular interests by playing off rival unions against each other, or by improvising

[70] Cf. Ben-Ami, *The Origins*, pp. 108–11.

[71] Cf. Aunós's works, *La organización corporativa y su posible desenvolvimiento* (Madrid, 1929); *La reforma corporativa*, pp. 129–39.

[72] See below, pp. 301–2.

[73] *The Times*, 25 July 1927.

[74] *Boletín del Sindicato Católico de Tipógrafos y Similares de Madrid*, Aug., Sept. 1928, Jan., Mar. 1929; García Venero, *Historia del nacionalismo vasco*, pp. 446–7.

[75] *El Joven Obrero. Portavoz de la Juventud Obrera y Campesina*, 5 Jan. 1929.

their own docile, yellow syndicates. Thus, Aunós rightly believed, the Comités Paritarios ran a very slight chance of becoming a gallery for contesting demagogues.

In 1927 and 1928, the corporative system was extended to two spheres beyond the twenty-seven of which the system had originally consisted. To the delight of tenants, a decree of 17 October 1927 set up the Corporative Organization of Lodgings. In October 1928, the Comités Paritarios of Work Done in the Home were set up.[76]

A major novelty in Aunós's machinery lay in the fact that it acquired a legislative and executive power. Once a shop-floor committee had reached a decision, and this had been approved by a Local Mixed Commission, it acquired the status of a law, the violation of which could be punished by the Comité Paritario itself with a 1,000 peseta fine. This was not an infrequently resorted-to practice, as employers were to become increasingly bitter at the fact that the Comités Paritarios tended to lean towards the cause of workers. As a whole, however, though certainly not comprehensively embracing all the workers and the employers in the country—there were about 652 arbitration committees to which 320,000 workers and 100,000 employers appealed to settle their disputes[77]—Aunós's machinery was nevertheless instrumental in consolidating labour relations along peaceful channels of negotiation.[78]

The Socialists had every reason to be the main defenders of the Comités Paritarios. Through the corporative organization the Dictatorship had been able to seal its alliance with the Socialist movement. It had granted them favourable labour contracts and had turned their unions into the main working-class organization in the country possessing 'a clear juridical personality'.[79] Such a juridical recognition of the UGT, argued the Socialist leader Saborit, was in itself sufficient reason for his movement 'to praise the Dictatorship'.[80]

Praise such as that coming from a member of the Unión Patriótica, who wrote in 1928 that 'there is not in all Spain a more numerous,

[76] Aunós, *La política social*, pp. 71–2. For tenants, see *Industria*, Dec. 1927.

[77] Aunós, 'Política social de la Dictadura y colaboración socialista', in *Anales de la Real Academia de Ciencias Morales y Políticas*, XVI, 1964, Madrid, p. 63.

[78] See a long list of labour disputes settled by the Comités Paritarios, Aunós, *La política social*, pp. 73–7.

[79] The Socialists' defence of the Comités Paritarios and the gains they drew from them have been discussed in more detail elsewhere; see Ben-Ami, *The Origins*, p. 110 ff.

[80] *Turbina*, March 1930.

disciplined, and conservative workers' organization than the Socialists', and that Spain owed to the combined efforts of Largo Caballero and Primo de Rivera the era of progress that it was enjoying,[81] was as reflective of the regime's satisfaction at its alliance with the Socialists as it was embarassing to the latter. The Socialists had to go to great pains to explain to their critics on the left and among the liberals that 'we are not friends of the Dictatorship' but rather 'its enemies who have accepted only that part of its deal that can favour the working class', and put it in a position 'to influence the way social legislation develops'.[82]

The gains stemming from the Socialists' collaboration with the Dictatorship were obviously also the consequence of the hostile, sometimes merely neutral, attitude of the regime towards other workers' organizations. Brutal repression, however, was never resorted to. Scores of Communists were arrested on several occasions in connection with some abortive plots. But then the Communist Party of Spain was hardly a meaningful enough power for the regime to strive to harness it to its chariot, or to make it a target of indiscriminate repression.[83]

Dictatorships are not the appropriate ground for the emergence of revolutionary syndicalism; Primo de Rivera's was no exception. Freedom of speech and association had always been indispensable for the growth of Anarchism and Anarcho-syndicalism in Spain. The CNT, which in 1923 was already exhausted by years of repression, staged nothing but a token demonstration of rebelliousness—an abortive strike—to protest against the seizure of power.[84] Nor did its unions display any meaningful opposition to Primo de Rivera's order that they must dissolve. In May 1924, more than 200 CNT militants were arrested, their meeting-places were closed, and their organ, *Solidaridad Obrera*, was banned.[85] Curiously, many of the members of Anarcho-syndicalist unions preferred to join the ranks of the Sindicatos Libres, rather than those of the 'collaborationist'

[81] *Unión Obrera*, 16 Nov. 1928.

[82] See the reports of Saborit's apologetic tour in the provinces, *El Socialista*, 13, 16, 18 Apr. 1929.

[83] Cf. Bullejos, *La Comintern*, pp. 55–63; Pérez Solís, *Memorias*, pp. 325–43. See also Pelai Pages, *Historia del partido comunista de España (desde su fundación en abril de 1920 hasta el final de la Dictadura de Primo de Rivera)* (Barcelona, 1978).

[84] Pestaña, *Lo que aprendí*, pp. 192–3; Alfaro Baratech, *El sindicalismo*, pp. 65–6.

[85] See Peiró's and Pestaña's letter from jail to *El Sol*, 10 July 1925. See also Ramos Oliveria, *Historia de España* (Mexico, 1952), vol. ii, pp. 472–3.

UGT.[86] Anarcho-syndicalists did manifest their existence through some of their periodical publications, some clandestine regional meetings, and even some independent industrial action. But it is self-evident that not until after the breakdown of the Dictatorship did the CNT return to life.[87]

That Primo de Rivera should have ostracized the Communists and the Anarcho-syndicalists is hardly surprising. A curious feature of his syndical policy, however, was that, being as it was, anti-Marxist and basically linked with the social teachings of the Church, it did not show a marked preference for the Sindicatos Libres and the Católicos. Notwithstanding the initial affinity of both these syndical groups with a strong-handed, non-liberal regime, Primo de Rivera's syndical policy hardly enabled them to challenge the hegemony of the Socialists. The almost exclusive domination of the Comités Paritarios, that were initially strongly welcomed by leaders of the Libres such as Padre Gafo,[88] and by the UGT aroused bitter feelings among both Catholic and Free syndicates. 'The employer avoids any contact with us . . . the authorities ignore us because of our insignificance; our voices are voices calling in the wilderness.'[89] Such were the terms used by the organ of a Catholic syndicate to express its frustration. Catholic syndicates blamed 'the manifest egoism of the employers' who preferred to accommodate themselves to the demands of the spoiled Socialist unions, rather than to the 'good', but officially unprotected, Catholic workers.[90] Unlike the Socialists, Catholic syndicates went out of their way to support the Comités Paritarios on *doctrinal* grounds. They viewed them as reflecting 'the collapse of the individualistic edifice of the French revolution', the victory of 'state interventionism' over 'the inhuman and brutal individualism of Spencer'.[91] No wonder that, given their ideological identification with the Dictator, they should have been so deeply frustrated by his refusal to support their demand—here they entirely coincided with the employers' view and with that of the Catholic *El Debate*—for a change in the system of election to the shop-floor committees, a change that would give representation to

[86] Pestaña, *Lo que aprendí*, p. 193.

[87] Cf. Brademas, pp. 25–43, Bueso, p. 272.

[88] *Boletín de Sindicato Católico de Tipógrafos*. Nov. 1928, Jan. 1929; Tusell, *Historia*, pp. 131–2.

[89] *Boletín del Sindicato Católico de Tipógrafos*, Oct. 1928.

[90] Ibid., March, May, June 1929.

[91] *El Eco del Pueblo. Comité Directivo de la Confederación Nacional de Sindicatos Católicos de Obreros*, 17 May 1928.

the minority unions. Primo would not even grant them a seat in the *Consejo de Trabajo* and in the *Instituto Nacional de Previsión* where the Socialists were generously represented. The Dictator would by no means sacrifice his alliance with the Socialists to please the Catholics who had, anyway, no revolutionary option.[92]

Indeed, by taming the 'red menace' and neutralizing the 'social danger' Primo de Rivera had, in a way reduced the importance of the Catholic syndicates as counter-revolutionary organizations. Not in vain did a contemporary write that, with no imminent social danger to fight, the Confederación Nacional Católico-Agraria drifted into a state that could be described as that of 'the anaemia of a giant'.[93] It seems very hard to refute the view expressed by Maximiliano Arboleya in 1930, that Primo de Rivera should take the blame for the fact that the Dictatorship spoiled a golden opportunity for Social Catholicism to establish a regime in its own exclusive image.[94]

The frustration of the Libres was as great as that of the Católicos. They accepted the Dictatorship as a heroic attempt to save the Spanish people from being 'dragged to the precipices of something similar to the hecatomb of Soviet Russia'.[95] They were everything the Dictatorship could have expected of a syndicate, 'apolitical . . . exclusively professional . . . practically confessional . . . supporters of neither 'catastrophic revolutionism nor political reformism'.[96] Yet they were amazed to see how the regime favoured in a most emphatic way the socialist unions that, at least in principle, were politically reformist, potentially revolutionary, and anything but confessional.[97]

But, to put things in their true proportion, one should not imply that the Dictatorship had tried to undermine the strength of the confessional syndicates. In spite of their complaints, the Libres had virtually tripled their membership—from 50,000 to 150,000[98]—under

[92] The whole issue was a central theme in *El Eco del Pueblo*, 31 May, 15 June, 15 July, 15 Aug., 31 Oct. 1928, 15 Apr., 15, 31 May, 30 June 1929, 15 Feb. 1930.

[93] Juan de Sahagún, 'Nuestra CNCA: La anemia de un gigante', in *Renovación Social*, no. 86, 15 May 1928, pp. 292–5, quoted in Montero, i, p. 88.

[94] Tusell, *Historia*, pp. 135–7.

[95] *Unión Obrera. Portavoz de la Confederación nacional de Sindicatos Libres de España*, 19 June 1926.

[96] Ibid., 25 Apr. 1925; see also *Unión Obrera. Justicia y Libertad. Portavoz de la Confederación nacional de Sindicatos Libres Profesionales*, 19 June 1926.

[97] Baratech, *El sindicalismo*, pp. 67–73.

[98] *La Vanguardia*, 24 Sept. 1929; Aunós, *La política corporativa*, p. 128; Baratech, *El sindicalismo*, p. 25.

the Dictatorship. And as the Socialists started to drift away from their initial alliance with the regime, the position of the Libres and the Católicos was further consolidated. Thus, for example, the optimism of the Catholic Syndicate of Printers in 1929 stood in striking contrast with its earlier frustration.[99] 1929 was also to be a year of vigorous activity by the Libres. Their National Confederation launched a campaign to organize small peasants and agricultural workers in order to represent them in the forthcoming rural Comités Paritarios; it extended its membership to the Employees of Commerce and Industry in Catalonia; and became the champion of the interests of Cenetista unions. To maintain the loyalty of their new recruits from the CNT, the Libres would not shrink from committing themselves to 'the tactics of direct action, the strike, and the boycott'. Following the model adopted by the Socialists, the Libres also now moved to set up their own Federaciones Nacionales.[100]

But in the final analysis, the Dictatorship was to profit neither from the strength of the Socialists nor from that of the Libres and the Católicos. It was a fundamental weakness of the regime that it lacked an organic working-class basis. The Socialist *point d'appui* was not immanent to the regime; it was a borrowed power whose support was conditional and for whom the Dictatorship was an avenue, not the terminal station, to another regime. Primo's natural working-class basis could have been found among the confessional unions and the Libres; but the Dictator failed to cultivate them accordingly. Instead of resting upon a workers' movement permeated with the philosophy of the regime and bent on defending it in its hours of crisis, Primo de Rivera helped to build a Socialist power that, if anything, was a reservoir for Spanish democracy, and, in any case, would not hesitate to break its *ad hoc* alliance with the Dictator once the latter could no longer deliver the goods.

2. *Inertia and Improvement*

It was a feature of the Dictatorship's social policy that, contrary to the favour it had shown to urban workers at the immediate expense of their employers, it exhibited a traditional, reactionary spirit in agrarian Spain. Primo de Rivera did not extend his social emphasis

[99] *Boletín del Sindicato Católico de Tipógrafos y Similares de Madrid, 1930* (Memoria de 1929).

[100] See the frequent reports on the Libres in *La Vanguardia*, 12, 23, 30, 31, Jan., 13, 17 Feb., 21 Apr., 25–27 Sept., 31 Dec. 1929.

to the countryside. No serious effort was made by the Dictator to tackle the social injustice inherent in *latifundismo*. He anticipated indeed the policy of Franco—with whom he shared a commitment to preserve intact the agrarian social structure—of 'solving' the agrarian problem by attracting the exasperated agrarian poor to the cities, rather than through a structural reform of the countryside. If Calvo Sotelo is to be believed, he had urged the Dictator to think of an agrarian reform that would divide the *latifundios* as the best way of doing away with 'the Spanish fear of the Communist phantom'.[101] But Primo de Rivera, the Andalusian landowner, could never bring himself seriously to contemplate such an idea. The land issue was hardly touched by the Dictatorship; its deference towards the landowners' interests was absolute.[102] It is therefore not surprising that the accession to power of Primo was the signal for his sympathizers among the Catalan landowners to start the eviction of troublemakers among their tenants, the *rabassaires*.[103]

However, some reforms were nevertheless initiated. Primo concentrated his efforts not on the colossal problem of landless labourers, but on an attempt to turn some of the tenant farmers into the owners of the land they tilled. As early as 1923, he had legalized the position of those small peasants who had squatted on state lands. In 1926, he set up a *Junta Central de Acción Social Agraria* to assist those tenants who were in a position to advance 20 per cent of the purchase price to buy the estates they cultivated, provided, of course, the landowners agreed to sell them. In this project the government invested only modest sums, however. Thirteen million pesetas were just enough to assist in the acquisition of 21,501 hectares where 4,202 farmers were to settle.[104] This was something of an achievement; but this new mechanism could not bring salvation to another 1.5 million tenants[105] who lacked any capital of their own. Nor was the pressure of small tenants on behalf of the introduction of a new lease law that should, among other things, assure that uncultivated land should be expropriated more fruitful. The

[101] Calvo, p. xi. Esperabe de Arteaga, 'El problema de la tierra', in *La Nación*, 17 Mar. 1928, demanded to divide the estates of more than 50,000 hectares for the benefit of small tenants.

[102] Primo in *ABC*, 1 Jan. 1928; he discarded the possibility of any meaningful agrarian reform.

[103] Edward Hansen, *Rural Catalonia Under the Franco Regime* (Cambridge University Press, 1977), pp. 71–3.

[104] Cristóbal de Castro, *Al servicio de los campesinos. Hombres sin tierra, tierra sin hombres* (Madrid, 1931), pp. 185–9.

[105] *La Nación*, 11 Mar. 1926.

principle of expropriation was anathema to the Dictator. And it was only in November 1929 that a law was promulgated that ensured longer leases and rent reductions in case of crop failure. Tenant farmers did not get a satisfactory deal from Primo de Rivera. This was due, they rightly argued, to 'the pressure of the big landowners who were being protected by the Dictatorship'.[106] An important initiative of Primo de Rivera was that concerning the *minifundista* land tenure—the *foros*—in poverty-stricken Galicia. He established the principle that those who worked the land could buy it, for which purpose *Cajas Provinciales de Crédito Rural* were set up.[107] But, as always, the whole enterprise was poorly endowed with funds, and the acute problem of the *foros* was to be bequeathed to the Republic, as unsolved as ever.

The gravity of Spain's agrarian problem was anything but alleviated by the Dictatorship. When Primo de Rivera stepped down from power there were still thirty-one million uncultivated hectares of land in Spain, and in many *pueblos de señorío* feudal customs still persisted. Land distribution, especially in the areas of large latifundia, was as appallingly unjust as ever. In a sample of twenty-seven provinces possessing altogether 19,648,497 hectares, an army of 1,75,000 landless labourers led a precarious life of seasonal work and starvation wages, another 142,000 people possessed tiny plots of between five and ten hectares, while the lion's share of the land was owned by the big landowners.[108] Social injustice as such, however, is not necessarily uneconomic. Experts such as Vizconde de Eza, the vice-president of the *Asociación de Agricultores de España*, would, in fact, argue that the excessive, and perhaps socially just, distribution of arable land into small plots was a major obstacle to the rationalization of Spanish agriculture.[109] The problem with Primo de Rivera was that he, who had committed his government to 'interventionist' enterprises of development in urban Spain, failed to launch any significant project that, even without touching the social issue, would develop, as Mussolini did

[106] *El Campesino. Órgano oficioso de la Liga Nacional de Campesinos*, Madrid, May 1931.

[107] *Gaceta de Madrid*, 26 June 1926. For a summary of Primo's land reforms, see Malefakis, pp. 436–8.

[108] Pascual Carrión, *La reforma agraria de la segunda república y la situación actual de la agricultura española* (Barcelona, 1973), pp. 37–42. Cristóbal de Castro, *Al servicio de los campesinos*, pp. 115–23.

[109] Eza examined twenty million hectares in 2,620 'términos'. See his findings in *Boletín de la Asociación de Agricultores de España*, Apr. 1930, pp. 175–6.

in Italy[110] the productive potentialities of agriculture. This was, after all, an indispensable condition for a balanced development of the national economy.

The regime's reactionary policies in the countryside should help to explain the fact that thousands of rural workers abandoned the UGT's rural sections during the Dictatorship.[111] These same policies had frustrated the efforts of Pablo Iglesias's disciples to bring about an extension to the countryside of the social benefits that they had been able to wrest from the Dictator on behalf of the workers in the cities. Indeed, the Socialists were aware that the disparity between their forces in the countryside and in the cities in favour of the latter reflected the unequal treatment accorded by the Dictatorship to rural and urban workers.[112]

A clear demonstration of Primo de Rivera's failure, or reluctance, to overcome the so-called 'traditional obstacles' in the countryside was his vain attempt to implement a decree of May 1928 extending the corporative organization to the countryside.[113] The *Confederación Nacional Católico-Agraria*, the *Liga Nacional de Campesinos*, and other landholders' associations exerted strong pressure on the government against the establishment of agricultural Comités Paritarios which, they feared, could become the Trojan horse through which Socialism would be able to infiltrate the countryside. Inherent in the idea of the Comités Paritarios was the principle that a distinction should be drawn between the interests of the workers and those of their employers. The CONCA could not accept this class concept, even though, as Aunós observed, the new corporative system was faithfully interpretative of its Social-Catholic doctrines.[114] The CONCA mainly objected to the clause in the decree that explicitly favoured the Socialists by conceding representation in the Comités Paritarios to minorities, which in rural areas were the Socialists, whereas in urban Committees where the Socialists were in the majority, no representation was provided for minorities.[115] But the Socialist euphoria at the decree—they envisaged themselves as changing the balance of forces in the countryside to the detriment of Catholic syndicates and landowner associations[116]—was short-lived. The determination of frightened

[110] Gregor, pp. 145–6, 276–7.
[111] For Socialist membership, see Ben-Ami, *The Origins*, pp. 109, 114.
[112] Sánchez Rivera in *El Socialista*, 5 July 1929.
[113] *Gaceta*, 20 May 1928.
[114] Aunós, *La reforma corporativa*, p. 138.
[115] *El Socialista*, 25 May 1928.
[116] Ibid., 26 May, 6 Nov., 7 Dec. 1928; 22 Feb., 9 Apr. 1929.

Catholics and landowners 'to prevent the revolution from using these powerful instruments [the Comités Paritarios] for its aims' finally bore fruit.[117]

The government succumbed to pressure, its dilatory tactics amounting to a virtual abolition of the decree. In spite of the indefatigable efforts of the Socialists to prevent the erosion of the government's professed policy of creating Comités Paritarios in the countryside,[118] these were not set up. This was a task to be taken up by Largo Caballero as the Republic's labour minister. Once again the Dictator had proved his deference towards the fundamental positions of the landowners and their Catholic allies in the countryside. The 'regenerationist' and social zeal that he seemed to be prepared to apply in the cities was not to be extended to rural Spain.

It is an interesting reflection on the Dictatorship's reactionary attitude to social issues in the countryside that, in spite of his unmistakably Catholic zeal, Primo de Rivera did not go out of his way in order to improve the material lot of the mass of parish and rural priests. Many of them lived in appalling conditions, their income frequently not differing from that of the average *bracero*. And there were cases in which priests supplemented their incomes by taking part-time jobs as day labourers.[119] This was how Anacleto Orejón, a priest from Palencia, described the situation in a letter to the Dictator:[120]

> The material conditions of the clergy in some dioceses, this one for example, are those of virtual misery. All the parishes lack the money for the most indispensable requirements of worship; at the homes of many priests you will not find the most necessary elements for subsistence . . . the rural priests simply cannot live materially; they hardly ever, if at all, get more than two pesetas as a contribution for holding mass . . . Baptisms, funerals, and weddings are not performed frequently, and even when they are, the fee is dreadfully low. The canons who oddly enough are categorized as part of the high clergy, hardly earn enough to make a very economical living, let alone a decent one as their social condition requires.

[117] *El Diario de Valencia* quoted in *El Socialista*, 1 June 1928. For the attitude of the CONCA, see Castillo, *Propietarios*, pp. 184–94.

[118] *El Socialista*, 19 Apr., 10 May 1929; 6 Feb. 1930.

[119] Pierre Lhande, 'Le Changement de régime en Espagne', *Études, Revue catholique d'intérêt général*, Paris, 5 May 1931. Cf. *The Times*, 6, 8 Dec. 1926, 18 Aug., 2 Nov. 1928.

[120] AHN, P.G. Leg. 326, Anacleto Orejón to Primo, 12 Mar. 1925.

But Primo would by no means consider radically correcting generations-old injustices, let alone remodelling rural society. Despite the permanent pressure of the clerical press, priests, the hierarchy, and Catholic syndicates,[121] the Dictator—who was not that thrifty when other fields of government expenditure were concerned—remained unshaken in his posture that his government could not revise in any radical way its expenditure policy to meet the demands of the lower clergy.[122] To be sure, the Dictator did authorize a certain improvement in the wages of about 3,313 parish priests who earned 1,500 pesetas a year (about four pesetas a day). From December 1926, their wages were to increase by 200 pesetas a year.[123] That this did not suffice to alleviate the conditions of the povery-stricken mass of lower priests is perhaps proved by the *juntas de defensa* they set up late in 1928 to continue their struggle for a decent living.[124]

* * *

As a whole, one might say that the standard of living of urban working-class families during the Dictatorship was stable with, in some cases, a slight tendency towards improvement, and in others—those of the unskilled and the unemployed—towards deterioration. The expansion of the economy and the grand schemes of public works helped to maintain an optimal level of employment. An Andalusian day labourer later recalled how the public works had generated 'a golden age'. 'Everything improved' during those seven years of the Dictatorship, said another. Then he remembered how 'people had work, earned money and lived better'.[125] Public works were crucial for the maintenance of working-class satisfaction. On the eve of the transition to civilian government and before the extraordinary budget had been created, *El Socialista* expressed its outrage at the 'frightening' dimensions of unemployment. In many industries, it said, more than 60 per cent of the workers had lost their iobs. 'Misery and unease had overtaken many proletarian homes', it concluded.[126] The Communist leader Pérez Solís expressed a similar preoccupation when he wrote of 'the intense crisis

[121] See hundreds of appeals in AHN, P.G. Leg. 326: Clero.
[122] *The Times*, 9 Apr. 1926.
[123] *La Nación*, 12 Oct. 1928.
[124] *The Times*, 2 Nov. 1928.
[125] Fraser, pp. 12, 15, 16.
[126] *El Socialista*, 1 May 1925.

of labour that is affecting almost every industry except the iron and steel industries'.[127] Yet unemployment was, after 1926, to be substantially eased by public works. Public works, claimed an organ of the industrialists, had contributed to the reduction of social tensions to a minimum.[128]

The per capita income in Spain showed a tendency towards stability and even improvement until 1925. After that, a mildly downward trend is discernible.[129] Coinciding as it did with the beginning of the development schemes of the regime, the depreciation of wages and the consequent maintenance of profit rates for entrepreneurs might look like—as was indeed the case under Fascism—one more bait proffered by the government to Spain's business community for its participation in the enterprise of modernizing the country.[130] But though it is true that wages, mainly those of unskilled workers, showed a downward tendency after 1925,[131] this was so only after they had substantially increased in the preceding years.

Wage per hour in industry[132]

	1914	*1920*	*1925*
State Industries	0.42 pts	0.76	0.96
Mining, Saltworks, Quarries	0.41	0.76	0.87
Metallurgy	0.54	0.95	1.11
Iron and other metal works	0.47	0.84	0.98
Chemical industries	0.41	0.76	0.89
Textile	0.37	0.69	0.79
Forest and Agricultural Industries	0.40	0.57	0.76
Building	0.42	0.79	0.98
Electric Industries	0.44	0.84	0.96
Food	0.41	0.75	0.86
Printing	0.52	0.90	1.15
Paper, Coal, Rubber, and Office Furniture	0.37	0.84	0.94
The Clothing Industry	0.40	0.71	0.85
Leather and Fur	0.41	0.69	0.84
Wood	0.47	0.87	1.00
Transport	0.48	0.87	1.03
Household goods	0.49	0.87	1.11
Ornamentation	0.46	0.85	1.05
Pottery and Ceramics	0.37	0.69	0.84
Glass and Crystal	0.56	1.02	1.28

127 *Lucha Social*, 16 Apr. 1925.

128 *Industria*, Jan. 1927, Jan. 1928. Cf. Maura, *Bosquejo*, pp. 187–8.

129 Paris Eguilas, *Factores*, pp. 438–9.

130 Cf. Gregor, pp. 194–9.

131 Iglesias, pp. 130–1; Tuñón, *El movimiento*, pp. 755–67.

132 *El Economista*, 21 Dec. 1929. Cf. Vicente Gay, 'Salarios y sueldos', in *La Nación*, 16 Mar. 1928. He claims that the wage index went up from 186 in 1920 (1914 = 100) to 216 in 1925.

Moreover, wage depreciation after 1925—it only affected 28 out of 52 professions recorded by an official source[133]—did not respond to a predetermined governmental policy. It was the improvement in the conditions of the urban workers, that was not extended to the countryside, as well as the attraction of public works, that had stimulated landless day labourers to leave the fields in an attempt to get more remunerative jobs in industry, 'thus augmenting the number of unemployed hands in the cities', and, consequently, putting pressure on wages. But even when, after 1925, wages started to go down, this was not always the case as far as skilled workers were concerned. There was also a marked difference between the various industries. Wages went up between 1925 and 1930 by 14 per cent in the state industries, by 11 per cent in the electric industry, by 5.16 per cent in the textile sector, by 2.3 per cent in mining, saltworks and quarries (wages in Asturias had trebled between 1914 and 1924, a period in which the cost of living of a miner's family 'merely' doubled[134]), and in the clothing industry, by 1.4 per cent in the food industries, by 0.9 per cent in leather and fur works, and by 0.8 per cent in ornamentation. Wages went down by 9.5 per cent in the printing industry, by 5.7 per cent in iron and other metal works, by 5.2 per cent in glass and crystal, by 3.4 per cent in metallurgy, by 3 per cent in the building sector, by 1.8 per cent in the wood works, and by 0.9 per cent in the transport sector.[135] But even in those branches where wages depreciated there were important regional variations. Thus, wages decreased in the metallurgical industry, but they increased in Biscay and Madrid. Indeed, in 1928, in the capital the hourly wage of workers in glass and crystal (between 1.34 and 1.03 pesetas), in metallurgy (1.50 pesetas), in leather workshops (1.50–0.62), in ironworks (1.37), in the transport system (1.31–0.87), and in the printing industry (1.53–1.12) was higher than the average wage in the same professions in 1925.[136] As a whole, there tended to be a difference between the higher wages in economically active regions such as Barcelona, Madrid, Biscay, Guipúzcoa, and Asturias, and those of the rest of the country.[137] In December 1928,

[133] Ministerio de Trabajo y Previsión, Dirección General de Trabajo, Sección de Estadísticas especiales de Trabajo, *Estadística de salarios y jornadas de trabajo referida al periodo 1914–1930* (Madrid, 1931), pp. lxxxviii–lxxxix.

[134] Consejo Nacional de Combustibles, *Dictámen oficial sobre industria hullera en Asturias* (Madrid, 1926), p. 16; wage per day in 1914—3.83 pesetas; 1924—9.39.

[135] *Estadística de salarios y jornadas*, op. cit., p. lxiii.

[136] 'El salario y la jornada en Madrid, 1928', *Anuario*, 1929, p. 506.

[137] Tuñón, *El movimiento*, pp. 755–67. For the better lot of skilled workers, see also Vicente Gay, 'Salarios y sueldos', *La Nación*, 16 Mar. 1928.

the teachers' association would even complain that the minimum wages decreed by the government for industrial workers were higher than those earned by teachers.[138]

The damaging effect that the tendency of wages of unskilled workers to decline was likely to have on living conditions was partly offset by a fall in the cost of living after 1925. The index of the cost of living for a working-class family in the city, which in October 1923 stood at 167.6 and which reached its highest average point in the period October 1925–March 1926 (180.8), that is when wages were also at their highest, resumed a downward trend in order to reach, by the end of 1929, the relatively low point of 165.5.[139] There was a clear tendency for the prices of the most basic food necessities to depreciate thanks to the government's policy of basic food-price control.[140] Special Committees of Supply were set up in every province to regulate the demand and offer of food items, as well as to supervise their prices.[141]

Average indexes can be misleading, however. Sharper fluctations in the price of certain commodities within short periods did take place to the detriment of the modest wage-earners. Thus, for example, while since March 1926 the index of the twelve items that formed the basic food basket of a working-class family had started on a generally downward trend, the price index of vegetables went up from a mean index of 167 for 1926 to 174 in January 1927, that of beverages from 170 to 179 (this was the result of the bad vintage in 1926), and the general index of foodstuffs rose from 183 to 188. The index of industrial products went up during the same period also by five points, but essential items such as coal, gas, and electricity rose sharply from 175 to 198.[142]

In other words, once one moves from the most basic food items to examine the price of industrial products and of a wider food basket than that which the statistics assumed would be consumed by a working-class family, one is bound to meet with higher prices. The price of industrial products—that had a more direct bearing on the

[138] AHN, P.G. Leg. 320; Rufino Carpena to Primo, 7 Dec. 1928.

[139] The index was based on twelve basic items; bread, cod, potatoes, chick-peas, rice, wine, milk, eggs, sugar, oil, beef, and lamb. It did not include clothing and housing, see *Anuario*, 1929: 'Coste de la vida del obrero', pp. 496–7.

[140] Velarde, *Política económica*, p. 201; *The Times*, 13 Apr. 1925.

[141] *Gaceta*, 4 Nov. 1923; Duarte, pp. 121–34.

[142] *The Economist*, 16 Apr. 1927. Not even *La Nación*, 22 Jan. 1927, could deny the high cost of living.

living conditions of the middle classes—had a tendency to increase under the protective umbrella of the Dictator's high tariffs. Also, the burdensome interventionist bureaucracy only contributed to the rise of the cost of production,[143] as well as of prices, as the Chamber of Commerce of Vigo angrily protested to the Dictator.[144] But the rise of industrial prices was discernible mainly until 1926, when wholesale industrial prices also started to go down. The wholesale food index, however, went up in a more steady way (though here also 1925 was the worst year, whence prices would return to milder indexes).[145]

This was so because for one thing, in spite of his policy of controlling basic food items, Primo de Rivera would not support what he called 'an excessive cheapening of essential commodities', because this would dangerously narrow the margin of profits of the producing sector.[146] For another, he had a simplistic and superficial notion of the cause of price rises. He attributed them to the malice of greedy merchants. He therefore tackled the problem mainly by inflicting arbitrary punishments on shopkeepers.[147] But these measures failed to touch the real cause of the problem which lay in the high brokerage gap, which sometimes consisted of more than a hundred per cent of the item's original price. Many merchants and shopkeepers would rather pay the fine imposed on them by Primo's inspectors, than give away their comfortable, arbitrary margin of profits. The middle men thus made fabulous profits at the expense of the average consumer. The only thing they cared for, as the critic of the Dictatorship, Dalmacio Iglesias, put it, was 'to get rich within four days in order to acquire cars and have mistresses with whom they could drink as much . . . champagne as they wished'. A major cause for the rise in prices, which Primo de Rivera failed to tackle, was the expensive internal transport fares, of which the main profiteers were the railway companies. It continued to be a constant feature of the Spanish market that the freight between Barcelona and Bilbao was still more expensive than that between Barcelona

[143] Cf. *The Economist*, 26 Nov. 1927; Benítez de Lugo, p. 60.

[144] *The Economist*, 29 Oct. 1927.

[145] Ceballos-Teresí, vol. 7, p. 353; *Anuario* 1929, pp. xxiv–xxv, 296–7; 'Los precios en España', in *El Financiero*, Nov. 1930, pp. 77–8. The wholesale index of industrial prices developed as follows: 1923—176; 1924—182; 1925—181; 1926—179; 1927—163; 1928—158; 1929—163. Food prices, 168; 183; 195; 183; 182; 176; 180.

[146] *El Sol*, 22 June 1924; Primo, *Intervenciones*, pp. 100–1.

[147] Such measures continued well into 1929; *La Vanguardia*, 5, 11, 19, 26 Jan. 1929.

and . . . Buenos Aires. The emergence of monopolies and trusts that suffocated free competition, as well as the over-bureaucratized machinery of economic regulation, were also unlikely to favour lower prices. Nor was the 'American-style' campaign of publicity and advertisements, what Primo described as the 'excessively luxurious commercial premises' that started to make their appearance in Spain, and the higher rents for commercial sites, to be paid for other than by the consumer. This was also true of the wide variety of taxes—dozens of them—levied upon industrialists and merchants by both the government and local councils. They were all bound to have their repercussion on prices.[148]

That 'social peace' was nevertheless maintained throughout the Dictatorship was due to the fact that the conditions of urban workers did not deteriorate in any dramatic way. The latent threat of unemployment, public works, the pacifying influence of the Comités Paritarios, and the fairly steady drop in the price of the most basic food necessities should also account for that.[149] It is perhaps significant that 33.2 per cent of the savers in a sample of five savings institutions in Madrid were defined as workers. Artisans and domestic servants also shared in the propensity for savings.[150] The relative satisfaction of the working class was also reflected in the marked decrease in the number of strikes during the Dictatorship in comparison with earlier as well as with later periods. Also the proportion of strikes that ended with the acceptance of the strikers' demands had increased,[151] but so had the proportion of strikes in which they lost their case.[152] The Comités Paritarios remained throughout the best alternative. The drop in the intensity of labour conflicts and tensions is evident. Between 1924 and 1928, 636 strikes with a total of 251,355 strikers were recorded, whereas in the couple of years that preceded the Dictatorship (1922–3) there were 952 strikes with a total of 240,039 strikers. Moreover, if the number of working days lost in all the strikes of 1924–8 was 3,774,773, that of the two years that preceded the Dictatorship was 5,699,593. With the fall of the Dictatorship, labour conflicts were to gain in intensity: 402

[148] For the causes of the rising prices, see Iglesias, pp. 90–2, 32–45, 64–9, 74–5, 96–9, 101–4, 109–29; Cambó, *La valoración*, p. 50. See Primo's attack on the luxury of commercial premises in Dionisio Pérez, p. 77.

[149] *Industria*, Jan. 1928, Oct. 1929.

[150] *Anuario* 1929, p. 533; José Francisco Formés, 'El ahorro popular en la Dictadura', in *Cuadernos*, pp. 275–6.

[151] This enraged a fanatic supporter of the regime, see Mask, pp. 124–5.

[152] Ceballos-Teresí, vol. 7, p. 349. Cf. *Anuario*, 1929, pp. xx–xxi.

strikes, in which 247,461 strikers took part and 3,745,360 working days were lost, took place in 1930 alone.[153]

The coercive authority of the Dictatorship cannot be the exclusive explanation of the fairly peaceful labour relations under Primo's rule. One case in which Primo imposed dictatorial coercion to 'solve' a dispute was that of the strike by the workers at the Barcelona International Exhibition, early in 1929. Too much was at stake, economic interests and, mainly, national prestige.[154] But it is a fact that whenever workers felt the need to strike there was nothing to stop them. In 1927 alone, 1,311,891 working days were lost in strikes at the forefront of which stood the building workers, the miners in Asturias and Biscay, and the textile workers in Barcelona, all of whom came out against the employers' attempts to increase working hours without a corresponding increase of wages.[155] The rising cost of living, mainly of foodstuff items, was also at the background of working-class protest.[156] The only restriction Primo would insist on having in relation to labour conflicts was that he would not accept political strikes, and would not allow the press to stir up passions by reporting regularly on strikes.[157] Encouragement would be given, however, to the official press to report extensively on strikes in other countries.[158] Such was also the standard device of Francoism for stressing the 'social peace at home'.

An additional explanation of the substantial drop in strikes during the Dictatorship lies in the conciliatory relations that were established between the strongest union in the country, the UGT, and Primo's government, the manifest social orientation of the regime, and the latent danger of unemployment. At a certain stage, the Asturian miners, under Llaneza's reformist leadership, would even agree to a virtual wage reduction in order to save the Spanish coal-mines, as well as their jobs, from an imminent catastrophe due to the competition of British coal.[159] Not in vain did the government hail this magnificent display of 'civic responsibility, so alien to any reprovable revolutionary action' by Spanish *obrerismo*.[160] And when the government decided to tax workers' wages, admittedly only the

[153] *Boletín del Banco Urquijo*, Sept. 1929; *Industria*, Oct. 1929; *Anuario*, 1931.

[154] *El Sol*, 20–2 Jan. 1929.

[155] *Industria*, Oct. 1929.

[156] *The Economist*, 2 Jan. 1926.

[157] Primo in *La Nación*, 9 Apr. 1928.

[158] *La Nación*, 1 Oct. 1928, opened a special column on strikes outside Spain. It claimed (15 May 1926) that the parliamentary system was an obstacle to the quick solution of the British coal strike.

[159] *Hojas Libres*, Nov. 1927; *The Times*, 19, 20 Oct. 1927; Saborit, *Asturias y sus hombres* (Toulouse, 1964), pp. 218–19.

[160] *La Nación*, 4, 8 Oct. 1927.

higher ones (above 3,250 pesetas per year), the employers, especially as after 1928 redundancies and wage freezes became a common practice, thought it was a highly unjust step.[161] But the workers' reaction, though occasionally reflected in strikes,[162] was surprisingly 'restrained', to use Calvo Sotelo's expression.[163] *El Socialista*, writing from the perspective of a socially and politically turbulent year, 1930, referred to the Comités Paritarios and the preferential treatment that the workers got there, as being a major reason for the 'social peace' enjoyed under the Dictatorship.[164]

* * *

Spanish society was coming to a turning-point during the 1920s. One might perhaps say that processes that had started earlier under the impact of the Great War were given renewed momentum by the Dictator's policies. The economic 'boom' had increased wealth, technological potentialities, and urbanization. The country's population increased in the decade of the twenties by 10.7 per cent (an increase of 2.3 million inhabitants)[165] and, though still an essentially agrarian-based society, Spain was increasingly acquiring urban features. The towns of over 10,000 inhabitants increased their population by an impressive figure of two million, and those of over 100,000 inhabitants by a not negligible one million, capital cities, whose population increased during the twenties by 30 per cent, getting the lion's share of the growth. On the other hand, the population of towns of less than 10,000 inhabitants remained virtually at a standstill. In 1930, 42 per cent of the population of Spain lived in towns of more than 10,000 inhabitants.[166] It is to a drop in the death-rate (19 per thousand in the twenties in comparison with 23.5 per

[161] *Industria*, Feb. 1928, *ABC*, 20 Feb. 1928, supported this view.

[162] *The Times*, 18 Jan., 1–3, 8 Feb. 1928.

[163] Calvo, pp. 126, 169. See also the exquisite tone of protest of *Bolétin de la UGT*, Feb., Mar. 1929.

[164] *El Socialista*, 12 June 1930.

[165] Amando de Miguel, *La pirámide social española* (Barcelona, 1977), p. 26. *Anuario*, 1929, p. xx-xxi. The crucial year, however, was 1930, because of a great return of emigrants then. If only the years 1923–9 are considered, the population increase was 5.2% (1,122,000 people). In 1930 alone, 800,000 people were added to the register.

[166] Díez Nicolás, p. 19. For the capitals, see also *Anuario*, 1929, pp. xx–xxi, and that of 1930 as quoted in Lacomba, *Ensayos sobre el siglo xx Español* (Madrid, 1972), p. 46. The population of the capitals increased in the years of the Dictatorship by over 10%. Again, the crucial year was 1930; the capital's population increased then by 13.47% in relation to 1929.

thousand in the previous decade) rather than to a meaningful increase in the birth-rate that the population growth should be attributed.[167] In fact, the birth-rate had descended to European standards, from 34.5 per thousand in the first decade of the century to 29.2 per thousand in the twenties.[168] Primo de Rivera's incentives to prolific families—he was thus following Mussolini's example[169]—failed to change the overall trend.

The flight from the Spanish countryside seemed to be reaching alarming proportions, especially for a regime that had frequently indulged in ruralist oratory. A contemporary critic of the Dictatorship blamed the process of urbanization for the 'desertion of the countryside', which, he said, was reaching 'frightening proportions'.[170] So much so that the government had to set up special *Juntas de Reintegración al Campo*, to resettle those who had left their rural communities on account of what Primo de Rivera called 'the excitements, the excessive desire to satisfy earthly appetites'. But he failed where Franco succeeded. The Caudillo would be able, in the forties, to reverse the trend by an authoritarian policy of resettlement in the countryside. Primo, however, was either unable, or unwilling, to elaborate a similar device. He had to reconcile himself with reality. 'The city', he said, 'offers today to the people of the countryside temptations such as they would never find in the fields.'[171] This was not only the case with landless day labourers in the destitute regions of Andalusia and Extremadura, but also among medium-sized and small landowners and tenants in the traditionally stable rural communities of Old Castile. The burden of taxation and harsh tenancy contracts combined with the attractions of the cities were all blamed by the representative of the *Liga Nacional de Campesinos* in the National Assembly, Sr. Monedero, as responsible for 'the increasing depopulation of the countryside, which further exacerbates the problems of the working classes in the cities and in industrial centres. It creates an unnecessary agglomeration of workers in urban centres. At the same time, it complicates the situation in the fields by creating a shortage of hands there.'[172]

Clearly, thanks to the relative prosperity, the lion's share of the

[167] De Miguel, *La pirámide*, pp. 22–4.

[168] *Anuario*, 1929, pp. 32, 38–9; Lacomba, *Ensayos*, p. 33.

[169] See the decree of 21 July 1926 in Bravo Morata, *La Dictadura*, ii, pp. 141–2.

[170] See the declarations of an Asambleista from Palencia in Primo, *Intervenciones*, p. 157.

[171] Ibid., pp. 146–51.

[172] *Diario de Sesiones de la Asamblea Nacional*, 23 Nov. 1927.

demographic movement in Spain during the twenties was confined to the national territory. The number of Spaniards who emigrated to both the Old and New World descended from 86,920 in 1924 to 55,554 in 1925, to 45,182 in 1926, and to 43,867 in 1927. With the start of economic difficulties in 1928, this descending trend started to be reversed with 48,555 people leaving the country that year. In 1929, the number went up to 81,343. But emigration was partly, and sometimes completely, balanced out by a rather steady number of immigrants: 1925–53,819; 1926–56,761; 1927–55,578; 1928–57,695; 1929–57,392.[173]

The provincial capitals became, obviously, the natural home of emigrants from the agrarian hinterland. *El Economista* was to write in 1929 of the spectacular proletarization of Madrid that had taken place in the last years.[174] 104,244 out of the 809,400 inhabitants (not of the work-force) of Madrid, that is about 13 per cent, were defined as workers.[175] The capital's population increased by about 27 per cent (from 750,000 to 952,000) between 1920 and 1930.[176] This should help to explain the acute housing shortage in Madrid after 1925. The 13,964 apartments built in the capital between 1925 and 1930 fell short of meeting the needs of the 119,823 people that were added to the city's population in the same period.[177] Density in the proletarian quarters of Madrid was now becoming an acute problem. In one such quarter, for example, 321 'houses of vicinity' lodged about 66,500 people in what was described as painfully overcrowded conditions.[178] The population of Barcelona increased even more spectacularly (by about 41 per cent, that is from 710,355 to 1,005,039) than that of Madrid.[179] The *ciudad condal* was described as undergoing 'a peaceful invasion' by an 'army of foreigners', who were threatening the Catalan people with 'demographic decadence'.[180] The entire movement of internal migration in the twenties amounted to a flight of about 1,169,000 people from the countryside to the cities, as compared with 878,000 in the previous decade.[181] It is also

[173] Cf. *Boletín del Banco Urquijo*, July 1929, p. 516, *Anuario*, p. 39; Javier Ruiz Almansa, 'La población en España', in *Revista Nacional de Economía*, Jan. 1930.

[174] *El Economista*, 21 Sept. 1929.

[175] *Anuario*, 1929, pp. 17, 504.

[176] Ibid., 1929 (pp. 16–17), 1931.

[177] Aviv, pp. 142–3.

[178] 'El fomento de la vivienda. Un problema social', *La Nación*, 22 Aug. 1928.

[179] It should be noted, however, that as far as the growth of these two capitals was concerned the dramatic year was 1930. In 1929, the population of Madrid was 824,927, and that of Barcelona, 881,275; see *Anuario*, 1929, pp. 16–17.

[180] De Miguel, *La pirámide*, pp. 124–5, dwelling on Vandellós.

[181] Alfonso Barbancho, *Las migraciones interiores españolas. Estudio cuantitativo desde 1900* (Madrid, 1967), p. 43.

evident that the more economically active cities such as Barcelona, Madrid, Valencia, Zaragoza, and Bilbao were the main centres to which emigrants tended to gravitate (their migratory balance was favourable by 280,032; 238,436; 65,381; 20,496; 33,396, respectively). But also in basically agrarian provinces such as Badajoz, Málaga, Valladolid, Córdoba, Granada, Salamanca, Seville, and Jaén, the capitals tended to attract part of the flight from the rural hinterland.[182] Even Galicia had experienced a growth in its urban population and a decrease in its agrarian habitancy.[183]

The Dictator's expansionist economic policy had also accelerated the process of de-archaization of Spain's social structure. Thus, for example, the proportion of the work-force employed in agriculture decreased from 57.3 per cent in 1920 to 45.51 per cent in 1930, while that employed in industry and the service sector went up from 21.90 per cent to 26.51 per cent and from 20.81 per cent to 27.98 per cent respectively. In fact, in proportional terms, the intensity of the transformation of the social fabric in the twenties almost matched, and in some aspects even surpassed, that which took place during the Francoist boom. One is surprised to discover, for example, that the twenties witnessed an increase of 4.57 per cent in the proportion of the work-force employed in industry, that is 1.35 per cent more than during the thirteen years of the Francoist boom (1960–73). In absolute terms the work-force increased in the twenties by 10.17 per cent (from 7,962,400 to 8,772,500).[184] Likewise, the fall in the rate of illiteracy in the twenties was the highest in the century until the sixties; 8.7 per cent for men and 9.15 per cent for women.[185] The number of children in primary schools had increased by about 23 per cent between 1924 and 1930.[186]

As for the middle classes, there exist indications as to the acceleration of their expansion under the Dictatorship. The number of taxpayers registered as industrialists and merchants increased from 416,777 in 1923 to 679,598 in 1928, a rise of about 63 per cent.[187]

[182] Ibid., appendix after p. 148.

[183] Vicente Risco, p. 79.

[184] Cf. *Estadísticas Básicas*, p. 369; *Anuario*, 1976, p. 285. Martínez Cuadrado, *La burguesía*, p. 113, claims the population employed in industry increased in the twenties by 580,209, and that of the services by 787,764. The latter seems to be an exaggerated figure. Using a different classification of the work-force, H. Paris Eguilas, p. 423, proposes a drop of 480,923 in the active agricultural force, an increase of 1,129,069 in that of industry, commerce, and transport; and 262,199 in the services and liberal professions.

[185] *Anuario*, 1929, 1931; José Ruiz Almanza, 'La población en España', p. 397; A. Guzmán Reina, *Causas y remedios del analfabetismo en España* (Madrid, 1955), p. 15.

[186] *Estadísticas Básicas*, p. 391.

[187] *Anuario*, 1929, p. 387.

Though part of this sudden build-up of the Spanish bourgeoisie might have been an artificial growth that could be attributed to more effective methods against tax evasion, there are grounds for thinking that an authentic growth also took place. For instance, the number of trade marks solicited in each of the years of the Dictatorship was higher than that of any previous period (3,609 in 1920; 4,257 in 1923; 4,488 in 1924; 4,334 in 1925; 4,247 in 1926; 4,357 in 1927; 5,941 in 1928; and 4,648 in 1929). The influx of students to business schools, whose population went up by 27 per cent in four years compared with an increase of only 6 per cent in the five years prior to 1923, was also a reflection of the renewed proliferation of business and of job opportunities in banking, industry, commerce, and in the administration of public works.[188]

People seemed to be more curious and to travel more than ever before as the number of commuters per year using the rail system increased by about 3.5 million in the first three years of the regime (Spanish rails were to transport in 1928 13,592,646 tons of merchandise more than in 1923); it dropped to lower figures later only because of the spectacular development of the road system and the increase by 400 per cent in the number of cars that made use of it. The frequent preoccupation of the press and the authorites with regulations concerning road traffic was a sign of the new times.[189] The car was starting to be viewed by contemporaries not just as a luxurious status symbol, but as a functional means of communication. And as the well-off people tended to leave the congested cities for their suburbs, the car became even more vital.[190] Private consumption of electricity also now showed a sharp increase, as the treasury claimed that its revenues from taxes on the private use of electricity increased by 33 per cent in the first four years of the Dictatorship.[191] Consequently, the number of telephones almost tripled during the same period. Between 1925 and 1929 the number of inter-city telephone conversations in Spain went up by more than 300 per cent, from 3 million to 10 million.[192] The radio and the movies

[188] Ibid., pp. 566–7.

[189] *La Nación*, 20 Dec. 1928; *El Debate*, 9 Mar. 1929; and Enrique La-Gasca, 'La circulación en Madrid', *La Nación*, 1 Nov. 1929.

[190] *La Nación*, 14 Sept. 1927.

[191] For data on railways, cars, and electricity, see *Anuario*, 1929; *Boletín de la Cámara de Transportes Mecánicos*, Apr. 1928. For the upsurge of commercial advertisements of electrical items (including washing-machines), see Juan Carlos Llorente, 'Producción y distribución de la energía eléctrica durante la década 1920–1930', in *Cuadernos*, p. 548.

[192] *Estadísticas Básicas*, p. 290, Bravo Morata, *La Dictadura*, ii, pp. 169–72.

became a widespread commodity. *Radiomanía* had completely changed the patterns of domestic life.[193]

The capital, Madrid, acquired the external aspects of a modern city.[194] Its underground, the construction of which was started in 1919 but was completed during the Dictatorship, transported thirty-seven million people in 1924. On the surface, 5,000 taxis circulated in Madrid early in 1928, and the Ayuntamiento had by then decided to limit their number because of the acute traffic problems.[195] It was in the twenties that the car jams, the huge football stadiums (that of Chamartín was inaugurated in 1924), and the system of hire purchase supported by endless advertisements made their appearance in the biggest centres, mainly Madrid and Barcelona.[196] It was during the Dictatorship that, alongside dozens of minor public buildings, modern and costly constructions appeared in the capital such as the Círculo de Bellas Artes in Alcalá Street (10 million pesetas), the Telephone Company building (32 million pesetas), the Palacio de la Prensa, and the Palacio de la Música in the Gran Vía, the new ministries, and scores of new theatres, such as the Alkazar, the Infanta Beatriz, and the Avenida. In 1929, a new municipal museum and a modern, ostentatious bullring were inaugurated, the preparations were started for the construction of the Barajas airport, and the two-million-peseta monument to Cervantes was erected in the Plaza de España.[197] A British newspaper wrote in 1929 that 'Spanish cities had abandoned the inertia of the past'.[198]

This was even true of some remote, backward villages where 'new winds' had now started to blow:

> Air, light, water were at long last being introduced in places where they had never penetrated before . . . Nakedness has brought with it the habit of swimming and the abuse of luxury . . . The indecency of the tango and savagery of the Charleston have also made their appearance . . . From here there is only one short step left to the 'dancing', the cabaret and the music-hall, and the step was made. The cinema and the theatre only aggravated the evil . . . Pornography, blasphemy and sexual passion . . . the dirty novel, the gallant review, the indecorous postcard have all combined

[193] *Radio Técnica*, Barcelona, 1929; *Radio y Luz*, March 1931; Bravo Morata, *La Dictadura*, ii, pp. 67–77. See the entertainment reviews *Komedias y Komediantes* and *Ars*.

[194] *La Petite Gironde*: 'Madrid, une capitale moderne' quoted in *La Nación*, 27 Oct. 1928.

[195] *La Nación*, 24 Mar. 1928.

[196] Bravo Morata, *La Dictadura*, vols. ii, iii, *passim*.

[197] F. Bravo Morata, *Historia de Madrid* (Madrid, 1967), vol. ii, *passim*.

[198] *Daily Chronicle*, quoted in *El Socialista*, 29 Dec. 1929.

to poison the very foundations of Christian families. Priapus was being worshipped instead of Jesus, and Astarte instead of the Virgin.[199]

'Life', as a French traveller in search of the poetic, immobile Spain noted, was 'penetrating the provinces, where some of the footpaths that looked poetic to Théophile Gautier have turned into roads furrowed with cars.[200] The Dictatorship was viewed by contemporaries as an era of crude materialism, one that did not care much for altruistic ideals.[201] Urban Spain was overwhelmed by the temptations of economic development as 'administration' and 'prosperity' replaced 'politics'.[202] Stock-exchange deals that carried the dreamy prospect of immediate enrichment, a passion for sport, especially soccer[203]—the legendary goalkeeper Zamora was the hero of the masses in the twenties, and the withdrawal of politics from the public interest, such was the *panem et circenses*[204] deal of Primo de Rivera.

The democratic enemies of the Dictator might have unduly fallen back on fatalism. Some of them underestimated the extent to which the Dictatorship had, by its own policies, eroded its prospects of survival. The pressures inherent in economic growth and in the social changes that the Dictatorship had accelerated presented a challenge to the non-democratic foundations of *Primoderriverismo*. The regime's inability to absorb and integrate the processes of change it had unleashed constituted a threat to its viability, let alone to political 'immobilism'. In Portugal, Salazar was to resist industrialization as a way of curtailing a possible erosion of his autocratic system.[205] In fact, such an approach was frequently taken by military rulers as a relevant device for consolidating their hold on the population.[206] An autocracy can of course perpetuate itself also by resorting to terror and brutal repression; but Primo de Rivera's was not a bloodthirsty regime. Unable or unwilling to resort either to mass

199 A. Samblancat, *El aire podrido. El ambiente social de España durante la Dictadura* (Madrid, 1930), pp. 42–3.

200 Verax, p. 523.

201 *El Presidencialista*, Jan., Aug. 1928.

202 Marcelino Domingo, *¿Qué espera?*, p. 142.

203 Pedro Rico, *El 'sport' en España* (Madrid, 1930); Cambó, 'La pasión del futbol', in *El Debate*, 24 Feb. 1929. For the sport cult, see also an article in *El Sol*, 25 Mar. 1928. See the soccer review *Tanto*, 1929. The public hero in Valencia in the last days of January 1929 was not the romantic rebel Sánchez Guerra, but the teams that were to contest the soccer cup final in the Levantine capital a few days later. *The Times*, 4, 5 Feb. 1929.

204 Gabriel Alomar in *El Progreso*, 8 May 1929.

205 Gallagher, 'Controlled Repression in Salazar's Portugal', *JCH*, vol. 14, no. 3, 1979, p. 393.

206 Luttwack, pp. 175–81.

repression or to mobilizing fully-fledged fascist practices of government, it was inevitable that the Dictator should create a vacuum of authority that his democratic enemies were only too eager to fill. There is no doubt that in the later years of Francoism, there was a more complete congruence between the structure and attitudes of society and democratic norms than in the late twenties. Nevertheless, *Primoderriverismo* had experienced, albeit on a lower scale, similar tensions to those that took place in the Spain of the sixties and the seventies when the incompatibility between the developing society and economy on the one hand and political autocracy and immobilism on the other created a crisis of identity for Francoism, and, in the last analysis, was virtually responsible for its ultimate breakdown. The growth of wealth and urbanization as well as the steady process of de-archaization of the social structure in the 1920s were increasingly becoming incompatible with autocratic norms of government. This is how a contemporary observer of the Spanish scene chose to put it, in the aftermath of Primo de Rivera's fall:

> The new status of the town worker and the effect on the peasants of the building of thousands of miles of roads and railways were bound to have a great effect on the future. Roads meant motor-buses, this meant more movement and freedom for the country people. It meant also that they would want a higher standard of living. Nothing would be the same in Spain again after General Primo fell. He had launched great schemes of modernization in a feudal country and there would be much political fruit in addition to economic changes.[207]

It was precisely to this relation between socio-economic and political change that Gregorio Marañón had made reference, a year before the breakdown of the Dictatorship, as likely to lead to far-reaching political transformation: 'The time is ripe in Spain for the most profound transformations that the country's social and political structure has ever undergone. In fact, these transformations are taking place at this very moment . . .[208]

These transformations were to come to full political fruition only with the establishment of the Second Republic in 1931. But before the breakaway of the urban middle classes, the army, and the Socialist movement from their alliance with authoritarian politics became a key factor in the institution of the 'bourgeois' republic, it

[207] H. Buckley, *Life and Death of the Spanish Republic* (London, 1940), p. 26. For the political consequences of the Dictatorship, see Ben-Ami, *The Origins*.

[208] *El Socialista*, 16 Dec. 1928.

had been highly instrumental in frustrating the Dictator's drive to legitimize his rule, and hence in critically narrowing the Dictatorship's prospects of survival. This predicament is the underlying subject of the last two chapters.

CHAPTER IX

The Breakdown of the 1923 Alliance

1. *Disenchanted Entrepreneurs and Proprietors*

The gradual withdrawal of support of considerable sections of the middle classes from the Dictatorship could not be concealed. It is not, as some analysts claimed, at some time in the middle of 1929 that this divorce between the regime and its bourgeois basis had started.[1] It was a phenomenon that manifested itself throughout Primo de Rivera's rule when different sections of the middle classes—never a homogeneous lot—took issue, at different times, with those of the Dictatorship's policies that had, in their view, put their respective interests in jeopardy. The senior republican militant, Alejandro Lerroux, was broadly right when he observed late in 1926 that big business, the powerful bankers, the big landowners, 'in sum, all those who represent highly important vested interests' could not be counted upon as a reservoir of support for those who, like himself, were determined to overthrow the Dictatorship.[2] But though the divorce between these sectors and the regime was more emphatically exposed in 1929, their disenchantment with the Dictatorship started at an earlier stage. Now, however, it was mainly the smaller entrepreneurs, the modest merchants, industrialists, and shopkeepers who did not wait until the famous boom had started to show signs of exhaustion in order to join the choir of protests against Primo de Rivera's regime.

Though the protective umbrella was certainly welcomed by the textile magnates of Catalonia and by the mining and heavy industrial concerns of the north, the tariff issue was a divisive one.

There was always a sector of the economy that would protest against the protection accorded to a commodity which it needed at a cheaper price. Thus, for example, the paper industry, whose profits rocketed under the Dictator's protective umbrella,[3] was certainly

[1] Maurín, pp. 48–9, 83; A. Nin, *Los problemas de la revolución española* (Ruedo Ibérico, 1971), p. 47.

[2] Lerroux's letter of 2 Oct. 1926 in Romanones Archive, Leg. 2, No. 32.

[3] For the profits of the Papelera, see above, p. 258.

happy with the high tariff walls erected against imported paper.[4] But this was not the case with book publishers and newspaper owners, who, for obvious reasons, wanted to demolish that wall. They wanted to share with the paper industry the advantage of having low tariffs for imported raw material.[5] On the whole, this seemed to be a consistent policy of the Dictatorship, to apply protective tariffs for the defence of the final Spanish product, while substantially reducing them for the raw material needed for its production.[6]

Nor was the government's consistent policy of reaching international trade agreements evenly palatable to the different sectors of the economy. On the whole, they were welcomed, and indeed strongly demanded, by that part of agriculture that depended on exports, namely the olive-growers and the orange- and wine-exporters. But they were seen as highly damaging by industrialists. There was here a most emphatic clash of interests between the fervent protectionist views of such organizations as the *Fomento de Trabajo Nacional*, the powerful association of Catalan big business, and the free-trade demands of, say, the agriculturists of Levante 'who live[d] off exports'.[7] The commercial treaty with France was warmly acclaimed by the orange-exporters and the wine-producers, who could not fail to see the promising prospects that lay in the French market. But the textile magnates of Catalonia strongly opposed, ineffectively, however, the treaty as likely to open the gates of Spain to French industrial products.[8] The agriculturists of Levante had been campaigning for some time in favour of the extension of the policy of commercial treaties to other industrial countries such as Belgium, Switzerland, and Germany. And when such treaties were finally concluded, it was not surprising that the industrial sector, whose exporting potentialities were slight, and whose ability to compete for the Spanish market with imported goods was hardly more promising, set out to combat them vehemently.[9] Its agitation, however, was somewhat superfluous. The

[4] AHN, P.G. Leg. 442: Sindicato Libre de Obreros Papeleros de Villalba demanded even higher protection.

[5] A pamphlet edited by *ABC*, in AHN, P.G. Leg. 442.

[6] See above, p. 262–4, on the case of raw cotton and textile products. Primo tried to apply the same principle to the car industry, see AHN, P.G. Leg. 442: 'Fábrica de automóbiles la Hispano-Suiza', 3 Feb. 1924.

[7] AHN, P.G. Leg. 330: a protest by Levantine agriculturists against the views of the Fomento, 11 Feb. 1924.

[8] AHN, P.G. Leg. 330: reactions to the treaty with France, Feb. 1924.

[9] AHN, P.G. Leg. 330: Protests from the Liga Vizcaína de Productores (2 Aug. 1924); from Barcelonian industrialists (29 Dec. 1924) and others.

import of industrial products went down from an index of 355 in 1923 to 310, 201, 199 in the following years. It increased again in 1927, when the public works came into effect, to 247; a trend that was maintained in the last two years of the regime (289,274).[10]

But the protectionist zeal was not evenly shared by all the non-agricultural sectors of the Spanish economy. It certainly was the preferred slogan of the protected monopolies and big business, companies such as Explosivos, Papelera, Minas del Rif, Basconia, and Altos Hornos, for whom the Dictatorship was a golden era of rocketing profits.[11] But the lesser industrialists and manufacturers who ran no chance of competing with the favoured, greater concerns faced in many cases the danger of virtual extinction. As the small industrialists and manufacturers of Galicia claimed in October 1927, conditions of fair competition could be created only when new policies were applied, namely a drastic reduction of tariffs, and the imposition of special taxes upon those industrial magnates who profited most from protectionism.[12] Merchants were especially enraged by the government's protectionist policy that limited the volume of their activities, raised artificially the level of prices, and narrowed the margin of their profits.[13] They usually found themselves, therefore, on the same side of the fence as the exporting sector of agriculture. This coalition of interests was best exemplified in the orange region of Valencia. As early as October 1923, it was clear to the president of the Valencian Chamber of Commerce and Navigation that 'the recent [protectionist] tariffs do nothing but favour in an excessive and unjust way the powerful interests that have been monopolizing our economy for a long time . . . The consequences can only be the ruin of our international commerce, especially our export.'[14]

Merchants and shopkeepers were of course also highly disturbed by what they viewed as the government's demagogic crusade of penalizing them for allegedly fixing excessively high prices for the commodities they traded in. The root of the problem lay not in their margin of profits, they would argue, but in the high protective tariffs and in government interventionism.[15] But the Dictator insisted on

[10] *Anuario*, 1929, p. xxiii.

[11] See above, p. 258.

[12] *The Economist*, 29 Oct. 1927.

[13] *Boletín de la Cámara de Comercio de Madrid*, Oct. 1923, and subsequent numbers; *El Mercantil*, 21 Apr. 1926.

[14] Joaquín Juliá, *El protectionismo y sus resultados* (Madrid, 1924), p. 11.

[15] *Boletín de la Cámara de Comercio de Madrid*, Oct. 1923. See also the protest of the Círculo Madrileño de la Unión Mercantil, 26 Feb. 1926, in Maura, *Bosquejo*, p. 153.

putting the blame for rising prices at the door of the merchants themselves. Accusing them of moving into 'the abominable sphere of politics' in order to combat him, he said that 'the excessive luxury' of their shops and sites was responsible for the rocketing cost of living.[16]

Moving from protectionism to interventionism, a similar distinction can be drawn between big business and the monopolistic concerns on the one hand, and the lesser industrialists and merchants on the other, as to their reaction to the government's 'interventionist' policies. Interventionism was usually seen by the smaller producers, shopkeepers, and merchants, as a device engineered for the benefit of big business, and was therefore rejected for 'invading a terrain' that, for the sake of economic prosperity, should be closed to all official obstruction.[17] The favour shown by the government towards big business was seen by people who were anything but dogmatic liberals as 'a doctrine that contradicts the principle of economic freedom'. 'Free competition', claimed the Superior Council of the Chambers of Commerce, Industry, and Navigation late in 1925, 'is an indispensable condition for a better quality, and a cheaper one, of production.' A policy 'that shielded the big monopolies' was bound to have diametrically different results.[18] A similar protest came later, in August 1929, from the smaller producers of cork, when the government contemplated the creation of a monopoly in that industry.[19] The organ of the industrialists in the area of Madrid had earlier castigated the government for creating the Regulating Committee of Industrial Production. It was an obstacle to 'the free play of economic laws', to the 'free competition among individual activities'. And when the government granted the petroleum monopoly to a consortium of Spanish banks, the same industrialists rejected it in the name of 'the thesis of the freedom of industry' as against 'the conscious interventionism of the state'.[20] These Spanish latecomers to the doctrines of *laissez-faire* resorted to liberal doctrines in a desperate attempt to survive in a system dominated by favouritism and the protection of one sector of industry (the larger enterprises) to the detriment of the other. Late in 1928, a deputy at the National Assembly summed up the effects of the 1924 Law of Assistance to National Industries in the following way: 'Those who benefit from

[16] Maura, *Bosquejo*, p. 153.

[17] Cf. Ben-Ami, *The Origins*, p. 27.

[18] *Bolétin de la Cámara Oficial de Comercio e Industria de Sabadell*, Nov. 1925.

[19] *La Vanguardia*, 6 Aug. 1929.

[20] *Industria*, Dec. 1926, Aug. 1927.

this law are not those who have built up their business in a silent, dignified way, with the help of nothing but their work, honesty and industry. No, the beneficiaries are those who have the right relations, power, means, contact with the authorities; those who are used to enjoying favours and the prodigality of the system.'[21]

Such was also the spirit of the protest of the *Confederación Gremial Española*, an association of small producers which in 1923 had been outspoken in acclaiming Primo's seizure of power,[22] against state interventionism. 'The activities of the regulating committees of national production and the concession of generous monopolies', it claimed, 'are an impediment to the development of our national industry.'[23]

Among the smaller urban property-owners there was a great deal of discontent at the restrictions put by the government upon 'the faculty of free disposal' of their property. Why should rural property-owners be absolutely free to fix their rents, while their urban counterparts were subject to endless restrictions?, they asked. Urban proprietors were especially disturbed by the increase in municipal taxes as well as by a recent decision to set up Comités Paritarios to regulate the relations between themselves and their tenants, precisely the kind of set-back that their rural counterparts were spared by the government.[24] Luis Saínz de los Terreros, the president of the property-owners in Madrid, claimed that it was precisely because of such governmental restrictions that people were no longer ready to invest in urban property, and the construction industry was, therefore, approaching a state of almost total paralysis. As in the case of industry, so also in the field of constructions, the smaller entrepreneurs were being pushed out of the market by the bigger companies whom the state and the municipalities had contracted to build, under fabulously favourable conditions, cheap housing.[25]

Spanish entrepreneurs had at long last discovered Cobdenist liberalism. The conservative *ABC* made itself the spokesman of this new mood when it welcomed Calvo Sotelo's resignation. In the name of 'economic freedom', it now expected the end of the

[21] Conde de Lizarraga quoted in Colectivo de Historia, 'La Dictadura de Primo de Rivera y el bloque de poder en España', in *Cuadernos Económicos de I.C.E.*, 1976/1978, p. 209. [22] See above, p.84 [23] *La Vanguardia*, 10 Nov. 1929.

[24] See above, p.302

[25] *Boletín de la Cámara Oficial de la Propiedad Urbana*, Feb., Nov., Dec. 1929; Jan. 1930.

monopolies. Earlier, the same newspaper attacked 'the absurd theory' according to which a country should produce everything at any price, as was the pretension 'of a sordid protectionism of business and privilege'.[26] The Superior Council of the Chambers of Commerce and Industry put this in the clearest terms possible, when it addressed the government early in 1929: 'The Government has long abandoned its harmonizing function. It now invades a terrain which, for the sake of the natural requirements of economic life, ought to remain closed to any official intervention.'[27]

It was no surprise that the immediate liberalizing steps taken by General Berenguer, Primo's successor, should have been warmly welcomed, especially by merchants and the smaller businessmen. The abolition of the Regulating Committee of Industrial Production, the Committee for the Control of Supplies and Prices, and the strict norms that regulated exports—'all of which had been a constant hindrance to progress'—was seen as a grand step 'towards the normalization of national life'. The merchants and the smaller industrialists conceded that protection and intervention might have assisted national industry to a certain degree; what they did not doubt was that both had inflicted 'untold damage' upon their class.[28]

Interventionism was unbearable to the modest businessmen, especially as they claimed to be paying with their taxes the bill for the government's protection of the bigger concerns. Such was the spirit of the petition handed, late in 1929, to Calvo Sotelo by 'the modest industrialists and property-owners' of the province of Burgos.[29] State intervention was not only, as the *Círculo de la Unión Mercantil e Industrial* put it when reacting to the creation of the Regulating Committee of Industrial Production, a blow to 'the major generator of wealth, private initiative', and 'an *étatisme* that is bound to result in an undue rise in prices'.[30] It was also a costly affair in the sense that it increased the government's expenditure, to which the business sector was increasingly asked to contribute. The wide variety of local and national taxes that the business sector had to comply with had become a stumbling-block that 'fatally hinders

[26] *ABC*, 22 Jan. 1930; 24 Mar. 1929.

[27] *Boletín de la Cámara Oficial de Comercio, Industria y Navegación de Málaga*, Feb. 1929.

[28] *Boletín de la Cámara Oficial de Comercio e Industria de Lérida y su Provincia*, Jan., Mar. 1930.

[29] *Boletín de la Cámara Oficial de Comerico e Industria de la Provincia de Burgos*, Oct.–Dec. 1929.

[30] *Folletín*, p. 324.

the normal development of production'; such was the message that the Superior Council of Chambers of Commerce, Industry, and Navigation tried to bring home to Calvo Sotelo upon his accession to the ministry of finance. But the variety of indirect taxes which the new minister imposed upon industry, such as the excise—'a hateful tax levied upon commodities', to borrow Dr Johnson's Dictionary definition—and stamp taxes, as well as his tax on income and profits, gave the industrialists the feeling of being 'defrauded' by the government.[31]

If anything, Calvo's measures against tax evasion further alarmed the modest entrepreneurs. They therefore rejected in loud and bitter terms, the new law that obliged them to run sales diaries. 'It is a permanent nightmare of merchants and industrialists', complained one of their representative organs, 'to be presented as the only defrauders of the treasury', despite being those who had to suffer 'the full weight of the tax reforms'. As if to prove the allegation of the modest entrepreneurs about the regime's symbiotic relations with big business, the government had stipulated that the big commercial concerns should be exempt from the obligation to run a sales diary. Instead of suffocating the economic potentialities of the small and medium-sized businessmen through 'intervention' and taxation, and since it looked rather reluctant to shift the fiscal burden over on to the shoulders of its powerful friends, the government was asked to resort to a policy of financial cuts and retrenchment.[32]

To be sure, Calvo Sotelo had tried to shift the burden of taxation on to the big landowners and proprietors. He failed. But the very attempt was sufficient to arouse a wave of panic and suspicion as to the social orientation of the Dictatorship among the owning classes. Calvo's 'sensational decrees' of January 1926 fixing a deadline of three months after which the property of those who failed to disclose the true taxable value of their property would be confiscated, were, according to the liberal *El Sol*, tantamount 'to a real revolution in the system of property'. It is not surprising, then, that the new measure was vehemently combated by such landowners as the Dukes of Alba, Fernán Nuñez, Villahermosa, and Medinacelli, as

[31] *Industria*, June, July 1926; March 1927.

[32] For the protests against the sales diary, see *Boletín de la Cámara Oficial de Comerico e Industria de Lérida y su provincia*, Dec. 1925–Feb. 1926; Maura, *Bosquejo*, p. 482. *La nación*, 9, 10 July 1926, found some entrepreneurs who supported the new measure.

well as by the powerful associations of proprietors all across the country. They were said to be 'in a state of profound malaise, alarm, and uncertainty'. Always defended by the Spanish state to the detriment of an army of destitute landless labourers, they suddenly discovered the sacred liberal principle of non-intervention by the state, or, for that matter, the sanctity of the Roman Law of use and abuse. An Andalusian property-owner wrote to Calvo Sotelo following the promulgation of the controversial decree: 'You are leading a frontal attack against property. Any measure that does not respect the right of use and abuse, the *jus abustere* of the Roman Law, is aimed at suffocating private property.'[33] The landowners' and urban proprietors' vehement campaign against Calvo's 'bolshevik' onslaught on the sanctity of private property succeeded in deterring the Dictator from implementing the relevant decrees.[34] For the small and medium-sized farmers of the *Liga Nacional de Campesinos*—themselves anything but pleased with a reform that 'infringed upon sacred rights and upset the tranquillity needed for the exploitation of the land'—the whole affair only proved the existence of the close affinity between the regime and the powerful economic interests. It also reasserted in their eyes the obvious fact that the big landowners had 'much taxable property to conceal'.[35]

The powerful proprietors had won the day.[36] But their minds could never again be fully set at rest. They would always be suspicious as to the social orientation of the regime.

> The privileged families of the old regime could not bear that the general . . . should have picked up the popular desire for the establishment of a new state. How did Calvo Sotelo dare, with his decrees of 1926, to tax the concealed wealth under the threat of expropriation? How could the Dictator be so audacious as to claim in an article in *ABC*, at the end of 1927, that he planned to carry out agrarian reform in 1928? What is all this socialist innovation of the Comités Paritarios about? None of these sorts of measures had ever been agreed upon (when they decided to support the coming of the Dictatorship).[37]

[33] Calvo, p. 128.

[34] For the landowners' campaign, see *El Sol*, 3 Apr. 1926; Maura, *Bosquejo*, p. 315; Calvo, pp. 126–8; *El Debate* and *ABC*, Jan.–Mar. 1927; Velarde, 'los terratenientes contra Calvo Sotelo', in *Sobre la decadencia*, pp. 193–5.

[35] *Folletín*, p. 317.

[36] See also Pemartín, *Los valores*, p. 183; Aunós, *Calvo Sotelo*, pp. 81–2.

[37] *Acción Española*, 16 Mar. 1933, pp. 102–3.

The now fashionable rejection of 'interventionism' was not exactly a piece of doctrinal liberalism for the landowners either. Rather it was their way of demanding an alleviation of the burden of taxation.[38] The economics of development were acceptable to them only so long as they did not have to pay the bill. Thus, the authority given to the municipalities to levy taxes of their own, and the special tax of 5 per cent imposed upon all the products of the land, were the cause of an unyielding campaign by landowners.[39] Their liberalism was applied very selectively. Phrases such as 'private initiative is the uterus of progress' were taken from the speeches of President Hoover and from the precepts of the Hansabund for strictly opportunist use. They therefore denounced as 'unfortunate interventionism' all governmental measures that regulated the price of agricultural products. But the kind of 'interventionism' embodied in high tariffs for imported agricultural products would always be welcome, indeed clamoured for. But since 80 per cent of the Spanish industrial products were consumed by the agrarian hinterland, it was in the interest of landowners to demand the government's 'intervention' against the 'ultra-protectionism' enjoyed by industry.[40] When faced with the crisis of over-production, the wheat-growers did not hesitate to clamour for state intervention, which they were only too happy to accept when it came in the form of a decree fixing minimum prices for wheat.[41] And when the olive-growers of Andalusia underwent a similar crisis, it was for the government's intervention that they appealed desperately.[42]

But when Primo de Rivera thought of some mild attempt to remedy the social injustice in the countryside, this was violently rejected by agriculturists as 'unbearable intervention' against sacred property rights. It was, for example, inadmissible from the point of view of landowners that the municipalities should have forced them, under the threat of a fine, to employ day labourers even when they did not have any productive work to offer them.[43] They likewise objected to Primo de Rivera's efforts to curb their attempts to put down rural wages through the importation of cheap labour from

[38] *Boletín de la Asociación de Agricultores de España*, May 1929; *La Época*, 22 Jan. 1929.

[39] *Boletín . . . de Agricultores*, Feb. 1929; *El Imparcial*, 15, 21 Feb. 1929.

[40] *Boletín . . . de Agricultores*, Apr., May 1929.

[41] *La Época*, 16 July 1929.

[42] *Boletín . . . de Agricultores*, Oct. 1929. See also 'Nuestra riqueza aceitera', *La Época*. 18 Jan. 1930.

[43] Aunós, *España en crisis*, p. 289.

outside municipal boundaries. The tax he levied upon the importation of cheap labour was combated as an arbitrary encroachment upon their sacred freedom.[44] At the same time, the Catalan landowners' association, *Instituto Agrícola de San Isidro*, came out in angry terms against the government's project to regulate tenancy contracts in such a way as to guard the tenants against arbitrary eviction, guarantee them contracts of long duration, and compensate them for whatever improvements they might have introduced on the land. All this was tantamount, in the eyes of the landowners, to 'throwing the property-owner out of his own house . . . sacrificing a whole social class on the altar of an illusory ideal . . . annulling the personality of the proprietor'. The reform proposals were attacked by landowners' representatives in the National Assembly as no less than a 'bolshevik' onslaught on their rights.[45]

The tide against 'interventionism' gained momentum in 1929. As early as January 1929, the Dictator had to come out in a special article against what he called 'the exaggerated repudiation of interventionism'.[46] Now, however, it was not only the very modest producers, but also the representatives of higher interests that had profited in the past from interventionism, that started to see in free enterprise and economic freedom a relevant formula of salvation.[47] The Federation of National Industries, a group of Basque and Catalan heavy industrialists, for example accused the government of 'suffocating private initiative', of 'guarding too zealously Spanish capital from industrial risks . . .'[48]. Why should the government, asked the Conservative *La Época* in despair, intervene also in those companies which did not have any state capital?[49]

Clearly, businessmen expected that a substantial reduction of government enterprises would entail a meaningful alleviation of the burden of taxation they had been inveighing against. It was because of high taxation, claimed the directors of the Río Tinto mines—the company's tax payments rose from £ 107,000 in 1923 to £ 403,000 in 1928[50]—that despite an improvement in sales and benefits, the company was compelled to pay lower dividends to its shareholders.[51]

[44] *Boletín . . . de Agricultores*, Feb. 1929.

[45] Ibid., June–July 1929; Baldomero Argente, 'Los proyectos agrarios', *El Imparcial*, 1 Aug. 1929.

[46] *La Nación*, 26 Jan. 1929.

[47] *The Economist*, 23 Nov. 1929.

[48] *El Economista*, 31 Aug. 1929.

[49] *La Época*, 9 Jan. 1929.

[50] Charles Harvey, *The Río Tinto Company* (Penzance, 1981), p. 256.

[51] *The Economist*, 27 Apr. 1929.

The government's insistence on maintaining the so far steady growth of its revenues from taxation at a time when economic uncertainties were looming was evident cause for alarm among the so-called 'moneyed people'.[52]

Big business was alarmed not because of state interventionism as such, but because the state was no longer an efficient agent of economic prosperity; in other words, its 'intervention' ceased to be efficient and desirable. Their resentment was mainly due to the monetary crisis,[53] and to what they viewed as an excessively heavy burden of taxation,[54] which they expected would be alleviated once the government had reduced its expensive economic bureaucracy and drastically cut its social and developmental enterprises.

First and foremost it was perhaps the costly social orientation of the regime which businessmen came increasingly to resent. The workers were being viewed as the spoiled children of a regime which had 'multiplied the advantages of social legislation' at the expense of the greater taxpayers.[55] The Federation of National Industries, the very same association of Basque and Catalan producers of steel and electricity, which in 1923 had urged the Dictator to launch a programme of public works in order to activate their industries,[56] now explicitly demanded an outright suspension of all schemes of public works. It furthermore expressed its 'preoccupation . . . with the rhythm, always more accelerated, of the government's social policy'. Any measure, it concluded, that tended to put more taxes on industry was a step towards 'extinguishing or slowing down the spirit of initiative and competition'.[57] Public works that were once referred to as an incentive to industry were now seen, as a protest of the Madrid Chamber of Industry put it, as fuelling inflation, and consequently deranging business.[58] The government was not unaware of the anxieties of the business community as to its social

[52] The treasury's revenue from direct taxation increased from 1,169,938,992 pesetas in 1928 to 1,203,081,680 in 1929, the yield of the indirect taxes went up from 1,308,405,570 pesetas to 1,363,650,366, see *Anuario*, 1929, pp. 353, 359.

[53] See below, pp. 346–9

[54] 'Hay que desgravar los tributos', *La Época*, 22 Jan. 1929.

[55] *La Época*, 21 Jan. 1929.

[56] See above, p. 251.

[57] *El Economista*, 31 Aug. 1929. One should emphasize that government expenditure was not reduced in 1929; see p. 340. If anything, the ordinary budget of the ministry of labour went up in 1929; see *Anuario*, 1929, p. 358. In 1929 the state issued 1,162,500,000 pesetas worth of bonds. This was more than the issue of any other previous year; see *Folletín*, pp. 840–1; *El Financiero*, Nov. 1930, p. 15.

[58] *ABC*, 18 Jan. 1930.

emphasis. *La Nación* tried, therefore, to set the businessmen's minds at rest:

> The socialism of the Dictatorship does not disregard, nor does it intend to weaken or run down, the right of property. It only canalizes and organizes it in such a way that it can fulfil high social functions . . . [Our aim is] to prevent the avaricious exploitation by capital as well as the violence and coercive actions of labour . . . There is, then, in the enterprise of the Dictatorship no cause for alarm whatsoever.[59]

Significantly, the most bitter opposition to the Comités Paritarios in 1929 came from the employers. They exemplified to them the increasingly unacceptable social emphasis of the regime. Employers' corporations,[60] aided by the Catholic and conservative press, launched a campaign of demolition, or at least reform, of the Comités Paritarios. *El Debate* claimed that as a Social-Catholic organ it condoned the corporatist principle;[61] but the way this was being applied in Spain threatened to create 'a state within a state'.[62] Similar views were put forward by the conservative *La Época* and *ABC*.[63] As in the case of the employers, Social Catholics had initially welcomed the Comités Paritarios.[64] It was when they realized that they had consolidated the Socialists' strength, not infrequently at the expense of Catholic Syndicates and the Libres, that they took up the cudgels for doing away with the system as conceived by the regime.[65]

In order to break the Socialist hegemony in the Comités Paritarios, and put an end to the practice whereby labour disputes were consistently being decided in favour of the workers (mainly through the intervention of the State delegate), the nationwide employers' organization, *Asociación de Estudios Sociales y Económicos*, proposed that the elections for the Committees should be direct and on an individual, rather than corporative, basis so that unorganized workers could also be elected.[66] It was precisely such an atomization of the working class that Aunós was determined to avoid in the first place. His view entirely coincided with that of the Socialists who

[59] *La Nación*, 30 Aug. 1929.

[60] See the case of the Huelva Mineowners' Association, in Harvey, p. 255.

[61] *El Debate*, 25 Apr. 1929.

[62] Ibid., 22 Jan, 29 Dec. 1929.

[63] *ABC*, 12 Jan. 1929; *La Época*, 12, 21 Jan. 1929. *El Socialista*, 22 Sept., 31 Oct. 1928, 1 Jan. 1929, refers to the views of the press that opposed the Committees.

[64] Montero, vol. i, p. 59, Aunós, *La política social*, p. 33.

[65] For examples of Socialist victories over Catholics and Libres in both Madrid and Biscay, see *El Dependiente*, Sept. 1928.

[66] *El Socialista*, 3 Jan. 1929.

rejected the employers' demand as a shrewd device to fill the Committees with 'non-associated workers' who could be easily manipulated into becoming 'the accomplices of the employers' class'.[67] The employers also demanded, through the League of Industrial and Commercial Defence, that the state should share the financial burden of the Committees.[68] The Superior Council of Chambers of Commerce of Spain joined the chorus of bitterness and protest with a complaint at the Committees' assuming functions that were not directly related to 'social relations'. In other words, they demanded that the Committees should only deal with questions of arbitration and conciliation and refrain from assuming legislative functions.[69]

However, Aunós was adamant. He would meet none of the employers' demands. On more than one occasion he assured the Socialists of his determination to keep the system intact.[70] 'The efficiency of the Comités Paritarios has been proved beyond any doubt', he responded to the complaints of the Madrid Chamber of Commerce, 'by their constant labour of pacification.' 'It is thanks to them', he continued, 'that the recent labour disputes in Seville and Valencia have been settled, and that the number of strikes recorded in 1928 is the lowest since 1905, in itself a year of only 87 strikes.'[71] Aunós later castigated Spanish capitalists for their obfuscation. In their bitter struggle against the Comités Paritarios, he wrote, 'they had moved to the revolutionary camp with their weapons and equipment, namely with their capital, in order to exploit the most vulgar demogogic passions against the Dictator'. They failed to realize, he deplored, that the Comités Paritarios were a key instrument in Primo de Rivera's revolution from above that alone could avoid an 'anti-capitalistic revolution', 'a catastrophic and anarchic revolution from below', the main victims of which would be the possessing classes themselves.[72] The latter failed to force a reform of the system. Neither were the attempts of many employers to sabotage the work of the Committees more successful.[73]

[67] Ibid., 12 Nov. 1927, 12 Apr. 1929.

[68] *La Vanguardia*, 27 Apr. 1930. See also the manifesto of the Madrid Chamber of Commerce in *El Socialista*, 12 Jan. 1930.

[69] For the complaints of the employers, see *Boletín de la UGT*, Mar. 1929; *Industria*, Oct. 1928, March, Dec. 1929. *La Época*, 12 Jan. 1929, summed them up.

[70] *Boletín de la UGT*, Mar. 1929; Aunós in *ABC*, 13 Feb. 1929.

[71] *El Socialista*, 12 Jan. 1930. See also Aunós in *España Comercial. Órgano de Propaganda de los Intereses del Comercio, Industria y Trabajo*, Sept. 1928.

[72] Aunós, *España en crisis*, p. 294.

[73] For such an attempt, see *Boletín Oficial de la Sociedad General de Obreros Gasistas, Electricistas, Teléfonos, Aguas y Similares de Madrid*, June 1928.

It did not take long also for the Catalan bourgeoisie to feel alienated from the Dictatorship. Its greatest gains from the new regime were obvious. Primo erected on their behalf the highest tariff walls in Europe.[74] The sharp drop in social crimes under the law-and-order Dictatorship (1919–23 = 253 dead, 382 injured, 100 unharmed; 1923–8 = 3 dead, 15 wounded, 13 unharmed)[75] was obviously also highly welcome to the Catalan business community.

Yet, not all the facets of the regime's socio-economic deal were always palatable to Catalan business. As early as the beginning of 1924 growing resentment was discernible among Catalan employers at the rapid fall in the exchange value of the peseta and at the consequent rise in the prices of foodstuffs, both of which created mounting pressures from labour.[76] The Catalan bourgeoisie, which in 1923 had 'invited' the Dictatorship to curb the unions, could not be too happy now with the regime's policy of institutionalizing a system of support and encouragement for organized labour. This was a sensitive issue especially in the textile industry, which in 1926 fell into a deep crisis. The factory-owners argued now that the crisis was due to the high wages they were being compelled to pay to their workers and to their being under strict obligation to comply with the eight-hour day.[77] By then the employers had new cause to worry: the high exchange rate of the peseta that was maintained throughout 1927 and the first half of 1928. Such a high rate put increasing strains on the exporting capacity of the textile sector; and before long enormous stocks had been accumulated, prices dropped, and unemployment increased. The government, on the other hand, did not rush to abide by the National Federation of Textile Industries' demand for export premiums to alleviate the crisis.[78] The result was that the value of the textile exports dropped by about 110 per cent between 1925 and 1928 (from 75,435,912 pesetas to 35,967,400).[79]

Nor was the unyieldingly anti-regionalist, indeed unitary, approach of the Dictator to the political aspirations of the Catalans[80] exactly instrumental in endearing his regime to the Catalan bourgeoisie.[81]

[74] *The Economist*, 26 Nov. 1927, 23 Nov. 1929.

[75] *La Vanguardia*, 11 Apr. 1929; *La Nación*, 29 Apr. 1929.

[76] *The Times*, 11 Mar. 1924.

[77] Ibid., 26 Aug. 1926.

[78] Pedro Corominas, 'La crisis económica en Cataluña', in *Hojas Libres*, 1 May 1927.

[79] In terms of volume, the drop was from 3,082,541 kg. to 2,483,341; see *Anuario*, 1929, p. 217.

[80] See above, pp. 194–202.

[81] I have discussed this issue elsewhere; see Ben-Ami, *The Origins* pp. 60–7, 163–5.

In private circles, bourgeois Catalans were heard to say that they had placed Primo in power, and he had betrayed them. It was now up to them to hurt him in return.[82]

Conspicuously, it was Cambó, the opulent leader of the Lliga, who became the most vocal interpreter of both the economic and political frustrations of his class. In the process of his confrontation with the regime, he set out to elaborate yet another opportunistic platform for a new *modus vivendi* between Spain and Catalonia, the dictatorial solution having failed so resoundingly. Not only had the Dictatorship fallen short of institutionalizing a new state that could secure the consolidation of an orderly society and polity, but it had also failed to shield effectively the economic interests of the Catalan bourgeoisie. Cambó's political disappointment with the Dictatorship was to be clearly expressed in his *Las dictaduras*, published in 1929. But he did not wait for that year of crisis to reveal his frustration at the regime's financial and monetary policies. In his *La valoración de la peseta*, a book based on articles he had started to publish in 1927, this personification of Catalan capitalism accused the government of encouraging speculation on the peseta, and consequently making life unbearable for the business sector, which had to adapt itself constantly to the chaotic and frequent fluctuations in the exchange rate of the currency. It is significant, however, that rather than pointing to a strictly economic solution to the problem, Cambó advanced a political clue. Only a democratic regime that would end the political uncertainties and eliminate extremist options either on the right or on the left could stabilize the peseta and restore business confidence.[83]

Cambó was here clearly anticipating the withdrawal of support of the Spanish bourgeoisie from the Dictatorship, and its move, out of a sober instinct of self-preservation, towards democratic postures. The Dictatorship had been in a way the expression of the Lliga's rebellion against the Spanish democratic state and 'Castilian' society. Now Cambó coined a new catchword: concord. The policy of 'let Spain sink so long as Catalonia is saved', that seemed to have motivated the Catalan upper bourgeoisie in 1923, had definitely gone bankrupt, according to Cambó.[84] 'Isolation leads nowhere', agreed *La Veu de Catalunya*.[85] It should not be surprising that

[82] FO 371/11936, Rumbold to Chamberlain, 7 May 1926.

[83] Cambó *La valoración*, pp. 99–111, 113–27. For the crisis of the peseta, see below, pp. 194–202.

[84] Cambó, *Por la concordia* (Madrid, 1927).

[85] Quoted in *La Epoca*, 7 Aug. 1929. See also Valls i Taberner, 'Moralitats i reflexions', in *La Veu de Catalunya*, 1 Jan. 1929.

Cambó, one of the only 'old politicians' towards whom Primo de Rivera showed any respect, should have been described by the Dictator, by the end of 1927, as somebody 'whose patriotism has been proved to be of doubtful quality'[86] and whose public activities should be strictly limited and supervised.[87]

2. *1929: The Economy, A Question of Confidence*

(a) *An Economic Crisis? The Times* wrote late in September 1928 that in Spain 'economics will in the end supply the measure by which the success or failure of the Dictatorship is gauged'.[88] For a regime that viewed prosperity and development as its greatest achievement, such an argument indeed carries much weight. The Dictatorship's final débâcle, however, though it coincided with the beginning of the Great Depression, was very much conditioned by political imperatives. Rather than a catastrophic 'crash', the Spanish 1929 economic crisis was one of financial and monetary mismanagement. Indeed, contemporary economic analysts observed at the time that the eclipse of the Dictatorship represented a completely opposite tendency to the ascending movement of the economy.[89]

Notwithstanding the 'economic miracle' it had experienced under Primo de Rivera, Spain remained fundamentally an agrarian country that produced most of its own basic food necessities. She did not depend on mass importation of foodstuffs, and her main exports were agricultural. Her mines produced most of the coal, albeit of a low quality, and iron she needed. She had obviously to import industrial products, including vital agricultural machines. Yet, owing to the rather self-contained character of its economic structure, the foreign-trade volume was modest in relation to the national wealth. The favourable or adverse balance of trade, and monetary depreciation, which though they could have serious internal repercussions, lacked the dramatic importance to the general internal welfare in Spain that it had in a country like England, whose food and very life were inextricably bound up with foreign trade and world finance. A report of the Bank of Spain in 1934 summed up the Spanish depression as 'a notably less profound phenomenon than the world depression.

[86] *The Times*, 21 Nov. 1927.

[87] Pabón, *Cambó* vol. ii, pt. I, pp. 554–5. See also the official attacks on Cambó following the publication of his articles on the peseta, *La Nación*, 11 Dec. 1928.

[88] *The Times*, 29 Sept. 1928.

[89] For example, Ceballos-Teresí in *El Financiero*, Nov. 1930, p. 10.

It paralleled the latter neither in its beginnings nor in its end, nor in its most substantial and typical vicissitudes.'[90]

Rather than a 'crash', 1929 represented in Spain 'the highest point in an ascending movement' of economic expansion.[91] This was, moreover, reflected in the fact that the industrial sector was able to mobilize in 1929, through its bond issues, a record sum of public money (1,076,970 million pesetas) that surpassed that of any other previous year.[92] The rise in Spain's index of industrial production in 1929 (one source speaks of 14 per cent; another of 8 per cent) was higher than that of some of the most important industrial countries, such as the USA (7.2 per cent), Belgium (0.1 per cent), Germany (1.4 per cent), England (6 per cent) and Sweden (0.9 per cent). Spain ranked with France (9.4 per cent), Canada (8.1 per cent), and Japan (11.3 per cent). Only the Soviet Union stood far ahead of any other western economy with an industrial growth of 24.3 per cent.[93] Likewise, the number of bankruptcies in Spain was insignificant in comparison with that of the industrial countries.[94] A comforting picture could also be formed from the index of production per capita. It increased steadily, showing a decline in the industrial field only after 1932.[95] 1929 proved to be an exceptionally good year for industrial production. Altogether, the profits of a sample of five heavy industrial concerns (Altos Hornos, Española de Construcciones Navales, Duro-Felguera, Siderúrgica del Mediterráneo, Maquinista Terrestre y Marítima) rose by 17 per cent in 1929.[96]

Getting down to particular industries, the increase in output is further underlined. The production of ingot iron increased by 14.9 per cent in relation to the previous year. 1929 was the best year of the whole period of the Dictatorship as far as the production of ingot iron was concerned. Such was also the case in the steel industry: an increase of 20 per cent compared with 1928. 1929 was also a successful year in the production and exportation of iron ore

[90] Banco de España, *Ritmo de la crisis económica española en relación con la mundial* (Madrid, 1934), p. 354.

[91] *El Financiero*, Nov. 1930, p. 10.

[92] 'Valores emitidos en 1929', *El Financiero*, Nov. 1930, p. 15.

[93] *Anuario*, 1931, p. 731; Lefaucheux, p. 152.

[94] *Anuario*, 1931, pp. 335–6.

[95] Vicens Vives, 'El moviment obrer a Espanya de 1929 a 1936 en relació amb la crisi económica', in *Serra D'Or*, 2ᵉ epoca, iii, no. 2, Feb. 1961, p. 29. Cf. David Ruiz, 'Repercusión de la crisis de 1929 en España. Consideraciones en torno', in *Hispania* (Madrid), xxviii, no. 109 (1968), pp. 337–52; Banco de España, *Ritmo*, pp. 336–8.

[96] Hernández Andreu, 'Algunos aspectos de la depresión', *Cuadernos*, p. 397.

(an increase of 6 per cent compared with 1928).[97] The same was true of coal production, which reached its peak in 1929, increasing by 10 per cent in relation to the previous year.[98] The overall value of the production of the mining industry in Spain reflected this ascending trend: it rose by 28 per cent and 13 per cent in relation to 1927 and 1928 respectively. This did not respond only to a depreciation of the peseta, but also to an increase in real output, from 28,653,945 tons in 1928 to 30,366,969 in 1929.[99] Moreover, the mining industry employed in 1929 5,847 more workers than in 1928 (163,367 compared with 157,520).[100] The production of electric energy and the number of new power-stations in 1929 surpassed that of any previous year. And, as Perpiñá Grau observed at the time, the hydroelectric business in Spain 'reached a really distinctive flowering' in 1929, thanks largely to foreign investments.[101]

Even a key branch such as the cotton industry that went through a serious crisis of over-production and had, therefore, to dismiss superfluous workers and to abolish overtime for the 125,000 workers still employed in the industry was said to have scored record exports in 1929. During the first nine months of the year, the cotton branch of the textile industry exported 86 per cent more than during the same period in 1929. The exports in the last quarter of 1929 doubled in relation to the parallel period in 1928. The crisis was mainly one of over-production, and this, in its turn, was the result of a substantial modernization of machinery.[102]

True, the abolition of the extraordinary budget by the end of the year was to mark a change in the so far generous policy of public works. But the impact of such a change was not felt before the fall of the Dictator.[103] Significantly, in addition to the 1,556,800 tons of cement produced in Spain in 1929, an additional quantity of 217,085 tons had to be imported in order to cope with the non-diminishing

[97] Barreiro, 'La industria minero-siderúrgica española', *Revista de Economía*, Jan. 1930, pp. 70–4.

[98] *Estadísticas Básicas*, p. 186.

[99] *Anuario*, 1931, pp. 138–9.

[100] *El Financiero*, Nov. 1930.

[101] Perpiñá, 'Cómo se racionaliza España en 1929', 'La industria eléctrica en España', in *El Financiero*, Nov. 1930, pp. 11–13, 51–5. For the absolute figures, see *Estadísticas Básicas*, p. 188: 1927—707,200 kWh; 1928—865,000; 1929—937,000.

[102] *Boletín del Comité Regulador de la Industria Algondonera*, Dec. 1929, pp. 445–9; P. Gual Villalví, 'La augustiosa situación de la industria algodonera nacional', *El Financiero*, Nov. 1930, pp. 16–18.

[103] According to the relevant decree, the new policy was to come into effect only on 31 December 1929.

needs.[104] It is also noteworthy that the issue of public bonds in 1929 reached the highest figure since 1922: 2,336,170,000 million pesetas, of which the state was responsible for 1,162,616,400 (in 1928 only 800 million) pesetas.[105]

In agriculture, as in the cotton industry, the crisis was one of over-production, and hence of a drastic depreciation of prices. The wheat harvest, for example, was optimal. Spain produced in 1929 400,000 tons more than it needed for its national consumption. Also exceptionally good were the harvests of common rye, barley, and oats.[106] Over-production and the import of foreign cereals in the first half of the year (the 1928 frost had severely damaged the crops) combined to produce a sharp depreciation of prices to the detriment of the Castilian farmers, who clamoured vociferously for a hermetic ban on imported cereals.[107] The crisis was shared by olive-growers, the export of whose products decreased by more than 60 per cent though their harvest was the highest of the decade. This also entailed a drastic drop in prices.[108] Also, the wine industry was badly hit by a French ban on the import of foreign wines, at a time when the Spanish production of wine went up from 22 million hectolitres in 1928 to 24.9 million in 1929.[109] Especially detrimental to the wine-producers in Spain was the American ban on alcohol.[110] There was also a drop of 19 million pesetas in the export of oranges, and about 20 million in that of rice (from 59 to 39 tons).[111] Yet a more effective control on the import of agricultural products and a certain increase in exports still accounted in 1929 for a narrowing of the trade deficit in cereals, vegetables, and greens by 55,249,000 pesetas as compared with the situation in 1928.[112]

Indeed, Spain's export volume in 1929 was the second highest

[104] 'La industria de cemento en España', *El Financiero*, Nov. 1930, pp. 122–3.

[105] 'Valores emitidos en 1929 comparados con el decenio 1919–1928', *El Financiero*, Nov. 1930, pp. 13–16.

[106] *El Economista*, 23 Nov. 1929; 'La agricultura y la ganadería españolas en 1929', in *El Financiero*, Nov. 1930, pp. 108–17.

[107] *Boletín de la Asociación de Agricultores de España*, Jan., Feb. 1930.

[108] *La Vanguardia*, 27 Mar., 19 Nov. 1929; *El Debate*, 23 Oct. 1929. For the good harvest, see Ministerio de Trabajo y Previsión. Dirección General de Acción Social, *La crisis agraria andaluza de 1930–31. Estudios y documentos* (Madrid, 1931), p. 11. For the agitation among the olive-growers, see 'Los olivareros de la provincia ante la persistente baja en el precio del aceite', *Boletín de la Cámara . . . de Lérida y su Provincia*, May–June 1929.

[109] *El Financiero*, Nov. 1930, pp. 108–17.

[110] *The Times*, 19 Apr. 1929.

[111] Hernández Andreu, 'Algunos aspectos de la depresión', *Cuadernos*, p. 386.

[112] *El Financiero*, Nov. 1930, p. 115.

since 1910. A drop of 267,943,000 pesetas worth of imports in relation to 1928 and a not-negligible increase of exports (2,112,948,000 pesetas for 1929; 1,895,282,000 pesetas in 1927) brought down the trade deficit to 624,000,000 pesetas in comparison with 821,513,000 in 1928.[113]

(b) '*The Battle for the Peseta*'. 'The 1929 crisis' in Spain was almost exclusively related to the depreciation of the peseta, or rather to its instability. It was the state of the national currency that shook the confidence of economic circles and of the whole regime. The crisis of the peseta, however, was not due to strictly economic reasons. Political uncertainty and a crisis of confidence in the regime were no less important in determining the fluctuations of the national currency.

The troubles of the peseta went back to the end of the Moroccan war. Primo de Rivera's victory in the Riff, the narrowing of the trade deficit,[114] the political assurances involved in the transition to civilian rule, and the successful conversion of the floating debt that ensued, enhanced the general confidence in Spanish finances. The widespread impression abroad that the peseta was about to be forced back to par with gold unleashed a speculative movement. It started in January 1927 with the massive flow of foreign capital into Spain and the acquisition by foreign banks of huge sums of pesetas. Not surprisingly, the quotation of the peseta was thus raised artificially to just under 28 pesetas to the pound sterling, thus nearly restoring it to its gold parity of 25.22 pesetas to the pound. There was only slight economic justification for such an estimate. In February 1927, for example, the Spanish wholesale price index stood at 180 as against 143 for Great Britain.[115]

Primo de Rivera and his finance minister, however, did not stop in order to evaluate the shaky foundations of the peseta's sudden rise; they preferred to see it as 'the symbol of the economic resurgence of the nation'.[116] 'Gold parity for the peseta! Long live Spain!', such was now the chauvinistic mood that overwhelmed the government,

[113] Cf. 'El comercio exterior de España', in *El Financiero*, Nov. 1930, p. 92; *Anuario*, 1931, pp. 174–5; Villanueva; *¿ Qué?*, pp. 127–9.

[114] It dropped from 659,600,000 million pesetas in 1925 to 542,430,000 in 1926; see *Comercio Exterior de España, 1901–1956. Datos del Instituto Nacional de Estadística*, Madrid, 1958, p. 29.

[115] For this speculative movement, see José Tallada, *Economía Monetaria espanyola* (Barcelona, 1930), p. 81; Luis Olariaga, *La Intervención de los cambios en España* (Madrid, 1929), pp. 23–8.

[116] Primo in *Folletín*, p. 575.

as Primo later acknowledged.[117] This hasty commitment to reach gold parity for the peseta further fuelled speculation. A colossal sum of between 700 and 1000 million pesetas invaded the country during those days, as foreign speculators rushed to buy cheap pesetas that they expected were likely soon to be traded in their gold value.[118]

The first six months of 1928 exposed the situation in all its nakedness as the peseta drifted gradually, but persistently, from its speculative level, and the flight from it became evident. Calvo Sotelo tried deperately to dam the avalanche: 'There is no economic motive for this depreciation of the peseta, since Spain has its public finances completely balanced, and it lives with an exiguous amount of paper currency.'[119]

But by the middle of 1928, 'the manipulations of international speculation', to use the standard rhetoric of the regime, no longer played the central role in determining the fate of the peseta.[120] Political uncertainties, high internal prices, and an excess of imports of 886 million pesetas in 1928 as compared with 689 millions the preceding year combined to move the peseta down from its artificial value.[121] Furthermore, with an authentic budgetary deficit of 1,066,931,998 pesetas for 1928,[122] a year for which Calvo Sotelo claimed a surplus of 183 million,[123] one could hardly expect that the peseta could be easily stabilized. Nobody took too seriously Calvo Sotelo's boastful declarations about the 'conclusive and eloquent testimony of the healthy state of our public finances'.[124]

Rather than diminishing, government expenditure had, if anything increased during the last three years of the Dictatorship, and the budgetary deficit was clearly widening. The financial strain the government was under looks especially heavy when the expenditure of the extraordinary budget is also taken into account.

The revenues provided for by the ordinary budgets (the extraordinary budget was all expenditures) consisted of 3,258,518,000 pesetas in 1928, and 3,399,771,082 in 1929. In other words, when

[117] Pabón *Cambó*, vol. ii, pt. II, p. 566.

[118] Calvo, p. 186; Olariaga, *La intervençión*, pp. 25–6.

[119] *El Sol*, 21 June 1928.

[120] Lefaucheux, p. 15.

[121] Olariaga, *La intervención*, pp. 65–71; Iglesias, pp. 47–9; *El Economista*, 20 July 1929. Primo conceded that the adverse trade balance added to the precariousness of the peseta; *La Nación*, 10 Oct. 1929.

[122] Maura, *Bosquejo*, p. 296.

[123] *Folletín*, p. 819. Primo claimed a similar surplus, in *La Nación*, 10 Oct. 1929.

[124] *Folletín*, p. 819.

	1927	*1928*	*1929*
Ordinary budget	3,139,441,153	3,257,590,079	3,365,360,970
Extraordinary budget	449,661,581	462,709,600	465,068,600
Railways budget	500,000,000	500,000,000	500,000,000
Budget of Confederations	50,000,000	50,000,000	50,000,000
Tourism			25,000,000
Total expenditures	4,139,106,734	4,270,299,679	4,405,429,170

Calvo Sotelo was boasting of a surplus in 1929, he was actually faced with a deficit of 1,005,658,508 pesetas, which he had to cover by issuing public loans.[125] The government's decision, in November 1929, to abolish the extraordinary budget was tantamount to its recognition that a drastic reduction of expenditure was necessary as a pre-condition for the stabilization of the peseta.[126] But it is important to stress that, in practice, the expansionist budgetary policy of the government continued intact until its very last days in office. High expenditure entailed a rise in internal prices, and this put further obstacles in the way of a possible stabilization of the peseta, as critics such as Cambó urged the government to realize. But the regime could never reconcile itself to the idea that for it to be able to save the peseta it would have to give up its image as the modernizer of Spain's infrastructure and the generator of prosperity, however fictitious this might be.

Whatever the reasons, speculators started a panic escape from the peseta to sound currencies. This further worsened the position of the peseta.[127] It does also seem that Deterding, the American petrol magnate, did in fact, as the Spanish authorities alleged, mount a vindictive campaign against the Spanish currency in retaliation for the exclusion of western companies from the petrol monopoly.[128] But one should, nevertheless, be careful not to exaggerate the role of the oil companies in the misfortunes of the peseta. It is doubtful whether they possessed the power to influence the international money market to an extent that must place on them the lion's share of the blame for the troubles of the Spanish

[125] For the data on the budgets, see *Folletín*, pp. 821–3.

[126] The relevant decree was heralded in the summer, *El Economista*, 8 June 1929; but was issued only in late November, *La Nación*, 21 Nov. 1929.

[127] *Boletín del Banco Urquijo*, Apr., July, Sept. 1929, Feb. 1920. Cambó, *La valoración*, pp. 28–9.

[128] Deterding confessed this to the Spanish foreign minister in August 1930, see FO 371/15041, a report dated 5 Aug. 1930.

currency. Nor is it conceivable that Spain should have been so high on the agenda of Shell and Standard, as the nationalist subscribers to the theme of 'international conspiracy' would have liked us to think.[129]

By mid 1928 the government had precipitately intervened through its Foreign Exchange Committee with a highly unrealistic target, that of achieving gold parity for the peseta.[130] National pride and the prestige of the regime were unnecessarily committed in a purely financial issue; and the failure to improve the performance of the peseta would thus imply the failure of the entire system. For Calvo Sotelo, an unstable peseta, or one stabilized at a devalued rate, a device which even Mussolini had adopted in his 'quota novanta',[131] was 'incompatible with the fatherland's vigour'.[132] In the past, the regime's spokesmen were themselves quick to point to the soundness of the peseta as indicative of the Dictatorship's strength.[133] They therefore knew only too well what the weakness of the currency would now mean in the eyes of the public.

The resources placed at the disposal of the Foreign Exchange Committee enabled some measure of defence to be presented against 'bear raids' on the peseta; and the year of 1928 closed with the sterling rate at 29.87 pesetas, a slightly better rate than that which had prevailed at the start of intervention.[134] The Committee, however, would never have enough money to cope with the colossal quantity of pesetas in foreign hands. Its efforts were bound to have a limited effect.[135] The government's timetable was, by its own choice, excessively reduced. It wanted quick results to show to anxious public opinion which had become accustomed to expect from the government economic acts of magic.

In January 1929, the government appointed a special committee of experts and representatives of economic interests, all headed by the eminent economist Flores de Lemus, to explore the possibility of returning to the gold standard. But in its final report the commission warned that no parity of the peseta should be attempted before the balance of payments was improved and stabilized and before public finances were put in order. The commission's proposal

[129] Cf. *El Economista*, 8 June, 29 July 1929; Salvador Canals, *La crisis exterior de la peseta* (Madrid, 1930), pp. 125–6.

[130] 500 million pesetas in gold were put at the disposal of the Committee, *Gaceta*, 26 June 1928.

[131] Gregor, pp. 146–7.

[132] *El Economista*, 26 Oct. 1929.

[133] *La Nación*, 16, 23 June 1926.

[134] *The Economist*, 28 Dec. 1929.

[135] Tallada, pp. 88–90.

was basically a deflationist one; a reduction of public expenditure was indispensable.[136]

But the government was adamant. A short time after the commission had submitted its report, it resumed its policy of artificially bolstering the peseta. This device had been temporarily suspended in the aftermath of the Ciudad Real mutiny as the government seemed to be at the end of its resources.[137] But the result of this abandonment of defensive measures was that between February and June 1929 the peseta deteriorated from 31.16 to the pound to 34.30. Hence the decision of July to resume, with the assistance of massive foreign credits, the artificial support for the peseta.[138]

Yet government intervention that aimed at maintaining the exchange at a level bearing no relation to comparative price levels not only exhausted its foreign credits but also acted as nothing more than an unsuccessful temporary palliative. At the moment that the government froze their intervention, as they did in October, the rate drifted immediately (from 33 to 35).[139] The activities of the Foreign Exchange Committee, Calvo Sotelo was finally compelled to recognize, 'entail sacrifices for which no compensation is forthcoming'.[140] It is true that a low exchange rate was positively advantageous to exports, especially now that the fruit-exporting season was approaching. It likewise helped the Spanish coal-miners. But it does not seem that such considerations were the reason for the abandonment of intervention. This responded more to a mood of weariness and despair rather than to sound economic considerations, as can indeed be gathered from Calvo Sotelo's concluding remarks: 'The total revaluation of the peseta is a beautiful ideal; as beautiful as it is impossible now, and God knows for how many years.'[141]

(c) *'The Riot of the Moneyed People'*. In December Calvo Sotelo engaged in one of his final financial adventures, only to discover that the regime no longer inspired confidence among the *clases adineradas*. To repay the now depleted foreign credits, he issued at par a new loan consisting of 350 million pesetas of 6 per cent Gold Treasury bonds. The avowed object of the loan was to place the government in possession of sufficient foreign currencies to repay

[136] A summary of the report in the account of a member of the Commission, Tallada, pp. 81–9.

[137] *El Debate*, 20 Feb. 1929.

[138] *The Economist*, 28 Dec. 1929; Calvo, pp. 195–6.

[139] *El Economista*, 19 Oct. 1929; *The Economist*, 28 Dec. 1929.

[140] *La Nación*, 12 Oct. 1929.

[141] *El Economista*, 26 Oct. 1929.

the July credits and to leave a balance in hand.[142] Calvo Sotelo was confident that both the favourable conditions of the loan and the 'patriotism of Spanish capitalism' would crown this new enterprise with success. The disillusion was as great as the expectations. The well-to-do classes had definitely abandoned the regime as Calvo Sotelo had finally to realize: 'Many rich Spaniards, aristocrats, and big businessmen pretended to be deaf to the government's appeal. Some even refused to listen, others pretended to be only partially deaf . . .'.[143] The Bank of Spain refused to let the government use its gold reserves to back the loan. The latter only enhanced the value of the pound, as many banks seized upon the favourable terms of the loan in order to take loans in foreign currency abroad.[144] 'The hope that the gold loan might produce an immediate favourable reaction' of the peseta 'has been frustrated', concluded the *Boletín del Banco Urquijo*.[145]

By the end of December 1929, Primo de Rivera publicly admitted the bankruptcy of his monetary policy. And though he was still able to produce optimistic utterances—on 11 January he promised to a highly anxious business community that 'we are to take the peseta bull by the horns'[146]—the government had fallen back on fatalism. By mid January, within a few days only, the peseta dropped to 40 to the pound. A rate of 40 was something of an indigestible reality. And Calvo Sotelo, who only recently had been seriously taken aback by the refusal of the Bank of Spain to back his loan, was now completely exhausted.[147] On 21 January, Calvo resigned amid rumours about a national government with Cambó, the Catalan financial expert, as premier. 'The Cambó share', wrote a contemporary, 'went up at least as fast as the pound sterling.'[148]

There can be hardly any doubt that the troubles of the peseta were closely linked to the political crises and uncertainties of 1929.[149] 'The price of the national currency reflects the current quotation of

[142] *La Nación* 5, 6, 12 Dec. 1929.

[143] Calvo, p. 214. He reiterated this accusation against Spanish capitalism in *ABC*, 19 Aug. 1930. There is no ground to sustain *El Imparcial*'s (21 Dec. 1929) view about 'the immediate success' of the loan. Banks, foreign and local, were the main subscribers; see Canals, *La crisis*, pp. 102–3.

[144] *The Times*, 21, 23, 28 Dec. 1929. For the Bank of Spain, see Villanueva, *¿Qué?*, p. 178.

[145] *Boletín del Banco Urquijo*, Feb. 1930, pp. 98–100.

[146] *The Times*, 13 Jan. 1920.

[147] For the peseta at 40!, see Villanueva, *¿Qué?*, pp. 143–4, 178.

[148] *ABC*, *El Sol*, 22 Jan. 1930. The last quotation in Villanueva, *¿Qüé?*, p. 76.

[149] See also Chapter X.

the political regime', explained Benítez de Lugo. And when Calvo Sotelo had finally to resign in despair, he did it acknowledging that 'so long as we do not stabilize Spain politically, it would be a waste of time to attempt monetary stabilization'.[150] One has only to look at the repercussions upon the rate of exchange of such events as the Ciudad Real mutiny and the student riots,[151] in order to refute Primo's claim, made in early January, that the troubles of the peseta were not at all connected with political uncertainties.[152] The economy, and with it the stock exchange, was simply becoming a highly sensitive seismograph of political developments, and 'the mere rumour about an attempt to disturb public order' was 'enough to cause the country the loss of millions'.[153]

But there was no way the financial and political situations could be disentangled from each other. Indeed, the Dictator's surprising decision, in May 1929, to give in to the demands of the rebellious students[154] was due to his awareness of the economic damage they were causing. Even the demonstrative election of oppositional figures by the Madrid Bar Association as its representatives in the National Assembly had devastating effects on the peseta.[155] Significantly, on the two occasions that the government had decided to suspend the operations of its Exchange Committee, it did it under the impact of the set-backs inflicted upon the peseta by the opposition: Ciudad Real in January and the elections to the Assembly in October. The blunt rejection by the 'old *políticos*', in the winter of 1929, of Primo's invitation to them to join the Assembly further accelerated the fall of the peseta.[156] The 'politicians'' attitude also had an influence upon the decision of Sr. Vergara, the governor of the Bank of Spain, to withdraw his support from Calvo's monetary policy. The Bank of Spain, and more precisely the private interests represented in it, had consistently refused to mobilize its gold reserves for the defence of the peseta.[157] The Bank of Spain was essentially a private institution, hence its dissociation from the government's

[150] Calvo, pp. 195, 292, 354.

[151] Ibid., pp. 279–80, 286–7; *Boletín del Banco Urquijo* Feb. 1929; *The Times*, 5 Feb. 23, 26 Apr. 1929.

[152] *El Sol*, 9 Jan. 1930. A similar declaration he gave a year earlier, *La Nación*, 5 Dec. 1928.

[153] *La Vanguardia*, 3 Feb. 1929. For the reaction of the stock exchange to the Ciudad Real mutiny, see *La Época*, 30 Jan. 1929.

[154] See below, p. 354.

[155] Eduardo Ortega, in *España*, 18 Nov. 1929; Calvo Sotelo, pp. 196–8.

[156] F. Villanueva, *El momento constitucional* (Madrid, 1929), pp. 135–7.

[157] Luis Olariaga, *La política monetaria en España* (Madrid, 1933), p. 118.

monetary policies reflected the loss of confidence in the political prospects of the regime by the banking system. Private bankers as a whole opposed an artificially high exchange rate for the peseta on the grounds that this might accelerate the flight of capital out of Spain.

The government's wavering approach towards the issue of constitutional reform[158] was not instrumental either in improving the precarious position of the peseta. The *Boletín del Banco Urquijo*, which understandably monitored with great anxiety the financial and monetary situation, put the main blame for the precariousness of the national currency upon 'psychological factors'. And it stated specifically that the persistent declarations of the government that the present regime was of 'an interim nature', rather than inspiring confidence, encouraged the flight of capital.[159] This analysis was accepted not only by what one might claim were biased Spanish analysts, such as the conservative *ABC*.[160] It was also subscribed to by foreign observers such as the French economist Daniel Rieu,[161] and *The Times*. 'Finance experts are at a loss', wrote the latter when the peseta drifted to 38.80 to the pound. The determining factor in the fall of the Spanish currency, it concluded, was 'more moral than material'.[162] The power of a Dictatorship, indeed of every regime, is, if anything, likely to be jeopardized by doubt. So long as political uncertainty as to the future of the regime prevailed,[163] capital would persist in its 'abstentionist' attitude.

Throughout the financial crisis of 1929, the crucial predicament of the regime was further underlined, that was how to finance development projects and social enterprises without raising against itself the anger of either the business community and the landowners, who resented having to finance public expenditure with their own taxes, or the working class. It ended up by alienating both.

As the financial failures of the regime became evident, the loss of confidence of the moneyed people in its political future was further underlined. But the whole affair was a vicious circle, as the economic association of *Amigos del País* of Barcelona explained in a

[158] See Chapter X. [159] *Boletín del Banco Urquijo*, July 1929, Feb. 1930.

[160] *ABC*, 29 Dec. 1929. [161] See his views in Villanueva, *¿Qué?*, p. 130.

[162] *The Times*, 9 Jan. 1930. On 10 June 1929 it wrote that the steady depreciation of the peseta 'must obey causes that are a mystery'.

[163] For an account of the widespread political bewilderment in 1929, see Hipólito Finat Rojas, *¿Cuál es el horizonte político de España? Reflexiones del hombre de la calle* (Madrid, 1929).

public manifesto.[164] The regime's lack of political prospects, it claimed, did not equip it to inspire confidence in the money-market. But the confidence among the 'alarmed' and 'panic-stricken Spanish capitalists' could be restored only through a political stabilization that was not forthcoming. Indeed, the only real way out of the impasse was, as the directing boards of seven powerful Catalan economic associations put it in a collective appeal to the government, for the Dictatorship to give way to a new 'national government'.[165]

Though the preoccupation with the peseta exchange was 'for the first time shared by all social classes'[166] it was the business community that protested most vociferously. Stabilization, both monetary and political, was vital to business. The fluctuations in the peseta rate became the nightmare of businessmen who, as in the case of Catalan industry, depended on imported raw material and machinery.[167] Primo de Rivera, who came to power with the acclamation of the Catalan business community, was now accompanied to his downfall by the outcry of the very same community against the 'aggravation of the exchange problem'.[168] The Superior Council of the Chambers of Commerce, Industry, and Navigation of the country protested against the derangement of business in angry terms:

> There is profound alarm produced by the fact that the oscillation of the peseta is no longer a daily phenomenon, but rather an hourly one. The gravity of the situation justifies the nervousness of the great mass of producers and merchants. The situation is especially detrimental to the latter. The fluctuations in the international rate of the peseta do not allow them to adopt a firm position either when buying or when selling abroad. They find it impossible to secure themselves against a probable breakdown when they decide upon a certain business deal.[169]

The constant drop of prices on the stock exchange throughout 1929 constituted a daily vote of no confidence in the regime by the middle

[164] The text is in Villanueva, *¿Qué?*, pp. 132–6.

[165] *La Vanguardia*, 12, 13 Jan. 1930. The protest was subscribed to by the Chamber of Commerce and Navigation, the Chamber of Industry, the Chamber of Property, the Barcelona Economic Association of Amigos del País, the Instituto Agrícola Catalan de San Isidro, The Banker's Syndicate, the League of Industrial and Commerical Defence.

[166] Ibid., 12 Jan. 1930.

[167] *The Economist*, 23 Nov. 1929; Villanueva, *¿Qué?*, pp. 124–5.

[168] *La Vanguardia*, 12 Jan. 1930.

[169] *Boletín de la Cámara Oficial de Comercio, Industria y Navegación de Málaga*, June 1929.

and entrepreneurial classes.[170] Had not *La Nación* itself claimed in 1926 that the high quotation of shares and bonds was indicative of the 'vital rhythm' of the Dictatorship?[171] This 'vitality' was then fading out. Though the overall value of bonds and stocks issued in 1929 was still the highest of the whole Dictatorship, it was nevertheless clear that the second half of 1929 witnessed a sharp, even dramatic, drop in the issue of stocks and bonds compared with the first half of the year.[172] The excessive abundance of money in 1928 was now replaced by scarcity and inhibition. Businessmen were highly disturbed by the scarcity of money, which raised the cost of production. In this context, the government's decision, early in 1929, to put up the bank rate from 5 to 6% came as 'a painful surprise to the world of business'.[173] 'A reduced volume of business', 'laxity', 'an expectant attitude', such was the predominating mood in the money-market. Occasional improvements would occur, especially following what looked like determined steps by the government towards stabilizing the peseta, but 'psychological factors' would always reassert themselves to the detriment of business.[174] In October and November, the situation seemed to be beyond repair. 'Business is reduced, money shows a chronic contraction; it simply lacks the incentive for reactivation and hence for improving quotations.'[175] The Wall Street 'crash' had no direct impact upon the Spanish market, but it was obviously anything but instrumental in remedying the general malaise in the Spanish stock exchange.[176] The loan in gold issued by the government by the end of the year momentarily improved the situation. But then it was the oncoming political crisis of the regime that reasserted itself to produce 'an unease that reflects itself in a direct and indirect emigration of capital'.[177] Summing up the trend of the money-market in 1929, a specialized financial organ wrote:

> 1929 has been in our money-market one of marked depression produced both by extrinsic and internal causes . . . In the internal field [one should

[170] *Bánco de Crédito Local. Memoria leída en la junta general de accionistas celebrada el día 31 de Marzo de 1930; Memoria del ejercicio de 1929*, p. 11; Araquistain, pp. 250–3.

[171] *La Nación*, 27 May 1926.

[172] *El Financiero*, Nov. 1930, p. 13; 1,492,660,000 pesetas worth of bonds were issued in the first half of the year; 843,510,000 in the second half.

[173] *Boletín de la Cámara Oficial de Comercio e Industria de la Provincia de Lérida*, Jan.–Mar. 1929. The relevant decree is in *Gaceta*, 18 Dec. 1928.

[174] *Boletín del Banco Urquijo*, Feb., Mar., July, Sept. 1929, pp. 135, 253, 378, 505.

[175] Ibid., Nov. 1929, pp. 605–6.

[176] Ibid., Dec. 1929, pp. 665–6.

[177] Ibid., Feb. 1930, p. 100.

mention] the persistent devaluation of our currency . . . the excessive weight of the burden of taxation, state interventionism in industrial activities that restricts the freedom of production and development, the nervousness of money, whose owners refuse to invest it because of the political insecurity of the dictatorial regime.[178]

The flight of capital from Spain, as the French economist Daniel Rieu observed in November 1929, responded to the search of the owning classes for a politically stable atmosphere to shield their investments.[179] Not even the small and medium saver was inclined to risk his money. As early as February 1929, bankers advised the finance minister that their clients were no longer investing in government stocks as willingly as before.[180] It was hardly surprising that the first reaction of the stock exchange to Primo de Rivera's fall was one of 'optimism'. The first two weeks of February 1930 were to witness 'an improvement and an overall favourable tendency in the money-market'.[181]

In a book published at the time of the peseta's misfortunes, Cambó expressed his class's disenchantment with the financial and monetary policy of the regime. He did not leave any doubt that, in his view, it was futile for a regime that no longer inspired the confidence of the business community to attempt monetary stabilization. The man who represented an entire section of society which in 1923 had vociferously clamoured for a dictatorship, had now moved to embrace the view that Primo de Rivera had reached the end of his political itinerary.[182] CHADE, a giant electric concern of which Cambó was a major shareholder, was constantly losing ground on the stock exchange,[183] and he was in no mood to suggest that a new lease of life be given to the ailing Dictatorship.

As far as the strictly economic issue was concerned, Cambó accused the government's nationalistic vanity of being responsible for keeping the currency's rate at an artificial value. Devaluation, he argued, should not be regarded as tantamount to national humiliation, as Calvo Sotelo tended to think. He shared the view of economic experts such as Daniel Rieu and Benítez de Lugo that it was the government's intervention that was responsible for the harmful incompatibility between the foreign and the internal value

[178] 'La bolsa de Madrid en 1929', *El Financiero*, Nov. 1930, pp. 55–66.
[179] Rieu in Villanueva, *¿Qué?*, pp. 127, 137.
[180] *The Times*, 20 Feb. 1929.
[181] *Boletín del Banco Urquijo*, Mar. 1930, p. 19.
[182] Cambó, *La valoración*, *passim*.
[183] *El Financiero*, Nov. 1930, pp. 56–66.

of the peseta. Cambó was obviously sensitive to the fact that the depreciation of the peseta put up the cost of the import of the raw materials that were vital for Catalan industry. But whatever rate was decided upon, it was the industrialists' demand to see it *stabilized*.[184]

The way Cambó, and indeed most of those who criticized the regime from the viewpoint of the needs of business, proposed out of the impasse was tantamount to demanding that the Dictatorship ceased to be what it was, a highly interventionist and 'developmental' regime. Cambó explicitly praised Mussolini's economic policy for favouring private initiative; while Primo stifled it.[185] He called for a radical change in priorities and indeed in the entire structure of the dictatorial economy. He believed that a deflationary policy was now needed that would cut down wages and benefits, reduce taxes and tariffs, suppress monopolies and other kinds of government intervention, and stimulate private initiative. Above all, it was budgetary stringency—the main sufferers from which might be the humble classes—that Cambó demanded. The inflationary extraordinary budget should be abolished, and with it the 'frenetic' expenditure on public works.[186] Cambó's colleagues in the Catalan business community did not oppose public expenditure on doctrinal grounds. They were anything but doctrinaire. What they resented was having to pay with their taxes for public projects. Not even when the project was intended to favour them directly—such as, for example, the pretentious international exhibition held in Barcelona—were they willing to pay the bill.[187]

* * *

In the end, however, it was perhaps the image of the Dictatorship created by the professional middle classes, journalists, lawyers, students, and intellectuals which prevailed, discredited the regime, and undermined its prestige beyond repair.[188]

The rebellion of the universities and the intelligentsia against Primo de Rivera has been studied elsewhere.[189] Here we should

[184] Cambó, *La valoración*, pp. 34–5, 48–52, 96.

[185] Cambó, *Las dictaduras*, pp. 116–17.

[186] For the call for deflationary economics, see Cambó, *La valoración*, pp. 57–9; *Boletín del Banco Urquijo*, Feb. 1929, Feb. 1930.

[187] *La Vanguardia*, 22 Mar., 11 Oct. 1929, 10 Jan. 1930.

[188] Cf. Ramiro de Maeztu, 'La lección de la caída', in *Liquidación*, pp. 145–51.

[189] Ben-Ami, 'La Rébellion universitaire en Espagne (1927–1931)', in *Revue d'histoire moderne et contemporaine*, July–Sept. 1979, pp. 365–90.

only underline the attitudes of the Dictator, and the meaning of that turmoil within the broader context of the challenges that were gradually building up, among the middle classes, against authoritarian policies.

It was up to a young generation of radical middle- and lower-middle class students[190] in the campuses to respond to the Dictatorial challenge. As elsewhere, student radicalism flourished along with the process of social change, and the consequent growth of the universities' population; it more than doubled during the Dictatorship (18,969 in 1922, 42,099 in 1929).[191] It is not surprising that student dissent should have gained in bellicosity especially in the last years of the Dictatorship, when the impact of 'modernization' was being felt more strongly. The student rebellion with its sub-culture and its challenge to orthodox values was a largely bourgeois phenomenon that responded to the widening generation gap, that has been everywhere a concomitant of modernization and change. Student activism was, to put it in the words of dismayed conservatives, the reflection of the 'collapse of paternal authority in urban society'.[192] Primo's cultural and educational fundamentalism proved to be entirely out of tune with the new atmosphere in the campuses.

Unlike his son, the founder of the Falange, Primo de Rivera did not represent the image of a youthful, vigorous renovator or revolutionary leader that could appeal perhaps to some intellectuals and students. His conceptual waverings and his eventual failure to become a political architect prevented him from attracting figures like, say, Ortega, who had been also preaching, throughout the Dictatorship, a regime based on a strong executive and a parliament devoid of real authority.[193] Nor did Primo establish the kind of dynamic totalitarian regime that could have appealed to a fascist like Giménez Caballero. José Antonio was an intellectual, and some of his mentors were to be found in the lecture hall. His father, however, did not make the slightest effort to harness the intelligentsia to his regime. A man of action, he despised the 'semi-intellectuals',[194] men of letters and words. 'I feel a mixture of pity and contempt for these gentlemen',[195] he was to say. The playwright Benavente was not followed by many

[190] 'El estudiante como fuerza social', in *Nueva España*, 2 Jan. 1931.

[191] Cf. *Estadísticas Básicas*, p. 426, *Anuario*, 1929, pp. xx–xxi, Bravo Morata, *La Dictadura*, ii, p. 63.

[192] *ABC*, 12 Apr. 1931. Cf. R. Flacks, *Youth and Social Change* (Chicago, 1967), p. 6.

[193] Ortega in *El Sol*, 29 June, 3l, 12, 19 July 1924; 12, 15 Mar. 1925.

[194] *El Sol*, 23 Apr. 1926.

[195] Ibid., 15 July 1924.

men of letters in his praise of the Dictatorship as a very welcome 'government of force', a positive, 'vertebrate' regime.[196]

It is indicative of the anxieties of the professional middle classes in 1929 that the FUE (the republican Federation of University Students) should have now centred its opposition against the regime upon a struggle for the abolition of article 53 of the Callejo reform on education, which allowed Augustinian and Jesuit Colleges to confer academic degrees.[197] Nor was an additional decree which allowed ex-artillery cadets to continue their studies at the university palatable to the students.[198]

The proliferation of university degrees posed a serious threat to middle-class employment, and was bound to bring about a decline of incomes at a time when the economic 'boom' was showing signs of weariness. The FUE's character as reflected in its campaign against article 53 was one which a sociologist would have called a 'transgressive' organization, that is one that combined ideological protest with 'role-seeking' orientation. The struggle of this new mass of students against article 53 was motivated not merely by altruistic concern for the preservation of the values of university life. The FUE evidently also reacted against the artificial increase in the number of degree-holders, which was bound to reduce job opportunities.[199] Significantly, the students who displayed the boldest opposition to the reform were those studying architecture, agronomics, road, and mining engineering,[200] that is, the professions that were most likely to suffer from the much-heralded cuts in expenditure on public works. The prospects were not more promising for medical students. Already in January 1927 they had petitioned the government to cut the number of students in the faculties of medicine because, while there was, they said, a superfluity of physicians in the country, 40 per cent of the students in Spain studied medicine.[201] The fears of 'vocational

[196] *La Nación*, 3 Dec. 1927.

[197] For the full text of the article, see Antonio Gascón, *Los hombres que trajeron la república: los estudiantes* (Madrid, n.d.), p. 31. It was inspired by the Bishop Leopoldo Eijó Garay. [198] FO 371/14164, Grahame to Chamberlain, 13 Mar. 1929.

[199] For the students' motives, see the Catholic *La Ciencia Tomista*, May–June 1931; and FO 371/14174, Grahame to Chamberlain, 13 Mar. 1929. For an elaboration of the concept of 'transgressive organization', see Frank Pinner, 'Western European Student Movements Through Changing Times', in Seymour Lipset and Philip Altbach (eds.), *Students in Revolt* (Boston, 1969), pp. 62–4. Cf. also D. Apter, *Ideology and Discontent* (The Free Press, 1964), pp. 28–30.

[200] Maura, *Bosquejo*, pp. 326–7, 332; *La Vanguardia*, 13–23 Mar. 1929; *The Times*, 22 Apr. 1929. [201] *The Times*, 28 Jan. 1927.

prospectlessness', however, just like political vocation, may stimulate students to call for sweeping radical changes.

I have studied elsewhere the virulent confrontation of the universities with Primo de Rivera in 1929,[202] and need not recapitulate its details. Suffice it to stress here its main impact upon the regime. The student rebellion struck at its very foundations. 'A minor issue' had turned into a national conflict, as Gabriel Maura noted in despair. The problem was not one of 'public order' as Martínez Anido would have liked to think ('Repress student movement! Report number of victims!', was his order to the police).[203]

The real force of a movement cannot be measured only by its numerical strength. The vigour and the dimensions of the reactions it provokes from its enemies is probably no less valid an indicator. Indeed, the Dictator was not unaware of the need to counter the FUE's mobilization against his rule by a similar effort on the right. The Unión Patriótica organized 'public opinion' to send millions of signatures in support of the Dictator; huge popular parades were organized in front of the General's residence; 'loyal' intellectuals voiced their adherence to the regime in public meetings, and economic entities praised the 'peace, order, culture, work, and progress' represented by the regime. At one stage, Primo de Rivera even tried to attract José María Sbert, López-Rey, and other FUE leaders into the ranks of the youth section of the UP. He thus hoped to harness 'tamed' student activism as a vehicle for controlled mobilization in support of his regime. But now open war was declared. The National Assembly of the UP youth called in April 1929 upon its members to keep away from 'the decadent and pessimistic intellectualism' of the universities, that Gomorrah of 'fictitious democracy'. At a youth congress precipitately convened in Zaragoza a few days later the Dictator could hardly conceal the fact that he was desperately looking for a juvenile answer to the student rebellion and to what he called 'pseudo-intellectualism'. 'If and when', he said, 'some bold rebel boastfully claims that youth is in a state of rebellion against me, you will stand up to contradict him.'[204]

But Primo de Rivera's eventual downfall, as the Italian organ *Critica Fascista* rightly pointed out,[205] owed much to the fact that

[202] Ben-Ami, 'La Rébellion', pp. 375–81.

[203] A. Gascón, p. 37.

[204] *Unión Patriótica*, 1 Apr., 15 May 1929; *Nueva España*, 18 Oct. 1930 (an interview with Sbert).

[205] Quoted in R. de Felice, *Mussolini il Duce, Vol. I. Gli anni del consenso 1929–1936* (Torino, 1974), p. 229.

Primoderriverismo was essentially a movement of quinquagenarians devoid of any meaningful support either in the campuses or among youth in general. When a dictator daily announces that he is rejuvenating and regenerating a country, he obviously faces an acute dilemma when the young generation and its mentors rise against him and the kind of state he is creating. The Dictatorship, according to the FUE militant López-Rey, failed to acquire even 'a semblance of the support of the young generation'.[206] In the end, Primo stepped down, entangled in the same reactionary spirit of mind that brought the Bishop of Lérida to exclaim, in the heat of the student riots, that 'the habits are being corrupted', and to ask in despair, 'From where did the perdition of Spain stem if not from these damned liberties, the stepdaughters of the revolution?'[207]

The University rebellion challenged the Dictator to muster his own forces, only in order to come up with a false sense of power. There was no solid ground for his boastful claim, following the huge and fabricated pro-regime demonstrations of mid April to the effect that 'the Church, the army, the navy, industry, labour, commerce, the banks, the civil service, the aristocracy, the taxpayers, in fact, everybody, even down to the poor and needy, with the sole exception of part of the university intellectuals and the majority of the press, are content with the Dictatorship'.[208]

La Nación claimed that 'the economic force' represented by those who demonstrated their solidarity with the regime in such an 'indescribable way' amounted to 'hundreds of thousands of millions . . .'.[209] The truth was, however, that, if anything, the student disturbances further eroded the confidence of business in the regime. The success of the pretentious international exhibitions in Seville and Barcelona was severely threatened by the unstable image of the regime as reflected in the recent riots. The seventy economic corporations in Catalonia, which were led by the *Fomento de Trabajo Nacional* and the League for the Defence of Industry and Commerce to issue a collective demand for 'a firm and robust public power' as the only guarantee for the success of the exhibitions,[210] represented the anxiety in business circles at the fact that even 'law and order',

[206] Cf. López-Rey, in Jiménez de Asua, *Juventud, Conferencia de Jiménez de Asua y réplica de José López-Rey* (Madrid, 1929), p. 149.

[207] *La Vanguardia*, 9 Jan. 1930.

[208] *The Times*, 16 Apr. 1929.

[209] *La Nación*, 15 Apr. 1929.

[210] *La Vanguardia*, 22 Mar. 1929. See another manifesto of virtually hundreds of economic entities in *El Imparcial*, 26 Mar. 1929.

the most fundamental advantage they could expect to derive from a Dictatorship, was no longer forthcoming. And when this was made quite clear, business circles simply put pressure on the government to give in to the students' demands 'in the interests of trade', as the Madrid Chamber of Commerce put it.[211] The conservative *ABC* also joined the business campaign for 'leniency' towards the students 'to guarantee the success of the exhibitions'.[212] And, indeed, it was the economic damage, combined with the government's fear that the disturbances might jeopardize the forthcoming meeting of the League of Nations in Madrid, that forced Primo de Rivera to reopen the campuses he had formerly closed.[213] To forestall troubles on the eve of the 1929–30 academic year, Primo de Rivera capitulated on what he thought was the crucial issue. On 24 September he decreed the suspension of article 53.[214]

A Dictatorship that gives in so absolutely to the pressures of non-manipulated public opinion certainly faces, to say the least of it, a crisis of identity. It is this inherently irreconciliable tension between 'autocracy' and 'opinion' that, in the last analysis, manœuvred the Dictator into a political cul-de-sac. A capitulating Dictatorship is a defeated one; the students were fully aware of this maxim. Indeed, the Dictator's desperate concessions fell short of keeping the students out of the street. The winter term witnessed them rioting again.[215] On 28 January, Primo de Rivera was to hand in his resignation to the king with student clamour still echoing in his ears. Just as in Argentina in 1930 the decision of the military to oust Irigoyen was forced upon them by university agitation that aroused public opinion to an emphatic anti-government position,[216] so the FUE's agitation in Spain acted as a powerful catalyst in Primo's fall. It was not at all impossible, as the British ambassador observed at the time,[217] that the Dictator's fateful appeal for support addressed to his fellow generals on 26 January 1930[218] was made in a moment of depression caused to a large extent by the recent student demonstrations.

[211] *Boletín Oficial de la Cámara de Comercio de Madrid*, Apr.–May 1929.
[212] *ABC*, 7 May 1929. [213] *El Sol*, 22 May 1929; *The Times*, 21, 23 May 1929.
[214] *Gaceta*, 24 Sept. 1929.
[215] López-Rey, *Los estudiantes frente a la Dictadura* (Madrid, 1930), pp. 273–310; *Nota Oficiosa. Últimas noticias del movimiento escolar*, 24 Jan. 1930, in Romanones Archive, Leg. 2, No. 44.
[216] R. Walter, *Student Politics in Argentina* (New York, 1968), p. 92.
[217] FO 371/15040, Grahame to Henderson, 28 Jan. 1930.
[218] See below, p. 386.

The significance of both student activism and the growth of republican feelings in the country was that they represented a drive to substitute the politics of democratic mobilization for the old system of patronage and clientele and its stifling substitute, the Dictatorship. For the middle classes, especially the liberal professions, republicanism was the vehicle by which they could manifest their political independence. But republicanism came also to represent a wide and heterogeneous public in its hope of finding a remedy to particular social and economic grievances. It started to embrace, and give expression to, the urban petty bourgeoisie, small entrepreneurs threatened with the breakdown of their business under the burden of taxation and the regime's favouritism towards the big monopolistic concerns, and merchants who had to reduce the scale of their deals because of the Dictatorship's high tariff policy. Significantly, free trade and the defence of the smaller concerns against the expansionism and the protectionist priorities sponsored by big business were standard articles on the platforms of most republican parties. The latter were also attractive to the professional classes, especially in the provincial capitals, where the teacher, the physician, the engineer, and the lawyer found it increasingly difficult to make a decent living because of both the rising prices and, especially in 1929, the strain on job opportunities. 'To go to the pawnshop' was a regular practice for middle-class housewives eager to maintain the external appearances of a 'decent' standard of living. In a bid to regain his popularity among the lower middle classes, Primo financed in 1926, with state money, the release of their possessions in pawn. But these were soon to find their way back to the pawnshops.[219] Lawyers were especially shocked by the lawless procedures of the Dictatorship, teachers by the clerical hegemony in the educational system as well as by their dreadfully low wages, and engineers by the visible prospect of a near end to the era of public works which, given the popular appeal of republicanism, they had every reason to expect would be resumed by the Republic. But the crisis of confidence in the old order was also shared by many in the so-called 'conservative classes'. Indeed, as in France where the Thiers and the MacMahons had made possible the advent of the Third Republic, so in Spain republicanism came to mean for ex-monarchist members of the *clases acomodadas* the institutionalization of an orderly democracy as a barrier against the 'red menace' that they were afraid might be

[219] Bravo Morata, *Historia de Madrid*, ii, p. 93.

unleashed by the blunders of the monarchy and by the Dictatorship's failure to establish a new, viable political consensus.[220]

3. *The Seed-bed of a* 'Contre-Brumaire'

For a *coup d'état* to be a bloodless affair it is essential for the military to be united. And although, upon his seizure of power, Primo de Rivera was an almost isolated gambler hardly enjoying the active support of a handful of officers, his peaceful take-over was made possible by the army's acquiescence in his rebellion. But this temporary unity of the military was very much conditioned by the king's role in the *coup d'état*. Had the king refused to give his blessing to the 'pronouncer', it is highly probable that the army would have been divided between a majority of officers loyal to the king and a minority supporting the rebellious general.

But the cohesion of the 'military family' could not be maintained for long. An increasing alienation of the military from Primo de Rivera became evident once social order was no longer under imminent threat, the Moroccan problem had been solved, and the king started to exhibit unequivocal signs of unease with the Dictatorship. True, the army was not exactly the loser from Primo's budgets. The fact is often overlooked that about 43% of the much-publicized extraordinary budget (1,509,208,000 pesetas), that is almost as much as the sum that went to public works (1,600,000,000), was invested in military modernization.[221] But the transition to a civilian regime late in 1925 and the Dictator's determined drive to substitute as his power-base a new constitutional framework and a wide civilian movement for the bayonets and the crown had increasingly dissociated his regime from the image of an elementary praetorian system. The erosion of the military basis of his Dictatorship was further enhanced by Primo de Rivera's tactless encroachment upon the professional sensibilities of the military corps. Furthermore, the effect of his policies on the army was such that increasing sections of the officer corps started to move away from the monarchy towards an alliance with the liberal forces in the country. Primo had definitely undermined, for the immediate future, the praetorian basis of autocratic politics in Spain.

[220] For republicans and republicanism, see Ben-Ami, *The Origins*, Chapter I.

[221] *Gaceta*, 13 July 1926. The army's and the navy's ordinary budgets, however, had been constantly, and substantially, decreasing after 1924; cf. *Anuario* 1929, pp. xxvi–xxvii: Army, 1924—602,172,000; 1928—374,393,000. Navy, 1924—284,985,000; 1928—161,023,000.

To be sure, Primo de Rivera did not let slip any opportunity to stress that his regime enjoyed the full support of the military. It was the army as a corporate body, he said in December 1923 to the officers of the garrison of Madrid, which had assumed the task of governing the country.[222] But, as he explained in July 1924, it was his intention to use this 'unanimous' military support in order to make a smooth transition to a civilian system, and then return the army to its barracks.[223] Such a transition was necessary if only because the Dictator's claim about the 'unanimity' of military support did not carry much conviction. It was in order to make them accomplices to his dictatorial rule that he constantly reminded his fellow officers that 'you rebelled on the 13th of September through my voice'.[224] After the transition to civilian government was completed, he boasted in a speech to an *Upetista* audience at Alcalá de Henares that, if and when his regime was threatened by a meaningful opposition, he would not hesitate, as he did on 13 September, to call to his side the army 'now silent in its barracks'.[225] He did exactly that late in January 1930. The army, however, bluntly refused to salvage his uncertain rule.[226]

As it turned out, even Primo's bid to enhance the effective strength and organization of the army brought him into collision with vested interests in the various corps, and had therefore the adverse effect of further undermining his military support. 'The time has come', he said 'to reorganize the army leaving only those units that are essential to the defence of the nation.' To the superfluous officers he proposed a not very appealing deal. They would either become redundant or be employed 'in adequate [civilian] patriotic jobs', such as for example, *delegados gubernativos*.[227] The institution represented by the latter, however, was at the time of Primo's declaration grossly inefficient and overstaffed, with a waiting-list of *pretendientes* at least as long as the number of *delegados* in service.[228]

In spite of the opposition of vested military interests, the dream about the reduction of army cadres started to materialize under Primo de Rivera. After the Moroccan war, he repatriated most of the soldiers who had taken part in it.[229] By the end of the Dictatorship,

[222] *The Times*, 10 Dec. 1923.

[223] *Folletín*, p. 154.

[224] *A los Señores Generales, jefes y oficiales del Ejército y Armada*, 1 Sept. 1924, in Romanones Archive, Leg. 63, No. 75.

[225] *La Nación*, 26 Apr. 1926.

[226] See below, pp. 386–7.

[227] *Folletín*, p. 375; *El Sol*, 2 Dec. 1925.

[228] Mola, p. 1028; Lerroux, *Al servicio*, pp. 283–4.

[229] *La Nación*, 25 Sept. 1926. By then 12,000 soldiers were repatriated.

the army's size had been reduced by as much as 30 per cent.[230] The data for 1928–9 show that in 1929 there were 3,565 officers fewer in active service than in 1928.[231]

Of course, a reduction of army cadres was likely to enhance its efficiency as a fighting force, as was the case with the reform of the navy.[232] This reform abolished the navy's autonomous classifying junta, and forced some officers into early retirement.[233] Also for the sake of efficiency, Primo reduced in August 1929 the teaching staff of all military academies in Spain.[234] But nobody wanted efficiency at the expense of his own job. Not many superfluous infantry officers, for example, were happy with Primo's proposal that they should become schoolteachers in small provincial towns.[235] The Dictator's early promise to the army that 'no heavy sacrifices would be demanded of the army; it would not be reduced, though a reform in its organization would be carried out'[236] seemed to many officers, whose careers had been affected by his reforms, a great deception. Their personal sacrifice was too heavy for them to bear. 'We are being severely discriminated against by this shameful regime which the navy has never supported', wrote a committee representing 600 naval officers who were likely to be affected by Primo's reforms.[237]

If the support of the armed forces was indeed crucial to Primo de Rivera's rule, one can hardly conclude that he was excessively careful in cultivating it. The erosion of the military basis of his dictatorship was, if anything, aggravated by his patronizing and frequently arbitrary interference in the internal life of the various corps. An especially devastating effect upon his chances of enjoying the unanimous support of this 'caste' was produced by the Dictator's interference with matters of promotion.[238]

Clearly, the high command was being 'contaminated' with

[230] *Anuario*, 1931, pp. 506–7. According to *The Times*, 3 Jan. 1927, the size of the army was fixed at 184,636 in 1927. Payne, *Politics*, p. 241, says it was 130,000 by the end of the regime. For the reduction of army cadres, see also *Hojas Libres*, 1 Sept. 1927.

[231] *Anuario*, 1931, p. 490; *Estadísticas Básicas*, p. 474.

[232] Carlos Ibáñez de Ibero, *Historia de la marina de guerra española* (Madrid, 1939), pp. 232–5.

[233] *The Times*, 15 Jan. 1929.

[234] Ibid., 13 Aug. 1929.

[235] Ibid., 18 Jan. 1929.

[236] See his speech to the infantry officers at the Madrid garrison in ibid., 10 Dec. 1923.

[237] *Anónimo del Comité de la Armada dirigido a Sánchez de Toca con motivo de la supresión del Estado Mayor Central*, in Romanones Archive, Leg. 63, No. 44.

[238] López de Ochoa, pp. 78–102; Payne, *Politics*, pp. 224–6. See a great number of examples in Primo's letters; Armiñán, *Epistolario*, pp. 77, 88–9, 115, 131, 220, 241, 250.

insubordination. General Weyler was certainly not the only one to have spoken of the need to return to 'liberal principles' as in itself a good reason for the Dictator to relieve him from duty.[239] General Aguilera, the president of the military high tribunal, formed part, from the very early days of the regime, of a military camarilla working against Primo de Rivera. Especially disturbing to the Dictator was Aguilera's insistence on reviving the issue of 'responsibilities' so as to put Primo's early announcement to the test.[240] The military as a whole were not altogether happy with the idea of having officers, among them prestigious figures such as Berenguer and Cavalcanti, again brought before military tribunals. On the other hand, for Primo de Rivera to shelve the 'responsibilities' dossier would have meant bowing to criticism so persistently put forward that precisely this was the *raison d'être* of the *coup d'état*, to stifle the clamour for 'responsibilities'. The solution found to the dilemma was reflected in the lenient verdicts passed on the defendants. General Tuero and Colonel Sirvent were condemned to a year's imprisonment, and Colonel Lacanal to only six months. General Cavalcanti was acquitted outright.[241] In General Berenguer's case, an amnesty immediately followed the sentence of the high court relieving him of his military duties. But Berenguer did not reciprocate the Dictator's goodwill, and he was reported to be meeting at frequent intervals the enemies of the regime.[242]

But the king's favour protected military dissidents such as Berenguer and Cavalcanti. Alfonso desperately needed a power base in the army to counter the Dictator's influence, and shake his monopoly over the armed forces. After being amnestied, Berenguer was assigned to be the captain-general of Galicia. And during the artillery crisis he was appointed as the head of the king's military household, an excellent position in the midst of the military anti-Primo royal camarilla.[243]

Indeed, it was from within that same camarilla that the first anti-Primo conspiracy had originated in September 1924. Led by General Cavalcanti, a member of the famous quadrilateral and now the head of the king's military household, this conspiracy clearly

[239] *The Times*, 8 Oct. 1925; *España Avanza. Órgano mundial de las ciudadanías hispano-americanas*, 16 Sept. 1928.

[240] FO 371/9490, Howard to Curzon, 20 Dec. 1923.

[241] See reports on the 'responsibilities' trials in *The Times*, 15 Jan., 26 Feb. 1924.

[242] FO 371/15040, 29 Jan. 1930.

[243] Juan de la Cierva, p. 314; *The Times*, 28 Mar. 1925.

indicated how the monarch had been working among the higher command to secure his own power-base even if that meant undermining the Dictator's hold on the army.[244]

But Primo's troubles were not just with the royalist camarilla. For example, in October 1925, the buds of a new movement of *Juntas de defensa* of junior officers seemed to be emerging in Barcelona. Like the royal clique, they expected the king to give legitimacy to their rebelliousness; but unlike their senior counterparts, they were motivated by a deep frustration at what they viewed as the failure of the Dictatorship to become a truly military regime, that is a regime unyieldingly committed to the advancement of the army's corporate interests. They likewise protested against the arbitrary way in which 'the Primo de Rivera–Martínez Anido camarilla' had monopolized the distribution of favours to their men in the army at the expense of those whom they disliked. In a clandestine manifesto the members of this embryonic Junta castigated 'the so-called military directory' for failing to meet the corporate aspirations of the officer corps. There can be little doubt that the purpose of this group was to revive the notorious Juntas as a means of pressure against a regime that, though it was called military, fell far short of adequately remedying the grievances of junior officers. 'The glorious days must return', they concluded, 'when our *Juntas de defensa* inspired respect for the Spanish uniform.' A month later, this same self-styled *Junta nacional de defensa* appealed to the garrisons of the peninsula to rally around 'the august figure' of the king in order to put an end to the Dictatorship. It was not the army that ruled Spain, they said, but 'a faction' of it 'working in collaboration with adventurers of the *Unión Patriótica*, who had only been lured to join it by promises of booty'.[245]

One of the first liberal officers to perceive that only by force could Primo de Rivera be overthrown was Colonel Segundo García of the aristocratic cavalry corps to which General Cavalcanti also belonged.[246] It did not augur well for the regime's capacity to rely on the army that the military plotters were found to have been closely linked with liberal politicians and even with some 'anti-dynastic and revolutionary elements'.[247] One of the ominous results of Primo's

[244] *El Sol*, 24 Sept. 1924; Villanueva, *La Dictadura*, pp. 133–4; FO 371/11936, Rumbold to Chamberlain, 16 Sept. 1926.

[245] See reports on this movement in *El Carbayón* (Oviedo), 9 Oct. 1925; FO 371/11096, Gurney to Chamberlain, 12 Dec. 1925.

[246] López de Ochoa, pp. 108–9; *The Times*, 13, 14, 20 Nov. 1925.

[247] FO 371/11096, Gurney to Chamberlain, 19 Nov., 9 Dec. 1925.

policy was to push growing sections of the army towards a closer collaboration with liberal politics. It was now, during the Dictatorship, that sections of the army set out to restore the old nineteenth-century alliance between liberalism and the military.[248]

It was upon such an alliance that the so-called *Sanjuanada* plot was to evolve. Whereas so far military plotters had acted on their own to supplant a disappointing directory with their own brand of military monarchism, the Sanjuanada clearly demonstrated, as was also to be shown in the artillery crisis, that the Dictatorship had unconsciously unleashed a democratic movement within the army. The army, as the manifesto of the 'pronouncers' written by the Reformist leader Melquiades Álvarez stated, could no longer tolerate its identification with a regime that despoiled the people of its rights, and had therefore decided to return to its liberal traditions and fight for an outright restoration of constitutional normalcy.[249]

The Sanjuanada was not the last attempt by an alignment of civilian and military discontent to do away with the Dictatorship. Late in September 1927, about two hundred officers and their civilian allies were arrested for preparing a *coup* they planned to launch on precisely the day when the National Assembly was first scheduled to meet.[250] The wide spectrum of political figures that joined this plot reflected more than anything the determination of some army circles to get rid of the Dictator even if that meant accepting compromising political deals.[251]

In July 1928, the security police were again put on alert to prevent the materialization of a *putsch* engineered, this time, by artillery officers.[252] Whereas in the first years of his rule Primo was even ready to invent conspiracies against his regime in order to underline its indispensability for the safety of Spain, now, when the pressures against the Dictatorship were mounting and the threats to its continuation were real, he resorted to the opposite tactic, that of minimizing the importance and the impact of the periodic plots. 'In reality the attempted *coup* lacked any real importance. A few little groups in Barcelona, and others in Valencia, nothing more', such

[248] Lerroux, *Al servicio*, p. 286; López de Ochoa, pp. 115, 16.

[249] See accounts on the Sanjuanada in *Ejército y Armada*, and *ABC*, 26 June 1926; López de Ochoa, pp. 109–16. The manifesto is in Marco Miranda, pp. 71–6.

[250] *La Nación*, 4 Oct. 1927; Maura, *Bosquejo*, p. 236; FO 371/12717, Rumbold to Chamberlain, 3 Oct. 1927, reporting a conversation with Primo.

[251] See the report of one of the civilian participants, Bartolomé y Mas, in *Folletín*, pp. 640–4.

[252] Maura, *Bosquejo*, p. 287.

was now his reaction.[253] But the credibility of his official notes had been increasingly eroded by the continuous attempts against his regime. 'Primo de Rivera deceives himself as to his personal credibility if he really believes that people attribute too much value to his word.' This was how the French *L'Œuvre* reacted to the now standard official denial of rumours about a conspiracy, this time centred on the Getafe military airfield.[254]

When there was no arbitrariness to engender discontent, it was Primo de Rivera's drive to impose a uniform rule of promotion throughout the army that, while infringing upon the traditional prerogatives of élite corps such as the artillery and the engineers, produced military agitation and even rebellion. As a general policy, Primo de Rivera succumbed to the criterion of the Africanistas against promotion by seniority.[255] This was a reversal of attitude on his part. In 1923, he strongly opposed promotion by merit, a system so dear to the fighting African army and so detrimental to the interests of the penisular 'juntero' army, of whose leaders Colonel Nouvilas was to be the first secretary of the military directory. In 1924, under the pressure of the Africanistas whose goodwill was crucial to the survival of his regime at precisely the moment when the Moroccan war was approaching its critical stage, the Dictator completely abandoned the 'juntero' criterion of promotion by seniority.[256]

This change of criterion was to have fatal consequences for the cohesion of the army and the stability of the regime. Significantly, so long as the military directory remained in office, Primo de Rivera shrank from implementing his reform. It would have been interpreted as the vindictive, partisan policy of one section of the army against another. Enacted, as it was, by the civilian directory, it could more convincingly be presented as a national policy. None the less, the cleavages opened within the army by the dispute over the system of promotion were to put the most serious question mark so far on the regime's claim that it possessed solid military support. The test case did not take long to materialize. On 9 June 1926 Primo de Rivera imposed promotion by merit upon all the army. The reaction of the artillery corps, whose officers were zealously committed to the system of seniority, was one of total rejection.[257]

[253] *La Nación*, 13, 14 July 1928.
[254] Quoted in *Hojas Libres*, 1 May 1927.
[255] See his letter to the Duke of Tetuan, 23 June 1925, in Armiñán, *Epistolario*, pp. 241–2.
[256] Mola, p. 1025.
[257] For a detailed survey of the artillery crisis, see Payne, *Politics*, pp. 238–40.

In 1926, with economic prosperity high on the agenda, and the charisma of the Caudillo of Alhucemas still undimmed, the rebellion of the artillery lacked the necessary *ambiente*. Its main significance lay in that it underlined the separation of the artillery corps, and indeed of the higher classes of society from which that corps was picked, from the Dictatorship. Especially significant was the officers' claim that an abyss had been opened between themselves and the monarchy, and that an increasing number among them viewed themselves as the military reservoir of an eventual republican movement in Spain. The Dictatorship, they stressed, no longer represented, assuming that it ever had, the army. Rather, it was 'the rule of an audacious minority which has usurped power'.[258] It should be emphasized, however, that it was out of purely personal grievances, rather than because of any deep political conviction, that officers in the artillery and elsewhere were turning to republicanism.[259]

Moreover, essentially middle- and lower-middle-class people, the military—as was the case in 1917 and in the post-war crisis—could not but share the economic malaise of their civilian counterparts. This is how a contemporary analyst described the mood of the army during the twilight of the Dictatorship:

> The increasing economic malaise of the whole middle class affected the military as well . . . Generals were increasingly becoming uneasy under the pressure of their officers who, though still considered as the only support of the regime, were strongly influenced by undercurrents of protest, every day more aggressive, stemming from friends and relatives who voiced recriminations against them either for having encouraged the formation of the Dictatorship or for not taking up the cudgels for its overthrow. In many provincial capitals, military circles . . . were degenerating into political clubs, in which personal and collective grievances, jointly exhumed with those of the nation, were creating an ambience identical to that which had produced the *juntas de defensa* first, and the *coup d'état* later.[260]

Whatever the reasons for the alienation of sections of the army from the Dictatorship, the regime's main preoccupation concerning

[258] *A nuestros compañeros del ejército y al país*, 24 Nov. 1926; *Ideales del cuerpo de artillería*, in Romanones Archive, Legs. 2, no. 36; 28, no. 52. For the 'republicanization' of the artillery corps, see also 'El conflicto artillero' in *Hojas Libres*, Apr., Sept., 1927, Jan. 1928; and FO 371/11936, Rumbold to Chamberlain, 8 Nov., 2 Dec. 1926.

[259] Cf. Queipo de Llano, *El general Queipo de Llano perseguido por la Dictadura* (Madrid, 1930), pp. 46–52, 68, 70; Lerroux, 'Carta dirigida a Francisco Morayta de Ciudad Real', in Romanones Archive, Leg. 2, no. 45. [260] Maura, *Bosquejo*, p. 359.

the military increasingly became that of 'extirpating from the army any shade of dissidence'.[261] The need for urgency in taking such action was brought home to the regime, among other things, by an inquiry run in 1928 by Martínez Anido, showing that most officers opposed the continuation of the Dictatorship.[262] 'I count upon you to see to it that commanding officers and military governors obtain knowledge as to what officers are thinking and how they are acting', thus ran one of the secret circulars of Primo de Rivera to the Army's high command.[263]

But, whatever the Dictator's capacity to police the activities of military dissidents may have been, the fact was that the military basis of the Dictatorship had been seriously eroded. His sense of the increasing alienation of his fellow officers from his regime was more likely to infiltrate his utterances in private. 'I believe that I am not isolated', he wrote to Sanjurjo concerning his reaction to the Sanjuanada, 'but if I am to perish, I'll go down fighting.'[264] Furthermore, as both the Sanjuanada and the agitation in the artillery corps had proved, military opposition had the tendency to drift easily towards political protest. Primo de Rivera should take the blame for what Gabriel Maura later called 'the loss of monarchist cohesion in the army'.[265] Deeply divided, and for some time eager to withdraw from 'politics', the best posture the army could take to avoid a civil war was one of abstention. This it did in January 1930, thus paving the way for the Dictator's fall, and in April 1931, thus making way for the second Republic.[266]

[261] Ibid., p. 225.
[262] Payne, *Politics*, p. 244.
[263] *The Times*, 5 Feb. 1930.
[264] Primo to Sanjurjo, 2 July 1926, in Armiñán, *Epistolario*, p. 366.
[265] G. Maura and Fernández Almagro, *¿Porqué cayó Alfonso XIII?* (Madrid, 1948), p. 395.
[266] Ben-Ami, *The Origins*, pp. 247–8.

CHAPTER X

Trial and Débâcle

'Breves et infaustos populi amores'
Tacitus, *Annales*, II. 41.

1. *The Frustrated Search for Political Legitimacy*

(a) *In a Blind Alley*. Unfortunately for the Dictator, the financial crisis and the alienation of the middle classes occurred simultaneously with, and indeed were largely conditioned by, the collapse of his experiment in acquiring political legitimacy. Though the government had never officially endorsed the Assembly's constitutional project, the regime's spokesmen and supporters defended it against its calumniators. Especially appealing to them was the draft's breach with 'the notorious suffragist democracy'.[1] This view was entirely endorsed by the regime's organ, which did not hesitate to proclaim the incompatibility between its present support for a non-liberal constitution and its position in the past that the 1876 constitution should not be abrogated. 'We have changed our view', it confessed.[2] As for Primo, even if the draft were not amended, he hoped it would be 'the flag' around which all those would gather who saw in it 'the emblem of our illusions and our hopes'.[3]

Yet the fate of the Assembly was to be decided by the generally hostile reaction that its constitutional draft aroused. This document, which was presented in July 1929 to a free debate in the press, with the intention of submitting it to a formal plebiscite at a later date, was rejected out of hand by the vast majority of public opinion. The public resented the way that the king and his Dictator were breaking with the ancient Spanish tradition that sovereignty resides in the Cortes with the king. Both Conservatives and Liberals attacked the new constitution's disregard for the basic principles of parliamentarism and national sovereignty. They dismissed it as a 'utopian

[1] Juan de Castilla, Vicente Gay, and Pemán in *La Nación*, 17 Aug., 9, 10, 11, 13 Sept., 31 Oct. 1929.
[2] *La Nación*, 26, 27 July 1929.
[3] Ibid., 8 July 1929.

and fantastic conception of reactionary politics'. Whatever the nature of the proposed constitution, both the spokesmen of 'old politics' and the republicans insisted that the Dictatorship lacked the necessary legitimacy to lead the transition to 'normalcy'. A constitution prepared by a dictatorial parliament was inadmissible. Primo de Rivera was thus manœuvred into a vicious circle. He wanted to institutionalize a new legitimacy of his own making, but he was denied the right to do so because his rule was not 'legitimate'. Not even on the extreme right did the Dictator find support for his ill-fated constitution. The Carlists failed to see in it the provisions for a Christian monarchy and society; the Catholic syndicates' bitterness at the regime's symbiotic relationship with the Socialists prevented them from actively supporting the draft, while *El Debate*, almost the mouthpiece of the Dictatorship in its early years, could hardly conceal its lukewarmness. *La Vanguardia*, the usually pro-regime organ of the *españolista*, conservative opinion in Catalonia, summed up the public debate on the constitution with the suggestion that the whole idea be dropped.[4]

Stuck with a constitution that hardly anyone, including himself, was ready to fight for, the Dictator made it plain that the regime was ready for reconciliation with its enemies even if that entailed the shelving of its constitutional project in favour of a more liberal document. It seemed as though some kind of liberal dictatorship that would divide the opposition and attract wider popular support now became the circumstantial formula for survival.

The invitation to join the Assembly that was extended to the ex-premiers, representatives of royal academies, universities, Bar associations, ex-presidents of parliament, and members of the UGT[5]—all foci of opposition to the regime—reflected the stress under which the Dictator had been operating since the summer of 1929. In the past he had boasted that 'the forever extinguished' voices of the *políticos* should never be heard in the Assembly. Now he desperately appealed to them to help him prepare 'the juridical settlement that would determine the political future of the patria'.[6] He even promised the Socialists that those who had been in the past political prisoners would also be allowed to be deputies.[7] All this was a needless 'capitulation' by Primo de Rivera, claimed his supporters.[8] But to make his invitation even more palatable to his

[4] The negative response to Primo's constitution was surveyed by the author in his *The Origins*, pp. 19–20, 166–7.

[5] The relevant decree is in *Gaceta*, 30 July 1929.

[6] Maura, *Bosquejo*, p. 347.

[7] *Gaceta*, 30 July 1929.

[8] *La Vanguardia*, 25 July, 18 Aug. 1929.

enemies, the Dictator explained that the constitutional draft under consideration, which they opposed, had not at all been endorsed by the government. And, to prevent the immediate collapse of his strategy of *rapprochement*, he extended, late in August, the time-limit for the acceptance of his invitation to early October.[9]

Although the government had let it be clearly understood that in accepting the seats offered the new members would in no way be considered as thereby adhering to the views of the regime,[10] the 'rejectionist' response was fatally discouraging for the Dictator.[11]

There was, of course, also a limit to the concessions that Primo de Rivera was ready to make in order to pave the politicians' way back to the fold—among other things, he promised to Romanones that Alba, the man who had been presented as the incarnation of wickedness, and whose 'crimes' were the very reason for the *coup d'état*, would be allowed to return to Spain.[12] The guarantees that some of the *políticos* demanded as the indispensable condition for them to join the Assembly were tantamount to a reinstitution of democracy.[13] But Primo de Rivera, whose rule had rested on the demagogic manipulation of a presumed incompatibility between parliamentary democracy and Spain's destiny, would rather step down from office than admit the bankruptcy of his political philosophy.[14]

The *retraimiento* of the dynastic parties reflected an anti-Dictatorial contumacy that strongly underlined the political impasse into which the regime had manœuvred itself. Primo de Rivera's failure to enlist the support of other sectors besides the circles of *Upetistas* and, hence, the exposure of his increasing political isolation were plainly reflected in the rebellion led by the Conservative ex-premier Sánchez Guerra in January 1929. Both in its aims and in its composition this conspiracy underlined the democratizing effects that the struggle against the Dictatorship had on the opposition. That Primo de Rivera's authoritarian constitution was unacceptable to dynastic politicians and their liberal allies was no surprise. The novelty lay in

[9] *Boletín de la Asamblea Nacional*, Aug.–Oct. 1929, vol. iii, pp. 169–70.

[10] *Gaceta*, 30 July 1929.

[11] For the various demonstrative elections, see Villanueva, *El momento constitucional*, pp. 123–33; *El Imparcial*, 2, 25 Oct. 1929; *España*, 18 Nov. 1929. For the Dictator's angry reaction, see also *La Nación*, 27 Sept., 5 Oct. 1929.

[12] Romanones to Alba in García Venero, *Santiago Alba*, p. 267.

[13] *Informe del Marqués de Alonso Martínez sobre la asistencia a la Asamblea de los ex-presidentes de las Cámaras*, in Romanones Archive, Leg. 68, No. 24.

[14] Cf. *La Nación*, 13, 14 Aug. 1929.

that they were now ready to embark upon a more democratic enterprise than that embodied in the Canovite system. The minimum programme they subscribed to demanded the outright convocation of a constituent Cortes. Not even the curtailment of the King's power would now be discarded.[15]

The conspiracy ended in a melodramatic fiasco. But it was in his role as martyr in the struggle against absolutism, rather than as leader of a farcical rebellion, that Sánchez Guerra would be able to inflict a serious blow on Primo de Rivera's regime. His arrest and subsequent trial struck at the very foundations of the Dictatorship and the throne. 'Poor chancellor of iron, your lot is cast', exclaimed a clandestine leaflet on the morrow of Sánchez Guerra's arrest.[16]

There can be little doubt that the main impact that this whole affair had upon King Alfonso was that of bringing home to him the message that, unless he got rid of the Dictator, the erosion of the monarchy's position even in traditionally loyal zones would become an irretrievable phenomenon. The ex-prime ministers who met the king, by mid March, to urge him to return immediately to 'constitutional normalcy'[17] were by no means out of tune with his mood.

There was a lesson for Primo de Rivera too. The trial at which Sánchez Guerra was acquitted by a military tribunal of six generals amounted to a recognition that a rebellion against an unconstitutional government was unpunishable. That a military court should have passed such a verdict augured ill for the Dictator.[18]

The Sánchez Guerra affair brought to the surface the great dilemma of the regime. Should it now resort to repression or continue in its so far frustratingly unsuccessful attempts to reach some kind of constitutional legitimacy? Or should it simply quit the scene? A wavering combination of all these possible alternatives manifested itself throughout the months that followed Sánchez Guerra's arrest.

For some time now, the Spanish police had been drifting towards the practices of a political police in a totalitarian state. On the first hint of trouble brewing, the police would hasten to lay hands on the list of suspicious officers and civilians which, since 1923, had, if anything, grown exceedingly long. Its technical skill had improved

[15] Sánchez Guerra, *El movimiento revolucionario de Valencia (relato de un procesado)* (Madrid, 1930), pp. 30–3. E. Ortega, 'El frente único' in *Hojas Libres*, Nov. 1927.

[16] *Noticiero del Lunes (Sobre Sánchez Guerra y Primo de Rivera)*, in Hemeroteca Municipal de Madrid, A/1711.

[17] *The Times*, 13 Mar. 1929.

[18] For the trial, see *España*, 18 Nov. 1929; Villanueva, *El momento*, pp. 142–56.

and its tactics acquired a touch of toughness and sophistication. The fact that it was able to frustrate whatever conspiracies had been engendered by the enemies of the regime was certainly reflective of its efficiency. The Dictator had also been financially generous with his police services. He increased their budget—the Guardia Civil's excluded—by about 62 per cent.[19] The arbitrary punishments inflicted on the supposed enemies of the regime lacked, admittedly, the bestial nature of totalitarian punishments. But some imitations were nevertheless attempted. Following the arrest of some conspirators in late September 1927, the government announced that these people had committed 'an extraordinarily grave crime, a crime of *lèse-patrie*'. They were, therefore, to be 'denied their citizenship, their goods would be totally confiscated, and their names and titles would be taken off the national census'.[20]

In spite of fervent speeches of support for the regime and against 'those who damage national prestige', [21] and in spite of the government's boastful announcements that thousands of telegrams of support were flowing in from all the country,[22] there was an evident loss of nerve in official circles in the aftermath of the Ciudad Real mutiny.

The government initially opted for repression. It was to measures such as the 'concession of extraordinary powers to the government to remove and substitute any officials', rather than to allegedly 'favourable public opinion', that the regime resorted in order to secure its position. The loyal chief of the Civil Guard, General Sanjurjo, was immediately moved to Valencia where he was given *carte blanche* to restore order. The government was empowered to dismiss, exile, and suspend the salary of any public official who expressed views hostile to the regime. Every newspaper in the country was from now on to leave one-sixth of its space for official use.[23] A decree of 9 February closed down all the social and intellectual clubs where opponents of the regime used to meet.[24] And, in order to curb the dangerous, and evident, contamination of the

[19] *Folletín*, pp. 230, 278.

[20] Ibid., p. 640.

[21] *Diario de Sesiones de la Asamblea Nacional*, no. 39, 31 Jan. 1929. See also leading articles in *Ejército y Armada*, 30 Jan. 1929; *El Debate*, 1 Feb. 1929, and, of course, *La Nación*, 30, 31 Jan., 1, 3, 5 Feb. 1929.

[22] *La Nación*, 18 Feb. 1929 claimed that 1.5 million people expressed their support in the government through '49 kg. of telegrams'.

[23] For these measures, see *Gaceta*, 4 Feb. 1929; *La Nación*, 4 Feb. 1929; Cambó, *Las dictaduras*, pp. 42–3.

[24] *Gaceta*, 9 Feb. 1929.

army by 'evil ideas', its officers and soldiers would receive special lectures on military discipline and on 'the supreme duty of never involving the name of the fatherland in seditious action of a political character'.[25] Primo now also decreed the total dissolution of the artillery corps, which had been the main core of Sánchez Guerra's supporters in the army.[26] The artillery was, as far as Dictator was concerned, beyond redemption. It contained 'buds of bolshevism' and it had inflicted upon the nation 'irreparable damage'.[27]

In Primo de Rivera's concept, then, the Sánchez Guerra affair had only underlined the necessity of a dictatorship. It proved to him that 'the evils, the weaknesses and the misunderstanding that this regime had come to remedy, are still there'. He therefore declared, in a fit of anger, 'a halt in the march towards normalcy'. The transitional process of which he had been talking for some time was frozen.[28]

As both the hard-line decrees of early February and the decision of early November to freeze the transitional process indicated, Primo de Rivera seemed, in the aftermath of the events of Ciudad Real, to be toying with the idea of a return to purely dictatorial practices. Furthermore, deeply disappointed by the lack of spontaneous reaction by the Unión Patriótica and the Somatén to the news of the rebellion,[29] and, since the middle of 1929, increasingly baffled by the hostile reaction to his constitutional projects, he set out to reorganize the UP in what evidently looked like hours of isolation for the regime. Determined to fight back, the Dictator went out to muster his forces.

A credible mobilization of a party is possible either along democratic or totalitarian lines. Primo decided now to toy for a while with the latter in a desperate and short-lived bid to salvage his regime from falling into political amorphousness. It was, indeed, as an immediate reaction to Sánchez Guerra's rebellion that Primo de Rivera took steps towards bringing the UP nearer than ever to the totalitarian model of the party as an instrument of terrorism and internal surveillance. He cast upon the UP and the Somatén the task of assisting the government in tracing its enemies by preparing files on political suspects. Both institutions were turned into 'centres of investigation and civic information'.[30]

[25] *Diaro Oficial del Ministerio del Ejército*, 1 Feb. 1929.
[26] *La Nación*, 20 Feb. 1929; Villanueva, *¿Qué?*, pp. 20–2.
[27] Primo in *El Debate*, 20 Feb. 1929.
[28] *La Nación*, 5 Nov. 1929; Villanueva, *¿Qué?*, pp. 20–2.
[29] Calvo, p. 333.
[30] *Gaceta*, 4 Feb. 1929, *La Nación*, 19 Apr. 1929.

Later, when it became evident that the Assembly's constitutional project was being rejected by the public, the Unión Patriótica was immediately mobilized by Primo de Rivera to propagate throughout the country the constitutional draft with the Dictator's personal amendments.[31] The peak of this campaign was achieved in a grand gathering, in mid September 1929, at the Madrid Cinema Monumental, from where the proceedings were relayed to 600 groups of the UP all over the country and even abroad. Constitutional reform was imperative, explained the Dictator at that meeting; it was time now for a change of which the UP must be the instrument, he added. Simultaneously with that central meeting, 1,500 propagandists were sent to the provinces to spread the message about the inadequacy of the 1876 constitution.[32]

Now, however, it was too late for the exhausted Dictatorship to acquire legitimacy through a totalitarian bid. The latter was nothing but a brief episode that vanished without making any impact. As the reality of the approaching end of his rule became clear to the Dictator, the idea of 'change' was being replaced with one of survival. The UP was, consequently, conceived, in the last days of 1929, as a political party ready to defend, in case of the total débâcle of the regime, the Dictatorship's 'achievements' and its collaborators, lest they be exposed to the dangers of future political upheavals.[33]

Consequently, a reorganization of the party was decided upon within the framework of Primo de Rivera's plan to hold municipal and provincial elections as a possible step towards 'political normalcy'.[34] He expected the UP to win those elections. A census of the party members was therefore started, instructions for internal elections to the UP's local, provincial, and national organs were issued; and a departmental subdivision of youth, workers, women, and general sections was initiated.[35] *El Socialista* and *El Sol* were quick in protesting against the official support and stimulus that the UP was getting with an eventual electoral contest in view.[36] Clearly, the regime seemed to be determined not to step down, or, for that matter, give political liberties to the other parties, before the UP had completed its organizational process and was ready to face,

[31] *The Times*, 30 Aug. 1929.

[32] For the campaign, see AHN, P.G. Leg. 33: Barcelona, 18 Aug. 1929; *La Nación*, 16 Sept. 1929.

[33] *La Nación*, 22 Jan. 1920; 31 Jan. 1930.

[34] For Primo's latest 'transitional' plans, see below pp. 378–82.

[35] *Unión Patriótica*, 1, 18 Jan. 1930. *La Nación*, 2, 3 Jan. 1930.

[36] *El Socialista*, 25 Jan. 1930; *El Sol* quoted in *La Nación*, 22 Jan. 1930.

unprotected, the electorate.[37] Always too hasty in drawing analogies with Fascism, Primo de Rivera explained to the Italian ambassador that this overall reorganization of the UP would enable it, in the future, to be based upon the *ordinamenti fascisti*.[38]

It does seem, however, that Primo had seriously come to the conclusion that, as the situation was approaching in which the UP would no longer be in a position to profit from the heat of official favour, it would have to rely in future on an authentic *élan*, on strict discipline, and on a greater organizational cohesion. Its reorganization was necessary, as Primo himself pointed out, because 'even the best Dictatorship' must end sometimes, and the life of one man is too precarious a basis upon which to build the future of a nation.[39]

But a party of personal clients, dependent upon the individual power of their beneficent patron, the UP's life was as precarious as the Dictator's; its decline was determined by the very failures of the regime that had brought it to life and shielded it thereafter.

(b) *The Collapse of Primo's Working-Class Strategy*. Unfortunately for the Dictator, by the end of 1929, his spoiled children, the Socialists, had also deserted him. In fact, they played a most decisive role in the collective *coup de grâce* that the social and political forces in the country inflicted upon his regime by refusing to give legitimacy to his constitutional schemes. It does not seem, however, that the Socialists decided to jump on the opposition's bandwagon because of any dramatic deterioration in the conditions of the working class. Their motives were mainly political.

True, economic difficulties were building up and a greater crisis was looming on the horizon. The Socialists had every reason to be worried by the ominous signs about an imminent change for the worse in the economic prospects of the regime. The increasing financial difficulties of business, and industry in particular, certainly heralded a strain on job opportunities.[40] But there was no indication, on the eve of the fall of the Dictator, of massive unemployment or economically motivated popular unrest. The shadow of unemployment that started to fall over Spain in the closing months of 1929 was not of more disturbing dimensions than the degree of unemployment

[37] 'La reorganización de UP', *La Nación*, 20 Jan. 1930.

[38] Primo said that to the Italian ambassador: *I Documenti Diplomatici Italiani*, seventh series, 1922–35; vol. viii, Medici to the minister of foreign affairs, 15 Nov. 1929, no. 156, pp. 175–7.

[39] *The Times*, 20 Jan. 1930.

[40] D. Berenguer, *De la Dictadura a la República* (Madrid, 1946), p. 10; Maura, *Bosquejo*, p. 364.

that had existed throughout the years of the Dictatorship. 'The unemployment question is not a vital one in Spain', observed a contemporary analyst. And even agricultural unemployment was eased by the recruiting of labourers under contract for South America, France, and the West Indies.[41] The work involved in the international exhibitions of Barcelona was also instrumental in saving thousands of workers, mainly from the province of Murcia, from unemployment. 15,000 of them moved to the *cuidad condal*, 'the promised land', with their families.[42] Later in the year, some public works, such as the Madrid underground and the new ministries, had just ended. Yet the building of the new Ciudad Universitaria was in full swing.[43] And, although by the end of 1929 the regime seemed determined to embark upon a policy of budgetary cuts, its decision to abolish the extraordinary budget was designed to come into effect only on 31 December 1929.[44] It was precisely the decision of the Berenguer government to put into practice the almost posthumous deflationary intentions of its predecessor that started seriously to fuel unemployment in Spain. 1929 ended the way it had started, as a relatively peaceful year in labour relations, in no way comparable with the explosion of strikes that were to accompany the following year.[45]

It is also notable that 1929 was the first year after 1925 to show an increase of the per capita income in Spain. It rose from 1,349 pesetas in 1928 to 1,372 in 1929.[46] But data on workers' wages is hardly available or too sporadic, and in any case not always very reliable. Wages also varied from province to province, and there was moreover a great disparity between those of the skilled and the unskilled worker. In the case of the former, 1929 did not represent a marked deterioration, and in some cases there was even an improvement, at least as far as the situation in some of the provincial capitals was concerned, and according to official data.[47]

[41] Department of Overseas Trade, *Economic Conditions in Spain*, June 1930, pp. 23, 45. Cf. Banco de España, *Ritmo*, pp. 352–3.

[42] Bravo Morata, *La Dictadura*, ii, pp. 120–2.

[43] *Boletín de la Cámara Oficial de la propiedad Urbana de Madrid*, Jan. 1930. The government had allocated 130 million pesetas to the project, see Pemartín, *Los valores*, p. 470.

[44] See p. 340.

[45] Cf. Ben-Ami, *The Origins*, pp. 24–5; 131–2. Admittedly, many of the 1930 strikes were political, that is of the kind that was forbidden by the Dictatorship.

[46] Hernández Andreu, 'Algunos aspectos de la depresión . . .', *Cuadernos*, p. 400. Paris Eguilas, *Factores*, pp. 438–9, proposes a more substantial rise, from 2,534 to 2,896 pesetas.

[47] 'Tipos medios de jornales de algunos oficios en las capitales de España', in *Anuario*, 1929, pp. 507–8.

But all this tells only the bright part of the story. A study of nineteen provinces carried out by *El Economista* in December 1929 showed the dreadfully low wages that prevailed for the lowest-paid sections of the working class. In the mines of Sama, Mieres, and Siero (Asturias) there were workers who earned 1.25 pesetas per day; in Villacosa, the maximum wage was 4 pesetas. In the mines of Bilbao, the skilled blast-furnace workers earned 4.50 pesetas, while the loaders of ore took home between 3 and 4 pesetas, and women and children between 2 and 2.50 pesetas. The overseers in the mines of Huelva earned between 6.50 and 10 pesetas, but the foundry workers only between 3.75 and 7. Men in the coal-mines of Belmez earned between 2.50 and 6 pesetas; and in the mines of Ciudad Real, wages oscillated between 2 and 4 pesetas. Blast-furnace workers in the mines of Linares earned 3 pesetas per day.[48]

There was some consolation, however, in the fact that the post-1925 downward trend of wages of unskilled workers was partly offset by a drop in the cost of living.[49] There was a clear tendency towards a depreciation in the price of basic food necessities, while the price of industrial products witnessed a slight upward tendency. Though, unlike the depressed economies of the West, Spain did not witness a massive drop in wholesale prices,[50] it would none the less be right to claim that since 1926 the trend of prices in Spain had been one of depreciation, a process that was maintained in 1929, 'thanks to the excess of production both of agricultural and industrial products'.[51]

It is fairly clear that Barcelona was, as far as a working-class family was concerned, a more expensive city than Madrid. But this did not reflect itself in any meaningful rise in prices during 1929. In fact, eight out of the fifteen basic items examined by the statistics department of the ministry of labour[52] were cheaper in Barcelona in December than in January as compared with only three such items in Madrid, though the general level of prices was lower in the capital than in the *ciudad condal*. In each case, the discernible trend was one either of stability of prices or of a slight depreciation or rise. Taking the two cities together, in twenty cases prices fell or remained

[48] *El Economista*, 21 Dec. 1929. Cf. Harvey, p. 260 (on the Río Tinto miners).

[49] See above p. 306.

[50] Banco de España, *Ritmo*, pp. 333, 354.

[51] 'Los precios en 1929', *El Financiero*, Nov. 1930, p. 77; *Anuario*, 1929, pp. 296–7.

[52] Cf. 'Coste de vida del Obrero', in *Boletín de Estadística. Ministerio de Trabajo y Previsión. Servicio General de Estadística*, Madrid, 1929; *Anuario*, 1929, pp. 496–7.

stable, and in nine cases they rose in relation to January but not always in relation to other months of the year. When *The Times* wrote in March 1929 that 'the cost of living is in some ways the most serious of the Dictator's problems'[53] it was not referring to the price of basic food necessities. The trend described above for Barcelona and Madrid is, as a whole, applicable to other provincial capitals throughout the country.[54] More probably, *The Times* referred to the evident influence of the system of monopolies and high tariffs upon the price of industrial products,[55] and indeed upon the cost of living of the middle classes. The latter, rather than the workers, were the major 'rebels' of 1929. It is highly remarkable that the Dictatorship did not face any serious problems either in the destitute south or in the industrial belts, at least not as serious as those posed by lawyers, students, journalists, and politicians.

Probably the most serious opposition to the continuation of the Socialist flirtation with the Dictatorship came from the Miners' Syndicate of Asturias. Conditions in the mines, never too good, had deteriorated since 1927 when a drop in demand for Spanish coal forced the closure of some pits, and was the cause for the dismissal of 3,077 workers and for making another 1,785 redundant. But in spite of the evident worsening conditions of the Asturian miners, a process that was responsible for the increasing militancy of the workers, the reformist leadership of the Asturian Miners' Syndicate (SMA) remained adamant in its refusal to adopt revolutionary tactics.[56] As late as the end of 1929, the SMA's policy was described by one of its leaders, González Peña, as one of 'utmost discretion'. To 'shun any strike action' and to rely on 'government measures' continued to be the SMA's strategy until, at least, the end of the Dictatorship.[57] Moreover, though it is fairly clear that the XIIth Congress in July 1928 had brought home to the Socialist leadership the message of the growing alienation of those sections of the working class, such as the Asturian miners, that were most severely hit by the economic crisis, it is nevertheless evident that this fell short of changing the tactical postures of the UGT's national leadership towards the Dictatorship. The non-collaborationist motion of Teodomiro Menéndez, posing as the champion of the miners, was

[53] *The Times*, 13 March 1929.
[54] See above, note 52.
[55] Cf. *The Times*, 31 Jan., 20 Feb. 1929.
[56] Shubert, 'Una revolución . . .', pp. 106–7, 111, 112.
[57] González Peña in *El Socialista*, 31 Dec. 1929.

overwhelmingly rejected (5,064 against 740!). It is difficult to accept that the conditions of the Asturian miners in 1929 had a direct bearing on the Socialists' eventual decision to 'betray' the Dictator. The miners had known even more difficult times before 1929,[58] a year in which, rather than casting the shadow of unemployment, the mining industry in Spain had created 5,847 new jobs.[59]

As was shown above, the wages in both the Asturian mines and the mines of the Bilbao area were anything but enviable. But, as elsewhere, the decline in the cost of living helped to offset this adverse trend. A glimpse at the cost of basic food items for working-class families in mining districts around Oviedo and Bilbao will show a clearly downward trend of prices throughout 1929. Eight out of fifteen such items were cheaper in Oviedo by the end of the year than at the beginning. Three out of the remaining seven were maintained at a fairly stable level, and only four had gone up in price. In Bilbao, seven items were cheaper, four maintained stability, and four had gone up. But in one of the latter cases, the price of beef, it still was substantially lower than in Oviedo or indeed than the average national price for that item. Also lamb, bacon, and cod were all reasonably cheap items in Bilbao.[60]

Whatever economic difficulties there were during the twilight of the Dictatorship, the latter remained until its very last days a regime emphatically attentive to the needs of the working class. Nobody in the Socialist camp thought seriously of an immediate alternative to Primo de Rivera that would be more favourable to the working class. The orthodox economy of the Berenguer government and its abandonment of its predecessor's social orientation were soon to prove that Primo de Rivera was better than any other available alternative, short of a social Republic.

Considerations of a political nature were uppermost in the Socialists' minds when they decided to turn down Primo de Rivera's invitation to join the National Assembly. Nowhere in the internal debates of the UGT over the issue of the Assembly did economic arguments come up to support an 'abstentionist' attitude.[61]

[58] The challenge of the Miners' Syndicate to 'collaborationism', has been studied elsewhere, see P. Preston, *The Coming of the Spanish Civil War*, pp. 8–12; Ben-Ami, *The Origins*, 112–13, 117. D. Ruiz, *El movimiento obrero en Asturias*, pp. 191–200.

[59] *El Financiero*, Nov. 1930.

[60] 'Coste de vida del obrero', *Boletín de Estadística. Ministerio de Trabajo y Previsión. Servicio General de Estadística*, Madrid, 1929.

[61] See the proceedings of the debates in *Boletín de la UGT*, Aug. 1929.

Already in 1927, the UGT had rejected the invitation to join the Assembly on the ground that the government did not allow it to designate its own representatives.[62] The Socialists' attitude did not change in 1929 when the Dictator, overwhelmed by difficulties, accepted their conditions and invited them to elect their own delegates to the Assembly. The reason for the bold anti-collaborationist posture that was now taken by the Socialists should be looked for in their growing awareness that the Dictatorship was a politically exhausted cause that they could no longer exploit to their benefit. Indeed, it became clear to them that only if they dissociated themselves from Primo's ailing regime would they be able to avoid the adverse political repercussions that its imminent breakdown was likely to have upon its collaborators. The growing resentment in the army, Sánchez Guerra's 'revolution', and the student disturbances proclaimed from every corner the Dictator's isolation. Political wisdom suggested the desertion of Primo de Rivera and, in the process, the acquisition of the merit for, and the highly reputable halo of, having contributed to the breakdown of his regime. The immediate political future augured well for the Dictator's enemies, and ostracism to his friends. The Socialists, moreover, had a blemished record of collaboration with the Dictator which they were now anxious to disavow.

Consequently, the National Committee of the UGT decided, in the middle of August 1929, to reject the Dictator's invitation. The verdict was not unanimous. But the view prevailed that, as Largo rationalized, the Dictatorship was an ailing regime and the Socialists should therefore abstain from assuming the undignified role of injecting it with a new lease of life. By joining the Assembly, explained Largo, 'we legitimate and prolong its life indefinitely'. Such a step, Saborit followed suit, would be tantamount 'to drowning ourselves *politically* without any glory whatsoever'.[63] Largo clearly wanted the movement to shift its emphasis from the strictly professional and unionist orientation it had been following in the last years to one which was national and political. 'The political structure of Spain is about to change', he said in October 1929, 'and we must play a principal role . . . in that transformation.'[64] But this did not

[62] Ibid.

[63] See the debate in the National Committee in *Boletín de la UGT*, Aug. 1929, pp. 8–11.

[64] *Boletín de la UGT*, Oct. 1929, See also his article 'Temores infudados', in ibid., May 1929.

mean that the Socialists should now *actively* fight the Dictatorship. Largo was never too eager to put in jeopardy the carefully built Socialist power, however sublime the goal might have been. To *abstain* from supporting the uncertain regime was for him a daring revolutionary move.

And indeed it was. The Dictator was most seriously taken aback by the new Socialist posture. Their abstention was a fatal set-back to his desperate attempts to acquire political legitimacy. His whole working-class strategy had simply collapsed before his eyes, and he blamed the Socialists for acting as 'politicians', while he had always expected them to limit themselves to strictly professional action.[65] The conservative *La Vanguardia* was probably over-impressed by the Socialists' decision, and it predicted that they would now abandon their evolutionary tactics for one of rebellion.[66] Clearly, the shift in their tactics had drastically limited the Dictatorship's prospects of survival.

2. *The Death-throes of an Embarrassed Dictator*

(a) *A Xerxes in Search of a Themistocles*. Overwhelmed by accumulating difficulties, the Dictator definitely lost his self-confidence and, consequently, embarked upon a series of confusing and frequently contradictory schemes of transition. The repressive measures decided upon after the Valencia affair, which in fact institutionalized a police state in Spain, reflected the collapse of the myth of 'popular support'. Primo de Rivera was now heard to complain too frequently about his ill health and about the necessity to shorten the preparatory work which would enable him to relinquish power peacefully. On the other hand, the fear that his rule might end in an abrupt, undignified way, throwing the country into political chaos was a permanent challenge to him not to step down before he had institutionalized a new legality. In effect, Primo's major political aim throughout the last months of 1929 was that of relinquishing power in an orderly way.

Undoubtedly, physical and mental fatigue were largely accountable for Primo's growing, though never fully consistent, desire to go.[67] More persistent rumours of Primo's will to retire started in

[65] *El Socialista*, 14, 17 Aug. 1929. The Socialists were definitely bent on overthrowing the Dictatorship, see Dr Mouriz, '¿Hasta cuando?', in *Almanaque de El Socialista*, 1930.

[66] *La Vanguardia*, 18 Aug. 1929.

[67] See Primo's letter of 12 Dec. 1925 to Quiñones de León, in Calvo, pp. 334–5.

1928 when he planned to marry a certain upper-class lady, Ms Castellanos, and retire with her to lead a secluded life.[68] Simultaneously, he thought of advising the king to form a civilian government on the basis of the Unión Patriótica, 'without my own participation, because I think I have the right to rest'.[69] But neither the marriage nor the political transition materialized. The opposition, he said, had interpreted his transition plan as a sign of weakness and had consequently mounted a campaign of defamation against the regime, and the UP in particular. The nation, he concluded, was not yet ready to accept a political transition that would respect the legacy and the institutions of the Dictatorship.[70]

The Dictator was fully aware that the worst thing for the country would be 'an intestate succession'.[71] In October 1928 he put forward a new plan. He then promised that a biennial budget for the years 1929–30 was soon to be submitted for the approval of the National Assembly. The latter was to continue its deliberations on constitutional reform so that by 1931 the nation might be provided with a constitution.[72] But the immediate effect of Sánchez Guerra's rebellion was to strengthen for a while the Dictator's determination to stick to his post. He promised, in February 1929, that 'I will remain at my post until I have fulfilled my obligations to the Spanish nation', the main one being that of establishing 'a constitution of a type suitable for the proper government of Spain'.[73]

The idea of preparing elections for the transition to a government that would rule under the new constitution was sometimes spoken of. But the Dictator was reluctant to accept it. It would have been to ratify a system which, as he said in a speech in Zaragoza at the end of March 1929, should be abolished 'to be succeeded by a truer and more national one'.[74] Though under Mussolini's advice Primo seemed to have toyed for a while with the idea of holding elections to a new parliament, he finally gave in to the pressure of the UP on behalf of a manipulated plebiscite as the best way to secure a controllable transition.[75] New laws, however, would be needed to run 'truer' elections some time after the plebiscite.

[68] *La Nación*, 23 Apr. 1928.
[69] A letter to Quiñones de León, 10 June 1928, in Calvo, p. 335.
[70] *Unión Patriótica*, 15 June 1928; *The Times*, 9 June 1928.
[71] *La Época*, 25 Mar. 1929.
[72] *La Nación*, 3 Oct. 1928.
[73] Ibid., 16 Feb. 1929; *La Razón* (Buenos Aires), 20 Feb. 1929.
[74] *El Imparcial*, 26 Mar. 1929.
[75] Calvo, pp. 336–7; *La Nación*, 1 Apr., 13 July 1929.

It is from the parliament that was expected to emerge from a long and gradual process of transition that the king would designate his new government. Though he promised to lead the entire transitional process, Primo said he would be absent from this constitutional government because, as he put it, 'he who has governed a long time dictatorially would never be able to abide by the legalistic scrupulosity that is required once a new regime is born'.[76] Primo de Rivera was never unaware of his weaknesses, nor did he ever lack sincerity.

The set-back that he suffered by the rejection of the constitution by most shades of public opinion compelled the Dictator, in the summer of 1929, to readjust his plan once more to the changing circumstances. In August he proposed a more abridged schedule of transition.[77]

But the last months of the Dictatorship were the political death-throes of an embarrassed Dictator. None of his schemes of transition seemed to have aroused a favourable reaction. The ice was melting and he was definitely making for the shore before his footing gave way. He desperately looked for a golden bridge upon which to carry out his retreat. No Themistocles was available, however, to provide this retreating Xerxes with such a bridge. Just like the royal dictator of Yugoslavia, King Alexander, the Spanish Dictator discovered to his dismay that it was easier to destroy a regime than to erect a new one. Alexander had finally decided to grant a new constitution.[78] Primo would not be allowed to go that far, if only because he had a king, and a very domineering one, close behind his shoulders.

On 4 November 1929, following upon Sánchez Guerra's acquittal, Primo de Rivera returned for a while to a position of fictitious confidence. In a stroke of anger, he then declared a halt in the process of transition. 'No more timetables!', he exclaimed.[79]

But a few days later he again returned to the 'fixing of timetables'. Moreover, he now definitely gave up his earlier wish to lead the transition to the new regime personally. At a government business dinner at the Lhardy restaurant, in mid December,[80] the Dictator discussed with his colleagues his latest plan. Its main message was the need 'to cut short the life of the Dictatorship by the appointment, by the king, of a transitional government, of neither a dictatorial

[76] *Unión Patriótica*, 1 Mar. 1929.

[77] *La Nación*, 12 Aug. 1929.

[78] Sforza, pp. 134–5.

[79] *La Nación*, 5 Nov. 1929.

[80] For a full account of this meeting and the plan that emerged from it, see Calvo, pp. 342–9; *La Nación*, 10, 11 Dec. 1929.

nor a constitutional nature, headed by a civilian of a rightist cut'. He had Guadalhorce in mind.[81]

Primo de Rivera's major expectation of the transitional government was that it should shield his collaborators from the possible unleashing, by a hostile government, of an anti-dictatorial vindictive campaign. More than anything, the ailing Dictator wanted desperately to avoid the emergence of a government that might seek legitimacy by demolishing the work of his regime. It is in this context that he now also demanded that the reorganization and reinforcement of both the UP and the Somatén be speeded up. Indeed, he expected himself to be the eventual president of the UP. This was a task, he said, 'I have no doubt I would be elected to'. To avoid an uncontrolled democratization, he also stipulated that the members of the new Ayuntamientos and Diputaciones should be half-elected on a corporate basis and half-appointed by the transitional government.

Though determined to step down, Primo de Rivera still expected his successors to abide by his political testament. He did not give up hope that the 'new order' would be the product of 'an integral national Chamber' in which thc working class, he was careful to stress, would have a proper representation. 'Discipline and order' would be the major pillars of the new system. Because

> to open the door, even a bit, to those who want a laic Spain, or preferably an impious one; to a regime of property only slightly short of Communism; to the abolition of hierarchic respect; to an anti-social and extravagant science; to a purely civil, or rather immoral, family, would mean, given the state of cultural deficiency and civic immaturity of the masses, to launch the country into a revolution . . . A regime based upon majorities is as absurd as a personal system—they are both tyrannies.[82]

Though he was evidently in dire straits, Primo de Rivera insisted on maintaining a façade of self-confidence. Let no one be deceived, he warned, 'the Dictatorship will not go by an *espanta*, as they say in the bullfights jargon'. Not until he had established a 'serious and secure' political arrangement would he leave office. Until then, he promised, he would stay in his post 'whatever the cost'.[83]

But reality could not be concealed altogether. Nor did the Dictator's fictitious display of confidence convince his enemies that his regime was not 'exhausted'.[84]

[81] Calvo, p. 338.
[82] Quoted in Calvo, p. 346.
[83] *La Nación*, 16 Dec. 1929.
[84] *El Sol*, 31 Dec. 1929.

The last days of Primo de Rivera's rule were then to be dominated by a desperate search for a dignified outlet from the cul-de-sac in which he found himself. A return to the old political system would have been tantamount to a resounding failure of his entire enterprise. 'Do not worry, the *other* regime will not return', he pledged.[85] But, in reality, he was hardly in a position to determine the political future of Spain by means of a positive policy of his own choice. The most he could do was to speed up the passage by the National Assembly of legislation concerning 'public order' and an authoritarian press law.[86] This was his last-moment contribution to the materialization of his immediate goal, i.e. a *Primoderriverismo* without Primo de Rivera.

Otherwise, the Dictator was not even in a position to rally his followers around his immediate political designs, and present a coherent front *vis-à-vis* the king. The Lhardy plan was not too enthusiastically endorsed by the government. Nor was the UP that happy with the idea that it might have to face, unprotected, an electoral contest. It feared elections might result in a 'displacement of hierarchies'.[87] The ministers were especially worried at the possibility of having another prime minister to lead the transitional process. They collectively appealed to Primo to stick to his post until the transitional process was completed, even if that meant his having to face the verdict of the polls and 'fight democratically *à la* Tardieu or *à la* Briand'.[88] This view did not coincide with that of some people in the UP. Eager to succeed, at long last, to the Dictatorship, they visualized a transitional government in which the official party should have the upper hand.[89]

(b) *'Primo de Rivera, No!', or to Sacrifice a Dictator for the Sake of a King*. As in the case of Primo's rise to power, so in his downfall it was again the king who came to play the crucial role. Alfonso was now, more than ever before, looking desperately for a return to solid constitutional ground. The Dictator's sequence of transitional plans had become an unbearable nuisance to him. Indeed, the way in which Primo de Rivera fixed for himself timetables was seen by the king as an affront to his sovereignty, a blow to his prerogative to designate and unseat prime ministers. But when Primo was busy

[85] Ibid., 1 Jan. 1930.
[86] *El Imparcial*, 15 Jan. 1930.
[87] Calvo, p. 340.
[88] Ibid., pp. 353–4.
[89] *La Nación*, 26 Dec. 1929; Cf. Calvo, p. 334.

producing transitional plans, new every morning, in the antechambers of the royal palace all sorts of manœuvres to get rid of the Dictator were being engineered.[90] The king, who had been contemplating such a move for some time now, was further stimulated to act by his assessment, indeed an accurate one, that the political uncertainty and the continuation of the Dictatorship were seriously undermining military discipline,[91] not to mention the position of the monarchy.

At a cabinet meeting on 31 December, Alfonso did not fail to realize than an incoherent government led by a bewildered Dictator stood before him with a patched-up plan. The king, moreover, understood that in spite of the façade of solidarity they tried to erect, the government did not support, or at best was divided about, the Lhardy plan.[92] The shrewd and experienced Alfonso did not fail to grasp that the psychological moment for Primo de Rivera's 'Bourbonization' was at last approaching. He acted, however, cautiously; and at the above-mentioned meeting he asked for a few days to think over Primo's plan. 'That day the death sentence of the Dictatorship was signed', observed Calvo Sotelo[93] who, a fortnight later, overwhelmed by financial difficulties, was to anticipate, by his own resignation, that of his master.

But to Primo's credit, one must admit that he did not fall back on fatalism. The dismissal of Calvo Sotelo and his replacement by a personal friend of the king, the Conde de los Andes, was yet another desperate step in the Dictator's fight for political survival. It was a conscious attempt by the general to placate the monarch. De los Andes's good relations with Mauristas and Conservatives, Primo might also have thought, would help him to build a bridge of understanding with such political forces.[94] The king, however, would not be satisfied by the personal sacrifice of Calvo Sotelo. Nor was he too happy with the Dictator's frequent allusions to the support that he presumed to enjoy from wide sectors of opinion and from the army. Such boastful claims only widened the abyss between the two men, as they responded to a political philosophy that was unacceptable to the king, that is, that power rested with 'opinion', the *palacio de oriente* no longer being its source.

Yet, whatever the Dictator's presumptions, he had no serious

[90] Aunós, *España*, pp. 311–13.

[91] Villanueva, *¿Qué?*, pp. 68, 71.

[92] *The Times*, 1 Jan. 1930; Pabón, *Cambó*, vol. ii, pt. I, p. 587.

[93] Calvo, pp. 350–2.

[94] *Folletín*, pp. 868–71.

popular backing to resist the king's will. The Unión Patriótica was in the midst of a precipitate process of reorganization. Its membership, according to the Dictator himself, had shrunk from about 1.3 million in 1927 to about 700,000 in late 1929;[95] and many of its branches were, for every practical purpose, in disarray.[96] As for 'public opinion' and the 'classes', had not Primo de Rivera himself explained in an almost fatalistic mood, after his fateful meeting with the king on 31 December that

> the aristocratic classes . . . hate me . . . The conservatives refuse to support the Dictatorship . . . Nor do those who maintain the strongest affinities with the Church . . . assist the Dictatorship, or applaud its plans. The banks and industry . . . the patronal class . . . the civil service . . . the press . . . as well as other sectors . . . do not support warmly the Dictatorship . . . In fact, they unconsciously join those who claim that it is exhausted.[97]

Nor did the embarrassed Dictator find consolation in the army during his last days in office. 'It was common knowledge that something was wrong with the military . . . the conflict with the artillery ended by being a conflict with the entire army.'[98] The unpopularity of the regime affected the army as its supposed supporter. Persistent rumours circulated everywhere with regard to military unrest, and clandestine leaflets that circulated among the garrisons spread the virus of discontent and indiscipline.[99]

Primo might have liked to dismiss such protests as confined to isolated *tertulias* of the younger officers. It is, moreover, evident that the Moroccan army was far less, if at all, contaminated by anti-dictatorial propaganda than the units of the peninsula. A victorious army, whose cherished criterion of promotion had been institutionalized by the Dictator, it did not harbour any essential reservations against the regime. But Primo could certainly not ignore the grave significance of the military plot that was being prepared under the leadership of General Goded during the very last days of his rule. A *contre-brumaire*, to use an expression of Napoleon Bonaparte, was brewing in the southern garrisons.

[95] Dionisio Pérez, p. 297.

[96] See the case of that of Barcelona, AHN, P.G. Leg. 46: 'Informe sobre la UP de Barcelona', 20 Apr. 1929, by Gassó y Vidal.

[97] *ABC*, 1 Jan. 1930. Even *El Debate*, 29 Dec. 1929, urged him now to step down.

[98] Villanueva, *¿Qué?*, pp. 68, 71.

[99] Ibid., p. 68. Such a document is quoted in *El Liberal* (Murcia), 9 Aug. 1929. See also *Las Juntas de defensa. A los pocos lectores de la Nación*, Aug. 1929: Romanones Archive, Leg. 2, No. 25. For the agitation among the officers at the Barcelona garrison, see also Bueso, p. 274; *La Vanguardia*, 7 Nov. 1929.

Supported by the garrisons of Málaga and Granada[100] and by frustrated naval officers in the ports of the south, and subject to increasing pressure from hot-headed anti-Primo officers such as Ramón Franco,[101] Goded posed a serious challenge to the Dictator. Moreover, the sanguine attitude of the Captain-General of Seville, the Infante Don Carlos, towards the plotters might indicate that he was by no means unconnected with the conspirators. It was in his interest and that of his brother-in-law, the king, to confront the Dictator in the boldest possible way with the sad reality that he no longer enjoyed the support of the army.

Surely, for the king, Goded's conspiracy should have been invented if it was not really there, as it gave further strength to his strategy of getting rid of the Dictator, lest a revolutionary movement should sweep away both the Dictatorship and the monarchy. It is, indeed, not at all impossible that the Infante D. Carlos and the king had encouraged this bizarre conspiracy—bizarre at least in the sense that its existence was common knowledge and the press wrote freely about it—as a blackmailing device against the Dictator. Furthermore, it is noteworthy that the execution of the conspiracy was said to have been 'postponed' only because of persistent rumours about an imminent change of government, this time with the king's favourite, the chief of his military household, General Berenguer, as prime minister.[102] It was likewise significant that Primo de Rivera should have demanded the outright dismissal of D. Carlos as an accomplice in the Andalusian conspiracy, and that the king should have refused to carry it out.[103]

The initial reaction of the Dictator to the 'Andalusian conspiracy' was to display a certain degree of self-confidence, however fictitious. When asked, on 25 January 1930, by a correspondent of *ABC* to comment on the news that a *coup d'état* was about to be staged by the garrisons of Andalusia, he preferred to play down the importance of the whole affair. But he was clearly not unaware of the manœuvre that was being prepared to get rid of him. Addressing himself as much to the king as to the conspirators, he added: 'I am ready to step down only if somebody, in good faith, comes to substitute me. What I am by no means ready to do is to allow power to be snatched

[100] For the agitation in Andalusian garrisons, see *La Época*, 31 Dec. 1929; FO 371/14161, Grahame to Henderson, 31 Dec. 1929.

[101] Ramón Franco, *Deciamos ayer* (Madrid, 1931), p. 48.

[102] Villanueva, *¿Qué?*, p. 167.

[103] González Ruano, pp. 134–5, Villanueva, *¿Qué?*, pp. 178–9.

from me, because this would unleash symptoms of anarchic decomposition.'[104]

But, unimportant as the Dictator might have liked to make out Goded's conspiracy to be, he nevertheless accepted its challenge and precipitated a desperate attempt to put to an open test the army's support, and at the same stroke, to disactivate the king's manœuvres against him. Depressed, ill-humoured, and overwhelmed by the renewed student disturbances, he appealed on 26 January to his fellow generals to convey to him whether he, who had assumed power 'by the proclamation of the military, still deserves the confidence of the army and the navy'. He added that if the answer was negative, then 'within five minutes' he would hand his resignation to the king, since it was the king who, 'interpreting the will of the military', had given him the power in the first place.[105]

Now, however, 'the will of the military' proved to be a broken reed. Primo's appeal to the generals was an attempt at an impossible counter *coup d'état*, this time against the king. Primo's claim that 'military opinion is the source of my rising to power' was an affront to the crown and a violation of the old political framework whereby the king was the supreme source of power. In effect, the Dictator's appeal to the army was an unprecedented consultation in the annals of praetorian politics since the establishment of the liberal monarchy. A monarchist *coup* against the will of the king was an inconceivable contradiction in terms. The army was in no position categorically to decree the continuation of the Dictatorship because, as two contemporaries put it, 'it does not share either with the king or with the people the right to appoint or unseat governments'.[106] And even if they would not have been deterred by their deference towards established norms, the generals as a whole were anything but willing to stage a new bid for power, this time a purely military one. A dissociation of the army's prestige from Primo's sinking boat, that was what they wanted most at this stage, if only because it was possible that Primo's overthrow might enable the army to start healing the divisions that had been developing in its ranks in the last years.[107]

Furthermore, the king's careful cultivation of his personal relations

[104] *ABC*, 26 Jan. 1930.

[105] *El Sol*, 26 Jan. 1930.

[106] Berenguer, pp. 28–30, Villanueva, *¿Qué?*, pp. 172–4.

[107] Such an analysis was frequently made elsewhere by generals when they decided to oust a military ruler, see Nordlinger, pp. 140–7.

with the army's high command paid off well on this occasion. Most of the generals to whom Primo had appealed were either intimate friends of the king or extremely loyal to him as both the sovereign and, no less important, the commander-in-chief of the army.[108] Not even intimate friends of the Dictator such as the Captain-General of Catalonia, Emilio Barrera, the chief of the Civil Guard, General Sanjurjo, and the high commissioner in Morocco, Gómez Jordana, were now ready to back him. They all reiterated in their responses their total subordination to the king and to whatever government enjoyed his confidence.[109] Barrera even rebuked the Dictator for inviting an already agitated and increasingly divided army to interfere in politics. He wrote:

This appeal of yours to the army is a very grave affair, as it amounts to an additional *coup d'état*. If you enjoy the king's support then there is no need for you to ask for the army's backing. But if you lack the confidence of the crown you are not entitled to appeal to the army . . . It is tantamount to saying that every government should henceforth demand the army's approval . . .[110]

Alfonso was furious at the tactless attempt of the Dictator to transfer the royal prerogative to the barracks;[111] and he did not lose any time in seizing the opportunity of again putting himself in the position of the interpreter of the national will.[112] As such, he expected the Dictator to quit immediately. Surprisingly, however, Primo was still reluctant to unseat himself. But all the cards were in the king's hands. The Dictatorship which he had sanctioned in order to save his crown had now to be sacrificed for the same purpose.

Primo had yet to be persuaded to resign, for he still could not bring himself to do so of his own free will. The king placed the task of convincing the Dictator that all options, bar resignation, were tightly closed to him upon the new finance minister, the Conde de los Andes. But Primo had still to be advised by his intimate friend, the Minister of the Interior, Martínez Anido, against trying to resist before he finally handed his resignation to the king on the afternoon of 28 January 1930.[113]

[108] Ana de Sagrera, p. 348, gives a complete list of the generals approached by Primo and their relations with the king.

[109] See an example of such an answer in Berenguer, p. 17. See also *The Times*, 28 Jan., 1 Feb. 1930.

[110] Julio Milego, *El general Barrera (de Cataluña al 10 de Agosto)* (Madrid, 1936), pp. 97–101. He was thus expressing the views of the officers under his command: *La Vanguardia*, 28 Jan. 1930.

[111] Villanueva, *¿Qué?*, pp. 174–5.

[112] *El Debate*, 29 Jan. 1930; Cortés-Cavanillas, *Alfonso XIII*, pp. 136, 292.

[113] Ossorio y Gallardo, *Mis memorias* (Buenos Aires, 1946), pp. 153–4.

The most striking thing about the last days of the regime was the almost total isolation of the Dictator. At no moment did he contemplate doing with the UP what he had frequently done in the past, that is to mobilize it in an attempt to outplay the king. And the UP, as a truly governmental party, would not move unless ordered to do so. Essentially, the UP was the private clientele of its leader. The general recognition of the regime's lack of prospects and the widespread feeling that Primo could no longer deliver the goods had on the party members exactly the same effect that it had on other sections of society, the business sector and the Socialists, for example. They all sought to dissociate themselves from, and look beyond, the Dictatorship. Primo de Rivera's mood oscillated between fatalism and occasional displays of decisiveness. He could not be counted upon to provide effective leadership for his party. The UP, its members knew, had also become extremely unpopular with the public, especially after the royal decrees of 3 and 4 February which turned it into a virtual police organization of petty informers. The hostility towards the Dictatorship was, if anything, increased by the royal order of 4 February 1929 which threatened to exile any public servant who uttered criticism against the regime. Such practices had existed from the early days of the Dictatorship. Now, however, they were made part of the machinery of the state. At the end of nearly seven years the image radiated by the regime was that of a Dictator, physically a wreck of his former self, but still sitting squarely on the safety-valve of state, held in position by an increasing number of stays and chains.

As early as a fortnight before Primo's resignation, even his vociferous mouthpiece, *La Nación*, seemed to have abandoned him. It succumbed to the view that the end of the regime was imminent. It looked at it all as a painful but irreversible process. *La Nación* simply ceased to regard itself as the unyielding champion of the Dictatorship. As early as 14 January it wrote an almost official farewell to, indeed an obituary of, the outgoing regime.[114] A fortnight earlier, it had even acknowledged that the people did not want the Dictatorship to be consecrated as a permanent system of government, 'because it knows that such a thing is impossible'.[115] *La Nación*'s report on Primo's resignation was given with the most astonishing equanimity.[116]

[114] *La Nación*, 14 Jan. 1930. ('de una situación a otra'), 16 Jan. 1930. By this time the paper's front page was no longer concerned with political news; this was relegated to the back pages. [115] Ibid., 27 Dec. 1929. [116] Ibid., 29, 30 Jan. 1930.

As in the case of Mussolini, Primo's fall was determined to a great extent by the role of the king and the army. Curiously, the impact of Primo's 'Bourbonization' upon the Duce and other Italian Fascists was that of reinforcing their ineradicable fear of a possible bid by Vittorio Emmanuele to dissociate himself from Fascism. Therefore, when the Spanish monarchy passed away in 1931, the Fascists were only too eager to stress the moral: the fate of the Italian monarchy, like that of its Spanish counterpart, was inextricably bound up with the fate of the Dictatorship—*simul stabunt o simul cadent*.[117]

In the last analysis, however, it would be wrong to attribute either to the king or to the generals the exclusive responsibility for the overthrow of both the Spanish Dictator and his Italian counterpart. Such a claim would constitute a neglect of the civilian momentum unfolded by Primo's rule, as well as a minimizing view of the political and economic difficulties that had, in the first place, created the pre-conditions either for his 'Bourbonization' or for the withdrawal of support from the military. Primo de Rivera had never enjoyed the unanimous support of the army, nor was he 'made', as is sometimes argued, exclusively by his fellow generals. He was the product of a political and social crisis, the spokesman of powerful civilian forces, not merely the champion of the army's interests. By 1929, however, the 1923 civilian alliance had disintegrated, and the acquiescence of the army had been eroded beyond repair. When, in the twilight of his rule, Primo appealed to the generals, he was already a defeated man. They only administered the *coup de grâce*. The Dictatorship was not overthrown by the will of one person, it was rather 'suffocated by the intellectuals, the business circles, the students, the depreciation of the peseta, and the general restlessness. It ended because it could no longer go on.'[118] Unsustained by either mass coercion or a fanatically dedicated political movement, Primo's Dictatorship succumbed to the mounting challenge of its enemies.

A wreck who was to die within a couple of months in a second-rate hotel in Paris, Primo de Rivera went, immediately after he handed in his resignation, back to his desk to write his swan song. It was a pathetic and, as usual, intimate official note in which he insisted on underlining the fearful message that in Spain, 'the true freedom . . . ought to be always accompanied by civil guards'.[119]

[117] Cf. De Felice, *Mussolini*, pp. 100, 129–30.

[118] Ossorio y Gallardo, *Incompatibilidad* (Madrid, 1930), p. 21.

[119] *La Nación*, 29 Jan. 1930. The government's official communiqué presented Primo's ill health as the reason for his resignation: *El Debate*, 29 Jan. 1930.

Indeed, during his last months in power he had made it plain that he expected his successors to be people of a civil-guard mentality, figures such as General Barrera, Martínez Anido, and La Cierva.[120]

Primo's views on the succession coincided with those of the king on one essential point. Both discarded the possibility of an immediate succession by the 'políticos'. King Alfonso realized that these were now still alienated from him and were, anyway, disorganized and confused as to what really remained of their political following after seven years of ostracism.[121] Until the 'políticos' could again be used as 'an instrument of government', the king opted for an interim reliance on a 'bayonet with a civil touch'. General Dámaso Berenguer, in the king's own words 'a military with prestige both in the army and among civilians',[122] was the ideal choice. The king's reliance on Berenguer was probably not a last-minute insight. There were indications that Alfonso had been using the head of his military household in order to make Primo wonder whether his position in the army was not being undermined.[123] The Dictator, in desperation, was thus goaded into addressing the high command directly. It may well be that he was deliberately manœuvred by the king into a trap.

The transition to the 'new regime' could not have been smoother. Primo himself did not put any obstacles in the way of the new government. He urged his civil servants to abide by the new government, and even assist it; and though obviously deeply concerned, they followed the general's lead. The ministers resigned respectfully, and so did some of the civil governors, such as Miláns del Bosch in Barcelona. Yanguas Messía immediately left his post as the president of the National Assembly.[124] It was not easy for all sorts of 'patriotic' corporations, such as some UP branches and associations of Catholic ladies, to swallow the bitter pill; they vainly exhorted the Dictator not to give way to the new government.[125]

That the 'transition' was to be disrespectful, indeed vindictive, towards the labour of the Dictatorship was made clear by the very initial measures of the new government. Clearly, Berenguer thought to acquire legitimacy in the eyes of the nation by systematically demolishing Primo de Rivera's work.[126] Primo de Rivera had also

[120] La Cierva, *Notas*, p. 305; Maura, *Así*, pp. 44–5. [121] Berenguer, p. 32.

[122] Cortés-Cavanillas, *Alfonso XIII*, p. 293; Villanueva, *¿Qué?*, pp. 166–7.

[123] FO 371/15040, Grahame to Henderson, 4 Feb. 1930.

[124] For the transition process, see *La Vanguardia*, 31 Jan., 1 Feb. 1930; Alcalá-Galiano, *The Fall of a Throne*, pp. 22–74. [125] *La Vanguardia*, 28 Jan. 1930.

[126] Ben-Ami, *The Origins*, p. 23.

every reason to lament the absence from the new government of any of his ex-ministers, in spite of his explicit appeal to Berenguer not to exclude them out of hand. The ex-Dictator was also shocked by the appointment of a bitter enemy of his regime, Santiago del Valle, to the conspicuous job of prosecutor-general. 'I am sure that he is going to wrap us up in paper', was Primo's reaction as he conveyed it to his ex-ministers.[127]

To defend his achievements and to shield his collaborators from what evidently looked like an attempt to reach legitimacy by sacrificing the dictatorial lamb, Primo de Rivera took up the cudgels, on the morrow of his resignation, to speed up the reorganization of the UP and make it ready to struggle for power. In a speech before the UP's national committee, on 29 January, he gave high priority to the preparations for the forthcoming elections; they were, he said, the major immediate task of the party.[128] Indeed, it can be asserted that Primo de Rivera was the initiator of the *Unión Monárquica*, in which he said he was more than ready to collaborate,[129] and which was officially to be founded by the ex-ministers of the Dictatorship only after the general's death.[130]

But gradualist, democratic practices were totally alien to the spirit and the character of the ex-Dictator. He lacked the patience and the health needed for the long-range political strategy, or for building a party in the wilderness of the opposition. This was probably the reason that, a few days after his resignation, Primo's burning desire 'to serve Spain again' manifested itself in an awkward bid for power, an absurd attempt to reverse the flow of events. He was in Barcelona, on his way to a self-imposed exile in Paris, when the memories of 'that heroic night' of the 12th–13th of September 1923 came again to his mind, and made him toy with the idea of playing it all again, with the assistance of old friends such as Sanjurjo and Barrera. But the reasons that had brought about his downfall did not vanish overnight. What did vanish outright for lack of support and of an appropriate *ambiente* was this venturous idea about a reversion of the 13th of September. No garrison in the country, not even that of Barcelona under his friend General Barrera, would stage an anti-royalist *coup d'état* on behalf of a

[127] Ana de Sagrera, pp. 351, 353.
[128] *Unión Patriótica*, 4 Feb. 1930.
[129] See his manifesto in *Unión Patriótica*, 18 Feb. 1930. He also appealed to La Cierva to join the new party; see La Cierva, *Notas*, p. 306.
[130] For the origins and the creation of the UM, see S. Ben-Ami, 'The fore-runners of Spanish Fascism: Unión Patriótica and Unión Monárquica', in *European Studies Review*, vol. 9, no. 1, Jan. 1979, pp. 60–1.

frustrated, lonely man, and without the support of a meaningful section of civilian society.[131]

Primo's abortive bid for power was a response to his sudden and lucid grasp of his political blunders, and hence to a renewed determination to correct them. A few days after his resignation, he analysed in a conversation with Aunós the reasons for the failure of his regime. He should have drawn up, he said, a constitution before anything else and submitted it immediately to a vote of the people.[132] The lack of legal framework and his frequent allusions to an imminent return to 'normalcy' were the greatest enemies of the Dictatorship. In the view of Italian Fascists, *Primoderriverismo* collapsed because it was not a coherent dictatorship, or, to put it in other words, it fell short of being a truly Fascist system. Therefore, as Mussolini was eager to point out, the débâcle of the Spanish Dictatorship should by no means be interpreted as a set-back to Fascism. 'We are not responsible for these people abroad, even if they claim to be our sympathizers', he concluded.[133] The moral for Fascism was clear: to invigorate its own dictatorship rather than indulge in liberalizing experiments *à la* Primo de Rivera.[134] In the end, both friends and opponents would agree, Primo failed in the crucial test of a leader of a revolution, that of converting an adventure into a regime.[135] The adventure, therefore, ended in melancholy.

[131] See accounts of this frustrated attempt in E. Aunós, *Semblanza política del general Primo de Rivera* (Madrid, 1947), pp. 65–6; Berenguer, pp. 78–9; Mola, pp. 234–5.

[132] Aunós, *Semblanza*, pp. 62–4; Aunós, *Calvo Sotelo*, pp. 62–4.

[133] Quoted in M. Michaelis, *Mussolini and the Jews* (Oxford University Press, 1978), pp. 47–8.

[134] De Felice, *Mussolini*, p. 131.

[135] See also the view of the Duce's brother, Arnaldo Mussolini, in *The Times*, 1 Feb. 1930.

CONCLUSION

If one must do the job of a political scientist and classify *Primoderriverismo* in relation to other dictatorships, it would seem that the nearest 'model' into which it can be fitted is that of the royal dictatorships in the Balkans in the inter-war period. Some interesting analogies can also be drawn with the regime of Pilsudski and his successors in Poland as well as with Salazar's *Estado Novo*. Undoubtedly, Primo's rule represented a higher and more sophisticated stage of authoritarianism than the elementary and ideologically amorphous one that underlined the policies of the Portuguese military dictatorship that preceded the advent of *Salazarismo*.[1]

Yet there is certainly truth in Lequerica's view that the Spanish Dictatorship was an essay of authoritarian political methods that have been employed elsewhere—in Italy, presumably—in a more definitive way.[2] Unlike Fascism, and more convincingly, Nazism, that aspired to a totalitarian control of society on the basis of an all-embracing ideology, the dictatorships mentioned above were ideologically syncretic, and they never attempted to control society, or even the political system, in a totalitarian way. Primo de Rivera would have certainly subscribed to Salazar's condemnation of the totalitarian state as 'essentially pagan, incompatible by its nature with the character of our Christian civilization'.[3] These were not totalitarian dictatorships. Nor were they, however, elementary authoritarian systems, or regimes based on the simple principle of 'halt or I shoot!'. Dwelling on traditional precepts, they responded more to the need to control change than to that of constructing an entirely new society.[4] Franco was later to refer to Primo's Dictatorship as a transitional stage between the era of pronunciamientos and that of the 'organic' systems.[5]

[1] Cf. Tom Gallagher, 'The Mystery Train: Portugal's Military Dictatorship 1926–1932', in *European Studies Review*, vol. 11, no. 3, July 1981, pp. 325–53.

[2] Lequerica quoted in E. Vegas Latapié, *El pensamiento*, pp. 41–2.

[3] Salazar, p. 231. For the non-totalitarian socio-economic views of Salazar, see H. Wiarda, *Corporatism and Development, The Portuguese Experience* (The University of Massachusetts Press, 1977), pp. 175–6.

[4] E. Nolte would have brought these regimes under the category of pre-fascist, traditional systems that responded more to the need to defend the past than to that of erecting an entirely new state; see Nolte, *Three Faces of Fascism* (London, 1965), pp. 13–15.

[5] Charles Delzell (ed.), *Mediterranean Fascism* (New York, 1971), pp. 290–1.

When Dictators such as Primo de Rivera, Pilsudski, Rydz-Śmigly, Metaxas, Călinescu, Antonescu, Stojadinović, and Salazar came to power they exhibited apprehension towards mass mobilization; indeed their rise to power was, in a way, a defensive reaction against uncontrolled politicization. Yet, all of them realized very soon that bayonets and decrees could hardly be used as exclusive instruments of government in countries that had just tasted the experience of a short, but sometimes intensive, process of politicization. They therefore fell back on practices of mobilization. But they did so as a way of moulding and manipulating public opinion. Their instruments were official parties such as Călinescu's Front of National Revival, Pilsudski's Non-Partisan Bloc for Co-operation with the Government, Rydz's Camp of National Unity, Metaxas's National Youth Organization, Stojadinović's Yugoslav Radical Union, Salazar's União Nacional, and, of course, Primo de Rivera's Unión Patriótica.[6] Unlike in Fascism and Nazism, these parties were not used as instruments for the seizure of power; they were conceived as a means of keeping it.[7] But by their commitment to mass mobilization, albeit a measured and controlled one, and to the ritual of democracy they manifested a departure from elementary authoritarian practices of government.[8] Grasping the fact that their countries were in the midst of a process of transition from systems based on manipulation to the politics of mobilization, they opted for the control of the latter rather than simply turning the clock back. The army, therefore, could not be conceived as the exclusive basis of power, but as one of its pillars, the other being 'organized' civil opinion.[9]

In these parties—all essentially governmental creations—one can

[6] See ibid., p. 332 for a comparison between Pilsudski's party and the União Nacional.

[7] Linz, 'Una teoría del régimen autoritario', pp. 230–1, views this as a fundamental difference between what he calls authoritarian systems and totalitarian regimes. Dollfuss (his Vaterland Front is a case in point) and Franco are 'authoritatrian'.

[8] Renzo de Felice, p. 55, sees mobilization as the principle that divides conservative authoritarian systems from Fascism. Similar views are proposed by Barrington Moore, 'Totalitarian Elements in Pre-Industrial Societies', in *Political Power and Social Theory, Six Studies* (Harvard University Press, 1958), pp. 59, 80; and Franz Neumann, pp. 244–5.

[9] For the various movements, see E. Weber, 'Romania', in Weber and Rogger (eds.), pp. 554–5, 559–67; Henry Roberts, pp. 206–35; Cliadakis, pp. 101–7; and C.M. Woodhouse, *Modern Greece. A Short History* (London, 1977), pp. 229–37; J.B. Hoptner, pp. 121–4; Antony Polonsky, *Politics in Independent Poland. The Crisis of Constitutional Government* (Oxford University Press, 1972), pp. 237–47, 419–35; F. C. C. Egerton, pp. 188–94.

easily recognize all the verbiage and trappings of the 'new order' in Europe. Fascism, a theory of conflict and revolution, was institutionalized and sterilized by basically conservative dictators, who distrusted the radical right just as they did mass democracy, but were either unable or unwilling to embark upon purely and simply military dictatorships.

Thus, for example, it would seem that in Spain the emergence in 1922 of a modern rightist party such as the *Partido Social Popular* was a threat to the old order just as much as radicalization of the Anarcho-syndicalist unions, or the fact that parliament was starting to exercise its sovereign functions with greater conscientiousness and energy than at any time since the Restoration. Consequently, Primo's institutionalization of the UP should also be viewed as an attempt to tame and domesticate the potential dynamism of both the fascist *La Traza* group in Barcelona and the nucleus of Social Catholics that had founded the party in the first place. It should not be surprising that these elements were gradually to realize that their aspiration to create a party in their own image had been frustrated by the Dictatorship. *Acción Nacional* and later the *Ceda* were to be the products of such a frustration. In an article in April 1927, *La Nación* acknowledged that there were people who had been disappointed by the too 'mild enthusiam' of the UP and expected it to be 'more active and agitative'. But their pressure was successfully resisted, as the regime did not want 'a party of agitators'.[10] It was only to be expected that a genuine fascist such as Ernesto Giménez Caballero should have felt alienated from Primo's regime.[11]

A similar suspicion existed between Salazar and Rolão Preto's blueshirts. The latter's 'youthful exaltation, their power cult, their belief in direct action, and their drive to mobilize the masses behind one leader' were anything but palatable to Salazar, and he did not lose time in disbanding them.[12] Likewise, in Yugoslavia the more authentic fascism of the *Ustaše*, whose recruiting ground was among the 'typical' strata of society upon which fascism had relied elsewhere, stood in apparent contrast to the Stojadinović brand of

[10] *La Nación*, 5 Apr. 1927.

[11] Pastor, p. 34. Among those disappointed by Primo's watery fascism one can find the two most truly fascist spirits in his entourage, Ramiro de Maeztu and Aunós. For the former, see above pp. 184–5; for the latter, see Aunós in *Acción Española*, vi (1933), pp. 31–2.

[12] Cf. Wiarda, *Corporatism*, pp. 78–9.

'establishment fascism'.[13] Also, in Greece the '4th of August regime' of Metaxas, though it had institutionalized many of the trappings of fascism, could hardly stomach the ultra-rightism of groups such as the Sidera Terini of General Pangalos or the Nationalist-Socialists of George Mercuris. A case in point is also the fundamental divergency that existed between Pilsudski's regime and that of his even more radical successors on the one hand, and more authentically fascist groups such as the National Party, the Camp for Great Poland, and the Falanga.[14] The same was of course true of the unbridgeable abyss that lay between the youthful, mystical, and violent fascism of Codreanu's *Legion of the Archangel Michael* and the Carolist dictatorships, however ready they were to adopt some of the external trappings of fascism. The Străjeri's parades were a pale imitation of the irresistible exaltation of the Legionnaires. And the creation by General Ion Antonescu, in September 1940, of the *National Legionary State* was, as in the case of the Falange in Franco's Spain, tantamount to the domestication of the Legionnaire revolutionary spirit. It was harnessed to serve a paternalistic, authoritarian regime.[15]

It was a feature of these official parties that were created by decree that they never really developed a genuine mass following. As was also the case with Trujillo's Partido Dominicano,[16] and Nasser's National Union,[17] both founded some time after the seizure of power,[18] they mainly became the instrument for the popularization of official policies, and a device to surround the new regime with a semblance of public acquiescence. In most cases, they were a springboard to positions of power and influence. The ideological glue and the drive to consolidate the 'revolution' were far less strong, except perhaps among a leading group of ideologues and activists, than the eagerness to take refuge in the government's shadow. The social and political background of their followers was inevitably eclectic. Pilsudski's BBWR was not unique in that it rested on new

[13] Cf. Pribicevic in *The Identification of Pre-Fascist Elements*, pp. 62–4; Stephen Graham, *Alexander of Yugoslavia, Strong Man of the Balkans* (London, 1938), pp. 127–39.

[14] S. Andreski, 'Poland', in Woolf (ed.), *European Fascism*, pp. 175–83.

[15] Weber, 'Romania', pp. 552–66; Henri Prast, *Destin de la Roumanie* (Paris, 1954), pp. 111–36.

[16] Cf. Wiarda, *Dictatorship*, pp. 74–80.

[17] Keith Wheelock, *Nasser's new Egypt. A Critical Analysis* (London, 1960), pp. 53–4, 62–3, 70–2.

[18] Cf. Nordlinger, pp. 112–7, on the practice of some praetorian rulers of setting up 'parties from above'.

technocrats, deserters from conservative parties, ex-Socialists like himself, Catholics, people of the centre, and sections of the minorities in Poland. Pilsudski and Primo de Rivera were not alone in opening their respective parties to 'all men of goodwill'. All the official parties that have been mentioned here would have made their own the following recruiting principles of Salazar's National Union:

> Men of every creed, from every sphere of thought and action, of every class, have agreed to put away their differences and have found in the fundamental principles of the União Nacional a common ground in which all Portuguese can meet and collaborate . . . The União Nacional was established on a ground sufficiently broad in outlook to admit all Portuguese of goodwill, irrespective of their political or religious creeds, provided only that they accept the existing institutions and are prepared to defend the principles of our national reconstruction.[19]

Such popular support, however, could be generated and retained only as long as official favour and encouragement were guaranteed. Parties from above would not outlive the regimes that had created them.

But it is not only by their resort to popular support that these 'transitional dictators' should be seen as breaking away from primitive *Caudillismo*. Though they might have started as the champions of a given status quo, they nevertheless approached in varying degrees the threshold of a 'new state'. Some of them, like Metaxas, the admirer of 'Roman totality' as opposed to 'Greek individualism and intelligence', Stojadinović, Trujillo, Primo de Rivera—more discernibly the leading ideologues of the UP—developed the mental apparatus of idealists in search of *Weltanschauung*, and moved away from old conservative loyalties.[20]

The very fact that the previous multi-party system was replaced by a state party around one indisputable leader represented a definite breach with the past. In Yugoslavia, the decision of Prince Paul to get rid of Stojadinović stemmed from the very reasons that had brought the Italian foreign minister, Ciano, to admire the Serbian *Vodja* as 'fascist by virtue of his conception of authority, of the state, and of life'. His utter disregard of parliamentary practices

[19] Salazar, pp. 109, 113, 133.

[20] Cf. Wiarda, *Dictatorship*, pp. 102–23; Cliadakis, pp. 97–101, Hoptner, *passim*. Salazar came to power with an established world-philosophy, see Egerton, pp. 102–17.

of government could no longer be tolerated by the crown. The *führerprinzip* that in the case of Primo de Rivera, Metaxas, and Stojadinović threatened to relegate the king, their original source of legitimacy, to a secondary position amounted to a political change that the old political class could not comply with. Both Metaxas and Primo de Rivera complemented their breach with the political past by their vindictive campaign against old conservative and liberal politicians.[21]

To further guarantee that 'decaying' parliamentarism would not be revived, additional measures had to be taken. In a law of 9 February 1938, Metaxas had institutionalized the move to the hierarchic, corporatist state. Such a state was about to be created by the generals who succeeded Pilsudski in power. Far more radical than Pilsudski, they launched an attack against 'the myth of seymocracy' according to which the nation is reflected in, and represented by, parliament. The State, the Nation, and the *Wodz* (leader) became the key to Poland's cohesion and destiny. A drive to restructure the state, economics, and society along corporatist lines was substituted for the politics of liberalism.[22]

A greater social emphasis than that which the parliamentary right was ready to contemplate would also seem to be a demarcation line between the past and the present. Primo de Rivera had anticipated by a generation Perón's *Justicialismo*. His 'favourable' treatment of the working class and populist proclivities were increasingly unpalatable to the business sectors. Marxism would become a thing of the past once the essence of its message, great developmental projects and social improvements, was absorbed by the nationalist state—such was the hope that underlined the social policies of Primo de Rivera, Pilsudski's successors, and Metaxas.

Salazar's social message, however, was anything but exciting. His was the conception of returning to the medieval corporatist structure of society, and of preventing social change. His *Estatuto Nacional do Trabalho* and the vertical syndicates which it allowed were nothing but the bureaucratic instruments of social discipline. But then, the Spanish Dictatorship was unique in the degree of favour

[21] For Metaxas's breach with the old parties, see Cliadakis, pp. 92, 107–12. For the tension between Stojadinović and the regent, see Balfour and Mackay, *Paul of Yugoslavia* (London, 1980), pp. 159–60.

[22] For how Pilsudski's successors developed the idea but not the reality of Fascism, see Edward Wynot, *Polish Politics in Transition. The Camp of National Unity and the Struggle for Power 1935–39* (University of Georgia Press, 1974), p. 73 ff.

that it showed, and independence that it gave, to the unions even though, at least on principle, they still subscribed to a socio-political philosophy fundamentally opposed to the Dictator's. Moreover, Salazar's orthodox budgetary approach, his house-keeping mentality, so diametrically different from the lavish and generous expenditures policy of Primo de Rivera, underlined his unique brand of social immobilism. Change, whether controlled or not, was for the Portuguese dictator anathema, as it was likely to carry on its wings untold threats to the stability of Portuguese Christian society.[23] A devout Catholic, and essentially committed to a stable Christian society, Primo de Rivera was nevertheless far more ready than Salazar to embark upon 'a revolution from above'.

In many senses, however, this was a *révolution manquée*. Primo had shattered the foundations of the old regime without enthroning a new state, thus leaving behind him a dangerous vacuum of power. He might have saved, as the conservative *ABC* claimed,[24] Spain from anarchy; he certainly restored public order and brought a 'dignified' end to the Moroccan war, and he greatly advanced the modernization of Spain. But, as is not unusual in dictatorships, he had also suffocated the civic spirit by his centralistic and paternalistic policies, thus betraying the most essential elements of the 'regenerationist' myth, which he claimed to have embodied. He might not have precipitated the degeneration of Spanish administration, but his new brand of *caciquismo* and favouritism was certainly not instrumental in purifying the system of its pathological deficiencies. A burning issue such as 'responsibilities' for which he had promised a quick solution was shelved, and indeed bequeathed almost intact, even aggravated, to his successors, to the detriment of the monarchy. Some of the problems that his panegyrists claimed that he had 'solved' proved simply to have been temporarily frozen. For they erupted, on the morrow of his resignation, more serious than ever. Such were, for example, the presumed 'disappearance' of anarchism,[25] the 'elimination' of the Catalan problem,[26] the

[23] Wiarda, *Corporatism*, pp. 128–55. Antonio Ferro, *Salazar, Portugal and her Leader* (London, 1935), pp. 206–12, on 'poor citizen in a wealthy state'.

[24] *ABC*, 29 Jan. 1930. For a similar summary, see *España Militar, Revista Profesional de la Escala de Reserva del Ejército*, Feb. 1930.

[25] On the very day of Primo's fall, Pestaña exposed the fallacy of such a claim, see *El Socialista*, 28 Jan. 1930.

[26] The UP's leader in Barcelona, Gassó y Vidal, did not think that the Catalan problem was 'solved'; AHN, P.G. Leg. 330: Barcelona, 18 Nov. 1929.

'balancing' of the budgets, the 'restoration' of the unity of the army. In fact, he had shattered to so-called 'harmony of the military family' as no one had done before him.

In an 'unconscious', dialectical way, Primo de Rivera was a major promoter of the cause of Spanish democracy. The effects of his policies upon the military are a case in point. The Second Republic was undoubtedly made possible by the attitude of the very army which Primo de Rivera had not ceased to claim unanimously stood behind him. The army was certainly not Republican in 1931. But the experience of the Dictatorship had shown the military that the philosophy of the barracks was not an adequate instrument of government, and head-on policies would not solve complex economic and social problems. It was, moreover, during the Dictatorship and its immediate aftermath that important sections of the army had definitely renewed the old nineteenth-century alliance between liberalism and the military. The army of 1931 had lost the 'monarchist cohesion of the past'. Neither among the generals nor at the level of local garrisons would candidates be found to stage a last-ditch defence of the monarchy. The army of 1931 was too divided to be able to take a positive stand towards the crisis of the monarchy. 'Abstentionism' seemed to be the best way to avoid not only a confrontation with the people, but also the possibility that soldiers might have to fire upon their brothers in arms. Though the post-Primo de Rivera army was anything but a revolutionary militia, republicanism, and democratic currents had made probably more headway in its ranks than in those of the army that is supposed to be the armed shield of democracy in the post-Franco era. Moreover, in the minds of many Spanish officers today, Francoism is still a fresh model of unity, progress, and order to long for and to wish to transfer from the realm of nostalgia to practical politics. In 1931, however, the military looked at their recent authoritarian model, Primo de Rivera's Dictatorship, as a highly discredited affair that did not deserve nostalgic embraces, let alone a bid for revival.

That such a bid proved to be a historical impossibility was also due to the substantial social and economic changes brought about by the Dictatorship. Primo de Rivera had improved Spain's industrial potentialities, he had enhanced its urbanization, as well as the conditions for a de-archaization of its social structure. True, emotionally and socially attached to the landowning classes, the Dictator refused to consider meaningful agrarian reform. A fanatic protection of industry and of the olive- and wheat-growers, to the detriment of the merchants, special favour shown towards big capital combined with a less forthcoming approach towards smaller concerns, a determination to protect the urban workers at the expense of their employers, and a great reluctance to extend to the countryside the social benefits and legislation he had decreed for the urban proletariat—such were the socio-economic foundations of *Primoderriverismo*.

They were not entirely devoid, however, of a drive to break away from conservative loyalties and traditions, even in the countryside. His taxation policy and his budgetary priorities reflected an attempt to shift the balance towards a betterment of the masses' lot, even when this meant alienating the 'moneyed people'. Primo de Rivera's commitment to a populist orientation as well as his schemes of development had enhanced and strengthened the position of the Spanish proletariat, certainly of the organized sections of it. The irony was that he, who had seized power, in the first place, in order to defend an antiquated social system against its enemies on the left, soon realized that the best defence Spanish capitalism could hope for lay in a certain degree of social change, however controlled and limited. This was a 'revolution from above' that came to avoid that from 'below'. In the process he alienated both the defenders of stagnation, who were expected to pay for the regime's social emphasis, and the champions of a real, far more radical change of the social structure. Entangled in this predicament, he stepped deep into oblivion.

This he did, however, not before laying the foundations of the 'new state' later to be erected by the aggressive right of the thirties. The general, who came to power with nothing but 'parenthetical' intentions, found himself gradually developing the mental apparatus of an idealist in search of a *Weltanschauung*. Many of his policies can certainly be found in the teachings of the traditionalist, non-democratic strands of opinion that had existed in Spain since the French revolution. Primo de Rivera's, however, was the first regime in Spain to combine such legacies with the lessons of contemporary dictatorships and those of what he and his ideologues thought was the anti-liberal *Zeitgeist*, in an attempt to create a New State entirely divorced from the formulas of the parliamentarian right which had monopolized political life in Spain since the 1830s. Primo's 'new deal' was imbued with an unequivocal negation of liberalism and parliamentarism. It advanced a social approach that viewed the care for the popular classes as a mission that should be accomplished through a corporatist reorganization of labour relations; it advocated an economic policy based on control, planning, and *dirigisme* to a scale never attempted before; and it defended a political system based on direct democracy (through the plebiscite), organic as opposed to individual suffrage, a strong executive, and a single official state party that should hold the monopoly of key administrative posts as well as of the political and ideological truth.

Retrospectively, the very failure of Primo de Rivera perhaps constituted a great lesson for the radical right of the Republic as well as for the architects of the Francoist regime; it taught them how to avoid the Dictator's mistakes in the process of building a New State. Primo de Rivera might after all have been a political architect, albeit by default.

BIBLIOGRAPHY

ALL major and public archives contain collections of cuttings from the Spanish and foreign press, as well as pamphlets and political tracts. These are not included in the present bibliography but are referred to in the notes of this book.

I. MANUSCRIPT SOURCES

1. *Public Archives*

Archivo Histórico Nacional, *Sección de Gobernación, Serie A*, 1923–30.
Archivo Histórico Nacional, *Sección Presidencia del Gobierno*, 1923–30.
Public Record Office, *Diplomatic Despatches from Spain*, May 1923–Feb. 1930.
The Italian Documents Collection, St. Antony's College, Oxford.

2. *Private Papers*

José Ortega y Gasset's Archive (Madrid).
Maura Archive (Madrid).
Romanones Archive (Madrid).
Santiago Alba Archive (Madrid).
Unamuno Archive (Salamanca).

II. PRINTED SOURCES

1. PRIMARY SOURCES

A. *Printed Documents*

Anuario Estadístico de España, 1929–31.
Armiñán, José Manuel y Luís, *Epistolario del dictador* (Madrid, 1930).
Avance estadístico de huelgas correspondiente al primer semestre de 1923 (Madrid, 1924).
Banco de España, *Ritmo de la crisis económica española en relación con la mundial* (Madrid, 1934).
Berwick y Alba, Duque de, *Catálogo histórico y bibliográfico de la Exposición Internacional de Barcelona 1929–1930*. Publicado bajo la dirección del Excmo Sr. Duque de Berwick y Alba, Director de la Real academia de la historia, Tomo I (Madrid, 1931).
Boletín de Estadística (Ministerio de Trabajo y previsión, Servicio General de Estadística, Madrid, 1929).
Boletín de la Asamblea Nacional, 1928–9.
Boletín de Información Social del Ministerio de Trabajo y Previsión (Madrid, 1919–30).
Boletín de Legislación Social, 1926–9.
Cámara Oficial de la Propiedad Urbana de Barcelona, *Las recientes disposiciones del Directorio encaminadas a impulsar la construcción de viviendas económicas* (Barcelona, 1924).

Comercio exterior de España, 1901–1956. Datos del Instituto Nacional de Estadística (Madrid, 1958).

XII Congresso del Partido Socialista Obrero Español, 28 de Junio al 4 de Julio de 1928 (Madrid, 1929).

Consejo de Economía Nacional, Sección de Defensa de la Producción, *Prontuario de disposiciones protectoras de la producción e industrias nacionales* (Madrid, 1926).

Consejo Nacional de Combustibles, *Real decreto regulador de la obligación de consumir carbón nacional impuesta a las industrias protegidas* (Madrid, 1927).

Consejo Nacional de Combustibles, *Dictámen oficial sobre industria hullera en Asturias* (Madrid, 1926).

Delzell, Charles (ed.), *Mediterranean Fascism* (New York, 1971).

Diario de Sesiones de la Asamblea Nacional, 1927–30.

Diario de Sesiones del Congreso de los Diputados, July–September 1923.

Díaz-Plaja Fernando, *La España política del siglo XX en fotografías y documentos. Tomo Segundo: De la Dictadura a la guerra civil (1923–1936)* (Barcelona, 1970).

Estadísticas Básicas de España 1900–1970 (Confederación española de cajas de ahorro, Madrid, 1975).

Franco, Francisco, *Discursos y mensajes del jefe de estado, 1955–1959* (Madrid, 1960).

Gaceta de Madrid, 1923–30.

García Nieto, María Carmen, *et al.*, *Bases documentales de la España contemporánea.* Vol. V (La crisis del sistema canovista 1898–1923); Vol. VI (Expansión económica y luchas sociales 1898–1923); Vol. VII (La Dictadura) (Madrid, 1972–3).

I Documenti Diplomatici Italiani, seventh series, 1922–35.

Las responsabilidades políticas de la Dictadura. Un proceso histórico. Los alegatos de Calvo Sotelo. La defensa de Primo de Rivera. El voto particular de Casanueva. La sentencia (Madrid, 1933).

Legislación sobre la jornada máxima de 8 horas (Instituto de Reformas Sociales, Sección de Legislación y Publicidad, Madrid, 1924).

Memoria de la actuación del Consejo de Economía Nacional en el año 1927 (Madrid, 1928).

Ministerio de la Gobernación, Dirección General de Administración, *Estadística de la beneficencia particular en España correspondiente a los años 1926 al 1928 inclusive* (Madrid, 1930).

Ministerio de Trabajo y Previsión. Dirección General de Acción Social, *La crisis agraria andaluza de 1930–31. Estudios y documentos* (Madrid, 1931).

Ministero de Trabajo y Previsión. Dirección General de Trabajo. Sección de Estadísticas Especiales de Trabajo. *Estadística de salarios y jornadas de trabajo referida al periodo 1914–1930* (Madrid, 1931).

Número de huelgas que ha tenido conocimiento el Instituto de Reformas Sociales desde 1905 a 1920 (IRS, Madrid, 1920).

Pérez, Dionisio, *La Dictadura a través de sus notas oficiosas* (Madrid, 1930).

Primo de Rivera, Miguel, *Intervenciones en la Asamblea nacional del General Primo de Rivera. Prólogo de José de Yanguas Messía* (Madrid, 1930).

Publicaciones Patrióticas, *La Asamblea Nacional. Biografía y retratos de los 400 Asambleistas y numerosos datos del mayor interés* (Madrid, 1927).

Servicio Nacional de Crédito Agrícola, *Folleto comprensivo de las disposiciones legales y formularios a los fines de la divulgación del servicio, ley, reglamento y reales decretos referentes al crédito agrícola* (Madrid, 1927).

Unión Patriótica, Estatutos y reglamento para su régimen (Madrid, 1927).

B. *Press*

A. NATIONAL NEWSPAPERS

ABC (monarchist daily), 1923–30.

El Debate (conservative, Jesuit daily), 1923–30.

El Imparcial (Liberal daily), 1923–30.

El Sol (liberal organ), 1923–30.

El Socialista (the PSOE's organ), 1923–30.

Folletín de El Sol, 1923–30.

La Época (Conservative organ), 1923–30.

La Nación, 1925–30 (official organ).

La Vanguardia (*españolista*, conservative organ, Barcelona), 1923–30.

B. OTHER POLITICAL ORGANS

Acción Española, 1932–33.

Almanaque de 'El Socialista', Madrid, 1923–30.

Amor Patrio. Periódico inspirado en el programa de Unión Patriótica (selected numbers).

Boletín de la Asociación Patriótica Española, Buenos Aires, 1928.

El Carbayón, Oviedo (selected numbers of 1925).

El Cruzado Español, 1929.

El Día de Cuenca, February 1924.

El Diario Universal (Romanonista organ), September–November 1923.

El Diluvio, Barcelona.

El Liberal (selected numbers).

El Liberal, Murcia (selected numbers).

El Noticiero (Cáçeres), November 1927.

El Presidencialista. Órgano de la Juventud Republicana Presidencialista de España, Madrid, 1928.

El Progreso (Republican organ), 1927–9.

España. Informaciones y comentarios actuales, Paris, 1929.

Heraldo de Aragón, June 1923.

Heraldo de Madrid (selected numbers).

Hojas Libres, Hendaye, 1927–9.

Hojas Libres (edición especial), October, 1928.

Hojas Libres (Extraordinario), Bayonne.

La Acción (Maurista daily), 1923.

La Defensa. Por Dios y Por la Patria, Madrid (selected numbers).

La Libertad, liberal daily (selected numbers).

La Nación. Edición semanal para America, 1926–9.

La Rioja, Logroño (selected numbers).

La Veu de Catalunya, the Lliga's organ (selected numbers).

La Voz, September 1923.

Nueva España, 1930–1.
Patria Española. Todo por Dios y Para Dios. (Revista descriptiva, con censura eclesiástica), 1928.
Región, Oviedo (selected numbers).
Republicano. Órgano del Centro Republicano Español, Rosario de Santa Fe, 1927–8.
Solidaridad Obrera (Anarcho-syndicalist organ), 1923.
Unión. Órgano de la Unión Patriótica de Mataró, 1926.
Unión Patriótica, 1926–30.

C. FOREIGN PRESS

The Economist, London, 1923–30.
The Times, London, 1923–30.

D. CORPORATIVE ORGANS

Acción Católica de la Mujer, 1930–1.
Banco de Crédito Local, *Memoria leída en la junta general de accionistas celebrada el día 31 de Marzo de 1930. Memoria del ejercicio de 1929.*
Boletín de la Administración Local, Madrid, 1925–6.
Boletín de la Asociación Oficial de Vecinos e Inquilinos de Madrid, 1925.
Boletín de la Cámara de Comercio de Madrid, 1923–9.
Boletín de la Cámara Oficial de Comercio, Industria y Navegación de Málaga, 1927–30.
Boletín de la Cámara Oficial de Comercio e Industria de Sabadell, 1925.
Boletín de la Cámara Oficial de Comercio e Industria de Lérida y su Provincia, 1925, 1926, 1929.
Boletín de la Cámara de Transportes Mecánicos, 1928–31.
Boletín de la Cámara Oficial de Industria de la Provincia de Madrid, 1923–9.
Boletín de la Cámara Oficial de Comercio e Industria de Burgos, 1928–9.
Boletín de la Cámara Oficial de la Propiedad Urbana, 1923–30.
Boletín de la Juventud Católica Española, 1929.
Boletín de la UGT, 1929.
Boletín del Banco Urquijo, 1923–30.
Boletín del Comité Regulador de la Industria Algodonera, 1929.
Boletín del Sindicato Católico de Tipógrafos y Similares de Madrid, 1925–9.
Boletín del Sindicato Católico de Tipógrafos y Similares, Memoria de 1930.
Boletín Oficial de la Acción Católica Española, Toledo, 1929.
Boletín Oficial de la Asociación de Agricultores de España, 1923–9.
Boletín Oficial de la Cámara de Comercio de Madrid, 1923–9.
Boletín Oficial de la Sociedad de Obreros Gasistas, Electricistas, Teléfonos, Aguas y Similares de Madrid, 1928.
Caridad. Revista mensual con licencia y censura de la autoridad eclesiástica, 1929.
Ciencia Tomista, Madrid, 1929–31.
Confederación Gremial Española, Memoria de 1925.
Correspondencia de España, businessmen's organ (selected numbers).
Diario Oficial del Ministerio del Ejército, August 1926, 1929.
Miercoles Ciudadanos. Semanario independiente, 1927.
Ejército y Armada, military daily, 1923–30.

El Arsenal del Predicador, Revista mensual dedicada al clero, 1929.
El Campesino. Órgano oficioso de La Liga Nacional de Campesinos, 1929–31.
El Dependiente Español. Órgano de la Federación Nacional de Dependientes de Comercio, Industria y Banca, 1928.
El Eco del Pueblo. Órgano del Comité Directivo de la Confederación Nacional de Sindicatos Católicos de Obreros, 1928–30.
El Eco Patronal, Madrid, 1928–9.
El Ejército Español, military daily, 1923–30.
El Joven Obrero, Bilbao, 1929.
El Joven Obrero. Portavoz de la Juventud Obrera y Campesina, 1929.
El Licensiado del Ejército. Semanario independiente, Madrid (selected numbers).
El Magisterio Castellano. Revista de Instrucción Pública, 1924.
El Magisterio Español, 1929.
El Mercantil. Diario independiente de las 12 de la mañana (selected numbers).
El Mercantil. Diario independente de la tarde. Monitor de los intereses materiales de la nación, 1928.
El Mercantil Patronal. Órgano de la Defensa Mercantil Patronal, 1925–6.
El Soldador, 1929.
España Agraria, Madrid, 1928–9.
España Comercial. Órgano de propaganda de los intereses del comercio, industria y trabajo, 1926–9.
España en Africa, 1927–30.
España Militar. Revista Profesional de la Escala de Reserva del Ejército, 1929–30.
Indústria. Revista de economía, derecho, organización y técnica industrial. Órgano de la Cámara Oficial de Industria de Madrid, 1923–30.
Juventud, 1928–30.
Juventud (Revista Semanal), Alicante, 1930.
La Calle. Periódico católico popular (selected numbers).
La Correspondencia Militar, military organ (selected numbers).
La Lectura Dominical, 1926.
La Turbina, 1929.
La Unión. Revista de las damas españolas, Madrid, 1929.
La Unión Ferroviaria. Órgano del Sindicato Nacional Ferroviario, 1929.
La Voz del Cantero. Órgano de la Sociedad de Canteros y Similares de Madrid, 1928.
Lucha Social, 1925.
Memoria. Cámara de Comercio y Navegación de Barcelona, 1930.
Revista Hispano-Africana. Liga Africanista Española, 1925–9.
Senara, Semanario defensor de los intereses morales y materiales de Ciudad Rodrigo, 1926.
Somatén. Boletín Oficial, 1928–30.
Unión Alcoholera Española, *Concepto de las causas productoras de la crisis vitivinícola actual y de la memoria presentada al Consejo de Economía por la comisión nombrada por el gobierno para su solución* (Madrid, 1926).

Unión General de Trabajadores (Semanario), 1926–7.
Unión Matronal, 1928–9.
Unión Mercantil, Málaga (selected numbers).
Unión Obrera. Portavoz de la Confederación Nacional de Sindicatos Libres de España, April, June 1925–1926.

E. REVIEWS AND MAGAZINES

Actividad Financiera, 1925–9.
Actualidad Española. Revista de cultura, arte, literatura y espectáculos, 1927.
Álbum Primo de Rivera. Suplemento artístico de la revista 'El Iman' (Barcelona).
Ars. Programa de los espectáculos de S.A.G.E. Palacio de la Música, 1927–9.
Asociación Anticomunista Internacional (Secretariado Español de la 'Entente Internationale Contre la III Internationale'), Madrid, 1929.
Audencia Pública, 1927–9.
Blanco y Negro, 1929.
El Economista, 1927–30.
El Financiero, Nov. 1930 (no. extraordinario dedicado a 1929).
España Avanza. Órgano mundial de las ciudadanías hispano-americanas, Madrid, 1928.
Estampa, 1929.
La Actualidad Financiera, 1923, 1925–6.
La España de Hoy. Periódico editado en español, francés, alemán e inglés, para propagar en todo el mundo el resurgimiento actual de España, 1929.
La España Nueva, 1929.
Mundial Financiera. Revista de banca, bolsa, seguros, ferrocarriles, minas, electricidad, obras públicas, hacienda, e industrias, Madrid, 1925–8.
Radio Técnica, 1929.
Radio y Luz, 1929.
Tanto, 1930.

C. *Literary Works*

Bastos Ansart, Francisco, *Pistolerismo (historia trágica)* (Madrid, 1935).
Buckley, Ramón, and Crispin, John (eds.), *Los Vanguardistas Españoles, 1925–1935* (Madrid, 1973).
Colección Novela Política (Madrid, 1931).
Fernández de la Reguera, and March, Susana, *Episodios nacionales contemporáneos: La Dictadura, I. El Directorio Militar (1923–25); II. El Régimen Civil (1926–1930)* (Barcelona, 1969–71).
FRU-FRU (a series of pornographic novels from the twenties kept in the Hemeroteca Municipal de Madrid).
Novela Política (Madrid, 1930), Hemeroteca Municipal de Madrid, 364/5.
Novela Roja (Madrid, 1931), Hemeroteca Municipal de Madrid, Carp/18.

D. *Memoirs and Accounts of the Protagonists*

Alba, Santiago, *Para la historia. Artículos publicados en Mayo 1930 por 'El Sol'*.

——, *Después de la Dictadura. El Pensamiento político de Don Santiago Alba* (prólogo de Franceso Netti, Valladolid, Imprenta Castellana, 1930).

Albiñana, José María, *Después de la Dictadura. Los cuervos sobre la tumba* (Madrid, 1930).

Alcalá-Zamora, Niceto, *Memorias (segundo texto de mis memorias)* (Barcelona, 1977).

Aunós y Pérez, Eduardo, 'La economía social del ministerio de trabajo', *Revista de Acción Social*, no. 5 (Oct. 1928).

——, *Calvo Sotelo y la política de su tiempo* (Madrid, 1941).

——, *La reforma corporativa del estado* (Madrid, 1935).

——, *'Política social de la Dictadura y colaboración socialista'*, *Anales de la Real Academia de ciencias Morales y Políticas*, XVI, 1964, Madrid.

——, *La organización corporativa y su posible desenvolvimiento* (Madrid, 1929).

——, *El golpe de estado del general Primo de Rivera y sus primeras disposiciones de orden social* (Madrid, 1944).

——, *Semblanza política del general Primo de Rivera* (Madrid, 1947).

——, *La política social de la Dictadura* (Real Academia de Ciencias Morales y Políticas. Discurso leído por el Excmo Sr. D. Eduardo Aunós en el acto de su recepción pública, y contestación del Excmo Sr. Marqués de Güad-el-Jelú el día 23 de Mayo de 1944) (Madrid, 1944).

——, *Primo de Rivera soldado y gobernante* (Madrid, 1944).

——, *Itinerario histórico de la España contemporánea (1808–1936)* (Barcelona, 1940).

——, *España en crisis 1874–1936* (Buenos Aires, 1942).

Avance de la provincia de Barcelona en el último quinquenio de septiembre de 1923 a igual fecha de 1928 (Barcelona, 1929).

Ayats Surribas, José, *El problema de Cataluña ante la Asamblea Nacional Consultiva* (Barcelona, 1930).

Ayuntamiento de Molíns del Rey. Cuatro años de actuación. Memoria de la gestión realizada durante el cuatrienio 1924–1927, redactada por el secretario de la corporación municipal D. Feliciano Baratech Alfaro (Barcelona, 1928).

Azaña y Díaz, Manuel, *Obras Completas* (Mexico, 1966–7).

Balcells, Albert (ed.), *El arraigo del anarquismo en Cataluña 1926–1934* (Madrid, 1973).

Baldomero, Argente, *La tregua aduanera y la organización de la paz* (Madrid, 1930).

Berenguer, Dámaso, *De la Dictadura a la República* (Madrid, 1946).

Blasco Ibáñez, Vicente, *Alfonso XIII Unmasked. The Military Terror in Spain* (London, 1925).

Bottai, Giuseppe, *Esperienza Corporativa* (Roma, 1929).

Bueso, Adolfo, *Recuerdos de un cenetista* (Barcelona, 1976).

Burgos y Mazo, Manuel, *El verano de 1919 en Gobernación* (Cuenca, n.d.).

——, *La Dictadura y los Constitucionalistas*. 4 Vols. (Madrid, 1934–5).

Calvo Sotelo, José, *Mis servicios al estado. Seis años de gestión. Apuntes para la historia* (Madrid, 1931).

Calvo Sotelo, José, 'Orientaciones económicas y tributarias', *Curso de ciudadanía. Conferencias pronunciadas en el Alcazar de Toledo, Marzo de 1929* (Depósito Geográfico e Histórico del Ejército, s.a.).

——, *Discurso del ministro de hacienda (estudio económico y de la hacienda pública española en el momento actual)* (Diciembre 1928).

Cambó, Francisco, *A la solución autonomista del problema catalán* (conferencia en la Real Academia de Jurisprudencia y Legislación, 29 de Noviembre, 1918).

——, *La valoración de la peseta* (Madrid, n.d.).

——, *Por la concordia* (Madrid, 1927).

——, *España, Cataluña y la nueva constitución* (Buenos Aires, 1929).

——, *Las Dictaduras* (Barcelona, 1929).

——, *Actuació regionalista; a proposit d'un article de don Gabriel Maura Gamazo* (Barcelona, Lliga Regionalista, 1915).

Chapaprieta, Joaquín, *La paz fué posible. Memorias de un político* (Barcelona, 1972).

Cierva y Peñafel, Juan de la, *Notas de mi vida* (Madrid, 1955).

Costa, Joaquín, *Reconstitución y Europeización de España* (Huesca, 1924).

Cueto, Juan, *Cuentos al nuncio. Sobre derivaciones republicanas de los sucesos de Vera* (Madrid, 1933).

Curso de ciudadanía. Conferencias pronunciadas en el Alcazar de Toledo, Marzo 1929. Prólogo del General Primo de Rivera (Depósito Geográfico e Histórico del Ejército).

Domingo, Marcelino, *¿Qué es España?* (Madrid, 1925).

——, *¿Qué Espera el Rey?* (Madrid, 1930).

E.T.L., *Por pueblos y aldeas. De las memorias de un delegado gubernativo* (Madrid, 1928).

Estelrich, Joan, *Catalunya endins. Un examen de consciencia colectiva en temps terbols* (Barcelona, 1930).

——, *La qüestió de les minories nacionals* (Barcelona, 1929).

Eza, Vizconde de, *Mi responsabilidad en el desastre de Melilla como ministro de la guerra* (Madrid, 1923).

——, *Resultados de la reforma agraria en Europa* (Asociación Española para el Progreso de las Ciencias, sesión del día 22 de Mayo 1929).

Félix Huerta, José, *Sobre la Dictadura* (Madrid, 1930).

Franco, Ramón, and Ruiz de Alda, J., *De Palos a Plata* (Madrid, 1926).

García Benítez, José, *Tres meses de dictadura obrero-ateneista* (Madrid, 1931).

Gil Robles, José María, *No fué posible la paz* (Barcelona, 1968).

Goicoechea, Antonio, *La crisis del constitucionalismo español* (Madrid, 1926).

Gómez Fernández, Ramiro, *De la oposición al poder. La Dictadura me honró encarcelandome* (Madrid, 1930).

Güad-el-Jelú, Marqués de, *Contestación al discurso leído por el Excmo. Sr. D. Eduardo Aunós en el acto de su recepción pública, el día 23 de Mayo de 1944* (Real Academia de Ciencias Morales y Políticas, Madrid, 1944).

Güal Villalví, Pedro, *Memorias de un industrial de nuestro tiempo* (Barcelona, 1922).

Hoyos y Vinent, José María, *Mi testimonio* (Madrid, 1962).
Hurtado, Amadeu, *Quaranta anys d'advocat. Historia del meu temps* (Barcelona, 1964).
Iglesia Celedonio, de la, *La censura por dentro* (Madrid, 1930).
Informe del Marqués de Alonso Martínez sobre la asistencia a la Asamblea de los ex-presidentes de las Cámaras.
Jiménez de Asua, Luis, *Política, figuras, paisajes* (Madrid, n.d.).
——, *Notas de un confinado* (Madrid, 1930).
——, *Al servicio de la nueva generación* (Madrid, 1930).
——, *Juventud. Conferencia de Jiménez de Asua y réplica de José López-Rey* (Madrid, 1929).
Kindelán Duany, Alfredo, *Ejército y política* (Madrid, 1947).
Largo Caballero, Francisco, *Presente y futuro de la UGT* (Madrid, 1925).
——, *Mis recuerdos. Cartas a un amigo* (Mexico, 1954).
Lerroux, Alejandro, *Para un periódico de America. Colaboración o revolución* (Hemeroteca Municipal de Madrid, A/1685).
——, *La pequeña historia* (Buenos Aires, 1945).
——, *Al servicio de la República* (Madrid, 1930).
López Ochoa y Porteundo, *De la Dictadura a la República* (Madrid, 1930).
López-Rey, J., *Los estudiantes frente a la Dictadura* (Madrid, 1930).
Lorenzo Pardo, M., *La Confederación del Ebro. Nueva política hidráulica* (Madrid, 1930).
Lucía Lucía, Luis, *En estas horas de transición* (Valencia, 1930).
Maeztu, Ramiro de, *Defensa de la hispanidad* (Valladolid, 1938).
——, *El nuevo tradicionalismo y la revolución social* (Madrid, 1959).
——, *Liquidación de la monarquía parlamentaria* (Madrid, 1957).
——, *Con el directorio militar* (Madrid, 1957).
Marco Miranda, Vicente, *Las conspiraciones contra la Dictadura* (Madrid, 1930).
Maura, Duque de, *Discurso ante la Real Academia Española, el 18 de enero de 1929* (Madrid, 1920).
Maura Gamazo, Gabriel, *Dolor de España* (Madrid, 1932).
——, *Recuerdos de mi vida* (Madrid, n.d.).
Maura Gamazo, Miguel, *Así cayó Alfonso XIII* (Barcelona, 1962).
Mola Vidal, Emilio, *Obras Completas* (Valladolid, 1940).
Noguera, Enrique, *Genética, eugenesía y pedagogía sexual. Libro de las primeras jornadas eugénicas españolas* (Madrid, 1934).
Ortega y Gasset, Eduardo, *España encadenada. La verdad sobre la Dictadura* (Paris, 1925).
Ossorio y Gallardo, Ángel, *Incompatibilidad* (Madrid, 1930).
——, *Una crisis del sentido conservador* (Madrid, 1925).
——, *Mis Memorias* (Buenos Aires, 1946).
——, *La España de mi vida* (Buenos Aires, 1941).
Pemán, José María, *Mis almuerzos con gente importante* (Barcelona, 1970).
——, *El hecho y la idea de la Unión Patriótica* (Madrid, 1929).
——, *Poema de la bestia y el ángel* (Madrid, 1939).
Pemartín, José, *Los valores históricos de la Dictadura española* (Madrid, 1928).
Pérez Baró, Albert, *Els 'feliços' anys vint. Memóries d'un militant obrer 1918–1926* (Palma de Mallorca, 1974).

Pérez Solís, Oscar, *Memorias de mi amigo Oscar Perea* (Madrid, n.d.).

Pestaña, Ángel, *El terrorismo en Barcelona* (Tarragona, 1920).

——, *El terrorismo en Barcelona seguido de principios, medios y fines del sindicalismo en Cataluña. El sindicalismo en Cataluña por Angel Pestaña y Salvador Seguí* (Conferencias dadas en Madrid el día 4 de Oct. de 1919) (Barcelona, 1978).

——, *Lo que aprendí en la vida* (Madrid, n.d.).

Pradera, Victor, *Al servicio de la patria. Las ocasiones perdidas por la Dictadura* (Madrid, 1930).

Prieto, Indalecio, *De mi vida, recuerdos, estampas, siluetas, sombras . . .* (Mexico, 1968–70).

——, *Discursos fundamentales* (prólogo de Edward Malefakis) (Madrid, 1975).

——, *Palabras al viento* (Mexico, 1969).

——, *Con el rey o contra el rey* (Mexico, 1972).

Primo de Rivera, Miguel, *Conferencia del General . . . de 8 de Marzo de 1919* (Madrid, 1919).

——, *El pensamiento de . . . Sus notas, artículos y discursos. Prólogo de José María Pemán* (Madrid, 1929).

——, *Opinión emitida ante un redactor del periódico 'El Ejército Español' con motivo del orden público en los actuales momentos* (Guadalajara, 1919).

——, *Disertación ciudadana* (Conferencia pronunciada en el Alcazar de Toledo, Marzo de 1929).

——, *Recuperación de Gibraltar* (1917).

——, *La obra de la Dictadura. Sus cuatro últimos artículos* (Madrid, 1930).

——, *Actuación ciudadana que corresponde al ejército, 26 de Octubre de 1927* (Madrid, 1927).

Queipo de Llano, Gonzalo, *El General Queipo de Llano perseguido por la Dictadura* (Madrid, 1930).

Romanones, Conde de, *Las responsabilidades políticas del antiguo régimen 1875–1923* (Madrid, n.d.).

——, *Notas de una vida 1912–31* (Madrid, 1947).

Ruiz de Alda, Julio, *El viaje del hidroplano 'Plus Ultra' de Palos a Buenos-Aires* (Conferencia pronunciada el 23 de abril de 1926, en el Teatro de la Princesa de Madrid).

Saborit, Andrés, *Asturias y sus hombres* (Toulouse, 1964).

——, *Julián Besteiro* (Mexico, 1961).

Saínz Rodríguez, Pedro, *Testimonio y recuerdos* (Barcelona, 1978).

Sánchez Guerra, José, *Al servicio de España. Un manifiesto y un discurso* (Madrid, 1930).

Sánchez Guerra, Rafael, *El movimiento revolucionario de Valencia (Relato de un procesado)* (Madrid, Barcelona, Buenos Aires, 1930).

Salazar, Antonio de Oliveira, *Doctrine and Action. Internal and Foreign Policy of the New Portugal 1928–1939* (London, 1939).

Suñer, Enrique, *Los intelectuales y la tragedia española* (Burgos, 1937).

Tedeschini, Federico, *Discursos y cartas sobre Acción Católica Española* (Santiago de Compostela, 1958).

Unamuno, Miguel de, *De Fuerteventura a Paris* (Paris, 1925).

Valdeiglesias, Marqués de, *1875–1949: La socıedad espanola vista por el Marqués de Valdeiglesias, Crónicas recogidas por Mercedes Escabor y Kirkpatrick* (Madrid, 1957).

Valverde, José Tomas, *Memorias de un alcalde* (Madrid, 1961).

Vinent, Marqués de (Hoyos y Vinent, Antonio), *El primer estado. Actuación de la aristocracia antes de la revolución, en la revolución y después de ella* (Madrid, 1931).

E. *Contemporary Accounts and Studies*

Aguirre de Carcer, Manuel, *Glosas del anõ 23* (Madrid, 1924).

Alcalá Galiano, Álvaro, *The Fall of a Throne* (London, 1933).

Andrade, Benito Mariano, *Castilla ante el separatismo Catalán* (Madrid, 1921).

Araquistain, Luis de, *El ocaso de un régimen* (Madrid, 1930).

Armiñán Oriozola, José Manuel y Luis, *Francia, el dictador y el moro. Páginas históricas* (Madrid, 1930).

Ayala Pérez, Ramón de, *Escritos políticos* (Madrid, 1967).

Ayensa, Emilio, *Vista de la causa seguida contra el Sr. Sánchez Guerra* (Madrid, 1929).

Baelen, Jean, *Principaux traits du développement économique de l'Espagne de 1914 à l'avènement du directoire militaire* (Paris, 1924).

Barango-Solís, Fernando, *Un movimiento revolucionario: de los sucesos de Ciudad Real al proceso Sánchez Guerra* (Barcelona, 1929).

Baratech Alfaro, F., *El sindicalismo español en el momento actual* (Barcelona, 1929).

——, *Los sindicatos libres en España. Su origen, su actuación, su ideario* (Barcelona, 1927).

Barreiro, Luis, 'La industria minero-siderúrgica española', *Revista Nacional de Economía*, Madrid, January 1930.

Bekaert, Maurice, *L'Espagne et le directoire* (Brussels, 1924).

Benavides, Manuel, *El último pirata del mediterráneo* (Barcelona, 1934).

Beneyto Pérez, Juan, and Costa Serrano, José Maria, *El partido* (Zaragoza, 1939).

Benítez de Lugo, Félix, *Obra económica, financiera y monetaria de la Dictadura* (Madrid, 1930).

Bermis, F., *Consecuencias económicas de la guerra* (Madrid, 1923).

Blanco, Carlos, *La Dictadura y los procesos militares* (Madrid, 1931).

Blas Vives, *La política arancelaria de España* (Madrid, 1928).

Brunet, Manuel, 'L'eglesia Catalana durant la Dictadura', *La Veu de Catalunya*, 3 May 1930.

Buckley, Henry, *Life and Death of the Spanish Republic* (London, 1940).

Bueno, Manuel, *España y la monarquía. Estudio político* (New York, 1925).

Cabanellas, Guillermo, *Militarismo y militaradas (Acotaciones de la historia político-militar de España)* (Madrid, 1933).

Campo, Isidro, del, *Lo que no ha dicho Romanones. Cartas abiertas al general Primo de Rivera* (Madrid, 1925).

Canals, Salvador, *Spain, the Monarchy and the Constitution* (London, 1925).
——, *La crisis exterior de la peseta* (Madrid, 1930).
Capella, Jacinto, *La verdad de Primo de Rivera. Intimidades y anécdotas del dictador* (Madrid, 1933).
Carrión, Pascual, *La reforma agraria de la segunda república y la situación actual de la agricultura española* (Barcelona, 1973).
——, *Los latifundios en España. Su importancia, origen, consecuencias y solución* (Barcelona, 1972).
Casas Pérez, José, de las, *El régimen y sus hombres. Lo que me han contado a mí* (Madrid, 1926).
Casas Ramos y Moraleda, *Dos años de directorio militar* (Madrid, 1925).
Cascón, Miguel, *Luz sin sombra. El Marqués de Comillas* (Comillas, 1926).
Castro, Cristóbal de, *Al servicio de los campesinos. Hombres sin tierra, tierra sin hombres (Ensayo sobre la nueva política agraria en Europa y su aplicación en España)* (Madrid, 1931).
Castro y Hernández, Magdaleno de, *Nacionalismo, humanismo y civilización (La constitución interna de España y la ideología catalanista)* (Madrid, 1922).
Ceballos-Teresí, J. G., *Economía, finanzas, cambios. Historia económica, financiera y política de España en el siglo XX* (Madrid, 1932).
Correas, Juan Francisco, *El bolchevismo en España* (Madrid, 1920).
Cortés-Cavanillas, Julián, *La Dictadura y el Dictador. Rasgos históricos, políticos, y psicológicos* (Madrid, 1929).
——, *Alfonso XIII. Vida, confesiones y muerte* (Barcelona, 1966).
Costedoat-Lamarque, Jean, *La Question agraire en Andalousie* (Paris, 1923).
Cuartero, José, *Veinte años de política española. Sus mejores artículos en 'ABC' 1917–36* (Madrid, 1947).
Daye, F., *En Espagne, sous la Dictature* (Brussels and Paris, 1925).
Denjean, François, 'Le Mouvement revolutionnaire en Espagne', *Revue de Paris*, xxviii, 1 Nov. 1921.
Department of Overseas Trade, *Economic Conditions in Spain*, June 1930.
Díaz del Moral, Juan, *Historia de las agitaciones campesinas andaluzas* (Madrid, 1973).
Díaz-Retg, Enrique, *España bajo el nuevo régimen. Cinco años de gobierno Primo de Rivera. 1923–Septiembre–1928* (Madrid, 1928).
Domingo, Marcelino, *Una dictadura en la Europa del siglo XX* (Madrid, 1929).
Duarte, Fernando, *España: Miguel Primo de Rivera y Orbaneja (Dos palabras por prólogo de Benito Mussolini)* (Madrid, 1923).
Dudon, Paul, 'Le Dictateur espagnol, Miguel Primo de Rivera'. Extract from *Études*, vol. 203, 20 Apr. 1930, no. 8.
Durán y Ventosa, Luis, *Los políticos* (Barcelona, 1928).
Dwelshauvers Georges, *La Catalogne et le problème Catalan* (Paris, 1926).
Farfán de los Godos, G., and González, G. de Santiago, *Por los fueros de la verdad. Aclaraciones necesarias para la historia de los sucesos de Valencia* (Madrid, 1930).
Farré Morego, José María, *Los atentados sociales en España* (Madrid, 1922).

Fernández Díez, Gregorio, 'La economía Castellana ante la Dictadura', *Revista Nacional de Economía* (Madrid, January 1930).

——, Gregorio, *La orientación nacionalista de la economía* (Barcelona, 1927).

Finat Rojas Hipólito, Marqués de Carvajal, *¿Cuál es el horizonte político de España? Reflexiones del hombre de la calle* (Madrid, 1929).

Foix, Pedro, *Los archivos del terrorismo blanco* (Madrid, 1931).

Fontán Palomo, José, *El somatenista español* (Barcelona, 1924).

Francos Rodríguez, José, *La mujer y la política españolas* (Madrid, 1920).

Gandarías, Manuel, *Perfiles síquicos del Dictador Primo de Rivera y bosquejo razonado de su obra* (Cadiz, 1929).

García Gallego, Jerónimo, *La quiebra de nuestro sistema político y la gestación de un régimen nuevo* (Madrid, 1928).

García Queipo de Llano, Genoveva, and Tusell Gómez, Javier, 'Texto inédito contra la Dictadura de Primo de Rivera (por Azaña)', *Historia 16*, 6, no. 58, Feb. 1981, pp. 27–41.

García-Menéndez, B., *La España rural (hambre de tierra y sed de justicia)* (Madrid, 1931).

Garcitoral, Alicio, *Breviario de la Dictadura. Política* (Barcelona, 1928).

Gascón, Antonio, *Los hombres que trajeron la República — Los estudiantes* (Madrid, n.d.).

Gasset, Rafael, *La humanidad insumisa. La revolución rusa. El problema social en España* (Madrid, 1920).

Glorias de la raza. La voz del pueblo y el raid Huelva–Buenos Aires (Madrid, 1926) (prólogo de Díaz-Retg, Enrique).

Graell, Marcelino, *Resumen de la situación económica de España. Surgimiento de la clase media* (Barcelona, 1923).

Granada, Eduardo, *Una página de la historia de España escrita por los propios actores (Sánchez Guerra, acusado, procesado y absuelto). Los caballeros y la política* (Barcelona, 1929).

Graudel, J., *Le Monopole du pétrole en Espagne* (Paris, 1935).

Hernández Mir, Francisco, *Del desastre a la victoria (1921–26). El Rif por España* (Madrid, 1927).

——, *Del desastre a la victoria (1921–26). Del Rif a Yebala* (Madrid, 1926).

——, *La Dictadura en Marruecos. Al margen de una farsa* (Madrid, 1930).

——, Un crimen de lesa patria. La Dictadura ante la historia (Madrid, 1930).

Iglesias, Dalmacio, *Política de la Dictadura. La carestía de la vida: sus causas y remedios (programa económico para cualquier partido)* (Barcelona, 1930).

Jordán, Francisco, *La dictadura del proletariado* (Madrid, 1920).

Jover Mirá, Manuel, *La España inmortal* (Madrid, 1930).

Juliá, Joaquín, *El protecciónismo y sus resultados* (Madrid, 1924).

Laure, A. M. E. (Lieut.-Col.), *La Victoire franco-espagnole dans le Rif* (Paris, 1927).

López Nuñez, Álvaro, 'Previsión y seguros sociales', *Curso de Ciudadanía. Conferencias . . . en el Alcazar de Toledo . . .* (1929).

López Rienda, Rafael, *El escándalo del millón de Larache* (Madrid, 1922).

Madariaga, Salvador de, 'Spain and Russia: a Parallel', *New Europe*, 30 Aug. 1917.
Madrid, Francesc, *Els exiliats de la Dictadura. Reportatges i Testimonis* (Barcelona, 1930).
Malaparte, Curcio, *Técnica del golpe de estado* (Barcelona, 1958).
March, José María, *El Somatén, su origen y naturaleza, su historia y organización. La salvación de España* (Barcelona, 1923).
Mares, Roland de, 'Les Étapes de la Dictature espagnole' in *Revue de Paris*, 1 Dec. 1927.
Marín del Campo, Rafael, *La política del porvenir* (Madrid, 1928).
Martí Jara, Enrique, *El Rey y el pueblo* (Madrid, 1929).
Martínez de la Riva, Ramón, *Las jornadas triunfales de un golpe de estado. Historia del movimiento militar llevado a cabo en España con todos sus detalles, anécdotas, documentos, retratos, comentarios, fotografías etc* (Madrid and Barcelona, 1923).
——, *La España de hoy* (Madrid, 1926).
'Mask', *Hacia la España nueva. Pasado, presente y porvenir del directorio militar* (Madrid, 1925).
Maura Gamazo, Gabriel, *Jurados mixtos para dirimir las diferencias entre patronos y obreros y para prevenir y remediar las huelgas* (Madrid, 1901).
——, *Bosquejo histórico de la Dictadura* (Madrid, 1930).
Maurín, Joaquín, *Los hombres de la Dictadura* (Madrid, 1930).
Meseguer y Costa, José (Bishop of Lérida), *Catecismo de la doctrina cristiana* (Lérida, 1929).
Montagut, J. (Canónigo), *El Dictador y la Dictadura* (Barcelona, 1928).
Moreno Duarte, Francisco de, *Disertación Somatenista* (Zaragoza, 1928).
Morón, Gabriel, *El partido socialista ante la realidad política de España* (Madrid, 1929).
Mousset, Albert, *L'Espagne dans la politique mondiale* (Paris, 1923).
Navarro Canales, Luis, *La cuestión religiosa en el anteproyecto constitucional* (Madrid, 1929).
Navas, Miguel, *Los socialistas españoles y la dictadura militar* (Buenos Aires, 1929).
Nin, Andrés, *Los problemas de la revolución española* (Ruedo Ibérico, 1971).
——, *Las dictaduras de nuestro tiempo* (Madrid, n.d.).
Olariaga, Luis de, *La intervención de los cambios en España* (Madrid, 1929).
——, *La crisis siderúrgico-metalúrgica en España* (Madrid, 1932).
——, *La política monetaria en España* (Madrid, 1933).
Oller Piñol, J., *Martínez Anido, su vida y su obra* (Madrid, 1943).
Ortega y Gasset, Eduardo, *Annual. Relato de un soldado e impresiones de un cronista* (Madrid, n.d.).
Ortega y Gasset, José, *Obras completas. Escritos políticos, II (1922–33).* (Revista de occidente, Madrid, 1969).
——, *El tema de nuestro tiempo* (Madrid, 1923).

Pardo González, Cándido, *Al servicio de la verdad. Las juntas de defensa militares . . . La Dictadura del segundo Marqués de Estella* (Madrid, 1930).
Pascazio, Nicola, *La rivoluzione di Spagna. Dittatura, monarchia, repubblica, rivoluzione* (Rome, 1933).
Pemartin, José *¿Qué es lo nuevo?* (Madrid, 1940).
Perucho, Artur, *Catalunya sota la Dictadura (Dades per a la historia)* (Badalona, 1930).
Posada, Adolfo, *España en crisis* (Madrid, 1923).
Prat de la Riba, E., *Los jurados mixtos para dirimir las diferencias entre patronos y obreros y para prevenir o remediar huelgas* (Madrid, 1901).
Primo de Rivera, José Antonio, *Obras completas* (Madrid, 1942).
Pyrene, *Antiespañolismo. Marxistas y separatistas contra España* (Zaragoza, 1935).
Rato Sastrón, Antonio, *Consideraciones acerca de la implantación de los comités paritarios en las industrias* (Conferencia pronunciada el 30 de marzo de 1927 en la Cámara Nacional de Industrias Químicas, Barcelona).
Revesz, Andrés, *Mussolini, el dictador en pyjama* (Madrid, n.d.).
——, *Frente al Dictador* (Madrid, n.d.).
Revuelta Martín, Agustín, *Ventajas que la sindicación católica reporta a la clase agraria* (León, 1928).
Rico, Pedro, *El 'sport' en España. Amateurs y profesionales* (Madrid, 1930).
Risco, Vicente, *El problema político de Galicia* (Madrid, Barcelona, and Buenos Aires, 1930).
Riumbau Lazcano, Martín, *El levantamiento militar, sus causas y efectos* (Palma, 1923).
Rodríguez, Villamil, José María, *Muerto el Dictator (impresiones periodísticas)* (Valladolid, 1930).
Royo Villanova, Antonio, *Bolchevismo y sindicalismo* (Madrid, 1920).
——, *Intervención en la discusión de la memoria del Sr. Roig Ibánez 'sobre el porvenir político de España' en la Academia de Jurisprudencia* (Madrid, 1929).
Ruimar Cándido, *¿Quién mató a Meco?* (Ateneo de Madrid. Conferencias pro-responsabilidades, 13.6.23, Madrid).
Ruiz Albeniz, Victor (el Tebib Arrumi), *Estado actual del problema de España en Marruecos y medios prácticos para resolverlo* (Conferencias dadas en el Ateneo de Madrid los días 29 y 31 de Mayo de 1922).
——, *Las responsabilidades del desastre. Ecce homo* (Madrid, 1922).
——, *Tanger y la colaboración franco-española en Marruecos* (Madrid, 1927).
Ruiz Almansa, Javier, 'La población de España', *Revista Nacional de Economía* (Madrid, January 1930).
Saldaña y García, Quintiliano, *El momento de España (Ensayos de sociología política)* (Madrid, 1929).
——, *Al servicio de la justicia. La orgía aurea de la Dictadura* (Madrid, 1930).

Samblancat, Ángel, *El aire podrido. El ambiente social de España durante la Dictadura. Acto en cuatro misterios* (Colección 'Visiones Políticas y Sociales', Madrid, 1930).
San Martín Losada, Eduardo, *Sueldos, haberes, y gratificaciones del ejército* (Madrid, 1927).
Saseras y Batlle, José María, *Dos años de directorio militar (homenaje a Primo de Rivera)* (Barcelona, 1925).
Sforza, Carlo, *European Dictatorships* (London, 1932).
Siurot, M., *La emoción de España. Libro de cultura patriótica—popular* (Madrid, 1924).
Solá Cañizares, F. de, *Luchas sociales en Cataluña 1812–1934* (Madrid, 1970).
Soriano, Rodrigo, *A los hombres con verguenza* (Manuscript in Romanones Archive, Leg. 57, no. 20).
——, *España bajo el sable* (Santiago de Chile, 1926).
Tallada, Josép María, *Economía monetaria espanyola* (Barcelona, 1930).
Tarduchy, Emilio, *Psicología del Dictator y caracteres mas salientes, morales, sociales y políticos de la Dictadura* (Madrid, 1929).
Thomas, Hugh (ed.), *José Antonio Primo de Rivera. Selected Writings* (London, 1972).
Un Español Neutral, *Réplica al Conde de Romanones sobre las responsabilidades del antigo régimen* (Madrid, 1925).
Vázquez Campo, Ángel, *Hacia la reforma constitucional española* (Madrid, 1929).
Verax, 'Quelques maîtres du destin: Le Général Primo de Rivera', *Revue des deux mondes*, Paris, 1 June 1928.
Villanueva, Francisco, *El momento constitucional* (Madrid, 1929).
——, *Crónica de actuaciones públicas y privadas para salir de la Dictadura de España* (Madrid, 1929).
——, *La Dictadura militar* (Madrid, 1930).
——, *¿Qué ha pasado aquí?* (Madrid, 1930).
Xuriguera, Ramón, *Els exiliats acusens* (Barcelona, 1930).
Zancada, Práxedes, *Los problemas constitucionales de España* (Madrid, 1930).
Zurano Muñoz, Emilio, *Hagamos patria. La voluntad en acción (cultura, educación, trabajo)* (Madrid, 1927).

2. Secondary Sources

'A Century of Conservatism'. A Special issue of the *Journal of Contemporary History*, vol. 13, no. 4, Oct. 1978.
Alastos Doros, *Venizelos, Patriot, Statesman, Revolutionary* (London, 1942).
Alexander, J. Robert, *The Peron Era* (New York, 1965).
Allardyce, Gilbert, 'What Fascism Is Not: Thoughts On the Deflation of a Concept', in *American Historical Review*, vol. 84, no. 2, Apr. 1979.
Alonso, José Ramón, *Historia política del ejército español* (Madrid, 1974).
Alzaga Villaamil. Oscar, *La primera democracia cristiana en Espãna* (Barcelona, 1973).

Aracil Rafael, and García Bonafé (eds.), *Lecturas de historia económica de España*, Vol. II (Barcelona, 1977).
Armiñán, Luis de, *Weyler* (Madrid, 1946).
Athenian, *Inside the Colonels' Greece* (London, 1972).
Aviv, Aviva and Isaac, 'Ideology and Political Patronage: Workers and Working-Class Movements in Republican Madrid 1931–34', in *European Studies Review*, Vol. 11, no. 11, Oct. 1981.
Bainville, Jacques, *Dictators* (London, 1937).
Balcells, Alberto, *El sindicalismo en Barcelona (1916–1923)* (Barcelona, 1965).
Balfour, Neil, and Mackay, Sally, *Paul of Yugoslavia* (London, 1980).
Barager, Joseph (ed.), *Why Peron Came to Power* (New York, 1968).
Barbancho G., Alfonso, *Las migraciones interiores españolas. Estudio cuantitativó desde 1900* (Madrid, 1967).
Barrington Moore, 'Totalitarian Elements in Pre-Industrial Societies', in *Political Power and Social Theory. Six Studies* (Harvard University Press, 1958).
——, *Social Origins of Dictatorship and Democracy. Lord and Peasant in the Making of the Modern World* (Boston, 1967).
Barzini, Luigi, *The Italians* (London, 1966).
Bec, R., *La Dictature espagnole* (Montpellier, 1935).
Bécarud, Jean, and Laponge, Gilles, *Los anarquistas españoles* (Barcelona, 1973).
Ben-Ami, Shlomo, *The Origins of the Second Republic in Spain* (Oxford University Press, 1978).
——, 'The Forerunners of Spanish Fascism: Unión Patriótica and Unión Monárquica', *European Studies Review*, vol. 9, no. 1, Jan. 1979.
——, 'La Rébellion universitaire en Espagne (1927–1931)', in *Revue d'histoire moderne et contemporaine*, July–September 1979.
——, 'The Catalan and Basque Movements for Autonomy', in Y. Dinstein (ed.), *Models of Autonomy* (New Brunswick, 1982).
Benavides,D., *El fracaso social del catolicismo español. Arboleya Martínez, 1870–1951* (Barcelona, 1973).
Benítez Toledo, José María, *Una política española del petróleo* (Madrid, 1936).
Blinkhorn, Martin, *Carlism and Crisis in Spain 1931–1939* (Cambridge University Press, 1975).
——, 'Spain: The "Spanish Problem" and The Imperial Myth', in *Journal of Contemporary History*, vol. 15, no. 1 (1980).
Boyd, Carolyn, *Praetorian Politics in Liberal Spain* (The University of North Carolina Press, 1979).
Brademas, John, *Anarcosindicalismo y revolución en España (1930–37)* (Barcelona, 1974).
Bradley Wells, Warre, *The Last King. Don Alfonso XIII of Spain* (London, 1934).
Brand Burch, Betty (ed.), *Dictatorship and Totalitarianism* (Toronto, New York, and London, 1964).
Bravo Morata, Federico, *Historia de Madrid* (Madrid, 1967), Vol. II.

Bravo Morata, Federico, *La Dictadura* (Madrid, n.d.), 2 Vols.
Brenan, Gerald, *The Spanish Labyrinth* (Cambridge University Press, 1964).
Bruguera, F. G., *Histoire contemporaine d'Espagne* (Éditions Ophrys, 1953).
Busquets, Julio, *El militar de carrera en España* (Barcelona, 1971).
Cárcel Ortí, Vicente (ed.), *La Iglesia en la España contemporánea (1808–1975)* (Madrid, 1979).
Carr, Raymond, *Spain 1808–1939* (Oxford, 1970).
——, 'Spain, Rule by Generals', in Howard, Michael (ed.), *Soldiers and Governments* (London, 1957).
Carr, Stephen, 'Industry and Society: Barcelona 1914–1923' (Oxford D.Phil thesis, 1979).
Carocci, Biampiero, *La Politica Estera dell'Italia Fascista (1925–1928)* (Bari, 1969).
Castillo, Juan José, *El sindicalismo amarillo en España. Aportación al estudio del catolicismo social español (1912–1923)* (Madrid, 1977).
——, *Propietarios muy pobres. Sobre la subordinación política del pequeño campesino* (Madrid, 1979).
Center for Mediterranean Studies. American Universities Field Staff, *The Identification of Pre-Fascist elements in Certain Modern Societies. Summary of Seminar Proceedings* (Rome, n.d.).
Cierva, Ricardo de la, 'La dialéctica de las bofetadas', *Historia y Vida*, March 1969.
Cimadevilla, Francisco, *El general Primo de Rivera* (Madrid, 1944).
Cliadakis, C. Harry, 'Greece 1935–1941: The Metaxas Regime and the Diplomatic Background to World War II' (Ph.D. dissertation, New York University, Oct. 1970).
Clogg, Richard, and Yannopulos, George (eds.), *Greece under Military Rule* (London, 1972).
Cobban, Alfred, *Dictatorship, Its History and Theory* (1971, first edition, 1939).
Colectivo de Historia, 'La Dictadura de Primo de Rivera y el bloque de poder en España', *Cuadernos Económicos de I.C.E.*, 1976/78.
Cotorruelo, Agustín, *La política económica de la vivienda en España* (Madrid, 1960).
Cuadernos Económicos de I.C.E. no. 10, 1979 (A special issue on the Dictatorship).
Cuenca, José Manuel, 'Miguel Primo de Rivera a escala histórica', *Historia y Vida*, iii, no. 22, 1970.
Cuesta Garrigos, Ildefonso, 'Los grandes bancos españoles. Su evolución (1922–1943)', *Moneda y Crédito*, Dec. 1944, no. 11.
De Felice, Renzo, *Mussolini il Duce, Vol. I: Gli anni del Consenso 1929–1936* (Turin, 1974).
——, *Fascism. An Informal Introduction to its Theory and Practice. An Interview with Michael A. Ledeen* (New Jersey, 1977).
Dedijer Vladimir, *et al.*, *History of Yugoslavia* (McGraw–Hill Book Company, 1974).

Díaz Nosty, Bernardo, *La irresistible ascención de Juan March. Notas previas para una investigación biográfica* (Madrid, 1977).
Díez Nicolás, Juan, *Tamaño, densidad y crecimiento de la población en España 1900–1960* (Madrid, 1971).
Douglas, W. Foard, 'The Forgotten Falangist: Ernesto Giménez Caballéro', *Journal of Contemporary History*, vol. 10, no. 1, January 1975.
Dunmore, Timothy, *The Stalinist Command Economy. The Soviet State Apparatus and Economic Policy 1945–1953* (London, 1980).
Duverger, Maurice, *Les Partis politiques* (Paris, 1951).
Egerton, F. C. C., *Salazar, Rebuilder of Portugal* (London, 1943).
Emmerson, Donald (ed.), *Students and Politics in Developing Nations* (London, 1968).
Esteban-Infantes, Emilio, General, *General Sanjurjo* (Barcelona, 1958).
Ezcurra, Luis, *Historia de la radiodifusión española. Los primeros años* (Madrid, 1974).
Fernández Almagro, Melchor, *Historia del reinado de Alfonso XIII* (Barcelona, 1934).
Ferro, António, *Salazar, Portugal and its Leader* (London, 1935).
Finer, S. E., *The Man on Horseback. The Role of the Military in Politics* (New York, 1962).
Flacks, Richard, *Youth and Social Change* (Chicago, 1967).
Fleming, Shannon and Ann, 'Primo de Rivera and Spain's Moroccan Problem, 1923–27' in *Journal of Contemporary History*, vol. 12, no. 1, 1977.
Fontana, Josép, and Nadal, Jordi, 'Spain 1914–1970', in Cipolla, Carlo (ed.), *The Fontana Economic History of Europe*, vol. 6, part 2 (Fontana Books, 1976).
Forcadell, Carlos, 'El asesinato del cardenal Soldevila', *Tiempo de Historia*, iv, no. 47, Oct. 1978.
Franco Salgado-Araujo, Francisco, *Mis conversaciones privadas con Franco* (Barcelona, 1976).
Fraser, Ronald, *The Pueblo, A Mountain Village on the Costa del Sol* (London, 1973).
Fusi, Juan Pablo, *Política obrera en el país vasco* (Madrid, 1975).
Furneaux, Rupert, *Abd-el-Krim* (London, 1967).
Galinsoga, Luis de, *Centinela de Occidente. Semblanza biográfica de Francisco Franco* (Barcelona, 1956).
Gallagher, Tom, 'Controlled Repression in Salazar's Portugal', *Journal of Contemporary History*, vol. 14, no. 3 (1979).
——, 'The Mystery Train: Portugal's Military Dictatorship 1926–1932', *European Studies Review*, vol. 11, no. 3, July 1981.
Gallego, José Andrés, *El socialismo durante la Dictadura 1923–30* (Madrid, 1977).
Ganivet, Ángel, *Spain: An Interpretation* (London, 1946).
García, Canales, M., *El problema constitucional en la Dictadura de Primo de Rivera* (Madrid, 1980).
García Delgado, José Luis, *Origenes y desarrollo del capitalismo en España. Notas críticas* (Madrid, 1975).

García Escudero, José María,'El final de la monarquía liberal: Primo de Rivera y Alfonso XIII', *Arbor*, 1953.

García Venero, Maximiano, *Historia del nacionalismo vasco* (Madrid, 1969).

——, *Santiago Alba, monárquico de razón* (Madrid, 1963).

——, *Torcuato Luca de Tena y Álvarez-Ossorio. Una vida al servicio de España* (Madrid, 1961).

——, *Historia del nacionalismo catalán* (Madrid, 1967), Vol. II.

——, *Historia de las Internacionales en España*, Vol. II *(1914–36)* (Madrid, 1957).

Garriga, Ramón, *Juan March y su tiempo* (Barcelona, 1976).

Gay de Montellá, R., *Valoración hispánica en el mediterráneo* (Madrid, 1952).

Gerschenkron, Alexander, *Continuity in History and other Essays* (Harvard University Press, 1968).

Gómez-Navarro Navarrete, José Luis, *Unión Patriótica. Aproximación al estudio de un partido dictatorial* (Memoria de licenciatura, Universidad de Madrid, 1979).

González Calbet, María Teresa, *Aproximación al estudio de la Asamblea Nacional Consultiva de Primo de Rivera (1927–1930)* (Memoria de Licenciatura, Facultad de Filosofía y Letras, Madrid, 1976).

González Ruano, César, and Tarduchy, Emilio, *Sanjurjo (Una vida española del novecientos)* (Madrid, 1933).

González Ruano, César, *Miguel Primo de Rivera. La vida heróica y romántica de un general español* (Madrid, 1935).

Goodspeed, D. J., *The Conspirators. A Study of the Coup d'État* (London, 1962).

Graham, Stephen, *Alexander of Yugoslavia. Strong Man of the Balkans* (London, 1938).

Greene, Nathanael (ed.), *Fascism, an Anthology* (New York, 1968).

Gregor, James, *Italian Fascism and Developmental Dictatorship* (Princeton University Press, 1979).

Guzmán Reina, A., *Causas y remedios del analfabetismo en España* (Madrid, 1955).

Halstead, Charles and Carolyn, 'Aborted Imperialism: Spain's Occupation of Tangier 1940–45', *Iberian Studies*, vol. vii, no. 2 (Autumn 1978).

Hansen, C. Edward, *Rural Catalonia Under the Franco Regime. The Fate of Regional Culture since the Spanish Civil War* (Cambridge University Press, 1977).

Harries-Jenkins, Gwyn, and Van Doorn, Jacques, (eds.), *The Military and the Problem of Legitimacy* (Sage Studies in International Sociology, Beverly Hills, London, 1976).

Harrison, Joseph, *An Economic History of Modern Spain* (Manchester University Press, 1978).

——, 'Catalan Business and the Loss of Cuba 1898–1914', in *Economic History Review*, Second Series, vol. xxvii, no. 3, Aug. 1974.

Harvey, Charles, *The Río Tinto Company. An Economic History of a Leading International Mining Concern 1873–1954* (Penzance, 1981).

Herrero, Javier, *Los origenes del pensamiento reaccionario español* (Madrid, 1973).
Hibbert, Christopher, *Benito Mussolini, a Biography* (London, 1962).
Hoptner, J. B., *Yugoslavia in Crisis 1924–1941* (New York, 1962).
Howard, Michael (ed.), *Soldiers and Governments: Nine Studies in Civil–Military Relations* (London, 1957).
Huntington, Samuel, and Moore, Clement (eds.), *Authoritarian Politics in Modern Society: The Dynamics of Established Party Systems* (New York, 1970).
Ibáñez de Ibero, Carlos, *Historia de la marina de guerra española* (Madrid, 1939).
Jelavich, Charles and Barbara (eds.), *The Balkans in Transition. Essays on the Development of Balkan Life and Politics since the Eighteenth Century* (University of California Press, 1963).
Jelinek, Yeshayahu, 'Storm-troopers in Slovakia: TheRodobrana and the Hlinka Guard', in *Journal of Contemporary History*, vol. 6, no. 3, 1971.
Joaniquet, Aurelio, *Calvo Sotelo. Una vida fecunda, un ideario político, una doctrina económica* (Santander, 1938).
——, *Alfonso Sala Conde de Argemí* (Madrid, 1955).
Johnson, J. John (ed.), *The Role of the Military in Underdeveloped Countries* (Princeton University Press, 1962).
Jutglar, Antoni, *Els burgesos catalans* (Barcelona, 1966).
Kautsky, John, *The Political Consequences of Modernization* (New York, 1972).
Lacomba, Juan Antonio, *Introducción a la historia económica de la España contemporánea* (Madrid, 1969).
——, *La crisis española de 1917* (Madrid, 1970).
——, *Ensayos sobre el siglo XX español* (Madrid, 1972).
Lalcona, F. Javier, *El idealismo político de Ortega y Gasset* (Madrid, 1974).
Lee Wolff, Robert, *The Balkan in Our Times* (Harvard University Press, 1967).
Lefaucheux, Pierre, *La Peseta et l'économie espagnole depuis 1928* (Paris, n.d.).
León-Ignacio, José, *Los años del pistolerismo* (Barcelona, 1981).
Linz, Juan, 'Una teoría del régimen autoritario: el caso de España', in S. Payne (ed.), *Política y sociedad en la España del siglo XX* (Madrid, 1973).
——, 'Una interpretación de los regímenes autoritarios', *Papers. Revista de Sociología* (Universidad Autónoma de Barcelona), no. 8 (1978).
——, 'Spanish Cabinet and Parliamentary Elites: from the Restoration to Franco', Unpublished paper.
——, 'The Party System of Spain, Past and Future', in Seymour Lipset and Stein Rokkan (eds.), *Party Systems and Voter Alignments* (New York, 1967).
Luttwak, Edward, *Coup d'État. A Practical Handbook* (Penguin Books, 1969).
Lyttleton, Adrian, *The Seizure of Power. Fascism in Italy 1919–1929* (London, 1973).

Lyttleton, Adrian (ed.), *Italian Fascisms: From Pareto to Gentile* (New York, 1975).

Madariaga, Salvador de, *España, ensayo de historia contemporánea* (Buenos Aires, 1964).

Malefakis, E. Edward, *Agrarian Reform and Peasant Revolution in Spain. Origins of the Civil War* (Yale University Press, 1970).

Martín, M., *El colonialismo español en Marruecos* (Paris, 1972).

Martínez Cuadrado, Miguel, *Elecciones y partidos políticos de España 1868–1931* (Madrid, 1969).

——, *La burgesía conservadora (1874–1931)* (Madrid, 1976).

Mas i Perera, Pere, 'Quaranta-cinc anys després. Antecedents catalans de l'adveniment de la dictadura de Primo de Rivera', *Xaloc* (Mexico), v, no. 26.

Maura, Duque de, y Fernández Almagro, Melchor, *¿Porqué cayó Alfonso XIII?* (Madrid, 1948).

Mayer, Arno, *Dynamics of Counterrevolution in Europe* (New York, 1971).

McClelland, J. S. (ed.), *The French Right from de Maistre to Maurras* (New York, 1971).

Meaker, H. Gerald, *The Revolutionary Left in Spain, 1914–1923* (Stanford University Press, 1974).

Melograni, Piero, 'The Cult of the Duce in Mussolini's Italy', *Journal of Contemporary History* vol. 11, no. 4, 1976.

Menéndez Pidal, Ramón, *Los españoles en la historia* (Madrid, 1971).

Miguel, Amando de, *La pirámide social española* (Barcelona, 1977).

Miguel, A. de, and Oltra, B., 'Bonapartismo y catolicismo. Una hipótesis sobre los origenes ideológicos del franquismo', in *Papers. Revista de Sociología* (Universidad Autónoma de Barcelona), no. 8 (1978).

Milego, Julio, *El General Barrera (De Cataluña al 10 de Agosto)* (Madrid, 1936).

Molas, Isidre, *Lliga Catalana. Una historia política de Catalunya de 1901 a 1936, a través de les vicissituds del partit catalanista de mes llarga tradició* (Barcelona, 1972).

Montero, R. José, *La CEDA. El catolicismo social y político en la II república* (Madrid, 1977).

Moreno, Andrés, 'El mercado de capitales en España', in *Moneda y Crédito* Dec. 1954.

Morodó, Raúl, 'La proyección constitucional de la Dictadura: la Asamblea Nacional Consultiva', *Boletín de Ciencias Políticas*, no. 13–14, August–December 1973.

——, 'El 18 de Brumario español. La Dictadura de Primo de Rivera', *Triunfo*, no. 572, 15 Sept. 1973.

Mosse, L. George, 'Caesarism, Circuses and Monuments', in *Journal of Contemporary History*, vol. 6, no. 2, 1971.

Mulhacén, Marqués de, *Política mediterránea de España 1704–1951* (Madrid, 1951).

Muntanyola, Ramón, *Vidal i Barraquer, el Cardenal de la paz* (Barcelona, 1971).

Nadal Jordi, Vicens i Vives Jaume, Casimir Martí, 'El moviment obrer a Espanya de 1929 a 1936 en relació amb la crisi econòmica' in *Serra D'or*, 2ᵉ època, iii, no. 2, Feb. 1961.
Nadal, Jordi, *La población española* (Barcelona, 1971).
Nordlinger, Eric, *Soldiers in Politics. Military Coups and Governments* (New Jersey, 1977).
Nolte, Ernest, *Three Faces of Fascism* (London, 1965).
Neumann, Franz, *The Democratic and the Authoritarian State. Essays in Political and Legal Theory* (The Free Press, Glencoe, Illinois, 1957).
Offer, Avner, *Property and Politics 1870–1914* (Cambridge University Press, 1981).
Oneto, José, *La noche de Tejero* (Barcelona, 1981).
Organski, A. F. K., *The Stages of Political Development* (New York, 1965).
Pabón, Jesús, *Cambó* (Barcelona, 1969).
——, *La revolución portuguesa (de Don Carlos a Sidonio Paes)* (Madrid 1941).
Paris Eguilaz, Higinio, *Factores del desarrollo económico español* (Madrid, 1957).
——, *El movimiento de precios en España* (Madrid,1943).
Pastor, Manuel, *Los origenes del fascismo en España* (Madrid, n.d.).
Payne, Stanley, *Politics and the Military in Modern Spain* (Oxford, 1967).
——, *Falange. A History of Spanish Fascism* (Stanford University Press, 1962).
Payne, Stanley (ed.), *Política y sociedad en la España del siglo XX* (Madrid, 1978).
Payne, Stanley, 'Catalan and Basque Nationalism', in *Journal of Contemporary History*, vol. 6, no. 1, 1971.
——, 'Spanish Conservatism 1834–1923', in *Journal of Contemporary History*, vol. 13, no. 4 (1978).
Paz, Abel, *Durruti. Le peuple en armes* (Bordeaux, 1972).
Peers, Allison, *Catalonia Infelix* (London, 1937).
Peirats, José, *La CNT en la revolución española* (Ruedo Ibérico, 1971).
——, *Los anarquistas en la crisis política española* (Buenos Aires, 1964).
Pelai Pages, *Historia del partido comunista de España (desde su fundación . . . hasta el final de la Dictadura de Primo de Rivera* (Barcelona, 1978).
Pérez Ledesma, Manuel, 'La Dictadura' (I and II)', *Cambió 16*, no. 98, 1.10.73, no. 99, 8.10.73.
Peripiñá Grau, Román, *De estructura económica y economía hispana* (Madrid, 1952).
Petrie, Charles, *King Afonso XIII and his Age* (London, 1963).
Pike, B. Frederick, *Hispanismo, 1898–1936. Spanish Conservatives and Liberals and their Relations with Spanish America* (University of Notre Dame Press, 1971).
Polonsky, Antony, *Politics in Independent Poland. The Crisis of Constitutional Government* (Oxford University Press, 1972).
Poulantzas, Nicos, *Fascisme et dictature* (Paris, 1970).
Prast, Henri, *Destin de la Roumanie* (Paris, 1954).
Preston, Paul, *The Coming of the Spanish Civil War* (London, 1978).

Preston, Paul, 'Spain', in Woolf, S. J. (ed.), *Fascism in Europe* (London, 1981).
Ramos Oliveira, Antonio, *Historia de España* (México, 1952).
——, *Politics, Economics and Men of Modern Spain 1808–1946* (London, 1946).
Ramirez, Luis, *Vie de Francisco Franco, régent du royaume d'Espagne par la grâce de Dieu* (Paris, 1966).
Ratcliff, F. Dillwyn, *Prelude to Franco* (New York, 1957).
Roberts, L. Henry, *Rumania. Political Problems of an Agrarian State* (Archon Books, 1969).
Rogger, Hans, and Weber, Eugen (eds.), *The European Right. A Historical Profile* (University of California Press, 1966).
Roldán, Santiago, *et al.*, *La formación de la sociedad capitalista en España 1914–1920* (Madrid, 1973).
Roldán, S., García Delgado, J. L., *La consolidación del capitalismo en España 1914–1920* (Madrid, 1973).
Romano, Julio, *Weyler, el hombre de hierro* (Madrid, 1934).
Romero Maura, Joaquín, '*La rosa de fuego*' (Barcelona, 1974).
Rossinyol, Jaume, *Le Problème national catalan* (Paris, 1974).
Rothschild, Joseph, *Pilsudski's Coup d'État* (Columbia University Press, 1966).
Rubio Cabeza, Manuel, *Crónica de la Dictadura* (Barcelona, 1974).
Ruiz González, David, 'Repercusión de la crisis de 1929 en España. Consideraciones en torno', in *Hispania* (Madrid), xxviii, no. 109 (1968).
——, *El movimiento obrero en Asturias* (Oviedo, 1968).
Sagrera, Ana de, *Miguel Primo de Rivera. El hombre, el soldado, el político* (Jerez de la Frontera, 1973).
Salazar, Rafael, 'Perfil humano de Primo de Rivera', *Historia y Vida*, iii, no. 22 (1970).
Salvemini, Gaetano, *Under the Axe of Fascism* (London, 1936).
——, *The Origins of Fascism in Italy* (New York, 1973).
Sarti, Roland (ed.), *The Ax Within. Italian Fascism in Action* (New York, 1974).
Scholl, S. (ed.), *Historia del movimiento obrero cristiano* (Barcelona, 1964).
Sencourt, Robert, *Spain's Uncertain Crown. The Story of the Spanish Sovereigns 1808–1931* (London, 1932).
Seton-Watson, Christopher, *Italy from Liberalism to Fascism 1870–1925* (London, 1967).
Seton-Watson, Hugh, 'Fascism, Right and Left', *Journal of Contemporary History*, vol. I, no. 1, 1966.
Shubert, Adrian, 'Una revolución de autodefensa: La radicalización de los mineros de Asturias 1921–1934', in *Sistema. Revista de Ciencias Sociales*, Jan. 1982.
——, 'Oil companies and Governments: International Reaction to the Nationalization of the Petroleum Industry in Spain: 1927–1930', in *Journal of Contemporary History*, vol. 15, no. 14 (1980).
Stepan, Alfred, *The Military in Politics. Changing Patterns in Brazil* (Princeton University Press, 1971).

Sternhell, Zeev, *La Droite révolutionnaire 1885–1914. Les origines françaises du fascisme* (Paris, 1978).

Tal, Uriel, *'Political Faith' of Nazism Prior to the Holocaust* (Annual Lecture of the Jacob M. and Shoshana Schreiber Chair of Contemporary Jewish History. University of Tel Aviv, 14 June 1978).

——, *Structures of German 'Political Theology' in the Nazi Era* (Second Annual Lecture of the Jacob M. and Shoshana Schreiber Chair of Contemporary Jewish History. University of Tel Aviv, 16 May 1979).

Talmon, Jacob, *The Rise of Totalitarian Democracy* (Boston, 1952).

Thompson, William, *The Grievances of Military Coup-Makers* (Beverly Hills, 1973).

Tuñón de Lara, Manuel, *El movimiento obrero en la historia de España* (Madrid, 1972).

——, *Historia y realidad del poder* (Madrid, 1967).

——, '1929: El último año de la Dictadura', *Boletín Informativo del Seminario de Derecho Político*, Salamanca, no. 32 (1964).

Turner, Henry (ed.), *Reappraisals of Fascism* (New York, 1975).

Tusell, Javier, *La crisis del caciquismo andaluz (1923–1931)* (Madrid, 1977).

——, *Historia de la democracia cristiana en España* (Madrid, 1974).

Vallotón, H., *Alfonso XIII* (Madrid, 1945).

Varela Ortega, José, 'El proteccionismo de los trigueros Castellanos y la naturaleza del poder político de la Restauración', *Cuadernos Económicos de I.C.E.*, no. 6, 1978.

Vegas Latapié, Eugenio, *El pensamiento político de Calvo Sotelo* (Madrid, 1941).

Velarde Fuertes, Juan, *Política económica de la Dictadura* (Madrid, 1973).

——, *Sobre la decadencia económica de España* (Madrid, 1969).

——, Vilar, Sergio, *Fascismo y militarismo* (Barcelona, 1978).

Viver Pi-Sunyer, C., *El personal político de Franco (1936–1945)* (Barcelona, 1978).

Voltes Bou, Pedro, 'Enfoque Barcelonés de la política económica del gobierno de Primo de Rivera', *Cuadernos de Historia de Cataluña*, Barcelona, no. 3 (1970).

Walter, R., *Student Politics in Argentina* (New York, 1968).

Weinstock, Stefan, *Divus Julius* (Oxford University Press, 1971).

Weiss, John, *The Fascist Tradition, Radical Right-Wing Extremism in Modern Europe* (New York, 1967).

Wheeler-Bennett, J. W., *The Nemesis of Power. The German Army in Politics 1918–1945* (London, 1967).

Wheelock, Keith, *Nasser's New Egypt. A Critical Analysis* (London, 1960).

Wiarda, J. Howard, *Dictatorship and Development. The Methods of Control in Trujillo's Dominican Republic* (University of Florida Press, Gainesville, 1970).

——, *Corporatism and Development: The Portuguese Experiment* (Amherst, 1977).

Winch, Donald, *Economics and Policy. A Historical Survey.* (Collins/Fontana, 1972).

Woodhouse, C. M., *Modern Greece. A Short History* (London, 1977).
Woolf, S. J.(ed.), *European Fascism* (London, 1968).
Woolman, David, *Rebels in the Rif* (Stanford, 1968).
Wynot, Edward, *Polish Politics in Transition. The Camp of National Unity and the Struggle for Power 1935–1939* (University of Georgia Press, 1974).
Yaavetz, Zvi, 'Levitas Popularis', *Atene e Roma*, 1965, n.s. 10, III.
Ybarra, Javier de, *Política Nacional en Vizcaya* (Madrid, 1947).

Index